Martin D. Joachim
Editor

Historical Aspects of Cataloging and Classification

Historical Aspects of Cataloging and Classification has been co-published simultaneously as *Cataloging & Classification Quarterly*, Volume 35, Numbers 1/2 2002 and Volume 35, Numbers 3/4 2003.

Pre-publication REVIEWS, COMMENTARIES, EVALUATIONS . . .

"MORE THAN A NOSTALGIC LOOK AT PAST GLORIES, this book points the way to the future of cataloging. Martin Joachim has pulled together a series of chapters that PROVIDES A SOLID GROUNDING IN THE PRINCIPLES OF CATALOGING around the world, while simultaneously pointing out challenges that face those attempting to provide bibliographic control to multicultural, multi-format, highly specialized materials."

Carol G. Hixon, MS
Head
Cataloging Department
University of Oregon

Historical Aspects of Cataloging and Classification

Historical Aspects of Cataloging and Classification has been co-published simultaneously as *Cataloging & Classification Quarterly*, Volume 35, Numbers 1/2 2002 and Volume 35, Numbers 3/4 2003.

Cataloging & Classification Quarterly™ Monographic "Separates"

Below is a list of "separates," which in serials librarianship means a special issue simultaneously published as a special journal issue or double-issue _and_ as a "separate" hardbound monograph. (This is a format which we also call a "DocuSerial.")

"Separates" are published because specialized libraries or professionals may wish to purchase a specific thematic issue by itself in a format which can be separately cataloged and shelved, as opposed to purchasing the journal on an on-going basis. Faculty members may also more easily consider a "separate" for classroom adoption.

"Separates" are carefully classified separately with the major book jobbers so that the journal tie-in can be noted on new book order slips to avoid duplicate purchasing.

You may wish to visit Haworth's Website at . . .

http://www.HaworthPress.com

. . . to search our online catalog for complete tables of contents of these separates and related publications.

You may also call 1-800-HAWORTH (outside US/Canada: 607-722-5857), or Fax 1-800-895-0582 (outside US/Canada: 607-771-0012), or e-mail at:

getinfo@haworthpressinc.com

Portraits in Cataloging and Classification: Theorists, Educators, and Practitioners of the Late Twentieth Century, edited by Carolynne Myall, MS, CAS, and Ruth C. Carter, PhD (Vol. 25, No. 2/3/4, 1998). *"This delightful tome introduces us to a side of our profession that we rarely see: the human beings behind the philosophy, rules, and interpretations that have guided our professional lives over the past half century. No collection on cataloging would be complete without a copy of this work." (Walter M. High, PhD, Automation Librarian, North Carolina Supreme Court Library; Assistant Law Librarian for Technical Services, North Carolina University, Chapel Hill)*

Cataloging and Classification: Trends, Transformations, Teaching, and Training, edited by James R. Shearer, MA, ALA, and Alan R. Thomas, MA, FLA (Vol. 24, No. 1/2, 1997). *"Offers a comprehensive retrospective and innovative projection for the future." (The Catholic Library Association)*

Electronic Resources: Selection and Bibliographic Control, edited by Ling-yuh W. (Miko) Pattie, MSLS, and Bonnie Jean Cox, MSLS (Vol. 22, No. 3/4, 1996). *"Recommended for any reader who is searching for a thorough, well-rounded, inclusive compendium on the subject." (The Journal of Academic Librarianship)*

Cataloging and Classification Standards and Rules, edited by John J. Reimer, MLS (Vol. 21, No. 3/4, 1996). *"Includes chapters by a number of experts on many of our best loved library standards. . . . Recommended to those who want to understand the history and development of our library standards and to understand the issues at play in the development of new standards." (LASIE)*

Classification: Options and Opportunities, edited by Alan R. Thomas, MA, FLA (Vol. 19, No. 3/4, 1995). *"There is much new and valuable insight to be found in all the chapters. . . . Timely in refreshing our confidence in the value of well-designed and applied classification in providing the best of service to the end-users." (Catalogue and Index)*

Cataloging Government Publications Online, edited by Carolyn C. Sherayko, MLS (Vol. 18, No. 3/4, 1994). *"Presents a wealth of detailed information in a clear and digestible form, and reveals many of the practicalities involved in getting government publications collections onto online cataloging systems." (The Law Librarian)*

Cooperative Cataloging: Past, Present and Future, edited by Barry B. Baker, MLS (Vol. 17, No. 3/4, 1994). *"The value of this collection lies in its historical perspective and analysis of past and present approaches to shared cataloging. . . . Recommended to library schools and large general collections needing materials on the history of library and information science." (Library Journal)*

Languages of the World: Cataloging Issues and Problems, edited by Martin D. Joachim (Vol. 17, No. 1/2, 1993). *"An excellent introduction to the problems libraries must face when cataloging materials not written in English. . . . should be read by every cataloger having to work with international materials, and it is recommended for all library schools. Nicely indexed." (Academic Library Book Review)*

Retrospective Conversion Now in Paperback: History, Approaches, Considerations, edited by Brian Schottlaender, MLS (Vol. 14, No. 3/4, 1992). *"Fascinating insight into the ways and means of converting and updating manual catalogs to machine-readable format." (Library Association Record)*

Enhancing Access to Information: Designing Catalogs for the 21st Century, edited by David A. Tyckoson (Vol. 13, No. 3/4, 1992). *"Its down-to-earth, nontechnical orientation should appeal to practitioners including administrators and public service librarians." (Library Resources & Technical Services)*

Describing Archival Materials: The Use of the MARC AMC Format, edited by Richard P. Smiraglia, MLS (Vol. 11, No. 3/4, 1991). *"A valuable introduction to the use of the MARC AMC format and the principles of archival cataloging itself." (Library Resources & Technical Services)*

Subject Control in Online Catalogs, edited by Robert P. Holley, PhD, MLS (Vol. 10, No. 1/2, 1990). *"The authors demonstrate the reasons underlying some of the problems and how solutions may be sought. . . . Also included are some fine research studies where the researchers have sought to test the interaction of users with the catalogue, as well as looking at use by library practitioners." (Library Association Record)*

Library of Congress Subject Headings: Philosophy, Practice, and Prospects, by William E. Studwell, MSLS (Supp. #2, 1990). *"Plays an important role in any debate on subject cataloging and succeeds in focusing the reader on the possibilities and problems of using Library of Congress Subject Headings and of subject cataloging in the future." (Australian Academic & Research Libraries)*

Authority Control in the Online Environment: Considerations and Practices, edited by Barbara B. Tillett, PhD (Vol. 9, No. 3, 1989). *"Marks an excellent addition to the field. . . . [It] is intended, as stated in the introduction, to 'offer background and inspiration for future thinking.' In achieving this goal, it has certainly succeeded." (Information Technology & Libraries)*

National and International Bibliographic Databases: Trends and Prospects, edited by Michael Carpenter, PhD, MBA, MLS (Vol. 8, No. 3/4, 1988). *"A fascinating work, containing much of concern both to the general cataloger and to the language or area specialist as well. It is also highly recommended reading for all those interested in bibliographic databases, their development, or their history." (Library Resources & Technical Services)*

Cataloging Sound Recordings: A Manual with Examples, by Deanne Holzberlein, PhD, MLS (Supp. #1, 1988). *"A valuable, easy to read working tool which should be part of the standard equipment of all catalogers who handle sound recordings." (ALR)*

Education and Training for Catalogers and Classifiers, edited by Ruth C. Carter, PhD (Vol. 7, No. 4, 1987). *"Recommended for all students and members of the profession who possess an interest in cataloging." (RQ-Reference and Adult Services Division)*

The United States Newspaper Program: Cataloging Aspects, edited by Ruth C. Carter, PhD (Vol. 6, No. 4, 1986). *"Required reading for all who use newspapers for research (historians and librarians in particular), newspaper cataloguers, administrators of newspaper collections, and–most important–those who control the preservation pursestrings." (Australian Academic & Research Libraries)*

Computer Software Cataloging: Techniques and Examples, edited by Deanne Holzberlein, PhD, MLS (Vol. 6, No. 2, 1986). *"Detailed explanations of each of the essential fields in a cataloging record. Will help any librarian who is grappling with the complicated responsibility of cataloging computer software." (Public Libraries)*

AACR2 and Serials: The American View, edited by Neal L. Edgar (Vol. 3, No. 2/3, 1983). *"This book will help any librarian or serials user concerned with the pitfalls and accomplishments of modern serials cataloging." (American Reference Books Annual)*

The Future of the Union Catalogue: Proceedings of the International Symposium on the Future of the Union Catalogue, edited by C. Donald Cook (Vol. 2, No. 1/2, 1982). *Experts explore the current concepts and future prospects of the union catalogue.*

Historical Aspects of Cataloging and Classification

Martin D. Joachim
Editor

Historical Aspects of Cataloging and Classification has been co-published simultaneously as *Cataloging & Classification Quarterly*, Volume 35, Numbers 1/2, 2002 and Volume 35, Numbers 3/4 2003.

The Haworth Information Press
An Imprint of
The Haworth Press, Inc.
New York • London • Oxford

Published by

The Haworth Information Press®, 10 Alice Street, Binghamton, NY 13904-1580 USA

The Haworth Information Press® is an imprint of The Haworth Press, Inc., 10 Alice Street, Binghamton, NY 13904-1580 USA.

Historical Aspects of Cataloging and Classification has been co-published simultaneously as *Cataloging & Classification Quarterly*, Volume 35, Numbers 1/2 2002 and Volume 35, Numbers 3/4 2003.

The development, preparation, and publication of this work has been undertaken with great care. However, the publisher, employees, editors, and agents of The Haworth Press and all imprints of The Haworth Press, Inc., including The Haworth Medical Press® and Pharmaceutical Products Press®, are not responsible for any errors contained herein or for consequences that may ensue from use of materials or information contained in this work. Opinions expressed by the author(s) are not necessarily those of The Haworth Press, Inc. With regard to case studies, identities and circumstances of individuals discussed herein have been changed to protect confidentiality. Any resemblance to actual persons, living or dead, is entirely coincidental.

Cover design by Jennifer Gaska.

Library of Congress Cataloging-in-Publication Data

Historical aspects of cataloging and classification / Martin D. Joachim, editor.
      p. cm.
    "Co-published simultaneously as Cataloging & classification quarterly, v. 35, nos. 1/2 2002 and v. 35, no. 3/4, 2003.
    ISBN 0-7890-1980-9 (hard : alk. paper)– ISBN 0-7890-1981-7 (pbk: alk. paper)
    1. Cataloging. 2. Classification–Books. I. Joachim, Martin D., 1938- II. Cataloging & classification quarterly.

Z693.H57 2003
025.3–dc21

                2002155233

Indexing, Abstracting & Website/Internet Coverage

This section provides you with a list of major indexing & abstracting services. That is to say, each service began covering this periodical during the year noted in the right column. Most Websites which are listed below have indicated that they will either post, disseminate, compile, archive, cite or alert their own Website users with research-based content from this work. (This list is as current as the copyright date of this publication.)

(continued)

*Special Bibliographic Notes related to special journal issues
(separates) and indexing/abstracting:*

- indexing/abstracting services in this list will also cover material in any "separate" that is co-published simultaneously with Haworth's special thematic journal issue or DocuSerial. Indexing/abstracting usually covers material at the article/chapter level.
- monographic co-editions are intended for either non-subscribers or libraries which intend to purchase a second copy for their circulating collections.
- monographic co-editions are reported to all jobbers/wholesalers/approval plans. The source journal is listed as the "series" to assist the prevention of duplicate purchasing in the same manner utilized for books-in-series.
- to facilitate user/access services all indexing/abstracting services are encouraged to utilize the co-indexing entry note indicated at the bottom of the first page of each article/chapter/contribution.
- this is intended to assist a library user of any reference tool (whether print, electronic, online, or CD-ROM) to locate the monographic version if the library has purchased this version but not a subscription to the source journal.
- individual articles/chapters in any Haworth publication are also available through the Haworth Document Delivery Service (HDDS).

For Professor Emeritus David Kaser,
who instilled in me a love for library history

Historical Aspects
of Cataloging and Classification

CONTENTS

ABOUT THE EDITOR

Martin D. Joachim, MA (classical languages and literatures), MA (library science), is Principal Cataloger at the Indiana University Libraries, where he was head of the cataloging department for eleven years. He has been active in the American Library Association and has chaired or served on various committees. He has also been involved in the Program for Cooperative Cataloging (PCC) and serves as a national trainer for NACO, the name authority component of the PCC. Mr. Joachim has managed three grant-funded cataloging projects. A member of the editorial board of *Cataloging & Classification Quarterly* since 1985, Mr. Joachim has published in various library, microform, and history journals and edited *Languages of the World: Cataloging Issues and Problems*, published by The Haworth Press, Inc. in 1993.

Introduction

Martin D. Joachim

This collection of essays considers the historical aspects of cataloging and classification throughout the world and throughout the centuries. This volume on historical topics includes articles from many countries that illustrate not only the differences but also the commonalities in their histories. In this volume there are twenty-seven articles by thirty-two authors from ten countries (Argentina, Australia, Botswana, China, Costa Rica, Germany, Iran, Japan, Mexico, and the United States) on six continents. Of the thirty-two authors, fifteen are practicing librarians, eleven are library educators, two are retired librarians, two are library school students, and two are non-librarians. They represent national, state, university, and special libraries. The articles have been divided into three categories: general works on cataloging rules, individual countries or regions, and special formats or topics.

The authors have written on a wide variety of topics from the general (for example, cataloging rules, classification schemes, Western influence on cataloging worldwide, issues dealing with specific formats of materials, the importance of providing access to unique materials, development of online systems, and histories of cataloging in many countries) to the specific (for example, Alaskan native languages and cultures, development of the law classification at the Library of Congress, book collectors of imperial Spain, and the cataloging of sexual materials). There is much fascinating and important information contained in these twenty-seven articles, and the reader will learn much from them.

The success of a volume such as this depends on many individuals in addition to those who have written articles. I have called upon fellow members of the Editorial Board of *Cataloging & Classification Quarterly* for advice and

[Haworth co-indexing entry note]: "Introduction." Joachim, Martin D. Co-published simultaneously in *Cataloging & Classification Quarterly* (The Haworth Information Press, an imprint of The Haworth Press, Inc.) Vol. 35, No. 1/2, 2002, pp. 1-2; and: *Historical Aspects of Cataloging and Classification* (ed: Martin D. Joachim) The Haworth Information Press, an imprint of The Haworth Press, Inc., 2003, pp. 1-2. Single or multiple copies of this article are available for a fee from The Haworth Document Delivery Service [1-800-HAWORTH, 9:00 a.m. - 5:00 p.m. (EST). E-mail address: getinfo@haworthpressinc.com].

suggestions in identifying potential authors from throughout the world. They were unhesitatingly kind and helpful. I wish to express my gratitude to Michael Carpenter (Louisiana State University), Ruth Carter (Editor-in-Chief of *Cataloging & Classification Quarterly*), Peter Haddad (National Library of Australia), Felipe Martínez-Arellano (National Autonomous University of Mexico), Monika Münnich (University of Heidelberg), John Riemer (UCLA), Richard Smiraglia (Long Island University), Elizabeth Steinhagen (University of New Mexico), and Dajin Sun (Yale University). Several of these colleagues have written articles for this volume. In addition I thank James Cole of Iowa State University and Rahmat Fattahi of Ferdowsi University (Mashhad, Iran) for their advice. And finally, I express my appreciation to the Indiana University Libraries in general and to two colleagues in particular: Mechael Charbonneau for her assistance with some of the articles in this volume from Spanish-speaking countries and to Steven Hendren for his guidance, patience, and good humor in helping me with the illustrations and graphics that accompany many of the articles.

GENERAL WORKS ON CATALOGING RULES

Forging the Anglo-American Cataloging Alliance: Descriptive Cataloging, 1830-1908

Virgil L. P. Blake

SUMMARY. This paper discusses the development of descriptive cataloging from 1830 to 1908 and focuses on the careers of Antonio Panizzi, Charles Coffin Jewett, and Charles Ammi Cutter and the development of the American Library Association (ALA) and the Library Association of the United Kingdom (LAUK). It analyzes the various rules and codes put forth by both Americans and British librarians and the eventual cooperation between the United States and the United Kingdom. *[Article copies available for a fee from The Haworth Document Delivery Service: 1-800-HAWORTH. E-mail address: <getinfo@haworthpressinc.com> Website: <http://www.HaworthPress.com> © 2002 by The Haworth Press, Inc. All rights reserved.]*

Dr. Virgil L. P. Blake, Professor at the Graduate School of Library and Information Studies, Queens College, CUNY, has taught cataloging for many years (E-mail: VirgilBF@cs.com).

This paper is dedicated to Dr. H. Gordon Stevenson.

[Haworth co-indexing entry note]: "Forging the Anglo-American Cataloging Alliance: Descriptive Cataloging, 1830-1908." Blake, Virgil L. P. Co-published simultaneously in *Cataloging & Classification Quarterly* (The Haworth Information Press, an imprint of The Haworth Press, Inc.) Vol. 35, No. 1/2, 2002, pp. 3-22; and: *Historical Aspects of Cataloging and Classification* (ed: Martin D. Joachim) The Haworth Information Press, an imprint of The Haworth Press, Inc., 2003, pp. 3-22. Single or multiple copies of this article are available for a fee from The Haworth Document Delivery Service [1-800-HAWORTH, 9:00 a.m. - 5:00 p.m. (EST). E-mail address: getinfo@haworthpressinc.com].

KEYWORDS. Antonio Panizzi, Charles Coffin Jewett, Charles Ammi Cutter, American Library Association, Library Association of the United Kingdom, descriptive cataloging, cooperative cataloging, cataloging rules

INTRODUCTION

For current (and many not so current) students of cataloging, the dominance of an international standard of cataloging rules is a given. However, in historical terms, this is a comparatively recent development. Librarians have been confronting the challenge of compiling a complete and accurate record of their holdings since 2000 B.C.[1] Our current situation owes its existence, primarily, to three individuals–Antonio Panizzi, Charles Coffin Jewett, and Charles Ammi Cutter. In this paper, the efforts of these three men and two fledgling professional societies, the American Library Association (ALA) and the Library Association of the United Kingdom (LAUK), in forging the Anglo-American cataloging alliance will be examined. The joint publication of the Anglo-American code of 1908 represents the conclusion of this first phase of the creation of an international code now under the aegis of the Joint Steering Committee for the Revision of AACR.

This paper limits itself to descriptive cataloging. What is of interest here are two problems: first, creating a bibliographic description of an item based on its physical characteristics according to some prescribed formula and, second, determining where the resulting description should be filed. In current parlance this is ascertaining both what the access points are and how they are to be recorded. Panizzi, Jewett, and Cutter would be familiar with these issues if they were defined as problems of entry and heading. What is not of concern here is subject cataloging. This is defined, for purposes of this paper, as determining subject headings to be appended to a bibliographic record based on its content and assigning a classification number to represent an item's primary topic.

BEGINNINGS

As Strout[2] indicates, catalogs up to the nineteenth century tended to be the works of individuals and varied widely in quality. As long as collections remained small and demands for the books in them remained modest, there was little pressure for very sophisticated catalogs. But if either of these factors changed and the need to retrieve books in a speedy fashion increased, there would be a crisis. And that is what developed at the British Museum.

The most recent catalog of the British Museum had been completed in 1819 under the direction of Sir Henry Ellis, Principal Librarian, and Rev. H. H. Baber, Keeper of the Department of Printed Books. It was a seven volume printed book catalog organized alphabetically by author. It had no subject index. To this had been added another twenty-two volumes of manuscript entries since 1820. There had been an attempt to create a classified catalog begun in 1826 by T. Hartwell Horne, but this had been abandoned. By the 1830s the British Museum was "a disorganized and random collection of books catalogued by indigent clergymen and other part-time drudges."[3] In the midst of all this, Antonio Panizzi, former Italian revolutionary and lawyer, was appointed as an extra assistant librarian in 1831.

In 1833 the impatient trustees of the British Museum ordered a new printed book catalog. Baber, who had succeeded Ellis as principal librarian, hoped that this could be done following the system that he and Ellis had devised for the 1813-1819 catalog but had no one supervising the project. He was also limited by the trustees' decision that the catalog be completed letter by letter and not shelf by shelf.

With little progress in the offing, the House of Commons, in 1836, appointed a select committee to investigate the British Museum, including the sad state of its catalog. Witnesses complained about the inability to find books. Others argued strongly for a classified catalog. Alphabetical catalogs were defended. "Surely such great interest in the minutiae of cataloging has never been displayed at any time by scholars, readers or government."[4] As a result, Baber appointed Panizzi Keeper of the Department of Printed Books in 1837. Panizzi inherited both the cataloging project and the impatience of the trustees.

Panizzi was an advocate of the alphabetical catalog. He was quickly asked to submit a report on the state of the catalog and a copy of the Ellis-Baber rules used in creating the 1819 book catalog. His response indicated that there had been little progress made since 1834 and that he could find no copy of the sixteen Ellis-Baber rules to share with them. He did agree, however, that a detailed set of rules governing the creation of the new catalog was required. But Panizzi was not going to be given much leeway in that regard. Mindful of the fallacies of the oral tradition, the trustees insisted that the rules by which the catalog was to be created be approved by them. Panizzi was given, however, permission "to draw up a complete set of rules for their consideration."[5]

The objective of this new set of rules was clear–"to standardize the format of the bibliographic records and to assure that enough detail was included to differentiate one record from another."[6] The ninety-one rules were devised by Panizzi and a committee of librarians including J. Winter Jones, Thomas Watts, Edward Edwards, and John Perry. Each of the members first considered the task as individuals. Then they met as a group and, where there were differences, the issue was settled by majority vote. Panizzi submitted a proposal of seventy-three rules, which the trustees expanded to ninety-one. The new code, "Rules for the Compilation of the Catalogue," was approved in 1839 and published in the first volume of the catalog itself in 1841.

Lehnus's[7] analysis of the ninety-one rules indicates that thirteen rules (XVIII-XXI) are devoted to description and thirteen rules (LIV-LXIX) focus on cross references. The subjects of sixty-one of the ninety-one rules are the twin problems of entry and heading. These ninety-one rules are based on three principles: (1) the data are derived from the item in hand, (2) the title page is the primary source of data, and (3) the title is to be transcribed exactly as it appears in the work. Virtually all aspects of personal author entry and heading are considered. Corporate bodies (with a number of exceptions) are entered under place but are not yet to be considered authors. There are a number of form headings–e.g., ACADEMIES, PERIODICALS, etc.–under which other types of publications are to be placed. The elements of description indicated are title (and edition when this is a part of that element), place, printer and date of publication. Panizzi advocated using the name as it appeared on the title page even for pseudonyms in those instances when the author's true identity was known. The apparent overemphasis on entry and heading is understandable since the "main concern of the 'Ninety One Rules' was the alphabetic arrangement of the printed book catalog of one library, in which related entries were grouped together under headings determined according to the principles enunciated in these rules."[8]

CROSSING THE ATLANTIC

Charles Coffin Jewett graduated from Brown University in 1835. He then attended Andover Theological Seminary and, while there, met Oliver A. Taylor, who was then preparing a catalog for the library there. Jewett became Taylor's assistant. The Andover Theological Seminary catalog was an alphabetical listing of the books in the collection to which, Ranz adds, Taylor intended to add a systematic index. "Certainly in America no previously published catalogue exhibited a comparable method and skill in discovering and listing the names of authors, the use of added entries and cross references, and in the accuracy and completeness of the bibliographic descriptions."[9] Jewett had been well educated by his participation in this project.

In 1841, as the ninety-one rules were being published, Jewett was appointed librarian and Professor of Modern Languages at Brown University. The library there had a collection of 10,000 volumes and was considered "one of the better collections in the country."[10] Nevertheless, this library had previously published only two catalogs: one in 1793 (2,173 volumes) and the second in 1826 (5,818 volumes). There was a need for a new catalog, and Jewett considered this to be his first responsibility.

The catalog of the Brown University Library was completed in 1843. Jewett "followed the plan of Mr. O. A. Taylor's Catalogue of the Theological Seminary of Andover."[11] Like Taylor's, this catalog consisted of an alphabetical "Descriptive Catalogue" and an alphabetical "Index of Subjects." In the preface to the catalog Jewett explained:

> In the Descriptive Catalog, the works are placed in alphabetical order under the names of authors, and the names themselves alphabetically arranged . . . anonymous works, of which I have been unable to ascertain the author, are placed under the most important word of the title, or subjects to which they relate.[12]

The index of subjects featured three types of entries: (1) under the most important word used in the title; (2) broad subjects, e.g., chemistry; and (3) specific subjects, e.g., photographs. "The index of subjects," Jewett said, "I have endeavored to arrange in such a manner as to answer the purpose of such an alphabetical index."[13]

This catalog represented an important advance for American cataloging since it was not a classified catalog, and Jewett was highly praised for this achievement. Shortly thereafter, Jewett was sent on a book-buying tour of Europe. He took full advantage of this opportunity and met both Panizzi and Edward Edwards and spent a considerable amount of time with them learning from two of those responsible for the ninety-one rules as much as he could. As Lehnus phrases it, "the first link in the chain that was discovered begins with Sir Anthony Panizzi of the British Museum. He knew personally Edward Edwards, who was also at the British Museum, and Charles Jewett, who, at the time of their meeting, was the librarian of Brown University in Providence, Rhode Island."[14] During this same period the role of a bequest to the United States was being debated.

James Smithson, upon his death in 1829, had willed his estate to his nephew, Henry James Hungerford. By the terms of Smithson's will, if his nephew should die childless, the remainder of his estate would go to the United States for the purpose of increasing and diffusing knowledge. Joseph Henry of the new Smithsonian Institution was given authority, in 1846, to appoint a librarian. Jewett was appointed to the position the following year. The seeds of conflict already existed. Henry felt that the Smithsonian should support research and publish the findings of the projects it funded. Jewett believed that the Smithsonian should assume the role of *de facto* national library and worked vigorously to bring about this end.

Jewett had two objectives in mind. At the Library Conference of 1853, he assured his audience "that the collection and publication of statistics of libraries, the increase and dissemination of bibliographic knowledge . . ."[15] would continue. But of far greater interest was his plan for a national union catalog through a system of stereotyping catalog entries first revealed in 1850. There were to be two printing plates. "The title of every book and of each distinct edition is stereotyped upon a separate plate. The author's name stands by itself."[16] The idea of separate stereotyping of individual entries would permit the creation of a general catalog with location symbols as well as the preparation of individual book catalogs for contributing public libraries. Either catalog forced him to confront the problem of rules, i.e., the formulation of the entries. Jewett outlined the Smithsonian Catalogue System thusly:

1. The Smithsonian Institution to publish rules for the preparation of catalogs.
2. Other institutions, intending to publish catalogs of their books, to be requested to prepare them in accordance with these rules, with a view to having them stereotyped under the direction of the Smithsonian Institute.[17]

In formulating these rules Jewett had two options. He could write an entirely new code for cataloging, or he could adapt one already in existence. Jewett opted for the second strategy. The rules, Jewett explained, "were formed after a careful study of those adopted for the preparation of the catalogue of the British Museum."[18]

Jewett, in his "On the Construction of Catalogs," created a code of thirty-nine rules, which were enhanced by exceptions and copious remarks. Neither of these features was found in Panizzi's ninety-one rules since that code was meant for the catalog of a single library. London points out that this code was better organized than Panizzi's and can "neatly be divided into four parts: I. Titles, i.e., bibliographic description (Rules I-XII); II. Headings (Rules XIII-XXIX); III. Cross References (Rules XXX-XXXI); IV. Arrangement (Rules XXXII-XXXIX)."[19]

Jewett did adopt some of the ninety-one rules verbatim. Rule IV (Early printed books without title pages . . .) is identical to Panizzi's Rule XX. In other cases, Jewett consolidated separate rules into one. Jewett's Rule XVIII (The following classes of persons . . .) combined Rules IV, V, VI and VIII of the ninety-one rules. Some basic features recur: (1) cataloging data is to be elicited from the item in hand; (2) the reliance upon the title page as the primary source of information; and (3) the exact transcription of the title. The elements of bibliographic description are still title (with the addition of what is now called the statement of responsibility), place of publication, publisher (as opposed to Panizzi's printer), date of publication, and, another new element, size of the volume. Unlike Panizzi's, Jewett's rules mandated that, if the author used a pseudonym and his identity was known, the work be filed under the author's real name. Title entries in Jewett's code were entered under the first word in the title, not the first important word. Nor was Jewett as willing to use form headings such as ACADEMIES or PERIODICALS. Jewett's Rule XXII placed publications of academies under their own names. Periodicals (Rule VII) were placed under title. Only sixteen of the thirty-nine rules were devoted to the primary concern of Panizzzi: entry and heading. While that reflects a better balance between the two activities in descriptive cataloging, far more interesting is the order in which Jewett placed the rules. Description precedes entry and headings in this code–something that would not recur until 1978.

But the grand design was never to be. Shortly after the conclusion of the 1853 conference, Jewett overplayed his hand by demanding that 50 percent of the Smithsonian's budget be allocated for the national library he had outlined. His zeal led to insubordination, and in January 1855 Jewett was relieved of his duties as librarian. This marked the end of Jewett's role in forging the Anglo-American alliance.

Later that same year Jewett accepted a position as a cataloger at the Boston Public Library. By 1858 he was director. In that year the *Index to the Catalogue of a Portion of the Public Library of the City of Boston Arranged in its Lower Hall* was published. Many of the features of his cataloging rules for the Smithsonian Institute were retained, but there were some significant changes. He adopted a single alphabetical strategy, incorporating in one listing author, title, and subject entries. He used full entries and included in the description place of publication, date, and size (as had been the case in his proposed rules) under the author entry. In the case of second authors, titles, and subject entries, the bibliographic data was not as complete; and the user was expected to go to the more complete author entry if more detail was needed. Jewett, once again, chose to enter works by authors using pseudonyms under their real names when that could be determined. In addition to the author entry, "each volume was also entered under a subject heading and again under the first prominent word in the title."[20] There was another distinguishing mark to this catalog and its 1861 supplement. "Cross references were liberally and intelligently used, the contents of multi-volume works were listed in detail; bibliographic notes accompanied many of the titles; and bibliographic essays were prepared in many subjects."[21] While this represented a significant achievement for Jewett, there was an unanticipated event that moved the developing Anglo-American cataloging alliance forward. During this same period Charles Ammi Cutter worked at the Boston Public Library and "catalogued under the eye of Charles Coffin Jewett, the most eminent cataloguer of his day whose cataloging ideas Cutter thoroughly learned, especially those concerning author and title entry."[22]

LAYING THE FOUNDATION

Charles Ammi Cutter graduated from Harvard College in 1855. He had to wait a year before entering the Divinity School from which he graduated in 1859. From 1857 through 1859 Cutter worked as a student in the library of the Divinity School, but he never became the Unitarian pastor that was his expected career. In 1860 he became assistant to Ezra Abbot, librarian and chief cataloger of the Harvard College Library. Abbot was, at that time, working on the creation of a new catalog for the library. Abbot's planning called for two catalogs: an index of authors and an index of subjects. Abbot had also concluded that every volume should have at least one subject entry and more if they were warranted. More interestingly, he felt that the subject entry/entries should be based on the book's content, not significant words in its title. Abbot rejected the idea of a single alphabetical listing of subjects on the grounds that this strategy dispersed related topics solely on the basis of a letter. On the other hand, Abbot concluded, a classified catalog was too difficult for most users. He took the middle ground and planned to use an alphabetical-classed arrangement for his index of subjects. Cutter was intensely involved in the completion of this catalog. In his "The New Catalogue of the Harvard College Library," Cutter indicated that this was going to be a card catalog rather than the usual printed book catalog. Part One was to be an alphabetical list by author indicating "nor merely books and pamphlets, but all important memoirs and transactions of learned societies and in periodicals."[23] Cutter added, "The need for a catalogue of subjects does not admit of a moments doubt."[24] This is territory into which neither Panizzi nor Jewett tread and is beyond our scope here. His experiences at Harvard and the process of creating this catalog "provided Cutter with an excellent apprenticeship in librarianship."[25] This is clearer when one recalls that Cutter spent this same period working under Jewett at the Boston Public Library.

In 1868 Cutter, based on his extensive background, was named librarian at the Boston Athenaeum. At that time this library, like the Boston Public Library, had 70,000 volumes and was the third largest library in the United States. It also had a major problem in the form of the state of its catalog. Cutter's predecessor, William A. Poole, had begun to develop a new catalog in

1856 "that was to resemble in its general features the catalogue of the Mercantile Library Association of Boston."[26] Poole's Mercantile Library catalog was a printed book catalog with entries organized in a single alphabetical listing for authors, titles, and subject words derived from the titles. The entries were brief, i.e., the titles were not transcribed exactly. Many of the elements of description–place of publication, publisher, publishing date, collation–were included, but Poole relied on a series of abbreviations to impart the information. While all the entries were interfiled, there were no cross references, no contents notes, and no analytics.

Poole's effort at the Boston Athenaeum fared no better really. Poole himself did not exercise close supervision of the undertaking. Completing the catalog was placed in the hands of inexperienced assistants. With little progress apparent by 1862, "full control of the work was transferred to Mr. Charles R. Lowell."[27] Lowell worked diligently until his untimely death in 1870. Cutter inherited the project (as Panizzi had earlier), and it "was not an enviable inheritance. The work passed on to him was in poor repair."[28] Cutter examined the work done to that date and was severely disappointed in its quality. Cutter conceded that he "had been engaged chiefly upon a catalogue constructed of an entirely different plan (that of Harvard College Library)."[29] Despite that, he undertook the task "with the intention of making as few changes as possible. . . ."[30] The catalog of the Library of the Boston Athenaeum was a five-volume work that appeared between 1874 and 1882. Cutter made one major change in it. Prominent words from the title as the basis for subject access to items in the collection were rejected in favor of true subject headings based on an item's content. There were 6,000 subject headings created as well as a system of cross references from general subjects to subordinate topics to which they were related. Other unique features were contents notes to indicate individual works within a collective volume and analytical entries to indicate portions of a book that might be of interest to the reader. These are features that Jewett had employed at the Boston Public Library. Cutter's catalog, Ranz notes, "was immediately recognized as an outstanding piece of work."[31] It also "assured the predominance of the dictionary arrangement in American catalogues for years to come."[32]

The experience of completing this catalog and his previous experiences with both Abbot and Jewett also solidified Cutter's thinking concerning catalogs and cataloging. This led to the publication of his *Rules for a Printed Dictionary Catalog* as Part II of the U.S. Bureau of Education "Special Report on Public Libraries" in 1876. There would be three more editions by 1904, and *Printed* would disappear from its title. This is where Cutter laid out "the first principles for cataloging."[33]

The *Rules for a Dictionary Catalog* grew from 205 (1876) to 368 (1904).[34] Of these 368 only twenty-seven (Rules 161 to 188) were concerned with subject entries. Included in this manual is Cutter's classic statement of the objects and means of cataloging and 115 definitions of terms (both unprecedented). A basic premise for the descriptive aspects of cataloging was that the "heading for a bibliographic unit will be the person or corporate body chiefly responsible for the intellectual content of the work."[35] Carpenter argues that by stating "bodies of men are considered as authors of works published in their name or by their authority,"[36] Cutter went beyond the bounds established by Panizzi and Jewett and created the concept of corporate authorship. Cutter's rules reverted to the major concern of Panizzi, entry and heading. Jewett's proposed code had considered description first and then entry and heading. Cutter's concentration on "Entry: Where to Enter" and "Style: How to Enter" is nearly total. In the Cutter rules, entry is the topic of rules 1 through 160, and headings ("STYLE") is the subject of rules 197 through 351. Three hundred fourteen (92 percent) of the 341 rules not subject-related are taken up by these two concerns. Description for Cutter was an afterthought as it had been for Panizzi. Cutter, like Jewett, would enter both pseudonymous and anonymous works under the authors' real names if they could be determined. By the time Cutter published his rules, the form headings used by Panizzi, severely eroded by Jewett, disappeared entirely. Like Jewett, Cutter entered anonymous works whose authors could not be determined under the first word in the title not an article.

Cutter's rules were highly acclaimed upon their publication and have since become a vital part of descriptive cataloging. Hufford notes that it "was the last published code published by one man."[37] Maxwell also comments: "Influential though they were, Cutter's Rules did not win universal acceptance as a code for the construction of catalogs either in the United States or Great Britain."[38] Nor did the *Rules for a Dictionary Catalog* ever receive the imprimatur of the new professional associations emerging in both the United States or Great Britain.

FIRST STEPS TOWARD AN ALLIANCE

The year 1876 saw the birth of the profession of librarianship in America. Both Cutter's *Rules* and the first edition of the Dewey Decimal Classification appeared. *Library Journal* began publishing. Shortly after the Centennial Exposition closed, 103 librarians met in Philadelphia for the second national conference. From this platform the American Library Association was launched.

A major concern of the 1876 conference was the revival of Jewett's concept of cooperative cataloging. Led by the two major systematizers on the scene–Melvill Dewey and Charles Cutter–the new American Library Association created the Committee on Co-operative Indexing with the objective of recommending a uniform approach to cataloging. In January 1877 the committee published a proposed set of rules for comment and discussion. The hope was that the process would result in a set of cataloging rules endorsed by the association that would then be used by the leading libraries in the United States. It was not to be.

In March 1878 the Committee on Uniform Titles published its "Condensed Rules for Cataloging." The proposed code was derived from Jewett and featured first "the elements of bibliographic description: title, edition, imprint, collation and notes."[39] Only after these issues were resolved did the proposed set of rules consider "choice and form of entry."[40] This proposed code was closely tied to Cutter's *Rules*. Following the individual rules in this proposed set were annotations indicating the analogous rules in Cutter by rule number. The Committee asked for comments and surveyed "several dozen librarians and the next meeting of the full Committee on Co-operative Cataloging at the Boston Conference of 1879 approved it as published."[41] At that point, progress toward a uniform code of cataloging halted pending the results of similar efforts in Great Britain.

In 1877 British librarians met in a conference that ultimately led to the formation of their professional association: the Library Association of the United Kingdom. A delegation of sixteen prominent American librarians, including Charles Ammi Cutter, attended. As had been the case in Philadelphia the year before, cataloging was a major concern of these librarians. The third session of the conference "was devoted to seven papers in bibliography and cataloging."[42] In responding to these papers, Cutter endorsed both the card catalog and the dictionary arrangement of author-title-subject entries. Justin Winsor discussed the methods in use at the Boston Public Library to create an author-subject-title catalog for the main library and all of its branches. Poole extolled the glories of the catalog of the Chicago Public Library while Lloyd Smith discussed the general catalog of the Library Company of Philadelphia.

The fourth session of the conference featured four more papers on cataloging. These papers discussed: (1) catchword subject entries for American books, (2) cooperative cataloging, (3) a proposal for an international union catalog, and (4) creation of a general catalog of English literature. In sum, approximately one third of all the papers delivered at this conference concerned cataloging, bibliography, and subject cataloging (subject headings). Like their American counterparts, these British librarians were also very much interested in the concept of cooperative cataloging. The prerequisite for this was a common cataloging code–a task that was then undertaken.

The results of the British efforts were two editions of *Cataloging Rules of the Library Association of the United Kingdom* (LAUK), one in 1881, the second in 1883. Both versions followed the Jewett model–i.e., description preceded the twin issues of entry and heading. The 1881 edition consisted of forty-nine rules divided into six sections:

> 1. Title; 2. Volumes, Size, Place, Dates, etc.; 3. Language of Title and Imprint; 4. Contents and Notes; 5. Headings, Books are to be entered . . . (This is by far the longest section, it comprises rules 10-33); and 6. Miscellaneous.[43]

The 1883 edition was a little more compact: forty-eight rules in four sections with minor changes.[44]

Having seen what their British compatriots were up to, the Cooperation Committee of ALA resumed its efforts. In 1882 this committee resolved "to revise the American rules and bring them into harmony with the new LAUK rules and the 'Compendious Rules' of the Bodleian Library . . ."[45] In 1883 it published, in *Library Journal*, the "Condensed Rules for an Author Title Catalog." This code was not a detailed set of rules but only "the outlines of cataloging."[46] The "Condensed Rules" reverted to the structure employed by Panizzi and Cutter. The sequence in this proposed code was Entry (Rules 1a through 1z), Headings (2a through 2e), Titles (3a through 3z), Imprints (4a through 4h), Contents, Notes (5a), Miscellaneous (6a through 6f), and Arrangement (7a through 7h). Thirty-one of the sixty-seven rules were devoted to entry and heading. This emphasis is reminiscent of that of both Panizzi and Cutter. The 1883 proposed code retained the title page as the primary source of information and the exact transcription of the title. The elements of description were familiar–edition, place of publication, year of publication, collation (volumes/pages), and size. This proposed code closely adheres to the Jewett-Cutter model by applying the real names of authors to pseudonymous works if the authors were known. It is ironic that, while the committee's intentions were to be more closely aligned to their British colleagues, the "Condensed Code for an Author Title Catalog" was inverse in its structure to the LAUK codes of 1881 and 1883.

The "Condensed Rules" was not expected to be used by itself since it was not "detailed enough to provide a universal American Standard for cataloging. This code, as a result, simply joined Cutter's Rules and the English Codes as a source of advice and support for individual cataloguers."[47]

In 1886 Dewey expanded upon the 1883 ALA code. Two years later this enhanced code was published as "Rules for Author and Classed Catalogs as Used in the Columbia College Library." This became better known as the "Library School Card Catalog Rules." Poole, chair of the ALA Cooperation Committee, suggested at the 1889 conference "accepting Dewey's revised code prepared for the Columbia College Library except as it differed from the previous recommendations of the ALA."[48] Unfortunately, he linked this to a proposal to change the approach for corporate bodies. As a result, the committee was unable to resolve that issue, and the idea of melding the 1883 "Condensed Rules" and Dewey's "Library School Rules" was shunted aside.

There was yet another factor coming into play here. Klas Linderfelt, then of the Milwaukee Public Library, had set out to translate J. Dziatzko's *Instruction für die Ordnung der Titel in alphabetischen Zettelkatalog der Königlichen und Universitäts-Bibliothek zu Breslau* (1886). He came to the conclusion, however, that "a mere translation would be of little service."[49] Consequently, Linderfelt retained Dziatzko's original structure but added rules adapted from Cutter, the Bodleian Library, the British Museum, Jewett, the ALA and LAUK rules and Dewey's "Library School Rules." The result was "a digest of the accepted practices of the art and mystery of cataloging."[50] It was published in 1890 by Cutter under the title *The Eclectic Card Catalog Rules.* There were two parts to this code. Part I was concerned with author and title entries and references; and part II discussed transliteration, spelling foreign names, and related issues. What was novel about it was that Linderfelt organized it in a non-traditional fashion. The cataloger was to look at the item in hand and characterize it as single personal author, multiple author, collection, etc.; and, once it was categorized, the cataloger would be led to the appropriate rule for the situation revealed by the analysis of the item. It was similar to a programmed learning tool in vogue much later. This code was regarded as something very interesting, even helpful, but it made no real impact on the state of American cataloging.

As the nineteenth century was coming to a close, there had been significant gains in the state of the catalog since Panizzi's ninety-one rules. But one goal–the use of a uniform code by all libraries–was elusive. The degree to which this was the case was illustrated by a survey of 191 libraries conducted by W. C. Lane of the Boston Athenaeum in 1893. There were some interesting differences in the types of catalogs in these libraries. Lane's respondents indicated that "six had only an author catalog, fifteen an author and title only, eighty-nine a dictionary catalog, eight separate author and subject catalogs, fifty-seven author and classed catalogs, and five libraries only a classed catalog."[51] More interesting were the catalog rules used in these libraries. Lane found "eighty-five used Cutter's rules with or without modification, thirty-six

Dewey's Library School Rules, ten these two in combination, nine ALA rules, three Linderfelt's Eclectic Rules, two Jewett's Rules for the Smithsonian Institution, and thirty-nine made no report or said they followed no system."[52] Clearly much more needed to be done to meet the goal of cooperative cataloging espoused by Cutter and Dewey at Philadelphia in 1876.

A COMPACT AT LAST

In 1900 the idea of cooperative cataloging was resurrected, but any substantial progress in that regard was dependent upon having a national code that all libraries would use. The Lane survey had shown that there was no consensus on cataloging in the United States. The idea of forming "a bureau for cooperative cataloging and the printing of cards"[53] surfaced. At the Montreal conference of 1900, a new Catalog Rules Committee was established to "consider the cataloging rules in force, particularly those points on which American libraries have been unable to agree."[54] In December, ALA's Publishing Board appointed an advisory committee on Cataloging Rules. ALA was determined, it seemed, to attain its long-sought goal.

ALA never had to print cards for libraries. There was an agreement reached with the Library of Congress (LC) that committed that library to making printed cataloging cards available to American libraries beginning in 1901. LC itself had approved its own code for printed cards in 1898. This created a slight difficulty since there were some differences between the 1898 LC code and the 1883 ALA code. While ALA was willing to accept the LC cards in order to get the distribution of them to libraries, some accommodation was going to have to be made as the Catalog Rules Committee moved toward the completion of a new code that would replace the 1883 rules. In 1901 the committee decided that the new code would be designed to fit the needs of larger more scholarly libraries. There were specific discussions concerning typography and form of entry. It was also decided that "the variations on the part of the Library of Congress rules would be specified in notes."[55] In July 1901 the ALA Executive Board finally authorized the publication of ALA catalog rules for printed cards.

The Advisory Committee on Cataloging Rules met in March 1902. The objective was to "bring about uniformity between its revision of the ALA rules, the 4th edition of Cutter's *Rules for a Dictionary Catalog*, then to be issued, and a new edition of the Library School rules. . . ."[56] The committee quickly came to an agreement on all remaining outstanding issues. The committee's report was delivered to the ALA conference. After a long acrimonious debate the committee received approval for a draft that was printed by the Library of Congress as *A.L.A. Rules, Advance Edition.*

These proposed code rules were quite close to those adopted by LC in 1898, and the Library of Congress "accepted them about in toto. . . ."[57] The *A.L.A. Rules, Advance Edition* was regarded as a "preliminary report of the Committee, they (the rules) are still open to criticism and amendment."[58] The proposed code, it was reported, met Cutter's criteria of being for the public, not for catalogers themselves.

The eighty-one rules made some minor changes in the order of the elements of description. The title, as it appeared on the title page, was followed by edition, if it was present, place, publisher, date, and then collation. It opted to use the fullest form of an author's name and the author's real name for pseudonymous works when that could be determined. Kroger, a member of the committee, did indicate that "the small library need not elaborate the details of paging, illustrations etc."[59] and conceded that "a public library must find it more convenient to enter authors who write under pseudonyms under the pseudonym . . . ."[60] The most sweeping change noted by Kroeger was the treatment of books with multiple authors. In the era of printed book catalogs and handwritten card catalogs, the most complete entry was always found under the first author with briefer entries placed under the names of subsequent authors. The adoption of printed cards from LC permitted full entries under each of the authors since all copies of the card would be identical. The printed rules of the 1902 advance edition were issued to each subscribing library either in pamphlet or card form. In 1903 the Library of Congress added rules on collation and series notes. Throughout 1903 and 1904 cataloguers submitted comments and criticisms of the draft. By the end of 1904 "the materials for the new revision were sufficiently advanced to warrant the hope that a first edition might go to press in the course of the winter."[61]

British librarians were also actively considering the status of the LAUK rules that had been in place since 1883. At its 1902 meeting the Library Association of the United Kingdom was considering reprinting/revising the 1883 code. Jast argued that "the rules do not adequately answer to the practice and needs of today."[62] To support his contention, Jast indicated that the place of publication and edition, both mandated in the 1883 code, ought to "be regarded as optional."[63] He also pointed out that Cutter had stated that cataloging was based on principles but that he had failed to indicate what these were. Jast added that "if cataloging is a science, it must be reducible to principles, and if we can bring these out in our new code, arranging particular rules under wider rules from which they naturally flow, we shall have their mastery comparatively easy, and laid the foundation of an intelligent–the only intelligent–method of teaching cataloging."[64]

The LAUK began its revision process following that 1902 meeting. Shortly after that conference, Dewey contacted Jast and suggested that the two professional associations combine their efforts and work toward a common cataloging code. In the meantime Jast had written to H. Putnam at the Library of Congress to secure a copy of the 1902 ALA rules as the basis for the revision project then underway. The British Committee on Cataloging Rules did not see major differences between their thinking and the ALA draft code and recommended that the goal of a joint code be pursued.

At its September 1904 conference the LAUK officially accepted Dewey's proposal and sent Jast to the ALA conference in St. Louis to present the draft of the proposed code then being considered by the LAUK. The draft and the proposal for a joint code were accepted by ALA, and the Executive Council was authorized to see the project through. Specific responsibility was placed in the hands of the Catalog Rules Committee.

In 1905 the ALA Catalog Rules Committee met and accepted twenty-nine of the fifty-four rules in the proposed British code. A report of this action was then sent to the committee's British counterpart. Both the American and British committees continued their efforts throughout 1906. At its meeting the American committee's differences were narrowed to the point that plans for printing were under active consideration. Now that there was general agreement among themselves, the American committee sent a report to the Secretary of the Catalog Rules Revision Committee of the LAUK outlining its discussions and agreements. At its meeting that year the British committee was "of the opinion that the draft codes (English and American) have reached such a stage of agreement as to warrant printing as soon as possible, and we have been authorized by the Library Association to proceed with and conclude such further negotiations as may be necessary."[65] The British committee suggested that there be "two editions (English and American) but that the editions should as far as possible be identical in arrangement and wording, and where a divergence of opinion between the two committees exists with respect to a particular rule, such difference of opinion should be explained either in a note appended to the rule in question or by printing the two rules side by side showing which is which."[66]

The American committee then agreed to present its draft code to the Library Association at its annual conference in May 1907. This draft was adopted, and the committee was instructed to negotiate further "in order to harmonize any differences as to details still existing·between the British and American Committees. . . ."[67] J. C. M. Hanson, chair of the ALA committee, was sent to meet with British librarians in September, and "the two committees came to full agreement on all but 8 of the 174 rules."[68] The differences were minute and included the form of entry for a married woman author, the translations of foreign works, issues arising from changing names, title changes for periodicals, and similar very specific questions.[69] Then the Executive Council of ALA authorized the printing and publication of the joint code.

The result of this effort, *Catalog Rules: Author and Title Entries*, was very much in the Panizzi-Cutter mold. It was limited to author and title entries. Subjects were excluded from its scope. Like Cutter's rules, this code had fifty-eight definitions (pages xiii-xvi) before the main body of rules. The basic structure was very much in the Panizzi/Cutter tradition with entry and heading being resolved first. Personal authors were discussed first (rules 1 through 57), then corporate bodies (rules 58 through 111), title entries (rules 112 through 129), and finally miscellaneous (rules 130 through 135). Only then was the problem of description addressed (rules 136 through 166). The order of the elements of description was, by now, quite familiar: title, edition, place, publisher, date, collation, and series. References were treated next (rules 167 through 171) and, finally, capitals, punctuation and figures (rules 172 through 174). Like Panizzi's and Cutter's rules, the problems of entry and headings dominate this code, accounting for 135 of the 174 rules. Both Panizzi and Cutter would have been very comfortable with this result, Jewett less so.

EPILOGUE

Sixty-nine years after Panizzi's ninety-one rules, the Anglo-American cataloging alliance had been forged. Over the course of the next two decades, neither professional association took active steps to maintain the currency of the 1908 code. In the interim the Library of Congress found it necessary to make a number of "revisions, clarifications, and additions. . . ."[70] In 1930 the ALA Committee on Cataloging and Classification "suggested the advisability of a revision of the 1908 rules. . . ."[71] The dissolution of the alliance had begun.

REFERENCES

1. Ruth French Strout, "The Development of the Catalog and Cataloging Codes," *Library Quarterly* 26, no. 4 (October 1956): 255.

2. Ibid.

3. Michael Gorman, "Let Us Now Praise . . . ," *American Libraries* 11, no. 4 (April 1980): 201.

4. Strout: 268.

5. Nancy Brault, *The Debate on Panizzi's Rules in 1841-1849: The Issues Discussed* (Los Angeles: School of Library Service and the University Library, University of California, Los Angeles, 1972), 3.

6. Jon R. Hufford, "The Pragmatic Basis of Catalog Codes: Has the User Been Ignored?" *Cataloging & Classification Quarterly* 14, no. 1 (1991): 28.

7. Donald J. Lehnus, *A Comparison of Panizzi's 91 Rules and the AACR of 1967*, Occasional Paper, no. 105 (Champaign, Ill.: University of Illinois, Graduate School of Library Service, 1972).

8. Gertrude London, "The Place and Role of Bibliographic Description in General and Individual Catalogues: A Historical Analysis," *Libri* 30, no. 4 (October 1980): 256.

9. Jim Ranz, *The Printed Book Catalog in American Libraries: 1723-1900* (Chicago: American Library Association, 1964), 28.

10. Michael H. Harris, ed., *The Age of Jewett: Charles Coffin Jewett and American Librarianship, 1841-1868* (Littleton, Col.: Libraries Unlimited, 1975), 11.

11. Ibid., p. 28.

12. Ibid., p. 60.

13. Ibid., p. 61.

14. Donald J. Lehnus, *Milestones in Cataloging* (Littleton, Col.: Libraries Unlimited, 1974), 30.

15. George Utley, *The Librarians Conference of 1853* (Chicago: American Library Association, 1951), 57.

16. Charles Coffin Jewett, "The Smithsonian Catalogue System," in *The Librarians Conference of 1853,* 147.

17. Ibid.

18. Utley, 68.

19. London, 259.

20. Joseph A. Barome, *Charles Coffin Jewett* (Chicago: American Library Association, 1951), 116.

21. Ranz, 68.

22. Francis L. Miksa, ed., *Charles Ammi Cutter: Library Systematizer* (Littleton, Col.: Libraries Unlimited, 1977), 49.

23. Ibid., "The New Catalogue of Harvard College Library," 154.

24. Ibid., 156.

25. Francis L. Miksa, "Cutter, Charles Ammi (1831-1903)," in *Dictionary of American Library Biography,* ed. Bohdan Wynar (Littleton, Col.: Libraries Unlimited, 1978), 110.

26. Charles Ammi Cutter, "Librarian's Report on the Best Method of Copying Mr. Lowell's Catalog," in Miksa, ed. *Charles Ammi Cutter,* 172.

27. Ibid.

28. Ranz, 73.

29. Cutter, "Librarian's Report," 173.

30. Ibid.

31. Ranz, 75.

32. Ibid.

33. Charles Ammi Cutter, *Rules for a Dictionary Catalog,* 4th ed. (Washington: Government Printing Office, 1904), 3.

34. Margaret F. Maxwell, "The Genesis of the Anglo-American Cataloging Rules," *Libri* 27, no. 3 (1977): 239.

35. Ibid.

36. Michael Carpenter, *Corporate Authorship: Its Role in Library Cataloging* (Westport, Conn: Greenwood Press, 1981), 13.

37. Hufford, 31.

38. Maxwell, 239.

39. London, 266.

40. Ibid.

41. "Proceedings of the Boston Conference," *Library Journal* 4 (July/August, 1879): 299. As cited in Terry M. Heisey, "Early Catalogue Code Development in the United States, 1876-1908," *Journal of Library History* XI, no. 3 (July 1976): 218-248.

42. Budd Gambee, "The Great Junket: American Participation in the Conference of Librarians, London, 1877," *Journal of Library History* 2, no. 1 (January 1967): 28.

43. London, 267.

44. Ibid.

45. Heisey, 220.

46. Ibid.

47. Ibid.

48. Ibid., 221.

49. W.C. Lane, "Review of Eclectic Card Catalog Rules by Klas Linderfelt," *Library Journal* 16, no. 5 (May 1891): 148.

50. Ibid.

51. Heisey, 223.

52. Ibid.

53. Ibid., 226.

54. Paul S. Dunkin, *Cataloging USA.* (Chicago: American Library Association, 1969), 9.

55. *Cataloging Rules: Author and Title Entries,* compiled by Committees of the American Library Association and the (British) Library Association (Chicago: American Library Association, 1908), v.

56. Ibid., vi.

57. Alice B. Kroeger, "Cataloging and the New A.L.A. Rules," *Public Libraries* 8, no. 1 (January 1903), 20.

58. "Review of *A.L.A. Rules, Advance Edition*," *Library Journal* 27, no. 10 (October 1902): 904.

59. Kroeger, 20.

60. Ibid., 21.

61. *Cataloging Rules: Author and Title Entries,* vi.

62. L. Stanley Jast, "The Library Association Cataloging Rules," *The Library Association Record* IV, no. 2 (December 1902): 571.

63. Ibid., 580.

64. Ibid., 581.

65. *Cataloging Rules: Author and Title Entries,* vii.

66. Ibid.

67. Ibid., viii.

68. Kathryn Luther Henderson, "Treated With A Degree of Uniformity and 'Common Sense': Descriptive Cataloging in the United States, 1876-1975," *Library Trends* 25, no. 1 (July 1976): 231.

69. "Review of 'Catalog Rules: Author and Title Entries,' compiled by committees of the American Library Association and the (British) Library Association," *Library Journal* 33, no. 2 (December 1908): 524.

70. Wyllis E. Wright, "The Anglo-American Cataloging Rules: A Historical Perspective," *Library Resources and Technical Service* 20, no. 1 (Winter 1976): 36.

71. Ibid.

ADDITIONAL REFERENCES

"Condensed Rules for an Author and Title Catalogue," prepared by the Cooperation Committee, ALA. *Library Journal* 8, no. 9/10 (September/October 1883): 251-254.

Harris, Michael H. "Jewett, Charles Coffin (1816-1868)." In *Dictionary of American Library Biography,* edited by Bohdan S. Wynar. Littleton, Col.: Libraries Unlimited, 1978: 271-274.

Jewett, Charles Coffin. "On the Construction of Catalogues." In *The Age of Jewett: Charles Coffin Jewett and American Librarianship, 1841-1868*, edited by Michael H. Harris. Littleton, Col: Libraries Unlimited, 1975: 131-155.

McCrimmon, Barbara. "Whose Ninety-One Rules? A Revisionist View." *Journal of Library History* 18, no. 2 (Spring 1983): 163-177.

"Rules for the Compilation of the Catalogue." In *Foundations of Cataloging: A Source Book*, edited by Michael Carpenter and Elaine Svenonius. Littleton, Colorado: Libraries Unlimited, 1985: 3-14.

The Original 73 Rules of the British Museum:
A Preliminary Analysis

Michael Carpenter

SUMMARY. The well-known 91 rules of the 1841 British Museum catalog, adopted in July 1839, had an ancestor in a draft of 73 rules from
March 1839, a document that might be called the original rules of
Antonio Panizzi. The code, finally sanctioned by the British Museum
Trustees, has some substantial differences from the original draft, differences that seem to foreshadow later discussion on cataloging rules. In
this preliminary analysis, some of these differences are described. Additionally, the origin of the rules is discussed. *[Article copies available for a
fee from The Haworth Document Delivery Service: 1-800-HAWORTH. E-mail
address: <getinfo@haworthpressinc.com> Website: <http://www.HaworthPress.com>
© 2002 by The Haworth Press, Inc. All rights reserved.]*

KEYWORDS. Cataloging rules, Anthony Panizzi, British Museum
rules, British Museum, Department of Printed Books, Catalogue of
printed books in the British Museum

Michael Carpenter, MLS, MBA, PhD, is Associate Professor, School of Library
and Information Science, Louisiana State University, Baton Rouge, LA 70803-3920
(E-mail: LSCARP@LSU.EDU).

The author wishes to thank the Louisiana State University Council on Research for
funding some of the research for this paper. He also wishes to thank Mr. P. R. Harris of
the British Library not only for help in finding the document that is the subject of this
paper, but also for his valuable comments.

[Haworth co-indexing entry note]: "The Original 73 Rules of the British Museum: A Preliminary Analysis." Carpenter, Michael. Co-published simultaneously in *Cataloging & Classification Quarterly* (The
Haworth Information Press, an imprint of The Haworth Press, Inc.) Vol. 35, No. 1/2, 2002, pp. 23-36; and:
Historical Aspects of Cataloging and Classification (ed: Martin D. Joachim) The Haworth Information Press,
an imprint of The Haworth Press, Inc., 2003, pp. 23-36. Single or multiple copies of this article are available
for a fee from The Haworth Document Delivery Service [1-800-HAWORTH, 9:00 a.m. - 5:00 p.m. (EST).
E-mail address: getinfo@haworthpressinc.com].

On June 15, 1849, just weeks short of ten years after the Trustees of the British Museum had finally finished their revisions of cataloging rules composed by Antonio Panizzi (1797-1879), William Richard Hamilton (1777-1859), one of the members of the subcommittee responsible for the revisions, was testifying as a witness before members of the Commissioners Appointed to Inquire into the Constitution and Government of the British Museum. As chairman of the commission, Francis Egerton, the Earl of Ellesmere (1801-1857), asked Hamilton if he were aware of the differences between the system found in the 91 rules for the entry of anonymous works and that originally desired by Panizzi in the original set of rules. After saying that he could not [!] discern any true differences of opinion, Hamilton went on to say:

> ... I should beg leave to say once for all, that I have thought that the Library Committee or the Committee discussing the mode of making the catalogue, did a great deal more harm than good, and that it would have been much better for the Institution and the public if it had never interfered with the catalogue, and if Mr. Panizzi had been allowed to follow up the original suggestions made by himself and Mr. Baber, without interference on the part of the Trustees, except that they should have understood and sanctioned the general principles upon which he was proceeding; and for this reason, that Mr. Panizzi must naturally understand the subject much better than any, or all of the Committee.

Lord John Wrottesley, another of the commission members, then asked, "You would have left, therefore, almost the whole matter in the discretion of Mr. Panizzi?" Answer: "Yes; he was a professional man, and we were only amateurs."[1]

What were the original rules that the so-called amateurs modified? The only extant published source, specifically Panizzi's testimony to the commission of July 13, 1848, describes a set of 73 rules, a set of rules that previous writers on the origins on the 91 rules never found.[2] These 73 rules, printed without date, and titled *Alphabetical Catalogue of Printed Books. Rules to Be Observed in Preparing and Entering Titles*, were mislaid through having been incorrectly marked in the archives of the British Library's Department of Printed Books, until Mr. P. R. Harris, a then-retired Deputy Keeper of the Department of Printed Books, found them for the present writer on July 4, 1988. The document in hand, marked "2 copies of a revise AP" in Panizzi's handwriting, is twenty-eight pages long, of which the rules constitute the first eight pages; it is printed on extra-wide paper to facilitate the writing of revisions. An intermediate printing, containing 79 rules and some of the revisions of the Trustees, is yet to be found. Additionally, a marked-up copy handed in by Panizzi during his testimony has not been located.[3]

Following the first eight pages, which contain the text of the 73 rules, are 284 numbered examples on pages 9 though 17, plus a sample catalog article on Horace containing examples numbered 285-604, on pages 18 through 28. Some, but not all, of the entries from the first series of 284 examples are identified in the left margins of the rules so as to provide examples for them.

The rules themselves are printed in both italics and in Roman letters. The rules in italics, with one important exception relating to the cataloging of anonymously published works, contain the text of a set of sixteen rules (slightly modified in the case of Baber's rule XIII), originally drafted by the Rev. Henry Hervey Baber (1775-1869); these rules will be called the Baber rules in what follows. Baber, Panizzi's predecessor as the officer in charge of the Department of Printed Books (he had resigned from the Museum in 1837), had prepared these rules in an unnumbered version in 1834 and presented them in a report to the Trustees on April 26, 1834.[4] These rules were then numbered and written out in three fair copies on blue paper; only in December 1838 would they be committed to print.[5] A copy of the Baber rules is readily available in a 1954 essay by Frank Francis.[6]

Baber's rules deal with formation of headings for authors' names, the transcription of what we would today call the bibliographical description portion of the entry, the problems of dealing with anonymously and pseudonymously published works, and the editorship of works "which embrace the collected productions of various writers upon particular subjects." Baber's rules do not deal with references nor the publications of corporate bodies, while the instruction for foreign names seems to assume that publishing conventions respecting prefixes are stable in other countries.

The provision in Baber's rules that most bothered Panizzi was Baber's rule 13: "In the case of *anonymous works*, some prominent or leading word in the title to be selected as the heading to be prefixed to the title. If the author's name should be known, or conjectured, by the librarian, the same to be inserted at the end of the title, and included in brackets." The problem, as Panizzi realized, was the ambiguity in "some prominent or leading word." To resolve the matter and provide for certainty, he suggested following the procedure for entering anonymous works that Giovanni Battista Audiffredi (1714-1794) had used in his unfinished catalog of the Biblioteca Casanatense in Rome, namely choosing the first word not an article or preposition as the entry.[7] Of course, Audiffredi's procedure entails that the reader know the title he is seeking. Panizzi first communicated his suggestion to the catalogers verbally and hints at what he had done in a letter, transmitting a copy of Baber's rules to Josiah Forshall (1795-1863), the Secretary of the Trustees, on December 5, 1838.[8] Panizzi says:

> My opinion was that, for consistency's sake, the first word in the title (except an article or preposition) ought to be taken as the leading one under which to place anonymous publications. Mr. Baber and Mr. Cary differing from me on this point, my opinion was overruled; but I have very lately requested Mr. Garnett to prefer the first word for the principal entry for such works, giving, however, as many cross references as he may deem requisite from any other entry he thinks proper to make, by which means the rule originally adopted will not be materially departed from.[9]

When the standing committee looked at the matter on December 15, 1838, it requested Forshall to obtain Panizzi's written rule. At the same meeting, the committee members also caused Baber's rules to be printed with Panizzi's signature under date of December 18 [*sic*], 1838.[10] After a lengthy contest of wills with Forshall, in which Panizzi said that he was not about to sign the rules, and Forshall said that Panizzi should, Panizzi asked Richard Garnett (the elder, 1789-1850) on December 24 to verify what Panizzi had asked him to do, namely "whenever the least doubt might exist as to which might be deemed the leading word, it would be desirable to prefer the first word in the title, except an article or a preposition, giving as many cross-references as you might deem necessary from any of the leading words which might be taken to be the leading ones."[11] Garnett agreed.[12]

Because the trustees had dealt with the proposed rule for anonymous works in the January 5, 1839, meeting of the Sub-committee on the Department of Printed Books, Panizzi wrote again on January 10, suggesting, in slightly differently worded form, the adoption of his rule for cataloging anonymously published works. Sir Henry Ellis (1777-1869), the Principal Librarian (1828-1856), noted on Panizzi's memorandum that Panizzi's new rule was different from the procedures he had adopted in the Museum's so-called octavo catalog.[13] In their meeting of January 19, 1839, the trustees deliberated on Panizzi's draft and amended it to read as follows: "Whenever no heading word can be fixed upon in the title, the first word in the title except it be an article or preposition may be taken, and the work entered alphabetically under it, adding however as many cross references, as may be considered necessary from any other part."[14] This writer was unable to find a version of Baber's rules as thus amended by the Trustees; however, a copy of the rules as printed up with Panizzi's falsely ascribed signature dated December 18, 1836, does have a handwritten addition of the amended rule just quoted.[15] In fact, the italicized portion of the 73 rules containing the text of Baber's rules includes the new amendment, in italics, in its rule XXXIV.[16]

HOW THE RULES WERE COMPOSED

Four accounts of the composition of the rules by participants are extant, namely two by Panizzi and one each by Parry and Edwards.[17] Although it is the source of a romantic story about the composition of rules around sandwiches and glasses of Burgundy as the light of the day grew dim, Edwards' account should be set aside because Edwards had been fired at Panizzi's instigation in 1850; and by the time of the 1870 publication of his account, some thirty years had already passed. On the other hand, ten years had elapsed since the composition of the rules by the time Panizzi and Parry gave their accounts.

What is surprising is the timing; as it turns out, Panizzi composed the whole set of rules, and the committee of four—namely, Edward Edwards, John Winter Jones, John Humffreys Parry, and Thomas Watts that Parry and Edwards both identify—worked not on the draft rules themselves but on the revision of those draft rules to satisfy the Trustees committee.[18] In reply to a memorandum by Ellis, Panizzi wrote up a reply, consuming fifty-seven folio pages of manuscript, titled "Observations on the Report of Sir H. Ellis, Dated November 14, 1846," and signed by Panizzi on January 7, 1847.[19] In it Panizzi points out that on March 8, he requested the Trustees to allow him to draw up a set of rules (what turned out to be the draft of 73 rules) and submit them for the Trustees' approval; the Trustees approved the idea on March 9. Only nine days later, Panizzi presented the draft at the March 18, 1839, meeting.[20] Given that it took time to print the draft, the timing is amazing. Perhaps Panizzi already had something in hand; the available documents do not let us know. Did the committee members help Panizzi compose the original draft? Parry says the committee first met in March.[21] In referring to the 73 rules in his testimony, Panizzi says, "I was not able to prepare the whole at first."[22] Later in his answer to the same question, Panizzi also states that after the rules were printed in March, he "gave a copy to every gentleman in the house who understood the business, and who had the goodness to assist me, to have the advantage of their suggestions before submitting the rules to the Trustees." Panizzi then gives the names of several Museum employees who were not in the committee of four as having given him assistance. In question 4121, Panizzi has the following to say, and it is important in view of the timing:

> When we drew up these rules, easy as they may seem, my assistants and myself worked all the day long for weeks; we never went out of the Li-

brary from morning till night; sometimes we took a chop in my apartment, and worked the whole day and at night too, and on Sundays besides, to submit the rules from time to time, and with the utmost dispatch, *to the Sub-Committee of Trustees, altered as they ordered.* [Emphasis added]

The committee of four was working to deal with the Trustees' revisions, not compiling the original rules. Parry's statement is consistent with this; Parry says that the committee composed of catalogers and Panizzi met from March through July, the same time the Trustees were altering the rules.[23] Panizzi must have composed the 73 rules himself.

FEATURES OF THE RULES

To see what the Trustees' revision left out, and thereby clarify important differences between the 73 and the 91 rules, we should examine some of the 73 rules that have no counterpart in the 91 rules. Rule IX of the 73 reads:

Assemblies or corporate bodies (with the exception of Academies, Universities and Learned Societies, respecting which special rules are to be framed), to be considered as the authors of any act, vote, resolution, or other document purporting to be agreed upon, authorized or issued by them, no attention whatever being paid to the names of the officers who may have put their signature to such document.

As is well known, corporate bodies are not considered as authors in the 91 rules. Rule IX was changed into something resembling the form it had in the 91 rules during the first subcommittee meeting dealing with the 73 rules, March 20, 1839.[24] The examples listed for rule IX have the following headings:

ASSEMBLEE NATIONALE *Constituante, de France.*
COMMON COUNCIL [*of the City of London*].
COMMONS, *House of.*
     and
CONSEJO REAL [*of Castile*]

That these headings are for subordinate bodies is clear and, yet, completely unlike the pattern found in the 91 rules; and, aside from many Italian cataloging codes, in the majority of post-British Museum cataloging codes, the intent is for direct entry of subdivisions. In fact, the examples given in the Appendix for the version of the 91 rules found therein seem to provide for a major heading (the country), followed by the subordinate heading.

The use of geographical headings, of course, reaches its full-blown extent in the Academies section of the 91 rules in rule 80, where the primary division is the "four parts of the world" subdivided by independent governments alphabetically arranged and finally by the name of the cities within each government's jurisdiction alphabetically arranged. The origins of this seemingly bizarre arrangement seem to be completely independent of the 73 rules.

In the first of the British Museum catalogs, published in 1787, it would appear that the heading ACADEMIÆ is used only as a catchword for some anonymous works; only five items are listed under the heading, and none of them are the proceedings or transactions of an academy.[25] On the other hand, the entries for various societies under SOCIETY are organized by date of first publication of a particular society's publications, with subsequent publications of that society being listed chronologically immediately after the first publication of that society; this procedure means that one must know the beginning date of the society's first publication to find all the publications of the society. However, not all is lost; there is only one column's worth of society listings in the 1787 catalog.[26] Although the octavo catalog of 1813-1819 contains a greater number of society publications than the 1787 catalog, the procedure followed is much the same.

The catalog of a large portion of the British Museum collection published closest in time to the rules controversy is the catalog for the King's Library, a catalog of the books collected by George III and presented to the British nation by George IV.[27] Although complied shortly prior to the gift, this catalog is clearly influential in the development of the future British Museum catalog. In the King's Library catalog, although the academies heading is ACADEMIÆ et SOCIETATES, there is another heading, SOCIETY, which has a "see also" (*v. etiam*) reference to ACADEMIÆ et SOCIETATES. Although the SOCIETY heading uses an indiscernible ordering scheme, it does not follow the geographical arrangement in the major portion of the Academies section. Materials under the heading ACADEMIÆ et SOCIETATES occupy pages 6 through 31 of the King's Library catalog; the heading ACADEMICI et ACCADEMICI contains fifteen items on page 31; and, finally, the heading ACADEMICO et ACCADEMICO holds another fifteen items on page 31 and 32. Of these three headings, only ACADEMIÆ et SOCIETATES is arranged geographically. After two highly general works, there are several pages under the subheading MAGNÆ BRITANNIÆ ET HIBERNIÆ ANGLIÆ including the Royal Society's publications and, somewhat strangely, the Board of Agriculture's publications. The place names are listed in Latin, even though the preface to the catalog is in English.

The King's Library catalog does not use "periodicals" or "laws" as form headings, but it does use arbitrarily selected words as entry points for anonymously published works. Given the strange mixture of practices in the King's Library catalog, one should best conclude that the great divisions, such as Academies, Ephemerides, and Encyclopædias were in the process of development, possibly as result of pressure from influential members of the library's reading public to have some sort of classified catalog. If this conjecture has validity, one could easily see why Panizzi deferred the creation of rules to deal with "academies" in his 73-rule draft.

One provision found in the 73 rules that persisted into the 91 rules, but does not appear to have been a part of British Museum cataloging practice prior to the promulgation of the 91 rules, is the prohibition against double entry. Rule XLIX of the 73 rules provides: "No work ever to be entered twice at full length. Wherever requisite, cross-references to be introduced." Rule 54 of the 91 rules is identical. However, in the King's Library catalog, one can find several double entries of the sort just prohibited, the first being under the general heading "ACADEMIÆ et SOCIETATES" and the second being under the heading for the author.

With respect to bibliographical description, Rule XX of the 73 rules reads: "If it be found unnecessary to transcribe the title at full length, and the omissions extend to more than a few insignificant words, dots to be substituted to indicate the omission, more particularly in old and rare volumes, in which however, abridgments should be seldom resorted to." The examples listed include entries for three books with omissions marked; their imprint dates are 1624, 1791 (with its supplement of 1805), and a multi-volume work of 1734-1742. The entries for two books with lengthy titles and no marks of omissions in their catalog entries are dated 1531 and 1555. Rule XX was deleted at a meeting of the standing committee on June 29, 1839; however, one of its examples persisted through the first printing of the 91 rules and was explicitly deleted by members of the standing committee during a "cursory" examination of the rules on July 6, 1839.[28] One can speculate that the Trustees were trying to be consistent with the provision first found in the 1833 version of their Statute for the governance of the Museum to the effect that each keeper was to maintain a "full and accurate" catalog for the materials in his care.

HOW THE REVISION OCCURRED

At the time of the drafting of the 73 rules, and throughout the whole controversy resulting from the attempt to complete the 1841 catalog, the British Museum had an unusual managerial arrangement. A forty-eight-member Board of

Trustees consisting of three different classes of members had the ultimate responsibility for the affairs of the Museum; the three classes were official, the family, and the elected members. The twenty-three official trustees at the time consisted of various officers of the government and the Church of England, plus the presidents of the Royal Society, the College of Physicians, the Society of Antiquaries, and the Royal Academy. The nine family trustees consisted of representatives or heirs of some large donors to the Museum. The official and family members of the board chose the fifteen elected trustees. Finally, there was a Royal Trustee. Since a forty-eight-member board is unwieldy, the trustees, at their beginning in 1755, had selected fifteen of their number to be a standing committee; since membership in the standing committee was open, there were no further elections to the standing committee, and any member who showed up was part of the standing committee when it met.[29] It would appear from the records of attendance at trustees meetings that any three were competent to conduct business.[30] Of course, there were other committees such as those on the Department of Printed Books and on the Catalogue.

When summoned for a meeting, individual trustees had no idea as to the nature of the agenda because the Secretary, Josiah Forshall (Secretary, 1828-1850), did not include such information in the summons. In fact, Forshall was the only person who set the agenda for the trustees. Furthermore, the officers of the Museum, such as the Keepers of the various collections, had to transmit their questions not only through the Principal Librarian (essentially the director of the Museum), Sir Henry Ellis, but also through Forshall. Similarly, the trustees had to communicate through Forshall; as can readily be seen, Forshall had become the most powerful person in the institution.[31] Nor was this all; aside from the office of Principal Librarian, appointed by the Crown on the nomination of the Principal Trustees, virtually all employment within the Museum was within the gift of one of the three Principal Trustees (members of the Official Trustees), usually the Archbishop of Canterbury.[32] For this reason, an officer such as Panizzi had very little control over who would be working for him. And, finally, according to Harris, Forshall was subject to mental illness; in the latter part of the 1840s, Forshall had to stay off work for extended periods.[33] During the late 1830s, through his incorrect transcription of minutes from the trustees meetings, along with critical omissions, Forshall caused Panizzi to carry out courses of action with respect to the catalog that were clearly disastrous.

Given this background, it would be interesting to examine the attendance of the various trustees at the meetings when the revision of the 73 rules was underway. Since the ninth, and last, meeting was devoted solely to the acceptance of the 91 rules, only eight meetings were required for consideration of the rules. According to Panizzi's undated loose note, only one member of the group of trustees who had been appointed to revise the rules was present for the vote on final acceptance.[34] As can be seen from Table 1, no one individual was present at all the meetings that dealt with revision of the rules. By far the two most consistent trustees were Henry Hallam (1777-1859), a historian and an elected trustee (1837-1859), and William Richard Hamilton (also 1777-1859), a diplomat, former secretary to Lord Elgin and an elected trustee (1838-1858); each attended seven times. Hallam and Hamilton also attended the two-person meeting with Panizzi on April 24, 1839. The only other person to come anywhere near the attendance records of Hallam and Hamilton was Sir Robert Harry Inglis, Baronet (1786-1855), an elected trustee (1834-1855), an opponent of Catholic emancipation, a dedicated Tory, and an opponent of Panizzi in the 1847-1849 hearings. Because the meeting minutes, as printed in the Appendix, unfortunately do not disclose reasons for particular decisions, only the decisions themselves, it is hard to determine the reasoning of the trustees who participated in the rule revision.[35] Furthermore, those trustees who did testify during the 1847-1849 hearings did not disclose their reasoning about the rules.

As noted above, during the revision by the committees of the trustees, Panizzi and several catalogers were arriving at texts for the rules suitable for the trustees, performing an editorial function, as it were. The product that emerged from the revision is reprinted on pages 185 through 218 of the Appendix, and, like the 73 rules, is titled *Alphabetical Catalogue of Printed Books: Rules to Be Observed in Preparing and Entering Titles.*[36] The 91 rules themselves occupy the left-hand column of the page, while examples illustrating each rule are to be found in the right column. Thus printed, the rules extend through to page 197. Some of the examples present in the 73 rules are to be found in the text but now have a different appearance and often different headings, thanks to the rule revisions made by the Trustees. Following the rules is a new collection of entries for the Roman poet Horace on pages 198 through 218; this printing has little resemblance to the version found in the 73 rules. References from the secondary literature on Horace are now provided in the latter part of the article. The references at the head of the article are much fuller than used with the 73 rules. In the 73 rules, one is simply directed from Horace's heading (HORATIUS (QUINTUS FLACCUS)) to a collection of other authors identified by surname only, while in the 91 rules under Horace (now HORATIUS *Flaccus* (QUINTUS)), the references have surnames, abbreviated forenames, abbreviated titles, dates, size, but no pressmarks.[37]

TABLE 1. Trustee Participation in the Revision of the 73 Rules, 1839

Trustee Names	20-Mar Committee P/B	6-Apr Committee P/B	13-Apr Committee P/B	20-Apr Committee P/B	24-Apr Committee partial P/B	8-Jun Committee Standing	29-Jun Committee Standing	6-Jul Committee Standing	13-Jul General Meeting	Meetings Attended
Ashburton						x	x		x	3
Cadogan						x		x	x	3
Canterbury (Abp. of)									x	1
Cawdor			x	x		x	x			4
Halford			x			x				2
Hallam	x		x	x	x	x	x			7
Hamilton (Duke)							x		x	2
Hamilton (W. R.)	x	x	x		x	x	x	x		7
Harrowby			x			x	x	x		4
Inglis		x	x	x		x	x	x		6
London (Bishop of)			x				x	x		3
Northampton			x	x						2
Northumberland						x	x	x		3
Rutland									x	1
Shee				x				x		2
Stanley	x	x					x			3
Towneley			x	x		x	x		x	5
In Attendance	3	4	9	7	2	10	9	7	7	

P/B stands for the Sub-committee on Printed Books; the partial meeting of April 24 had too few members to conduct business. Aside from the church officials, the individual trustees are identified either by title or surname.

CONCLUSION

What did the revision accomplish? Clearly the 73 rules show some haste in being assembled. For example, the reference structure reflects older, more useless practice. The dropping of the marks of omission in the description is curious; perhaps the reasoning was to make the cataloger use the words of the original title more carefully than he might have otherwise; perhaps it was to satisfy the need for a "full and accurate" catalog, a requirement found for the first time in the 1833 Statute enacted by the Trustees for the Museum. The rules finally adopted for anonymous works were bound to cause trouble and, in the end, probably had the effect of helping to cause the abandonment of the British Museum catalog in its traditional form; the rules had become quite baroque through time. The Academies heading would not be dismantled until the early 1930s; and, even then, most, if not all, corporate bodies would be listed under the names of the places in which they were located following the successor provisions to rule 9 of the 91 rules.[38] In short, the revisions had made the catalog not an author catalog but a sort of name catalog with strongly classified elements. Not only was rule revision swift in 1839, but the amateurs wound up making a catalog quite different from the one originally envisioned in the 73 rules.[39]

REFERENCES

1. Great Britain. Commissioners Appointed to Inquire into the Constitution and Government of the British Museum, *Report of the Commissioners Appointed to Inquire into the Constitution and Government of the British Museum, with Minutes of Evidence, Presented to both House of Parliament by Command of Her Majesty.* Reports from Commissioners, 1850, v. 5. House of Commons Session (1850), v. 24. [Command paper] 1170. (London: printed by Williams Clowes and Sons for Her Majesty's Stationery Office, 1850). (Reprint: Irish University Press Series of British Parliamentary Papers. Education. British Museum, 3. Shannon, Ireland: Irish University Press, 1969), p. 774 (questions 10468 and 10469). The hearings in this document took place between July 10, 1847, and June 26, 1849. This report will hereafter be cited as: 1850 report. Because the 10933 questions are all numbered, particular locations of testimony will be identified by question.

2. 1850 report, questions, 4117-4124. The most important of the secondary sources is: A. H. Chaplin. *GK: 150 Years of the General Catalogue of Printed Books in the British Museum.* Aldershot, England: Scolar Press, 1987 (hereafter referred to as Chaplin), while the main "reference work" for the history of the library, the Department of Printed Books of the British Museum (since 1973, the British Library), is: P. R. Harris. *A History of the British Museum Library, 1753-1973* (London: The British Library, 1998), hereafter referred to as Harris. Unattributed factual information in this paper generally relies on Harris, *passim.*

3. Panizzi testimony, 1850 report, question 4117.

4. Great Britain. Commissioners Appointed to Inquire into the Constitution and Government of British Museum, *Appendix to the Report of the Commissioners Appointed to Inquire into the Constitution and Management of the British Museum* (London: printed by W. Clowes and Sons for Her Majesty's Stationery Office, [n.d., probably 1850], p. 102-103.) Hereafter cited as: Appendix. This document was issued in anywhere between 12 to 100 copies, depending on reports. The document contains 482 pages, of which "A Return of All Reports Made to the Trustees, Relative to the Catalogue of Printed Books, &c." occupies pages 97 through 358. The Appendix has no index or table of contents. This writer is aware of only two original copies of the Appendix, one in the British Library and the other in the Houghton Library at Harvard University.

5. Appendix, p. 167.

6. F. C. Francis, "A Reconsideration of the British Museum Rules for Compiling the Catalogues of the Printed Books–I," in *Cataloguing Principles and Practice: An Inquiry. Lectures Delivered at a Vacation Course of the University of London School of Librarianship and Archives in March 1953,* ed. Mary Piggott (London: Library Association, 1954). CLW Reprint Series, 3. Reprint ([S.l.] published for the College of Librarianship Wales by University Microfilms, 1970), pp. 26-49; the rules are reprinted on 32-33.

7. Giovanni Battista Audiffredi, *Bibliothecae Casanatensis catalogus librorum typis impressorum: Sanctissimo Domino Nostro Clementi XIII. dicatus . . .* (Romae: Excudebant Joachim, [et] Joannes Josephus Salvioni fratres, 1761-1788) 5 v. in 4 (Vol. 5 incomplete and without title page). A substantial discussion of the bases in Audiffredi for Panizzi's preference for using the first word not an article or preposition as the entry for an anonymously published work, as expressed in the 1850 report, can be found in Margherita Palumbo, "L'innovazione catalografica di Giovanni Battista Audiffredi," *Il bibliotecario* n. 15 (marzo 1988): 91-123.

8. Appendix, pp. 165-166.

9. Ibid., 166.

10. Ibid., 166-168.

11. Ibid., 171.

12. Garnett to Panizzi, December 24, 1838, loc. cit.

13. British Museum. Department of Printed Books. *Librorum impressorum qui in Museo britannico adservantur catalogus.* Sir Henry Ellis and H. H. Baber, eds. 7 v. in 8 Londini, 1813-1819.

14. Appendix, p. 173.

15. MS note on folio 96 (verso) DH 1/1, Department of Printed Books, British Library Archives.

16. Rule numbers in Baber's draft and in the 73 rule draft are identified by Roman numerals, while, for the 91 rules, they are identified by Arabic numerals.

17. Panizzi: 1850 report, questions 4097-4124, esp. 4117 (testimony of July 13, 1848), and Appendix, pp. 302-303 (from Panizzi, "Observations on the Report of Sir H. Ellis, dated November 14, 1846," January 7, 1847); Parry, 1850 report, questions 7311-7342 (testimony of March 9, 1849); and, Edward Edwards, *Lives of the Founders of the British Museum, with Notices of its Chief Augmentors and Other Benefactors, 1570-1870* (London: Treubner and Co., 1870) (reprint: New York: Burt Franklin, 1969), pp. 567-569.

18. Parry testimony, March 9, 1849, 1850 report, question 7311 and 7317.

19. Appendix, pp. 298-334.

20. Appendix, pp. 302-303.

21. Parry testimony, March 9, 1849, 1850 report, question 7317.

22. Panizzi testimony, July 13, 1848, 1850 report, question 4117.

23. Parry testimony, March 9, 1849, 1850 report, question 7317.

24. Rule 9, as finally adopted by the Trustees, reads: "Any act, resolution, or other document purporting to be agreed upon, authorized, or issued by assemblies, boards or corporate bodies, (with the exception of academies, universities, learned societies, and religious orders, respecting which special rules are to be followed), to be entered in distinct alphabetical series, under the name of the country or place from they acquire their denomination, or, for want of such documentation, under the name of the place whence their acts are issued." Although multiple sources exist for printings of the 91 rules, this quotation is taken from Appendix, p. 186.

25. British Museum. Department of Printed Books. *Librorum impressorum qui in Museo Britannico adservantur catalogus*, 2 unpaged volumes (Londini, 1787), columns ABR and ACC.

26. Ibid., v. 2, columns SOC and SOD.

27. British Museum. Department of Printed Books. King's Library. *Bibliothecæ regiæ catalogus* 5 volumes (Londini: excudebant Gul. Bulmer et Gul. Nicol, 1820-1829). Hereafter referred to as King's Library catalog.

28. Without having seen the 73 rules, Chaplin (p. 13) correctly surmised that rule XX had to do with omissions from lengthy titles.

29. "Report" [of the Commissioners] in 1850 report, pp. 1-44 (first sequence of pagination); the pertinent discussion is on pp. 3-8.

30. Appendix, pp. 5-49.

31. "Report," 1850 report, p. 8 (in the first sequence of pages).

32. 1850 report, Sir Henry Ellis testimony, question 181: "As regards the rest of the officers [except the Principal Librarian], down to the porter at the gate, they are appointed by the Archbishop of Canterbury, the Lord Chancellor, the Speaker of the House of Commons, or any two of them." As can be found in the British Library archives (series DH1, Panizzi's official papers), the Archbishop of Canterbury used blank forms that had already been signed by one of the other Principal Trustees.

33. Harris, pp. 159, 167, 170, 175.

34. British Library Archives. Official papers of Sir A. Panizzi: Royal Commission of 1848.9: Committee on Free Libraries. [Letterbox of unbound papers].

35. Appendix, pp. 219-227, *passim.*

36. The title of the rules at the head of the 1841 catalog is *Rules for the Compilation of the Catalogue.*; these rules also include italicized additions to the "original" 91 rules, printed in 1839.

37. A British Museum pressmark is what is known as a call number in the United States; bookcases are often called presses in England.

38. Chaplin, p. 116.

39. The writer hopes to present a publication of the text of the 73 rules and a further study of its origins and influence in the near future.

Principle Issues:
Catalog Paradigms, Old and New

Elisabeth de Rijk Spanhoff

SUMMARY. Recent attempts to assess the adequacy of AACR as a descriptive cataloging code for the online environment have focused attention on cataloging principles. This paper looks at some old and new attempts to isolate the fundamental principles underlying AACR. It considers catalog objectives, principles, and rules and looks at how these relate to one another. It analyzes the relationship of these principles and rules to the final product, the library catalog, pointing out differences (in this regard) between catalogs that are paper-based and those that are electronic. Finally, it comments on the present effort of the Joint Steering Committee for Revision of AACR to formulate a statement of principles to be included in a new introduction to AACR. *[Article copies available for a fee from The Haworth Document Delivery Service: 1-800-HAWORTH. E-mail address: <getinfo@haworthpressinc.com> Website: <http://www.HaworthPress.com> © 2002 by The Haworth Press, Inc. All rights reserved.]*

KEYWORDS. Cataloging rules, cataloging aims and objectives, cataloging main entry, Joint Steering Committee for Revision of AACR, International Conference on Cataloging Principles, Paris Principles, International Conference on the Principles and Future Development of AACR, Anglo-American cataloging rules evaluation

Elisabeth de Rijk Spanhoff is Coordinator of Technical Services, State Library of Louisiana (E-mail: espanhof@pelican.state.lib.la.us).

[Haworth co-indexing entry note]: "Principle Issues: Catalog Paradigms, Old and New." Spanhoff, Elisabeth de Rijk. Co-published simultaneously in *Cataloging & Classification Quarterly* (The Haworth Information Press, an imprint of The Haworth Press, Inc.) Vol. 35, No. 1/2, 2002, pp. 37-59; and: *Historical Aspects of Cataloging and Classification* (ed: Martin D. Joachim) The Haworth Information Press, an imprint of The Haworth Press, Inc., 2003, pp. 37-59. Single or multiple copies of this article are available for a fee from The Haworth Document Delivery Service [1-800-HAWORTH, 9:00 a.m. - 5:00 p.m. (EST). E-mail address: getinfo@haworthpressinc.com].

INTRODUCTION

I would like to consider the question, "What are the principles of AACR2?" This question has become the focus of a current project of the Joint Steering Committee for Revision of AACR. A discussion paper was submitted to the committee by Barbara Tillett, which formulates a statement of principles for a new introduction to AACR2. I would also like to comment on her discussion paper.

Catalogers show a tendency to return to first principles whenever they are seriously challenged. They revisit the intellectual foundations of cataloging, examine the structure and functions of the catalog, and ask whether it is still doing what it is supposed to do. In the late 1930s when LC cataloging arrearages and decline in production resulted in a "crisis in cataloging," and Hanson began to question the wisdom of author entry practices, Julia Pettee responded with her now classic article on the authorship principle in the Anglo-American cataloging tradition.[1] In the subsequent decades of code revision that culminated in the creation of the first AACR, Lubetzky examined the theoretical foundations of cataloging practice, and the International Conference on Cataloguing Principles issued its *Statement of Principles (Paris Principles)*, based in part on Lubetzky's theoretical work. Challenges of the 1980s included the "political and economic drive toward cooperation," the rise of library automation systems, and the conversion of paper to electronic files. The Conference on the Conceptual Foundations of Descriptive Cataloging convened at UCLA in 1987 to "discuss the impact of these forces on code development."[2]

Since the mid-1990s the greatest threat to cataloging has been the growth of the Internet, with its resources that are so much richer than the surrogates in most library catalogs and that resist traditional bibliographic control, its sophisticated search engines that compete with library catalog interfaces, and its ease of use and ready availability that lead searchers to consult it before the library catalog and draw people away from the library. Responses to these challenges have included the ALCTS Preconference, AACR2000, Chicago, 1995; the International Conference on the Principles and Future Development of AACR, Toronto, 1997; the Bicentennial Conference on Bibliographic Control for the New Millennium: Confronting the Challenges of Networked Resources and the Web, Washington, D.C., 2000; and, most recently, the OCLC Symposium, Reconceptualizing Cataloging, at ALA Midwinter, New Orleans, 2002.

What are the conceptual foundations of cataloging and where do principles fit in? It is generally agreed that questions about "the purposes of the catalog and the means to achieve these" are questions about the foundations of cataloging.[3] The purposes of the catalog, at least in the Anglo-American tradition, have been identified with the catalog objectives ("objects") first stated by Charles A. Cutter in 1876 and later adapted by the International Conference on Cataloguing Principles in 1961. Also referred to as the finding and gathering functions, they appear in the Paris Principles as follows:

> PP 2: The catalogue should be an efficient instrument for ascertaining
> 2.1 whether the library contains a particular book specified by
> (a) its author and title, or
> (b) if the author is not named in the book, its title alone, or
> (c) if the author and title are inappropriate or insufficient for identification, a suitable substitute for the title; and
>
> 2.2 (a) which works by a particular author and
> (b) which editions of a particular work are in the library.[4]

Cataloging principles express the means whereby the purposes of the catalog can be achieved. To use Lubetzky's words, they are "general directives whereby the objectives of cataloging can best be served."[5] Together, the objectives and principles underlie the cataloging code, and constitute its conceptual, or intellectual, foundation.

Are the intellectual foundations of cataloging fixed for all time or were they perhaps "built to justify the limits of old technologies," as Wilson speculated?[6] Should we then be willing to alter them as conditions change? The response from the library community is ambiguous. A common observation is that ". . . some of the present cataloguing principles and rules are inadequate, less relevant, or irrelevant to the new electronic environment."[7] Yet at the same time, a recent conference devoted to examining these principles concluded that "the present explicit principles [of AACR2] are satisfactory, with the caveat that there is a need to change some terminology."[8] Few would argue against the need for periodic rule revision, yet there is a certain reluctance to admit that we should alter the principles upon which the rules are built. Gorman and Oddy recently identified four principles underlying AACR2 and added:

> These principles are as valid today and for the foreseeable future as they were when AACR2 was created. Any revision of AACR2 must recognize the centrality of these principles and will, therefore, be something that is different from AACR2 in degree rather than kind.[9]

Speculating on the direction code revision might take, Tillett wrote, ". . . I would also add an introductory section giving basic principles and guiding concepts upon which we have built library catalogs and will continue to build bibliographic systems."[10] Malinconico conceded that principles might be subject to change, but flatly denied technology's ability to drive that change. "[T]echnological advances have not had, and cannot have, any influence on the principles on which bibliographic control is based."[11]

USES OF "PRINCIPLE"

It is hard to know what to make of these sorts of claims, since the expression "cataloging principle" has been used to mean a number of different things. For early theorists, the authorship principle, expressed in the collective rules for main entry, was considered the basic principle underlying the code. It enabled catalog users to find wanted items and to see assembled all works of given authors under single forms of names used to represent them in the catalog. Thus it answered both the finding and gathering functions of the catalog. At least, that is how it was designed to work in a linear, fixed-display catalog. Traditional principles, such as this one, were tied closely to the form of the catalog and the arrangement of its entries. By way of accentuating their intimate connection to the structure and form of the catalog, Lubetzky would sometimes refer to authorship as the "method" and main entry as the "means" of achieving catalog objectives.[12] He preferred this to calling them "principles." In this he echoes Cutter, who also lists "author-entry with the necessary references" under "means" of meeting the catalog "objects" in his *Rules for a Dictionary Catalogue.*[13]

Principles have also included more general statements, such as Cutter's principle of convenience: "The convenience of the public is always to be set before the ease of the cataloger."[14] In AACR we find the "principle of integration," which calls for using the same general rules to describe all kinds of materials collected by libraries, regardless of media (rule 0.1). Another example is AACR's rule 0.24, which stated in part (before it was revised in 2001), that " . . . the starting point for description is the physical form of the item in hand. . . ." These general directives are similar in character to principles recently proposed by Svenonius, such as her "principle of representation," which says that "descriptions should be based on the way an information entity describes itself," or the "principle of standardization," which states that "descriptions should be standardized, to the extent and level possible."[15] These and others like them are general principles for the design of bibliographic systems with only tenuous, if any, connection to catalogs of a particular structure. One could hardly describe them as "means" or "methods" for achieving catalog objectives.

The *Statement of Principles* drafted by the International Conference on Cataloging Principles in 1961 (Paris Principles) exhibits yet another use of the term, very like the treatment of principles in the writings of Julia Pettee. In 1991 I noted her tendency to use the term "principle" variously to stand for objectives, principles, and even rules of cataloging.[16] The Paris Principles, an odd assortment of statements consecutively numbered 1-12 (with sub-sections), similarly blurs the distinction among these concepts. Statement number 1, for example, is not a principle at all but a comment about the principles. It tells us that what follows are principles of access, not principles of description:

> The principles here stated apply only to the choice and form of heading and entry words–i.e., to the principal elements determining the order of entries–in catalogues of printed books in which entries under authors' names and, where these are inappropriate or insufficient, under the titles of works are combined in one alphabetical sequence . . .

Statement number 2 lists the functions of the catalog, followed by general directives about the number and types of entries to be assigned to each cataloged item. Many of the remaining statements could easily be mistaken for rules one encounters in AACR2. For example, number 9 (Entry under Corporate Bodies) reads as follows:

> 9.1 The main entry for a work should be made under the name of a corporate body . . .
> 9.11 when the work is by its nature necessarily the expression of the collective thought or activity of the corporate body. . . .[17]

Compare this to AACR2:

> 21.1B2. General rule. Enter a work emanating from one or more corporate bodies under the heading for the appropriate corporate body . . . if it falls into one or more of the following categories:
> . . .
> c) those that record the collective thought of the body. . . .

The relationship of objective to principle and principle to rule was recently described as though one followed or should follow logically from the other:

First, a statement about the functions of the catalogue should be made. From the statement of these functions the principles on which a catalogue is based should be derived. From these principles, the cataloguing rules should then be developed.[18]

Of course, this is seldom how it works in practice, unless one is designing a system from the ground up. Svenonius herself takes this vantage point when she calls principles "guidelines for the design of a set of rules."[19] Lubetzsky was laying the foundation for a revision of the code, thus also adopting the designer point of view, when he characterized cataloging principles as "basic directives whereby the objectives of cataloging can best be served, considering both the efficiency of the catalog and the economy of cataloging."[20]

More often, however, we are working in the opposite direction. Pettee described principles as the products of a process of discovery: "The rules . . . were drawn up based, not on theory, but upon practices already fixed by usage . . . systematizing and coordinating rules . . . has resulted in bringing to light a few principles. . . ."[21] One might argue that we have the advantage over Julia Pettee these days because our code, AACR2, is based on an explicit statement of principles, the Paris Principles. We should no longer have to discover the principles in our rules. But is this true? The rules are not static; they are constantly revised. Can we be assured that revision will always result in a code that is consistent with our principles? That would be reassuring but hardly realistic.[22] So, unless our eye is on code redesign, it would be more appropriate to regard principles not as guidelines for the design of rules but as statements of the common intent of the rules.

USES OF PRINCIPLES

In short, when one is trying to assess claims about cataloging principles, it is helpful to consider the context in which the claims are made. Are the writers documenting existing practice, or are they considering the code's redesign? Are they talking about principles that are closely tied to the present form and structure of the catalog and that might reasonably be altered as we move from paper to electronic systems? I mean those principles we encountered in the writings of Lubetzky and Pettee and that I referred to as "traditional" principles (principles of access). Or are they considering general design principles that are likely to remain valid regardless of the physical form our bibliographic systems might take?

The appeal to traditional principles is often a way of stifling debate. It's like telling your opponent, "What you're suggesting undermines our rules. In case you have forgotten the principles they were built on, let me refresh your memory." Critiques of main entry are typically countered in this manner. An example of this strategy, as we have seen, was Pettee's response to the main entry debate of the 1930s. A more recent example occurred on the Toronto Conference electronic list in 1997. This discussion list had been organized prior to the conference to consider the papers and issues on the conference agenda. When persons on the list began to urge simplification of the cataloging process and questioned the necessity of main entry in the online environment, others responded with an urgent call for a "layman's introduction" to AACR2. This introduction, originally conceived as a brief (5 p.) statement of principles and purposes, might be used, it was proposed, to inform those outside the profession and to teach the uneducated or under-educated within the profession what "professional" cataloging was supposed to be about.[23]

This idea of a layman's introduction gained favor among the conference attendees and resulted in the formal "charge" by the Joint Steering Committee of drafting principles for an introduction to AACR2, a task assigned to Barbara Tillett. It was observed that the original AACR (1967) had included a statement of principles but that subsequent editions had omitted it. The recommendation was to "consider reinstating useful statements of principle for AACR1 that were dropped from AACR2." By the time the recommendation turned into a formal charge, its purpose had broadened: a statement of principles might serve as a useful guide in rule revision. It had become part of the general agenda: "The Conference reviewed the underlying principles of AACR, with a view to determining whether fundamental rule revision is appropriate and feasible and, if so, advising on the direction and nature of those revisions."[24] Within this context and agenda, what might we expect to find in such a list of principles? Statements expressing the common intent of present cataloging rules, relative to the traditional catalog objectives? Or design guidelines for the creation of a new or re-engineered code?

PRINCIPAL CRITICISMS OF AACR2

Many who have studied the underlying principles of AACR in the context of code redesign have concluded that cataloging standards (rules, principles, rarely, objectives) should change in response to changing technologies.[25] Fattahi states:

> . . . cataloging standards which are based on the concept of the traditional catalog need to be reassessed and redesigned in terms of their relevance to the new electronic environment. These standards must be recon-

structed and developed on a basis parallel to the development of the environment in which they are used.[26]

Their arguments are often based on the conviction that the current code no longer functions effectively in the electronic environment or is not structured optimally to take advantage of the potential benefits of automation.[27] It is often noted that the code was designed to produce a linear, alphabetical catalog and is less successful in catalogs that are non-linear and not limited to a fixed form of display. Fattahi comments:

> The principles underlying the structure of the catalogue and choice of entries in AACR2 include rules concerning the determination and construction of necessary entries for a linear, alphabetical catalogue of main entries, added entries, and references. An online catalogue based on such a linear approach has many problems in searching, retrieval, and display of bibliographic sources . . . the future AACR should take a new approach to the structure of the catalogue and the bibliographic record.[28]

The principles that are the focus of these comments tend to be what I have called the traditional principles. Fattahi's discussions, for example, deal with main entry, uniform titles, and uniform headings, all of which he recognizes as principles underlying AACR. From these and similar insights into the code's shortcomings have come many recent efforts aimed at analyzing our cataloging records and the data structures used to store and communicate them in the electronic environment. Both AACR and MARC have been subjected to logical analysis. A number of alternatives to the present structures have been investigated since the 1970s, either for bibliographic databases as a whole or for elements, such as access control (authority) records.[29]

Fidel and Crandall undertook one of the earliest structural analyses of AACR2, using the entity-relationship model. Their study is particularly interesting for the light it throws on several lively issues that have surfaced in the course of these various reengineering efforts, namely, the need for standards for OPAC displays and the role of the main entry. Their approach to the code involved assessing it as a "schema for database design," which is what AACR2 effectively amounts to in an automated environment. Their evaluation of AACR2 took the form of isolating the different design levels present in individual rules. Database design decisions occur on three levels: the conceptual, internal, and external. The conceptual level of design deals with the objects of the database–entities, such as publisher; attributes, such as the name of the publisher; relationships, such as published by; and the rules governing their creation and application. The internal design level concerns how the data are stored–the storage medium, the format, indexes and internal organization of the records. The external level pertains to the way the data is presented to those querying the database. It governs the particular views of the data–what is shown, how the data is arranged, the display format, and so on.

Their findings were not favorable. AACR2 was found "incompatible" with the principles of database design.[30] First, it violates the "principle of data independence," which requires that "decisions on the conceptual level should be independent of both the internal and external level." Second, it violates the "principle of rigorous data analysis," which states that, "decisions on the conceptual level should be made before those on the internal and external levels."[31] It does so, they concluded, by scattering rules that deal with the same level of database design and by mixing different levels of database design within a single rule. The result is confusion among the levels of design and poor organization of the rules. As the researchers pointed out, AACR2 makes no distinction between the internal and external levels of database design. These two levels are virtually identical in printed catalogs. (Filing rules play a role in the presentation of the data; but filing rules are not part of AACR2.) Not so in automated catalogs where the bibliographic data can be approached and displayed in a great variety of ways.

In printed catalogs, where the internal and external design levels are identical, author main entry, together with references and filing rules, is an effective means of meeting catalog objectives. In the online catalog they may or may not be effective, depending on the way external design decisions were made by the OPAC developer. If the electronic catalog delivered the same data in the same order as the paper catalog–in other words, delivered the entire record in a linear display following ALA filing rules–it would function as designed by the current rules. With any other arrangement and in the absence of rules governing the external level of design, the code cannot control what the catalog returns to the searcher. The OPAC designer is effectively in control. In short, without standard rules for display or presentation of bibliographic data in a database, the traditional principle(s) underlying the rules for entry cannot be relied on as effective means of meeting catalog objectives. It is generally agreed that present OPACs satisfy the finding objective very well, the gathering objective less well. For this reason, Carpenter likes to call them finding lists with indexes, not true catalogs.[32] Part of the problem stems from the fact that many OPACs deconstruct the catalog record. The searcher has no assurance which part of the record will be returned in a search or that the ordering of results will favor the collocation of works or the display of bibliographic relationships. Carlyle and Yee, who have both done significant studies of OPAC displays, agree that present OPACs collocate author and work records poorly. Yee complains, "The generations of library leaders that followed Lubetzky dropped the ball . . .

and allowed the development of OPACs that impede the user who seeks particular works much more than the card catalog ever did."[33]

Not surprisingly, many catalogers today deplore the lack of OPAC display guidelines. Despite the growing demand for standardization in OPAC output and display since Tillett's call for an ISBD for display in 1992,[34] our only significant accomplishment to date has been the production of draft guidelines, the product of the IFLA Task Force on Guidelines for OPAC Displays, formed in 1997.[35] These guidelines were drafted out of the realization that OPAC users were experiencing difficulties in dealing with a multiplicity of search interfaces, their lack of standardization, and the absence of guidelines for effective customization. They did not, says Yee, originate out of a perception of the code's structural deficiencies:

> We take current cataloguing rules and current MARC formats as a given in this document, and try to suggest better ways to use existing records in OPAC displays. We do not try to suggest ways that actual changes in cataloguing practice might help to improve OPAC displays, although we recognize that many potential solutions to OPAC display problems lie in changes in cataloguing practice.[36]

The deficiencies of the code do figure in Carpenter's vision of a re-engineered online catalog display. "More than catalog interface revision is required," he writes. "Rules would need to be changed." The justification he gives is very much in line with Fidel and Crandall's analysis:

> Cataloging rules have two aspects in their logic, aspects not clearly distinguished in any current code. The first aspect is the standard for the record structure: what type of information needs to be gathered? The second aspect is a display standard: what is a useful arrangement of the catalog? . . . Concentration on the aspect of a code as a display standard would not only give direction to the reengineering effort but also provide guidance in determining what should go into the record structure.[37]

It is sometimes observed that the concept of main entry is not really integral to AACR2 because Rule 0.5 gives libraries an alternative–the alternative of using alternate heading entries:

> It is recognized, however, that many libraries do not distinguish between the main entry and other entries. It is recommended that such libraries use chapter 21 as guidance in determining all the entries required in particular instances. . . .[38]

This has long been the position of Gorman.[39] In his latest analysis of AACR2 principles for the Toronto Conference, the Paris Principles, authorship, and main entry are conspicuously absent.[40] Here is their short list:

- That descriptions are to be formulated in accordance with the specifications of the International Standard Bibliographic Description (ISBD)
- that all media of communication are treated equally
- that descriptions are based on the bibliographic item
- that access points are to be derived from the nature of the work being cataloged, not the nature of the bibliographic entity being described.

Though Gorman speaks elsewhere of a "principle of authorship" and acknowledges main entry as an "organizational principle" of AACR2, they are not listed as principles here. One can appreciate his reluctance to include them since he's been arguing against main entry for years and, as he points out, ". . . the *principle* of authorship has been confused with a concept of catalogue organization–the 'main entry.' " But the two are not the same, he insists, "doing away with the idea of the 'main entry' as an organizational principle of the catalogue does *not* involve abandoning the principle of authorship. I hope that future revisions of AACR2 will contain wording that makes this point clear." As for authorship, he writes, "I believe the principle of authorship–the idea that one's first consideration on assigning access points/headings to a work should be to discover the author(s) of that work–is as valid today as it has ever been."[41] But if this is true–if the principle of authorship can survive the death of the main entry–and if it is still as valid today as it has ever been, then why not include it as a principle of AACR2? Is its tendency to be confused with the concept of main entry sufficient reason for excluding it?

Whatever the exact relationship between authorship and the main entry, analyses of AACR2, such as the structural analysis of Fidel and Crandall, strongly suggest that the concept of main entry is intimately bound up with the rules:

> The analysis of AACR2 from a database approach . . . shows that the role of chapter 21 is central to the cataloging code and, therefore, the structure of AACR2 is strongly determined by the concept *entry* (or access points), and in particular by that of *main entry*.[42]

Their findings support a study conducted earlier by Baughman and Svenonius.[43] Taking rule 0.5 at its word and adopting a highly practical approach, these authors proceeded to remove main entry language from chapter 21 only to discover that the rules became either nonsensical, overly complicated, or so problematic as to require guidelines before they could be applied.

PRINCIPLES OF AACR2

So what are the principles of AACR2? That this may not be a simple question is suggested by the conflicting answers we have already encountered. What does AACR itself say? AACR distinguishes "principles underlying rules for entry and heading" from "principles of descriptive cataloging." The former are discussed in the general introduction, the latter in the preface at the beginning of Part II. Principles of access are the more familiar of the two. They are what are usually thought of when we speak of "principles of AACR2." Authorship, main entry, the Paris Principles are all principles of access. To use the words of the Paris Principles, they govern the "choice and form of headings and entry words."

The principles of access underlying AACR and all of its revisions are the Paris Principles, with certain departures necessitated by a number of political and/or economic imperatives (AACR, p. 3). As we recall, these include a statement of catalog objectives. The intent of the rules based upon these principles is expressed in the summary below (AACR, p. 2), which also shows that the principle of authorship clearly underlies them:

> . . . the rules have been designed to meet the requirements of multiple-entry alphabetical catalogs in which all entries for particular persons or corporate bodies appear under a uniform heading or are related by references . . . Although the rules are oriented to multiple-entry catalogs, it has still been regarded as necessary to distinguish main entries from added entries . . . By prescribing what shall be the main entry, the rules respond to this necessity for a standard mode of identifying a work. They follow the principle, firmly established in modern cataloging and bibliography, that a work should be specified by its author and title or, if it lacks an author, by its title.

Besides these, AACR2R (p. 305) includes rule 20.1: "The rules in part II apply to works and not to physical manifestations of those works, though the characteristics of an individual item are taken into account in some instances." This is reflected in Gorman and Oddy's fourth principle.

Principles of description have not received the same amount of attention in library discussions as principles of access. In AACR, as in the Paris Principles, the statement of principles begins with a list of objectives:

The objectives of descriptive cataloging are: (1) to state the significant features of an item with the purpose of distinguishing it from other items and describing its scope, contents, and bibliographic relation to other items: (2) to present these data in an entry which can be integrated with the entries for other items in the catalog and which will respond best to the interests of most users of the catalog.

These objectives are then followed by principles dealing with "description of a perfect copy," "extent of description," "terms of description," "organization of the description," "documentation," and "style" (AACR, p. 189-90).

In the revision of AACR, some (but not all) of these principles have been replaced by the International Standard Bibliographic Description (ISBD), which prescribes the elements of description, their order, and their punctuation. The original objectives appear to be still valid. The second objective is restated in rule 0.1. The principle directing the cataloger to make an effort to describe a "physically complete copy" is now reflected in rule 0.24, which states in part that "the starting point for description is the physical form of the item in hand, not the original or any previous form in which the work has been published" (AACR2R, p. 8). This rule, however, has recently been revised. It is interesting to note that the Principles Group of the Toronto Conference disputed the status of rule 0.24 as a principle of AACR. They called it a "method of procedure," which, they said, was tied to the present arrangement of chapters in AACR2 and which "needs to be revised if AACR is revised."[44] In this connection, a JSC Format Variation Working Group was formed to assess the viability of basing the catalog description on the expression (a level between the "perfect copy," or manifestation, and the work). As anticipated by Gorman and Oddy, they uncovered the manifold difficulties of such an approach and quickly proposed a return to manifestation (item) level cataloging.[45]

NEW STATEMENT OF PRINCIPLES

So much for explicit statements of principle in AACR and AACR2. When we turn to Barbara Tillett's list of principles, which she prepared as a discussion paper for the Joint Steering Committee for Revision of AACR, we are confronted by something quite different. This is a little unexpected in view of the fact that these principles are destined for a new introduction to AACR2, at least part of whose purpose is to make explicit the intellectual foundations upon which the present code is built.

What are Tillett's principles?[46] She tells us that they are based on the "general principles for the design of bibliographic systems" that were identified by

Elaine Svenonius in her latest study.[47] Based upon Anglo-American cataloging practice, these consist of five principles and three sub-principles. It is instructive to note that they are all principles of description, not principles of access. They reformulate principles explicit in AACR or principles that are implicit but inform cataloging practice, such as Cutter's principle of user convenience. Tillett adapts them for her purposes, reduces their number (five principles and two sub-principles), broadens their scope to include "controlled forms of names for access," and then presents them as principles of description *and* access. Following is her list:

> Principle of user convenience
>> Decisions taken in the making of descriptions and controlled forms of names for access should be made with the user in mind.
>
> Principle of common usage (sub-principle)
>> Normalized vocabulary used in descriptions and access should accord with that of the majority of users.
>
> Principle of representation
>> Descriptions and controlled forms of names for access should be based on the way an information entity describes itself.
>
> Principle of accuracy (sub-principle)
>> Descriptions and controlled forms of names for access should faithfully portray the entity described.
>
> Principle of sufficiency and necessity
>> Descriptions and controlled forms of names for access should include only those elements that are bibliographically significant.
>
> Principle of standardization
>> Descriptions and controlled forms of names for access should be standardized, to the extent and level possible.
>
> Principle of integration
>> Descriptions for all types of materials should be based on a common set of rules, to the extent possible.

These principles are followed by a list of entities (e.g., works, expressions, manifestations, items, etc.), which are based on the entities identified in the document, *Functional Requirements for Bibliographic Records* (*FRBR*).[48] Tillett then adds a statement of catalog objectives, also taken from *FRBR*, expanded by Svenonius. Absent are all references to ISBD, to rule 0.24, and to the traditional principles of access represented by the Paris Principles. Why is this? The answer is not hard to find. "What I've captured here are the principles that guide the creation of rules," she writes, "and I recommend our using these in the new Introduction to AACR." What she and the committee are about is rule revision. In her words:

> As the 1997 JSC conference stressed, AACR is long overdue for a change to reflect the changed environment, to take advantage of the new technologies for online catalogs and Internet searching and access, to build on the conceptual models provided in the IFLA *Functional Requirements for Bibliographic Records (FRBR)*, and to finally exploit and provide guidance on authority control and bibliographic relationships.[49]

PRINCIPLE ISSUES

Tillett's principles and objectives support this agenda. They are built on the conceptual models of *FRBR*, but *FRBR* does not deal with catalog structures and records as defined in AACR2. The two do not even share the same premises. *FRBR* looks to the needs of "national bibliographic agencies." The *FRBR* study recommends "a basic level of functionality and basic data requirements for records created by national bibliographic agencies."[50] Compare this to AACR2's rule 0.1: "These rules are designed for use in the construction of catalogues and other lists in general libraries of all sizes." *FRBR* "makes no *a priori* assumptions about the bibliographic record itself, either in terms of content or structure."[51] AACR2 commits itself to a bibliographic record of a definite content and structure, the content and structure required by the ISBD.[52]

As for the catalog objectives presented by Tillett, these, too, are built upon the *FRBR* model, as she herself explains:

> *FRBR* lists objectives in terms of meeting users needs to *find, identify, select*, and *obtain*. Svenonius nicely updates and clarifies the "**objectives of a full-featured bibliographic system**" (on p. 15-17 she provides the historical perspective of Cutter's objectives, Lubetzky's objectives as reflected in the Paris Principles, and IFLA *Functional Requirements for Bibliographic Records (FRBR)* objectives), and she expands the *FRBR* objectives. I have paraphrased and added to Svenonius' objectives.[53]

FRBR "takes a user-focused approach to analyzing data requirements insofar as it endeavours to define in a systematic way what it is that the user expects to find information about in a bibliographic record and how that information is used."[54] These user expectations are not, however, discovered through research into user behavior but are stipulated for the purposes of the study. *FRBR*, in other words, *does* make *a priori* assumptions about user expectations. The catalog objectives answering to these presumed expectations do not, and are not meant to, restate the objectives in the Paris Principles. What's more, by the time Tillett gets through with augmenting them, they have moved considerably beyond traditional catalog objectives.

Her objectives cover just about everything a catalog could possibly do. Her objectives would probably do fine as objectives "of a full-featured bibliographic system," but they certainly won't do as an accurate reflection of the sort of catalog for which AACR was written. They go far beyond what is dealt with in the rules. For example, one of the objectives is to locate all resources on a given subject. Another is to acquire or obtain access to an item described (that is, to acquire an item through purchase, loan, and so on). Are we to suppose that AACR is now going to provide rules for subject assignment or the transfer of orders to publishers? Is it going to include interlibrary loan protocols? We know that modern library management systems are capable of doing all these things. But these capabilities are not the subject of descriptive cataloging, at least, not as we know it today.

Besides not describing the AACR we all know, Tillett's principles and objectives probably won't even do what the Principles Group of the Toronto Conference said they should do–namely, to relate to one another in such a way that we can derive principles from objectives and then develop rules from them. Tillett's objectives deal with access; her principles, despite their expanded application to "controlled forms of names," still are basically principles for description. It is hard to see how their relationship could follow this model, which was inspired by the old, traditional principles and objectives, as in the following example:

> Objective: PP 2: The catalogue should be an efficient instrument for ascertaining
>> 2.2 (a) which works by a particular author and
>> (b) which editions of a particular work are in the library.

> Principle: (paraphrase of principle 5): make an entry for each book under a heading derived from the author's name or from the title as printed in the book, and when variant forms of the author's name or of the title occur, an entry for each book under a uniform heading, consisting of one particular form of the author's name or one particular title, or, for books not identified by author or title, a uniform heading consisting of a suitable substitute for the title, and appropriate added entries and/or references.[55]

> Rule: 21.14A: Enter a translation under the heading appropriate to the original . . .

It is difficult to see also how Tillett's objectives and principles (even with the addition of the *FRBR* entities) could result in a catalog of the necessary structure to meet catalog objectives. In the absence of principles of entry, she certainly would need to add principles or guidelines for OPAC display. These guidelines, as we have seen, are being developed independently of this effort. It troubles me to think that the two efforts might run counter to each other, or, at best, run past each other. Already it is clear that the IFLA Task Force is working within the limits of AACR2, within the realities of the MARC format, and presupposing a system of main entry.[56] The JSC Committee, on the other hand, has its eye on fundamental rule revision, and the Tillett document is silent on the question of entry. The OPAC guidelines, if ever approved, could well stand as a companion document to AACR2. The principles document, on the other hand, would be more suitable as an introduction to a re-engineered AACR2 or an AACR3.

NOTES

1. Julia Pettee, "The Development of Authorship Entry and the Formulation of Authorship Rules as Found in the Anglo-American Code," in *Foundations of Cataloging: a Sourcebook*, eds. Michael Carpenter and Elaine Svenonius (Littleton, Colo.: Libraries Unlimited, 1985): 75-89.

2. Elaine Svenonius, ed., *The Conceptual Foundations of Descriptive Cataloging* (San Diego, Calif.: Academic Press, 1989), xiii.

3. Michael Carpenter and Elaine Svenonius, eds., *Foundations of Cataloging: A Sourcebook* (Littleton, Colo.: Libraries Unlimited, 1985), xii.

4. International Conference on Cataloguing Principles (ICCP), Paris, October 1961, "Statement of Principles," in *Foundations of Cataloging: A Sourcebook.*, eds. Michael Carpenter and Elaine Svenonius (Littleton, Colo.: Libraries Unlimited, 1985): 179.

5. Elaine Svenonius and Dorothy McGarry, eds., *Seymour Lubetzky: Writings on the Classical Art of Cataloging* (Englewood, Colo.: Libraries Unlimited, 2001), 133.

6. Patrick Wilson, "The Intellectual Foundations of Information Organization," *College & Research Libraries* 62, no. 2 (2001): 203-4.

7. Rahmatollah Fattahi, "AACR2 and Catalogue Production Technology: Relevance of Cataloguing Principles to the Online Environment," in *The Principles and Future of AACR: Proceedings of the International Conference on the Principles and Future Development of AACR, Toronto, Ontario, Canada, October 23-25, 1997*, ed. Jean Weihs (Chicago: American Library Association, 1998): 17.

8. Jean Weihs, ed., *The Principles and Future of AACR: Proceedings of the International Conference on the Principles and Future Development of AACR, Toronto, Ontario, Canada, October 23-25, 1997* (Chicago: American Library Association, 1998), 241.

9. Michael Gorman and Pat Oddy, "The Anglo-American Cataloguing Rules, Second Edition: Their History and Principles," in *The Principles and Future of AACR: Proceedings of the International Conference on the Principles and Future Develop-*

ment of AACR, Toronto, Ontario, Canada, October 23-25, 1997, ed. Jean Weihs (Chicago: American Library Association, 1998): 159.

10. Barbara B. Tillett, "Future Cataloging Rules and Catalog Records," in *Origins, Content, and Future of AACR2 Revised*, ed. Richard P. Smiraglia (Chicago: American Library Association, 1991): 111.

11. S. Michael Malinconico, "AACR2 and Automation," in *The Making of a Code: The Issues Underlying AACR2*, ed. Doris Hargrett Clack (Chicago: American Library Association, 1980): 27.

12. Svenonius-McGarry, 133, 284.

13. Charles A. Cutter, "Rules for a Dictionary Catalog: Selections," in *Foundations of Cataloging: a Sourcebook*, eds. Michael Carpenter and Elaine Svenonius (Littleton, Colo.: Libraries Unlimited, 1985): 67.

14. Ibid., 66.

15. Elaine Svenonius, *The Intellectual Foundation of Information Organization* (Cambridge, Mass.: MIT Press, 2000), 68.

16. E. de Rijk, "Thomas Hyde, Julia Pettee and the Development of Cataloging Principles; with a Translation of Hyde's 1674 Preface to the Reader," *Cataloging & Classification Quarterly* 14, no. 2 (1991): 37-8. In *The Intellectual Foundation of Information Organization* (p. 67), Svenonius notes the same tendency in the "literature of bibliographic description" generally.

17. ICCP, 181.

18. Weihs, 241.

19. Svenonius, *Intellectual Foundation*, 68.

20. Svenonius-McGarry, 133.

21. Pettee, 306.

22. Lubetzsky charged that the revision of AACR (AACR2) strayed from the sound principles of corporate authorship and author main entry as the basis for all entries (Lubetzky 1980, 16-25).

23. Those interested in tracing the development of this idea of a layman's introduction can follow the electronic list discussion, which is archived on the Toronto Conference home page at http://www.nlc-bnc.ca/jsc/intlconf.html. The original post was dated August 6, 1997.

24. *International Conference on the Principles & Future Development of AACR* Home page, 11 March 2002. See note 25 for URL.

25. Sherry L. Vellucci and Rahmatollah Fattahi (see full citations in Bibliographical References) both offer useful summaries of the issues involved. Fattahi's generous list of references, in particular, serves as a good introduction to the copious literature on this topic.

26. Rahmatollah Fattahi, "A Comparison Between the Online Catalog and the Card Catalog: Some Considerations for Redesigning Bibliographic Standards," *OCLC Systems & Services* 11, no. 3 (1995): 35.

27. Raya Fidel and Michael Crandall, "The AACR2 as a Design Schema for Bibliographic Databases," *Library Quarterly* 58, no. 2 (1988): 123-42.

28. Fattahi, "AACR2 and Catalogue Production Technology," 23.

29. See, for example, Tom Delsey, "Modeling the Logic of AACR, in *The Principles and Future of AACR: Proceedings of the International Conference on the Principles and Future Development of AACR, Toronto, Ontario, Canada, October 23-25, 1997*, ed. Jean Weihs (Chicago: American Library Association, 1998): 1-16; Michael Gorman, "Cataloging and the New Technologies," in *Foundations of Cataloging: A*

Sourcebook, eds. Michael Carpenter and Elaine Svenonius (Littleton, Colo.: Libraries Unlimited, 1985): 242-52; Michael Heaney, "Object-Oriented Cataloging," *Information Technology and Libraries* 14, no. 3 (1995): 135-53; Gregory Leazer, "A Conceptual Plan for the Description and Control of Bibliographic Works" (Ph.D. diss., Columbia University, 1993); and Barbara Tillett, "Access Control: A Model for Descriptive, Holding and Control Records," in *Convergence: Proceedings of the Second National Conference of the Library and Information Technology Association, October 2-6, 1988, Boston*, ed. Michael Gorman (Chicago: American Library Association, 1990): 48-56.

30. Fidel-Crandall, 133.

31. Ibid., 126.

32. Michael Carpenter, "Main and Added Entries," in *The Future of Cataloging: Insights from the Lubetzky Symposium, April 18, 1998, University of California, Los Angeles*, eds. Tschera Harkness Connell and Robert L. Maxwell, Chicago: American Library Association, 2000: 67.

33. Martha M. Yee, "Lubetzky's Work Principle," in *The Future of Cataloging: Insights from the Lubetzky Symposium, April 18, 1998, University of California, Los Angeles*, eds. Tschera Harkness Connell and Robert L. Maxwell (Chicago: American Library Association, 2000): 102. See also Allyson Carlyle, "Creating Efficient and Systematic Catalogs," 42-59.

34. Tillett, "Future Cataloging Rules," 113.

35. Martha M. Yee, "Guidelines for OPAC Displays" WWW Home page, [cited 16 January 2002]; available at http://www.ifla.org/IV/ifla65/papers/098-131e.htm.

36. Ibid.

37. Carpenter, "Main and Added Entries," 67.

38. AACR2.

39. Gorman-Oddy, 160. See also Ronald Hagler, "Access Points for Works," in *The Principles and Future of AACR: Proceedings of the International Conference on the Principles and Future Development of AACR, Toronto, Ontario, Canada, October 23-25, 1997*, ed. Jean Weihs (Chicago: American Library Association, 1998): 228.

40. Gorman-Oddy, 159.

41. Michael Gorman, "Seymour Lubetzky, Man of Principles," in *The Future of Cataloging: Insights from the Lubetzky Symposium, April 18, 1998, University of California, Los Angeles*, eds. Tschera Harkness Connell and Robert L. Maxwell (Chicago: American Library Association, 2000): 19.

42. Fidel-Crandall, 136.

43. Betty Baughman and Elaine Svenonius, "AACR2: Main Entry Free?" *Cataloging & Classification Quarterly* 5 (1984): 1-15.

44. Weihs, 242.

45. Jennifer Bowen, "JSC Format Variation Working Group Interim Report, October 8, 2001," JSC Current Activities WWW Home page [cited 11 March 2002]; available at http://www.nlc-bnc.ca/jsc/current.html. Others have commented: "Descriptions are of bibliographic items. . . . It is literally impossible to have a single description of two or more different bibliographic items. Once described, the cataloguer looks at the manifestation in the light of the work (an intellectual construct that, by its nature, cannot be described) in order to assign access points (including uniform titles) and create authority files. This process, which should be understood by anyone who has taken an introductory cataloguing class, clearly demonstrates that the idea of a 'master record' for several manifestations of the same work is cataloguing nonsense" (Gorman-Oddy,

163). Svenonius (*The Intellectual Foundation of Information Organization*, 109) also has difficulty with this idea. She writes, " . . . the document continues to be the springboard for description. More than just the momentum of tradition accounts for this; there simply is no alternative. Disembodied information, like the Cheshire cat, cannot be grasped or retrieved."

46. I am excluding Tillett's general design principles from consideration in this discussion; focus is on the more specific principles for bibliographic description.

47. Svenonius, *The Intellectual Foundation of Information Organization*.

48. IFLA Study Group on the Functional Requirements for Bibliographic Records, *Functional Requirements for Bibliographic Records: Final Report* (München: K. G. Saur, 1998).

49. Barbara B. Tillett, "Principles of AACR," JSC Current Activities WWW Home page [cited 11 March 2002]. Available at: http://www.nlc-bnc.ca/jsc/current. html.

50. IFLA Study Group, 2.

51. Ibid., 3.

52. The entities and attributes identified by *FRBR* are not drawn from AACR and were not meant to be. Some of the logical attributes resist mapping to ISBD elements. There are no ISBD elements for the title, extensibility, and revisability of an expression; no ISBD elements for the item identifier, exhibition history, scheduled treatment, and access restrictions, to give just a few examples (Appendix A).

53. IFLA Study Group, 5.

54. Ibid., 3-4.

55. International Conference on Cataloguing Principles, Paris, October 1961, "Statement of Principles," in *Foundations of Cataloging: A Sourcebook*, eds. Michael Carpenter and Elaine Svenonius (Littleton, Colo.: Libraries Unlimited, 1985): 180.

56. Martha Yee, who prepared the OPAC display guidelines, is a staunch defender of main entry. The Toronto Conference and Tillett's discussion paper carefully avoid the issue of main entry. Commenting on the present JSC effort, Margaret Maxwell ("Guidelines for a Future Anglo-American Cataloging Code," in *The Future of Cataloging: Insights from the Lubetzky Symposium, April 18, 1998, University of California, Los Angeles*, eds. Tschera Harkness Connell and Robert L. Maxwell (Chicago: American Library Association, 2000): 160) states, "At a minimum, because it remains the foundation document for AACR, the 'Statement of Principles adopted at the International Conference on Cataloguing Principles, Paris, October 1961,' should be summarized in this introduction. . . . I agree with Martha Yee's eloquent plea for keeping the principle of main entry as presented in an online discussion group on the Toronto Conference papers."

REFERENCES

Baughman, Betty, and Elaine Svenonius. "AACR2: Main Entry Free?" *Cataloging & Classification Quarterly* 5, no. 1 (1984): 1-15.

Bowen, Jennifer. "JSC Format Variation Working Group Interim Report, October 8, 2001." JSC Current Activities WWW Home page [cited 11 March 2002]. Available at http://www.nlc-bnc.ca/jsc/current.html.

Carlyle, Allyson. "Creating Efficient and Systematic Catalogs." In *The Future of Cataloging: Insights from the Lubetzky Symposium, April 18, 1998, University of California, Los Angeles*, eds. Tschera Harkness Connell and Robert L. Maxwell. Chicago: American Library Association, 2000: 42-59.

Carpenter, Michael. "Main and Added Entries." In *The Future of Cataloging: Insights from the Lubetzky Symposium, April 18, 1998, University of California, Los Angeles*, eds. Tschera Harkness Connell and Robert L. Maxwell, Chicago: American Library Association, 2000: 60-71.

Carpenter, Michael, and Elaine Svenonius, eds. *Foundations of Cataloging: A Sourcebook.* Littleton, Colo.: Libraries Unlimited, 1985.

Clack, Doris Hargrett, ed. *The Making of a Code: The Issues Underlying AACR2.* Chicago: American Library Association, 1980.

Connell, Tschera Harkness, and Robert L. Maxwell, eds. *The Future of Cataloging: Insights from the Lubetzky Symposium, April 18, 1998, University of California, Los Angeles.* Chicago: American Library Association, 2000.

Cutter, Charles A. "Rules for a Dictionary Catalog: Selections." In *Foundations of Cataloging: A Sourcebook*, eds. Michael Carpenter and Elaine Svenonius. Littleton, Colo.: Libraries Unlimited. 1985: 62-71.

_____. "Rules for a Printed Dictionary Catalogue." Pt. II of *Public Libraries in the United States of America: Their History, Condition, and Management.* Washington, DC: Government Printing Office, 1876.

Delsey, Tom. "Modeling the Logic of AACR." In *The Principles and Future of AACR: Proceedings of the International Conference on the Principles and Future Development of AACR, Toronto, Ontario, Canada, October 23-25, 1997*, ed. Jean Weihs. Chicago: American Library Association, 1998: 1-16.

Fattahi, Rahmatollah. "AACR2 and Catalogue Production Technology: Relevance of Cataloguing Principles to the Online Environment." In *The Principles and Future of AACR: Proceedings of the International Conference on the Principles and Future Development of AACR, Toronto, Ontario, Canada, October 23-25, 1997*, ed. Jean Weihs. Chicago: American Library Association, 1998: 17-43.

_____. "A Comparison Between the Online Catalog and the Card Catalog: Some Considerations for Redesigning Bibliographic Standards." *OCLC Systems & Services* 11, no. 3 (1995): 28-38.

_____. "Relevance of Cataloguing Principles to the Online Environment: An Historical and Analytical Study." Ph.D. diss., University of New South Wales, 1996. Also author's WWW Home page [cited 12 March 2002]. Available at http:// wilma.silas.unsw.edu.au/students/rfattahi/thes1.htm.

Fidel, Raya, and Michael Crandall. "The AACR2 as a Design Schema for Bibliographic Databases." *Library Quarterly* 58, no. 2 (1988): 123-42.

Gorman, Michael. "AACR2: Main Themes." In *The Making of a Code: The Issues Underlying AACR2*, ed. Doris Hargrett Clack. Chicago: American Library Association, 1980: 41-50.

_____. "AACR3? Not!" In *The Future of the Descriptive Cataloging Rules*, ed. Brian E. C. Schottlaender. Chicago: American Library Association, 1998: 19-29.

_____. "Cataloging and the New Technologies." In *Foundations of Cataloging: A Sourcebook,* eds. Michael Carpenter and Elaine Svenonius. Littleton, Colo.: Libraries Unlimited, 1985: 242-52.

_____. "Seymour Lubetzky, Man of Principles." In *The Future of Cataloging: Insights from the Lubetzky Symposium, April 18, 1998, University of California, Los Angeles,* eds. Tschera Harkness Connell and Robert L. Maxwell. Chicago: American Library Association, 2000: 12-21.

Gorman, Michael, and Pat Oddy. "The Anglo-American Cataloguing Rules, Second Edition: Their History and Principles." In *The Principles and Future of AACR: Proceedings of the International Conference on the Principles and Future Development of AACR, Toronto, Ontario, Canada, October 23-25, 1997,* ed. Jean Weihs. Chicago: American Library Association, 1998: 158-65.

Hagler, Ronald. "Access Points for Works." In *The Principles and Future of AACR: Proceedings of the International Conference on the Principles and Future Development of AACR, Toronto, Ontario, Canada, October 23-25, 1997,* ed. Jean Weihs. Chicago: American Library Association, 1998: 214-28.

Heaney, Michael. "Object-Oriented Cataloging." *Information Technology and Libraries* 14, no. 3 (1995): 135-53.

IFLA Study Group on the Functional Requirements for Bibliographic Records. *Functional Requirements for Bibliographic Records: Final Report.* Munchen: K. G. Saur, 1998.

International Conference on Cataloguing Principles, Paris, October 1961. "Statement of Principles." In *Foundations of Cataloging: A Sourcebook,* eds. Michael Carpenter and Elaine Svenonius. Littleton, Colo.: Libraries Unlimited, 1985: 176-85.

"International Conference on the Principles & Future Development of AACR." WWW Home page. [cited 11 March 2002]. Available at http://www.nlc-bnc.ca/jsc/intlconf. html.

Joint Steering Committee for Revision of AACR. "Joint Steering Committee for Revision of Anglo-American Cataloguing Rules." WWW Home page [cited 11 March 2002]. Available at http://www.nlc-bnc.ca/jsc/.

Leazer, Gregory. "A Conceptual Plan for the Description and Control of Bibliographic Works." Ph.D. diss., Columbia University, 1993.

Malinconico, S. Michael. "AACR2 and Automation." In *The Making of a Code: The Issues Underlying AACR2,* ed. Doris Hargrett Clack. Chicago: American Library Association, 1980: 25-40.

Maxwell, Margaret F. "Guidelines for a Future Anglo-American Cataloging Code." In *The Future of Cataloging: Insights from the Lubetzky Symposium, April 18, 1998, University of California, Los Angeles,* eds. Tschera Harkness Connell and Robert L. Maxwell. Chicago: American Library Association, 2000: 157-62.

Pettee, Julia. "The Development of Authorship Entry and the Formulation of Authorship Rules as Found in the Anglo-American Code." In *Foundations of Cataloging: A Sourcebook,* eds. Michael Carpenter and Elaine Svenonius. Littleton, Colo.: Libraries Unlimited, 1985: 75-89.

Rijk, E. de. "Thomas Hyde, Julia Pettee, and the Development of Cataloging Principles; with a Translation of Hyde's 1674 Preface to the Reader." *Cataloging & Classification Quarterly* 14, no. 2 (1991): 31-62.

Schottlaender, Brian E. C., ed. *The Future of the Descriptive Cataloging Rules.* Chicago: American Library Association, 1998.

Smiraglia, Richard P., ed. *Origins, Content, and Future of AACR2 Revised.* Chicago: American Library Association, 1992.

Svenonius, Elaine, ed. *The Conceptual Foundations of Descriptive Cataloging.* San Diego, Calif.: Academic Press, 1989.

_____. *The Intellectual Foundation of Information Organization.* Cambridge, Mass.: MIT Press, 2000.

Svenonius, Elaine, and Dorothy McGarry, eds. *Seymour Lubetzky: Writings on the Classical Art of Cataloging.* Englewood, Colo.: Libraries Unlimited, 2001.

Tillett, Barbara B. "Access Control: A Model for Descriptive, Holding and Control Records." In *Convergence: Proceedings of the Second National Conference of the Library and Information Technology Association, October 2-6, 1988, Boston,* ed. Michael Gorman. Chicago: American Library Association, 1990: 48-56.

_____. "Future Cataloging Rules and Catalog Records." In *Origins, Content, and Future of AACR2 Revised,* ed. Richard P. Smiraglia. Chicago: American Library Association, 1992: 110-118.

_____. "Principles of AACR." JSC Current Activities WWW Home page. [cited 11 March 2002]. Available at http://www.nlc-bnc.ca/jsc/current.html.

Vellucci, Sherry L. "Bibliographic Relationships." In *The Principles and Future of AACR: Proceedings of the International Conference on the Principles and Future Development of AACR, Toronto, Ontario, Canada, October 23-25, 1997,* ed. Jean Riddle Weihs. Chicago: American Library Association, 1998: 105-46.

Weihs, Jean, ed. *The Principles and Future of AACR: Proceedings of the International Conference on the Principles and Future Development of AACR, Toronto, Ontario, Canada, October 23-25, 1997.* Chicago: American Library Association, 1998.

Wilson, Patrick. "The Intellectual Foundations of Information Organization." *College & Research Libraries* 62, no. 2 (2001): 203-4.

Yee, Martha M. "Guidelines for OPAC displays." Paper presented at the 65th IFLA Conference, Bangkok, Thailand, 20-28 August 1999. Web page. [cited 16 January 2002]. Available at http://www.ifla.org/IV/ifla65/papers/098-131e.htm.

_____. "Lubetzky's Work Principle." In *The Future of Cataloging: Insights from the Lubetzky Symposium, April 18, 1998, University of California, Los Angeles,* eds. Tschera Harkness Connell and Robert L. Maxwell. Chicago: American Library Association, 200: 72-104.

INDIVIDUAL COUNTRIES OR REGIONS

Historical Perspectives
of Cataloguing and Classification in Africa

Stephen M. Mutula
Mashingaidze Tsvakai

SUMMARY. This paper discusses the historical perspectives of cataloguing and classification practices in Africa and looks at international cataloguing practices and their implications for African librarianship. The challenges facing libraries on the continent in the cataloguing and classification of Africana materials are discussed and some suggestions offered on how the situation may be improved. Efforts towards developments of bibliographic control in Africa are highlighted. *[Article copies available for a fee from The Haworth Document Delivery Service: 1-800-HAWORTH. E-mail address: <getinfo@haworthpressinc.com> Website: <http://www.HaworthPress.com> © 2002 by The Haworth Press, Inc. All rights reserved.]*

KEYWORDS. Cataloguing–history–Africa, cataloguing perspectives–Africa, cataloguing African materials, African local materials, bibliographic control of African materials

Stephen M. Mutula is a lecturer and Mashingaidze Tsvakai is an MLIS student, both with the Department of Library and Information Studies, University of Botswana, P.O. Box Private Bag 0022, Gaborone, Botswana (E-mail: mutulasm@mopipi.ub.bw and tsvakaim@yahoo.com, respectively).

[Haworth co-indexing entry note]: "Historical Perspectives of Cataloguing and Classification in Africa." Mutula, Stephen M., and Mashingaidze Tsvakai. Co-published simultaneously in *Cataloging & Classification Quarterly* (The Haworth Information Press, an imprint of The Haworth Press, Inc.) Vol. 35, No. 1/2, 2002, pp. 61-77; and: *Historical Aspects of Cataloging and Classification* (ed: Martin D. Joachim) The Haworth Information Press, an imprint of The Haworth Press, Inc., 2003, pp. 61-77. Single or multiple copies of this article are available for a fee from The Haworth Document Delivery Service [1-800-HAWORTH, 9:00 a.m. - 5:00 p.m. (EST). E-mail address: getinfo@haworthpressinc.com].

SUMMARY IN SETSWANA. Pampiri e e sekaseka ditso tsa go soboka mekwalo ka meono ya one jaaka go dirwa mon Afrika, e lebelela kafa tiro e e dirwang ka teng ko mafatshefatsheng le bokao jwa se mo go bao ba berekang mo motlobong ya dibuka. E sedimosa kafa MaAfrika ba sobokang le go rulaganya mekawalo yotlhe ee runtseng mono gae, Afrika. Dikgwetlo tse di lebanyeng MaAfrika mogo phutheng dibuka go di rulaganya le go di soboka ka meono ya tsone di a sekasekwa mme go fiwe dikgakololo gore tsela goka tsewa efe go tlhabololo tiro e. Pampiri e e nankola tse eleng tswelelo pele mo taolong ya rulaganya le go soboka dibuka mo Afrika.

DIKGANGKGOLO (KEYWORDS IN SETSWANA). Ditso, Thulagany le tshoboko–Afrika, Tebo ya Thulaganyo–Afrika, Thulaganyo ya dibuka tsa Afrika, Taolo ya thulaganyo ya dibuka–Afrika

INTRODUCTION

Generally there is limited information on cataloguing and classification practices in Africa, partly because most of what exists remains unpublished and there are poor publishing practices among African scholars compared to their Western counterparts. A search on the Internet, for example, reveals insignificant content by Africa's librarians not only in the area of cataloguing and classification but in the area of general bibliographic control. However, Africa's information environment is rich in resources; but most of these resources remain largely oral and not documented. Within this environment the process of cataloguing is considered the core area that defines the professional competence of any person who is called a librarian. It is generally believed that without cataloguing skills one does not qualify to be called a professional librarian. This belief derives from the importance of the library catalogue, the product of the cataloguing process. The objectives of the catalogue that were adopted as a standard by the International Conference on Cataloguing Principles in Paris in 1961 are still as valid today as they were at that time.

THE HISTORY OF CATALOGUING IN AFRICA

In Africa the use of the catalogue started with the alphabetical list of titles recorded in school exercise books. As libraries expanded, more details became necessary. The recording of works in exercise books was followed by the book catalogue, which was made available in libraries in multiple copies. This form of catalogue was preferable because it was easy to use and cheaper to produce and reproduce (Quigg 1968, 74). The book catalogue, of course, was not flexible when it came to inserting new material. Book catalogues were later replaced by card catalogues, which in Africa were either written by hand or printed. Card catalogues provided for easy insertion of new entries and withdrawal of others and is still much used today in Africa where many libraries are not computerized. Even for libraries which have been able to computerize and are also connected to the Internet, the book catalogue is still a common feature as a backup because of the instability of computer technology in the African environment, which is characterized by erratic power supply, poor technology support, and lack of computer skills. In addition, Africa's library professionals lag behind their colleagues in Western countries in making contributions to the Internet. In such situations there is little motivation for developing local bibliographic tools and standards for cataloguing. In general, African librarians are basically consumers of products on the Web, such as subject based information gateways, virtual libraries, portals, etc., that are largely produced in the West.

The concept of a library in Africa is a borrowed idea. Missionaries and colonialists from Western countries introduced libraries into Africa. The colonial masters promoted the use of libraries to facilitate reading and writing. The missionaries taught Africans literacy skills primarily so that they could read the Bible. They built schools and established libraries in order to keep materials that facilitated learning. Libraries in Africa, in the Western sense, are a direct result of the colonial heritage. For instance, libraries have existed in Nigeria for more than sixty years since the British started to settle there.

Most of the materials in African libraries are in the languages of the missionaries or the colonial rulers. In Nigeria and other parts of Africa, for example, the medium of instruction was English. In other African countries instruction was in French, Portuguese, or German. The African continent was divided into North, South, East, Central, and West Africa. Under these broad divisions individual countries were arranged in groups according to colonial preference. These divisions included British West Africa, French West Africa, German East Africa, and British Southern Africa. The political influence that the colonial powers wielded affected many aspects of life, including methods of acquiring, processing, and using information.

As a result, both the Library of Congress Classification (LCC) and the Dewey Decimal Classification (DDC), which are widely used on the African continent, are part of the colonial legacy. These classification schemes were further entrenched when most library professionals from Africa trained in Western countries, which largely use these classification systems. Today most information materials used in libraries on the continent, including biblio-graphic tools, are acquired from abroad; and so LCC and DDC continue to be used almost exclusively in both academic and public libraries. Despite the wide use of these classification schemes, they are inadequate for organizing African resources.

In Nigeria, Greaves (1980, 12) indicates that the growth of the volume of material known as Nigeriana is quite apparent. Nigeriana comprises all materials published in Nigeria as well as foreign publications with some connection to Nigeria. Today, despite the invisibility of African publications in international bibliographic tools, there are many works produced on the African continent. Materials in Africa include, for example, research publications and literary works of such African authors as 1986 Nobel Prize winner Wole Soyinka. There are also many documents from international organizations such as the United Nations Educational, Scientific, and Cultural Organization (UNESCO) and the World Health Organization (WHO). Other publications are written in native languages in a variety of areas including the social sciences, agriculture, imaginative writings, and others. Emerging local publishing companies such as Daystar Press in Ibadan are encouraging local authors to publish materials about Africa in local languages. Additionally, some publishing houses have arisen in connection with institutions of higher learning, especially universities, which are encouraging the output of publications from Africa. Such publishing houses are encouraging the publication of academic writing such as research publications, textbooks, and newsletters. There is also an increase in the number of bookshops, and governments are publishing more and more national and municipal documents. All of these efforts are producing many types of materials and are forcing librarians to catalogue and provide access to them.

In addition, many countries in Africa collect various publications under legal deposit, usually all the publications written in the countries themselves or written elsewhere about the countries. National libraries are required to catalogue legal deposit documents and keep them in the libraries of those countries. Each country, furthermore, is by law required to publish a national bibliography. The aim of the national library is to list information sources in a systematic manner to enable people to become aware of what information is available and where it can be located. Because information is shared internationally, cataloguers are compelled to be aware of international cataloguing and classification standards and practices.

After independence, most countries inherited the languages of their colonial rulers, especially those with most of the books in use coming from Britain and America; and the situation has not changed much several decades later. The current African elite, who hold influential political and professional posts within their own countries, are products of the Western education system and are largely inclined to the values of that system. The majority of people with little or no formal education, however, continue to speak the many different local vernacular languages in their own countries. Africa is, therefore, one of the most linguistically complex areas in the world. Nigeria, for example, has about three hundred languages. In the whole of Africa, there are more than 2,000 spoken languages.

Cataloguing practices in Africa have had a long history. Africa has information resources in the form of oral traditions, unpublished indigenous knowledge, and a multiplicity of other unpublished literature. Much of these resources cannot be accessed because they are not catalogued nor classified, and generally there is a lack of formal bibliographic tools to facilitate their access. In addition, the cataloguing rules and classification tools that do exist do not deal effectively with Africa's diversity of information resources, especially indigenous nomenclature, names, languages, etc. Africa has its own cultures, languages, and names, which cannot effectively be catalogued using Western cataloguing codes.

CHALLENGES OF CLASSIFYING AND CATALOGUING AFRICANA MATERIALS

Most African libraries use the Anglo-American Cataloguing Rules; and, as stated, LC and DDC are the major classification schemes with some libraries also using the Universal Decimal Classification (UDC). These schemes, however, do not adequately meet the needs for cataloguing of African materials.

The diversity of African languages and linguistic syntax makes the cataloguing of Africana materials difficult. For example, Arabic is widely spoken in parts of Africa, especially in East Africa and North Africa. The Arabic language has unique characteristics that are not widely used in roman scripts. Similarly, countries such as Eritrea and Ethiopia use Amharic to a large extent; in Somalia the Somali language is widely used. These languages pose problems because they are not modeled on an alphabetical system and roman numbering or scripting system. Most classification schemes, on the other hand, are modeled on an alphabetical and roman system of numbers and script and are not adequate for Africana materials of this nature. Custom classification as well as specialized training for cataloguers to handle Africana materials in languages that have unique number and script systems would be vital to enhancing the cataloguing and classification of such materials.

As stated before, most librarians in Africa trained in Western library schools and have largely internalized Western professional idiosyncrasies and have contributed considerably to the current problem of inadequacy of customized bibliographic tools to facilitate classification and cataloguing of Africana materials. Africa suffers from a lack of bibliographic tools, for example, that could help standardize the diversity of names. Other problems that make standardization of names important but difficult are the fact that African naming schemes are so complex. "African personal names," says Bein (1993, 97), "are as profuse, rich, and varied as African languages." For example, a first name in certain ethnic groups may be a surname in another. The problems of classification and cataloguing Africana materials are exacerbated by the fact that some names have certain meanings attached to them relating to events, people, spirits, or places; and providing an equivalent English word is difficult. In Setswana, for example, one English word may require a phrase or even a sentence when translated.

Another problem that faces cataloguers of Africana materials is the parallel provision of names and even subject headings. In South Africa, for example, before the multi-racial elections of 1994 that ushered in non-racial government, Afrikaans was the main language; and most materials in the exclusive white universities were in Afrikaans, and classifications tended to reflect this bias. However, with independence there is policy that requires provision of parallel names in other major languages in the country. This requires that tools in those languages be available to provide for these changes. Such tools, unfortunately, do not exist; and direct interpretation of a given word in Afrikaans into local languages can result in inaccuracies leading to difficulties in accessing the information needed. Other problems relate to lack of materials in certain disciplines. For example, many materials are being generated in the languages, social sciences, and humanities. Though these materials are mostly in English, which can effectively be catalogued and classified using existing international codes, those written in local languages cannot be adequately provided for. Additionally, there is a tendency to build strong collections in certain areas and not in others. This can pose a problem because of lengthy Cutter numbers, especially considering the fact that many names in Africa can be very common with variant forms. Cataloguing and classifying Africana materials suffer from the lack of name and subject authority tools. The problem of variant forms of names could be addressed if such tools were available to cataloguers.

There is also great variation in names of people from one country to another or even within the same country. In Kenya, for example, names like **Tina**, **Daina**, **Dina** and **Diana** are variants of the name **Dinah**. Similarly, names of Kenyan President **Daniel Arap Moi** have variant forms depending on the part of Kenya one comes from. In Western Kenya this name would be **Daniel Moi**, and in Central Province the name is **Daniel Wa Moi** while in Nyanza Province the same president is called **Daniel K'Moi**. These variations of the same name causes headaches for even the most experienced and professional cataloguers. Filing such variations in names can be varied. Should the surname of President Moi be filed as **Moi** or **Arap Moi** (**Arap** means **son of**) or **Wa Moi** or **K'Moi**? Furthermore, the diversity of ethnic groups in Africa leads to a multiplicity of names of peoples or tribes. For example, the Luo tribe in Kenya is referred to by the Luhya tribe as **Vavo** while the Luhya tribe refer to the Kikuyu tribe as **Vaseve**. These variations in personal names and ethnic names, along with frequent changes in geographic names, present difficulties, especially given the lack of African bibliographic tools to standardize these names.

There are many components of names, each with its own significance. Geographical names may change for political, social, or religious reasons. Government agencies change their names with the political climate. Additionally, African names appear in four different types: traditional, European, Christian, and Islamic (Bertelsen 1995); and these variations create complex naming patterns with regard to cataloguing and classification. This is exacerbated by the enormous numbers of groups and languages involved, thus making it difficult for a cataloguer to know even a fraction of the correct forms to be used for accurate cataloguing of personal names. In choosing names as access points, the cataloguer will find that AACR2 does not always provide firm ground on which to walk. Further, there can be several different spellings of the same name. In several parts of Africa, people change their names any time they like. Greaves (1980, 17) indicates that Nigerians have a tendency to use different names at different times in different places. As a result, many different people are known by the same name; and one person may be known by several names depending on the role he plays in life. Woman more often change their names after marriage, and these changes can result in confusion for a cataloguer.

The difficulties of diverse languages, as we have seen, present great challenges for cataloguers. The prevailing problems concerning language names and relationships in Africa are well articulated by Fivaz (1973, iii) in his observation that the field of Bantu language classification, for example, is a complex and difficult one in a number of aspects. Of the large number of languages involved, the vast geographical spread of the languages, the "wave-like" distribution of features, and the complexities of nomenclature are so well known as not to call for specific comment. Yet there is hardly any readily available comprehensive volume on language names and relationships in Africa to address the prevailing problem concerning such issues as parallel names arising from the diversity of African languages, variations in the same names from one ethnic group to another, and frequent changes of topographical names coupled with variations of spelling.

Kisiedu (1980, 65) also notes that Africana cataloguers suffer from lack of authoritative tools akin to the *Nation Union Catalogue* or the *British National Bibliography*; and, therefore, verifying names and access points becomes problematic. DDC and LCC do not sufficiently cover African materials, and LCC often scatters materials that could be collocated because of cultural, ethnic, and linguistic similarities (Kisiedu 1980, 65).

In African libraries there is much material that is largely unpublished and not catalogued and, therefore, inaccessible. For example, at the University of Ibadan in Nigeria, the works of famous people such as Herbert Macaulay and Henry Carr have not been catalogued to enhance access to them. In other university libraries in Nigeria, there are manuscripts that include unpublished theses. There are also collections of slides, films, gramophone records, and tapes (Greaves 1980, 13). These materials, if they were properly organised, could facilitate research not only in Nigeria but internationally.

The complexity of cataloguing Africana materials is not confined entirely to the African continent. A look at the cataloguing practices of the Northwestern University Library, for example, reveals that the use of DDC has to be modified to provide for Africana materials. For cataloguing materials on South Africa, the Dewey numbers fall in the following ranges for the subjects shown: **300–309** for social sciences, **320–329** for political science, **330–339** for economics, and **350–359** for public administration and military science. The use of **968** or **968.06** is limited to works about the history of South Africa. Works about South African race relations are classified in **305.8**. Works about apartheid are classified under **320.56**. These restrictions, though, do not apply to subdivisions of South Africa. For example, **963.4** is for Natal, which should ideally be treated in the same manner as single countries (Northwestern University).

Kisiedu (1980, 64) gives a vivid example of how the two major Western classification schemes are inadequate for handling African cultural characteristics. He observes that both LCC and DDC recognize division of the African continent into North, South, East, Central, and West Africa. Under these broad divisions countries are arranged according to colonial affinity in terms of British West Africa, German East Africa, etc. There is no regard for geographic contiguity or for historical or cultural affinity between one country and another. Within these regions there is a confusion of arrangements of towns, empires, or states. This policy has led to separation of countries from their immediate neighbours. For example, in the following sequence in the **960**s of

DDC, Tunisia and Libya are separated from Morocco and Algeria by Egypt, the Sudan, and Ethiopia:

961	**North Africa**
.1	**Tunisia**
.2	**Libya**
962	**Egypt**
.4	**Sudan**
963	**Ethiopia**
964	**Morocco**
965	**Algeria**

Note also that this arrangement assigns some countries whole numbers (e.g., **962** for Egypt) and others decimal numbers (e.g., **962.4** for Sudan).

The Library of Congress has likewise created inadequate classification numbers for many African countries. Many entire countries have only single numbers–e.g., **DT541** for Benin and **DT549** for Senegal.

WESTERN CATALOGUING PRACTICES AND IMPLICATIONS FOR AFRICAN LIBRARIANSHIP

Africa's libraries have not developed cataloguing codes for themselves but instead use those that have been developed in the West. But, as Kisiedu (1980, 50) notes, the Western codes used for cataloguing non-Western material have always presented problems that have emphasized the cultural differences as well as the unequal levels of technological advancement between the West and the Third World. Today most libraries in Africa use the Anglo-American Cataloguing Rules but in the past used the Anglo-American code of 1908 (AA code). The Anglo-American code of 1908 consists of the author and title entries that were compiled by committees of the [British] Library Association (LA) and the American Library Association (ALA). The 1908 code, the first international code, is also referred to as the joint code. It was meant to bring uniformity into the cataloguing practices of English-speaking countries. According to Quigg (1968, 25), it was influenced by other rules such as Cutter's rules, the Library of Congress rules, and the British Museum code. With the AA code, the full baptismal name of an author was the basis for cataloguing–obviously a problem for a continent with large non-Christian populations. Most African countries were colonized by Western powers in the last part of the nineteenth century, and during this time the Europeans imposed their own systems on the colonies. It was automatic that a country colonized by one of these powers would adopt and use the AA code.

The AA code treated the issue of corporate authorship unsatisfactorily and had many rules that were difficult to follow. Because of the problems faced when using the AA code, there was a demand for revision. In 1930 the Library of Congress appointed a committee to study its revision, and work was begun by the American Library Association with the cooperation of the [British] Library Association. A code drawn up in 1941 was highly criticized for being as equally confusing as the AA code. Consequently, another code was drawn up in 1949 that dealt with rules of entry. Although it basically followed the AA code and the ALA code of 1941, it had new features. For example, it prescribed that the main entry had to be established under the person or body chiefly responsible for the intellectual content of the book, literary work, music, etc. Intellectual responsibility was not confined only to the title page. It emphasized the concept of corporate versus personal authorships by giving more guidance on corporate authorship (Fattahi 2002). However, cataloguers, unhappy with the ALA code, continued to demand further revisions. Despite the revisions that were made in the codes, which were still deemed inadequate, Africa's libraries in some cases continued to use them for lack of resources to acquire revised tools. Today it is not uncommon to find African countries using old versions of discarded codes from the West because they have no financial resources to acquire new cataloguing tools.

The Anglo-American Cataloging Rules (AACR), prepared by the American Library Association, the Library of Congress, the [British] Library Association, and the Canadian Library Association, were adopted in 1967. Most libraries in Africa used these codes with modifications from one library to another. In AACR the primary criterion for determining authorship was intellectual responsibility. The governing principle was that an entry was to be based on various conditions of authorship and not on type of publication. Like its predecessors, however, this code also presented problems for African libraries in that it was meant to serve the Western community and ignored important aspects of African society and culture. Kisiedu (1980, 51) makes it clear in her article on Ghana that AACR did not pay attention to African names and their complexity. It was necessary for libraries to have staff that understood the many languages of African books; such language skills were not easily available. AACR was also criticized in that it was specifically meant for card catalogues and would not be very useful in a computerized environment.

In 1971 the International Standard Bibliographic Description (ISBD) was developed to specify requirements for the description of publications for the purpose of international communication. Many codes that followed after it were based on the stipulations of this standard. In 1978 three professional bodies, the American Library Association, the Canadian Library Association and the Library Association (UK), adopted the Anglo-American Cataloging Rules

(AACR2), which have undergone revisions in 1982, 1983, 1985, and 1987. Many libraries in Africa today use AACR2 but often lag behind in adopting new versions because of financial constraints in acquiring them (Fattahi 2002).

CONVENTIONAL CLASSIFICATION SCHEMES: IMPLICATIONS FOR AFRICANA MATERIALS

Many libraries and information centers in Africa use classified catalogues. Classification is defined by Intner and Weihs (1996, 136) as the act of systematically arranging sets of objects or phenomena. The most widely used classification schemes on the African continent, as already noted, are the Dewey Decimal Classification (DDC), the Library of Congress Classification (LCC), and the Universal Decimal Classification (UDC). Different libraries use different classification schemes according to their preferences. However, public libraries normally use DDC while universities generally use LCC. Although DDC and LCC have schedules of numbers and letters representing all topics in all disciplines in the universe of knowledge (Intner and Weihs 1996, 136), both, products of the United States, are biased towards that country and Western culture in general. This brings up the problem of compatibility with the African continent that Kisiedu (1980, 34) raises as regards the cataloguing codes: that they tend to overlook important aspects of other cultures when applied to the African context. Much African material cannot fit into the existing international classification systems. This lack demonstrates how imperative it is that Africa develop its own bibliographic tools and standards rather than rely on the West. DDC and LCC differ in a number of ways, primarily that LCC is larger and has many more classes than DDC's ten. LCC also has greater specificity than DDC. Some libraries in Africa have tried to develop specialized schemes to meet their local needs. Despite these efforts, the diversity of cataloguing standards poses challenges to the uniformity that is needed to promote exchange of bibliographic data. As African libraries increase their collections with local orientation, the problem of cataloguing arising out of deficiency in the existing bibliographic services is of great concern.

According to Schmierer (1989, 97), good management of cataloguing operations requires that many procedures that may be common to all cataloguing operations be implemented in exact relation to a particular library situation. With current technological developments, many libraries are planning to implement the integration of online databases with their catalogues, either by downloading selected records, such as analytics for serials held by the libraries or articles by faculty authors, or by the provision of workstations to provide access to the catalogue and to a whole range of other online databases. Africa's information infrastructure is hampered by lack of sufficient access to information technology, and this lack means that African libraries cannot always apply the computerized cataloguing processes that have brought increasingly exacting demands for precision and logic in the recording of bibliographic data.

As Africa's libraries look at ways to enhance the cataloguing practices of its information resources, it is important to recognise the importance of descriptive cataloguing as an integral part of the descriptive code. An integrated code is one that formulates a theory and practice of bibliographic description that is equally applicable to all types of material. Other aspects of integration that can be looked into include the catalogue for different types of materials. Existing codes are not designed to enhance the cataloguing of African resources, and so any attempt that focuses on the uniqueness of cataloguing African materials should address this deficiency.

PROBLEMS OF BIBLIOGRAPHIC CONTROL OF AFRICANA MATERIALS IN AFRICA

It is well documented that African research results are poorly covered by international bibliographic databases, and it is suggested that one percent of research work done in Africa appears in many of these databases. Sturges and Neil (1990, 20) suggest that over sixty percent of publishing in Africa is grey literature. This situation applies to theses as well. The unavailability of African theses and dissertations in major international databases is detrimental to African scholarship. For example, the absence of systematic compilation and indexing of postgraduate theses and dissertations in most African universities often means that the countries for which such research is primarily undertaken do not benefit fully from it. The majority of African countries have legal deposit laws, but often most grey literature is not covered.

In Africa most information is generated through indigenous knowledge systems (IKS). This "knowledge that is unique to a given culture or society" is not systematically documented (Indigenous Knowledge, 2002). Such information is transmitted through genealogies of families, classes, and groups and through myths and sacred texts such as rituals, prayers, etc. (Ndiaye 2001, 49). Such information is vulnerable to loss because it has not been recorded to facilitate accurate transmission. Within communities one finds assigned gatekeepers of specialist knowledge and trained, oath-bound professionals entrusted with the practice and ultimately the responsibility to impart the IKS to select individuals for apprenticeship. Such specialization can relate, for example, to fields such as smelting, the art of the smith in tool- and jewellery-making technologies, and traditional healing.

The lack of documentation of Africa's indigenous knowledge makes its acquisition and formal use in libraries difficult. This is further compounded by the fact that information professionals in African libraries have yet to fully acknowledge the existence of IKS as a fundamental area of importance. The theoretical basis for librarianship in Africa has assumed a total absence of local information sources and information transfer systems (Mchombu 1990, 7). Sturges and Neill (1990, 9) concluded that, though IKS is the primary source of information in rural areas, they have remained invisible to librarians as purveyors of book-linked and literacy-based information services because they are not formalized. Additionally, the elite in society have not acknowledged the value of IKS, and this fact has contributed to its neglect as a valid information system. Further, African librarianship has no formal training that would impart skills to librarians to facilitate the acquisition of local information held by individual villages. The absence of databases of unpublished oral information exacerbates the problem of acquiring and using indigenous information in libraries.

Africa, like the rest of the world, is faced with the problem of an information explosion. This problem is further aggravated by the fact that, as a result of colonization, the bulk of information on African cultures is not available in libraries though occasionally such material is available in libraries in Europe. Concern about accessibility of material on Africa, especially works published on the continent, has been felt for a long time. The International Conference on African Bibliography, held in Nairobi, Kenya, from 4-8 December 1967, addressed the problems of national bibliographies, bibliographical works concerned with African countries, writings on Africa produced outside of Africa, cataloguing, and classification.

One result of this conference was the development of the Library of Congress Field Office in Nairobi. This office has been involved in collecting publications from the following sources: commercial publishers and government and non-government organizations in Eastern, Central, and Southern Africa. The office publishes and distributes free accession lists, an annual directory of publishers, and an annual serial supplement. The accession list is bi-monthly and also includes publications from international organizations. It serves an important role in collection development. Most countries in Africa have national bibliographic agencies; but these agencies are bedevilled with inadequate legal deposit laws, lack of staff, inadequate funding, and lack of equipment to adequately undertake their mandate. In countries such as South Africa, Botswana, Uganda, Zimbabwe, Ethiopia, Kenya, Malawi, Uganda, Zambia, and Namibia, national bibliographies are produced but run several years behind schedule (Ng'an'ga 1998, 37).

In most libraries on the continent, collection development is hampered by lack of skills, policies that do not include indigenous resources, and inadequate bibliographic control of locally produced documents such as theses, government publications, research reports, technical reports, sound recordings, etc. In addition, funding is poor and tends to focus on Western resources. Further, most research that is sponsored by the private sector or non-governmental organizations remains unavailable in the custody of the funding organizations. Also, the lack of an effective reading culture and of an inquisitive reading populace discourages library professionals from collating locally generated resources because of lack of effective demand.

In Africa much effort is spent on creating bibliographies of materials obtainable from outside the continent and on maintaining authority files of foreign names. Other problems include incomplete coverage of existing bibliographic tools (which are irregular), poor quality of bibliographic records, and lack of standardization.

DEVELOPMENTS TO ENHANCE BIBLIOGRAPHIC CONTROL IN AFRICA

The Africana Subject Funnel Project began in spring 1995 as part of the Library of Congress's Subject Authority Cooperative project (SACO) component of the Program for Cooperative Cataloging (PCC). It is a project of the Africana Librarians Council Cataloging Committee. This funnel project concentrates on the creation of new subject headings and the changing or updating of old subject headings with the goal of providing greater and better access to Africana materials. To date, a wide variety of headings has been proposed and accepted, ranging from **Bible stories, Hausa** to **Ulundi (Kwazulu, South Africa), Battle of, 1879** (Library of Congress 2002; Program for Cooperative Cataloging, 2002).

A proposal from the Library of Congress to include African-American subject headings as part of the funnel project was discussed at the fall 1998 meeting of the Africana Librarians Council Cataloging Committee in Chicago. Committee members generally agreed that it was important to address this topic but acknowledged that they did not have the expertise or the manpower to take on this added responsibility. The committee agreed, however, that it would be willing to act as mentors if anyone was interested in starting a new funnel for this subject area (Africana Librarians Council 1998).

There are efforts to enhance bibliographic control of certain resources though these efforts are not coordinated. In South Africa and Egypt, for example, projects have been undertaken to computerize bibliographic information networks of theses and dissertations produced in each country. In South Africa a union catalogue of theses and dissertations completed in South African universities since 1918 is available online (Sabinet Online 2002). In Egypt theses and dissertations are available on the Ain Shams University Network (Association of African Universities 2002). This database includes dissertations done in Egypt as well as those done about Egypt from abroad or by Egyptians in other countries.

The Project for Information Access and Connectivity (PIAC) was convened in Nairobi, Kenya, in 1988 to plan a feasibility study for a pilot project to index, abstract, and distribute theses and dissertations completed in Africa universities. The Association of African Universities (ASUNET) in collaboration with PIAC has embarked on an initiative to build pilot databases of African theses and dissertations (DATAD). Similarly, Rhodes University in South Africa has developed the Electronic Theses and Dissertation Initiative in which it has built a database, accessible on the Web, of all dissertations submitted to that university (Ubogu 2000, 9; Rhodes University 2002).

These efforts demonstrate the appreciation of the problems of bibliographic control facing African libraries and the need to extend these efforts to cover other information resources.

CONCLUSION

The challenges of cataloguing and classification in libraries on the African continent were by and large shaped by the colonial legacy, which imposed foreign values to the local information environment. This foreign influence consequently created problems in cataloguing African documents. Africa's culture is diverse and different from Western cultural values. Classification schedules and cataloging manuals often fail to specify all languages used in individual African countries. As a result, gaps are created in cataloguing patterns and practices not only on the continent but also throughout the world. It is important for African librarians and linguists to strive to solve this problem at the continent level through participatory action before it can be taken to the international level for harmonization with existing widely used cataloguing standards. This is important in order to create an environment that enhances the design of bibliographic exchange formats and the regulatory practices essential for resource sharing.

In the past, information professionals, especially librarians, have not done much in developing bibliographic tools but have largely borrowed from Europe, not out of choice but because of colonialism. However, with the proliferation of works on Africa and in African languages, there is need for Africa to develop her own tools and standards to make it easier for libraries to catalogue the large reservoir of non-Western materials that exist on the continent. Cataloguing rules and practices are also changing with developments in information technology. Consequently, the widely used AACR2 code will inevitably need to undergo scrutiny and revision in order to remain responsive to the challenges of new information technology. Already some initiatives from Western countries and the United States of America are modeling AACR2 to meet the increasing demands of resources on the Internet. As Africa's librarians strive to come up with their own tools and rules to enhance the cataloguing of local materials, they need to be cognizant of the demands of new technology on cataloguing and classification. African efforts to enhance the cataloguing of local information materials must also take account of international rules and African reality.

REFERENCES

Aderibigbe, M. R., and D. J. E Udo. 1990. "L.C. Subclass PL8000-8844: A Case for Revision." *Cataloging & Classification Quarterly* 10:3: 77-90.

Africana Librarians Council Cataloging Committee. 1998. "Cataloging Committee Minutes, Oct. 29, 1998." [cited 30 March 2002]. Available at http://lcweb.loc.gov/rr/amed/catm298.html; Internet.

Association of African Universities. 2002. "Database of African Theses and Dissertations (DATAD)." [cited 5 May 2002]. Available at: http://www/aau.org/datad/; Internet.

Bein, Ann. 1993. "Cataloging of Materials in African Languages." In *Languages of the World: Cataloging Issues and Problems*, ed. Martin D. Joachim, 97-114. New York: The Haworth Press, Inc.

Bertelsen, C. D. 1995. "Issues in Cataloging Non-Western Materials: Special Problems." [cited 29 March 2002]. Available at http://www.vt.edu:10021/B/bertel/africana.html; Internet.

Fattahi, Rahmat. 2002. "Recycling the Past: Historical Development of Modern Catalogs and Cataloging Codes." [cited 15 March 2002]. Available at http://wilma.silas.unsw.edu.au/students/rfattahi/ch2.htm; Internet.

Fivaz, D. 1973. *Bantu Classificatory Criteria towards a Critical Examination and Comparison of the Language Taxonomies of Doke and Guthrie.* Communication no. 3. Grahamstown: Dept. of African Linguistics, Rhodes University.

Fivaz, D., and P. E. Scott. 1977. *African Languages: A Genetic Decimalized Classification for Bibliographic and General Reference.* Boston: G. K. Hall.

Greaves, Monica A. 1980. "Cataloging and Classification: The Nigerian Scene." In *Cataloging and Classification of Non-Western Materials: Concerns, Issues, and Practices*, ed. M. M. Aman, 12-30. Phoenix, AZ: Oryx Press.

"Indigenous Knowledge." 2002. [cited 30 March 2002]. Available at http://www.nuffic.nl/ik-pages/about-ik.html; Internet.

Intner, S. S, and J. Weihs. 1996. *Standard Cataloging for School and Public Libraries.* Littleton, Colorado: Libraries Unlimited.

Kisiedu, Christiana O. 1980. "Cataloging and Classifying non-Western Materials in Ghanaian Libraries." In *Cataloging and Classification of Non-Western Materials: Concerns, Issues, and Practices,* ed. M. M. Aman, 31-73. Phoenix, AZ: Oryx Press.

Kotei, S. I. A. 1972. "The Social Determinants of Library Development in Ghana with Reference to the Influence of British Traditions." M. Phil. thesis, University of London.

Library of Congress. 2002. "Follow-up to the Spring 1999 Workshop at the Library of Congress." [cited 30 March 2002]. Available at http://www.loc.gov/rr/amed/catfwk.html; Internet.

Mchombu, K. 1990. "Which Way African Librarianship?" Paper presented at the 56th IFLA General Conference, Stockholm, Sweden, 18-24 August 1990.

Ng'an'ga, J. 1988. "Bibliographic Control in Eastern and Southern Africa: State of the Art." In *Management of Information Services,* ed. Augustes Musana, 34-41. Bonn: German Foundation for International Development, Education, Science and Documentation Centre.

Ndiaye, A. R. 2001. "Oral Tradition: From Collection to Digitisation." In *Collecting and Safeguarding the Oral Traditions: An International Conference, Khon Kaen, Thailand, 16-19 August 1999,* eds. John McIlwaine and Jean Whiffin, 49-67. Munchen: Saur.

Northwestern University Library. Serial Cataloging Section. 2002. "Africana Cataloging Variant Procedures." [cited 12 March 2002]. Available at http://staffweb. library.northwestern.edu/serials/scp/scp97.html; Internet.

Program for Cooperative Cataloging. 2002. "SACO." [cited 30 March 2002]. Available at http://lcweb.loc.gov/catdir/pcc/saco.html; Internet.

Quigg, Patrick. 1968. *Theory of cataloguing,* 2d ed. London: Bingley.

Regional Research and Documentation Centre for Cultural Development. 1985. *International Thesaurus of Cultural Development: Sub-Saharan Africa.* Paris: UNESCO.

Rhodes University. "Rhodes University Electronic Theses and Dissertations Initiative." 2002. [cited 5 May 2002]. Available at http://www.ru.ac.za/library/theses/rutheses.html; Internet.

Sabinet Online. "The Union Catalogue of Theses and Dissertations (UCTD)." 2002. [cited 5 May 2002]. Available at http://www.up.ac.za/asservices/ais/gw/histcat2.htm; Internet.

Schmierer, H. F. 1989. "The Impact of Technology on Cataloguing Rules." In *The Conceptual Foundations of Descriptive Cataloging,* ed. E. Svenonius, 97-100. San Diego: Academic Press.

Sturges, R. P., and Richard Neill. 1990. *The Quiet Struggle: Information and Libraries for the People of Africa.* London: Mansell.

Ubogu, F. N. 2000. "Spreading the ETD Gospel: a Southern Africa Perspective." Paper presented at the third International Symposium on Electronic Theses and Dissertations: Applying New Media to Scholarship, University of South Florida, St. Petersburg, Florida, March 16-18, 2000.

Facts, Approaches, and Reflections on Classification in the History of Argentine Librarianship

Hechos, Enfoques y Reflexiones Sobre la Clasificación en la Historia de la Bibliotecología Argentina

Elsa E. Barber
Nicolás M. Tripaldi
Silvia L. Pisano

SUMMARY. Argentine library science literature reflects a diverse interest in the subject organization of library collections. Early writings looked at the need to organize one library in particular (the National Library methodical catalog of 1893); and, therefore, the central issue was the adoption of a practical model of library organization. However, the twentieth century inaugurated the era of library studies in the

---

Elsa E. Barber is Professor, Classification of Knowledge, Nicolás M. Tripaldi is Professor, Library Science History, and Silvia L. Pisano is Professor, Cataloging of Non-book Materials, all affiliated with Departamento de Bibliotecología y Ciencia de la Información, Universidad de Buenos Aires (E-mail: elsabarber@ciudad.com.ar; tripwal@dd.com.ar; and filolg@feedback.net.ar, respectively).
The editor wishes to express his gratitude and appreciation for Mechael Charbonneau, Head, Cataloging Division, Indiana University Libraries, for her assistance with the English translation of this article.

[Haworth co-indexing entry note]: "Facts, Approaches, and Reflections on Classification in the History of Argentine Librarianship." Barber, Elsa E., Nicolás M. Tripaldi, and Silvia L. Pisano. Co-published simultaneously in *Cataloging & Classification Quarterly* (The Haworth Information Press, an imprint of The Haworth Press, Inc.) Vol. 35, No. 1/2, 2002, pp. 79-105; and: *Historical Aspects of Cataloging and Classification* (ed: Martin D. Joachim) The Haworth Information Press, an imprint of The Haworth Press, Inc., 2003, pp. 79-105. Single or multiple copies of this article are available for a fee from The Haworth Document Delivery Service [1-800-HAWORTH, 9:00 a.m. - 5:00 p.m. (EST). E-mail address: getinfo@haworthpressinc.com].

strictest sense. It began an exchange of ideas about the advantages and disadvantages of decimal classification, and it resulted in the work of Carlos V. Penna by the middle of the century. This article is based on the analysis and interpretation of the primary sources, with the purpose of identifying the influences of European and American library thought on the development of the history of classification in Argentina in a period during which a national library identity began to develop. *[Article copies available for a fee from The Haworth Document Delivery Service: 1-800-HAWORTH. E-mail address: <getinfo@haworthpressinc.com> Website: <http://www.HaworthPress.com> © 2002 by The Haworth Press, Inc. All rights reserved.]*

KEYWORDS. Classification history, classification systems, Argentina

RESUMEN. La literatura bibliotecológica argentina refleja un interés diverso por la organización temática de las colecciones bibliotecarias. Los primeros escritos enfocan la necesidad de organizar una biblioteca en particular (Vg. el catálogo metódico de la Biblioteca Nacional de 1893) y, por ende, el punto central es la adopción de un modelo práctico de organización bibliotecaria. En cambio, el siglo XX inaugura la era de los estudios bibliotecológicos propiamente dichos. Se inicia con un intercambio de ideas sobre las ventajas y desventajas de la clasificación decimal y desemboca, a mediados de esa centuria, en la obra de Carlos V. Penna. El presente artículo se basa en el análisis e interpretación de las principales fuentes primarias con el fin de identificar las influencias del pensamiento bibliotecario europeo y norteamericano en el desarrollo de la historia de la clasificación en Argentina en un período en el que comienza a gestarse una identidad bibliotecológica nacional.

PALABRAS CLAVES. Historia de la clasificación, sistemas de clasificación, Argentina

INTRODUCTION

The history of Argentine library science has been a narrowly explored area of research. Without a doubt, it presents conflicting and controversial subjects as well as different approaches and methodologies. Even though most authors seem to agree that writings that deal with the historical qualify as "library literature," no one has yet investigated the theoretical foundations that would group a given work as falling under the rubric of "library science."

Some authors believe that works conceived independently to deal with a specific library and/or book industry problem represent library literature (Parada 2001, 110). In contrast, other researchers maintain that the only relative contributions to the library organization are works of library science and, therefore, by definition, works about Argentine library literature are scarce (Finó y Hourcade 1952, 269).

This critical issue is centered on an ontological plane: what is the essence of library literature (i.e., that which makes a work a library text) and, hence, when does its history start? For example, is a writer's scholarly discourse on the role of libraries in popular education of a library nature despite its doubtful scientific value? And if it is so, should we differentiate scientific library literature from other works deemed "pre-scientific" or "rhetoric?" On the other hand, in what category should a product of library activity–for example, a printed catalog–be included?

If we stand on a rigorous epistemological position, library literature is strictly represented by documents whose primary intent is the treatment of historical, theoretical, logical, and methodological library science problems. Unfortunately, this approach excessively limits the scope of Argentine library literature. The multiple questions and their possible answers to this issue are beyond the scope of this article. Despite the complexities, the viewpoints of existing analysis have been equally valid and have contributed to the development of Argentine library historiography.

The periodization of Argentine library history is generally divided into two broad categories: territoriality and nationality. According to the first category, the beginning of library phenomena took place during its colonial origins (Viceroyalty of the Río de la Plata). Within this category, two large periods existed: the era of the Hispanic domination and the era of independence (Sabor Riera 1974). This line of investigation sets the 1757 *Index Librorum Bibliothecae Colegiae Maximi Cordubensis Societati Iesus* as the first antecedent of library literature (Finó y Hourcade 1952). On the other hand, from the nationality perspective, library literature began during the 1810 independence movement. Thus, the first Argentine library documents are related to the foundation and inauguration of the Biblioteca Pública de Buenos Aires (Buenos Aires Public Library).

At present, studies on the history of Argentine librarianship are not exhaustive, and they are limited to a certain era or to a specific subject. This article does not limit itself to the arguments presented so far. Certain facts or phenomena related to classification (e.g., catalog filing, subject organization of a particular library, reflections on a particular classification system, theoretical studies about bibliographic classification, etc.) and their influence on Argentine librarianship are distinguished from the independent era to the mid-twentieth century. The importance of this period lies in the introduction of the main classification systems and the revelation of major trends of contemporary library thought related to the physical and subject organization of collections. A discussion on the historical evolution of the contemporary library thought from the second half of the twentieth century to the present in Argentina will have to be left for another opportunity.

NINETEENTH CENTURY BEGINNINGS

Libraries occupied a distinguished place in the Argentine independence process, and they have accompanied the political and cultural evolution of the country from its beginnings. One of the measures adopted by the first patriotic government was the creation of the Biblioteca Pública de Buenos Aires (announced in the periodical *Gazeta de Buenos Ayres*, no. 15, on September 13, 1810). The library was inaugurated almost two years later on March 16, 1812. Although there are no precise details about the technical organization of its collections, there are references to the creation of its catalog. One of its first librarians, Luis José Chorroarín, asked the government, in January 1812, for successive extensions for the library's grand opening; in one of them, he argued that there was the need to create the library's catalog (Sabor Riera 1974, 28).

Further convincing evidence of library technical operations appear in a document entitled *"Reglamento provisional para el régimen económico de la Biblioteca Pública de la Capital de las Provincias Unidas del Río de la Plata (Provisional Regulations for the Economic Regime of the Biblioteca Pública de la Capital de las Provincias Unidas del Río de la Plata)."* Its fourth article stipulates, among other issues, that "if anyone wishes to know about the books available upon any subject, he will be given the index so that he can examine it to his entire satisfaction."[1] This assertion is evidence of the probability of subject access to the collection and, therefore, the application of some classification criteria. Parada confirms this fact: "From a strictly library point of view, it is possible to point out the existence of certain professional practices. Firstly, the creation of author and subject indexes, recorded under the format of notebooks or books . . ."[2] What these sources do not reveal is the classification system being used. However, it is possible to conjecture that the arrangement responded to a series of subject categories created by the librarian. This follows from the report about the state of the library carried out by an ad hoc commission in 1833, which recommended the creation of a catalog "on the basis of an exact classification of the sciences."[3] Furthermore, it is known that books were shelved according to an established order even though it is not known what criteria were adopted. The goal of the Biblioteca Pública de Buenos Aires was to serve the cultural and educational policies of the revolution, with a "pragmatic employment of bibliographic resources."[4] Thus it is clear that technical organization was of secondary importance.

A significant library movement was propitiated by the promulgation of the *Ley de Protección de Bibliotecas Populares (Popular Libraries Protection Act)*. In effect, the *Ley Nacional no. 410* of 1870 constituted a milestone in the history of Argentine libraries. Its main purpose was to encourage the creation of new popular libraries and maintain the existing ones. It was inspired by similar legislation in the United States and Canada. The bill was sent to the Congress and endorsed by the President of the Republic, Domingo F. Sarmiento, and by his Minister of Culture, Justice, and Public Instruction, Nicolás Avellaneda, who asserted:

> Thus, the accompanying bill that the Executive Branch proposes to incite the creation of popular libraries is copied on the basis that, recommended by Horace Mann, they were adopted in most of the States of the Union, and it repeats almost literally the dispositions of a statute of High Canada . . .[5]

The project aroused harsh arguments in both Houses of the Legislative Branch (Tripaldi 1997, 27). Nevertheless, the Congress passed the law, which was promulgated on September 23 and regulated on October 29, 1870. Its second, third, and fifth articles highlighted the most important aspects of the new legislation. The second article established the creation of the Comisión Protectora de Bibliotecas Populares (Popular Libraries Protective Commission), comprised of five members and a secretary. The third article determined the specific functions of organizations responsible for inspection of libraries as well as the investment of funds to which the fifth article referred. The latter assigned a subvention equivalent to the amount that each library would remit to the Protective Commission. The total amount was then to be used for the acquisition of books.

The Protective Commission began publishing the *Boletín de Bibliotecas Populares (Popular Libraries Bulletin)* in 1872. This publication provided accounts of the accomplishments of the organization, reproduced the invoices of books sent to the provinces, and lists of libraries receiving funds. Furthermore, the *Bulletin* included articles of interest about educational issues concerning libraries and provided lists of recommended works for selection and acquisition.

Even though the Comisión Protectora de Bibliotecas Populares acted as a centralized agency for library acquisitions, it did not function in the same way regarding technical operations. Different issues of the *Boletín de Bibliotecas Populares* would publish, as models, statutes of libraries already established and regulations introduced by various Argentine political or cultural individuals. These documents contained suggestions about classification or arrangement of the collections, but they were not inclined to favor any particular system. In fact, proposals were notably disparate in their recommendations. The Commission (*Boletín* 1872a) proposed a bibliography or suggested works for acquisition by libraries in which bibliographic records were grouped in broad subject areas: philosophy, sciences and their application to the arts and industries; law, political science, social economy, and politics; history; geography, travel; literature; education; religion. Later the Commission compiled a new and more extensive list of bibliographic suggestions (*Boletín* 1874) but this time in strict alphabetical order by author. It is worth noting that the creation and printing of price lists of "useful books" was one of the duties that the Commission refused to delegate.

On the other hand, as already mentioned, model statutes or regulations were published to help guide new libraries or associations. Some of them had library implications. Dr. Joaquín Quiroga, for instance, who was a well-known public official from the province of Catamarca, introduced in 1872 a model statute for newly formed libraries. Chapter VI, article 25, subsection 3, referring to the duties of the librarian, states: "To maintain the good order of books and other publications or realia that the library shelves hold, be careful not to change its location, based numerical or alphabetical order, with which they are indicated in the respective catalogs."[6] The reference to the different types of materials, bibliographic and non-bibliographic, that a collection could contain is particularly interesting for this time period. The classification of the collection, however, remains ambiguous since the "numerical or alphabetical order" does not allude to any category in particular. Likewise, the phrase "respective catalogs" does not enlighten us as to their specific contents. Fortunately, other records were more descriptive regarding library practices. A singular case is the *Reglamento de la Biblioteca Popular de Baradero* (*Baradero Popular Library*

Regulation, Province of Buenos Aires). In its third article, it prescribes technical procedures:

> A catalog of all books numbered from 1 to 100, etc., of all volumes in-
> cluded in each section in which the library is divided; putting the same
> numeration in small stamps on the back of each volume. Sections will be
> designated in the catalog and on the shelves with the corresponding title
> and Roman numbers. These numbers will be placed in the stamp of each
> book, repeating them in all volumes that comprise the section designated
> by each one of those numbers. [7]

Undoubtedly, the "sections" reveal subject categories or semantic fields determined according to the content of the bibliographic items, given that such
sections were designated in the catalog and on the shelves with the "corresponding title." The word "title" is, in this context, a clear reference to the
subject matter.

Thus it is clear that the emphasis of Sarmiento's library administration policy, through *Law 419*, 1870, and its implementation through the Comisión
Protectora de Bibliotecas Populares, was on the propagation of libraries
throughout the Argentine territory and that there was a goal to increase the
number of available volumes and their circulation. A population otherwise excluded from formal education would have the benefits gained from the civiliz-
ing effects of reading. It is understandable, then, that the technical aspects of
the organization of library collections were not the primary consideration for
popular libraries protected by the government.

The case chosen to conclude this section is the opposite of what was stated
before. In effect, classification was seen as a scientific discipline, both in its
theoretical and in its practical phases. By the end of the nineteenth century
(1893), the Biblioteca Nacional Argentina (Argentine National Library) was
prepared to publish its *Catálogo Metódico de la Biblioteca Nacional* (*Methodical Catalog of the National Library*). The library's director, Paul Groussac,
had developed a classification system, a milestone in the history of Argentine
librarianship. Groussac wrote the preface to volume 1 (Sciences and Arts). The
text had two quite distinctive sections. First, there is a brief history of the
Biblioteca Nacional Argentina from its origins as the Biblioteca Pública de
Buenos Aires through its nationalization in the 1880s to Groussac's administration. The most remarkable topic of this article, however, is the section about
the outline of the classification adopted.

Theoreticians seek principles, generalities, and regularities–in a word, the
foundations on which all reality is based. Groussac, a rigorous and systematic

thinker, started from two closely related premises that he deemed substantial to any bibliographic enterprise: (1) the antinomy between the philosophical classification of human knowledge and bibliographic classification and (2) accessibility and maneuverability through the catalog (today we would speak of user friendliness, a term that would be an anachronism for that time).

Groussac criticized most bibliographers for confusing the plan of a subject catalog with a philosophical classification of the sciences or the systematic arrangement of a particular science, such as the taxonomic classification of Linnaeus. The author illustrates this confusion starting with positivistic philosophy. He demonstrates with the acuteness of a scholar how Bacon's, Comte's, and Spencer's classification of science, among others, used for a bibliography could become a true cryptography, even for the most learned user who was not lettered in positivistic philosophy. But where does the problematic core of this dichotomy narrow? Groussac solved it ontologically: " . . . there is another reason even more solid, from our special viewpoint; and it is the consideration of the very same structure of books, which are in the end our units, our scientific entities." [8] The topics that keep documents joined together cannot be separated, not even under philosophical justification.

The author's second premise has a pragmatic approach. The catalog is a work of the people–that is, a tool of fast and easy operation. In other words, the catalog should be self-explanatory. Groussac exposes this premise with lucidity:

> It is not his catalog, he that is responsible for instructing the readers, but his books; and the most he can aim for [referring to the bibliographer] is the simple and clear method that makes superfluous his personal intervention. His classifications must be the most usual and the ones that respond to natural and evident analogies. [9]

Now, how can these two principles meet in the coalescence of an adequate classification scheme for the subject catalog? In principle, according to Groussac, the system had to respond to a classification of partial analogy and be somewhat vague so that it could be complemented with notes and references to another one associated to it or similar. Secondly, the guideline to take into account in the organization of the plan's sections and sub-sections was the "criteria of generalization." The author forces this idea to its paroxysm: "For the bibliographer, if I am allowed to strain the thought a little bit more precisely, all animals that fly are birds, all that swim, fishes–as in Genesis" [10] Having set these basic principles that supported his conclusion, Groussac proposed not to part from the representation of the old faculties of knowledge and traditional organization when defining the main classes, no matter the order in which they are enumerated (herein lies an implicit criticism to ordinal systems). First-level subdivisions in his scheme responded to five categories: sciences and the arts, historical sciences, literature, and theology. The problem with subdivisions of main classes was solved in the same way: the criteria of generality, only that, in this case, because of being applied to the designation of subdivisions, Groussac called it "criteria of decreasing generality."

The influence of French bibliography and French bibliophilism on Paul Groussac was undeniable–namely due to Jacques-Charles Brunet's handbook (Brunet 1810). Brunet's influence was demonstrated in the preface of Groussac's *Methodical Catalog*, for example, when it was stated that sections were "almost the same" as Brunet's table. The figure of the French bookseller was also an object of criticism by Groussac: "Brunet's classic handbook is riddled with doubtful attributions, because of not having used the method of repetitions. It's true that he uses the one of notes and references in headings; but it is not enough, since the title is missing in another section."[11]

The resulting classification system was the object of countless objections; however, if it had detractors, it also had supporters (Simons 1934; Selva 1939). Moreover, it was adopted by different Argentine libraries: The Biblioteca del Congreso de la Nación (Library of the National Congress) and the Biblioteca del Jockey Club (Jockey Club Library) (Selva 1939, 243).

To conclude, it is not the purpose of this article to reproduce Groussac's classification system or to fall into descriptive redundancies of its different classes, yet we prefer to highlight the depth of his reflections about the foundations of a classification system for his time. His theoretical speculations opened a new phase in the history of Argentine librarianship in general and of classification in particular.

CLASSIFICATION IN THE CENTER OF THE DEBATE

During the first three decades of the twentieth century, two individuals, Federico Birabén and Juan Túmburus, through each of their works related to library organization, opened up the discussion about which classification systems were more convenient to adopt, both for library organization and for bibliographic work. They both were prominent figures in the professional field and organized academic and special libraries; both kept close links with politicians and educators of that time, and they collaborated in the development of educational projects for the instruction of librarians, especially Federico Birabén. Each of them embraced different stances on the issue, and they became well-known experts of their time. It is significant, then, to introduce the ideas that these authors shaped in their works to illustrate this period.

As early as 1904, a few years after the creation of the International Institute of Bibliography (1895), Federico Birabén explained his opinions on how an academic library in the city of Buenos Aires could be organized and made known the criteria that would need to be followed in order to realize this goal. He deemed classification a central activity; and even though he admitted that history recognized the existence of numerous "bibliographic systems" for the classification of documents, the initiative promoted by the Institute was for him " . . . the most worthy of receiving the attention of scholars, and even of captivating it . . . " [12] He recognized that the Dewey Decimal Classification System adopted by Brussels had three essential peculiarities that made it highly valuable:

> . . . (1) a truly scientific principle of bibliographic classification, from which a notable bibliographic nomenclature and notation is derived; (2) an actually practical system of bibliographic notation or writing; and (3) a wide and fruitful work method founded on international cooperation and even universal . . . [13]

Birabén maintained that this system was solid and comprehensive enough to extend its use outside the boundaries of bibliography in the strict sense, for example, to the field of library management. Likewise, he recommended taking it into account for the physical arrangement of works. Thus, he suggested the adoption of the bibliographic system, of its methodology and form of cooperation in order to resolve the problems related to library science. By supporting the Decimal System and the creation of the Oficina Bibliográfica Nacional (National Bibliographic Office), Birabén became the main advocate of the use of tools recognized at the international level and contributed to strengthening the concepts of normalization and universality that characterize modern librarianship.

In an opposite stance, it is worth analyzing the approach of Juan Túmburus, who through his writings achieved the most original contribution to the history of classification in Argentine librarianship. In his work *Apuntes de Bibliotecografía* . . . (*Notes on Bibliotecografía* . . . 1913, 747-48)–*bibliotecografía* is a branch of librarianship pertaining to the study of classification principles and systems–he made a review of classification systems and systematized them into the following typology:

Ancient:	Egyptian:	*Hieratic*		
		Demotic		
	Assyrian Babylonic:	*Topographic*		
	Hebrew-Theological			
	Alexandrian:	*Methodical* (Calimachus)		
		Canonic (Aristarchus)		
		Alphabetic (poetry)		
	Greeks:	*Aristotelian*		
		Hippocratic		
	Romans:	*Alphabetic* (Polion)		
		Tiranionic (Cicero)		
Medieval:	Cassiodorus:	*Trivium-quadrivioum*		
		Didactic		
	Cloistral:	*Theological–Pure*		
		Theologica –Mixed		
	Moriscan:	*Al Hakem*		
Contemporary:	Commercial:	*Pure:*	Manucio	
			Willer	
			Hinrish	
		Applied:	Gesner:	Martin
				Marchand
			Garnier:	Barbier
				Brunet
	Philosophical:	*Ideological:*	Locke	
			Bacon	
		Inductive:	Comte	
			Diderot and	
			D'Alambert	
		Deductive:	Descartes	
			Kant	
		Metaphysical:	Mabun	
			Camus	
			Merlin	
		A priori:	Ampère	
		Etymological:	Bentham	
	Impropios:	*Geographical:*	Local System	
			Topographic	
		Chronological	By epoch	
			Annual	
		Philological		
		Editorial		
	Neo-philosophical:	*Mixed*		
		Positivistic	Robin	
			Spencer	
			Trivero	

Utilitarian:	*Commercial:*	Pure:	Editors
			Booksellers
		Applied:	Brunet
	Numerical:	Rigid:	Dewey
			Schwartz
		Expansive:	Cutter
			Brown
	Onomastic:	By author	
		By subject	
		(dictionary systematic)	
Specialized:	*Scientific*:	Pure sciences	
		Applied sciences	
	Legislative		
	Pedagogic		
	Industrial		
	Sports, etc.		

Similarly, Túmburus created a periodization of classifications from ancient times to the nineteenth century:

- ***1st era or ancient era:*** from the VI Egyptian dynasty (3200 B.C.) to the destruction of the library of Alexandria (641 Christian era)
- ***2nd era or cloistral era:*** from the destruction of the library of Alexandria (641 Christian era) to the invention of the press by Gutenberg (1438 according to Lambinet)
- ***3rd era or philosophical and commercial era:*** from Gutenberg (1438) to J.-Ch. Brunet (1810)
- ***4th era or utilitarian, contemporary era:*** from J. Ch. Brunet (1810) to Dewey (1876) (Túmburus 1913, 749).

In this context he pointed out the reaction against the "philosophical systems" of *clasificación bibliotecográfica* initiated with the "utilitarian systems," among which he cited the one created by Jacques-Charles Brunet. He noted that these had had their time of popularity and Brunet's in particular had been adopted by some libraries in Latin America. He emphasized that, in spite of library congresses that were taking place, in order to define the aspects of uniformity or universality of classification unsuccessfully, Melville Dewey (1876) introduced his utilitarian Decimal Classification System, and " . . . it raised a true wasps' nest among the most renowned librarians from countries all over the world . . . "[14] He pointed out that Dewey's contribution was portrayed by Marcel Baudouin as "une géniale invention," which propitiated the

Belgian government acceptance, which ordered the creation of the International Institute of Bibliography (1895).

Túmburus evaluated the Institute's *Manuel du Répertoire bibliographique universel* and claimed that the Decimal Classification System could be useful for a bibliographic institute but not for a library since an institute works with cards and impersonal users while a library works with physical volumes and readers. As he indicated: "In bibliographic institutes the *reader* does not exist; there exist employees who serve remote clients and correspondents, while in libraries the *reader* is everything. The difference is enormous!"[15] On the other hand, he commented on the "expansion or dilution" and on the forced "contraction or condensation" to which subjects included were exposed.

Furthermore, he called attention to the inconvenience of applying the same criteria of universality to classification:

> Some time ago, it was discussed in some country of this world to legislate on '*clasificación bibliotecográfica*,' making mandatory the adoption of the Decimal Classification–*Creo quia absurdum est.*–Only to Nero, the most autocratic of emperors, could such an imposition have occurred. Classification goes together with science, and the latter does not admit limits determined *a priori*.[16]

Túmburus considered classification as a central issue in the library process and expressed that other areas of library activities could be normalized, but ". . . never classification. The latter, in countries all over the world, shouts: Freedom! Freedom! Freedom!"[17]

He stressed that the Germans had labeled the Decimal System with the term *Starre-system* meaning *rigid system* or *without flexibility*. According to Túmburus, the Germans also classified this system as cryptic:

> Another epithet not less expressive is *Rätselsystem* (puzzle) to demonstrate that if a reader is placed in front of the figure: 617.558.1.0897 (*acertotilis Bartolillo*) he is completely in the dark, and if he does not have the help of that little handbook of 2000 pages called *compendium*, he will never be able to puzzle out that number of eleven figures, which in decimal language means just *nephrectomy*.[18]

He also emphasized that other classifications, like Brunet's for instance, became popular by themselves, while the Decimal System needed international publicity to promote its application. This, according to Túmburus, had a counterproductive effect anyway because it led Europe to say that it was used in America and in America that it was used in Europe.

Based on the criticisms enumerated above, this author proposed what he named "reasoned specialized classification" (Túmburus 1913, 750). In fact, he didn't suggest adopting a certain classification scheme; when referring to a general library he recommended taking both a utilitarian classification as well as a philosophical one as guidelines. In a special library, on the other hand, he advised using a treatise on the subject of works to be organized as a starting point (Túmburus 1915, 51).

Túmburus introduced his classification system as a methodology to be followed, and he developed a series of general principles and procedures that explained the rules necessary for its implementation. Firstly, the librarian had to identify a "provisional classification key." To this effect two factors had to be taken into account: a principal or main one, the reader, and an accessory or secondary one, the kind of books that comprised the library–that is, the subjects contained in the collection. To allow for the main factor, it was necessary to meet two premises:

- acquired book–classified book
- detailed classification

By respecting the equation reader-subject, the librarian was ready to formulate the "classification key." The number of existent volumes guided the degree of expansion that was more suitable for the "provisional key." This was for Túmburus an open, flexible system that allowed for the intercalation of new sections and sub-sections. Thus, problems caused by the relationship of decimal classification systems to the proximity and hierarchy of subjects were balanced. The artificial "dilation-contraction" that he observed, as well as the impact on the shelving and physical management of the collection, was avoided. The system's economy was preserved due to the fact that " . . . except for the cases of relationship between two or more different subjects [. . .] only one methodical card should be enough."[19]

On the issue of procedures, in a later work, *El Bibliotecario Práctico* (*The Practical Librarian*) (1915), Túmburus asserted that:

1. When constructing the *clave de previsión* (reference to a provisional or tentative classification scheme), notes had to be taken on the main parts that comprised the subject to classify, placing them in columns to the left of the sheet, somewhat distanced from one another. The first degree of classification was obtained this way.
2. These parts were subdivided into main sections, which were registered leaving an indentation below the ones from the first degree. Thus, the second degree of classification was achieved.

3. This process continued until the more convenient subdivision for the library whose collection was being classified was found.
4. Each chosen term was given a correlative number ("number level"), which was put in a column to the right of the paper.
5. An alphabetical index of all terms with their classification number was constructed.
6. Cards that would make the "methodical catalog" started to be classified. The most significant word of the work's title was looked up in the index, and the corresponding number was written down on the card. In case of doubt, the book was consulted. If a specific section wasn't found, it was classified in the one that could enclose it, or a new sub-section was created and assigned a provisional *subcota* (a correlative number representing each of the subclasses of the classification scheme) that had to be taken into consideration for the final revision of the system.
7. Cards from the same *cota numérica* (a correlative number representing each of the classification scheme's classes, subclasses, and sections) were gathered and grouped under a "sectional card" placed higher than the rest of the cards. In the space that extended beyond the "sectional card," the "cota numérica" and the section title were written down.
8. The "methodical catalog" or subject catalog was formed, following the sectional cards' numeric and the cards' alphabetical order under each section (Túmburus 1915, 51-69).

As indicated by Túmburus, the handling of the "methodical catalog" was very simple for the user:

> Be it a reader or a bibliographic researcher who wants to read a book about *quartering*, whose author he doesn't know or he isn't concerned about. Let's consult the alphabetical index of our classification, and we'll see that next to the word *quartering* is written the *cota numérica* 113. Hence, we deduce that in the catalog there is a sectional card with the number 113 and with the label QUARTERING. Going to the card catalog, we see that one of its drawers has the same label: 101 to 150; there thus must be the bibliographic section 113 we are looking for. If we cannot find it, it must be because either there are no books on that subject in the library, or those books are quite few and hence, they will be in the section immediately below: 100, BILLETING.[20]

Regarding the order on the shelves, the appropriate criteria to use according to Túmburus (1915, 20), was the "aesthetics of the line"; thus he recommended following "the rigorous order of height." He explained in detail how to carry out this process, which the Germans called "mechanical location" and what

Túmburus called "leveling" or "location by size" (Túmburus 1915, 22). He described the disadvantages of the systematic location, which he considered unaesthetic because it didn't comply with size-leveling, inconvenient because it forced a continuous movement of books on the shelves, and costly because it required more room. On this subject, the words that follow are extremely illustrative:

> Systematic location does not concern the simple library, or any other; it is a primitive location, of a school boy who wants to form a library out of the fifteen books he managed to gather in his life. Let us imagine all the history books together on a shelf, all novels on another, all geography and travel books on another, and so on. The ignorant (in librarianship, it is understood) would exclaim: This is the way I want my library organized! But the librarian knows the consequences of such an eccentric system: Firstly, the oversize book next to the miniature one will be verified; and, secondly, the library will be in continuous movement, not so much for the inquiries, but for the movements caused by the entry of each new book to the library . . . "[21]

The concern of this intellectual for the organization of libraries generated a novel line of reflection that transcended even to the beginning of the twentieth century and was, as already pointed out, the most relevant theoretical contribution in the classification field within the field of Argentine librarianship.

MASTERS AND DISCIPLES

Both Federico Birabén and Juan Túmburus were pioneers of differing positions regarding the implementation of library and bibliographic classification systems. Because of their thoughts and actions, they excelled during their time and led current opinion among their contemporaries. Pedro B. Franco and Dr. Bernardo Lavayén were the most outstanding disciples for spreading and putting their ideas into practice.

As a Librarian at the Museo Social Argentino (Argentine Social Museum) and at the Ministerio de Obras Públicas de la Nación (Ministry of Public Works), Birabén taught a course on cataloging and classification issues, according to the standards and tables of the Institute of International Bibliography, between 1909 and 1910. Pedro B. Franco, who since 1913 was in charge of the Biblioteca del Museo (Museum Library) and from 1921 was responsible for the *Boletín del Museo Social Argentino* (*Argentine Social Museum Bulletin*), took this course. The Library and the *Bulletin* were organized in accordance with his professor's recommendations; Birabén introduced into South America the rules of the Institute in Brussels. Franco recognized the advantages of the decimal bibliographic classification introduced by Birabén and made them known in his work *Tablas Compendiadas de la Clasificación Bibliográfica Decimal* (*Concise Bibliographic Decimal Classification Tables*) (1932):

- *ideological* and *universal:* its symbols represent ideas, and it encompasses the totality of knowledge;
- *international:* its symbols are figures;
- *methodical, uniform,* and *symmetric* due to the rules that govern the creation of subdivisions;
- Indefinitely *extensive.*

To Franco, its elasticity made this classification a practical instrument for the subject organization of books on the shelves, given that "the aesthetics in the location of books in a library that really wants to be useful to the reader must be set aside . . . "[22] He gave an account of the repercussions that the bibliographic decimal classification had had in different fields, and he argued:

> The multiple advantages of such a system, which any reader of medium erudition in the field of bibliographic sciences and librarianship observes, arouses the interest of many people and organizations that continuously come to our Institute with the aim of studying the organization of their Library. In order to satisfy the want of all those who ask us, giving them the necessary instrument, this publication, which is unique in Ibero-America, has been created. [23]

One manifestation of the favorable consensus related to the use of the decimal classification in the local environment was published in the bibliographic journal *La Literatura Argentina* (*Argentine Literature*), and transcribed in the "Boletín del Museo Social Argentino," in 1930. Carlos Manacorda, a member of the *Concejo Deliberante* (a parliamentarian organization of the city of Buenos Aires), when addressing the granting of land for the Social Museum, supported this initiative in his speech:

> More than one of the councilmen sitting at the left in this room–I am certain–have been to the Library of the Argentine Social Museum, the only one . . . with a decimal classification system that allows finding the necessary information promptly. I remember that we went there with men who are active in the Socialist Party, some of which had already disap-

peared, looking for data about the Argentine agrarian problem, and I can say that we obtained the best information in the Argentine Social Museum Library. [24]

These demonstrations make it clear the sympathy that men belonging to the Socialist Party had towards the decimal system. Angel M. Gutiérrez, for instance, a scientist and member of that political party, was inclined towards the decimal model, which was attractive to those who embraced the "socialist library ideology" for being a system with an international orientation, scientific, and modern (Tripaldi 1997, 29). These testimonies are representative of the significance that the bibliographic decimal classification had in the country and emphasizes the will of its followers to subscribe to standards emanating from institutions of worldwide prestige, hence reinforcing the basic concepts on which the new trends in the field were upheld.

From a different perspective, Dr. Bernardo Lavayén, in his article "Estudio Bibliotecográfico, Sistema de Clasificación en General, El Sistema Indefinido" (*Estudio Bibliotecográfico*, Classification System in General, The Indefinite System, 1929), presented with an application for the position of library director at the Facultad de Ciencias Económicas, Universidad de Buenos Aires (School of Economic Sciences, University of Buenos Aires), took up again the ideas advocated by his professor Juan Túmburus; these were based both on his published as well as unpublished writings, especially the one entitled *Bases técnicas para un Instituto Bibliográfico Latino Americano* (*Technical Basis for a Latin American Bibliographic Institute*). He developed the methodology created by his mentor with some additions that facilitated its application in the library he aspired to manage. He transcribed judgments made by Túmburus, and he asserted the advantages of the "indefinite system":

- simplicity for classifying, for handling the repertoire by the readers and the library staff, and for placing wanted books either on the shelves or in the inventory;
- ". . . absence of a *key* . . . Here the key appears gradually, without ever being finished; casually, it is governed by rules of its own lack of definition, from where the name given to the system comes: 'Indefinite.' "[25]
- interpolation of other classifications, an exclusive advantage of this system, according to Lavayén;
- easiness for creating and publishing catalogs;
- potential for making references;
- capability for making the "launching" or "breaking down" of the different subjects of topics covered in the book, journal, periodical, conference proceeding, etc.;

- economy of the system;
- no need for alphanumeric characters (Lavayén 1929, 1045-46).

As Sabor Riera (1975, 122) observed, with the death of Birabén and Túmburus in 1929, a period in the history of Argentine library techniques was closed. However, the debate initiated by them leaves the doors open for future generations.

AFFIRMATION OF THE INFLUENCE
OF AMERICAN LIBRARIANSHIP

Ernesto Nelson, Argentine educator and professor, member of the North-American Cultural Institute, of the Association of Teachers of Spanish (U.S.A.), and of the Museo Social Argentino, having lived in the United States for several years, had the opportunity to admire the organization and the role that libraries played in the development of that nation. He communicated his observations in a lengthy work *Las Bibliotecas en los Estados Unidos* (*Libraries in the United States*)–published in 1927, re-edited and enlarged in 1929–in which he carried out a detailed analysis of library organization in the United States through the description of the public library's mission, its relationship with the state, its historical evolution, administration, education of professionals, sections or departments, extension activities for different kinds of users, etc. The author states the goal of his work:

> And, writing for his brothers in race, he has deemed it necessary to insist on the picture of that spirit of cooperation and trust exhibited by libraries in the United States; spirit that, to his judgment is that libraries in the Latin part of this continent are more in need, so that soon Schwill's hard statement stops being true, who referring to libraries in South America, says: "Only one criticism can be made to all of them, and it is the irritating lack of life of their administrations."

> Hence, if this book, written with a mixed feeling of admiration for some and faith in the progress of others, could contribute to stimulating even in a small amount to the library progress in countries speaking our language, the motives for this author would be fulfilled.[26]

In the chapter dedicated to classification, he gives a brief account of the Decimal System created by Melvil Dewey, the Expansive System of bibliographer C. A. Cutter, the Library of Congress Classification System, and the Brown System. In regards to the Decimal System, he specifies: "One of the most complete expositions of the Decimal Classification System has been done in our countries by the Argentine bibliographer and publicist Federico Birabén, ardent propagandist of the Decimal System in South America."[27] To J. Frederic Finó (1952, 10), a researcher of the history of librarianship, this work represented "a true call of attention" for Argentine librarians.

In the next decade, Manuel Selva, who had a high technical position at the National Library, introduced his work *Antecedentes, Sistemas de Clasificación e Indice Metódico de Catálogos* (*Antecedents, Classification Systems and Methodical Catalogs Index*), published in 1931 and cited by Hanny Simons (1934, 29). Selva argued then: " . . . the classification system adopted by Groussac was in its time and it will still be for many years the best for our country . . . "[28] In other words, in his professional opinion, he agreed with the classification criteria set by Groussac for the catalogs of the National Library:

> Following this doctrine, we have tried to keep the main subject groups– which also allows a certain cohesion between the new catalogs and the old printed catalogs. However, we have taken into account the indexes of the Library of Congress in Washington and those of the so-called "decimal" system.

> Without trying to give our opinion about how good it is or its efficacy, we must say that the test made to adopt the Dewey System in our Library did not have a happy result, which was proved both because of the artificial inclusion of some subjects in sections openly unsuspected, as for the inadaptability of our public to a system that requires previous training, which does not take place with the current system, in which the simplest scholarly knowledge is enough to find any science in the corresponding area.[29]

Some years later (1937), Selva was the coordinator and professor of the first course for librarians, organized by the Museo Social Argentino. He published the *Manual de Bibliotecnia* (*Handbook of Library Techniques*) in 1939 in which there was a shift in the original thinking of the author towards the Decimal Classification. In its preface written by Ernesto Nelson, he emphasized the value of this repertoire given that it started the integral study of library techniques in the country. He recommended that this work be consulted as a source of knowledge for managing libraries and fundamentally for the study of issues related to the content of books:

> In this field, our libraries will find great benefit in consulting the work of Mr. Selva, who provides a detailed description of the way the Decimal

System works, which is widespread in our country after the persevering efforts made many years ago by Federico Birabén . . . [30]

Congruent with the evolution of his ideas in librarianship, by 1940 Selva introduced a project to reorganize the library of the Asociación Médica Argentina (Argentine Medical Association), where he advised, on that occasion, the usage of the Decimal Classification.

The proliferation of publications on library topics, the increasing interest in the technical organization of libraries, the concern over the need for modernization in library education, and the existence of a group of individuals committed to the development of Argentine librarianship are the factors associated with a renewed library movement in the beginning of the 1940s. The professional environment seemed to be mature enough to welcome the book *Catalogación y clasificación de libros* (*Cataloging and Classification of Books*) (1945a), by Carlos Víctor Penna. Some colleagues, gathered in the Escuela del Museo Social Argentino (Argentine Social Museum School), believed that with this work there would be an end of a history of division among librarians and that it would start a successful era for the profession in Argentina by the "definitive" prevalence of the "new library doctrine" (Finó y Hourcade 1952, 276).

As a matter of fact, the goals stated by Penna were not that ambitious. The value of this work, to our understanding, is that of having answered to the demands of synthesis and systematization at that particular moment in the history of Argentine librarianship. This hypothesis is verified by the words of Penna: ". . . the idea of the author has been purely and exclusively to present in an organic manner all the general problems that classification and cataloging pose, and it can only be considered a contribution to this aspect of librarianship." [31] The author of the prologue of the book, Ernesto G. Gietz, highlighted the methodical exposition of the different stages of classification and cataloging processes that, according to him, were the fruit of the expertise acquired by the author at Columbia University in New York; the influence of American librarianship was decisive not only for Penna but also for Argentine librarianship.

The plan of this work was carefully organized. Depending on why it was consulted, it could meet the requirements of a practical handbook or of a textbook. Both aspects sought a pragmatic purpose: to mitigate the distressing reality of Argentine librarianship at that time. Penna also occupied himself in reflecting on additional works that same year (Penna 1945b). In the specific field of classification, the author addressed different issues from the concept of classification to the systematic catalog, passing through subject headings and call numbers. He described the systems of Cutter, the Library of Congress, and the decimal classification systems (Dewey and UDC); to the latter he devoted a special chapter–Buonocore indicated Penna as one of the supporters of the decimal system in Argentina (Buonocore 1948, 271). At the same time, his preference for Anglo-American authors of his time (Margaret Mann, W. N. Randall, W. S. Merrill, W. C. B. Sayers, among many others) is undeniable. This fact is made clear in the bibliography he cites at the end of each of the chapters. In summary, the book by Penna did not bring new knowledge to classification. This was not his purpose, but it taught in a structured manner its main issues, problems, and possible solutions.

CONCLUSIONS

The history of classification in Argentina is marked by the influence of different bibliographic and library trends, both European and American, throughout the various periods. In the nineteenth century, library policies centered on the creation of libraries, unfortunately to the detriment of their technical organization. This led to the application of diffuse classification systems, originally conceived for the collections of specific libraries. However, by the end of the period, there emerged the figure of Paul Groussac, who proposed a classification scheme for the National Library catalog under the influence of French bibliography, represented in this case, by Jacques-Charles Brunet. Groussac's system had a wide acceptance in Argentine libraries of his time.

In the first decades of the twentieth century, a controversy about classification systems resulted in a dialectical process between the affirmation of the Decimal Classification by Federico Birabén and the antithetical stance led by Juan Túmburus under the influence of the German library tradition, mainly through Julius Petzholdt, who was one of the first critics of the Decimal System in Europe. This argument encompassed, in fact, the issues about the goals of classification: the bibliographic order and/or the library order. For example, Túmburus' ideas gave the particularity of each library as a system preference over the universality of classification.

The overcoming of the duality surrounding the debate took place during the 1930s and 1940s when the ascendancy of American librarianship in the treatment of library materials (particularly with regard to Columbia University) was firmly established. This was especially true since Carlos Víctor Penna set a trend in teaching classification in Argentine library schools.

To conclude, it is worth emphasizing that within this historical sequence the theoretical reflection about the foundations of classification have not been left aside. Paul Groussac (1893) and Juan Túmburus (1913) speculated on the feasibility of a bibliographic classification and on the general principles of the division of classes and subclasses of knowledge.

NOTES

1. "Si alguno quisiese saber sobre los libros que hay acerca de alguna facultad, se le franqueará el índice para que lo examine a su entera satisfacción" (Parada 2000, 437).

2. "Del punto de vista estrictamente bibliotecario, es posible señalar la existencia de ciertas técnicas profesionales. En primer término, la elaboración de índices de autor y de materia, registrados bajo la forma de cuadernos o libros . . ." (Parada 2000, 431).

3. "Sobre la base de una exacta clasificación de las ciencias" (Groussac [1893] 1967, lvii).

4. "Empleo pragmático de los recursos bibliográficos" (Parada 2000, 429).

5. "Así, el proyecto adjunto de ley que el Poder Ejecutivo viene a proponeros para excitar la formación de las bibliotecas populares, está calcado sobre las bases que, recomendadas por Horacio Mann, fueron adoptadas en la mayor parte de los Estados de la Unión y repite casi literalmente las disposiciones de un estatuto del Alto Canadá . . ." (Argentina. Congreso. Cámara de Senadores 1870, 453).

6. "Mantener constantemente el buen orden de los libros i demás publicaciones u objetos que contengan los estantes de la biblioteca; cuidando de no cambiar su colocación, según el orden numérico o alfabético, con que estén señalados en los catálogos respectivos" (Boletín . . . 1872b, lxxxiv).

7. "Un catálogo de todos los libros con la numeración desde el 1 hasta el 100, etc., de los volúmenes que contenga cada sección en que la biblioteca se divida; poniendo la misma numeración en estampillas pequeñas en el dorso de cada volumen. Las secciones serán designadas en el catálogo y en los estantes con el título correspondiente y números romanos. Estos números serán puestos en la estampilla de cada libro, repitiéndolos en todos los volúmenes que comprenda la sección designada por cada uno de aquellos números" (Boletín . . . 1873, lxxxviii).

8. "Existe otra razón aún más sólida, desde nuestro punto de vista especial; y es la consideración de la estructura misma de los libros, que son, al fin y al cabo, nuestras unidades, nuestras entidades científicas" (Groussac [1893] 1967, lvii).

9. "No es su catálogo, el que está encargado de instruir á los lectores, sinó sus libros; y lo más á que pueda aspirar [se refiere al bibliógrafo], es el método claro y sencillo que torne supérflua su personal intervención. Sus clasificaciones deben ser las más usuales y las que respondan á las analogías más naturales y evidentes" (Groussac [1893] 1967, lviii).

10. "Para el bibliógrafo, si me es permitido esforzar un poco el pensamiento con tal de precisarlo, todos lo animales que vuelan son aves, todos los que nadan, peces—como en el Génesis" (Groussac [1893] 1967, lviii).

11. "El clásico manual de Brunet está plagado de atribuciones dudosas, por no haberse empleado el método de las repeticiones. Cierto es que usa el de las llamadas y referencias en los encabezamientos; pero no es suficiente, puesto que el título falta en otra sección" (Groussac [1893] 1967, lxv).

12. ". . . la más digna de ocupar la atención de los hombres de estudio, y hasta de cautivarla . . ." (Birabén 1904, 344).

13. ". . . (1) un principio verdaderamente científico de *clasificación* bibliográfica, del que se deriva un notable sistema de *nomenclatura* y *notación* bibliográficas; (2) un sistema realmente práctico de anotación ó *redacción* bibliográfica; y (3) un amplio y fecundo método de trabajo fundado en la *cooperación* internacional y aun universal" (Birabén 1904, 346).

14. "... levantó un verdadero avispero entre los bibliotecarios más caracterizados de todos los países" (Túmburus 1913, 737).

15. "En los institutos bibliográficos el *lector* no existe; existen empleados que atienden los clientes lejanos y los corresponsales, mientras que en las bibliotecas el *lector* es todo. La diferencia es enorme!" (Túmburus 1913, 739).

16. "Se ha hablado hace algún tiempo, en un país de este mundo, de legislar la clasificación bibliotecográfica, haciendo obligatoria la adopción de la clasificación decimal–*Creo quia absurdum est.*–Solo a Nerón, al más autócrata de los emperadores, podría ocurrírsele semejante imposición. La clasificación marcha con la ciencia y ésta no admite límites determinados *a priori*" (Túmburus 1913, 742).

17. "... nunca la clasificación. Esta, en todos los países del mundo, reclama a voces: Libertad! Libertad! Libertad!" (Túmburus 1913, 742).

18. "Otro epíteto no menos expresivo es el de *Rätselsystem* (acertijo) para demostrar que si un lector se halla frente al guarismo: 617.558.I.0897 (*¡acertótilis Bartolillo!*) se queda en ayunas, y si no tiene a la mano ese manualito de 2000 páginas llamado *breviario*, nunca logrará descifrar ese guarismo de once cifras, que en lengua decimal quiere decir simplemente *nefrectomía* ... " (Túmburus 1913, 743).

19. "... salvo los casos de relaciones entre dos o más materias distintas [...] una sola ficha metódica debe bastar" (Túmburus 1913, 755).

20. "Sea un lector ó un investigador bibliográfico que quiere leer un libro sobre *acantonamientos*, cuyo autor no conoce ó le es indiferente. Consultemos el índice alfabético de nuestra clasificación y vemos que al lado de la palabra *acantonamientos* está escrita la cota numérica 113. De ahí deducimos que en el fichero hay una ficha seccional con el número 113 y con la inscripción ACANTONAMIENTOS. Dirigiéndonos al fichero, vemos que en un cajoncito del mismo lleva la chapita: 101 á 150; allí, pues, debe hallarse la sección bibliográfica 113 que buscamos. Si no se encuentra, será porque en la biblioteca no hay libros que traten de ese tema, ó bien esos libros son muy pocos y entonces figurarán en la sección de grado inferior: 110, ALOJAMIENTOS" (Túmburus 1915, 69).

21. "La colocación sistemática no pertenece á la bibliotáctica simple ni á ninguna otra; es una colocación primitiva, de colegial que quiere dar forma de biblioteca á los quince libretes que logró juntar en su vida. Imaginémosnos todos los libros de historia juntos en un estante, todas las novelas en otro, todos los de geografía y viajes en otro, etc. El ignorante (de biblioteconomía, se entiende) exclamaría: ¡Así quiero yo arreglada mi biblioteca! Pero el bibliotecario conoce las consecuencias de este estrafalario sistema: en primer lugar se verificará lo del gigante al lado del enano y, secundariamente, la biblioteca se hallará de continuo en movimiento, no tanto por las consultas, como á causa de los desplazamientos ocasionados por cada nueva entrada de libros ... " (Túmburus 1915, 22).

22. "La estética en la colocación de libros en una Biblioteca que quiera en verdad ser útil al lector, ha de hacerse a un lado ..." (Franco 1932, 28).

23. "Las múltiples ventajas de tal sistema, que advierte cualquier lector de mediana ilustración en ciencias bibliográficas y en Biblioteconomía, despiertan el interés de muchas personas y entidades que acuden continuamente a nuestro Instituto a fin de estudiar la organización de su Biblioteca. Para satisfacer el deseo de cuantos nos consultan, dándoles el instrumento necesario, se hace esta publicación que es única en Iberoamérica" (Franco 1932, 5).

24. "Más de uno de los señores concejales que se sientan a la izquierda de este recinto–tengo la seguridad–han concurrido alguna vez a la Biblioteca del Museo Social Argentino, la única . . . con un sistema de clasificación decimal que permite en poco tiempo encontrar los datos que son necesarios. Recuerdo que allí concurrimos con hombres que militan en el Partido socialista, algunos de los cuales ya han desaparecido, buscando datos sobre el problema agrario argentino, y puedo decir que la mejor información la obtuvimos en la Biblioteca del Museo Social Argentino" (*Bulletin* . . . 1930, 453).

25. " . . . ausencia de *clave* . . . Aquí la clave va surgiendo paulatinamente sin estar nunca en su fin; la rigen casualmente las normas de su propia indefinición, de donde el nombre dado al sistema: 'Indefinido' " (Lavayén 1929, 1045).

26. "Y, escribiendo para sus hermanos de raza, ha creído necesario insistir en la pintura de ese espíritu de cooperación y de confianza que exhiben las bibliotecas de los Estados Unidos; espíritu que a su juicio es el de que más necesitadas se encuentran las bibliotecas en la parte latina de este continente, a fin de que pronto deje de ser verdad el duro juicio de Schwill, quien, refiriéndose a las bibliotecas sudamericanas, dice: 'Una sola crítica puede hacerse a todas, y es la irritante falta de vida de sus administraciones.' "

Si este libro, pues, escrito con un mezclado sentimiento de admiración por los unos y de fe en el progreso de los otros, contribuyese a impulsar, siquiera en pequeñísima medida, el progreso bibliotecario en los países de nuestra habla, los móviles del autor serían colmados" (Nelson 1927, iv-v).

27. Una de las más completas exposiciones del sistema de clasificación decimal ha sido hecha en nuestros países por el bibliógrafo y publicista argentino Federico Birabén, ardoroso propagandista del sistema decimal en la América del Sur" (Nelson 1927, 203).

28. ". . . la clasificación adoptada por Groussac fué en su tiempo y será todavía por muchos años la mejor para nuestro país . . ." (Simons 1934, 29).

29. "Siguiendo esta doctrina, hemos procurado–lo que además permite cierta cohesión entre los nuevos ficheros y los antiguos catálogos impresos–mantener los grupos principales de materias. Hemos, no obstante, tenido en cuenta los índices de la Biblioteca del Congreso, de Washington y los del sistema llamado 'decimal.'

Sin que con esto pretendamos opinar sobre su bondad o eficacia, debemos decir que el ensayo efectuado para adoptar el sistema Dewey en nuestra Biblioteca, no obtuvo un feliz éxito, lo que se comprobó tanto por la artificial inclusión de algunas materias en secciones abiertamente insospechadas, como por la inadaptabilidad de nuestro público a un sistema que exige preparación previa, cosa que no sucede con el actual, en el que los más simples conocimientos escolares bastan para ubicar cualquier ciencia en la rama que le corresponde" (Selva 1935, 7).

30. "En este terreno nuestros bibliotecarios encontrarán gran provecho en consultar la obra del señor Selva, quien detalla el funcionamiento del sistema decimal, ya bastante difundido en nuestro país después de los perseverantes esfuerzos desplegadas desde hace muchos años por el ingeniero don Federico Birabén . . ." (Nelson 1938, 5-6).

31. ". . . la idea del autor ha sido pura y exclusivamente la de presentar en forma orgánica todos los problemas generales que plantean la clasificación y catalogación, y sólo puede considerársela como una contribución a este aspecto de la biblioteconomía" (Penna 1945a, xix).

REFERENCES

Argentina. Congreso. Cámara de Senadores. *Diario de Sesiones . . .* 1870. Buenos Aires: Cámara de Senadores.

Birabén, Federico. "La Futura Biblioteca Universitaria: Lo Que Podría Ser: Segunda Parte: El Instituto Internacional de Bibliografía de Bruselas." 1904. *Revista de la Universidad de Buenos Aires* 1: 344-70.

Boletín de las Bibliotecas Populares. no. 1. 1872a. Buenos Aires: Comisión Protectora de Bibliotecas Populares.

Boletín de las Bibliotecas Populares. no. 2. 1872b. Buenos Aires: Comisión Protectora de Bibliotecas Populares.

Boletín de las Bibliotecas Populares. no. 4. 1873. Buenos Aires: Comisión Protectora de Bibliotecas Populares.

Boletín de las Bibliotecas Populares. no. 5. 1874. Buenos Aires: Comisión Protectora de Bibliotecas Populares.

Buonocore, Domingo. *Elementos de Bibliotecología.* 1948. 2a. ed. Santa Fe: Castellvi.

Brunet, Jacques-Charles. *Manuel du libraire et de l'amateur de livres.* 1810. Paris: Brunet.

Finó, J. F., and Luis A. Hourcade. "Evolución de la Bibliotecología en la Argentina 1757-1952." 1952. *Revista Universidad: Órgano de la Universidad Nacional del Litoral* 25: 265-99.

Franco, Pedro B. "Tablas Compendiadas de la Clasificación Bibliográfica Decimal: Para Aplicarse a Ciencias Sociales y Cuestiones Anejas: con las Bases Esenciales para La Organización Bibliográfica y Documentaria en General." 1932. *Boletín del Museo Social Argentino* 20, nos. 115-117: sec. Bibliografía, 1-32.

Groussac, Paul. *Historia de la Biblioteca Nacional.* Buenos Aires : Biblioteca Nacional, 1967. Originally published in *Catálogo Metódico de la Biblioteca,* t. 1, cap. ciencias y artes: prefacio (Buenos Aires: Biblioteca Nacional, 1893).

Lavayén, Bernardo. "Estudio Bibliotecográfico: Sistema de Clasificación en General: El Sistema Indefinido." 1929. *Revista de Ciencias Económicas* 17, no. 100: 938-957; 17, no.101: 1031-1046.

Nelson, Ernesto. *Las Bibliotecas en los Estados Unidos.* 1927. Biblioteca Interamericana, 6. Nueva York: Dotación de Carnegie para la Paz Internacional.

_____. Prólogo de *Manual de Bibliotecnia,* por Manuel Selva. 1939. Buenos Aires: Julio Suarez.

Parada, Alejandro E. *El Primer Antecedente de Literatura Bibliotecológica en la Argentina: La 'Idea Liberal Económica sobre el Fomento de la Biblioteca de esta Capital,' del Dr. Juan Luis de Aguirre y Tejeda (1812).* 2001. Buenos Aires: Sociedad de Investigaciones Bibliotecológicas. Reprint, Infodiversidad, vol. 3.

_____. "El Reglamento Provisional para el Régimen Económico de la Biblioteca Pública de la Capital de las Provincias Unidas del Río de la Plata (1812)." 2000. *Investigaciones y Ensayos, Academia Nacional de la Historia,* 50: 413-40.

Penna, Carlos Víctor. *Catalogación y Clasificación de Libros.* 1945a. Buenos Aires: Acme.

_____. *Ideas para una Colaboración Integral entre Bibliotecas Argentinas.* 1945b. Temas Bibliotecológicos, no. 2. Santa Fe: Instituto Social, Universidad Nacional del Litoral.

Sabor Riera, María Angeles. *Contribución al Estudio Histórico del Desarrollo de los Servicios Bibliotecarios en la Argentina en el Siglo XIX: Parte 1, 1810-1852.* 1974. Resistencia, Chaco: Dirección de Bibliotecas, Secretaría de Coordinación Popular y Extensión Universitaria, Universidad Nacional del Nordeste.

_____. *Contribución al Estudio Histórico del Desarrollo de los Servicios Bibliotecarios en la Argentina en el Siglo XIX: Parte 2, 1852-1910.* 1975. Buenos Aires: Dirección de Bibliotecas, Secretaría de Coordinación Popular y Extensión Universitaria, Universidad Nacional del Nordeste.

Selva, Manuel. *Guía para Fichado y Catalogación Conteniendo la Tabla de Materias del Catálogo Metódico y un Índice de Palabras-Clave.* 1935. Buenos Aires: Biblioteca Nacional.

_____. *Manual de Bibliotecnia.* 1939. Buenos Aires: Julio Suarez, 1939.

Simons, Hanny. "Algunos Aspectos de la Biblioteconomía." 1934. *Boletín. Universidad Nacional de La Plata* 18, no. 4: 37-70.

Tripaldi, Nicolás M. "Origen e Inserción de las Bibliotecas Obreras en el Entorno Bibliotecario Argentino: Fines del Siglo XIX y Primer Tercio del Siglo XX." 1997. *Libraria: Correo de las Bibliotecas* 1, no. 1: 22-37.

Túmburus, Juan. *Apuntes de Bibliotecografía: Notas Histórico-Bibliográficas sobre Clasificación.* 1913. Buenos Aires: Coni. Reprint.

_____. *El Bibliotecario Práctico.* 1915. Buenos Aires: La Semana Médica.

Standardization of Technical Processes in Central American Libraries

Alice Miranda-Arguedas

SUMMARY. This article discusses the standardization of technical processes in Central American libraries. Topics covered include tools used for document analysis, tools used to process documents, standards for document cataloging, development of collections on and by indigenous ethnic groups, means of access to collections of documents on and by indigenous ethnic groups, standards used for information processing, development of document databases, access to networks, need for training on information processing, and consortiums of Central American libraries. *[Article copies available for a fee from The Haworth Document Delivery Service: 1-800-HAWORTH. E-mail address: <getinfo@haworthpressinc.com> Website: <http://www.HaworthPress.com> © 2002 by The Haworth Press, Inc. All rights reserved.]*

KEYWORDS. Technical processing, Central America, document analysis, cataloging standards, collection development, indigenous ethnic groups, information processing, databases, networks, technical processing training, library consortia

---

Alice Miranda-Arguedas, MLS, is Director, School of Library Science, Documentation, and Information, National University of Costa Rica (Universidad Nacional).

Address correspondence to: Alice Miranda-Arguedas, Apdo. 86-3000, Heredia, Costa Rica (E-mail: amiranda@una.ac.cr).

[Haworth co-indexing entry note]: "Standardization of Technical Processes in Central American Libraries." Miranda-Arguedas, Alice. Co-published simultaneously in *Cataloging & Classification Quarterly* (The Haworth Information Press, an imprint of The Haworth Press, Inc.) Vol. 35, No. 1/2, 2002, pp. 107-123; and: *Historical Aspects of Cataloging and Classification* (ed: Martin D. Joachim) The Haworth Information Press, an imprint of The Haworth Press, Inc., 2003, pp. 107-123. Single or multiple copies of this article are available for a fee from The Haworth Document Delivery Service [1-800-HAWORTH, 9:00 a.m. - 5:00 p.m. (EST). E-mail address: getinfo@haworthpressinc.com].

RESUMEN. Este artículo se trata de la normalización de los procesos técnicos en las bibliotecas de América Central. Los temas cubiertos incluyen las herramientas para el análisis de documentos, las herramientas para procesar documentos, las normas para la catalogación de documentos, el desarrollo de colecciones sobre/de grupos étnicos indígenas, los medios de acceso a las existencias de los documentos sobre/de grupos étnicos indígenas, las normas para el procesamiento de la información, el desarrollo de base de datos documentales, el acceso a redes, la capacitación sobre procesamiento de la información, y los consorcios de bibliotecas centroamericanas.

PALABRAS CLAVES. Procesos técnicos, América Central, análisis de documentos, normas de catalogación, desarrollo de colecciones, grupos étnicos indígenas, procesamiento de la información, bases de datos, redes, capacitación sobre procesamiento de la información, consorcios bibliotecarios

INTRODUCTION

Central America is a multi-cultural region where social groups with varied ethnic origins and/or heritage come together. Some poets describe it as the belt of the Americas. The U.S. writer O. Henry stigmatized it as "the banana republics." With over 35 million inhabitants and an area of approximately 758,800 km^2 (522,300 km^2 in continental Central America), it is seen today as a link between the northern and southern parts of the continent. It was the home of Miguel Angel Asturias (Guatemala), the first Nobel Prize winner in literature in narrative written in Spanish, in 1967. Others include Oscar Arias (Costa Rica), who was awarded the Nobel Peace Prize in 1988; and Rigoberta Menchú (Guatemala), who also received the Nobel Peace Prize in 1990.

In the field of documentation, Central America has been a region with very little development. The late arrival of the printing press and the fact that there are very limited opportunities for the exchange of documentary material have made Central America a place with scant commercial intellectual production. It is interesting that in Costa Rica, it was not until October 14, 1824, that the idea of obtaining a printing press was a result of the constitutional congress. Nevertheless, the first constitution of Costa Rica had to be printed in San Salvador, in 1825 (Lines 1944, xix). At the present time, many of the cultural and intellectual records of the region are based on grey literature.

Although Central American libraries as they are known today began with the Spaniards in colonial times, the original peoples had *amoxcalli* (*amoxtli* = document, and *calli* = house), to conserve their manuscripts (codices). Most of these documents were destroyed by the Spaniards, and now all that remains about their culture is recorded in the buildings of the Mayans and in the petroglyphs that have been rescued.

Another important aspect to take into consideration is the high index of illiteracy found in this region, due to the limited number of teaching-learning centers and the late appearance of libraries. In Costa Rica, for example, the National Library was founded on October 13, 1888. At that time there were no librarians in the country, and the organization of the documents in the library depended on the intuition and practical experience of those in charge of the books. Something similar occurred in the rest of Central America. When new libraries were established, the same thing happened; they were organized with make-shift criteria and no standardization principles. It should be noted, however, that the reality of that period indicates that this situation was not uncommon then, except for the large libraries in powerful countries.

If a brief retrospective account is made of the use of international standards to organize documents in libraries, it must be remembered that the first Anglo-American code (*Catalog Rules: Author and Title Entries*) was published in 1908. In 1949 both *A.L.A. Cataloging Rules for Author and Title Entries* and *Rules for Descriptive Cataloging in the Library of Congress* appeared. Moreover, the first meeting on standardization in cataloguing processes, in which a number of countries participated, was the International Conference on Cataloguing Principles held in Paris in 1961; the results of this conference became known as the "Paris Principles." Since then, socialization regarding international standardization has increased in Central America. Another aspect to consider concerning the use of universal norms is related to the fact that the large libraries were able to obtain all the material published in their lines of interest. This enabled them to satisfy the demands of their target users without having to establish strategic alliances with other libraries in order to complement their collections of documents.

Today the needs for information have changed. The accelerated industrialized publishing process has increased the volume of document production to the extent that no library can store the memory of the world in one physical collection. This makes it more difficult for local collections to satisfy their users' demands. Because of this new reality, it has become more appropriate to promote standardization, the creation of collective catalogs, interlibrary loan systems, and library consortiums.

STANDARDIZATION IN CENTRAL AMERICA

The standardization process has gone beyond international agreements and has resulted in an extremely important event related to classification, interpretation, and the conformation of neutral ideas and procedures. For this reason, although standardization is based on universal principles, it must take local factors into consideration. In the standardization process, the norms consist of a set of documentary truths based on logical reasoning that must be applied continually and constantly. When the norms are established, the intention of the participants is that the standards will be positively accepted by the users for a better administration of the information. The structure of the norms depends on a systemic way of organizing processes and establishing a hierarchy for them. They comprise a documentary construct that will facilitate the physical and intellectual description of the documents.

When attempting to catalog a new document, librarians refer to both present and absent knowledge for use in the standardization process of the data to be included in the document records. The present knowledge is the application–in a document record–of all of the international norms that are written and registered in the international codes used. The absent knowledge includes all of the experiences, expertise, and knowledge accumulated by the librarian that come into play at the moment when decisions are made or the point of access assigned. This may refer to the author or subject, or it also occurs when unusual elements are transcribed in the document records that are not indicated explicitly in the document or mentioned in the codes.

In Central America, initial signs of standardization of the cataloguing processes are mentioned by Miriam Álvarez, the first professor of classification of the University of Costa Rica. She reported that in 1949, she attended a summer course for Central American librarians, in Panama. It was part of a university-degree program, taught by Fermín Peraza, Elena de Peraza, and Marietta Daniels-Shepard, all of whom had doctorates. There were over fifty participants from Central America, including, curiously enough, army colonels from El Salvador, Honduras, and Nicaragua. The course was sponsored by UNESCO and the University of Panama. The second part of the course was held in summer 1950; however, there were no longer so many participants. The second course emphasized cataloguing and classification. This initiative introduced the A.L.A. and LC codes of 1949 and the Dewey Decimal Classification (DDC) System in Central America. Keeping in mind that these codes were first published in 1949 and that the course in Central America on cataloguing and classification was held in 1949-1950, we can affirm that Central America became familiar with the international standardization process early on.

In 1955 Nelly Kopper-Dodero prepared a text on cataloguing, *Catalogación de libros*, to be used in a library science course at the University of Costa Rica (UCR). In the preliminary note, she indicates:

> The main objective pursued in the preparation of this text has been to explain, in a simple way, the most common cataloguing rules. It is based on the "Descriptive Cataloguing Rules" of the U.S. Library of Congress and the "Cataloguing Rules for Authors and Titles" of the American Library Association.

This text is one of the first two teaching units on cataloguing written in Costa Rica. The second was written for the same purpose: to be used in a library science course at UCR. The title, also *Clasificación de libros*, by Miriam Álvarez-Brenes, states in the preliminary note:

> This is only a compilation of data and tables taken from different books written by experts on the subject. I would be tremendously satisfied if these few sheets are able to awaken an interest in the books mentioned and if they are sought and studied by Costa Rican librarians.

In 1976 a workshop of the Central American Cataloguing Center (Reunión de Estudio del Centro Catalográfico Centroamericano) was held in Costa Rica, with the following objectives:

- Study and approve the standards to be developed, the plans and procedures for a center at the University of Costa Rica, with national and international purposes.
- Establish the details for cooperation with the University of Panama to exchange the catalog cards corresponding to the new books; and with Nicaragua, to provide cataloguing information (Universidad de Costa Rica. Biblioteca 1976, vi).

Librarians from Nicaragua, Guatemala, Panama, Puerto Rico, the United States of America, Colombia, and Mexico participated in the event. The Central American Cataloguing Center agreed to apply the following policies:

- DDC will be used. In some cases the LC classification system will also be used.
- Cataloguing will be done based on the Anglo-American code (revised edition), applying ISBD norms.

- The list of headings developed by Carmen Rovira and Jorge Aguayo and *Library of Congress Subject Headings* (eighth edition and later) will be used. In addition, other specialized lists and headings created by the library of the University of Costa Rica will also be used (Rojas and Kopper-Dodero 1976, 6).

Later, in 1980, at the meeting held on cataloguing (Reunión sobre Catalogación), in San José, Costa Rica, Nuria F. de González, a Panamanian cataloger, said: "In the libraries in Panama, mainly the Dewey Decimal System is used [. . . and] the *Anglo-American Cataloguing Rules* are applied in all the libraries" (UCR/OEA 1980, 5). At that same meeting, Orfylia Pinel stated that 62 percent of the libraries in Honduras that she had surveyed used the *Anglo-American Cataloguing Rules* (AACR), DDC, and the list of subject headings for libraries compiled by Rovira and Aguayo (UCR/OEA 1980, 4). Nelly Kopper-Dodero and María Julia Vargas reported that DDC was the most common classification used in Costa Rica, particularly the nineteenth English edition. All libraries used AACR, and 82 percent of them used the Rovira-Uguayo list of subject headings (UCR/OEA 1980, 2). In Nicaragua, according to René María Meyer-Araúz, "most libraries still do not have the necessary tools to process material technically. They provide services without having their collection classified according to established systems; this leads to control problems" (UCR/OEA 1980, 3). In Guatemala, according to Ofelia Aguilar-Pellicer, "until the late 1980s it was difficult to find two institutions which used the same standards, and if by chance one of these participated and cooperated in more than one network, it had to go over the records two or three times" (1999, 81). Until the end of the 1980s, El Salvador experienced a turbulent period, during which time libraries were considered to be enemy organizations, and thus standardization lacked priority.

In 1981 the National University of Costa Rica published the bulletin *Boletín de fichas catalográficas*, with the objective of "contributing to other national and international libraries and documentation centers in the cataloguing process" (UNA 1981, ii). The second summary of DDC has been included in the appendix of this bulletin to enable the users to become familiar with the system.

In 1982, the NORTEBI Center on Technical Standards for Libraries (Centro de Normas Técnicas Bibliotecológicas) of the University of Costa Rica/OAS decided to "disseminate information in Spanish on the field of cataloguing through its series *Actualidades catalográficas*" (UCR/OEA 1982).

In summary, studies on standardization carried out in Central America in the 1980s and 1990s mention the following deficiencies found in libraries:

- Limited collections of the increasing quantity of information produced and compiled in the region.
- The need to organize, in a systematized fashion, the collections developed in different types of libraries.
- The necessity to contribute to the conceptual rescue of the phenomena described in the studies carried out in the region so that they will contribute to the interpretation of these phenomena.
- A lack of action making it possible to compile and process rare and autochthonous collections that would make it easier to reaffirm local and regional cultural identity.
- Limitations regarding systematization and standardization of documents on/from Central America, therefore making the plurality of the region invisible.
- A lack of national systems of information policies, thus leading to the duplication of functions and actions as well as the failure to use common standards in libraries.

In March 1995 a seminar was held in Nicaragua on the development of tools for library development (Seminario sobre Herramientas para el Desarrollo de Bibliotecas). It was sponsored by the Latin American Committee of the International Federation of Library Associations (IFLA/LAC). The participants emphasized the deficient organization of information in libraries in Central American countries. In addition, they stressed the limited amount invested in human resources and in physical, technological, and documentary infrastructure. Emphasis was also given to the identification, organization, access, and availability of the intellectual memory of Central America and cataloguing processes in the region (Miranda 1998, 136).

In 1996 the Central American Board for Higher Education (Consejo Superior de Universidades Centroamericanas, CSUCA) carried out a regional diagnostic study on document information systems in Central American universities (*Diagnóstico regional de los sistemas de información documental de universidades centroamericanas*). It was observed that of 130 libraries surveyed, fifty-nine of them used only a thesaurus, whereas twenty-four used subject headings, and ten libraries used both tools; two used three or more methods to assign thematic access, and seventeen libraries did not indicate whether they used any tool or procedure to assign thematic categories to their documents (see Table 1).

The information summarized in Table 2 and the observations made at each university would indicate that less than 50 percent use DDC and LC classification systems. The remaining 50 percent use a consecutive numbering system or no numerical classification system at all.

TABLE 1. Tools Used for Document Analysis in Document Information Systems, by University (1996)

UNIVERSITY	UID	THESAURUS		LIST OF SUBJECT HEADINGS		THESAURUS AND SUBJECT HEADINGS		THREE METHODS OR MORE		NO RESPONSE	
		Abs.	%	Abs.	%	Abs.	%	Abs.	%	Abs.	%
USAC	15	3	20.00	3	20.00	-	-	-	-	3	20.00
UCB	2	1	50.00	1	50.00	-	-	-	-	-	-
UNAH	4	-	-	-	-	-	-	-	-	-	-
UPNFM	1	-	-	-	-	-	-	-	-	-	-
UES	11	4	36.36	1	9.09	-	-	-	-	1	9.09
UNAN-Managua	12	6	50.00	1	8.33	-	-	-	-	5	41.67
UNI	4	3	75.00	-	-	-	-	-	-	1	25.00
UNAN-León	5	4	80.00	-	-	-	-	-	-	1	20.00
UNA, Nicaragua	3	3	100.00	-	-	-	-	-	-	-	-
UNA, C.R.	16	3	18.75	3	18.75	1	6.25	1	6.25	2	12.50
UCR	21	19	61.29	15	48.39	12	38.71	1	3.23	-	-
ITCR	3	1	33.33	-	-	-	-	-	-	-	-
UNACHI	2	-	-	-	-	-	-	-	-	1	50.00
UP	21	12	57.14	-	-	-	-	-	-	3	14.29
Total	130	59	45.38	24	18.46	13	10.00	2	1.54	17	13.08

Adapted from: *Diagnóstico regional de los sistemas de información documental de universidades centroamericanas.* San José, C.R.: CSUCA, 1999. Tabla 23.
Key: USAC: *Universidad de San Carlos* (University of San Carlos, Guatemala); UCB: University College of Belize; UNAH: *Universidad Nacional Autónoma de Honduras* (National Autonomous University of Honduras); UPNFM: *Universidad Pedagógica Nacional Francisco Morazán* (Francisco Morazán National Pedagogical University, Honduras); UES: *Universidad de El Salvador* (University of El Salvador); UNAN-Managua: *Universidad Nacional Autónoma de Nicaragua en Managua* (National Autonomous University of Nicaragua at Managua); UNI: *Universidad Nacional de Ingeniería* (National University of Engineering, Nicaragua); UNAN-León: *Universidad Nacional Autónoma de Nicaragua en León* (National University of Nicaragua at León); UNA, Nicaragua: *Universidad Nacional Agrícola* (National University of Agriculture); UNA, C.R.: *Universidad Nacional* (National University of Costa Rica); UCR: *Universidad de Costa Rica* (University of Costa Rica); ITCR: *Instituto Tecnológico de Costa Rica* (Costa Rica Institute of Technology); UNACHI: *Universidad Nacional de Chiriquí* (National University of Chiriquí, Panama); UP: *Universidad de Panamá* (University of Panama).

Table 3 shows that of 130 libraries surveyed in Central America, 101 (77.69 percent) use *Anglo-American Cataloguing Rules* (2nd edition) (AACR2), and twenty-two of them do not use any type of code to standardize descriptive information or points of access by author and title. Aguilar-Pellicer adds: "At present there is no coordinating body enabling bibliographic records to be stored in a standardized way, using international parameters" (1999, 81).

Miranda-Arguedas (1999) has covered the situation existing in each of the Central American countries (see Tables 4 and 5). With the exception of El Salvador, which did not respond to the survey, the rest of the countries stated that they have used some document processing method. Honduras, Nicaragua, Costa Rica, and Panama explicitly reported that they use DDC. Honduras,

TABLE 2. Tools Used to Process Documents in Document Information Systems, by University (1996)

UNIVERSITY	UID	Dewey Decimal System		Library of Congress		Cutter		Alpha-numeric		Other		No response	
		Abs.	%	Abs.	%	Abs.	%	Abs.	%	Abs.	%	Abs.	%
USAC	15	2	13.33	-	-	2	13.33	1	6.67	1	6.67	11	73.63
UCB	2	1	50.00	-	-	-	-	-	-	1	50.00	-	-
UNAH	4	4	100.00	-	-	4	100.00	-	-	-	-	-	-
UPNFM	1	-	-	-	-	-	-	-	-	-	-	1	100.00
UES	11	4	36.36	-	-	2	18.18	-	-	-	-	5	45.45
UNAN-Managua	12	3	25.00	3	25.00	6	50.00	-	-	2	16.67	3	25.00
UNI	4	1	25.00	-	-	1	25.00	-	-	-	-	2	50.00
UNAN-León	5	2	40.00	-	-	3	60.00	-	-	1	20.00	-	-
UNA-Nicaragua	3	1	33.33	-	-	3	100.00	-	-	3	100.00	1	33.33
UNA, C.R.	16	13	81.25	-	-	13	81.25	-	-	4	25.00	3	18.75
UCR	31	14	45.16	2	6.45	16	51.61	-	-	10	32.26	16	51.61
ITCR	3	1	33.33	-	-	-	-	-	-	-	-	-	-
UNACHI	2	-	-	-	-	-	-	-	-	-	-	2	100.00
UP	21	2	9.52	1	4.76	2	9.52	-	-	-	-	18	85.71
Total	**130**	**48**	**36.92**	**6**	**4.62**	**52**	**40.00**	**1**	**0.77**	**22**	**16.92**	**62**	**47.69**

Adapted from: *Diagnóstico regional de los sistemas de información documental de universidades centroamericanas.* San José, C.R.: CSUCA, 1999. Tabla 20.

Costa Rica and Panama also indicated that they use AACR, among others. It may be observed in Table 5 that of the seven countries surveyed, five have indicated that they have some sort of catalog, either manual or computerized. These tables show that in Central America, efforts are being made to process information, and tools are used to make it possible to have access to it. Both Tables 4 and 5 show that there is a lack of information on the access and availability of information in El Salvador. With the additional observations made in the region, it has become even more evident that, in spite of the librarians' good intentions, the situation experienced in these countries is precarious with regard to the development of the collections in general and information processing in particular.

STANDARDIZATION IN CENTRAL AMERICA TODAY

At the present time, standardization is valuable because it facilitates data availability and access to it. The concern in Central America with applying standards in library processes is felt even more strongly with the new tenden-

TABLE 3. Standards Used for Document Cataloguing in Document Information Systems, by University (1996)

UNIVERSITY	UID	AACR2		Others		No response	
		Abs.	%	Abs.	%	Abs.	%
USAC	15	12	80.00	1	6.67	2	13.33
UCB	2	1	50.00	-	-	1	50.00
UNAH	4	4	100.00	-	-	-	-
UPNFM	1	1	100.00	-	-	1	100.00
UES	11	8	72.73	1	9.09	2	18.18
UNAN-Managua	12	9	75.00	-	-	3	25.00
UNI	4	2	50.00	-	-	2	50.00
UNAN-León	5	1	20.00	-	-	4	80.00
UNA-Nicaragua	3	3	100.00	-	-	-	-
UNA, C.R.	16	14	87.50	-	-	2	12.50
UCR	31	22	70.97	6	19.35	3	9.68
ITCR	3	3	100.00	-	-	-	-
UNACHI	2	2	100.00	-	-	-	-
UP	21	19	90.48	-	-	2	9.52
Total	130	101	77.69	8	6.15	22	16.92

Adapted from: *Diagnóstico regional de los sistemas de información documental de universidades centroamericanas.* San José, C.R.: CSUCA, 1999. Tabla 21.

cies of the Information Society although efforts here date back to the first publication of AACR. However, it is true that there has been insufficient interest in overcoming the deficiencies.

For many years the lack of formal and informal training programs has made it difficult to establish the mechanisms required to standardize the organization of library documents internationally. At the present time, initial collective efforts are being made to overcome these limitations. They have been motivated mainly by the fact that the development of the region depends on the availability of information and access to it.

In practice, it has been shown that standardization is an indispensable requirement for implementing the procedures necessary for international data exchange. The failure to standardize document description processes, catalogs, or databases has been an obstacle for the creation, in Central America, of collective catalogs and regionally inter-linked databases, which would make it possible to share information produced and compiled here. This is essential for the development of a nation and to affirm the identity of its citizens and peoples.

TABLE 4. Development of Collections on/by Indigenous Ethnic Groups in Central America in National Libraries* (by Country): Procedures and Standards (1998)

Country Norm/ Procedure	Belize	Guatemala	El Salvador	Honduras	Nicaragua	Costa Rica	Panama
Identification	– Legal deposit – Bibliographic searches – Agreements with distributors	No response	– Contact with specialized institutions in the Americas and worldwide – Departments of Indigenous Affairs – Museums – Inter-American Indigenous Institute	– Personal contacts – Catalogs of publications – Bibliographies – Information in the press	No response	– ISBN Law – ISSN Law – Law on Legal Deposit – Printing Law – Law on Author's Rights – National Archives Law	– Strict control of editors, bookstores and authors – ISBN agency – Legal deposit
Selection	Automatic selection of everything produced in the country	No response	No response	Policy of acquiring all documents published on Honduras	No response	All documents published nationally are acquired by the National Library to be conserved as national patrimony	All documents, as they are considered part of the National Bibliography
Acquisition	Donation Purchase**	No response	Donation	According to university procedures	No response	By means of pertinent legislation	– Legal deposit – Exchange – Purchase – Donation
Processing	All documents	Everything received	No response	AACR2 Dewey 20 Thesaurus UNBIS-UNESCO	Dewey	AACR Dewey LEM Cutter Thesaurus Dictionaries	AACR Dewey MARC (Database) Horizonte

* In Honduras, this refers to the Library System of the National Autonomous University of Honduras.
** If necessary.
Data provided by the directors of the libraries.
Source: Miranda-Arguedas, Alice. Los grupos étnicos indígenas centroamericanos. Geic: un encuentro ciberespacial. Heredia, C.R.:IFLA/UNA, 2001. Cuadro no. 1

TABLE 5. Means of Access to Collections of Documents on/by Indigenious Ethnic Groups in Central America in National Libraries, by Country (1998)

Country	Belize	Guatemala	El Salvador	Honduras	Nicaragua	Costa Rica	Panama
Dissemination							
Computerized catalogs		x		x		x	x
Card catalogs		x		x	x	x	
Printed catalogs							
Open collections	x						
Others			Personal interviews	Specialized bibliographies	National Bibliography	Document archives	– National Bibliography – Bulletin on acquisitions – Internet

Source: Miranda-Arguedas, Alice. *Los grupos étnicos indígenas centroamericanos, Geic: un encuentro ciberespacial.* Heredia, C.R.: IFLA/UNA, 2001. Cuadro no. 16.

An exploratory study carried out in Central America is summarized in the following tables, to show the level of standardization found in the most outstanding libraries (national, public, university, and school libraries). University libraries and, more recently, national libraries are making greater efforts to standardize their processes.

Table 6 presents a promising situation with regard to the use of DDC and AACR2. All of the countries, except Belize, which applies Library of Congress subject headings, use the lists of subject headings for libraries, *Listas de encabezamientos de materia* (LEM), published by the Colombian Institute for the Promotion of Higher Education (Instituto Colombiano para el Fomento de la Educación Superior, ICFES). Four of the six countries use the MARC (Machine Readable Cataloguing) format in at least one of their libraries. The *in sito* observation made at the main libraries in each country shows that the MARC format is found in all Central American countries. However, in some places it is used in a primitive way without a full awareness of the fact that the structure of the database can be adjusted to the fields of the MARC format.

Table 7 shows the blunt reality of Central America: the software used in the libraries is obtained through donations (as in the case of MicroIsis), or it is limited to licenses for which the libraries must pay only an insignificant amount (such as the system developed by the University of Colima, in Mexico, known as SIABUC, *Sistema automatizado de la Biblioteca de la Universidad de Colima*). If this situation is analyzed positively, it has contributed favorably to the creation of a Central American culture in automating libraries.

TABLE 6. Standards Used in Central America for Information Processing, by Country (2002)

Country / Norms	Belize	Costa Rica	El Salvador	Guatemala	Honduras	Nicaragua	Panama
AACR2	x	x	x	x	x	x	x
Dewey	x	x	x	x	x	x	x
Cutter		x	x	x	x	x	x
MARC	x	x	-	-	-	x	x
LEM	LCSH	x	x	x	x	x	x

Most of the countries also use other tools such as *Agrovoc*, OECD Macrothesaurus, *Guía Agris*, and BIREME descriptors (used in regional medical libraries).
Data provided by the directors of the national and university libraries in Central America.

TABLE 7. Software Used in Libraries in Central America, by Country (2002)

Country / Software	Belize	Costa Rica	El Salvador	Guatemala	Honduras	Nicaragua	Panama
MicroIsis	x	x	x	x	x	x	x
SIABUC	x	x	x	x	x	x	x
Oracle Libraries		x					
Absys							x
Libsys		x					

Data provided by the directors of the national and university libraries in Central America.

According to the data shown in Table 8, it is evident that libraries in all of the countries prepare databases on bibliographies, users, management, and theses. However, only Belize and Costa Rica reported having databases on national newspapers. This type of information indicates that it would be possible to prepare a collective database on Central American autochthonous information, either centralized or more feasibly by means of links between the Web sites of the Central American libraries.

Regarding access to networks in Central America, 100 percent of the libraries report that they have this type of service (see Table 9). This has become a positive stimulus for cultural and intellectual exchange in the region. The opportunity to exchange data simultaneously has made it possible to consider new projects and other types of joint actions to promote the development of the region.

When asked about the need for training in the region, all countries have indicated that training is required in cataloguing, databases, classification, index-

TABLE 8. Development of Document Databases in Central America, by Country (2002)

Country / Databases	Belize	Costa Rica	El Salvador	Guatemala	Honduras	Nicaragua	Panama
Bibliographies	x	x	x	x	x	x	x
Theses	x	x	x	x	x	x	x
National newspapers	x	x					
Users	x	x	x	x	x	x	x
Management	x	x	x	x	x	x	x

Data provided by the directors of the national and university libraries in Central America.

TABLE 9. Access to Networks in Central America, by Country (2002)

Country / Networks	Belize	Costa Rica	El Salvador	Guatemala	Honduras	Nicaragua	Panama
Local	x	x	x	x	x	x	x
International	x	x	x	x	x	x	x

Data provided by the directors of the national and university libraries in Central America.

ing, and software related to libraries (see Table 10). This not only makes the lack of formal and informal training evident but also implies that joint action is necessary to achieve better continuing education in the field of information.

When asked about their interest in belonging to a Central American library consortium for information exchange, both national and university libraries are willing to share resources and services (see Table 11). On the national level, initial efforts are being made to establish consortiums of public libraries, school libraries, and special libraries. This interest in coordinating work implies that the libraries involved must accept certain levels of standardization in technical processes, and the participants have responded positively.

CONCLUSION

Locally, the study of standardization has grown through the years as a sustainable movement in Central America but in a moderate and almost invisible way. At present, standardization has been favored by current developments related to globalization, which implies resource sharing. Rational planning in library processes implies a rational resource use. Therefore, standardization

TABLE 10. Need for Training on Information Processing in Central America, by Country (2002)

Country Training	Belize	Costa Rica	El Salvador	Guatemala	Honduras	Nicaragua	Panama
Cataloguing	x	x	x	x	x	x	x
Databases	x	x	x	x	x	x	x
Classification	x	x	x	x	x	x	x
Indexing	x	x	x	x	x	x	x
Software	x	x	x	x	x	x	x

Data provided by the directors of the national and university libraries in Central America.

TABLE 11. Consortiums of Central American Libraries, by Country (2002)

Country Consortiums	Belize	Costa Rica	El Salvador	Guatemala	Honduras	Nicaragua	Panama
National	x	x	x	x	x	x	x
University	x	x	x	x	x	x	x

Data provided by the directors of the national and university libraries in Central America.

becomes an essential element, as it systematizes processes, making them more dynamic, functional, and economical. The purpose of standardization is closely related to sharing resources. This will permit an economy of scale among participants. Its development will multiply the achievements and results of each individual member in the region. The development and detailed application of standardization principles lead to a change in the concept of a closed, isolated, conservative library system, which is only a place to store its resources.

The adoption of standards implies policies that should be carried out according to the depends on these people. Standardization is a way of establishing an agreement among participants. They assume internal configurations, depending on reciprocal relationships among different library systems. In these relationships everyone benefits, but at the same time each member must share available resources. Standardization is essential in modern society for library systems to be joint local forces enabling each library to become a player in the political arena so that it is able to insert itself into the Knowledge Society. Library consortiums are established because of the needs identified by their members as a strategy to share efforts and resources; and, so, their processes must be standardized.

REFERENCES

Aguilar-Pellicer, Ofelia. 1999. El Control bibliográfico en Guatemala. In *Control bibliográfico universal*, comp. Roberto Garduño Vera, 80-88. México, D.F: UNAM/CUIB.

Álvarez-Brenes, Miriam. 2002. Historia de la normalización en Costa Rica. Letter to the author, February.

_____. *Clasificación de libros*. San José, C.R.: UCR, 1955.

Cassalli, Mercedes. 2002. Historia de la normalización en Guatemala. Letters to the author, January-April.

Colindres, Carlos. 2002. Historia de la normalización en El Salvador. Letter to the author, January.

CSUCA. 1999. *Proyecto Red de Sistemas Integrado de Información Documental de Universidades Centroamericanas: Diagnóstico de los Sistemas de Información Documental de Universidades Centroamericanas*. San José, C.R.: CSUCA, 1999.

Escobar, Arlene. 2002. Historia de la normalización en Belice. Letter to the author, March.

Gómez, Ruth Velia. 2002. Historia de la normalización de Nicaragua. Letter to the author, April.

IFLA/ALP. 1995. Seminario para la Identificación y Evaluación de las Necesidades Bibliotecarias de Centroamérica y la Elaboración de Proyectos (1995: Nicaragua) *Memorias*. [Uppsala]: Uppsala University Library.

Jean-Francoise, Daisy de. 2002. Historia de la Normalización en Panamá. Letter to the author in Panamá, January.

Kopper-Dodero, Nelly. 1955. *Catalogación de libros*. San José, C.R.: UCR.

Lines, Jorge A. 1944. *Libros y folletos publicados en Costa Rica durante los años 1830-1849*. San José, C.R: UCR.

Miranda-Arguedas, Alice. 1999. El control bibliográfico en Costa Rica. In *Control bibliográfico universal*, comp. Roberto Garduño Vera, 89-104. México, D.F.: UNAM/CUIB.

_____. 1997-1998. La información y la comunicación en Centroamérica. *Istmica* 3-4: 134-142.

_____. 2001. *Los grupos étnicos indígenas centroamericanos, Geic: un encuentro ciberespacial*. Heredia, C.R.: IFLA/UNA.

Morales-Campos, Estela y Homero Quesada-Pacheco. 2000. *Normas utilizadas en los servicios bibliotecarios y de información en América Latina y el Caribe*. 2d ed. México, D.F.: Universidad Nacional Autónoma de México, Dirección General de Asuntos del Personal Académico.

Ochoa, Gloria. 2002. Historia de la normalización en Honduras. Letter to the author, April.

Sanabria-M., Víctor. 1992. *Datos cronológicos para la historia eclesiástica de Costa Rica*. San José, C.R.: Comisión Nacional de Evangelización y Cultura.

Universidad de Costa Rica. 1979. Instituto de Investigaciones Sociales. Centro de Documentación. *Técnicas documentales aplicadas en el procesamiento de la información*. San José, C.R.: UCR.

_____. 1978. *Información documental costarricense y centroamericana*. San José, C.R.: UCR.

Universidad de Costa Rica. 1979. Proyecto Centro Catalográfico Centroamericano. *Informe final*. San José, C.R.: UCR.

Universidad de Costa Rica. 1976. Proyecto Centro Catalográfico Centroamericano. Reunión de Estudio (1976: Costa Rica). *Informe final*. San José, C.R.: UCR.

Universidad de Costa Rica/OEA. 1982. Proyecto Multinacional de Normalización de Técnicas Bibliotecológicas. *Actualidades catalográficas*. San José, C.R.: UCR.

Universidad de Costa Rica/OEA. 1980. Taller sobre Centros Catalográficos para Centroamérica (1980: Costa Rica). *Informe final*. San José, C.R.: UCR.

Universidad Nacional (Costa Rica). Departamento de Biblioteca. 1981. *Boletín de fichas catalográficas*. Heredia, C.R.: UNA.

Historical Perspective
of a Union Catalog in Chile:
Authorities and Periodicals

Perspectiva Historica
del Catalogo Colectivo en Chile:
Autoridades y Publicaciones Periodicas

Elizabeth N. Steinhagen

SUMMARY. For almost 20 years, the National Bibliographic Network (Red Nacional de Información Bibliográfica (RENIB)) has been the driving force of library networking and resource sharing in Chile. Administratively dependent on the National Library (Biblioteca Nacional) and also physically located on its premises, RENIB has been very successful in bringing together librarians from most of the major Chilean libraries and in obtaining their cooperation for a number of important joint projects. The most important among these was the development of the national union catalog, which provides access to the holdings of all member libraries. An earlier project resulted in the online union list of periodicals, developed

Elizabeth N. Steinhagen, MA, MLS, is Head, Ibero American Resources Section, University of New Mexico General Library, Albuquerque, NM 87131 (E-mail: ens1@unm.edu).

The author wishes to express her gratitude and appreciation for all the information, formal and informal, and for the mostly internal background documentation she has received from RENIB in the course of several visits to Chile.

[Haworth co-indexing entry note]: "Historical Perspective of a Union Catalog in Chile: Authorities and Periodicals." Steinhagen, Elizabeth N. Co-published simultaneously in *Cataloging & Classification Quarterly* (The Haworth Information Press, an imprint of The Haworth Press, Inc.) Vol. 35, No. 1/2, 2002, pp. 125-135; and: *Historical Aspects of Cataloging and Classification* (ed: Martin D. Joachim) The Haworth Information Press, an imprint of The Haworth Press, Inc., 2003, pp. 125-135. Single or multiple copies of this article are available for a fee from The Haworth Document Delivery Service [1-800-HAWORTH, 9:00 a.m. - 5:00 p.m. (EST). E-mail address: getinfo@haworthpressinc.com].

125

jointly with the National Commission of Scientific and Technological Research (Comisión Nacional de Investigación Científica y Tecnológica (CONICYT)), which contains periodical records and detailed holdings data of twenty-four universities. As the bibliographic database was being planned, RENIB personnel anticipated the need for a centralized authorities database in order to maintain consistency and uniform standards. Participating libraries provided expert staff members who work jointly with RENIB in teams that build and maintain headings for names, subjects, series, uniform titles, and subdivisions and resolve conflicts. RENIB provided documentation and training and, especially, the organizational structure that now allows for continuing cooperation among institutions that, traditionally, had not worked together. *[Article copies available for a fee from The Haworth Document Delivery Service: 1-800-HAWORTH. E-mail address: <getinfo@haworthpressinc.com> Website: <http://www.HaworthPress.com> © 2002 by The Haworth Press, Inc. All rights reserved.]*

KEYWORDS. Chile, RENIB, union catalog, periodicals union list, authorities database

RESUMEN. La Red Nacional de Información Bibliográfica (RENIB) ha sido la entidad que ha impulsado el trabajo cooperativo entre las bibliotecas chilenas en los últimos 20 años. RENIB, con sede en la Biblioteca Nacional de Chile, ha logrado, en el curso de este tiempo reunir a personal de las bibliotecas más importantes de Chile y obtener su cooperación en la planificación e implementación de importantes proyectos colaborativos. Uno de los más importantes entre estos fué el establecimiento del catálogo colectivo nacional, que proporciona acceso en línea a los recursos de todas las bibliotecas miembros de RENIB. Un proyecto anterior fué la creación del catálogo colectivo de publicaciones periódicas, establecido y creado en colaboración con la Comisión Nacional de Investigación Científica y Tecnológica (CONICYT). Este catálogo contiene información detallada sobre los recursos de publicaciones seriadas existentes en 24 universidades chilenas. Al mismo tiempo, RENIB anticipó la necesidad de contar con una base de datos de autoridades en línea, indispensable para mantener la consistencia de los registros bibliográficos y de normas uniformes para su ingreso. Las instituciones miembros de la red proporcionaron el personal experto que trabajó en equipos con colegas de RENIB en la creación y mantención de encabezamientos para nombres, tanto personales como corporativos, materia, series, títulos uniformes y subdivisiones. Estos equipos también resuelven conflictos bibliográficos. RENIB sigue proporcionando la asistencia técnica, la documentación, y la capacitación a sus miembros; igualmente provee la estructura necesaria para asegurar una continuada cooperación entre las diversas instituciones.

PALABRAS CLAVES. Chile, RENIB, catálogo colectivo, catálogo colectivo de publicaciones periódicas, catálogo de autoridades

BACKGROUND

Among Latin American nations, Chile has one of the strongest traditions of bibliographic control, dating back to colonial times. In addition to earlier subject catalogs, the *Anuario de la Prensa Chilena* had been published by the National Library (Biblioteca Nacional de Chile) since 1887. In spite of an 1834 law of legal deposit, the *Anuario* did not include all Chilean publications; however, it survived, intermittently, until the 1970s. In those years, various national agencies recognized the need to resort to the new computer technology available for the compilation and distribution of a national bibliography. With support from these agencies, a project was begun in the early 1980s to automate bibliographic processing in Chile's major libraries, through the recently donated NOTIS library automation software and an IBM mainframe computer housed at the National Library.

ESTABLISHMENT OF RENIB

The National Bibliographic Network (Red Nacional de Información Bibliográfica (RENIB)) was established in August of 1984 by agreement between the Department of Education, the Directorate of Libraries, Archives and Museums–overseeing the National Library–and the Committee on Libraries of the Council of University Presidents (Consejo de Rectores). It was housed at the National Library and its main objective was to create a database of Chile's bibliographic resources and to improve access to that information through a common online public catalog (OPAC) and the production of a national bibliography. The project called for establishing an administrative and organizational structure, and major university libraries were invited to share the responsibility with the National Library to create a joint union database. This meant that certain policies, standards, and formats would need to be agreed upon for creating bibliographic records that all could use. Therefore, one of the first activities of the new organization was the setting up of technical committees, with specialists from member institutions integrated into working groups to oversee the development of processing standards and procedures that are the basis of bibliographic control. The common set of principles adopted by these groups were similar to those developed and followed by North American libraries, such as the *Anglo American Cataloging Rules*, 2nd ed., (in its translation into Spanish in 1987 as *Reglas de Catalogación Anglo Americana, 2a. ed.*), the MARC formats, the use of controlled vocabulary for authority headings, and serial holdings at the detailed level, following NISO standard Z39.44 level 4.

After establishing its connection to RENIB, each member library would be able to create its own database. This then could be accessed through the network's union catalog mounted on the NOTIS system or through its local online catalog. Members could contribute original catalog records for others to use and were committed to maintaining up-to-date information about their collections in the union catalog, or they could duplicate existing records for their own databases and also transfer records from other online files. The latter options eventually resulted in savings of staff time and resources–one of the principal advantages of shared bibliographic control.

At present, RENIB has about fifteen active members, ranging from the National Library, several large public libraries, the Chilean Library of Congress, the National Commission of Scientific and Technological Research (Comisión Nacional de Información Científica y Tecnológica (CONICYT)), as well as the major academic libraries in the country and the Chilean British Cultural Institute. There are also a number of associate libraries which subscribe to the databases but do not contribute bibliographic records.

The coordination of this large undertaking is in charge of RENIB personnel, who focus on setting joint policies via the various working committees. This also involves exhaustive training activities throughout Chile, development of new standards, and preparation and distribution of supporting documentation. User services such as off-line products and communications are also basic RENIB responsibilities.

DATABASES

At this time, there are seven bibliographic databases available on the RENIB server, determined mainly by format or special interest. These are:

- a **union catalog** of member libraries, containing monographs, serials, theses, maps, music, audiovisual materials, of approximately 750,000 records held in about 120 libraries (1985-2000);
- a **periodicals union catalog**, of close to 13,200 records and their detailed holdings at over 120 departmental libraries of twenty-four universities (1986-1996);
- the **catalog of the National Archives** of about 31,000 records (1987-);
- an **analytics catalog**, of about 120,000 entries, which contain bibliographic descriptions of papers in Chilean scientific and cultural serials, in addition to press reviews (1991-2000);
- a **union catalog of museum libraries**, with about 30,000 records of books, serials, exhibit catalogs, and other specialized information, with holdings of the National Museum of Fine Arts, the National Museum of Natural History, the National Museum of History, and the Regional Museum of the Araucania (1997-);
- the **catalog of the Chilean British Institute of Culture**, whose specialized collections support the academic program of the Institute for the teaching of English (ELTRIC), in addition to monographs, serials, periodicals, and audio-visual materials on British culture. It consists of about 9,000 bibliographic records (1997-);
- a **union catalog of public libraries** of about 43,000 records of books held in over 200 libraries.

The content of these catalogs adds up to a total of about 996,200 records, of which approximately 81 percent represent monographs, 8 percent manuscripts, and 5 percent serials, with the remainder containing the other formats.

AUTHORITIES DATABASE

In addition, an authorities database, designed to facilitiate the work of all members, is an essential resource. As is still the case today in some countries, there was no agreement among Chilean libraries on their cataloging practices and policies before the creation of the network. Therefore, it was essential that RENIB members work on reaching consensus in defining common standards, especially for an authority structure, that would ensure the consistency and integrity of the data and accurate retrieval by users. The authority database was begun in 1986, with about 19,000 subject headings derived from the *Lista de Encabezamientos de Materia Bibliográfica (LEMB)* obtained from Colombia, through ICFES (Instituto Colombiano para el Fomento de la Educación Superior). The machine-readable file of these headings, most of which had been translated into Spanish from the *Library of Congress Subject Heading, (LCSH)*, was loaded into a database; and other headings for subjects, names, series, uniform titles, and subdivisions, created by the National Library and the Catholic University, were added gradually.

This standardized database has now existed for about fifteen years, and it contains well over 600,000 records. The largest component by far is that for personal names, with about 309,000 records, followed by subject headings, corporate and geographic names, subdivisions, and references. These three types of headings–the authorities proper, the references and the subdivisions–reside in a MARC file and are not linked to headings in the bibliographic files. Therefore, a validation software had to be developed so as to maintain consistency among the various files. Member catalogers work online, adding headings, creating cross references, and, especially, adding English equivalents from *LCSH* and other thesauri. In recent years however, with more libraries, including the National Library, having brought up local systems, this activity has become more cumbersome.

The coordinating body of all authority file activity is an "authorities control team," officially established in 1991 and composed of librarians drawn from the major member institutions. This group had been working since 1988 on the details of standards and procedures followed for the creation of new headings and the maintenance of existing ones. Its members are also involved in resolving conflicts between institutions, in validating changes and in requesting global changes in bibliographic records as authority headings change in order to facilitate database maintenance. As necessary, the team will also include some experts in, for instance, Chilean law for advice on the creation of an authority structure of legal terminology. This was necessary because much of the legal terminology from *LCSH* could not be translated into Spanish since Chilean law is based on the Napoleonic code and not on the Anglo-Saxon system.

Sources for new authority records can vary. Subject authorities, as indicated, were drawn from the *LEMB* list and were considered provisional until they could be validated or modified, if needed. In addition, Library of Congress subject headings were routinely translated and added when needed for new bibliographic records; MeSH and agricultural subject headings were also accepted as sources and translated. Among the major problems with some of the translations was the need to use prepositions in Spanish, plural vs. singular form, the use of articles, or two subdivisions used under one term.

For personal and corporate name headings, as well as geographical headings and uniform titles and series authorities, the authorities team mandated the *AACR2R* rules in Spanish, as interpreted by the *Library of Congress Rule Interpretations (LCRI)*. Additional sources suggested were biographical dictionaries, *Webster's New Geographical Dictionary*, as well as other standard publications. To the degree possible, members were encouraged to use natural language when establishing subject headings; and, in general, they were required to follow LC policies and practices for establishing headings, as outlined in its *Subject Cataloging Manual.*

From the beginning, the maintenance of this database was and continues to be the joint responsibility of all members. All participants are encouraged to propose modifications to existing headings or to send corrections to the institutions responsible for their creation. If the latter do not agree with the suggested changes, the authorities control team must intervene, analyze the issue, and make a decision. In addition, manual and automated validations of terms are carried out at certain intervals, with headings error lists sent out to members for correction. In addition, files with new authorities are periodically exported to local systems, which then must be converted at the point of loading. Ideally, if the technology were more compatible, it should be possible to create authorities simultaneously for both the RENIB and the local files.

PERIODICALS UNION LIST

It is well known that the primary function of a serials union list is to facilitate resource sharing among libraries. They began their existence in the late 1800s with printed listings of serial titles and holdings of collaborating libraries, such as the *Gesamt-Zeitschriften-Verzeichnis* in Germany issued before World War I. In the United States, both the *Union List of Serials* and the *New Serial Titles* had been the mainstay for interlibrary loan activities for about three quarters of a century. In Chile, a similar effort was the *Anuario de Publicaciones Periódicas Chilenas*, published by the National Library from 1921 to 1939 and again in the early 1950s. It listed approximately 450 *revistas* (magazines) by title and by geographic location and subjects. As the most comprehensive bibliography in printed format of serials, it included house organs, comics, professional journals, religious publications, movie, and children's magazines as well as official, university, and learned societies' publications. In the long run, however, as all printed catalogs, it could not keep its contents updated.

It is with the advent of library automation and computer technology that union lists came into their own; and while their usefulness has rarely been questioned, some of the debate during the last decades of the twentieth century centered on issues such as standards, systems, increasing costs, and the politics of cooperation.

In the mid-seventies, CONICYT, the official ISSN center in Chile, was leading in the field of information and documentation and had published numerous subject listings of serials in areas such as biology, medicine, technology and the social sciences with holdings of the most important Chilean libraries. With the advent of RENIB and its union catalog in the mid-1980s, an agreement was signed to develop a special union list of periodicals pilot project. It called for the creation and the maintenance of an online periodicals list that would be cooperatively developed and maintained by RENIB and its member libraries. Before beginning this ambitious project, several steps needed to be undertaken. Workshops were held on the details of the MARC-S format for serial records, and on the NISO standard Z39.44 for holdings data, the latter document having been translated into Spanish by CONICYT in 1986. For recording the serial bibliographic data, members agreed on using the minimum format for description and *AACR2R*, level 1, augmented. Other background documentation was prepared and distributed to all participants.

UNION CATALOG PILOT PROJECT

The pilot project began with under 4,000 serial records held by twenty-four Chilean academic libraries, with bibliographic records copied from the Library of Congress' (LC) serials database. RENIB and CONICYT personnel participated in training, in record creation, in the translation into Spanish of English-language subject headings that these records contained and, especially, in the creation of about 14,000 holdings data following the NISO standards for detailed holdings. This latter activity was the most complex part of the project and was based on information contained on shelflist cards or Kardex™ cards sent in by the participating institutions. The lack of uniformity at the various libraries in the way their holdings had been recorded manually over the years caused enormous problems for the creation of the holdings file and contributed to numerous delays. The participants also needed to create approximately 2,000 additional original serial records based on information provided by the shelflist cards and other sources.

After the database was created, it was necessary to produce different lists for participants so that they could undertake revisions and corrections. These included bibliographic record corrections and validation, the correction of holdings data, the revision and standardization of personal and corporate names associated with the serial records, and, last but not least, the correction and de-duplication of title fields. At this time, notes were also added and/or translated into Spanish. In addition, close to 4,000 Dewey classification numbers were added to records that lacked them so as to produce listings by subject area. After the completion of all revisions and corrections, a sample tape was produced and output on microfiche for further revisions. Finally it was possible to produce a computer-output microfiche (COM) catalog of the periodicals union list, which was delivered to all participants in early 1989. In its online version the database contained information on current titles, their location in the libraries of the twenty-four participating universities, and their detailed holdings in each of the departmental libraries. At the time it contained information for about 12,000 periodical titles. In late 1989, CONICYT and RENIB signed another agreement with the purpose of continuing to build the periodicals union list and, especially, to maintain and to update it periodically.

According to this agreement, CONICYT and RENIB personnel were to update the database at the end of each calendar year. At the completion of the pilot project, several issues had surfaced. These included the need to continue working on the translation of subject headings and the creation of the related authority structure. In addition, approximately 35 percent of the serial titles needed to be standardized to be in agreement with the *AACR2R* rules, and other bibliographic data completed. In recent years, however, as members were building their own local databases with bibliographic and holdings information, the initial impetus to maintain and update the union list appears to have stagnated somewhat. Nevertheless, CONICYT continued to update the union list until about 1997, with the holdings of those special libraries that were not members of the network and that did not have local systems. RENIB member libraries, on the other hand, ceased to update their holdings in the union list in 1996 as their data was transferred to their own NOTIS files. They maintained these until 1998 when they migrated the information to their own local systems and continue to perform maintenance only locally.

THE FUTURE OF UNION LISTING

In recent years, given new developments in computer technology, the rise of commercial document delivery services, full-text availability on the Web, declining library budgets and concomitant staff attrition, the situation for union lists has become extremely complicated. Traditional manual updating and holdings maintenance, especially in two incompatible files, have become extremely expensive and staff-intensive. In addition, no library, especially in countries where exchange rates fluctuate wildly, can afford to continue subscribing to all periodical titles that it may need. As U.S. academic libraries periodically go through painful serial cancellations, the situation in Chile and other Latin American countries will be even more serious.

According to Walt Crawford of the Research Libraries Group (RLG), "Libraries have come a long way from the multi-part typed forms and manual record-keeping systems of the 1970s and before." However, in spite of, or perhaps because of, all the new technology available at this time, "resource sharing has become more important." He continues to say that, "One route to fast, cost-effective resource sharing involves regional cooperation, delivery systems, and union catalogs." With skyrocketing subscription costs, which have added another powerful argument in favor of more cooperation and resource sharing, union lists that contain accurate and up-to-date bibliographic and holdings information may still be an essential part of our future. But until local systems and union lists residing at other sites become more compatible and allow for simultaneous record maintenance, it will be difficult for libraries to justify the resources and staff time spent on this activity, especially if it is not of direct benefit to their own users.

CONCLUSIONS

RENIB has been very successful in its almost 20-year existence in establishing the union catalog and, especially, the above two important databases. However, according to some observers, its major accomplishments lie in its bringing together staff from a variety of libraries and in obtaining their active cooperation and their support for working together within internationally agreed-upon standards and parameters. By building on this framework of cooperation, several ambitious plans continue to be developed for expanding and improving services and for connectivity to other networks. Although most members began working with the NOTIS software as their local utility, several of the major universities, as well as the National Library, have migrated to other integrated systems. It is likely that the RENIB databases will also be migrated from NOTIS to the local system maintained by the National Library. This might also imply some structural and administrative changes at the network, but one can only hope that the tremendous effort and hard work of twenty-plus years succeed in retaining the standards developed as well as the spirit of collaboration. It will be a challenge but well worth it in the long run as no library in Chile, or elsewhere, can afford to go it alone.

BIBLIOGRAPHICAL SOURCES

Bloss, Marjorie C. "And in Hindsight . . . the Past Ten Years of Union Listing." *The Serials Librarian* 10, no. 3 (fall-winter 1986): 141-148.
"Comisión Nacional de Investigación Científica y Tecnológica (CONICYT)." Home page. [cited 19 April 2002]. Available at http://conicyt.cl/.

Crawford, Walt. "ILL: Peering into the Future." *American Libraries*: 31, no. 10 (Nov. 2000): 35-48.

Freudenthal, Juan R. "Information and Documentation in Chile: Progress Report. Bibliography 1974-1976." *Journal of the American Society for Information Science* (1980): 445-448.

Iglesias Maturana, Maria Texia, and Soledad Fernandez-Corugedo. "Chile: El Control y los Servicios Bibliograficos." Paper presented at Seminario Internacional sobre Control Bibliográfico Universal, 1998.

Maturana Salas, Isabel. "El Sistema de Autoridades en RENIB." Paper presented at Reunión Internacional de Usuarios de LEMB, Dec. 1989.

Red Nacional de Información Bibliográfica (RENIB). Home page. [cited 19 April 2002]. Available at http://www.renib.cl.

_____. Catálogo Colectivo de Publicaciones Seriadas. Assorted documentation.

_____. Various reports of the Authority Control Team (UCA)

_____. "Manual de Autoridades de Materia en RENIB," 1991.

_____. "Pautas para el Procesamiento de Analíticas." Feb. 1992.

_____. *Informa* no. 1-11 (Jan. 1988-Mar. 1992).

Sanz, Maria Teresa. Interview by Elizabeth N. Steinhagen with Maria Teresa Sanz, first Coordinator of the National Library, and Soledad Fernández-Corugedo, current RENIB Coordinator, Dec. 1999.

Saporta Levy, Victoria. "La Automatización en la Biblioteca National." Paper presented at V. Jornadas Bibliotecarias Nacionales, Jan. 1989.

Steinhagen, Elizabeth N.. "Bibliographic Control in Chile: Cooperative Efforts and Standardization." Paper presented at the 45th Seminar on the Acquisitions of Latin American Library Materials (SALALM) Conference, May 2000.

_____. "Cooperative Cataloging in Chile." Paper presented at 5th Conference of Librarians in International Development, Kansas City, MO, 1995. Available at http://slim.emporia.edu/globenet/kc/steist.htm.

_____. "National Bibliography in Chile." Term paper, UW-Madison School of Library and Information Science, Dec. 1976.

Walravens, Hartmut. "The Beginnings of Serials Union Listing in Germany." *The Serials Librarian* 35, no. 3 (1991): 131-140.

The Development of Cataloging in China

Suqing Liu
Zhenghua Shen

SUMMARY. With a long history, cataloging has evolved with changes in society, economy, and technology in China. This paper presents Chinese cataloging history in four parts, with emphasis on the last two parts: the founding of the People's Republic of China in 1949 and the development of cataloging after 1979 when China opened its doors to the world. Particularly important has been the rapid growth of online cataloging in recent years. The China Academic Library and Information System (CALIS), as a successful online cataloging model, is emphasized. Through investigation of the entire history of Chinese cataloging, three distinct features can be stated: (1) Standardization–switching from the Chinese traditional way to aligning with international standards, (2) Cooperation–from decentralized and self-supporting systems to sharing systems, (3) Computerization and networking–from manual operation to computer-based online operation. At the end of this paper, a set of means by which to enhance online cataloging and resource sharing is suggested. *[Article copies available for a fee from The Haworth Document Delivery Service: 1-800-HAWORTH. E-mail address: <getinfo@haworthpressinc.com> Website: <http://www.HaworthPress.com> © 2002 by The Haworth Press, Inc. All rights reserved.]*

Suqing Liu is Librarian and Zhenghua Shen is Research Librarian, both at Peking University Library (E-mail: liusq@lib.pku.edu.cn and shenzh@lib.pku.edu.cn, respectively).

[Haworth co-indexing entry note]: "The Development of Cataloging in China." Liu, Suqing, and Zhenghua Shen. Co-published simultaneously in *Cataloging & Classification Quarterly* (The Haworth Information Press, an imprint of The Haworth Press, Inc.) Vol. 35, No. 1/2, 2002, pp. 137-154; and: *Historical Aspects of Cataloging and Classification* (ed: Martin D. Joachim) The Haworth Information Press, an imprint of The Haworth Press, Inc., 2003, pp. 137-154. Single or multiple copies of this article are available for a fee from The Haworth Document Delivery Service [1-800-HAWORTH, 9:00 a.m. - 5:00 p.m. (EST). E-mail address: getinfo@haworthpressinc.com].

KEYWORDS. Cataloging history, online cataloging, resource sharing, China, CALIS

摘要 **(SUMMARY IN CHINESE).**　中国是一个文明古国，编目工作随着社

会、经济和技术的发展在不断演进，本文分四部分阐述了中国编目工作的发展历史，

侧重介绍了 1979 年中国改革开放以来编目工作的进程，特别介绍了近几年联机编目

工作的飞速发展。联机编目的介绍以中国高等教育文献保障系统（ CALIS ）的联机

合作编目系统为代表。纵观整个编目发展史，它呈现出以下几方面的特点：（ 1 ）标

准化—从沿袭传统到与国际标准保持一致；（ 2 ）合作化—从分散的各自独立的编目

模式转向合作共享的模式；（ 3 ）计算机网络化—从手工操作转向计算机实时联机编

目，文章的最后提出了联机合作编目发展的几点建议。

Chinese cataloging can be traced back to the sixth century B.C. and has evolved with changes in society, economy, and technology. This paper presents a chronological profile of cataloging history in China, with an emphasis on the development of online cataloging.

1. FROM ANCIENT TIMES TO EARLY TWENTIETH CENTURY

Being a country with an old civilization, ancient China had an abundance of classical books. Traditionally, Chinese intellectuals believed that proper governance of the people could be learned from the classics. Hence, the royalties of individual dynasties attached great importance to the collection, compilation, and preservation of books to the extent that it had become a rule to do so. The oldest bibliography can be traced back to the sixth century B.C. (the Spring and Autumn Period). Confucius, the greatest Chinese thinker and educator, sifted through the best books to compile *Liu Jing* (the *Six Classics*, 《六经》), which is an inventory of ancient literature. In the second century B.C., Yang Pu (杨仆) compiled *Bing Lu*, a booklist of arms and the military 《兵录》 that is the earliest specific bibliography in China's recorded history. *Qi Lue* (the *Seven Categories,* 《七略》), the earliest comprehensive classified bibliography in China, was compiled by Liu Xiang (刘向) and his son Liu Xin (刘歆) from 26 B.C. to 6 B.C. Even though it no longer exists, it has had far-reaching influence on cataloging and classification. The earliest extant bibliography, *Han Shu Yi Wen Zhi* (*Han history: Bibliography*《汉书 • 艺文志》) was compiled by Ban Gu around 80 A.D. In Wei Zheng's *Sui Shu Jing Ji Zhi* (*Sui Dynasty: Bibliography* 魏征《隋书 • 经籍志》), title main entry became a tradition in compiling bibliographies, and it has been carried on until today. The Manchurians fully adopted the Han culture in the Qing Dynasty; and starting with Emperor Kangxi, several attempts were made to collect books written throughout China. In the fifty-fourth year of Emperor Qianlong's reign (1789 A.D.), *Si Ku Quan Shu Zong Mu*, the largest bibliography with abstracts for Chinese classical books, was finished, from which the well-known Si Ku classification scheme was developed.

2. EARLY TWENTIETH CENTURY TO 1949

During this period Western cataloging theory was introduced into China, and modern Chinese cataloging began. In ancient Chinese bibliographies there were no main entry headings; all Chinese books were entered under title. Classifying and abstracting were treated as two important ways to reveal the contents of documents. This tradition continued until the nineteenth century when Western cultures were introduced into China, especially after the New Library Movement early in the twentieth century. Many Western cataloging theories and experiences came into China, notably dictionary catalogs and subject headings; as a result, the bibliography's form changed, progressing from book to loose-leaf to card. The dominant position of the classified catalog was overturned, and subject catalogs were added in some academic libraries for their Western collections. At the same time author added entries became popular.

The National Library of Beijing (the predecessor of the National Library of China) distributed catalog cards in 1931. This distribution marked the beginning of centralized cataloging in China.

3. MODERN TIMES (1949-1989)

After the founding of the People's Republic of China in 1949, many changes occurred in library operations. Cataloging progressed gradually from individualized to a centralized model, from a manual to an automatic operation. This evolution can be divided roughly into four stages.

3.1 The First Stage (1949-1957)

With the foundation of the People's Republic of China, the library universe in China had entered a new epoch. With the influence of the Soviet Union, the political aspects in cataloging were emphasized, and many cataloging institutions were reorganized based on a new social system. There are four distinguishing features of this period:

1. Library cataloging was done manually and individually nationwide.
2. There were no unified cataloging rules. Multiple rules existed in parallel for different languages. For example, *Cataloging Rules for Chinese Books*, compiled by Liu Guojun, the famous library pioneer and researcher in China, was used by most libraries for Chinese books. The rules of the Soviet Union were followed for Russian books, Anglo-American cataloging rules for Western language materials, Japanese rules for Japanese materials, etc.
3. A lack of catalogers impeded the fast development of cataloging.
4. Because cataloging theory and practice were learned primarily from the Soviet Union, Western influence represented by American libraries was diminished considerably compared to the situation before 1949. However, some academic libraries subscribed to LC cards for their Western books, a practice that helped in the standardization of cataloging.

3.2 The Second Stage (1958-1965)

Centralized cataloging and newly emerging cataloging rules were a feature of this stage. In late 1958 the National Library of Beijing, the Library of the Chinese Academy of Sciences, and the Library of the Chinese People's University established centralized cataloging groups for Chinese, Western, and Russian books. They issued cards either nationwide or in local areas. Over 4,500 libraries subscribed to cards from the National Library of Beijing for their Chinese collections, and cards could be delivered with books in some cities. These services ceased after the start of the Great Cultural Revolution in 1966 and did not resume until 1974. The advantages of centralized cataloging can be seen at least in four ways: shortening the time from acquisition to circulation, unifying of cataloging rules, enhancing cataloging quality in various aspects, and finally, saving costs and human resources. Some cataloging rules were adopted during this period, such as *Descriptive Rules for Chinese Books with Abstracts* (《中文图书提要卡片著录条例》), published in 1959, and *Descriptive Rules for Western Language Monographs* (《西文普通图书著录条例》), published in 1961. These rules allowed libraries to do their cataloging in a standard way, but national rules and standards were still greatly needed.

3.3 The Third Stage (1966-1978)

During the Great Cultural Revolution, cataloging work could not be performed in a standard way and was even terminated in some libraries. Some shared cataloging activities, such as centralized cataloging for Chinese and Russian books, were forced to cease. The scale of centralized cataloging for Western books was reduced although it survived. In 1974 and 1976 centralized cataloging for Chinese books was resumed in Beijing and Shanghai, respectively. In 1978 the National Library of Beijing cataloged 6,400 titles and distributed its services to many cities in northern China. There were two distinguishing features of this stage: (1) Cataloging was obstructed by the Great Cultural Revolution, and communication and exchange with foreign countries discontinued to a great extent, and (2) USMARC and ISBD were introduced into China in the late 1970s.

3.4 The Fourth Stage (1979-1989)

China has moved to reform cataloging practices since 1979. It became popular to learn and apply international cataloging rules and standards in Chinese libraries, thereby bringing cataloging into a period of modernization and automation.

1. Cataloging Standardization

In 1979 *Descriptive Cataloging Rules for Chinese Monographs* (《中文普通图书统一著录条例》) was published, which in part unified cataloging standards for Chinese monographs. In December of this year, the China Standards Technical Committee (CSTC), under the leadership of the National Standards Bureau of China, was set up and functions much the same as ISO/TC46. Since then, subsequent standards have been issued or published under the direction of CSTC:

- General Bibliographical Description GB3792.1-83 (《文献著录总则》)
- Bibliographical Description for Monographs GB3792.2-85
  (《普通图书著录规则》)
- Bibliographical Description for Chinese Antiquarian Books GB3792.7-87
  (《古籍著录规则》)
- Bibliographical Description for Cartographic Materials GB3792.6-86
  (《地图资料著录规则》)

- Bibliographical Description for Serials GB3792.3-85
  (《连续出版物著录规则》)
- Bibliographical Description for Non-book Materials GB3792.4-85
  (《非书资料著录规则》)
- Bibliographical Description for Archives GB3792.5-85
  (《档案著录规则》)

The prefix **GB** represents the national standard. In addition to these, other rules were also published. For instance, *Descriptive Cataloging Rules for Western Language Materials* (《西文文献著录条例》), published in 1985 and aligned with AACR2 but more concise, has been used for cataloging Western materials. All these standards unified the methods of describing a variety of documents in different languages. Under the leadership of CSTC, the Chinese translations of the ISBDs were published. These efforts helped to move cataloging standardization forward.

2. Cataloging Automation

Library automation started in the early 1980s in China. In 1986 the National Library of Beijing drafted the Chinese Machine Readable Catalog (CNMARC). In 1989 the decision was made that CNMARC be set up as the standard for Chinese materials and USMARC for Western-language materials. Since then, the National Library of Beijing has distributed MARC data throughout the country. CNMARC became the professional standard of the Ministry of Culture in China in 1995. Moreover, library automation systems were developed successfully. For example, ILAS (Integrated Library Automation System), developed by Shenzhen Library, has been used by more than 400 libraries in China. Computerized cataloging became the core part of integrated library systems. Many bibliographic databases came into existence and are providing the foundation for bibliographic resource-sharing in the near future.

3. The Availability of CIP

Cataloging in publication (CIP) was introduced into China in 1979 and was under the charge of the Ministry of Culture and Journalism and Publication Bureau, which took the responsibility for creating the national standards for Chinese CIP. As the result of this effort, GB12450-90 and GB12451-90 were issued as Chinese CIP standards by the China Technical Supervision Bureau in 1990 and put into effect as of March 1, 1991.

4. Summary of Pre-1991 Cataloging in China

The features of pre-1991 cataloging in China can be summarized as follows:

- Cataloging operation turned from manual and individualized to a centralized and shared model.
- The means by which bibliographic records were made available ranged from the book catalog to loose-leaves, cards, microfiches, and MARC records.
- The establishment of cataloging rules was based on content and language. Originally there were four categories of rules: Chinese, Roman-language, Japanese, and Russian. After the adoption of MARC formats, these four merged into two language categories: Chinese (including Japanese) and Roman (covering Russian). This practice was quite different from the Western world, there were no unique rules such as AACR to apply to all kinds of documents in various languages.
- Classified catalogs played an important role in China. There were different classification schemes, among them Si Ku classification, created in the Qing Dynasty; it has been a principal classification system for more than two centuries and is still used today by some libraries for their classical books. However, classifications schemes used by Chinese catalogers changed through decades of evolution, including traditional Chinese schemes, translated versions of foreign schemes, self-compiled ones, and foreign schemes such as Dewey Decimal Classification. The China Library Classification (CLC) was finally adopted by most libraries and is used today by about 95 percent of the libraries in China.
- Before the 1920s subject headings were generally not included with Chinese cataloging records; abstracts traditionally substituted for subject headings to reflect book contents. In the 1920s LCSH was adopted for the cataloging of Western materials. Realizing the importance of subject access, furthermore, Chinese librarians concentrated on developing their own subject systems. By the 1980s there was a general Chinese thesaurus (《汉语主题表》) from which subject headings were provided for MARC records. To date, there are more than 100 specific thesauri.

4. THE DEVELOPMENT OF ONLINE CATALOGING IN CHINA (1990-PRESENT)

4.1 Rapid Advances in Information Technology Facilitating Online Cataloging

In the 1990s, with the rise of the World Wide Web and the emergence of new information technologies, the library community was led to a period of excitement, creativity, and change. Web-based OPACs, Z39.50-based virtual libraries, and metadata schemes to describe electronic resources are some of the developments in recent years. These changes have brought both opportunities and challenges for libraries worldwide.

In China, computer networks have been booming since the mid-1990s. The first direct Internet link was established in 1993 by the Institute of High Energy Physics of the Chinese Academy of Sciences. Thereafter, a large number of computer networks at different levels emerged. The top four nation-wide computer networks are the first high speed network, CSTNet (China Science and Technology Network); the first nation-wide education and research network, CERNET (China Education and Research Network); the first commercial network, ChinaNet (China Internet); and the largest public economic information network, ChinaGBN (China Golden Bridge Network). Convenient network environments laid a good foundation for the creation of online cataloging in China.

4.2 Western Influences on Strengthening Cataloging

1. Introduction of Western Cataloging Rules and Information Standards

Along with the rapid growth of the economy and openness to the world beyond China, communications and cooperation between China and Western countries were strengthened in the 1990s. On the one hand, Western bibliographic utilities such as RLG and OCLC developed CJK (Chinese, Japanese, Korean) cataloging systems, which led to the opportunity for cooperative cataloging of Chinese language materials. For example, Peking University Library has been contributing its classical book records to RLIN. The National Library of China cooperated with OCLC in 1991 to create the Chinese National Bibliography of the Republican Era (1911-1949) database, which has been only partially completed due to funding problems. Nevertheless, this cooperative project has definitely benefited both sides. OCLC's WorldCat has been enriched, and Chinese librarians have learned much about Western cataloging practices.

On the other hand, a range of national standards for descriptive cataloging has been set up to align them with Western cataloging rules and ISBDs. As for MARC, two formats–CNMARC for Chinese materials and USMARC (MARC 21) for Western materials–exist concurrently. Presently, the most up-to-date information about Western cataloging rules, new information standards, and protocols, such as the Z39.50 protocol, XML, and metadata schemes, can be located in a timely fashion via the Web, thereby guaranteeing that Chinese cataloging can keep pace with the international advanced levels.

2. Adoption of Foreign Library Systems

Although most libraries already have library systems, most of them have been developed in-house, usually with inherent weakness in system design, user interfaces, and function integration. In an effort to gain successful experience from foreign library automation, some large libraries have purchased library systems from abroad through international competitive bidding. Thus, systems such as INNOPAC (Innovative Interfaces Inc), Horizon (Dynix Australia Pty Ltd.), and Unicorn (SIRSI) have been brought into China. They have their pros and cons, but indeed they have expanded the country's horizons and enlightened and enhanced the creativity to develop new technology-based library systems.

4.3 The Prelude to Online Cataloging

It is time-consuming and cost-ineffective to do cataloging individually; libraries have gradually come to realize that it is necessary to share resources through cooperative cataloging. Furthermore, economic pressures, together with the explosive proliferation of information resources and the advancement of enabling technologies, are amplifying the importance of resource sharing.

Centralized and cooperative cataloging played a vital role in bibliographic resource sharing in the early 1990s. For centralized cataloging operations, some organizations have combined acquisitions and cataloging and deliver books with MARC records to their participant libraries. These well-known companies include Shanghai Shen Lian Literature and Information Technology Co., Shanghai Xiang Hua Books Limited Co., and Beijing Tu Lian Co. Centralized cataloging does indeed release librarians from labor-intensive and costly work. But the one-to-multiple offline sharing model is usually limited to certain areas, either large cities or provinces, and is not a perfect model.

In Beijing, the first bibliographic network, APTLIN (an alliance of the Chinese Academy of Sciences, Peking University, and Tsinghua University), was established by the three libraries in 1993; this is the first distributed technology-based library bibliographic network in China, which aims to serve the research and academic community in the Zhongguan Cun area (known as the Silicon Valley of China). It features an online shared union catalog, OPAC, and acquisitions coordination. In fact, it was not a real-time online cataloging system. In 1991 the Zhujiang (Pearl River) Delta Public Library Automation Network (ZDNET) was launched jointly by the Zhongshan (Sun Yat-sen) Library of Guangdong Province and a dozen other public libraries in the same area. ZDNET consisted of three categories of libraries: provincial, municipal, and county. Provincial libraries are the network centers that provide database retrieval services and, in addition, contribute most of the records into the database. Online cataloging was planned at the beginning, but this service never actually came to fruition. The significance of these practices lay in accumulating experience in cooperation, administration, and services and thus paved the way for the coming of the online cataloging era.

4.4 Evolution of Online Cataloging in China

4.4.1 Startup Stage (1997-1999)

Traditionally, Chinese libraries can be divided into three types: public, academic, and special. Each type of library has attempted to explore the operation of online cataloging.

The Online Library Cataloging Center (OLCC), supported by the National Library of China, established a consortium for public libraries in October 1997. Being a three-level (national, provincial, and local) consortium, OLCC emphasizes unifying, planning, standardization, gradual progress, cooperative development, coordination of management, and resource sharing. In December 1998, its online cataloging component was put into practice. As the national center, OLCC takes the responsibility for creation and maintenance of the database, organization of member libraries, creation of standards, conducting training, and so forth. The provincial centers make efforts to facilitate the participation in OLCC.

Local libraries download bibliographic records and submit their own holdings to the OLCC database. There are some disadvantages to the OLCC model:

- Bibliographic records are created primarily by the National Library of China while other participants concentrate more on sharing than contributing.
- Only CNMARC records for Chinese materials are accepted.
- Its online cataloging software cannot perform simultaneous uploading and downloading, so batch processing is still the primary way to transmit data. However, efforts made by OLCC have contributed greatly to the standardization of cataloging of Chinese materials and to the accumulation of abundant data sources.

Realizing the importance of periodicals in scientific research, public libraries affiliated with the Chinese Academy of Sciences (CAS) devoted much attention to building a periodicals union catalog. At first it was available in print or CD-ROM but can now be accessed via the Web.

Online cataloging is one of the projects being planned and investigated by CAS libraries. This project has two advantages: advanced network environments (CSTNet) and unified administration. The weakness is that there is only one type of MARC format (CNMARC) used for all materials, so it encounters some difficulties in data exchange with USMARC-based data.

For libraries affiliated with the Chinese Academy of Social Sciences (CASS), the Online Cataloging Coordination Office was established in March 1999; the creation of this office marked the start-up of its online cataloging. The way by which the office developed and managed databases is special; in all, it operates three databases: a temporary database to store the data that need to be verified by experienced librarians, a preparatory database to collect verified data from all libraries but without having gone through a de-duplication process, and a formal database to hold data that have gone through de-duplication. Obviously, this model is not a real online cataloging system; the process is too complicated to access high quality data in a timely manner for member libraries. Additionally, CAS or CASS online cataloging projects serve mainly the institutes within their own systems; they are isolated from libraries in other systems.

In the academic library community, some efforts were made to expedite shared catalogs in the early 1990s. For instance, the Union Catalog Program for the National Social Science Information Center, funded by the State Education Commission, collected data from sixteen university libraries and provided access via the Web. CALIS (China Academic Library and Information System) is the online cataloging project that is the outstanding result of this program.

1. CALIS Profile. In November 1998 the Ministry of Education founded CALIS to develop a network-based system in which academic libraries could share resources and reduce costs. Based on CERNET, CALIS aims to create an online sharing system that includes online cooperative cataloging, Web-based OPAC searching, interlibrary loan, document delivery, database or e-journal purchase coordination, resource digitalizing, etc. Its detailed tasks are:

- Building a network-based information sharing system, replacing the old modes of individual and self-support systems
- Setting up specific databases, such as a Chinese rare book database, a dissertation database, etc.
- Purchasing foreign online databases to provide service around the clock
- Ensuring document support in Chinese at 95 percent and in foreign languages at around 80 percent.

CALIS is a three-level network ranging from the national center to regional center and further to individual academic libraries. The National Administrative Center, located at Peking University Library, is responsible for planning and implementation of the project. Four subject-oriented national centers are the Center for Science and Technology at Peking University, the Center for Engineering at Tsinghua University, the Center for Agriculture at China Agriculture University, and the Center for Medical Science at the Medical College of Peking University. The seven regional centers are the Southeast Center at Shanghai Jiao Tong University, the East Center at Nanjing University, the South Center at Zhongshan University, the Middle Region Center at Wuhan University, the Southwest Center at Sichuan University, the Northwest Center at Xi'an Jiao Tong University, and the Northeast Center at Jilin University. In addition, the Center for National Defense at Ha'erbing Institute of Industry was founded later. CALIS member libraries are spread throughout all of China. CALIS also stresses cooperation in data sharing with bibliographic utilities at home and abroad such as the National Library of China and OCLC.

  2. *CALIS Online Cataloging.* Online cooperative cataloging, as the core component of CALIS, operated before the establishment of CALIS itself. In October 1997 a conference on "Building a Western Language Union Catalog" was held at Wuhan University; this conference marked the initiation of CALIS online cataloging. It reached some agreements on descriptive cataloging rules and the usage of USMARC among academic libraries. Thereafter, some active preparation for online cataloging had been carried out from 1998 to 1999. RFP (Requirements for Proposal) writing was an important part of this preparation. In addition, some guidelines for contributing bibliographic records were created. The "Manual for CALIS Online Cooperative Cataloging" is one achievement that has become a necessary cataloging tool for academic libraries.

  In a summary, OLCC in public libraries and CALIS in academic libraries are the two main systems for online cataloging in China. CALIS online cataloging remains on the leading edge of library and information technology and shapes the future directions in this field.

4.4.2 Growth (2000-Present)

  Since 2000 online cataloging has migrated into a stage of expansion and growth in China. CALIS online cataloging stands out prominently in many aspects. In January 2000, its online cataloging software was tested and was ready for operation. On March 15, 2000, twenty-seven core member libraries held a seminar on online cataloging operations; after the meeting they began to submit records as part of the "CALIS Online Cataloging Pilot Plan." On March

29, 2000 Wuhan University uploaded the first original bibliographic record (control number is CAL#022000368254) into the CALIS database, and the CALIS online cataloging system was formally in operation. As of March 13, 2002, 184 member libraries have worked together to build a database of 1,357,123 bibliographic records with 2,981,531 holdings. In comparison to long-standing bibliographic databases such as OCLC WorldCat, CALIS is a small part; but the speed of its development has been astonishing.

1. Organization and Management of CALIS Online Cataloging. The governance of the CALIS online cataloging project consists of three levels: the Project Administrative Group, regional centers, and member libraries. The Project Administrative Group, located at Peking University, is responsible for the following:

- Developing and maintaining bibliographic databases to ensure their continuing viability;
- Disseminating documentation on the standards and guidelines for sharing of cataloging;
- Making policy and development plans;
- Providing product training, troubleshooting, technical support, and consultation.

The functions of the regional centers are:

- Serving as the mirror sites of central databases that physically run on the servers at Peking University Library and providing an ease-of-use and cost-effective way for regional libraries to download data from neighboring centers;
- Facilitating the participation of local libraries as authorized users of CALIS bibliographic database;
- Providing cost-effective training and consultation to local libraries;
- Serving as a channel for communication between CALIS and its member libraries.

Member libraries' commitment to CALIS online cataloging include:

- Contributing all current bibliographic records and holdings to CALIS;
- Creating bibliographic records conforming to the standards and guidelines adopted by CALIS;
- Being authorized to use CALIS records, systems, and services;
- Co-maintaining databases with CALIS and regional centers.

2. System Features. The CALIS online cataloging software is a functional and flexible system with the following features:

- The first Z39.50-based client/server online union cataloging utility in China;
- The first simultaneous online union cataloging system in China;
- The first UNICODE-support online union cataloging system that can cope with multiple languages, including Chinese, Japanese, and Western languages. In the near future, Russian, Korean, and other Eastern languages will be added;
- The first online union cataloging system that supports multiple MARC formats.

3. Operation Models. Based upon the localization and updating mechanisms of data, operation can be classified into three models:

- **Downloading records to local systems.** In this model cataloging is done by CALIS Z39.50 software, and records are exported and then transmitted into local systems, appropriate to those libraries that do not support Z39.50 access;
- **Capturing records into local systems.** Cataloging is still done by CALIS Z39.50 software, and records are captured into local system afterwards using the Z39.50 function of local systems;
- **Simultaneous local and central updating.** This procedure requires an advanced database system and cataloging process management, allowing real simultaneous update. CALIS has been cooperating with library vendors to enhance library system integration with Z39.50. One successful example is ILAS (Integrated Library Automation System, developed by Shenzhen Library). Currently, ILAS libraries can upload to and download from the CALIS bibliographic database directly by using their local system commands and procedures. One example of recent Z39.50-based software is the Hui Wen System developed by Nanjing University, which can support simultaneous uploading and downloading.

It is impossible to give a complete list of all operation models for individual libraries here; sometimes a mixture of these three models can be applied depending on the functionalities of different library systems.

4. Bibliographic Database. To run a comprehensive system like CALIS, a set of principles is necessary to maintain the database:

- **One single record principle**. For each title, only one record can exist in the database. In other words, all uploaded records are matched automatically against the existing database using basic match procedures to identify potential duplicates. Due to the complexity of resource and non-standardization of publication, duplicate detection programs tend to become more complex, especially in order to handle some specific problems; for instance, it is always a problem to check for duplicates involving multi-volume monographs that could be treated as a set or separately. Once records are confirmed as duplicates they are merged into a single bibliographic record. For those potential duplicates that cannot be detected by the software, they will be transferred to a human interference database waiting for further processing. The de-duplicate program helps to reduce the duplicates and improve the quality of the CALIS bibliographic database.

- **Merging records according to the priority of data.** In the CALIS bibliographic database, each record is assigned an identification number to identify the level at which the data quality is based; records with higher level data can override lower level data. The data level number is hidden from libraries and is used to merge records automatically. This mechanism serves as a way to manage data and ensure the quality of the database.

As in OCLC's WorldCat, bibliographic records in the CALIS database do not yet have real-time links to circulation data. Considering the importance of item availability for end-users, CALIS is currently exploring how to make a link to individual library systems to obtain real circulation information.

5. Database Quality Control. The CALIS bibliographic database is well known for its high quality, and the following measures are taken to enhance database quality:

- Setting up a quality control group consisting of experienced and accomplished catalogers from member libraries, who are authorized to process records in a human-interference database, correct errors, and report duplicates to CALIS;
- Authorizing some libraries to correct or update data contributed by the same level or lower level libraries;
- Automatically verifying and executing global data updating.

6. Membership and User Management. CALIS member libraries are categorized into different levels according to their responsibilities and the functions that they perform: A+, A, B+, B, C+, C, E+, E, G, etc. Different users have different priorities in database operation. A+ and A levels, for example, are responsible for managing data and for data quality control while B+ and B levels are the core members who contribute records into the CALIS biblio-graphic databases. E+ and E levels are non-academic libraries, and G level is for commercial cataloging centers or book vendors. The levels are changeable based on the performance of libraries. As of March 2002, there are ten libraries at B+ level, seventeen at B level, and more than 150 at C and six other levels. This distribution of levels embodies the CALIS principle of "Co-creation and Co-sharing."

4.4.3 Future Trends

Online cataloging provides the foundation for resource sharing; its en-hancement is an overarching priority for information services. Future objec-tives will focus on:

- Integrating and enhancing functions of existing cataloging utilities and their services.
- Implementing simultaneous local and central updating.
- Promoting continuing growth of bibliographic and holdings data.
- Integrating with other systems, such as ILL and reference. Regardless of geographical location, system types, or description standards, end users will be able to find and obtain information no matter where and how it is stored.
- Facilitating cooperation with other online cataloging systems, national and international.
- Developing the CALIS union catalog beyond a bibliographical utility into a globally networked, Web-based information resource where the end-user can access through the union catalog not only bibliographic and holdings information but also abstracts, full texts, images, sound files, etc.
- Exploring metadata schemes to describe electronic resources and ex-panding the coverage from classical to electronic resources, finally creat-ing a virtual union catalog globally.

4.5 A Brief Summary of Online Cataloging in Post-1990 China

There have been great advances in online cataloging in China since 1990. Highlights can be summarized as follows:

- **Rapid development.** It took less than two years from planning in 1997 to implementation in 1998.
- **High technology support.** Information technology and network envi-ronments have advanced to new stages with plans to implement online cataloging in China. Basically, system designs are based on distributed

processing technology (client/server model), which is better and more effective than the centralized-model (mainframe/terminals).

- **Funding by governments.** Both state and local governments gradually realized the importance of building an information highway and of a resource-sharing system. Some large projects or programs such as CALIS have been launched since the mid-1990s to promote resource sharing.

- **In-house systems existing first.** Most libraries already owned their in-house systems when online cataloging was implemented in China; this situation is different from other countries, especially the United States. For example, OCLC cataloging operations were in place earlier than many library in-house systems. On the one hand, in-house systems helped to accumulate data and provide experience in automation that can speed up the process of online cataloging. On the other hand, the existing data in diverse systems produces conflicts with cataloging codes and standards, operation, and management required by online cataloging systems. Harmonization between online cataloging systems and in-house systems has, therefore, been necessary.

REFERENCES

Bai, Yang, and Hongye Sha. "谈谈我国实行图书在版编目" ("Cataloging in Print in China"). In 文献编目论文选 (*Selected Papers of Document Cataloging*), edited by Jungui Huang and Dehai Lin, 109-118. Beijing: Bibliography and Document Press, 1992.

Cousins, Shirley. "Virtual OPACs versus Union Database: Two Models of Union Catalogue Provision." *The Electronic Library* 17, no. 2 (April 1999): 97-103.

He, Yang. "An Overview on Networking in Library and Information Services in China." Paper presented at the Networking the Pacific: An International Forum supported by British Columbia Library Association, Victoria, British Columbia, Canada, May 5-6 1995. Available at: http://www.idrc.ca/library/document/netpac/abs8.htm.

Hu, Guangxian. "中国社会科学院图书馆系统开创联机编目工作的回顾与现状" ("Development of Online Cataloging in Libraries of the Academy of Social Sciences"). 情报资料工作 (*Information Work*) 1 (2001): 34-36.

Huang, Jungui, and Dehai Lin. "文献编目实践与理论进展综述 (1949-1989)" ("A Survey of the Development of Cataloging Practice and Theory from 1949 to 1989"). In 文献编目论文选 (*Selected Papers of Document Cataloging*), edited by Jungui Huang and Dehai Lin, 1-31. Beijing: Bibliography and Document Press, 1992.

Liu, Jessica. "Review and Prospect for Centralized Cataloging in China." *Cataloging & Classification Quarterly* 28, no. 2 (1999): 57-64.

OCLC. "About OCLC." [cited 16 May 2002]. Available at: http://www/global.oclc. org/about/; Internet.

Online Library Cataloging Center, National Library of China. WWW home page. [cited 16 May 2002]. Available at: http://www.nlc.gov.cn/newpages/english/ cooperate/olcc.htm; Internet.

图书馆学情报学词典 (*Dictionary of Library and Information Science*), edited by Wenjun Zhou. Beijing: Bibliography and Document Press, 1991.

Wei, Fu Bender. "An International Effort: Cataloging Cooperation Between the National Library of China and OCLC: A case study of China Project." Paper presented at the International Conference on New Missions of Academic Libraries in the 21st Century, Beijing, China, October 25-28, 1998. [cited 16 May 2002]. Available at: http://library.brandeis.edu/beijing_conference/WeiBender.doc; Internet.

Wu, Pengpeng. "我国图书集中编目工作的历程与前景" ("The Development and Prospect of Centralized Cataloging in China"). In 文献编目论文选 (*Selected Papers of Document Cataloging*), edited by Jungui Huang and Dehai Lin, 104-108. Beijing: Bibliography and Document Press, 1992.

Wu, Weici, and Guiju Xu. "图书馆自动化与网络化之现状及展望" ("Present Status and Future Prospects of Library Automation and Networks"). *The Journal of Library Science in China* 25, no. 119 (1999): 42-46.

Xie, Qinfang, Suqing Liu, Xinping Bai, Yunpan, Pingping Yu, and June Zhang. "CALIS 联合目录—高校书目数据共建共享的成果" (CALIS Online Union Catalog–the Achievement of Academic Library Cooperation"). 大学图书馆学报 (*Journal of Academic Libraries*) 3 (2002): 9-13.

Yan, Lizhong. "编目工作的发展和目录著录的标准化" ("Cataloging Development and Bibliographical Descriptive Standardization"). In 文献编目论文选 (*Selected Papers of Document Cataloging*), edited by Jungui Huang and Dehai Lin, 90-103. Beijing: Bibliography and Document Press, 1992.

Yan, Yiqiao. "中美文献编目工作比较研究" ("Comparative Study of Sino-American Document Cataloging"). In 文献编目论文选 (*Selected Papers of Document Cataloging*), edited by Jungui Huang and Dehai Lin, 148-159. Beijing: Bibliography and Document Press, 1992.

Zheng, Yanning. "Status Report on Information and Library Operations in China." Paper presented at the 12th ASTINFO Consultative Meeting and Regional Seminar/Workshop on Information and Communication Technologies and Knowledge Management, Ulaanbaatar, Mongolia, Sept. 18-23, 2000. [cited 16 May 2002]. Available at: http://www.stii.dost.gov.ph/astinfo/jultosep2k/pg10_to_11.htm; Internet.

The Development of Descriptive Cataloging in Germany

Hans Popst

Charles R. Croissant (translator)

SUMMARY. This article discusses the development of descriptive cataloging in Germany and the evolution of cataloging principles. The *Instruktionen für die alphabetischen Kataloge der preußischen Bibliotheken* (*Instructions for the Alphabetic Catalogs of the Prussian Libraries*, known as the *Prussian Instructions*, or PI, for short) were published in 1899. The so-called *Berliner Anweisungen* (*"Berlin Instructions," Instructions for the Alphabetic Catalog in Public Libraries*) appeared in 1938. Discussion for reform of cataloging rules began in the 1950s and received impetus from the International Conference on Cataloging Principles in Paris in 1961 and from the International Meeting of Cataloging Experts in Copenhagen in 1969. Preliminary drafts of the new *Regeln für die alphabetische Katalogisierung,* RAK (*Rules for Descriptive Cataloging*) were issued between 1969 and 1976; the complete edition of the RAK was published in the German Democratic Republic (East Germany) in 1976 and in a slightly different version in 1977 for the

Hans Popst is Professor, Cataloging and Bibliography, Department of Archival and Library Studies, Bayerische Beamtenfachhochschule, Kaulbachstrasse 11, D-80539 München, Germany (E-mail: Popst@bib-bvb.de). Charles R. Croissant is Catalog Librarian, Pius XII Memorial Library, Saint Louis University, St. Louis, MO 63108 (E-mail: croisscr@slu.edu). He is a member of the American Translators Association, certified for German-to-English translation.

[Haworth co-indexing entry note]: "The Development of Descriptive Cataloging in Germany." Popst, Hans. Co-published simultaneously in *Cataloging & Classification Quarterly* (The Haworth Information Press, an imprint of The Haworth Press, Inc.) Vol. 35, No. 1/2, 2002, pp. 155-172; and: *Historical Aspects of Cataloging and Classification* (ed: Martin D. Joachim) The Haworth Information Press, an imprint of The Haworth Press, Inc., 2003, pp. 155-172. Single or multiple copies of this article are available for a fee from The Haworth Document Delivery Service [1-800-HAWORTH, 9:00 a.m. - 5:00 p.m. (EST). E-mail address: getinfo@haworthpressinc.com].

Federal Republic of Germany (West Germany). A version for academic libraries appeared in 1983, followed by a version for public libraries in 1986. Between 1987 and 1997, supplementary rules for special categories of materials were published. *[Article copies available for a fee from The Haworth Document Delivery Service: 1-800-HAWORTH. E-mail address: <getinfo@haworthpressinc.com> Website: <http://www.HaworthPress.com> © 2002 by The Haworth Press, Inc. All rights reserved.]*

KEYWORDS. Descriptive cataloging history, Germany, Austria, *Prussian Instructions*, PI, *Berlin Instructions*, *Rules for Descriptive Cataloging*, RAK

ZUSAMMENFASSUNG. Es wird die Entwicklung der alphabetischen Katalogisierung in Deutschland besprochen, sowie die Entwicklung der Grundsätze der Katalogisierung. Die *Instruktionen für die alphabetischen Kataloge der preußischen Bibliotheken* (bekannt unter dem Namen *Preußische Instruktionen,* oder PI) erschienen 1899. Die so genannten *Berliner Anweisungen (Anweisung für den alphabetischen Katalog der Volksbüchereien)* erschienen 1938. Diskussionen um eine Reform der alphabetischen Katalogisierung begannen in den 50er Jahren des 20. Jahrhunderts und erhielten Antrieb durch die Teilnahme an dem International Conference on Cataloging Principles (Paris, 1961) und dem International Meeting of Cataloging Experts (Kopenhagen, 1969). Vorabdrucke der neuen *Regeln für die alphabetische Katalogisierung,* RAK, erschienen zwischen 1969 und 1976; die vollständigen Ausgaben erschienen 1976 in der Deutschen Demokratischen Republik und 1977, in geringfügig unterschiedlicher Fassung, in der Bundesrepublik Deutschland. Eine Fassung für wissenschaftliche Bibliotheken, die RAK-WB, erschien 1983, gefolgt im Jahre 1986 von der Fassung für öffentliche Bibliotheken, RAK-ÖB. Zwischen 1987 und 1997 erschienen Sonderregeln für besondere Materialarten.

SCHLAGWÖRTER. Alphabetische Katalogisierung, Deutschland, Österreich, *Preußische Instruktionen*, PI, *Berliner Anweisungen*, Regeln für die alphabetische Katalogisierung, RAK

Throughout most of the nineteenth century, German librarians, in providing access to their collections, devoted most of their attention to the maintenance of systematic catalogs, also known as classified catalogs. The systematic catalog generally also provided the record of each volume's location–i.e., it functioned simultaneously as the library's shelflist. In most libraries of the period, such a systematic catalog was the library's sole catalog. The only other means of access to the library's books was in the form of an index to the systematic catalog in which authors' names and titles of anonymous works were listed in alphabetic sequence.

Yet as early as 1790, Albrecht Christoph Kayser (1756-1811), with his theory of the catalog,[1] had laid the foundations for the development of rules for descriptive cataloging. Kayser's ideas were put into practice beginning in 1820 at the then Königliche Hofbibliothek (Royal Library) in Munich. In 1850 these rules were for the first time committed to paper, albeit only in a hand-written manuscript. In these rules, two important aspects received treatment that differed significantly from today's cataloging principles: there was no provision for entry under the name of a corporate body, and titles were ordered according to "grammatical order" (*grammatische Wortfolge*–the principle that titles should be filed in an order determined by the most grammatically significant noun in the title, as explained below).

These characteristics were shaped in large part by the conventions of the German national bibliographies produced for the booksellers' trade, such as the works of Wilhelm Heinsius[2] (1768-1817) and Christian Gottlob Kayser[3] (1782-1857), as well as the various lists produced by the publishing house of J. C. Hinrichs[4] in Leipzig. Publications of corporate bodies were uncommon in the nineteenth century, and those that existed were seldom intended for the booksellers' trade. Booksellers did not consider it worthwhile to include such publications in their lists, and thus it was deemed unnecessary to provide for them in the rules. Following the principle of grammatical order, titles were ordered according to the most important noun in the title, which in many cases was not the first word of the title.

It was only much later, in 1911, that this *Münchener Katalogisierungsordnung*[5] (*Munich Cataloging Rules*), often referred to as MKO, first appeared in print. Long before then, however, Carl Dziatzko, then director of the University Library in Breslau (Wrocław, Poland) and a prominent classical philologist, requested a copy of the *Munich Rules*, revised them, and then distributed them in multiple copies, at first in 1874 by using a hectograph to make manuscript copies, then from 1886 on in printed editions.[6] Dziatzko's *Instructions* were used in university libraries in Prussia, namely in Königsberg, Münster, and Göttingen.

When the Royal Library in Berlin began, in 1892, to issue lists of its newly acquired printed books,[7] it was found necessary to publish as well the cataloging rules on which the lists were based.[8] The Royal Library's list was published using one side of each page only so that users could cut the pages apart, thus separating the entries for the individual books so that these could then be pasted to catalog cards–an early cataloging distribution service. In 1898 all the university libraries in Prussia became active participants in this undertaking.[9] The increasing number of participating libraries, the increasing number of titles to be registered, and the preliminary work on a printed "Prussian Union Catalog" all made it necessary to replace the Royal Library's brief instructions from the year 1892 with more detailed rules. This led to the creation of the *Preussische Instruktionen* (*Prussian Instructions*) or PI, which is the shortened name by which the *Instruktionen für die alphabetischen Kataloge der preussischen Bibliotheken*[10] (*Instructions for the Alphabetic Catalogs of Prussian Libraries*) were generally known.

Fritz Milkau, the official within the Prussian Ministry of Culture who was in charge of libraries, was deeply involved in the creation of the *Prussian Instructions*. A committee of experts reworked first Dziatzko's *Instructions*[6] (with regard to the filing of titles) and then the "Instructions" of the Royal Library in Berlin[8] (with regard to the structure of the bibliographic record), expanded both and merged them into a cataloging code. An expanded second edition of the *Prussian Instructions* appeared in 1908.[11]

In addition to being used in the Royal Library's list of new acquisitions, published from 1910 on under the title *Berliner Titeldrucke*[12] (*Berlin Printed Titles*), the *Prussian Instructions* were also used for the cooperative effort, involving a number of libraries, towards producing the *Prussian Union Catalog*.[13] Beginning with the ninth volume (the first of the entries beginning with the letter B), the *Prussian Union Catalog* was expanded to be the *German Union Catalog*.[14] By the 1930s, not just all Prussian libraries but also almost all the important German and Austrian libraries were cataloging according to the *Prussian Instructions*. The most important library that declined to adopt the *Prussian Instructions* (although it participated in the Prussian and German Union Catalog projects) was Munich's Royal Library, by this time known as the Bayerische Staatsbibliothek (State Library of Bavaria). The Bayerische Staatsbibliothek continued to use its *Münchener Katalogisierungsordnung*,[15] repeatedly amended, right up until 1982 when it adopted the new German cataloging code, RAK. Up until the appearance of Regeln für die alphabetische Katalogisierung–RAK[16] (*Rules for Descriptive Cataloging*–RAK), the *Prussian Instructions* were the definitive cataloging code in Germany and Austria and led to a significant degree of uniformity in cataloging in the two countries.

The *Prussian Instructions* were organized in two parts: Part 1 addressed, in paragraphs 1-29, the *Aufnahme der Titel,* or transcription of titles–i.e., the outward form of the catalog entries and the form for bibliographic description. Part 2 contained, in paragraphs 30-241, the rules for the *Ordnung der Titel,* or filing of titles, where this phrase was understood to mean choice of main and added entry, the rules for the formulation of headings, and the filing order of entries in the catalog. There were six appendices: (1) examples, (2) transliteration tables, (3) abbreviations used in the bibliographic description, (4) rules for the description of incunabula, (5) rules for capitalization, and (6) rules for cataloging maps.

Under the *Prussian Instructions*, headings for personal names of the modern era were established not according to the *Staatsbürgerprinzip*, or principle of national citizenship, but according to the *Sprachprinzip*, or principle of language. With regard to the formulation of headings, only one differentiation was made, namely between surnames including prefixes that were of either Germanic or Romance origin. For example:

> *Item in hand:* Wernher von Braun
> *Heading:* Braun, Wernher von *[name of Germanic origin]*

> *Item in hand:* Walter de la Mare
> *Heading:* La Mare, Walter de *[name of Romance origin]*

The special characteristics of the *Prussian Instructions* were the same as those of the *Munich Cataloging Rules* of 1850: no entries under corporate names and filing of titles according to grammatical order. These two peculiarities will now be illustrated through examples.

Under the *Prussian Instructions*, entries were generally made only under personal names and under titles of anonymous works. Works published by corporate bodies received main entry under their titles. In title entries, titles were filed in an order determined by the degree of grammatical dependency of the words in the title, with the most independent word given first position, followed by the next most independent word, and so on, for example:

> *Item in hand:* Jahrbuch der Deutschen Bücherei (Yearbook of the National Library of Germany)
> *Main entry:* Jahrbuch Buecherei deutschen
> (No added entry was made under the name of the corporate body, "Deutsche Bücherei.")

These rules also applied in cases where the work bore a generic title and the name of the corporate body was needed as a supplement to the title for the purposes of citation, for example:

> *Item in hand:* Mitteilungen / Staatliche Hochschule für Bildende Künste
> (Reports / State Academy of Fine Arts)

> *Main entry:* Mitteilungen Hochschule staatliche Kuenste bildende
> (No added entry was made under the corporate name "Staatliche
> Hochschule für Bildende Künste.")

There was one exception to the rule that corporate bodies did not receive entries: publications of commercial businesses–auction catalogs and the like received an entry under the name of the corporate body.

Catalogers of the present day will surely find it difficult to follow the reasoning that underlay the filing of titles according to grammatical order. Nevertheless, we will make the attempt to explain this process, using a number of examples. To begin with, the *Prussian Instructions* differentiated titles into three types: (1) Titles in "usual form," (2) Titles in the form of sentences, and (3) Titles of mixed form.

Regarding Type 1, titles in "usual form" consisted of nouns and other words that did not constitute a complete sentence. The most significant noun in the title (the *Substantivum regens*–i.e., the "ruling noun" or first grammatically independent noun) became the word according to which the title was filed (the *erstes Ordnungswort*). The further ordering of the title was determined by the degree of grammatical dependency of each of the remaining words in the title. Unimportant words such as articles, prepositions and conjunctions were ignored for the purposes of filing. Here are some examples:

Title on the item	Filing title
The old book	(1) Book old
Cumulative book index	(2) Book-index cumulative
Books and libraries	(3) Books libraries
New books	(4) Books new
Sammlung Göschen	(5) Göschen Sammlung
Journal of chemistry	(6) Journal chemistry
Journal of inorganic chemistry	(7) Journal chemistry inorganic

Example (2) above is meant to show that words that would be written as compound words according to the rules of German spelling are treated as a single word, regardless of the way they are treated in their language of origin. In this case, "Book-index" in the filing title counts as a single word, although in English "book index" is treated as two separate words. Example (5) is meant to show that when two nouns stand in apposition to each other, the second is chosen as the filing word.

Regarding Type 2: "Titles in the form of sentences" included not only complete sentences but also titles that contained no noun as well as titles in which the noun was dependent on a participle, an adjective, or an adverb. Such titles were filed word by word in the order in which the words were given in the item, with initial articles being ignored. Examples of Type 2, in filing order:

> Damned to fame *[the noun "fame" is dependent on the participle "damned"]*
>
> (The) family is the patient *[a complete sentence. The initial article is ignored for purposes of filing]*
>
> Here comes the sun *[complete sentence]*
>
> How to get rich *[the title contains no noun]*
>
> My song is a piece of jade *[complete sentence]*
>
> Naked among cannibals *[the noun "cannibals" is dependent on the adjective "naked"]*
>
> This is Cleveland *[complete sentence]*

Regarding Type 3: Titles in "mixed form" consisted of a combination of a title in "usual form" with a title in the form of a sentence. Each part of the title is arranged for filing according to the rules for its type, for example:

> *Item in hand:* The great minerals and how to identify them
> *Filing title:* Minerals great how to identify them *["The great minerals" is a title in "usual form." "How to identify them" is a title in the form of a sentence]*

These complex rules were invented by the leading librarians of the large German libraries of the day, who were almost always philologists and scholars of grammar; they were never fully understood by the average layperson. Thus it is understandable that when rules were developed for the catalogs of the *Volksbüchereien,* as public libraries were known at that time, the rules for filing titles were made much simpler. These rules for public libraries were introduced in 1938 and were known as the *Berliner Anweisungen*[17] (Berlin Directives). The Berlin Directives adopted the principle of "mechanical order" (simple word-for-word filing). According to the Berlin Directives, the examples in the table and others given above would file as follows:

> Books and libraries
> Cumulative book index
> Damned to fame
> (The) great minerals and how to identify them
> Here comes the sun
> Journal of chemistry
> Journal of inorganic chemistry
> New books
> (The) old book
> Sammlung Göschen

In the 1950s academic librarians also began to join in criticizing the *Prussian Instructions.* In particular, they wanted to reduce the strain on the user by getting rid of grammatical order for filing and replacing it with word-for-word filing, i.e., "mechanical order." At first, librarians did not wish to write new rules but just to reform the existing ones. In his excellent bibliography[18] Rudolf Jung gives an overview of the various moves for reform.

However, the long overdue reform was delayed by Hermann Fuchs, who wrote a commentary on the *Prussian Instructions* in 1955[19] that made the Prussian rules easier to understand and to apply, at least for librarians. It must be said that he failed to recognize the fundamental reason why libraries exist, namely to serve their patrons. As late as 1963, in his textbook *Bibliotheksverwaltung*[20] (*Library Administration*), he was able to say, with astonishing arrogance: "Alphabetic catalogs, originally created for internal use by librarians, are now accessible to a very broad spectrum of users, who are not trained in librarianship and often lack the requisite sureness in thinking in grammatical terms. These users are neither inclined, nor are they in many cases competent, to learn and to apply the complicated rules for grammatical order."

In view of this difficult situation, German librarians sought active participation in the discussions regarding the principles of descriptive cataloging that began around this time at the international level. They were already present at the Preliminary Meeting of the International Cataloging Conference in London, in 1959, where they presented papers of their own. They participated in the International Conference on Cataloguing Principles (ICCP),[21] in Paris, in 1961, and with one exception agreed to the principles enunciated there. The one exception was the principle of national citizenship in regard to name headings (Principle 12: Entry Word for Personal Names), which was also rejected by the American delegation. Despite this rejection, the principle of national citizenship was later adopted without reservation in the RAK.

The numerous alternatives offered in the ICCP's "Statement of Principles"[22] made it easier for the Kommission für Alphabetische Katalogisierung des Vereins Deutscher Bibliothekare (Commission on Descriptive Cataloging of the Association of German Librarians) to adopt the ICCP Principles as a basis for the writing of a new German cataloging code. Work on the two reforms that were most important for German libraries could now be started. In 1965 a "Partial Draft"[23] of the new *Regeln für die alphabetische Katalogisierung* (*Rules for Descriptive Cataloging*, RAK) was presented, containing rules for main and added entries under corporate bodies and for the filing of entries according to the sequence of words as presented in the item in hand. From 1966 on, the *Deutsche Bibliothek* (the national library of West Germany) used the "Partial Draft" for constructing the entries for the *Deutsche Bibliographie* (*German Bibliography*). The *Deutsche Bibliographie* was the first national bibliography in the world to be produced by means of computerized data processing, which of course made it necessary to abandon grammatical order in filing titles and change over to filing by the order presented in the item in hand.

The reform movement had as its goal the creation of a cataloging code that would be used throughout German-speaking Europe. To achieve this goal, the Commission on Descriptive Cataloging of the Association of German Librarians (the West German body) worked together with the Arbeitsgruppe Alphabetische Katalogisierung der Kommission für Katalogfragen des Bibliotheksverbands der Deutschen Demokratischen Republik (Working Group on Descriptive Cataloging of the Commission for Cataloging Questions of the Library Association of the German Democratic Republic, the East German body) from 1975 on. Beginning in 1976, the Kommission für Nominalkatalogisierung der Vereinigung Österreichischer Bibliothekare (Commission on Descriptive Cataloging of the Association of Austrian Librarians) also joined the project. The drafts of the new rules were organized into groups of paragraphs by topic and issued between 1969 and 1976 in preliminary versions as mimeographs of typescripts. Many libraries started using the new rules before the final draft of the code was published.

The International Meeting of Cataloguing Experts (IMCE)[24] took place in Copenhagen in 1969, just in time for its decisions to be taken into account in the new German rules. Thus the refinements of the "Statement of Principles" agreed upon in Copenhagen with regard to formulating headings in the original language of the person or body were incorporated into the new rules. In addition, the International Standard Bibliographic Description (ISBD)[25] was made the basis for the formal structure of catalog entries. With regard to the ISBD(M), it should be noted that RAK uses ISBD(M) for the description of serials as well as monographs, rather than applying ISBD(S).

The complete edition of the new Rules for Descriptive Cataloging (RAK) was published in the German Democratic Republic in 1976[26] and in a slightly different form in the Federal Republic of Germany in 1977. Austria adopted the form used in the Federal Republic of Germany. The RAK are organized in nine main sections, followed by several appendices and an index:

1. §§ 1-35: Basic concepts
2. §§ 101-197: General rules
3. §§ 201-208: General rules for headings
4. §§ 301-343: Personal name headings
5. §§ 401-487: Corporate body headings
6. §§ 501-527: Formulation of headings for titles and collective titles, as well as rules for uniform titles
7. §§ 601-696: Main and added entries
    under personal names (§§ 601-630)
    under corporate names (§§ 631-694)
    under titles (§ 695)
8. §§ 701-716: Determination of the form of a title for main or added entries under title
9. §§ 801-823: Filing rules for the entries

Appendices:
      1) Terms for languages and scripts and their abbreviations
      2) Templates for bibliographic descriptions of various classes of works
      3) Acronyms used to identify various elements of the bibliographic record
      4) Abbreviations
      5) Transliteration tables
Index

The basic concepts of RAK (Section 1), in contrast to the Glossary in AACR2, are organized systematically, so that the relationships between the various concepts can be made clearer. The determinations of the concepts, in the form of definitions, create a secure foundation for a consistent formulation of rules in the following sections. The distinction among works according to the number of authors and the number of works contained, a feature not found in other catalog codes, has proved especially useful:

Number of works	Number of authors	
	One author	More than one author
One work	**Einzelwerk** (Single work; in AACR2 terms, a work for which a single person or corporate body is responsible)	**Gemeinschaftliches Werk** (Cooperative work; in AACR2 terms, a work of shared responsibility)
Several works	**Sammlung** (Collection of works by a single author)	**Sammelwerk** (Collection of works by more than one author)

The RAK general rules (Section 2) contain statements on:

- the functions of the catalog, following the ICCP "Statement of Principles"[22]
- the external form of the catalog (i.e., whether card, list, etc.)
- categories of entry (i.e., main or added, references)
- the structure of the bibliographic description, the *Kopf* (head, or first line of the record) and the *Nebeneintragungsvermerk* (the record of added entries made, analogous to the "tracings" on catalog cards)

The general rules for headings (Section 3) contain those rules that apply both to titles and to names of corporate bodies. These rules address the treatment of abbreviations, of sequences of words involving apostrophes, hyphens and other signs, the treatment of spelling variations (e.g., catalogue vs. catalog), treatment of numerals, symbols and equations, and treatment of geographic names. The decisive point here is that all of these rules are formulated with a focus on producing a logical indexing sequence.

The rules for personal name headings, corporate headings, and title headings (Sections 4-6) are based on the principle of national citizenship for personal names of the modern era and on the principle of original language for other persons, for corporate bodies, and for uniform titles, following the ICCP Statement of Principles.[22] The RAK thus is more closely aligned with these international agreements than AACR2[27] is.

With regard to surnames that include a prefix, the RAK prescribes that the prefix is to be elided to the name to form a single word for the purposes of filing:

> *On the item in hand:* Wernher von Braun
> *Heading:* VonBraun, Wernher

This has caused problems in searching in online catalogs. The rule is to be changed so that the heading will now appear as:

New heading: Von Braun, Wernher

The use of angle brackets to identify qualifiers added to headings has also been recognized as problematic in computer catalogs. These qualifiers are similar in function to the "additions" prescribed by AACR2. For example, for corporate bodies with a specific physical location, a geographic name appearing as part of a name is detached from the name, then added back onto the heading as a qualifier in angle brackets:

> *Official form:* University of Birmingham
> *Heading:* University <Birmingham>

In the rules on main and added entry (Sections 7 and 8), the RAK prefers main entry under personal name over main entry under title, and then again main entry under title is preferred to main entry under a corporate body. For a work to receive main entry under a corporate body, the work must be "anonymous" (i.e., more than three people shared in its creation), the corporate body must be the *Urheber* (originator) of the work, and the name of the corporate body must appear in the title or be a necessary complement to the title. RAK thus decided to apply Principle 9.12 of the ICCP Statement of Principles,[22] whereas AACR2 decided in favor of Principle 9.11. For the sake of comparison, the text of these two principles is quoted here (minus parenthetical statements and footnotes):

> 9.1. The main entry for a work should be made under the name of a corporate body
>> 9.11 when the work is by its nature necessarily the expression of the collective thought or activity of the corporate body, even if signed by a person in the capacity of an officer or servant of the corporate body, *or*
>> 9.12 when the wording of the title or title page, taken in conjunction with the nature of the work, clearly implies that the corporate body is collectively responsible for the content of the work.

Since neither principle will always lead in practice to an unambiguous decision, the RAK seeks to clarify the problem by stating that only corporate bodies that function as *Urheber* (originators) can receive main entry. A corporate body is an *Urheber* when it–alone or in conjunction with other corporate bodies–either produces (*"erarbeiten"*) an "anonymous" work (or part of a work), or commissions (*"veranlassen"*) such a work, *and* also issues (*"herausgeben"*) the work. Additionally, a corporate body is an *Urheber* of an "anonymous" work when it is named in the title or other title information and fulfills certain formal or content-related criteria. In the case of both these rules, it is important to note that a corporate body can be the *Urheber* only of an "anonymous" work. It is immaterial whether the work is really anonymous–that is, the author(s) are not, in fact, known–or whether the work is defined by the rules as anonymous–that is, it has been written by more than three persons, or it is a serial. Some examples of cases where main entry as determined by RAK differs from main entry as determined by AACR2:

> *Item in hand:* Capital and equality : report of a Labour Party study group
> *Main entry:* Capital and equality
> *Added entry:* Labour Party <Great Britain>
>
> *Item in hand:* The journal of the Acoustical Society of America : JASA / American Institute of Physics
> *Main entry:* Acoustical Society of America: ¬The¬ Journal of the Acoustical society of America

The RAK contains numerous optional and alternative rules. The large number of optional rules, which allow individual libraries or library consortia to exercise their own judgment about the amount of detail they wish to include in the bibliographic description and about the number of added entries they wish to provide, certainly made it easier for many libraries to decide that they would change over to the new rules. A decision in favor of the new rules was easier to make because libraries were facing automation and were thus compelled to part with their old catalogs in any event. The alternative rules in RAK allowed for establishing headings for persons, corporate bodies, and uniform titles according to German-language usage and were intended for public libraries.

Although these optional and alternative rules promoted a rapid changeover to RAK, they also acted as a barrier to the easy exchange of records between libraries since each library developed its own "canon" of rules to apply. To meet this challenge, the *Kurzfassung der Regeln für die alphabetische Katalogisierung (*KRAK*) (Short Version of the Rules for Descriptive Cataloging)*[28] was developed for use in academic libraries and in the library consortia that were now coming into being in West Germany. KRAK was not, as the title would suggest, a short summary of the rules, but rather a list of those optional rules which a normal academic library was expected to apply. A poll was conducted to determine which options academic libraries in fact wished to apply, and the results of this poll led in 1983 to the publication of a version of

RAK specifically intended for use in academic libraries (*wissenschaftliche Bibliotheken*), the *Regeln für wissenschaftliche Bibliotheken*, or RAK-WB.[29]

In 1986 a second volume of the new RAK was published; this volume was intended for public libraries (*öffentliche Bibliotheken*) and was entitled *Regeln für öffentliche Bibliotheken,* or RAK-ÖB.[30] The RAK-ÖB is an abridged version of the RAK-WB and also contains alternative rules for small public libraries, rules which allow uniform titles, personal names, and corporate names to be established in their German-language forms.

Like the 1976 and 1977 editions of RAK published in East and West Germany, the RAK-WB and the RAK-ÖB contain rules only for books and periodicals in European languages. The East German edition of RAK, published in four parts in 1976, also received a number of supplements published between 1977 and 1989; these supplements contained corrections, additions, more precise statements of certain rules, transliteration tables, and additional rules for maps and for printed music and sound recordings. With the exception of the additional rules, these supplemental materials were incorporated into a new, thoroughly revised East German edition of RAK, which was published in 1989 and which, oddly, is designated as the "first edition."[31]

In West Germany special rules for music (the RAK-Musik)[32] were published in 1986. In the same year a draft of special rules for works contained within larger works (*Sonderregeln für unselbständig erschienene Werke,* or RAK-UW)[33] was issued. In 1987, special rules for maps appeared, the RAK-Karten.[34] The year 1994 saw the publication of special rules for audio-visual materials, microforms, and games, the RAK-AV.[35] These rules were expanded in 1996 and renamed RAK-NBM,[36] NBM being non-book materials. In 1997 a second edition of the RAK-Musik was published.[37]

The special rules contain only rules that (a) address a matter that is to be treated differently from the way it is treated in RAK-WB or RAK-ÖB, *and* (b) address topics that do not arise for print media.

As regards to the cataloging of maps (RAK-Karten), one significant difference here is that main entry is always made under the title, even when an author is present. The rules for audio-visual materials and non-book materials, RAK-AV and RAK-NBM, also lead in most (though not all) cases to main entry under title.

Soon after the publication of the authorized editions of the rules, it was recognized that some means were required for ongoing maintenance of the rules. Since it was not possible to issue frequent new editions of the rules, changes, supplements, and more precise formulations of rules were published in West Germany, from 1984 on, in the form of *RAK-Mitteilungen* (RAK reports) in the journal *Bibliotheksdienst.* Those rule revisions published up through 1986 applied to RAK-WB only; after 1986, such revisions applied to both RAK-WB and RAK-ÖB. During the 1990s drafts for the RAK-AV, RAK-Musik, and RAK-NBM were also published as *RAK-Mitteilungen*. The problem with this form of rule maintenance was that rule revisions appearing in the journal *Bibliotheksdienst* had to be photocopied and then cut and pasted into one's published copy of RAK. This was not only time-consuming, but it also meant that it was difficult to work with one's published copy of RAK.

Therefore, the second, revised edition of RAK-WB appeared in 1993 in the form of a loose-leaf publication.[38] This made it possible to distribute more efficiently those changes that had been planned to deal with the online catalog. To date three supplemental fascicles for the loose-leaf edition have been issued in 1995, 1996, and 1998. A fourth fascicle, containing the revised rules for dealing with prefixes in names, was scheduled to be published in 2002.

Rules for formulating name headings for personal names from countries with non-European languages appeared in draft form in the 1960s and 1970s, but for a long time no further work was done on these drafts. It was not until 1998, in the third supplemental fascicle for the RAK-WB loose-leaf, that authorized "Rules for Headings for Personal Names from Countries Using Arabic, Persian and Turkish Languages" (RAK-ISL) appeared, as Part 1 of Anlage 20 (Appendix 20).[39] Further rules for other cultural and linguistic regions are planned.

. Work on a new cataloging code, oriented to the online catalog, was undertaken from 1998 to 2000 by the Arbeitsgruppe Formalerschliessung der Konferenz für Regelwerksfragen (Working Group on Descriptive Cataloging of the Conference for Cataloging Code Questions) and from 2001 on by its successor organization, the Expertengruppe Formalerschliessung des Standardisierungsausschusses (Expert Group for Descriptive Cataloging of the Commission for Standardization). The working title of this new code is RAK2. The main points of the new code are: (1) it does away with the distinction between main and added entries; (2) it simplifies the rules; and (3) it moves closer to AACR2 for the purpose of making it easier to exchange bibliographic data. The work of the Expertengruppe is guided by the Arbeitsstelle für Standardisierung at the Deutsche Bibliothek. This Arbeitsstelle is the executive board of the Standardisierungsausschuss (Commission for Standardization), which is made up of representatives, with voting rights, from the German library consortia, the Austrian Library Consortium, the major German libraries (the Bayerische Staatsbibliothek, the Deutsche Bibliothek, and the Staatsbibliothek zu Berlin). A final voting member represents the public libraries.

The work of the Expertengruppe Formalerschliessung is currently on hold because the Commission for Standardization decided in December 2001 that, in principle, German libraries and German library consortia should strive to change over from RAK and its related data format, MAB2 (*Maschinelles Austauschformat für Bibliotheken, Version 2,* or Machine-Readable Exchange Format for Libraries, Version 2) to AACR2 and MARC21. A study has been planned to examine the parameters of the changeover, its consequences, and the required timeframe for the change, with particular reference to its economic impact on the organizations involved. In the context of this decision, only such modifications to RAK are to be made as are absolutely necessary and in line with international developments, and no more modifications are to be made after the end of the year 2003.

Does this mean that Germany will no longer have a cataloging code of its own? Emotions are running high at the grass-roots level. One waits with a certain sensation of tension to see what may happen next.

NOTES

1. Albrecht Christoph Kayser, *Über die Manipulation bei der Einrichtung einer Bibliothek und der Verfertigung der Bücherverzeichnisse* (Bayreuth,1790).

2. Wilhelm Heinsius, *Allgemeines Bücher-Lexikon oder Vollständiges alphabetisches Verzeichnis aller von 1700 bis . . . [1892] erschienenen Bücher,* 19 Bde. (Leipzig, 1812-1894).

3. Christian Gottlob Kayser, *Vollständiges Bücher-Lexikon, enthaltend alle von 1750 bis . . . [1892] in Deutschland und in den angrenzenden Ländern gedruckten Bücher,* 36 Bde. (Leipzig, 1834-1911).

4. See in particular: *Halbjahresverzeichnis der Neuerscheinungen des deutschen Buchhandels,* 292 Bde. (Leipzig, 1798-1944). Until 1915 these lists were published by Hinrichs.

5. *Katalogisierungs-Ordnung der K. Hof- und Staatsbibliothek München* (Munich, 1911). Cited as: *Münchener Katalogisierungsordnung, MKO.*

6. Carl Dziatzko, *Instruction für die Ordnung der Titel im Alphabetischen Zettelkatalog der Königlichen und Universitäts-Bibliothek zu Breslau* (Berlin, 1886).

7. *Verzeichnis der aus der neu erschienenen Litteratur von der Königlichen Bibliothek zu Berlin erworbenen Druckschriften* (Berlin, 1892).

8. *Instruction für die Herstellung der Zettel des alphabetischen Kataloges* (Burg bei Magdeburg, 1892). Also: *Instruction für die Aufnahme der Titel* (Berlin, 1892).

9. *Verzeichnis der aus der neu erschienenen Literatur von der Königlichen Bibliothek zu Berlin und den preussischen Universitätsbibliotheken erworbenen neueren Druckschriften* (Berlin, 1892-1909). From 1910 on, appeared under the title *Berliner Titeldrucke.*

10. *Instruktionen für die alphabetischen Kataloge der preussischen Bibliotheken und für den preussischen Gesamtkatalog: vom 10. Mai 1899* (Berlin, 1899). Cited as: *Preussische Instruktionen* or *PI.*

11. *Instruktionen für die alphabetischen Kataloge der preussischen Bibliotheken,* 2. Ausg. in der Fassung vom 10. August 1908 (Berlin, 1908). Also cited as: *Preussische Instruktionen* or *PI.*

12. *Berliner Titeldrucke* (Berlin, 1910-1944). Included a number of sub-series and cumulations, for single years and for ranges of years. From 1935 on, published under the title: *Deutscher Gesamtkatalog. Neue Titel.*

13. *Gesamtkatalog der preussischen Bibliotheken: mit Nachweis des identischenBesitzes der Bayerischen Staatsbibliothek in München und der Nationalbibliothek in Wien,* herausgegeben von der Preussischen Staatsbibliothek (Berlin, 1931-1935). Bd. 1-8 (Aa-Az).

14. *Deutscher Gesamtkatalog,* herausgegeben von der Preussischen Staatsbibliothek (Berlin, 1936-1939). Bd. 9-14 (Ba–Beethordnung). Bd. 15 (Beethoven–Belych) was published in 1979. No more published.

15. *Katalogisierungsordnung der Bayerischen Staatsbibliothek München,* Ausg. 1981 (Munich, 1981). Cited as: *Münchener Katalogisierungsordnung* or *MKO.*

16. *Regeln für die alphabetische Katalogisierung, RAK,* edited by Irmgard Bouvier, autorisierte Ausg., 1. Aufl. [authorized ed., 1st printing] (Wiesbaden, 1977). Cited as: *RAK.*

17. *Anweisung für den alphabetischen Katalog der Volksbüchereien,* Ausgabe für grosse Büchereien und Büchereischulen (Leipzig, 1938).

18. Rudolf Jung, *Die Reform der alphabetischen Katalogisierung in Deutschland 1908-1976: eine annotierte Auswahlbibliographie* (Köln, 1976). An updated continuation of this bibliography is available on the WWW: *Die Regeln für die alphabetische Katalogisierung: eine bibliographische Bestandsaufnahme (1965-1999),* erarbeitet und zusammengetragen von Martin Baumgartner . . . et al. (München, 1999) [cited 25 April 2002]; available at http://www.bib-bvb.de/fachbereich/RAKWWW.htm.

19. Hermann Fuchs, *Kommentar zu den Instruktionen für die alphabetischen Kataloge der preussischen Bibliotheken* (Wiesbaden, 1955).

20. Hermann Fuchs, *Bibliotheksverwaltung* (Wiesbaden, 1963), 119.

21. International Conference on Cataloguing Principles, Paris, October 1961, *Report* (London, 1963).

22. International Conference on Cataloguing Principles, Paris, October 1961, *Statement of Principles Adopted at the International Conference on Cataloguing Principles, Paris, October, 1961,* annotated ed. with commentary and examples by Eva Verona (London, 1971).

23. Verein Deutscher Bibliothekare. Kommission für Alphabetische Katalogisierung, "Regeln für die alphabetische Katalogisierung: Teilentwurf," *Zeitschrift für Bibliothekswesen und Bibliographie* Sonderheft 2 (1965).

24. Franz Georg Kaltwasser, "Das International Meeting of Cataloguing Experts, Kopenhagen 1969," *Zeitschrift für Bibliothekswesen und Bibliographie* 17 (1970): 1-17.

25. International Federation of Library Associations, *International Standard Bibliographic Description for Monographic Publications, ISBD(M),* 1st standard ed. (London, 1974). Published in a German edition under the title: *Internationale standardisierte bibliographische Beschreibung für Monographien: ISBD(M),* 1. Standard-Ausg., deutsche Fassung von Irmgard Bouvier, Materialien zur Katalogisierung, 1 (Berlin, 1974).

26. Bibliotheksverband der DDR. Kommission für Katalogfragen, *Regeln für die alphabetische Katalogisierung: RAK* (Berlin, 1976).

27. *Anglo-American Cataloguing Rules,* 2d ed., prepared by the American Library Association . . . et al., edited by Michael Gorman and Paul W. Winkler (London, 1978). Cited as: AACR2.

28. Deutscher Bibliotheksverband. Arbeitsstelle für das Bibliothekswesen, *Kurzfassung der Regeln für die alphabetische Katalogisierung: KRAK*, Vorabdruck, Materialien zur Katalogisierung, 5 (Berlin, 1976).

29. Deutsches Bibliotheksinstitut. Kommission für Alphabetische Katalogisierung, *Regeln für wissenschaftliche Bibliotheken: RAK-WB*, autorisierte Ausg., Redaktion, Bearbeitung und Register, Irmgard Bouvier, Regeln für die alphabetische Katalogisierung, Bd. 1 (Wiesbaden, 1983).

30. Deutsches Bibliotheksinstitut. Kommission für Alphabetische Katalogisierung, *Regeln für öffentliche Bibliotheken: RAK-ÖB*, autorisierte Ausg., redaktionelle Bearbeitung, Hans Popst, Regeln für die alphabetische Katalogisierung, Bd. 2 (Wiesbaden, 1986).

31. Bibliotheksverband der DDR. Kommission für Katalogfragen, *Regeln für die alphabetische Katalogisierung: RAK*, 1. Aufl., redaktionelle Bearbeitung und Register, Elisabeth Lotte von Oppen (Leipzig, 1989).

32. Deutsches Bibliotheksinstitut. Kommission für Alphabetische Katalogisierung, *Sonderregeln für Musikalien und Musiktonträger: RAK-Musik*, autorisierte Ausg., redaktionelle Bearbeitung und Register, Klaus Haller, Regeln für die alphabetische Katalogisierung, Bd. 3 (Wiesbaden, 1986).

33. Deutsches Bibliotheksinstitut. Kommission für Alphabetische Katalogisierung, *Sonderregeln für unselbständig erschienene Werke: (RAK-UW): Entwurf*, Einführung, redaktionelle Bearbeitung und Anlagen, Hans Popst, Regeln für die alphabetische Katalogisierung (Berlin, 1986).

34. Deutsches Bibliotheksinstitut. Kommission für Alphabetische Katalogisierung, *Sonderregeln für kartographische Materialien: RAK-Karten*, autorisierte Ausg., redaktionelle Bearbeitung, Peter Baader und Dietrich Poggendorf, Regeln für die alphabetische Katalogisierung, Bd. 4 (Wiesbaden, 1987).

35. Deutsches Bibliotheksinstitut. Expertengruppe RAK-AV, *Sonderregeln für audiovisuelle Materialien, Mikromaterialien und Spiele: RAK-AV*, loose-leaf ed., redaktionelle Bearbeitung, Hans Popst, Regeln für die alphabetische Katalogisierung (Berlin, 1994).

36. Deutsches Bibliotheksinstitut. Expertengruppe RAK, *Regeln für die alphabetische Katalogisierung von Nichtbuchmaterialien: RAK-NBM: Sonderregeln zu den RAK-WB und RAK-ÖB*, loose-leaf ed., redaktionelle Bearbeitung von Hans Popst (Berlin, 1996).

37. Deutsches Bibliotheksinstitut. Expertengruppe RAK-Musik, *Regeln für die alphabetische Katalogisierung von Musikdrucken, Musiktonträgern und Musik-Bildtonträgern: RAK-Musik: Sonderregeln zu den RAK-WB und RAK-ÖB*, loose-leaf ed., redaktionelle Bearbeitung, Erwin Hardeck (Berlin, 1997-).

38. *Regeln für die alphabetische Katalogisierung in wissenschaftlichen Bibliotheken: RAK-WB*, 2., überarbeitete Aufl. (loose-leaf ed.). Produced until 1990 by: Deutsches Bibliotheksinstitut. Kommission für Alphabetische Katalogisierung. Produced after 1991 by: Deutsches Bibliotheksinstitut. Expertengruppe RAK, edited by Hans Popst (Berlin, 1993-).

39. "Anlage 20: Regeln für die Ansetzung von Personennamen in Staaten mit aussereuropäischen Sprachen," *Regeln für die alphabetische Katalogisierung in wissenschaftlichen Bibliotheken: RAK-WB*, 2., überarbeitet Ausg., Teil 1: "Regeln für die Ansetzung von Personennamen in Staaten mit arabischer, persischer und türkischer Sprache (RAK-ISL)," compiled by Helga Rebhahn and Winfried Riesterer, edited by Klaus Haller. Pp. 467-490 of "Ergänzungs-Lieferung 3 (1998)" of the loose-leaf ed. (Berlin, 1998).

RAK or AACR2?
The Current Discussion in Germany on Cataloging Codes

Charles R. Croissant

SUMMARY. Discussion around the issue of cataloging codes has become heated in Germany since Germany's national committee on cataloging standardization announced in December 2001 that its goal would now be to pursue a migration to AACR2 and MARC. Like AACR2, Germany's current cataloging code, RAK, is based on the ISBD, but the two codes differ from each other in a number of significant ways. This paper compares German and Anglo-American cataloging practice, with particular regard to determining main entry, the treatment of corporate bodies and conferences, the treatment of personal name headings, and the treatment of multipart items. *[Article copies available for a fee from The Haworth Document Delivery Service: 1-800-HAWORTH. E-mail address: <getinfo@haworthpressinc.com> Website: <http://www.HaworthPress.com> © 2002 by The Haworth Press, Inc. All rights reserved.]*

Charles R. Croissant is Catalog Librarian, Pius XII Memorial Library, Saint Louis University, Saint Louis, MO 63108 (E-mail: croisscr@slu.edu).

The author wishes to thank Professor Hans Popst (Bayerische Beamtenfachhochschule, Munich) and Ms. Monika Münnich (Universitätsbibliothek Heidelberg) for their helpful comments, which contributed to the final form of this paper. This article is intended to complement Professor Popst's article in this volume on the development of descriptive cataloging in Germany.

This paper began life as a presentation made to the Catalogers' Discussion Group of the Western European Studies Section (WESS) at the ALA Midwinter Conference, January 21, 2002, in New Orleans.

[Haworth co-indexing entry note]: "RAK or AACR2? The Current Discussion in Germany on Cataloging Codes." Croissant, Charles R. Co-published simultaneously in *Cataloging & Classification Quarterly* (The Haworth Information Press, an imprint of The Haworth Press, Inc.) Vol. 35, No. 1/2, 2002, pp. 173-186; and: *Historical Aspects of Cataloging and Classification* (ed: Martin D. Joachim) The Haworth Information Press, an imprint of The Haworth Press, Inc., 2003, pp. 173-186. Single or multiple copies of this article are available for a fee from The Haworth Document Delivery Service [1-800-HAWORTH, 9:00 a.m. - 5:00 p.m. (EST). E-mail address: getinfo@haworthpressinc.com].

KEYWORDS. AACR2, RAK, cataloging codes, main and added entry, corporate body headings, personal name headings, treatment of multi-part items, analysis

ZUSAMMENFASSUNG. Seit dem Beschluss des Standardisierungs-sausschusses im Dezember 2001 wird in Deutschland leidenschaftlich über die Frage der Regelwerksmigration bzw. über die relativen Vorzüge von RAK und AACR2 diskutiert. RAK und AACR2 basieren beide auf ISBD, weisen aber signifikante Unterschiede auf. Der Autor geht auf diese Unterschiede ein, mit besonderem Bezug auf Haupt- und Nebeneintragungen, Eintragung unter Körperschaften und Kongressen, die Individualisierung von Personennamen, und die Erschliessung von mehrbändigen Werken.

SCHLAGWÖRTER. AACR2, RAK, katalogisierung, regelwerke, haupt- und nebeneintragung, individualisierung von personennamen, erschliessung von mehrbändigen werken

The current German cataloging code is entitled *Regeln für die alphabetische Katalogisierung, RAK*. The phrase *"alphabetische Katalogisierung"* (alphabetic cataloging) in the code's title is meant to distinguish these rules from rules for the other two types of cataloging practiced in German libraries: subject cataloging and systematic cataloging. "Alphabetic cataloging" corresponds in Anglo-American parlance to "descriptive cataloging" and refers to the construction of entries for an author/title catalog indexed in a dictionary sequence.

The discussion in Germany around the issue of cataloging codes has become very heated. Until fairly recently, it was assumed that work would go forward on a major revision of RAK ("RAK2"). In December of 2001, however, the national committee on standardization in cataloging (the *Standardisierungsausschuss*) announced that it planned to cease making revisions to RAK and that its goal would henceforth be to move in the direction of adopting AACR2 as Germany's cataloging code. It must be emphasized that the idea of changing cataloging codes is still in the discussion stages; any actual action towards this end is at least several years away. It has been decided that first a feasibility study must be conducted. A joint German-American team of librarians is currently preparing a German translation of AACR2, scheduled for publication in the fall of 2002; but this is purely a study document, meant to facilitate discussion of the differences between RAK and AACR2. It is not intended for actual use in cataloging in German libraries.

What lies behind the December announcement of the *Standardisierungsausschuss*? German libraries are experiencing a great deal of pressure toward some form of rule harmonization with the English-speaking world. A significant portion of the acquisitions of German academic libraries are English-language materials; I have seen estimates as high as 60 percent of all acquisitions by German academic libraries that are in English.[1] Other German librarians whom I have contacted consider that this figure is too high and that a more realistic figure of current acquisitions in English would be 40 percent for the average academic library.[2] Even at the 40 percent level, however, this would represent a significant portion of a library's collection.

For the vast majority of such English-language materials, bibliographic records already exist in OCLC or RLIN. Importing such records into German catalogs can be problematic, however. MARC is not widely used as a data format in Germany. For exchanging bibliographic data between libraries, there is the format known as MAB (*Maschinelles Austauschformat für Bibliotheken*, or Machine-Readable Exchange Format for Libraries). Within the local systems of German libraries, a variety of different data formats are used, and these formats often differ significantly from each other. There is, for example, the Pica format, developed in the Netherlands, and the *allegro* format, developed at the Technische Universität Braunschweig. A variety of other homegrown formats are also in use. When a MARC/AACR2 record is imported into a German system, the cataloger is faced with the problem of editing the record to conform to RAK or leaving it as is. Project REUSE,[3] a study of the use of MARC records in Germany conducted in 1998, showed that, often, records are left as is. In some cases, headings formulated according to AACR2 are close to, or even identical to, those formulated according to RAK. In other cases, however, headings show significant differences in their formulation. Allowing both RAK and AACR2 headings to coexist in the same catalog is clearly not an optimal situation.

RAK and AACR2 both grew out of the Paris Principles of 1961 and ISBD; so there is much that they share in common, particularly in terms of rules for physical description. But as the products of two distinctly different library communities, they diverge from each other in a number of significant ways. Differences occur particularly over choice of main entry, corporate main entry vs. title main entry, formulation of personal name headings, treatment of corporate main entry, and treatment of multi-part items. The differences between AACR2 and RAK, real and perceived, form a major part of the current discussion.

One area in which practice diverges widely involves the question of entries for corporate bodies, in particular the question of main entry under a corporate body. In the Anglo-American library community, we often speak in practice of corporate authorship. Historically, however, Anglo-American librarians have been rather more comfortable with the idea of a corporate body being considered an "author" of a work than have our European colleagues.[4] For example, the predecessor work to RAK, the "Prussian Instructions," made no provision at all for entry under a corporate body, with a single exception: commercial publications such as publishers' catalogs could be entered under the name of the firm. Perhaps as a concession to European sensibilities on this issue, AACR2 never actually uses the phrase "corporate authorship." In essence, it evades the question as to whether a corporate body is capable of authorship and speaks instead of works that "emanate" from corporate bodies.

In the German view, a corporate body is not capable of authorship. This view receives expression in the language itself. A personal author is referred to as a *Verfasser*. A corporate body, however, cannot be referred to as a *Verfasser*; rather, an entirely different word is used, namely *Urheber*, meaning an entity that causes something to be created. The word *Urheber*, however, excludes the idea of direct creation that is implicit in the word *Verfasser*.

AACR2 undertakes its consideration of main entry under a corporate body in the famous, or infamous, rule 21.1B2. First, it limits main entry under corporate body to works that "emanate" from corporate bodies and goes on to state that a work emanates from a corporate body "if it is issued by that body or has been caused to be issued by that body or if it originated with that body." What it means in actual practice to say that a work is "issued by" a corporate body or "originates with" a corporate body is not explicitly stated by the rules, so the matter is ultimately left to the cataloger's judgment. Then six categories of works are defined that receive main entry under the corporate body. The definitions of these categories basically require the cataloger to make a judgment about the nature of the contents of the work in hand. Rule 21.1B2 has certainly generated its share of controversy over the years; but, on the other hand, it must be said that most Anglo-American catalogers now appear to have accepted the six categories as the means by which decisions on main entry under corporate body shall be made though some may still harbor reservations regarding the underlying principle, or lack of principle, on which the rule is based. The six categories themselves are fairly straightforward in their definitions; the trickier question is probably the initial one of deciding whether or not a work "emanates" from a corporate body.

RAK takes a different approach to the question of corporate main entry. Like AACR2, it begins by limiting its consideration to works that emanate from a corporate body. Unlike AACR2, it offers explicit criteria for determining whether a work emanates from a corporate body. With a single exception (discussed below), these criteria make no consideration of a work's contents. Rather, they are what the Germans call "formal" in nature, i.e., they are concerned solely with the wording presented on the title page. If that wording makes it clear that the corporate body prepared the work, or commissioned it *and* issued it, then the corporate body is the work's *Urheber*. Essentially, this means that the corporate body's name must appear in one of the following places: at the head of the title, in the title itself, or in the imprint. Only in one instance do the contents of a work play a role in determining whether a corporate body is an *Urheber*: when the corporate body is named only in the title, but nowhere else on the title page. A corporate body that is named only in the title can be an *Urheber* only if (1) the body is referred to in the title as an active agent (as opposed to being simply the object under consideration) or (2) the contents of the work make it clear that the corporate body named in the title produced it.

But even if a corporate body is determined to be the *Urheber* of the work in question, it receives the main entry only when it is named in the title or when its name is a necessary complement to the title–i.e., the work's title is distinctive only when the corporate body's name is added to it. Thus, in contrast to AACR2, a work's contents play a role in determining corporate main entry only in one rather rare and limited instance. A corporate body that is an *Urheber* but that is not eligible for main entry can appear in the bibliographic record as an added entry.

In general terms, and considering all types of works, RAK's process for determining main entry can be expressed in terms of a decision tree.[5] In the following description, note in particular the definition assigned to the term "anonymous," which is distinctly different from the meaning commonly assigned to that word in English:

1. A work by one to three personal authors receives main entry under a person (the most prominently named author, otherwise the first-named author).
2. A work by more than three persons is considered an "anonymous" work.
3. If an "anonymous" work does not emanate from a corporate body, it receives main entry under its title.
4. If an "anonymous" work emanates from a corporate body, and the corporate body's name appears in the work's title or is a necessary complement to the work's title, the work is entered under the corporate body.
5. If the "anonymous" work emanates from a corporate body, but the corporate body's name does not appear in the title and is not a necessary complement to the title, the work receives main entry under its title.

The decision tree just described applies to RAK in its current form. In the projected second edition of RAK, "RAK2," one particularly epochal change would have been made: RAK2 planned to abandon the distinction between main and added entry. As has often been remarked, our practice of distinguishing between main and added entries is a holdover from the days of the card catalog, and has little if any real justification in the online-catalog environment. In the online catalog all headings attached to a bibliographic record become equal access points in that record, and it was intended that the new language of RAK2 should reflect that fact.

To return to current practice and the corporate body question: the perception in the German cataloging community is that, under AACR2, more works receive corporate body main entry than is the case under RAK. It is not clear from the available research whether or not this is actually the case. At any rate, German catalogers would like to reduce the number of cases when works receive main entry under a corporate body. Indeed, they would like to see a general reduction in the number of corporate body entries, whether main or added. There is a body of opinion in the German library community that feels that it is not an effective use of the cataloger's time to add corporate body entries to bibliographic records since corporate body headings are so little used in catalog searches. This point of view is likely to evoke a certain feeling of resistance from Anglo-American catalogers. Certainly, speaking for myself here as an Anglo-American librarian and cataloger, I consider corporate body headings a useful form of access, and I make frequent use of corporate body headings in searching for particular items, both in my own library's catalog and in catalogs that I search remotely.

The number of cases in which AACR2 prescribes entry under the name of a jurisdiction causes particular concern to RAK catalogers. Under RAK, constitutions and treaties are entered under jurisdictions, but laws (illogically, from an AACR2 point of view) are simply entered under their titles; an added entry under the jurisdiction is not made. AACR2 catalogers will surely wonder how, in that case, laws issued by a particular jurisdiction are brought together in the catalog. I have studied the portions of RAK that appear to apply to this question, but so far I have not found any indication that RAK does provide for collocation under the name of the jurisdiction. The prevailing feeling among German catalogers seems to be that users can be expected to use a law's title as their search key.

RAK's rules for entry under conference are complex and result in fewer works receiving main or added entries for conferences than is the case under AACR2. Some German librarians have noted that conference entries can be very useful access points, particularly in certain fields of study, and feel that more conference entries should be made than RAK currently allows.[6] It should be noted, however, that many other German librarians do not share this view.

A conference is eligible for use as an access point only when it is considered to be a corporate body; and, according to RAK, not all conferences are corporate bodies. For a conference to meet RAK's definition of a corporate body, it must contain in its name a concept representing the idea of a conference (i.e., its name must contain the word "Congress" or one of its cognates) and its name must include a grammatically linked statement of the subject treated at the conference. For example, if on the title page we see *Report of the Fifth International Congress of Musicology, Rome, Italy, January 10-12, 1999,* then the congress meets RAK's criteria for being a corporate body; and since the name of the congress appears in the title, the work receives its main entry under the name of the congress. Consider, on the other hand, a title page presentation as follows: International Society of Musicologists, Fifth Congress, Rome, Italy, January 10-12, 1999, *New Developments in Electronic Music.* Here the concept "Congress" is not grammatically linked to the subject, musicology; so this congress does not meet the definition of a corporate body. Since the name of the Society is not a necessary complement to the title, this work would receive its main entry under title. An added entry would be made under "International Society of Musicologists," but the additional information on the Congress would not be incorporated into the heading. Under AACR2, in contrast, the additional information on the Congress would be integrated into the heading, and the work would receive main entry under that conference heading. In the RAK record, the information on the date and location of the conference would merely appear as other title information. Many in the AACR2 world will feel that this practice eliminates an access point that is potentially beneficial to users, especially those who happen to know the date or location of the conference they seek and would like to use that information in refining their search.

AACR2 has been criticized by some German librarians for being casuistic, i.e., creating special rules for special circumstances, while RAK is praised for its fidelity to a strictly logical structure. German librarians would certainly point to AACR2's rule for determining main entry under a corporate body as an example of AACR2's casuistic nature. A further case in point might be found in the differing treatment of sound recordings of popular music that bear a collective title. Mindful of the different conditions of authorship and intellectual responsibility pertaining to sound recordings as compared to books, AACR2 created the category of main entry under principal performer for sound recordings that contain music by one or more composers but which have a collective title and which prominently feature a particular performer or performing ensemble. Such recordings under AACR2 receive main entry under the name of the performer or the performing ensemble. True to its logical principles, and to the decision tree for determining main entry presented above, RAK assigns such recordings to the category of "anonymous works" and gives them main entry under title. While some may regard AACR2's policy as casuistic, others may see in it an agreeable example of flexibility and willingness to accommodate a set of circumstances that are distinctly different from those surrounding the authorship of printed books. American librarians would probably also see in AACR2's policy a willingness to accommodate the expectations of the catalog's users; for example, a user searching for recordings by ABBA probably expects to see the name ABBA appear prominently at the head of the displayed records rather than be hidden away among the added entries at the foot of the record.

Personal name headings are another area of divergent practice. Particularly in American catalogs, we have been accustomed for more than a century now to distinguish between different persons who happen to bear identical names, usually by adding dates of birth and/or death to persons' headings. In RAK and only in a very few special circumstances are any additions at all made to personal name headings–i.e., name headings are normally not "individualized" to distinguish between different persons bearing the same name. Most personal name headings in German catalogs are what we would consider to be undifferentiated name headings, covering a number of persons whose names happen to be identical. This difference in practice is bound to have major consequences in the future if we seek to implement the international sharing of authority files.

The following example illustrates the consequences to the user of this divergent practice for name headings: we have, on the one hand, the famous German author and Nobel Prize winner, Thomas Mann. On the other hand, we have the American Thomas Mann, a librarian at the Library of Congress who in recent years has written several highly regarded books on methods of library research. Our user is seeking works by Thomas Mann the librarian. Say that he or she accesses the OPAC of the Library of Congress and performs an author search on **Mann, Thomas**. She will next see a brief display of author headings, among which are **Mann, Thomas, 1875-1955** (with 378 associated records) and **Mann, Thomas, 1948-** (with eight associated records). She can recognize that **Mann, Thomas, 1875-1955** is unlikely to be the author that she seeks. She clicks on **Mann, Thomas, 1948-** and sees a list of eight titles, all authored by Thomas Mann the librarian and dealing with some aspect of library or information science.

Now let us take our user to Göttingen, Germany, and allow him to repeat this search in GBV (Gemeinsamer Bibliotheksverbund, a joint OPAC for academic libraries in the seven northern German states). He performs an author search on **Mann, Thomas**, and is taken directly to a list of 1,775 titles. Most of these, of course, are works by the German writer Thomas Mann; others are works by other German authors who happen to be named Thomas Mann. But somewhere among them are three works by the American librarian Thomas Mann; I was able to confirm the presence of these three works by doing title searches. If the user has only his author's name but happens not to know, or to have forgotten, the titles of works by Thomas Mann the librarian, his only recourse is to scroll through the list of 1,775 titles. He can limit the search to works in English, but even after doing so, there remains a list of 920 titles for him to scroll through.

Perhaps the most vexing question between the two cataloging communities is the question of hierarchical structure in records for multipart items: for which level of the work (the whole, or its parts?) shall records be created? And if records are created for both the whole work and for its parts, how shall these records be related to each other? This is as much a question of divergence in the structure of data formats as it is a question of having different cataloging codes. RAK requires that a record be made for each part of a multipart work. AACR2 certainly presents the option of preparing individual records for parts, in "Chapter 13, Analysis," but whether or not to do so is left to the cataloger's judgment. More seriously, from the German point of view, the MARC record does not provide a means for hierarchically linking part and whole records in the way that Germans are accustomed to linking such records in their own catalogs. There are ways in which MARC might be adapted for hierarchical links (by using the **773** and **774** fields, for example, although they were not really designed for this purpose), but there has been no serious attempt in the United States to do so.

Some of the problems associated with the treatment of multipart items arise because Anglo-American librarians and German librarians divide up the bibliographic universe in slightly different ways. Where Anglo-Americans, for example, perceive an entity designated as "collection," German librarians see two entities: the *Sammlung* (a collection of works by a single author) and the *Sammelwerk* (a collection of works by two or more authors). A *Sammlung* always receives entry under the author's name. A *Sammelwerk* can be either *begrenzt* (finite) or *fortlaufend* (open-ended, continuing). A finite *Sammelwerk*, when it has no collective title, is entered under the heading for the most prominently featured work, or for the first-named work. When a collective title is present, the item is entered under the collective title. With the continuing *Sammelwerk*, or *fortlaufendes Sammelwerk*, we reach those types of items we designate as "series" or "serials."

Certainly in Anglo-American cataloging practice, we tend to think in terms of two entities, the monographic series and serial publications (although it should be noted that in the AACR2 glossary, the terms "serial" and "series" are not particularly distinct from each other; it is also odd that the definition under "serial" mentions "numbered monographic series" but excludes unnumbered monographic series). The Germans divide up the series/serial territory a little differently. They define *fortlaufende Sammelwerke* as including the *Zeitung* (newspaper), Zeitschrift (a journal appearing at regular intervals), zeitschriftenartige Reihe (a journal-like publication, but appearing irregularly), and the *Schriftenreihe* (monographic series). But one particular category of work for which AACR2 allows series treatment is excluded from the German notion of "series." A multipart work by a single author cannot be treated as a series, since in German terms only *Sammelwerke*, i.e., collections of works by more than one author, are eligible for series treatment. A multipart work by a single author is a *Sammlung*, not a *Sammelwerk*. RAK, therefore, does not have a form of series entry that corresponds to our name-title series entry, i.e., our **490/800** access point. In the AACR2 world, we view the name-title series entry as a useful means for collocating the individual parts of a multipart work by a single author. The German library community has followed a different path in this regard and uses the hierarchical record structure to achieve this end.

In German practice a bibliographic record is created for each part of a multipart work (*Stücktitelaufnahme*), and a record is created for the work as a whole (*Gesamtaufnahme*). The *Stücktitelaufnahmen* contain the complete bibliographic information for their respective parts; the *Gesamtaufnahme* gives a record of the available *Stücktitelaufnahmen*. Essentially, in cases where we make a comprehensive record for a multi-volume work, we will have a single bibliographic record with multiple item records. The German catalog, in contrast, will have multiple bibliographic records, linked hierarchically. In the German context, this is seen as useful for sharing data within a consortium, particularly in the context of interlibrary loan.

German librarians seem much more inclined to think in terms of hierarchical relationships between bibliographic records than their American colleagues. This surely stands in some kind of connection to the nature of scholarly publishing in Germany, which delights in a complexity and variety of series statements (*Abteilungen,* subseries, supplements, *Sonderbände,* etc.) unsurpassed by any other language group. The "bibliographic universe" of the English-speaking world is a fairly "flat" universe in comparison to the German one. And while it may be said that "you don't miss what you have never known," even those American librarians who have become familiar with the

German methods of hierarchical linkage do not always evince a strong interest in making use of these techniques in American library catalogs.

It would appear that German librarians have little awareness of (or perhaps appreciation for?) our Anglo-American practice of analysis. The difference seems to be that in the German environment the rules demand that an analytic record shall always be made for every part of a multipart item. In the Anglo-American community, the question of whether to make an analytic record is left to the cataloger's judgment–i.e., if a particular cataloger in a particular library feels that the needs of his patrons require better access to the parts of a multipart item, then individual records for the parts are made. If this level of access is not felt to be essential in the context of a particular collection, then a single record is made for the item as a whole (although in such a case, conscientious catalogers will normally give a contents note that lists the titles of the individual parts).

When the Anglo-American cataloger does produce analytic records for the parts of a multipart item and includes in those records a properly formulated, uniformly applied series statement, that series statement surely functions as effectively as the Germans' embedded computer link in bringing together the records for the parts of a multipart item. The real stumbling block, from the perspective of German librarians, occurs in the case of multipart items that the AACR2 cataloger decides not to analyze. Again, the difference in practice results from a very real difference in outlook. The German librarian enunciates a principle–"Every title shall have its own record"–and proceeds to apply that principle universally. The question of actual utility to the user is secondary to the application of the principle although it is assumed that it *is* useful to the user for each title to have its own bibliographic record. The AACR2 cataloger, by contrast, operates on a pragmatic basis and makes case-by-case decisions. The AACR2 cataloger normally asks himself, "In what ways is a user likely to search for this record, and what access points do I need to provide to accommodate the user's probable attempts at access?"

The difference in outlook becomes striking in the case of a multipart item where the individual parts have titles that depend for their meaning on the title of the work as a whole. This is the kind of situation where an AACR2 cataloger will normally not create analytics, whereas the German cataloger is bound by his rules to create individual records for each part. The example that follows is drawn from a message sent to the RAK catalogers' listserv by Ms. Gunilla Jonsson of the Royal Library of Sweden; for convenience, I have taken the liberty of translating the title page information into English. The item in hand is a two-volume work. Both volumes bear the comprehensive title: *The monastery church of Rheinau.* Then each volume bears an individual title and statement of responsibility:

> Vol. 1. *The building and its restoration* / compiled by Marion Wohlleben ;
> with contributions by Peter Albertin.
> Vol. 2. *The organs and their restoration* / Friedrich Jakob.

Note that the titles of the parts depend for their meaning on the comprehensive title *The monastery church of Rheinau.*

The AACR2 cataloger can choose between two options (not having seen the item myself, I am not hazarding a guess as to considerations of main entry; from the German cataloging records for this item that I have viewed, it is not clear whether any of the named authors received a main entry or whether they were given added entries):

- Create a single record with a contents note:

  245 04 The monastery church of Rheinau.
  505 0   v. 1. The building and its restoration / compiled by Marion Wohlleben ;
  with contributions by Peter Albertin--v. 2. The organs and their restoration /
  Friedrich Jakob.

- Create individual records for each volume. In this case, I would most likely make use of subfields **n** and **p** in the **245**:

  Record 1:
  245 04 The monastery church of Rheinau. $n Vol. 1. $p The building and
  its restoration / compiled by Marion Wohlleben ; with contributions by
  Peter Albertin.
  Record 2:
  245 04 The monastery church of Rheinau. $n Vol. 2. $p The organs and
  their restoration / Friedrich Jakob.

If the AACR2 cataloger opts to create a single record, he or she will most likely not create separate records for the parts; conversely, if individual records for the parts are created, the AACR2 cataloger is unlikely to make a comprehensive record for the work as a whole.

The RAK cataloger does not need to make a choice between Options 1 and 2. Under RAK it is clear that three records should be made: a comprehensive record for the whole (*Gesamtaufnahme*), plus individual records for the two parts (*Stücktitelaufnahmen*). The *Stücktitelaufnahmen* are linked to the *Gesamtaufnahme* by embedding the ID number of the *Gesamtaufnahme* in the *Stücktitelaufnahmen*.

From the RAK perspective, neither of the AACR2 options is satisfactory. Option 1 does not provide the descriptive information about the individual volumes that German catalogers would expect to see and does not provide for controlled access to the titles of the parts. Option 2 does not provide for a comprehensive record that would link the records for the parts.

Fostering an increased level of genuinely informed discussion between the two cataloging communities could well bear useful fruit. For example, AACR2 might profitably adopt the explicit provisions of RAK for determining when a work "emanates" from a corporate body. We would then be spared a certain amount of agonizing over and second-guessing our decisions. This was pointed up in an exchange on the AUTOCAT discussion list during the first two weeks of April 2002. A German cataloger wrote to the list to inquire why the bibliographic record for AACR2 has a main entry under title; from his reading of Chapter 21.1B2, he would have expected the work to have a main entry under the Joint Steering Committee. Most Anglo-American catalogers who responded to this question seemed to agree that AACR2 didn't clearly fall into any of the six categories; therefore it was appropriate to give AACR2 main entry under title. But at least one Anglo-American cataloger wrote in to say that he thought that, after all, a case could be made for assigning main entry to the Joint Steering Committee. Most of us can probably recall from our own experience similar instances of indecision. Under RAK, this particular instance is clear-cut: the wording of the title page makes it clear that the Joint Steering Committee is the *Urheber* of the work, i.e., that AACR2 emanates from the JSC. But the JSC is not named in the title (only in the statement of responsibility), nor is the JSC's name a necessary complement to the title. Therefore the work is entered under its title, and an added entry is made for the JSC.

As I reflect back over the experience I have gained while working on the translation of AACR2 into German, several thoughts come to mind: AACR2 was created by and for English speakers. It was never intended as an international standard. It is thus inappropriate to fault it for failing to embody certain aspects that various communities around the globe consider ought to be present in an international standard. AACR2 has always been intended to produce cataloging records that meet the needs of English speakers. It cannot, or should not, be adopted "as is" by another language community. The translation of AACR2 into another language is only a first step; before it can be used in a non-English-speaking community, it requires extensive rewriting. It contains elements that are relevant only within an English-speaking context; such elements need to be modified or entirely replaced with elements that are similarly relevant to the language environment in which it is to be used. At that point, it really ceases to be the "Anglo-American Cataloging Rules." In the context of globalization and information sharing, it may be desirable to have a truly international cataloging code. Whether such a code can actually be achieved is another matter, of course. Certainly, it would have to arise out of the work of a truly international group of experts.

If German and Anglo-American librarians do indeed wish to pursue some form of rule harmonization, it would certainly be helpful for the AACR2 community to take note of German criticisms of AACR2. If they do, they will expect that German librarians also be willing to listen to Anglo-American criticisms of RAK. Ultimately, for productive rule harmonization to occur, both communities must attempt to step outside the boundaries of their national practice and examine, with an open mind and an avoidance of prejudice, the practices of the other community.

NOTES

1. Universitätsbibliothek der Technischen Universität Graz, Austria, "*Internationalisierung von Regelwerken zur formalen Erschliessung* (Internationalization of cataloging codes for descriptive cataloging)," [cited 3 May 2002]; available at http://www.cis.TUGraz.at/tub/Publikationen/Ausbildung/Elena/inhalt.htm; Internet.

2. Personal communication to the author from Professor Hans Popst, Department for Library and Archive Studies, Bayerische Beamtenfachhochschule in Munich.

3. "Project REUSE: Aligning international cataloging standards," [cited 3 May 2002]; available at http://www.oclc.org/oclc/cataloging/reuse_project/newsummary.htm; Internet.

4. C. Sumner Spalding, "The Life and Death (?) of Corporate Authorship," *Library Resources & Technical Services* 24 (Summer 1980): 197.

5. Klaus Haller and Hans Popst, *Katalogisierung nach den RAK-WB*, 5. überarbeitete Aufl. (München; New Providence: K.G. Saur, 1996), 181.

6. Luise Hoffman., "*Stand der Regelwerksdiskussion aus der Sicht eines Verbundes: Vortrag . . . am 28.5.1996* (The status of the discussion on cataloging codes from the perspective of a library consortium)," Hochschulbibliothekszentrum des Landes Nordrhein-Westfalen, [cited 3 May 2002]; available at http://www.hbz-nrw.de/wir/publika/publika.html; Internet.

Historical Aspects
of Cataloging and Classification in Iran

Poori Soltani

SUMMARY. This article consists of three parts: (1) Introduction, (2) Cataloging and classification of manuscripts, and (3) Cataloging and classification of printed matters in Iran. In the introduction, after a short review of Iranian libraries, the historical background of *Fihrist* is touched upon. In the second section, the historical development of cataloging of manuscripts is discussed, emphasising the catalogs of manuscripts of the Parliament, Astani Qods, and the National Library as examples. In the third section, the history of cataloging and classification of printed books in modern times is reviewed: This event was initiated in Iran through formal and informal courses taught mainly by foreign lecturers. The initiation of the MLS degree at the University of Tehran and the establishment of TEBROC paved the way for standard rules and methods. With the amalgamation of TEBROC in the National Library, modern ways and means were developed more rapidly, hence computerization of cataloging, CIP, and IRANMARC. *[Article copies available for a fee from The Haworth Document Delivery Service: 1-800-HAWORTH. E-mail address: <getinfo@haworthpressinc.com> Website: <http://www.HaworthPress.com> © 2002 by The Haworth Press, Inc. All rights reserved.]*

KEYWORDS. Iran, cataloging, classification, manuscripts, TEBROC, National Library of Iran, library education

Poori Soltani, MLS, is Senior Research Librarian, National Library of Iran (E-mail: poorisoltani@yahoo.com).

[Haworth co-indexing entry note]: "Historical Aspects of Cataloging and Classification in Iran." Soltani, Poori. Co-published simultaneously in *Cataloging & Classification Quarterly* (The Haworth Information Press, an imprint of The Haworth Press, Inc.) Vol. 35, No. 1/2, 2002, pp. 187-207; and: *Historical Aspects of Cataloging and Classification* (ed: Martin D. Joachim) The Haworth Information Press, an imprint of The Haworth Press, Inc., 2003, pp. 187-207. Single or multiple copies of this article are available for a fee from The Haworth Document Delivery Service [1-800-HAWORTH, 9:00 a.m. - 5:00 p.m. (EST). E-mail address: getinfo@haworthpressinc.com].

چکیده

این مقاله از فهرستنویسی کتابهاي چاپي تشکیل شده است. مقدمه شامل سه قسمت مقدمه, فهرستنویسي نسخ خطي, و نگاهي کوتاه به تاریخچه کتابخانه در ایران و بحث تاریخي در مورد کلمه "فهرست" است. در قسمت دوم سیر تاریخي تدوین فهرستهاي خطي با اشاره به اولین فهرستها, از جمله فهرست کتابخانه مجلس شوراي ملي, آستان قدس رضوي, و کتابخانه ملي مورد بحث قرار مي گیرد. در قسمت سوم تاریخچه فهرستنویسي و رده بندي کتابهاي چاپي به سبک نوین بررسي مي شود. در این زمینه به نقش کلاسهاي کوتاه مدت کتابداري, تاسیس رشته فوق لیسانس کتابداري در دانشگاه تهران, و نیز تاسیس مرکز خدمات کتابداري و چگونگي استاندارد کردن قواعد فهرستنویسي و رده بندي اشاره شده است. ادغام مرکز خدمات کتابداري در کتابخانه ملي منشاء فعالیتهاي چشمگیرتري از جمله کامپیوتري کردن فهرستنویسي, اجراي فهرستنویسي پیش از انتشار و تدوین مارک ایران شد.

INTRODUCTION

Historians have long spoken of the existence of libraries in pre-Islamic Iran. The first to give us a valuable account of such libraries and whose book *Al-Fihrist* (*The Catalog*) has survived is Ibn-Nadim (10th cent.). He states that in order to preserve knowledge for future generations, Iranians wrote on the bark of a special tree called *khadang* (*peuplier blanc*) and kept these writings in safe places immune to earthquakes. Thus the library of Saruyeh Jey in Isfahan came into existence. Ibn-Nadim says that he himself had seen the books of this library, which had been removed and brought to Baghdad.[1] There have been other libraries such as Gondi-Shapur University Library and the libraries in Ctisphun and Samarqand.

In addition, fire-temples had libraries attached to them, which were unfortunately destroyed by various invasions.[2] During the Islamic era, from the eighth century on, great libraries flourished everywhere. All mosques and seminary schools had libraries. Cities such as Nishapur, Marv, Saveh, Shiraz, and Rey had such famous libraries that people came from far away to use them.[3] It is not, however, my intention to elaborate on the history of libraries in Iran. Much has been written on this topic in Persian, Arabic, and European languages. But the fact that such libraries existed implies the existence of some sort of catalogs. The library of Sahib Ibn 'Abbad in Rey is said to have had a catalog of ten volumes.[4] Maqdasi (10th cent.) states that he had seen the library of Azod al-Dowleh in Shiraz in which books were arranged by subject and each subject was kept in a different room and each room had catalogs according to the title and author.[5] Avicenna, the librarian of Nuh-Ibn Mansur Samani, had used the Royal Library in Bukhara and states that among the books listed in the catalog were many titles that no one knew.[6] Here also books were kept on shelves according to subject. There are many references to catalogs of personal and private libraries in reference books and historical and social accounts.

In fact, the first time we hear of the word *fihrist* (catalog) is in the second century after Islam when Ma'mun (776-833), the Abbasid Caliph, asks the Iranian scholar, Hasan Ibn-Sahl (8th cent.): "Which Iranian book is the best?" and receives the answer *Javidan-i-Khirad (Perennial Wisdom)*. Ma'mun demands the *fihrist* from his library. To his astonishment he discovers that the book does not exist in his library.

The oldest catalog to survive, however, as noted above, is *Al-Fihrist* of Ibn-Nadim, which is, in a way, a bio-bibliography of all books in existence at his time. It is arranged in ten broad subjects, each one divided into more specific subjects, sometimes up to eight divisions, with each division at times further classified into subdivisions. Under each subdivision books are listed under the names of the authors. Ibn-Nadim often gives valuable information about the authors and social and cultural conditions of their times.

From the eleventh to the nineteenth centuries, there also exist several catalogs; these are primarily personal catalogs, which were compiled by individual authors or for them. Biruni's *Fihrist*, which is a list of the books written by

Abu-Reyhan Biruni (11th cent.), is one such example. Ibn-Tavus also compiled a list of his own books (13th cent.),[7] which still exists.[8]

Upheavals and invasions in Iran for more than ten centuries, however, affected the pace of library development. In the nineteenth century, during the Qajar Dynasty's relationships with the West, for the first time a European-style college, Dar-al-Fonun, was established, in which Austrian professors were employed to teach. Its library with Persian, Arabic, and German documents was cataloged and arranged on the shelves by accession numbers. Later, in 1937, these documents came to constitute the core collections of the National Library of Iran.

CATALOGING OF MANUSCRIPTS

Early in the twentieth century libraries began to be recognized again as sources of information and as places where the written heritage of the country had been preserved. Iranians looked back to their past fame, veiling their present backwardness with the pride of the past. Librarians looked at their collections and took pride in precious manuscripts, adorned with marvelous illustrations and miniatures. Thus they began to introduce these sources to scholars as well as to the public by printing their catalogs. With the victory of the Constitutional Revolution in 1906, the publication of newspapers and books flourished; and the age of enlightenment began, bringing some noticeable social and cultural changes, which were more or less influenced by the West. Some new public and government libraries were also established, and the existing silent libraries began to become active and people started to use them more often. The Library of the Parliament was officially inaugurated in 1925 though the proposal of its establishment dates back to 1909.[9] Arbab Keykhosrow, a member of Parliament, under whose supervision the library functioned, states that he himself listed the following documents in the accession book of the library: 183 Persian, 185 Arabic, 9 Turkish, 855 French, 21 English, 20 Russian, 75 German, and 17 Italian. These volumes, together with a donation in 1912 of 1091 volumes by Ehtesham al-Saltaneh, Head of Parliament (first and second round), comprised the core collection of the Majlis (Parliament) Library.[10]

Yet there is no trace of cataloging until 1926, when the first catalog of the Majlis Library was published; it included both printed works and manuscripts.[11] The introduction of this catalog reveals how much the compiler, Yusof E'tesami, had been influenced by Western ideas. He gives reference to Diodorus Siculus, the Greek historian. He speaks of some Western catalogs such as those of J. T. Zonker, August Müller, and many others. He also cites as examples the catalogs of the Bibliothèque nationale, the Bodleian Library (Oxford), and the British Museum. He discusses the classification systems of Melvil Dewey, Charles Cutter, James Brown, and the Library of Congress. He eventually concludes that subject catalogs rather than classified ones are preferable. Although he lists the manuscripts alphabetically by title because they were so few (only 216 titles), he does list printed books by subject. It is interesting to note that he lists the subjects alphabetically (according to the Persian alphabet), and under each subject books are arranged alphabetically by title. Altogether thirty-eight subject categories exist, the list of which is given at the beginning of the text.[12] The second volume of the catalog, also by Yusof E'tesami, came out in 1933 and excludes printed materials but includes the 216 manuscripts of the previous volume plus an additional 492 for a total of 708 manuscripts. The third volume, by Ibn-Yusof Shirazi, appeared in 1939; in the introduction he stresses the need for the catalog. He lists books under seven broad subjects, but gives more information about each volume.[13]

Also in 1926 the Library of Astan-i-Qods, with a historical heritage of some seven centuries, published a catalog of its collection in three volumes. In each volume manuscripts and printed books are separately arranged under broad subjects. Under each subject, books are arranged alphabetically by title. Under each manuscript title the following information is provided: language, author and dates, sponsor,[14] a few words of the first and last lines, date of the manuscripts, style of calligraphy, number of lines on each page, the donor, number of pages, and length and width of the pages. In some cases additional information about the authors and the books is provided in summaries, but this is never as informative as the content of Ibn-Nadim's *Al-Fihrist*. Almost all the catalogs prepared around this period provide more or less the same information, and most of them consist of both manuscripts and printed books. It should also be mentioned that until the 1950s most efforts to catalog manuscripts were motivated by the individual interests of catalogers and were not part of an organized project to provide control and access to manuscript holdings in Iran's libraries.

As noted, the second volume of the catalog of the Parliament Library consisted of manuscripts only. Gradually it became customary for libraries to publish catalogs only of their manuscripts. There are two main reasons behind this decision. First, printed books became superfluous and inexpensive and could be found in bookshops as well as in different libraries. Second, manuscripts were unique at each library and thus valuable as well as looked upon as the precious scholarly heritage of the country. So in the twentieth century many catalogs of manuscripts were published. Through tracing their development, one can identify signs of modern cataloging. Thus when in 1986 Ali Ardalan was assigned to revise the above-mentioned three volumes of the Astan-i-Qods catalogs by separating the manuscripts from the rest, he rearranged and edited the volumes and corrected a large number of mistakes and inconsistencies as well as misprints. Yet he found no mistakes in the subject classification.[15]

TOWARDS STANDARDIZATION

The National Library of Iran was officially inaugurated in 1937. Among its collections, a part of which came from the ex-library of Dar al-Fonun, donations from the Royal Library, and other sources, there were many manuscripts, which by 1956 totaled 4,157.[16] Before this time there had been some efforts to catalog the manuscripts, but none was ever published. In 1956 Iraj Afshar, presently one of Iran's most famous librarians, bibliographers, and scholars, who had just returned from a UNESCO course on librarianship,[17] became the head librarian and tried to set forth rules and regulations for the cataloging of manuscripts. He organized a committee of scholars and bibliographers. This committee eventually designed a worksheet of two sides (30 × 32 cm.). One side belonged to the bibliographic information of the manuscript, and the other side was for manuscriptology[18] in which all the distinctive features necessary for the recognition of a copy are listed. (See Figure 1.)

Abdollah Anvar, one of the committee members and also one of the most outstanding of Iranian researchers, was assigned to do the work. The first volume describing 500 manuscripts was published in 1964. Other manuscript catalogers followed this pattern. The catalog of Persian and Arabic manuscripts in the National Library of Iran eventually comprised ten volumes; all were published between 1965 and 1979 under the direction of Mr. Anvar and described more than 5,000 manuscripts. In 1995, inspired by AACR2, Chapter 4, and in order to bring about maximum consistency, the Cataloging Department of the National Library of Iran designed another worksheet that could be used in a computer format. (See Figures 2 and 3.)

Since then, this format has been used at the National Library of Iran. On 1-2 May 2000 a seminar on manuscripts was organized by and held in the Library of the Parliament with the cooperation of the National Library of Iran and the National Museum of Malek. Mr. Habibollah Azimi, the head cataloger of the Manuscript Department of the National Library, presented the format, asking for conformity among all manuscript catalogers. The matter is still open to further discussion.

FIGURE 1

نام کتابخانه

فهرست نسخ خطی ، فارسی ، عربی و ترکی

نسخه شناسی

شماره اختصاصی   شماره کتاب

اندازه جلد   اندازه نوشته   عدد اوراق   عدد سطور

نوع خط   نوع و رنگ کاغذ

نوع تزیینات جلد

تزیینات وتصویرات داخلی

تاریخ تحریر   نام کاتب   محل تحریر

اهدا تحریر   حواشی کتاب

یادداشتهای مهم مربوط به سرگذشت و تاریخ نسخه

توضیحات

نام کتابخانه

فهرست نسخ خطی ، فارسی ، عربی و ترکی

کتابشناسی

زبان

اسم کتاب   اسم مؤلف   اسم مترجم

زبان تألیف یا ترجمه   اهدا شده به   موضوع کتاب

فصول و ابواب کتب ناشناخته

آغاز کتابهای ناشناخته

پایان کتابهای ناشناخته

مرجعی که کتابهای مهم و نادر چاپ نشده در آنجا وصف شده است

FIGURE 2

کاربرگه کتابخانه ملی جمهوری اسلامی ایران
نسخه‌های خطــی

فهرستنویس		تاریخ
		سرشناسه
		عنوان و عنوان فرعی
		تکرار نام نویسنده مانی، محشی مترجم، کاتب وغیره

	تاریخ کتابت	محل کتابت	وضعیت کتابت
قطع	اندازه سطور	سطر	برگ	صفحه شمار

آغاز نسخه

انجام نسخه

خط — نوع کاغذ

ترئینات متن و جلد

نسخه‌شناسی

حواشی اوراق نسخه

مهرها و تملک و غیره

فرسودگی، ناقص بودن صفحات

امتیاز نسخه

FIGURE 3

معرفی کتاب شامل: زبان، تاریخ تالیف، چاپ و توضیحات ضروری	
یادداشتها و ملاحظات	
موضوعها در مستندموضوعی	
بود / نبود ۱	
بود / نبود ۲	
بود / نبود ۳	
بود / نبود ۴	
بود / نبود ۵	
بود / نبود ۶	
شناسه‌های افزوده در مستندمشاهیر	
بود / نبود الف	
بود / نبود ب	
بود / نبود ج	
بود / نبود د	
بود / نبود ه	
بود / نبود و	
بود / نبود ز	
شماره نسخه شماره پیشین شماره دیویی	شماره در خواست کتابخانه ملی

GENERAL CATALOGING AND CLASSIFICATION

Although Iran has a long history of libraries dating back to pre-Islamic times, such as the University of Gondishapur, the Public Library of Saruyeh Jey in Isfahan, and many libraries of the Islamic era, modern librarianship is fairly new in Iran. Due to the cultural relationship between Iran and Western countries, which essentially developed after the Constitutional Revolution (1906), Iran underwent major social changes. Students were sent abroad to be educated, printed publication increased, more modern schools succeeded the traditional learning institutions (*maktab khaneh*), and libraries flourished everywhere. Yet no concrete effort was made for the cataloging and classification of library materials. Books were usually arranged on shelves by size, accession number, or at best by broad subjects; and within each subject the arrangement was by accession number, making retrieval even more difficult. In libraries there were usually card catalogs. The existence of card catalogs was new and was considered fairly modern since most libraries had their holdings listed in accession books only. Even today the tradition of accession books continues in some libraries for peculiar financial reasons.

During the 1930s and 1940s there were hardly any major cultural transformations because of existing political conditions. Yet in 1938 the first course in librarianship was offered; and sixty students, who were either library employees or elementary or high school teachers, took part. The duration of the course was 120 hours; the lessons included alphabetizing, introduction to librarianship, history of librarianship, manuscripts, history of writing and calligraphy, literary style, and report writing. All the lecturers, except one, were Iranians and taught in Persian. None of them were professional librarians but rather scholars and men of fame. They were all familiar with Western culture, and some had been abroad. Ibn-Yusef, a manuscript cataloger, was one of the teachers. Rules for alphabetized categorization were taught by Salma Moqaddam, the French wife of Dr. Mohsen Moqaddam, one of the most famous archaeologists of Iran and a professor in the Faculty of Fine Arts, University of Tehran. In fact, he also helped his wife during the lessons, acting as her translator. Each participant received a library certificate. The course was set up by the Ministry of Culture, which was in charge of cultural and educational affairs.[19] Although cataloging was not taught as an independent subject, there were references to it during some of the lessons.

About 1940 Dr. Mohsen Saba, who had been trained as a librarian at the Bibliothèque nationale in Paris, became the librarian at the National Bank of Iran. He introduced the use of the card catalog; and in order to disseminate the idea, he published the cards in the form of a book catalog.[20] In 1941, just before the Second World War, which was also very significant in terms of East/West relationships, another course in librarianship was offered in which Dr. Saba and Dr. Mehdi Bayani, the founder and head librarian of the National Library of Iran, taught.[21] Between 1940 and 1950 card catalogs were introduced to libraries in Tehran University and also in the library of the National Iranian Oil Company, headed by Ms. Evlin Anna Mary Vartani, a professional librarian who had been educated in the United States and had returned to Iran in 1952.

For the first time,(in 1952, the University of Tehran (established in 1934), invited Josef Stumvoll from Austria and Mary Gaver from the United States to come to Iran to teach a five-month course in librarianship. In this course cataloging was given recognition as one of the independent lessons. Then in 1953 the first book in Persian on technical services librarianship was published.[22]

A year later in 1954 Susan Akers, former dean of the University of North Carolina Library School, continued to teach this course for another seven months at the University of Tehran.[23] Among her lectures, which still exist in the National Library of Iran in mimeograph, in both English and Persian, are several relating to cataloging and classification. She taught cataloging and classification in detail and lectured on the Dewey Decimal Classification (DDC). Several sessions were assigned to these topics.

In 1956 Fraune Dorfer, an Austrian librarian, was invited to Iran through UNESCO and taught a course on library science and collection management. Some mimeographs of his lessons also exist in the National Library of Iran. In all the lectures he presented, the main emphasis was on cataloging and classification. By this time there was a need for the development of librarianship in Iran, and efforts were made to promote the profession. From 1957 to 1964 librarianship became one of the elective courses at the Teachers' Training College. Iraj Afshar taught the course during this seven-year interval. He also published the national bibliography of Iran, *Kitabha-ye Iran* for ten years (1954-1963).[24] In the bibliography books were arranged according to the main divisions of DDC. The compiler acknowledges that he manipulated some sections relating to Iran, especially Iranian literature.

Under the supervision of Dr. Naser Sharifi[25] in 1960, another course was taught at the Teachers' Training College. The course was team-taught by Dean Farnsworth from the United States and Iraj Afshar. In the same year, for the first time, a type of centralized cataloging appeared. The Teachers' Training College printed and published catalog cards (7.5 × 12.5 cm.) to be used in all faculties of the University of Tehran as well as all other libraries requesting them. Following (Figure 4) is an example of these cards:

FIGURE 4

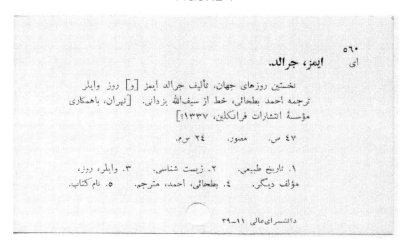

This is the main unit card. The rest are identical, each having appropriate added entries and subjects printed above the main entry. Card numbers are printed at the bottom, including year and accession number. This card-printing project seems to have lasted for only one year since all the cards have the same date of 1339 [1960]. At the top right-hand corner of the card, the DDC number and author mark are printed. The information has been printed on durable card stock of superior quality with beautifully selected print fonts. Never again were such elegant cards published in Iran. The cataloging on these cards shows that it conformed to the existing rules at that time.

In 1962 the Children's Book Council offered some classes for children's librarians. These classes, which were taught for four years, presented simple instruction in cataloging and classification as well as general and special services for children. During the 1960s the necessity and importance of librarianship grew, and its study flourished in libraries. By this time many librarians had been trained in the courses described above, and those who went abroad for training gradually returned. So in 1964 when a course was offered again for the university librarians in the Faculty of Science at the University of Tehran, it was taught entirely by Iranians.

Those who had come back from abroad were managing the libraries. They blended imported modern ideas with touches of Iranian cultural heritage and made use of them in their libraries. Technical services had become of utmost importance. Some special or governmental libraries even bought catalog cards from the Library of Congress for their non-Persian/Arabic books. Through these cards many librarians learned a great deal about cataloging and classification, the author of this paper being one of them. The Library of the Central Bank of Iran, which was established in 1960 and possessed the collection of the National Bank of Iran, was headed by Ms. F. Goharian, a professional librarian educated in the United States; it was at the time one of the best-organized libraries in Iran. The latest edition of DDC, in addition to Library of Congress subject headings, was used. The library bought catalog cards from the Library of Congress, used AACR, and possessed many other tools, such as the *National Union Catalog (NUC)* of the United States. This article's author was employed there in 1963 and was trained to be a cataloger.

OFFICIAL EDUCATION

The establishment of a master's degree in library science was proposed in 1964 to the chancellor of the University of Tehran by Iraj Afshar, then the head librarian of the Central Library of the university. It took two years for the proposal to be realized.[26] At that time Ms. Margaret Hopkins worked in the Central Library of the University of Tehran as a consultant. She had come to Iran through the Fulbright Program. Ms. Iran Daqiq, who had been sent to England to be trained as a librarian, had returned and became the head of the Technical Services Department of the Central Library.

Ms. Hopkins helped Iraj Afshar in writing the proposal for the master's degree. The duration of the degree program was two academic years. Ms. Alice Lohrer, lecturer at the University of Illinois School of Librarianship, came to Iran through the Fulbright Program to organize and teach courses for the degree. The head librarian of the Department, Mrs. Farangis Omid, had already obtained her MLS in the United States and was active in the field.

Of course, cataloging and classification were also among the courses; but Ms. Lohrer, who was not a cataloger, did not teach these subjects. This author was one of the students in this degree program[27] and, having been trained by the head librarian of the Central Bank of Iran, was quite familiar with the development of technical services abroad, as were some others who were already using and applying Western methods in their libraries. Ms. Hopkins and Elizabeth Russell, another American who came later, tried to teach those courses.[28] As soon as I graduated in 1968, I was asked to teach the cataloging and classification course, and I taught it until 1979.

TEBROC

The Tehran Book Processing Center (TEBROC) was established in 1968. Dr. John F. Harvey, an information scientist who came to Iran through the Fulbright

Program to take the place of Ms. Lohrer in the MLS degree program, wrote the plan for the center. He gave the outline of his plan to me for review and comments. I found the proposal relevant and useful. The plan had been written for the Ministry of Culture, directly responsible for the National Library. Yet the Minister was not disposed to its implementation. The plan was subsequently presented to the Ministry of Science and Higher Education; and after several sessions, the minister, Dr. M. Rahnema, agreed to its establishment as a sister organization to the Iranian Documentation Centre (IRANDOC).

TEBROC was founded with the intention that it would be a major force in the development of Iranian libraries. In order to fulfill this mission, TEBROC was to provide professional and technical services, especially cataloging, classification and consulting services, to all types of libraries and institutions under contract. TEBROC furthermore undertook special research projects in devising national standards.

To carry out these functions, TEBROC employed a pool of highly skilled post-graduate professional librarians, who could take advantage of new ideas developed abroad and make their services widely available to Iran's rapidly developing libraries. In addition, TEBROC supervised a bibliographic center that received national bibliographies, book reviews, who is who's, biographies, books and periodicals pertaining to library and information sciences in Iran and many other countries. This collection enabled TEBROC to aid librarians in book selection and acquisition as well as cataloging, classification, and research.

In preparing books for its customers, TEBROC employed the most recent and thorough cataloging and classification policies and procedures. The Anglo-American Cataloging Rules and Library of Congress subject headings were used for all books except those in Persian and Arabic. Since both the LC and DDC systems were used, each TEBROC catalog card offered customers a choice of classification schemes. Because standard cataloging and classification tools had been created basically for works in English or in the Latin alphabet, TEBROC attempted to satisfy its own needs by translating, adapting, and creating tools particularly suited to Iranian works or those in Arabic script. Therefore, one of the great undertakings of TEBROC was the cataloging of Persian books.

A special Iranian adaptation of the Anglo-American Cataloging Rules was gradually developed. As shortcomings in certain rules were encountered, decisions were made for adapting them to fit better into the Iranian environment.[29] A Persian list of subject headings was also prepared based on the subject matter of books cataloged. These subject headings, which were at first maintained in a card file, were later printed in a single volume for national use.

Special Iranian expansions of DDC and LC were prepared for subjects relating to Iran: Iranian languages, literature, history, geography, philosophy, and Islam. Two systems of Iranian author marks were prepared, one based on Cutter-Sanborn and the other based on the Library of Congress system.

The Tehran Book Processing Center also maintained the *National Union Catalog* and published six volumes, containing records from eight outstanding libraries of Iran. This publication was increasingly useful in facilitating the exchange of knowledge and inter-library loan. A union catalog of Persian and Arabic books was separately compiled and contained records from more than eighty major libraries of Iran. This catalog was kept on cards and still exists as such. The process stopped after the Islamic Revolution.

TEBROC also had a teaching function. It ran two one-month library workshops each year for the benefit of the staff of Iranian libraries; the senior staff of TEBROC offered courses at the University of Tehran, Faculty of Education, Department of Library Science. TEBROC consisted of five departments and one library research group. The departments were cataloging, classification, planning, selection and acquisition, and bibliography.

The members of the research group articulated and implemented all the expansions of DDC, LC, and other library tools. The first director of TEBROC was Mr. Abbas Mazaher (MLS), a professional librarian educated in the United States. Dr. Harvey became the consultant of both TEBROC and IRAN DOC and stayed until 1976. The author has headed the Library Research Group ever since.

TEBROC standardized the process of cataloging and classification, and all of its cataloging and classification tools[30] were used for the arrangement of most libraries. The National Library of Iran was the last one to adopt and use these standard tools. In 1983 TEBROC, along with its staff and collections, was transferred to the National Library of Iran. The first task of the staff at the National Library was to get the *National Bibliography of Iran* published according to the guidelines of UNESCO. The first volume came out in 1986 and was widely recognized and acclaimed by professional librarians and researchers.[31] It is a classified catalog, more or less similar to the *National Bibliography of Australia*, which was in fact adopted as the model. It has been published in the same style ever since.

When TEBROC was transferred to the National Library of Iran, almost all the necessary tools for cataloging and classification had already been published. In TEBROC we always exchanged ideas with and took the advice of the Library of Congress and Forest Press before introducing any of the revisions and expansions in DDC or LC classifications in the sections dealing with Iran.

During its ten years of existence, TEBROC has published about thirty titles of reference works and textbooks on technical services and librarianship resulting from research projects.[32] In addition to the classification expansions, two major publications should also be mentioned: a name authority list and a list of Persian subject headings.[33] Both are kept on cards and are updated daily and continue to be published at irregular intervals by the National Library of Iran.

The most important function of TEBROC, which was extremely influential as far as cataloging and classification are concerned, was the publication of printed catalog cards. Publication started almost six months after the establishment of TEBROC in 1969. Many libraries became customers and bought sets of unit cards. (See Figure 5.)

FIGURE 5

صدرالدین شیرازی، محمدبن ابراهیم، ۱۰۵۰ق.
[الاسفارالاربعه (فارسی)]
علم‌النفس یا روانشناسی صدرالمتالهین، ترجمه و تفسیر از سفرنفس
کتاب اسفار، نگارش جواد مصلح. تهران، دانشگاه تهران، ۱۳۵۲-
ج. (انتشارات دانشگاه تهران، ۱۳۸۳؛
ص.ع. و مقدمه به انگلیسی، Jawad Mosleh. The Psychology of Sadral-Dîn Shîrâzî...
نام دیگر کتاب " الحکمة المتعالیه فی‌المسائل الربوبیه" است.

(ادامه روی برگه بعد)
م۵۳-۳۸۵۷

مرکز خدمات کتابداری

صدرالدین شیرازی، محمدبن ابراهیم...علم‌النفس یا...۱۳۵۲-
(برگه ۲)

۱.روانشناسی- متون قدیمی تاقرن ۱۴ق. ۲.نفس. ۳.فلسفه
اسلامی. الف.مصلح، جواد، مترجم. ب.عنوان. ج. عنوان،
روانشناسی صدرالمتالهین. د. عنوان، الاسفارالاربعه. ه. عنوان،
الحکمة المتعالیه فی‌المسائل الربوبیه. و. عنوان، حکمت صدر-
المتالهین.

۵۴۱الف۴۳ص/B ۷۵۳ ۱۸۱/۰۷
۱۳۵۲ فت/الف۴۸۲ص
۱۳۵۲

مرکز خدمات کتابداری م۵۳-۳۸۵۷

From the beginning it was decided to use the third level of AACR. So full cataloging was used and each card had both LC and DDC class numbers for the benefit of libraries using either classification scheme. The Library of Congress catalog card was the model, but we offered author marks for DDC numbers as well.

After the founding of the Library School, the establishment of TEBROC constituted a real turning point in the history of librarianship in Iran, especially in the field of technical services.[34]

THE NATIONAL LIBRARY OF IRAN

As far as classification and cataloging are concerned, the National Library continued TEBROC's role in serving the country's libraries. Pursuant to TEBROC's revision and expansion of Iranian languages and literature in the Library of Congress classification,[35] the National Library has begun to publish translations and alphabetical rearrangements of individual authors in the LC classification. So far French **PQ** and American **PS** have been completed, and the literatures of some other countries are at hand. Research has been done on expanding the Iranian educational institutions section of the LC classification, and the National Library has been in contact with the Library of Congress on this proposal.[36] Adaptation of AACR, which had started at TEBROC, and the process of making decisions on cards continued at the National Library. The results were published after necessary revisions.[37] These works have gone through multiple revisions.

Three major innovations have taken place at the National Library of Iran in recent years. First is the beginning of computerization of cataloging in 1995 and the printing of catalog cards in response to individual requests. The library, which is situated in eight buildings scattered throughout Tehran, is to date about 60 percent computerized. The various locations do not have network connections although most of them are equipped with computers. Some activities, such as maintenance of the library's name authority file, are carried out both manually and electronically. The authority file is issued in hard copy as well as on CD. State-of-the-art technology will be available in the new building (about 100,000 square meters) of the National Library, which is scheduled for opening in early 2003.[38]

The second major innovation was government legal approval in 1996 to institute a Cataloging in Publication (CIP) program. Such an idea had, in fact, existed for about three decades. The first institution to use CIP was the University of Tehran. Iraj Afshar, the head of the Central Library and the University Press, launched the program by pre-cataloging publications of the University of Tehran and gave free sets of catalog cards to any faculty members of the university who requested them. Libraries not attached to the university had to purchase them. The program started in 1997 and lasted for three years. A catalog card was prepared for each title and was added before the title page in each published work. See Figure 6 below:

FIGURE 6

There were occasional instances of publications with CIP data before the CIP law was enacted. For example, a 1970 publication from Khaniqah-i Ne'matollahi has a catalog card printed on the verso of the title page. It should be noted that both the University of Tehran and Khaniqah-i Ne'matollahi actually provided catalog cards although they had no classification numbers.

In 1974 the problem of CIP and its development in the West was discussed in an article in *The Iranian Library Association Bulletin*, which stressed the necessity and usefulness of CIP for Iranian libraries.[39] After the Islamic Revolution, however, the matter was forgotten for awhile. But before the 1990s, some libraries headed by professional librarians adopted CIP. The Central Library of the Plan and Budget Organization (starting in 1363 [1984]), the Library of the Ministry of Foreign Affairs (starting 1991), and the newly established institution of the University Press were among the institutions that began to provide CIP. Some of these institutions brought their publications to the National Library of Iran and asked that CIP be provided. For a number of years this was done unofficially. At last an attempt was made to secure legal approval for CIP. The Deputy Director of the National Library, Dr. Fariborz Khosravi, worked to persuade the Cultural Revolution Council to permit addition of CIP. When eventually it was approved (5.12.1375 [24 February 1997]), it took nearly a year before the official announcement could be made. In the meantime attempts were made to get the agreement of other libraries, especially in the provinces, to cooperate with the National Library. Regulations concerning the use of CIP were written and distributed to all publishers. The Ministry of Culture and Islamic Guidance cooperates with the National Library to implement CIP for all publications. In 1380 (21 March 2001-21 March 2002), almost 90 percent of Iranian publications received CIP. Full cataloging was provided with subject headings, added entries, LC and DDC numbers, and author marks.

Finally, the third major innovation is the establishment of a committee to work on Iran-MARC, based on UNIMARC. The committee began its research in 1998, and an Iran-MARC manual for monographs has been printed. Several private companies and firms are now trying to implement and adapt the Iran-MARC format in the library software that they produce.

CONCLUSION

In the area of technical services, Iran is far ahead of other Middle Eastern and Islamic countries. Basic tools have been published to deal with all aspects of descriptive cataloging, subject analysis, and indexing as well as manuals to explain their use. AACR2 and DDC (abridged edition) have been translated into Persian. In recent years there has been a proliferation of books published on the use of the Internet, networking, and application of computers in libraries as well as library automation in general. Major reference tools include bibliographies, directories, and dictionaries such as the *National Bibliography of Iran* (which is published in hard copy and on CD), the annual *Directory of Periodicals and Newspapers*, and the *Persian Cultural Thesaurus*. National standards for both technical and public services exist for most types of libraries: university, special, libraries for the blind, prison libraries (at hand), and so forth. Iran is paving the way toward the realization of universal bibliographic control (UBC) and universal availability of publications (UAP).

REFERENCES

1. Muhammad ibn-Ishaq Ibn-Nadim, *Al-Fihrist*, translated by M.Reza Tajaddod. (Tehran: Chapkhaneh BankBazargani Iran, 1346 [1967]), 433-439.

2. Rokneddin Homayun-Farrokh, *Tarikh-cheh Ketab Khaneh-ha-i Iran va ketabkhaneh ha-i Omumi* (Tehran: Ettehad, 1344 [1965]), 11-17.

3. Ibid.

4. Yaqut ibn-'Abdollah Yagut Homavi, *Mo'jam al-Boldan* (Tehran, Adadi, 1965).

5. Muhammad ibn-Ahmad Maqdasi, *Ahsan al-Taqasim*, translated by Alinaqi Monzavi (Tehran: Shirkat Mu'alefan va Mutarjiman, 1361 [1982]), 668-669.

6. Alinaqi Monzavi, "Tarikh Fihristnigari dar Iran," *Karaneh* 1 (Spring 1373 [1994]): 17-47.

7. Ibid., 34-35.

8. Etan Kolberg, *Ibn Tawus and His Library,* translated by Ali Qarai and Rasul Ja'farian (Qom: Kitabkhaneh Ayatollah Mar'ashi, 1371 [1992]).

9. *Brief History of Iranian Majlis Library and Document Center* (Tehran: Iranian Majlis Library and Documentation Center (IMAL DOC), 1996), 5.

10. Ibid., 12-14.

11. Ibn-Yusof E'tesami, *Fihrist Kitabkhaneh Majlis* (Tehran: Matba'eh Majlis, 1305 [1926]).

12. Ibn-Yusof E'tesami, *Fihrist Kitabha-I Majlis Shora-ye Melli* (Tehran: Matba'eh Majlis, 1311 [1933]).

13. Ibn-Yusof Shirazi, *Fihrist Kitabkhane Majlis Shora-ye Melli* (Tehran: Matba'eh Majlis, 1318-1321 [1939-1942]).

14. A sponsor was the person for whom or by order of whom a manuscript had been written. Kings, rulers, governors, officials, etc., usually ordered calligraphers to copy documents for them. The names of these persons, if known, are included in the descriptions of the manuscripts.

15. Sayyed Ali Ardalan Javan, ed., *Fihrist Kotob Khatti kitabkhaneh Markazi Astan Qods Razavi,* 2nd ed., vol. 2 (Tehran: Mu'asseseh Chap va Intesharat-i Astan Qods Razavi, 1365 [1986]), 9-20.

16. M. Pour Ahmad Jakctadji, *Tarikhcheh Katabkhaneh Melli Iran* (Tehran: Ketabkhaneh Melli Iran, 1357 [1978]), 42.

17. Iraj Afshar [Letter to the Editor], *The Iranian Library Association Bulletin* 13: special issue (1349 [1970]): 86.

18. By "manuscriptology," I mean information peculiar and unique to the manuscript at hand. I have coined the word for the Persian *Noskheh shenasi* (نسخه شناسی): the study of the manuscript that one is studying. It is different from the bibliographic information that may be similar in different manuscripts of the same work. There are two areas examined in the cataloging of manuscripts: *Kitab-shenasi* and *Noskheh shenasi* (bibliography and manuscriptology).

19. Ziya'oddin Sajjadi, "Nakhostin Kelas Ketabdari dar Iran," *The Iranian Library Association Bulletin* 5:1 (spring 1972): 27-30.

20. Mohsen Saba, *Fihrist Ketabha-ye Bank Melli Iran* (Tehran, 1325 [1986]).

21. "Pasokh bi Khanandigan," *The Iranian Library Association Bulletin* 13: special issue (1349 [1971]): 83-86.

22. Mohsen Saba, *Osul-i fan-i Kitabdari . . .* (Tehran: University of Tehran, 1332 [1953]).

23. Amuzish Kitabdari Jadid in Iran," *The Iranian Library Association Bulletin* 3 (Winter 1349 [1970]): 37-44.

24. The first two volumes were entitled *Kitab-Shenasi-ye Iran.*

25. Naser Sharifi obtained his Ph.D. in librarianship from Columbia University in 1958, returned to Iran, and then went back to the United States and later became dean of the Pratt Institute. For further information, see *Who's Who in the World,* 14th ed., 1977, p. 1322.

26. Iraj Afshar, [Letter to the Editor], *The Iranian Library Association Bulletin* 3: special issue (1349 [1971]): 85.

27. Thirteen students, who were already working in different libraries in Tehran, were eventually graduated, the author being one of them. This MLS program has continued and is run by Iranian lecturers.

28. Ms. Russell was not a cataloger. At the time I was taking her course, I was working at the Library of the Central Bank of Iran as a cataloger. Most questions in class were answered by me; and as soon as I graduated, I was chosen to teach cataloging for the same MLS course.

29. A compilation of these decisions was published as *Manual of Cataloging Rules*, 3rd ed., edited by Mandana Sadigh-Behzadi (Tehran: National Library of the Islamic Republic of Iran, 2000). Text in Persian.

30. These tools include revision and rearrangement for the needs of Iranian libraries of sections of DDC and LC classification relating to Iran. Tools with Dewey revisions include *Iranian Languages* (2nd ed., 1998), *Iranian Literature* (2nd ed., 1998), *History of Iran* (3rd ed., 1999), *Islam* (3rd ed., 2002), and *Geography of Iran* (4th ed., 2000). Revised LC classification schedules include *Class PIR: Iranian Languages and Literature* (2nd ed., 1997), *Class DSR: Iranian History* (3rd ed., 2000), and *Class BP: Islam* (2nd ed., 1997). Other TEBROC publications include works on author numbers, which were based on *Cutter-Sanborn Three-Figure Table* and LC's system of creating author numbers. A textbook entitled *Technical Services* (8th ed.) was published in 1999, and subject heading lists were also compiled by TEBROC. University, governmental, and special libraries were foremost among types of libraries to use these tools for organizing their libraries.

31. For further information see: Poori Soltani, "*Iranian National Bibliography: an Approach to New Standards*," *International Cataloguing and Bibliographic Control* 18:8 (April/June 1989): 30-33.

32. For further information see: Poori Soltani, *TEBROC's Research Function* (Tehran: TEBROC, 1974).

33. Fershteh Mowlavi, ed., *The Name Authority List of Authors and Famous People*, 2nd ed. (Tehran: National Library of The Islamic Republic of Iran, 1997); Poori Soltani and Kamran Fani, eds., *List of Persian Subject Headings*, 3rd ed. (Tehran: National Library of the Islamic Republic of Iran, 2002).

34. For further information see: Poori Soltani, "TEBROC: History and Impacts on Iranian Librarianship," in *Trends in International Librarainship: A Festschrift Honouring Anis Khurshid* (Karachi: Royal Book Company, 1991).

35. See note 30.

36. For further information see: Poori Soltani, "Translation and Expansion of Classification Systems in the Arab Countries and Iran," *International Cataloguing and Bibiliographic Control* 25, no. 1 (Jan./Mar. 1996): 13-16; Poori Soltani, "Major Subject Access in Iran" in *Subject Indexing: Principles and Practices in the 90's: Proceedings of the IFLA Satellite Meeting Held in Lisbon, Portugal, 17-18 August 1993*, 94-108 (München: Saur, 1995).

37. See note 29.

38. For more information on the National Library, see its Web site at: http://www.nli.ir. Furthermore, about 80 percent of the major libraries in Iran, especially those in universities, are computerized. Although public libraries lag far behind in computerization, the Board of Trustees of Public Libraries, nevertheless, publishes a monthly journal *Namayeh* (نمایه), which indexes all major periodicals of Iran; this index is available in hard copy and on CD.

39. Zahra Shadman, "Fihrist-nevisi-ye Pish as Intishar," *The Iranian Library Association Bulletin* 7, no. 3 (Autumn 1353 [1974]): 37-43.

Cataloging in Japan: Relationship Between Japanese and Western Cataloging Rules

Tadayoshi Takawashi

SUMMARY. In 1943 the Japanese League of Young Librarians published Nippon Catalog Rules (NCR1942) based on ALA 1908, and adopted the author main-entry system for Japanese and Western materials. After World War II, the Japan Library Association (JLA) compiled and published NCR1952, based on ALA 1949 and LC 1949 but maintained the author main-entry system. The main-entry system was then replaced by an alternative heading method, which came to be known as the Description-Independent-System (DIS). NCR1965 adopted the main entry principle, which was based on the Paris Principles of 1961. NCR1977 was compiled and published by the JLA Cataloging Committee and based upon a "no-main-entry principle." Then in 1987, the Committee published the standard edition of the rules, which was completely compatible with the International Standard Bibliographic Description (ISBD). NCR1987R was published in 1994 and NCR1987R01 in 2001, which included revised "Chapter 9: Computer Files," devised according to ISBD(ER). *[Article copies available for a fee from The Haworth Document Delivery Service: 1-800-HAWORTH. E-mail address: <getinfo@haworthpressinc.com> Website: <http://www.HaworthPress.com> © 2002 by The Haworth Press, Inc. All rights reserved.]*

Tadayoshi Takawashi, BE, is Professor, Faculty of Education, Tokyo Gakugei University, 4-1-1 Nukui-Kitamachi, Koganei 184-8501, Tokyo, Japan (E-mail: takawasi@u-gakugei.ac.jp).

[Haworth co-indexing entry note]: "Cataloging in Japan: Relationship Between Japanese and Western Cataloging Rules." Takawashi, Tadayoshi. Co-published simultaneously in *Cataloging & Classification Quarterly* (The Haworth Information Press, an imprint of The Haworth Press, Inc.) Vol. 35, No. 1/2, 2002, pp. 209-225; and: *Historical Aspects of Cataloging and Classification* (ed: Martin D. Joachim) The Haworth Information Press, an imprint of The Haworth Press, Inc., 2003, pp. 209-225. Single or multiple copies of this article are available for a fee from The Haworth Document Delivery Service [1-800-HAWORTH, 9:00 a.m. - 5:00 p.m. (EST). E-mail address: getinfo@haworthpressinc.com].

209

KEYWORDS. Nippon Cataloging Rules, NCR, Description-Independent System, DIS, Japanese-Western relations

抄録 (ABSTRACT).　ALA1908 に基づく青年図書館員連盟の「日本目録規則 1942」が 1943 年に刊行されるまで、和漢書および洋書の双方に著者基本記入が採用されることはなかった。第二次世界大戦後、日本図書館協会は著者基本記入方式を維持した ALA1949 と LC1949 に基づく「日本目録規則 1952」を編纂し出版した。しかしながら、すぐに何人かの目録担当者が基本記入方式の長所に疑問を抱き「記述独立方式」として知られるようになった alternative heading 方式を主張するようになった。こうした中で、「日本目録規則 1965」は、「パリ原則」による基本記入方式を採用した。何回かの全国会議の後、日本図書館協会目録委員会は、「非基本記入方式」に基づく「日本目録規則 1977（予備版）」を編纂し出版した。その後、目録委員会は、ISBD に完全に一致した「日本目録規則 1977」の本版を 1987 年に出版した。1994 年には、「日本目録規則 1987R」が出版され、ISBD（ER）に従って第 9 章コンピュータ・ファイルを改訂した「日本目録規則 1987R01」を 2001 年に出版した。

キーワード**(KEYWORDS).**　日本目録規則 NCR 記述独立方式

1. CATALOGING RULES OF THE NATIONAL DIET LIBRARY (NDL)

Many Japanese libraries such as the National Diet Library (NDL) and university libraries that have both Japanese and Western materials use different cataloging rules according to language. Japanese materials are cataloged according to the Nippon Cataloging Rules (NCR) while ALA Rules and successive codes have been used for Western materials. When the NDL opened in 1948, Dr. Robert B. Downs, director of the library of the University of Illinois, recommended to the technical processing services of NDL that the library follow the practice of many American research libraries in separating Japanese and Western materials by language.[1] Dr. Downs also recommended using the revised edition of the *Nippon Catalog Rules 1942* (NCR1942)[2] for Japanese materials and both the *A.L.A. Cataloging Rules for Author and Title Entries. 2d ed.* (ALA 1949)[3] and the *Rules for Descriptive Cataloging in the Library of Congress* (LC1949)[4] for English materials.

NDL began to use the *Nippon Cataloging Rules 1952* (NCR1952)[5] in April 1953 and in 1971 the *Nippon Cataloging Rules 1965* (NCR1965),[6] which were based on the Paris Principles of 1961. At that time, the Machine Readable Cataloging (MARC) format was under development in the United States and Europe. Finally, the International Standard Bibliographic Description (ISBD), an international framework for description was formally adopted by IFLA in 1971. In Japan ISBD was partially adopted as well as a no-main-entry system for NCR1977[7] in contrast to the Western tradition. NCR1977 was applied to JAPAN/MARC in 1977. After NCR1987,[8] which was the standard edition of the NCR1977 preliminary new edition, was published, it was not immediately adopted by NDL. Then in 1998 NDL adopted NCR1987R[9] according to the revision of JAPAN/MARC.

For Western materials NDL used both ALA 1949 and LC 1949 from 1948 to 1968 when AACR1[10] was adopted. Since 1986 AACR2[11] has been used.

2. NIPPON CATALOGING RULES (NCR)

2.1 Nippon Cataloging Rules 1942 (NCR1942)

Japan had simplified cataloging rules compiled by the Japan Library Association (JLA), but there were no standardized cataloging rules until 1942. In 1929 the League of Young Librarians established the Committee of Cataloging Rules to standardize the rules, which were completed in 1942 and published in 1943.

NCR1942 adopted the principle of main entry for the first time in Japan. Before NCR1942, a title main-entry system had been used for almost all cataloging rules in Japan. The method to record a title first in a bibliography, for example, had been traditionally used in Japan from early times. During the Meiji Era (1868-1912), the cataloging rules adopted in libraries were based upon the practice of a title main-entry system. When JLA compiled new cataloging rules, there was disagreement about whether Japanese libraries should adopt a system of title or author main entry. In 1932 this so-called "main entry dispute" arose and was eventually resolved in favor of those who supported the practice of an author main-entry system. During this dispute, the League of Young Librarians strongly supported the main-entry principle.

NCR1942 dealt with books but not with non-book materials. Similar in structure to ALA1908,[12] it consisted of rules for entry, title, and description. There were no rules for subject cataloging and filing. "Entry" was divided into "main entry" and "added entry," and main entry consisted of headings and description. Headings consisted of author, title and miscellaneous rules; and author headings consisted of personal and corporate names. For the first time in Japan, cataloging rules were based on cataloging theory and adopted main-entry principles. NCR1942 had a great impact on Japanese libraries. It was not until after World War II, however, that the idea of NCR1942 was fully realized.

2.2 Nippon Cataloging Rules 1952 (NCR1952)

The recommendation of Dr. Downs to maintain separate collections of Japanese and Western materials was influential in the birth of NCR1952, which evolved to become the standard cataloging code in Japan. In his recommendation Dr. Downs stated:

> For Oriental books, the above works (American Library Association's *Cataloging Rules for Author and Title Entries* and Library of Congress *Rules for Descriptive Cataloging*) are too limited. The most nearly satisfactory tool for this purpose appears to be the Nippon Catalog Rules (1943), worked out over a period of about ten years by the League of Young Librarian's Committee of the Cataloging Rules. This compilation attempts to cover the cataloging of both Oriental and Occidental books. For the latter it is too incomplete to be relied upon. For Oriental books, however, especially if revised and expanded, it is the consensus that the NCR is well suited. It has an important advantage over earlier Japanese codes of being based on authors rather than titles. A committee of the Japan Library Association is now engaged in a revision of the Nippon Catalog Rules. It is recommended that the National Diet Library cooperate with this committee to complete the revision as promptly as possible, and that the Library then adapt the new NCR as its standard for the cataloging of books in Oriental languages.[13]

In response to Dr. Downs's recommendation, the Cataloging Committee of JLA started in 1948 to revise NCR1942. The first Cataloging Committee meeting was held in August 1949, and the Committee devised the new rules based on consultation with NCR1942; *ALA Catalog Rules: Author and Title Entries* (ALA draft code 1941); ALA1949; *Rules for Descriptive Cataloging in the Library of Congress* (1947draft); Vatican Library *Rules for the Catalog of Printed Books* (1948); and other bibliographic standards.

The committee first discussed the structure of the cataloging rules of NCR1942, which was based on ALA1908. The word "description" was not used in either ALA1908 or NCR1942. As stated above, deliberations on NCR1952 were based on consultation with ALA1949 and LC1949. NCR1952 differed from NCR1942 in that "headings" and "description" were clearly distinguished in NCR1952. NCR1942 had been used for both Japanese materials and Western materials although it was more suitable for Japanese materials. NCR1952 focused on Japanese materials while rules for Western materials were simplified.

The rules for NCR1952 used the main entry system. For example, an author's real name was generally used. If names changed, the latest ones were established as the headings. If, however, authors continued to use their former names and those names were more popular than the latest ones, the former names were established. Corporate bodies could also be established as main entries. If abbreviations or popular names also existed, the established headings were the complete corporate names. Description meant only description of books. There were no rules for non-book materials.

2.3 Nippon Cataloging Rules 1965 (NCR1965)

After publication of NCR1952, the Cataloging Committee compiled and published *Commentary on Nippon Cataloging Rules 1952* to provide for beginners interpretations for understanding the rules. In 1955 a new Cataloging Committee was formed. The objectives of the committee were as follows:

- To deliberate the questions about NCR1952, especially the DIS;
- To create a revised edition of NCR1952, if necessary;
- To complete NCR including the rules about serials and other non-book materials, which were lacking in NCR1952.

The International Conference on Cataloging Principles in Paris (Paris Principles) in 1961 was influential in the revision of NCR1952. Because the Paris Principles dealing with the selection and forms of headings and entry words were approved, the Cataloging Committee entirely rewrote NCR sections on selection and form of headings and entry words in the new Cataloging Rules. The Committee made two drafts and held hearings on the new rules, which were subsequently published as NCR1965.

NCR1965 prescribed using the same cataloging rules for both Japanese and Western materials. NCR1965 introduced the "objectives of the catalog," which consisted of what Cutter and Lubetzky had advocated for the Paris Principles. Before and after NCR1965, there was no statement of objectives in NCR.

In Japanese cataloging rules, headings are usually given in *kanji* (Chinese characters), so that *kana* (the Japanese-style phonetic alphabet) must be added to the kanji in a double-decker arrangement. This rule was also included in NCR1965, which also prescribed how to deal with serials, maps, and music. In 1979 a supplement was published dealing with microforms, audio discs and tapes, slides and films, motion-picture films, and videotapes. Rules for entry in NCR1965 were based substantially on authorship; however, there were some rules that prescribed how to select main-entry headings according to type of work.

As for personal names, NCR1952 had prescribed as a fundamental principle the use of an author's real name rather than a pseudonym. NCR1965 required using names as they appeared in an author's works. Corporate authorship was also recognized though the form of a corporate name structured as a name-entry heading might differ from the form appearing in the author statement in the description. The concept of main entry for cataloging ended with NCR1965.

3. PUBLIC LIBRARY MOVEMENT
IN JAPAN AND TECHNICAL SERVICES

Japan witnessed the birth of the Library Law in 1950 that established the idea of library activity comparable to that of the United States and many European countries. Because of post-war financial difficulties, however, library service was still focused on preservation as in pre-war time; and appropriate circulation services could not be developed.

Most Japanese had an image that libraries would be located in quiet places and that they would serve only those who visited them. The reading rooms in these libraries were often little more than study halls that were usually occupied by students studying for entrance examinations. A turning point in the service of libraries came with the publication of *Chūshō toshi ni okeru kōkyō toshokan no un'ei (Management of Medium and Small Public Libraries)*[14] by the Japan Library Association in 1963. In this book, the authors insisted that prefectural libraries supplement rather than substitute for local libraries. At that time prefectural libraries predominated in Japan. The authors also stated that libraries should increase funding for acquisitions for materials to serve a broader base of users. Moreover, reader registration should be simplified and more user-friendly. In 1965 a new public library was opened in Hino, the Hino City Library. The librarian was one of the authors of the book.

The old system of libraries in Japan was entirely changed, and new services were developed. Where there were no buildings or library facilities, people were served by bookmobiles. There was an increased awareness that public library service should focus on book circulation. To support increased book circulation, libraries felt that it was important that books should be available for everyone at anytime and anywhere. There was substantial increase in financial support for libraries.

As a result of increased support and services, Hino City Library achieved a remarkable registration rate increase in circulation. This success greatly surprised other public libraries and librarians in Japan. Since then, public library service in Japan has come to focus heavily on circulation. The demand for human resources became so great that librarians and staff had to be moved to public services from technical services. Because of decreased technical services staffing, technical services operations were simplified. The pendulum was now swinging in the reverse direction. Technical services were being neglected.

It would be safe to say that many public libraries in Japan did not have their own catalogs until the introduction of computers and their use as cataloging tools. We understand that bibliographic information is as integral to library service as drinking water is to our lives. Bibliographic information is required whenever users visited libraries to check out books or to seek reading advice and reference service. On the contrary, it must be acknowledged that there were librarians who did not recognize the need for cataloging and classification. How could they pursue their business as librarians in such a condition?

Under these circumstances, computers began to be used for circulation transactions to handle the flow of library users. Consequently, computers came to be used for cataloging and entry of bibliographic information into databases. From these database entries, computer-generated catalogs were created. However, computers were not sufficiently capable of producing catalogs in *kana* (the Japanese syllabary) but instead only in *katakana* (Japanese phonetic letters).

With the availability of high-performance computers at low cost and access to various MARC formats, Japanese public libraries started in 1980 to use computerized catalogs. At that time the main stream of cataloging was gradually changing from original cataloging to copy cataloging. Now almost all university and public libraries have online public access catalogs (OPACs). This increase in the use of OPACs resulted in advocacy by public service librarians for more user-friendly access in library catalogs. And so an alternative cataloging method, the Description-Independent System (DIS), was developed.

4. DESCRIPTION-INDEPENDENT SYSTEM– NO-MAIN-ENTRY PRINCIPLES

After NCR1952, which was based on the main-entry principle, was published, many librarians questioned the merits of a main-entry system and advocated an alternative method, the Description-Independent System (DIS). DIS was fundamentally a system employing alternative headings.[15,16] The main advocate of DIS was Koichi Mori, who challenged the main-entry principle in a 1955 paper entitled "Separation of Heading and Description."[17] His opinion was supported by many librarians in Western Japan (Osaka and other neighboring regions), and the theory of DIS was gradually made more sophisticated and became an established system. According to Mori, DIS was suitable for the use of small- or medium-sized libraries that maintained multiple-entry catalogs by reproducing unit cards. Mori argued that it was meaningless to record a main entry in a catalog that contains author, title, and subject cards with the same amount of bibliographic information.

In a catalog of Japanese materials, headings (access points) and descriptions in bibliographic records are usually recorded in *kanji* (Chinese characters). In order to file and retrieve entries, *kana* (the Japanese syllabary) or the alphabet (romanization) must be written above the *kanji* heading to provide for filing and retrieving entries in sequence (see Figure 1).

In other words, both *kanji* and *kana* (or romanization) must be used in a double-decker arrangement. In Western materials this double-decker format does not exist. In Japanese materials a heading for an added author and title may be shown only in the *kana*, or romanized form, written above the *kanji* main-entry heading, with the corresponding author's name or title in *kanji* in the description underlined in red (in the card catalog). The Japanese were forced to do this since there was usually insufficient space left on the unit card for another set of double-decker headings. Such an added entry card (Figure 2) looked peculiar to users since *kana* or romanization are usually written parallel to each other, as shown in the case of the main-entry card in Figure 1. For added author entries, the main-entry heading was not an appropriate second-order filing element, as was the same in the case of Western materials.

Features of DIS

- A unit card is comprised of a description and tracings. There are no main-entry headings (see Figure 3). Needed headings are recorded in the tracings. Headings are recorded on the upper part of the reproduced unit card. Cards with author headings are filed in an author catalog, title headings in a title catalog, and subject headings in a subject catalog. In such a system there is no concept of main entry.
- The formatting of a title main entry on a 3 × 5 unit card uses a hanging indention and is different from that of an author main entry. In DIS, where there is no concept of main entry, there is only one formatting required on unit cards. Thus, standardization in the formatting of the description is achieved. Also, all headings can be typed at the same indention and standardized.

FIGURE 1. Author Main-Entry Card

Takayama, Masaya	...Romanization of main heading
高山　正也	...Main heading (in *kanji*)
図書館概論　／ 高山正也、岩猿敏生、石塚栄二共著	...Title
東京 ： 雄山閣出版, 1992	... Imprint
237 p ; 21 cm. -- （講座図書館の理論と実際 ; 1)	...Series (in parenthesis)
ISBN 4-639-01087-7	...ISBN
1. Iwasaru, Toshio　2. Ishizuka, Eiji	...Romanization of added author heading
3. Toshokangakugaironn	...Romanization of title

FIGURE 2. Added Author Entry

Iwasaru, Toshio	...Joint author (added entry)
Takayama, Masaya	...Romanization of main heading
高山　正也	...Main heading (in *kanji*)
図書館概論　／ 高山正也、<u>岩猿敏生</u>、石塚栄二共著	...Title
東京 ： 雄山閣出版, 1992	...Imprint
237 p ; 21 cm. -- （講座図書館の理論と実際 ; 1)	...Series (in parenthesis)
ISBN 4-639-01087-7	...ISBN
2. Iwasaru, Toshio　2. Ishizuka, Eiji	...Romanization of added author heading
3. Toshokangakugaironn	...Romanization of title

FIGURE 3. DIS Card

図書館概論　／ 高山正也、岩猿敏生、石塚栄二共著	...Title
東京 ： 雄山閣出版, 1992	...Imprint
237 p ; 21 cm. -- （講座図書館の理論と実際 ; 1)	...Series (in parenthesis)
ISBN 4-639-01087-7	...ISBN
1. Takayama, Masaya 2. Iwasaru, Toshio　3. Ishizuka, Eiji	...Tracing
3. Toshokangaku gairon	

Advantages of DIS

- A unit card is created without headings, a procedure which is practical, efficient, and even theoretical.
- There is no longer need to be distressed over choice of main entry, the difficulties and contradictions of which are well known.[18]

Disadvantages of DIS

- The main entry heading (usually author heading) is used for an author (or book) number, but there is no indication in DIS as to the source of the author number. However, the author's name recorded in the first tracing can be used for the book number.
- DIS is effective for creating a multiple-entry but not effective for a single-entry catalog.

DIS has been the source of great dispute between those who support it and those who support the main-entry system based upon the Paris Principles. As stated above, NCR1965 adopted the main-entry system in spite of DIS. It was not until the 1970s that the Cataloging Committee of the Japan Library Association seriously began to think about adopting DIS in the compilation of a new NCR.

5. NIPPON CATALOGING RULES (NCR1977): CATALOGING CODE BASED ON THE NO-MAIN-ENTRY PRINCIPLE

In 1970 the Japan Library Association held the first National Conference on Processing, which focused especially on new cataloging rules and principles. At this conference, the Cataloging Committee of JLA proposed a "no heading unit card system" (NHUCS), which was a compromise between the main-entry principle and DIS (see Figure 4).

According to NHUCS, the descriptive part of the bibliographic record was to be created independently of the heading, and all the headings were to be recorded as tracings, including the "main entry heading," which was recorded in the first position without numbering (Figure 4). This proposal was taken as being applicable for both the main-entry principle and DIS.

On the other hand, the Study Group on Processing of the Nippon Association for Librarianship had been working on the draft of a cataloging code since 1969, based upon a no-main-entry principle. It came out in 1974 as the "Library Cataloging Rules (Draft)."[19] Though not compiled officially, the "Draft"

FIGURE 4. NHUCS Card (Unit Card)

図書館概論 ／ 高山正也、岩猿敏生、石塚栄二共著	...Title
東京 ： 雄山閣出版, 1992	...Imprint
237 p ; 21 cm. --　（講座図書館の理論と実際 ; 1）　...Series (in parenthesis)	
ISBN 4-639-01087-7	...ISBN
Takayama, Masaya.　1. Iwasaru, Toshio　2. Ishizuka, Eiji	
3. Toshokangaku gaironn 4. Toshokanjohougaku	
5. 010	

(Takayama, Masaya before numbered tracings is the main entry heading.)

appears to have been the first code in the world that adopted the no-main-entry principle. The "Draft" greatly influenced the making of NCR1977.

The main features of the draft are as follows:

- It is based upon the no-main-entry principle. Therefore, there is no record of main entry even in the tracing, unlike DIS.
- It is devised primarily for the use of divided catalogs, not dictionary catalogs.
- It considers a physical unit as the unit of description.

Most small- and medium-sized public libraries and school libraries in Japan had only title catalogs and shelflists, not classified catalogs. These libraries did not welcome the author-main-entry principle in NCR1965, which had been based upon the Paris Principles. Because public libraries in Japan grew enormously after 1965, public libraries generally received large shipments of books at a time. The catalogers who had to deal with all these books welcomed the "Draft," which maintained the physical unit as a bibliographical one.

After several national conferences, the JLA Cataloging Committee compiled and published NCR1977, based upon the no-main-entry principle. Instead of recording the main-entry heading in tracings, as in NHUCS, a Description Unit Card System (DUCS) was adopted in which there was no main-entry heading, not even as a tracing (Figure 5).

NCR1977 was a code dealing mainly with new Japanese books published after the Meiji Era (1868-1912) and was comprised of a series of comparatively concise rules. Its target libraries were small or medium in size, developed from the 1960s to the 1970s, which had rather small collections and usually placed emphasis on the acquisition of newly published Japanese books. Catalogers in university and research libraries, however, wanted a code

FIGURE 5. DUCS Card (Unit Card)

図書館概論　/ 高山正也. [ほか] 共著	...Title
東京 ： 雄山閣出版, 1992	...Imprint
237 p ; 21 cm. --　（講座図書館の理論と実際 ; 1)	...Series (in parenthesis)
ISBN 4-639-01087-7	...ISBN
1. Toshokangaku gaironn　a1. Takayama, Masaya.	
s1. Toshokanjohougaku　　① 010	
"a" = author.　"s" = subject heading.	
① = classified heading.	

with more detailed rules that could also be applicable to the large collections of foreign books in their libraries. In addition, they thought the present code was not adequate for sophisticated users in pursuit of more complicated bibliographical information. These libraries at that time used NCR1977 for new Japanese books, another code for the books published before the Meiji period, and AACR2 for foreign books.

NCR1977 was established as the standard cataloging code in Japan and was utilized for both Japan/MARC and the *Japanese National Bibliography*. Catalogers wanted to be rid of this complicated situation and longed for a MARC-oriented new code more rigidly consistent with international standards such as ISBDs. Under these circumstances, the appearance of NCR1987 was hailed. The JLA Cataloging Committee began to revise the code (NCR1977), which was in only a preliminary edition. The Committee was aiming to compile such rules as would be completely compatible with both ISBDs and UNIMARC. The claim in the preface that NCR1977 was compatible with the ISBDs was not necessarily true. For example, ISBD punctuation is not used in the code. The committee published the first draft of the standard edition in 1984, the second in 1985, and the third in 1986. The new edition, NCR1987, was published in September 1987.

Since the adoption of NCR1977 in Japan, great importance has been attached to the finding-list function of the catalog while the collocation function has been treated lightly. In addition, the principle of uniform heading for authors has been adopted even though the creation of uniform headings is not generally prescribed. Rules for the choice and form of heading were to be simplified. For example, in the assignment of a corporate heading, it was prescribed that the name of a higher body be chosen even though a work was published by a body subordinate to it. This rule caused inconvenience, especially for large libraries and for research libraries. In the new NCR1987, an option was provided that allowed the addition of a subordinate body to the corporate heading. Though limited to anonymous classics, sacred scriptures, and musical works, application of uniform titles is also provided as an option.

6. NIPPON CATALOGING RULES 1987 (NCR1987)

NCR1987 was compiled and published as a revision to NCR1977, which was known as a code based on an alternative headings system and also on the physical unit principle, contrary to the work unit principle predominant in Western countries. It prescribes that each cataloging object should be a physically separate item. Consequently, NCR1977 is a cataloging code deemed different from the traditional Western sense of cataloging. The targets of these cataloging rules were Japanese and Western materials. NCR1987 followed the no-main-entry principle established in NCR1977 but used ISBD punctuation; its targets are Japanese and Western materials.

A distinguishing feature of NCR1987, incorporated in preparation for online catalogs, is its provision for bibliographic hierarchy. The provision in question is "mainly devoted to showing how bibliographic data is [sic] organized at different levels in a record."[20] Integral to the concept of bibliographic hierarchy is that the work, not the physical piece, be taken as the basic unit of description. This is another distinguishing feature of NCR1987 since NCR1977 views a physical unit as the basis for description.

The concept of bibliographical hierarchy is required in the computerized cataloging age for the purpose of displaying bibliographic information in context. In a card catalog, the format of input and output is almost the same; therefore, the concept is not necessary. The Cataloging Committee defined **bibliographic unit** as "a unit that is defined as a set of data elements belonging to same bibliographic level and constituting a bibliographic record with or without other units of a different bibliographic level."[21] The bibliographic hierarchy then is constructed of the following units:

> 1.1 Basic bibliographic unit
> > Monographic bibliographic unit (Figure 6)
> > Serial bibliographic unit
> 1.2 Collective bibliographic unit (Figure 7)
> 1.3 Component part unit (Figure 8)
> 2　Physical unit: "a unit that describes a physically independent part of a larger item (Figure 9)

In the case of a physical unit, a numeric or another designation (usually a volume number) has been added for each physical part as an independent

FIGURE 6. NCR1987 Monographic Unit, Normal Style (Unit Card)

```
学校図書館と児童図書館 / 塩見昇、            ...Title:School libraries and ...
間崎るり子共著
東京 : 雄山閣、    1976
265p ; 24 cm. – (日本図書館学講座 / 椎名六郎[ほか]編 ; 5) ...Series in parentheses
内容 : 第1部 :   学校図書館 / 塩見昇著. –               ... Contents
第2部 :   児童図書館 / 間崎るり子著
t1.Gakko toshokan to jido toshokan                    ...Tracings
a1.Shiomi, Noboru a2.Masaki, Ruriko
s1.学校図書館(Gakko toshokan)
s2.児童図書館(Jido toshokan)
①   017   ②   016.8
```

FIGURE 7. NCR1987, Collective Level (Unit Card)

```
日本図書館学講座 / 椎名六郎[ほか]編
東京 / 雄山閣, 1975-1978
10 冊 ; 24cm
1:図書館概論 / 椎名六郎、岩猿敏生著
                ·
                ·
                ·
10 : 図書および図書館史 / 小野泰博著
```

FIGURE 8. NCR1987 Analytical Level (Unit Card) (Component Part Unit)

```
児童図書館 / 間崎るり子著. – (日本図書館
学講座 ; 5 : 学校図書館と児童図書館 /
塩見昇、間崎るり子共著. – 東京 : 雄山閣、
1976
265p. ; 24cm. – 第2部. – p. 155-263)
```

FIGURE 9. NCR1987 Physical Level (Unit Card)

COSMOS 下 / カール・セーガン著 ; 木村繁訳　　… Author: Carl Sagan
東京 : 朝日新聞社, 1980　　　　　　　　　　　下 = "No.2 of 2"
383p. ; 20cm

t1. Kosumosu　a1. Sagan, Carl.　A2. Kimura, Shigeru.

bibliographic data element because, without this designation, it would not be possible to identify each physical part of the larger item. The physical unit is used in the following cases: (1) to show publishing information for a multi-volume publication within a given period and (2) to show holdings for local housekeeping and for reporting to union catalogs.[22]

The National Center for Scientific Information System (NACSIS) used NCR1987 to compile NACSIS-Cat, a Japanese bibliographic utility for university libraries. The structure of "Description" preceding "Headings" reflects actual cataloging procedures and conforms to that of AACR2. Features of NCR1987 include:

- NCR1987 contains rules for filing.
- NCR1987 contains rules for subject cataloging (subject headings and class number as headings).
- NCR1987 is compiled for organizing not only an author and a title catalog but also a subject catalog and/or classified catalog.

7. NCR1987R, NCR1987R01

NCR1987 was followed by a revision in 1994 (NCR1987R) and another revision in 2001 (NCR1987R01).[23] NCR1987R had three chapters under construction ("Graphic materials," "Three-dimensional artifacts and realia," and "Manuscripts"), which are included in NCR1987R. NCR1987R01 includes revised Chapter 9 dealing with Computer files according to ISBD(ER).

8. CONCLUSIONS

The cataloging rules in Japan have been especially affected by various cataloging rules in Anglo-American libraries. Paul S. Dunkin has stated that, as automobiles in the first stage imitated the style of carriages, MARC also imitated the style of card catalogs.[24] But in the age of OPACs, we have to establish better cataloging rules that take into consideration how library patrons utilize computers to gain access to information. We do need bibliographic information to assist library users in identifying and retrieving information more precisely and immediately. Now metadata is under consideration in various forms. Whatever form it takes, I would like to insist that it provide a variety of relevant information for users.

It is high time to focus on the "no-main-entry-system" to enhance the function of computerized cataloging system.

There are some librarians who argue that they no longer need knowledge of classification and cataloging because OPAC record creation in Japan is being outsourced. I question how librarians can call themselves professional without understanding bibliographic information, an essential component of the library and its services–the lifeblood of the library and its services.

REFERENCES

1. Robert B. Downs, *Report on Technical Processes, Bibliographic Services, and General Organization* (Tokyo: General Headquarters, Supreme Commander for the Allied Powers, Civic Information and Education Section, Educational Division, 1948).

2. League of Young Librarians, *Nippon Catalog Rules 1942* (Osaka: F. Mamiya, 1943).

3. American Library Association, *A.L.A. Cataloging Rules for Author and Title Entries,* 2d ed. (Chicago: American Library Association, 1949).

4. Library of Congress, Rules for Descriptive Cataloging in the Library of Congress (Washington: Library of Congress, 1949).

5. Japan Library Association. Cataloging Committee, *Nippon Cataloging Rules 1952* (Tokyo: Japan Library Association, 1953).

6. Japan Library Association. Cataloging Committee, *Nippon Cataloging Rules 1965* (Tokyo: Japan Library Association, 1965).

7. Japan Library Association. Cataloging Committee, *Nippon Cataloging Rules*, Preliminary new ed. (Tokyo: Japan Library Association, 1977). Referred to as NCR1977.

8. Japan Library Association. Cataloging Committee, *Nippon Cataloging Rules*, 1987 ed. (Tokyo: Japan Library Association, 1987). Referred to as NCR1987.

9. Japan Library Association. Cataloging Committee, *Nippon Cataloging Rules,* 1987 ed., 1994 rev. (Tokyo: Japan Library Association, 1994). Referred to as NCR1987R.

10. *Anglo-American Cataloging Rules* (Chicago: American Library Association, 1967).

11. *Anglo-American Cataloguing Rules,* 2d ed., ed. Michael Gorman and Paul W. Winkler (Chicago: American Library Association, 1978).

12. American Library Association, *Catalog Rules: Author and Title Entries* (Chicago: American Library Association, 1908).

13. Downs, 12-13.

14. Japan Library Association. *Chūshō toshi ni okeru kōkyō toshokan no un 'ei (Management of Medium and Small Public Libraries)* (Tokyo: Japan Library Association, 1963).

15. John Friedman and Alan Jeffreys, "Cataloguing and Classification in British University Libraries: A Survey of Practices and Procedures," *Journal of Documentation* 23 (Sept. 1967): 224-246.

16. Alan Jeffreys, "Alternative Headings," *Catalogue & Index* 8 (Oct. 1967): 4-5.

17. Koichi Mori, "Separation of Headings and Description," *Toshokan-kai* 7 (Dec. 1955): 195-201.

18. Andrew D. Osborn, "Relation between Cataloguing Principles and Principles Applicable to Other Forms of Bibliographic Work," in *Report* [of the International Conference on Cataloguing Principles, Paris, 9th-18th October 1961], eds. A. H. Chaplin and Dorothy Anderson (London: Organizing Committee of the Conference, 1963): 125-137.

19. Nippon Association for Librarianship. Study Group on Processing, "Library Cataloging Rules (Draft)," *Toshokan-kai* 26 (Dec. 1974): 109-117.

20. Shojiro Maruyama, "Descriptive Cataloging and Cataloging Rules in Japan," *International Cataloging: Quarterly Bulletin of the IFLA International Programme for UBC*, 15.3 (1986): 29.

21. Ibid.

22. Ibid.

23. Japan Library Association. Cataloging Committee, *Nippon Cataloging Rules*, 1987 ed., 2001 rev. (Tokyo: Japan Library Association, 2001). Referred to as NCR1987R01.

24. Paul S. Dunkin, *Cataloging U.S.A.* (Chicago: American Library Association, 1969), 149.

Cataloging and Classification History
in Mexico

Filiberto Felipe Martínez-Arellano

SUMMARY. This article discusses cataloging and classification history in Mexico and how cataloging and classification have evolved according to the changes that libraries and library science have experienced on both a national and international level. The first part of the article refers to the first half of the twentieth century, detailing the origins of cataloging and classification history. The second part presents discussion of the development and consolidation of both cataloging and classification during the second half of the twentieth century. The article also discusses subject headings, automation, centralization, and union catalogs in Mexico. It discusses past difficulties in creating a union catalog at a national level and the advantages of automated systems in helping to develop this needed union catalog. The article discusses the need to resume publication of the *Bibliografía Mexicana*. One of the main problems that Mexican libraries have faced is a scarcity of librarians adequately prepared to perform cataloging and classification of their collections. This lack of librarians is even more acute in the Mexican states. There are insufficient numbers of students in library schools to provide

Filiberto Felipe Martínez-Arellano, PhD, is Director, Center for Research in Library Science, National Autonomous University of México (E-mail: felipe@servidor. unam.mx).

[Haworth co-indexing entry note]: "Cataloging and Classification History in Mexico." Martínez-Arellano, Filiberto Felipe. Co-published simultaneously in *Cataloging & Classification Quarterly* (The Haworth Information Press, an imprint of The Haworth Press, Inc.) Vol. 35, No. 1/2, 2002, pp. 227-254; and: *Historical Aspects of Cataloging and Classification* (ed: Martin D. Joachim) The Haworth Information Press, an imprint of The Haworth Press, Inc., 2003, pp. 227-254. Single or multiple copies of this article are available for a fee from The Haworth Document Delivery Service [1-800-HAWORTH, 9:00 a.m. - 5:00 p.m. (EST). E-mail address: getinfo@haworthpressinc.com].

227

the staffing that libraries demand not only for cataloging and classification but also for many other library activities. *[Article copies available for a fee from The Haworth Document Delivery Service: 1-800-HAWORTH. E-mail address: <getinfo@haworthpressinc.com> Website: <http://www.HaworthPress.com> © 2002 by The Haworth Press, Inc. All rights reserved.]*

KEYWORDS. Cataloging, classification, subject headings, union catalogs, centralized cataloging, cataloging automation, Mexico

RESUMEN. Este artículo presenta la historia de la catalogación y clasificación en México. Menciona como la catalogación y clasificación han evolucionado en nuestro país de acuerdo con los cambios que las bibliotecas y la bibliotecologia han experimentado como producto de la problemática nacional e internacional. En la primera parte se hace referencia a los inicios de la catalogación y clasificación durante la primera mitad del siglo veinte. El desarrollo y consolidación de la catalogación y clasificación en México tuvo lugar durante la segunda mitad del siglo veinte, lo cual es abordado en una segunda parte. Este artículo también hace referencia a la problemática de los encabezamientos de materia, la automatización, la centralización y los catálogos colectivos en México. Algunos de los puntos discutidos en el artículo son los siguientes: Es un hecho que no ha sido posible la creación de catálogos colectivos a nivel nacional. La elaboración de la "Bibliografía Mexicana" debe ser continuada. Los sistemas de automatización tienen una serie de ventajas para desarrollar los catálogos colectivos que el país requiere. Uno de los principales problemas que las bibliotecas mexicanas han enfrentado es la falta de recursos adecuadamente preparados para llevar a cabo la catalogación y clasificación de sus colecciones. Esta falta de bibliotecarios es más acentuada en los estados. Aún en nuestros días, el número de estudiantes de las escuelas de bibliotecología es insuficiente para cubrir las demandas de las bibliotecas, no sólo en catalogación y clasificación, sino en otras muchas actividades.

PALABRAS CLAVES. Catalogación, clasificación, encabesamientos de material, catálogos colectivos, catalogación centralizada, catalogación automatizada, México

Diverse methods, procedures, tools, systems, and standards have long affected cataloging practice and principles. In recent years the use of computers and new information technologies in cataloging and classification activities have brought about substantial changes. As in other countries, cataloging and classification in Mexico have evolved; and they have also been modified by the changes that libraries and library science have experienced from national and international settings.

The main objective of this article is to show how cataloging and classification in Mexico have evolved, to show what the factors are that have induced cataloging and classification development, to describe what the environment of cataloging and classification changes have been, and to learn how cataloging and classification have progressed in Mexico so that Mexican librarians understand the foundations of library practices in addition to bringing out opportunities to improve them.

THE BEGINNINGS:
THE FIRST HALF OF THE TWENTIETH CENTURY

The emergence of library science in Mexico began at the start of the twentieth century, and its development has continued throughout the century. During the first half of the century, several important events contributed to the confirmation of library science in Mexico. "The National Library began to have its peculiar nature; public libraries were thought of as a support to popular culture; library associations were created. In addition to the European point of view, American library science, the leader in many aspects, became known. The first Mexican librarians were to study abroad, and they supported the learning of the new generation of librarians. They also introduced changes in library services; library science schools, with a formal curriculum, were established" (Morales Campos 1988, 1-3).

Certainly, during the first half of the twentieth century, the development of library science in Mexico was highlighted by the establishment of a large number of libraries, particularly public libraries, and a constant concern to train people to organize the newly created libraries to offer modern services. In this context library science education played an important role. Librarian training was carried out by both informal and formal courses in the first schools of library science schools. In librarian training, the teaching of cataloging and classification played a leading role.

On April 14, 1915, the Academia de Bibliografía [Academy of Bibliography] was created and assigned to the Biblioteca del Pueblo [People's Library] in Veracruz City. Its objective was "to prepare capable employees for the study and organization of libraries in the country and for the unification of guiding criteria for all bibliographic institutions of the Republic." In order to attain this objective, Mr. Agustín Loera y Chávez gave a course to government libraries and archives employees that included twenty-five conferences on classification (Morales Campos 1988, 5).

Afterwards, "the necessity of having trained personnel and the wish to improve the functioning of libraries in the country, as well as library technical processes, led to the creation of the first school for librarians" (Morales Campos 1988, 5). Thus, on June 24, 1916, the Escuela Nacional de Bibliotecarios y Archiveros [National School of Librarians and Archivists] was created; the school lasted only until 1918. During its short life it had two curricula. The first one, in 1916, lasted one year and the second between 1917 and 1918 for two years. The first curriculum contained the following courses: library and archives organization, cataloging, library and archives classification, study of the book, Latin, French, and English. The two-year curriculum offered eleven courses that included bibliography and cataloging, palaeography, and the second courses of Latin and English" (Morales Campos 1988, 5-6).

The second attempt at establishing a school for librarians took place on April 25, 1925, when the Escuela Nacional de Bibliotecarios [National School of Librarians] was inaugurated. This school was administered by the Departamento de Bibliotecas de la Secretaria de Educación Pública [Department of Libraries of the Ministry of Public Education]. Unfortunately, this school also had a fleeting life, functioning only during its foundation year. "The subjects which made up the curriculum were study of the book, classification, cataloging, book selection, library organization, bibliography, and reference" (Morales Campos 1988, 8).

In addition to the efforts for the creation of library schools during the first half of the twentieth century, many non-curricular courses were conducted throughout the country. Their purpose was to prepare the employees needed for Mexican libraries, and courses included subject cataloging and classification.

In an analysis of curricular and non-curricular courses that were available from 1916 to 1945 in Mexico, Morales Campos (1988, 14-18) found that the most frequent subjects were librarianship, bibliography, cataloging, and classification. Likewise, these courses were divided into three main groups: technical subjects, foreign language courses, and cultural subjects. The technical subjects group had at its core five types of courses: cataloging, classification, bibliography, librarianship, and study of the book. Included in the cataloging courses were cataloging systems, catalog types and arrangement, bibliographic entries, and standardized rules of entry. The classification courses included classification systems, Dewey Decimal Classification (DDC), and classification methodology.

It can be seen, therefore, that the history of cataloging and classification in Mexico is tightly linked with the history of library science education. The main goal was to prepare librarians with the adequate knowledge to organize the libraries that were created at that time. A technical focus was given to library science education during the first half of the twentieth century.

DEVELOPMENT AND CONSOLIDATION: THE SECOND HALF OF THE TWENTIETH CENTURY

The definitive establishment of schools of library science in the second half of the twentieth century marks the beginning of library science development in Mexico. The efforts to create a school that would train the librarians that our country needed were rewarded on April 5, 1945. On that date the Escuela Nacional de Bibliotecarios y Archivistas [National School of Librarians and Archivists] was established under the administration of the Secretaría de Educación Pública [Ministry of Public Education]. This school exists today under the name Escuela Nacional de Biblioteconomía y Archivonomía [National School of Library and Archive Sciences].

Rodríguez Gallardo (1998, 192) points out that the subjects included in the first curriculum of this school "basically tended to train students in the technical area with a great humanistic culture." The subjects that comprised the initial curriculum were: cataloging I, II, III; classification I, II; subject headings I, II; foundations of library service; introduction to librarianship and to the library and its environment; bibliography; reference sources, book selection, and reference service; book history; advanced Spanish; Mexican history; cultural history I, II; Latin I, II, III; and English I, II.

Moreover, in 1952, the Ciudad Universitaria, the main campus of the largest Mexican university, the Universidad Nacional Autónoma de Mexico (UNAM) [National Autonomous University of Mexico], was inaugurated. This occurrence marked the beginning of a support cycle for university libraries and the starting of specialized libraries development (Tecuatl Quechol 2000, 39). The inauguration of Ciudad Universitaria led to an increase of UNAM schools and their libraries. Therefore, there was an increased need for trained employees in library science. Furthermore, the first Jornadas Mexicanas de Biblioteconomía, the annual Mexican Conference on Library Science, held in 1956, featured discussions on the need for having trained library science professionals to manage libraries.

In this context, on January 12, 1955, a project for the establishment of the Colegio de Biblioteconomía y Archivonomía [Librarianship and Archival College], actually the Colegio de Bibliotecología [College of Library Science], was submitted to UNAM authorities. The goal of this project was to resolve the problem that had confronted the university for many years: how to provide thirty-six university libraries with adequate staff for effective operation (Solís Valdespino 1980, 12).

The first Library Science College curriculum included thirty-six courses with four of them in the technical areas: classification and subject headings, cataloging 1, cataloging 2, and special problems of cataloging. In 1958 four courses were added to the curriculum, of which two were in technical areas: technical services of the book and Library of Congress Classification (Rodríguez Gallardo 1998, 222-225).

As can be observed, library education in Mexico featured strong emphasis on cataloging and classification, which continues to be an important part of the curricula of these two schools and in the four schools of library science schools that were established afterwards in Mexico (Martínez Arellano, 2000).

Mexico is a country characterized by a strong centralism that has influence in the social, economic, cultural, educational, and library areas. As mentioned, UNAM is the largest institution of higher education in the country, and its library system is the one that has the greatest influence in library practice, including cataloging and classification activities.

The number of UNAM students is around 250,000, a number that represents approximately thirty-five percent of the population in Mexican public and private universities (Ornelas & Levy 1991). Also, nearly sixty percent of research in Mexico is carried out in this higher education institution by first-level researchers in their respective disciplines (Adelman & Ortega Salazar 1995). The UNAM library system, comprised of approximately 140 libraries, is coordinated by a General Direction for Libraries, which was established in 1966. One of the functions of the General Direction is to carry out, in a centralized way, the cataloging of materials that UNAM libraries acquire–approximately 120,000 titles per year, of which 50,000 are new titles with the remaining ones being added copies acquired by the same or another library in this large system (García López 2000, 74).

Other significant occurrences in the history of library science in Mexico with relevance to understanding the evolution of cataloging and classification evolution in this country are revival of public libraries due to the establishment in 1983 of a National Plan for Public Libraries and the foundation of the Centro Universitario de Investigaciones Bibliotecológicas (CUIB) [University Center for Library Science Research] at UNAM in 1981.

On August 2, 1983, the National Plan for Public Libraries was set up to create the Public Libraries National Network, which has opened more than 6,000 libraries around the country. This library network, under the administration of the Consejo Nacional para la Cultura y las Artes [National Council for Culture and the Arts], is coordinated by a General Direction for Libraries that provides collections, according to the local user needs, to all the Mexican public libraries. Likewise, the General Direction for Libraries performs the centralized cataloging and classification of these collections and sends them to public libraries throughout Mexico ready for service.

The CUIB has its background in a research program initiated in 1988 at the UNAM General Direction for Libraries. It was established on December 14, 1981; and one of its goals is to carry out research dealing with diverse aspects of library science, among them cataloging, classification, storage and retrieval languages, and standardization in bibliographic organization.

CATALOGING

Cataloging practices in Mexican libraries have been greatly influenced by standards, methods, and procedures used in American libraries. This influence stems in part from the geographical proximity of Mexico and the United States as well as to easy access to the specialized literature produced in the neighboring country, but also it is a consequence of the preparation that the first professional librarians in Mexico received in American universities. These first librarians were founders and professors of the first Mexican schools of library science where, as has been previously mentioned, there was a strong emphasis in the teaching of cataloging and classification.

Cataloging standards taught in library science schools in Mexico and later applied in Mexican libraries were the same employed in most of the foreign libraries. Referring to the cataloging standards utilized in the first half of the twentieth century, Chávez Campomanes (1947, 245) mentions the following: "In our country, with the exception of some old libraries that used their own criteria to catalog their books, and others that adopted the French rules, libraries have been following for more than forty years the North American rules."

In spite of the fact that libraries in our country used the North American rules, particularly the *ALA Catalog Rules: Author and Title Entries* (1941) and the *A.L.A. Cataloging Rules: Author and Title Entries* (1949), their inconsistent application led to diverse problems. Chávez Campomanes (1947, 245), for example, points out the following:

Unfortunately, a complete unification in rules application has not been accomplished since, in some libraries, cataloging rules are used in the same way they were imposed a long time ago. In others they are applied according to criteria from people with very weak preparation; in others necessary adaptations and changes, additions and corrections have not been done from the original standards to the latest publication; and in some others Library of Congress printed cards are copied. A lack of uniformity is also noted in the margins, spacing, and other card aspects but mostly in subject headings. This lack of uniformity has not allowed the implementation of cooperative cataloging programs, which would bring great advantages to our libraries and avoid job duplication that would save money and effort and would make possible cataloging standardization in our libraries.

As has been stated, one of the great problems confronting cataloging in Mexico during the first half of the twentieth century was a scarcity of properly prepared librarians, a situation that precipitated the need for training librarians through non-formal courses and the sending of scholarship students abroad, particularly to U.S. library schools.

The creation of libraries in Mexico increased greatly from 1920 to 1924, a period in which José Vasconcelos was Minister of Public Education. Vasconcelos organized the Secretaría de Educación Pública [Ministry of Public Education] in three great departments: Scholarly Issues, Fine Arts, and Libraries. Certainly, the impulse that the creation of libraries received during the Vasconcelos period was notable, but also there was concern about preparing librarians to take care of the new libraries. In an official report, cited by Rodríguez Gallardo (1986, 65), it was pointed out: "The Department has sent two technicians so that they can study the best classification systems in New York City." The scholarship students who were sent to study in the United States were María Teresa Chávez and Juana Manrique de Lara, both of whom had a profound influence on cataloging and classification practices and in teaching in our country, particularly Chávez (Rodríguez Gallardo 1986, 65).

María Teresa Chávez Campomanes studied at the Pratt Institute Junior Undergraduate Library School (Morales Campos 1988, 24). After her return, Chávez Campomanes was an untiring promoter of the Escuela Nacional de Bibliotecarios [National School of Librarians], promoting her posture since the Primer Congreso Nacional de Bibliotecarios [First National Congress of Librarians], held in 1927 (Rodríguez Gallardo 1998, 170). Once the Escuela Nacional de Bibliotecarios y Archiveros [National School of Librarians and Archivists] was established, María Teresa Chavéz Campomanes, who had attained a leadership role in the area of cataloging, was a member of its first professors group (Tecuatl Quechol 2000, 15). She was also a member of the professors group that founded the UNAM Colegio de Bibliotecología [College of Library Science] (Rodríguez Gallardo 1998, 222). In both schools María Teresa Chavéz Campomanes taught cataloging courses for many years.

As a learning tool for her cataloging classes, Chávez Campomanes prepared a didactic tool titled "Catalogers and Classifiers Manual" (Morales Campos 1988). This manual became a basic reference work for catalogers and library science students. Esther Gama, a student of Professor Chávez Campomanes, was interviewed by Morales Campos (1988, 59) and points out the following memories related to this manual: " . . . and for cataloging (Professor Chávez) used to give us her notes that she elaborated in folded sheets of paper, using mimeograph; the first one to learn the card-making, and the second one to learn the rules that she had adapted."

The use of North American cataloging standards (*A.L.A. Cataloging Rules*), as noted, was adopted by Mexican libraries in the mid-twentieth century. Besides the arguments mentioned by Chávez Campomanes (1947, 245), Zamora Rodríguez (1947, 256) argued Mexican librarian participation in the making of this code:

> The main problem that has to be solved, if a (national) uniformity is to be reached for making catalogs in our country, is the adoption of a cataloging code, either the American Library Association one (later on called ALA code) or the Vatican one.

> We keep up our advocacy for the ALA code, because it is the one that has had more influence in libraries from the Occidental world, in library catalogs, in indexes, in bibliographies, and in printed reference works, and because at the current time, a new revision of it is being made, with the purpose of reaching greater international acceptance, and because in this time, Latin American librarians' opinions are being considered through the Committee of Cooperation with Latin American Cataloguers and Classifiers created since the end of 1953, to which the one who writes this paper is proud to belong.

Regarding the cataloging rules used in Mexico during the second half of the twentieth century, Morales Campos (1984, ix) mentions the following:

> During the last 25 years, the main libraries in Mexico–public, specialized, and university–have used as a standard to catalog their monographic collections the 1949 A.L.A. Cataloging Rules for Author and Title Entries, the 1967 Anglo-American Cataloging Rules, and in the last years, the revised chapter VI of the Anglo-American Cataloging Rules,

edited in 1976 by the UNAM Instituto de Investigaciones Bibliográficas. [Institute for Bibliographic Research]

Although Mexican librarians have made use of cataloging codes generated and adopted at an international level, sometimes these codes were not used at the same time as in other places due, among other reasons, to the language barriers. Regarding this problem, Morales Campos (1984, ix) points out:

> The 1949 American Library Association (ALA) code had plenty of followers in Mexico. Up to 1970, when the 1967 Anglo-American cataloging rules translation into Spanish was published, library science schools continued teaching the 1949 rules. In fact, the Spanish translation that Doctor Ma. Teresa Chávez C. has done as an educational tool for the learning of cataloging had a strong influence. Likewise, due to our librarians' limitations in reading English, new generations continued applying the 1949 code; and once a routine application of the 1967 Anglo-American cataloging rules, whose Spanish version was published in 1970 by the Organization of American States, the Chapter VI revision had already started.

To talk about cataloging in Mexico during the second half of the twentieth century, one must mention Gloria Escamilla, who was professor of many Latin American and Mexican catalogers. Gloria Escamilla González was one of the first-generation students from the UNAM Colegio de Bibliotecología [College of Library Science]. After concluding her studies in 1961, she received a scholarship from the Organization of American States that allowed her to study at Catholic University in Washington, D.C., and to work at the Library of Congress. Professor Escamilla had been interested in cataloging since her work at LC. The goal of her experience there was to learn the organization, procedures, routines, and management of bibliographic information in a library of that magnitude and to apply this knowledge in a smaller one like the Biblioteca Nacional de México [National Library of Mexico]. Her relationship with AACR emerged first as a cataloging student and afterwards as a professional interested in the application of the rules. She had studied with María Teresa Chávez at the time the ALA rules were used and later when AACR was adopted (Lira Luna 1999, 21).

Gloria Escamilla became a cataloging professor at the UNAM Colegio de Bibliotecología upon her return from Washington in 1963, a position she held until her death in 2001. The textbooks that she wrote to support the learning of cataloging–*Interpretación catalográfica de los libros* [*Cataloging interpretation of books*] (1979) and *Manual de catalogación descriptiva* [*Manual of descriptive cataloging*] (1981)–became classic works for catalogers and are still used. In addition, her translation "Chapter VI" of the *Anglo-American Cataloging Rules*, published in 1976, became a basic reference work for Mexican catalogers in spite of the polemics that they caused. Her participation in international discussions on cataloging was also important, as can be seen in this citation:

> In the development of rules, experiences from different nations have been considered. Although it is clear that most of them have been from the United States and England, there have been committees where we have been asked to express our opinions regarding diverse aspects that we have found. When I was in cataloging, in technical processing [at the National Library], I took part in some of those meetings with some contributions.

> I took part in studies of standards with the hope of getting new editions. That means the new edition does not come from the nothingness; they come from contributions of librarians who are working with current problems. (Lira Luna 1999, 21)

At this point it can be seen that most Mexican libraries use the Anglo-American Cataloging Rules to organize their materials; however, their interpretation and application have been inconsistent. One explanation for this inconsistency is the scarcity of librarians emerging from library schools; then cataloging sometimes has to be done by personnel from other disciplines, who are not trained in cataloging.

Bearing in mind the necessary standardization of AACR application and the need for updating of cataloging information, the Mexican Cataloging Group, sponsored by the "Centro Universitario de Investigaciones Bibliotecológicas" [University Center for Research in Library Science], was formed in 1984. One goal of this group was "to be a forum for Mexican catalogers to share experiences and projects that would contribute to the daily technical work improvement and to cataloger self-improvement" (Solís Valdespino 1984). As a result of this group's meetings, a set of recommendations has been printed in a publication entitled *The Problems of Entry of Personal Authors, Geographic Names, Corporate Authors, and Uniform Titles in Five Technical Processing Units in México City* (Solís Valdespino 1984). Regretfully, this group's activities did not continue.

CLASSIFICATION

As in many other countries, classification systems used in Mexican libraries have been mainly Dewey Decimal Classification (DDC) and Library of Congress Classification (LCC). Likewise, discussions about the adoption of a particular system or about the change from one system to another have been similar to those worldwide. At the beginning of the twentieth century, the use of DDC became popular in Mexican libraries. Díaz Mercado y Santamaría (1945, 45), in a speech given to the III National Congress of Librarians, held in 1944, pointed out:

> Once the Melvil Dewey Classification was known in Mexico, there immediately appeared a reasoned movement in favour of this classification . . . In fact, Mister Fernando Pérez Ferrari, Groups Head of the Mexican Commission for the 1900 Universal Exhibition of París, addressed Mister Fernández Leal, at that time Minister of Promotion, saying in a letter of October 27, 1899, the following:

> As soon as the printed brochure that included three different articles about the Decimal Classification for libraries was finished, I tried to give it the most possible circulation in the country so that this very useful system would be known and to make popular its use in public libraries.

At the beginning of the twentieth century, Mexican libraries began to use DDC; however, in many libraries, the Brussels Decimal Classification was adopted because it was considered a more complete variation of DDC. Díaz Mercado y Santamaría (1945) mentioned in a speech given in 1916 at the Third National Congress of Librarians that the National Library of Mexico adopted the Brussels Classification as a substitute for the Namur System. A number of libraries, mainly governmental, adopted this classification system although there were also some from the National University of Mexico. Proposed was "the adoption of the Brussels International Institute Classification system for all the libraries ruled by the Federal Government and for the ones that, for any reason, were considered as incorporated or recognized by the National Executive" (p. 23). The Díaz Mercado and Santamaría proposal was adopted as a resolution of the Congress.

In 1956 Tobías Chávez, head of the UNAM Library Department and professor of the UNAM Colegio de Bibliotecología, criticized the adoption of this resolution: "In Mexican governmental libraries, the Melvil Dewey Decimal system, amplified and punctualized by the Brussels International Bibliography Institute, should be adopted" (Chávez 1957, 232). Chávez states in his criticism: "From this conclusion, in my opinion, the part that says 'amplified and *punctualized* by the Brussels International Bibliography Institute' should be suppressed. The Dewey system was, in fact, amplified in Brussels so it could be applied to museums, archives, and other similar institutions. It was also *punctualized* through the use of new symbols–(O) (.) "." = + - X–and others. However, these new symbols unnecessarily complicate the system as it was first thought of for libraries. In our library field it is almost absurd to complicate what in the beginning was smooth; and if it became complicated, it was for possible extra-library uses" (Chávez 1957, 232). Additionally, Chávez (234) proposed the following:

> The institutions that involve several coordinated libraries should exclusively work with the Dewey Decimal system . . .
>
> It is recommended that all the remaining libraries of the country use the Dewey system, since this would make easier the formation of bibliographic consortiums and the librarian preparation in all aspects . . .
>
> Independent libraries that have a considerable part of their collection classified with the Brussels system or with the United States Library of Congress system could continue using the adopted system.

Tobías Chávez's position represents a break with the European influence on library science and classification in Mexican libraries and the beginning of North American systems and adoption of standards, considered more pragmatic.

Textbooks used in the first schools of library science, such as the Escuela Nacional de Bibliotecarios y Archiveros, were centered on DDC. An example of such educational materials is the one elaborated by Juan B. Iguíniz, *Instructions for the Writing and Formation of Bibliographic Catalogs According to the Melvin Dewey System Adapted by Hispano-American Libraries* (Iguíniz 1954, 15), which was published by the National Library in 1919 (Morales Campos 1988, 59). Another work for the learning of this classification system is Chávez Campomanes mimeographed notes entitled "Melvin Dewey Decimal Classification, adapted by Doctor Ma. Teresa Chávez, course professor; tables" (Morales Campos 1988, 59).

It is important to point out that in the Tobías Chávez document the Library of Congress Classification system was mentioned for the first time. Regarding this classification system, Zamora Rodríguez (1975, 307) states: "[I]n our country, the Congress Classification was implanted for the first time in 1942 at the Anthropology and History National Institute Library. By 1955 there were already three more libraries with that classification: a specialized library (the Cardiology Institute Library) and two university ones (the UNAM Central Library and the UNAM Physics Institute Library)."

As can be observed, the adoption of LCC in Mexican libraries has taken place since the 1950s. One of its main proponents is Professor Pedro Zamora Rodríguez, who did his library science studies at Louisiana State University. In referring to the Zamora work, Salas Estrada (1983, 20) states: "In March of 1954, he occupied the position of head of Technical Processes at the Central Library and was the most important promoter for the adoption of Library of Congress Classification as the official one for this library system [UNAM libraries]." It should also be mentioned that Zamora Rodríguez was one of the professors who founded the UNAM Colegio de Bibliotecología.

In a paper presented at the VI Mexican Conference on Library Science, Zamora Rodríguez (1975, 307) pointed out that after nineteen years since the adoption of LCC at UNAM, there had been a considerable increase in the number of libraries that also used this classification system. Among the libraries that had adopted it were 100 of the most important in the country in the pure and applied sciences, libraries belonging to great and prestigious institutions of higher education, such as UNAM and the National Polytechnic Institute. As in other parts of the world, the adoption of the LCC system was necessary because of the need for cataloging and classification and the lack of specialized personnel for these activities. Zamora Rodríguez stated:

> It has been demonstrated that the use of Library of Congress Classification is cheaper than the Decimal Classification. This low classification cost, together with centralized cataloging or shared cataloging programs, the use of the National Union Catalog, the catalogs . . . of library systems like UNAM's, and also the future possibility of MARC use in Mexico make the Congress classification highly recommended as the most convenient for our bibliographic centers of higher education and research institutions in the future. (p. 309)

It can thus be seen that the most widely used classification systems in Mexico in the second half of the century are the Dewey Decimal Classification and the Library of Congress Classification. Public libraries, coordinated by the Public Libraries National Network, use DDC. Other important libraries that use DDC are the National Library of Mexico and the Library of El Colegio de México, the most important in social sciences and humanities. As the result of a survey conducted among university libraries in Mexico in the 1980s, Martínez Arellano, García López, and Briseño Gómez (1992, 115) learned that 227 libraries used DDC, 270 LCC, one the Universal Decimal Classification (UDC), and 32 their own classification; 280 libraries did not respond to the survey. The survey also shows that the majority of libraries using LCC are found in the capital city. Moreover, it states that "a great majority of university libraries use the Dewey Decimal Classification; however, many of them are adopting Library of Congress Classification due to the advantages in its use, represented by the existence of diverse catalogs and mechanisms that can be used as tools for classification tasks, such as cataloging in publication (CIP), the LIBRUNAM data base, the United States Library of Congress National Union Catalog, and the Bibliofile database" (115-116).

Commenting on the problems of applying LCC in Mexican libraries, Abell Bennett (1975, 324) points out that the main difficulty was the inadequate preparation of library science students. There was a lack of mastery of English and an absence of manuals or guides to support the learning of this classification system. Years later, Roberto Abell contributed to the solution of this problem when he was adviser of Martínez Arellano (1979) and Garza Avalos (1979) studies, which were carried out in the research program of the UNAM General Direction for Libraries. Years later, when Roberto Abell became part of the CUIB research team, he was responsible for a series of manuals to support the learning and management of Library of Congress Classification in Mexican libraries. Following are some of the manuals that have been produced to facilitate the acquisition of these skills:

- *Some Problems in the Management and Application of L. C. Classification in Latin American Materials* (Martínez Arellano 1979).
- *Introduction to Science Classification: Class Q of the Library of Congress System* (Garza Avalos 1979).
- *Management and Application of the Library of Congress Classification in History: Classes C, D, and E-F* (Abell Bennet 1988).
- *Manual for Management and Application of the Library of Congress Classification in Geography, Anthropology, and Recreation: Class G* (Abell Bennett 1989).
- *Manual for Management and Application of the Library of Congress Classification in European Law: Class KJ-KKZ* (Abell Bennett 1992).
- *Management and Application of Tables for Latin American Law in L. C. Classification* [Also available on compact disc] (Martínez Arellano & Abell Bennet 2002).

With the goal of discussing and analyzing problems inherent in the use of Library of Congress Classification, Abell Bennet and Garza Avalos (1989), under CUIB sponsorship, called together Mexican classifiers for a series of meetings in 1985 and 1986. The discussions concluded with the creation of a group to study proposals for modifying LCC. One of the products of this group was the Martínez Arellano work (1987) about classification of Mexican educational institutions.

It is important to point out that the online catalog (LIBRUNAM) of the UNAM General Direction for Libraries is used as a support tool for cataloging in many Mexican libraries. Records may include both LCC and DDC (García López 2000, 76).

SUBJECT HEADINGS

One of the major problems that Mexican libraries have faced during the twentieth century is the lack of a subject headings list that adequately responds to their needs. A first attempt to make such a list that would be useful for the organization of materials in Mexican libraries was carried out by Juana Manrique de Lara. In 1934 he published *Lista de encabezamientos de materia para catálogos diccionarios* [*Subject Headings List for Dictionary Catalogs*]. In spite of this work, however, a lack of uniformity on catalog cards, particularly in subject headings, remained a problem during the first half of the twentieth century. As it has been previously mentioned, Chávez Campomanes (1957, 245) punctuated this fact in the First Conference on Library Science when she pointed out that many LC cards were used as they were with headings in English.

The problem of lack of uniformity in subject headings in Mexican libraries has also been pointed out by Datshkovsky (1957, 236):

> Due to the fact that we did not still have a complete list in Spanish to specify ample subject headings, in library catalogs there is a notable lack of uniformity in their use. In some libraries can be found subject headings based on instructions of the classification manual [the Manrique de Lara one perhaps, since none is indicated], in others the ones that the cataloger thinks are most adequate, and in others headings in English.

Certainly the insufficiency of trained librarians to adequately perform cataloging tasks and the easy accessibility of LC cards during the first half of the twentieth century meant that Mexican catalogers did not worry about creating subject heading lists according to local needs.

Since the 1950s, however, Mexican libraries began to compile their own lists, based on LC subject headings. In speaking of this practice, Datshkovsky (1957, 236), at that time head of the Technical Department of the Mexico Library, the largest and most important public library in the country, stated:

> To achieve our goal, we took as a base the 5th and last edition of the subject headings list used in the dictionary catalog of the Library of Con-

gress in Washington because we considered it the most complete among the ones that had been published in English. Our work has not only been a literal translation of terms or expressions, even though in many cases isolated words unavoidably have to be translated, but also an interpretation of the words or expressions has been made to fit them to the readers' needs, although perhaps giving more importance to those of public libraries than specialized ones.

At the same time, the Organization of American States, through the Colon Commemorative Library of the Pan American Union (Unión Panamericana), undertook a project (1957, 239) "to compile and to publish one of the indispensable manuals for library technical organization, an authorized Spanish subject headings list, with the purpose of easing the interpretation of material that technically is organized in libraries, using as basic works for the compilation of such a list other lists published in Spanish and English and subject headings lists used in important Latin American libraries." As a result of this project, the *Lista de encabezamientos de materia para bibliotecas* [*Subject Headings List for Libraries*], compiled by Carmen Rovira and Jorge Aguayo, was published in 1967.

This subject headings list was also based on the *Library of Congress Subject Headings (LCSH)*, but local terms were incorporated. A second edition of this subject headings list was published in 1985 by the Instituto Colombiano para el Fomento de la Educación Superior (ICFES) [Colombian Institute to the Promotion of Higher Education] and a third one in 1998 by the Luis Angel Arango Library of the Banco de la República de Colombia [Bank of the Republic of Colombia].

Another effort at producing a subject headings list suitable to local needs was done by the National Library of Mexico. Escamilla González (1985, 35) states: "It has been since 1962 when the National Library of Mexico began to create its authorities system to ease the management of information that was processed to serve as a basis for a national system, which would later on be integrated into an international authorities system."

As a result of the authority work accomplished at the National Library of Mexico in 1967, this institution published its "Subject Headings List" compiled by Gloria Escamilla González, which has since come to be known as the "Escamilla List." This work was based on a translation of *LCSH*; however, many local terms were also included. Since its appearance, this list has been adopted by the majority of Mexican libraries for the subject cataloging of their collections. A second edition published in 1978 continues to be used in the majority of Mexican libraries.

As previously mentioned, there were updated editions of the *Subject Headings List for Libraries*, compiled by Carmen Rovira and Jorge Aguayo; however, its use did not become popular among Mexican libraries, which preferred to use the "Escamilla List." One possible explanation for this situation is that the "Escamilla List" incorporated a major number of terms according to the Spanish spoken in Mexico.

Another notable endeavor to create a tool to facilitate subject cataloging work in Mexican libraries is the authority subject catalog of the UNAM General Direction for Libraries. The Technical Department of this institution, like many others in Mexico, decided to translate subject headings taken from *LCSH* to expand on its own authority catalog. Each time a bibliographic record was taken from the *National Union Catalog*, the subject headings were translated into Spanish and incorporated into the authority catalog. At the present time, this authority subject catalog includes nearly 100,000 subject headings. However, there is a lack of synonyms (see references) and hierarchical structures (broader, narrower, and related terms). It was not until 1989 that a project was initiated to turn this translated list into a real authority catalog, which is in process (García López 1999, 216). This authority subject catalog will be the basis for generating the subject headings list that Mexican libraries need.

Another Mexican library that has based its authorities work on translations from *LCSH* is "El Colegio de México" [The College of Mexico] Library; the most important list is of humanities and social sciences in Latin America. Since 1945, this library has used as its subject list *Subject Headings: Castilian-English, English-Castilian,* compiled by Ione Marion Kidder and used in Caracas at the National Library of Venezuela (Vela de la Sancha 1983, 67). This list of subject headings has been constantly enhanced with updates from *LCSH*, the "Escamilla List," and the "Rovira List." At present, this subject authority catalog has approximately 5,000 records (Quijano-Solís, Moreno-Jiménez & Figueroa-Servín 2000).

El Colegio de Mexico Library, together with a university libraries group, has begun a project to create a subject authority catalog in the humanities and social sciences (Quijano-Solís, Moreno-Jiménez & Figueroa-Servín 2000). This project has the support of LC and the Mexico-U.S. Fund for Culture. The project is developed around a database that contains the 5,000 authority records (authors, subjects, and local geographic names) of "El Colegio de Mexico" Library. At the end of this project, it is expected that the humanities and social sciences areas of Mexican libraries will have a Spanish subject headings database to support the cataloging of their collections.

AUTOMATION

The last twenty-five years of the twentieth century are characterized by the rise of automation and the application of new technologies in cataloging and classification. The most outstanding development in Mexico was the creation of the LIBRUNAM database. LIBRUNAM (from Spanish *libro* = book and the Spanish acronym for Universidad Nacional Autónoma de Mexico) was created in 1978 with the goal of expediting cataloging and classification of materials acquired by the UNAM library system where the Technical Department of the UNAM General Direction for Libraries is the centralized agency. The UNAM union catalog of approximately 359,000 records created until 1977 were integrated into the LIBRUNAM database, and it has annually increased with the titles acquired and cataloged in the library system (Martínez-Arellano & Ramírez Nieto 1990). In 2000, LIBRUNAM had grown to approximately 730,000 records. To automate LIBRUNAM records, the MARC format was used; but it was modified according to local needs and characteristics resulting in a version called MARC-DGB. These modificationa are explained in detail in the work *Manual de codificación para catalogadores* [*Codification manual for catalogers*] (Martínez Arellano and García López 1989).

After the creation of the LIBRUNAM database, other automation systems were created for catalog records management. In 1990, in addition to LIBRUNAM, there were LOGICAT, SIABUC, BIBLOS, and CDS/ISIS (Flores y Rodríguez Reyes 1991).

LOGICAT was the second Mexican experience in cataloging automation. It was derived from LIBRUNAM since one of LIBRUNAM's creators developed this new system, oriented to library technical, reference, and administrative processes (Flores y Rodríguez Reyes 1991). In the years following its creation in 1983, LOGICAT was used to produce catalog cards, bibliographic records, lending records, and bookshelf labels with book classification (Martínez-Arellano, García López & Briceño Gómez 1992). In 1990 LOGICAT was used in fifty libraries (Flores and Rodríguez Reyes 1991) and by 1992 in 150 libraries (Martínez-Arellano, García López & Briceño Gómez 1992).

SIABUC, an acronym for Sistema Integral Automatizado de Bibliotecas [Integrated Library System], was created in 1984 by Colima University as a support tool for technical and administrative library functions. This integrated system included the following modules: acquisitions, bibliographic analysis, reference, collection control and lending, and statistical information (Flores y Rodríguez Reyes 1991). Since its creation, SIABUC use has been popular, particularly to support cataloging and classification activities. In 1990 it was reported that SIABUC was used by seventy Mexican libraries and two abroad, in Ecuador and Costa Rica (Flores and Rodríguez Reyes 1991). By 1992, the number had increased to 150 libraries (Martínez-Arellano, García López & Briceño Gómez 1992).

BIBLOS was a system developed to generate a database that would allow the making of catalog cards to be sent together with the books to each library of the Public Libraries National Network. The BIBLIOS database was also reproduced on compact disc and it was sent to public libraries to support the cataloging of locally acquired materials (Martínez-Arellano, García López & Briceño Gómez 1992).

With regard to CDS/ISIS, Flores and Rodríguez Reyes (1991, 185-186) state:

> This system was developed by UNESCO and it is a microcomputer version for the ISIS system prepared by the International Organization of Labor and for MINISIS developed by the Canada IDRC . . . this is an information retrieval system specifically created for bibliographic and textual information management and its distribution is free. Because this system does not require standardization in cataloging records, its use in Mexican libraries has brought about countless problems.

Garduño Vera (1996, 179) reported in 1995 that the number of users of these various systems were as follows: LOGICAT in 357 libraries, SIABUC in 200, Microbiblos in 20, and Microisis in 464. Also, in 1988, LIBRUNAM became the first catalog produced on compact disc. Armendáriz Sánchez (1996) noted in a paper presented at the XXVI Mexican Conference on Library Science that a large number of libraries from 1990 to 1995 produced their catalogs on compact disc.

At present, large libraries, including the UNAM General Direction for Libraries, have opted for the acquisition of integrated systems instead of continuing the development of their own local systems. This decision eliminates the need for expensive local development and specialized human resources. For example, many large libraries in Mexico are currently using the ALEPH system.

CENTRALIZATION AND UNION CATALOGS

In Mexico, as in other libraries throughout the world, librarians have come to realize that centralization of cataloging and classification can result in a shorter time for performing these activities, cost reduction, and elimination of duplicate work. In proposing the establishment of a National Bibliographic

Centre, for example, Ocampo (1957, 179) emphasized these advantages of centralized cataloging.

Likewise, when discussing cataloging activities at the National Autonomous University of Mexico, Zamora Rodríguez (1957, 255) pointed out:

> The centralized cataloging process was initiated at the UNAM in the year 1927 by the Libraries Technical Department [which in 1966 became the General Direction for Libraries]. By 1954, when the Technical Processes Department was created as an integral part of the Central Library, its main functions were to select, to acquire, to register, to classify, and to catalog all the bibliographic material acquired by the Central Library and the 40 departmental libraries at the University.

Zamora Rodríguez was among the first advocates of a UNAM centralized cataloging system, the most important in the country taking into account the number of libraries in the system. He continues:

> When in 1954 the Technical Processes Department of the Central Library began the classification and cataloging of its collections, as well as the works that UNAM acquired for its 40 departmental libraries, we immediately noticed that the work was of a great significance for library science in Mexico; thus this work had to be planned and developed in such a way that it should satisfy not only current needs of university libraries but also future ones. (Zamora Rodríguez 1957, 258)

Indeed, the UNAM union catalog eventually became the most important and the most influential for cataloging activities throughout Mexico. LIBRUNAM was produced on microfiche in 1981 and, for easier access by Mexican libraries, on compact disc in 1988. Because a large number of Mexican libraries do not have enough librarians with proper training to carry out cataloging and classification activities, the development of centralized activities at UNAM meant that for many libraries, particularly those of the state universities, LIBRUNAM would become the main tool to support cataloging and classification. A study carried out by Martínez Arellano (1990) to test LIBRUNAM's value as a support for cataloging bibliographic materials in state university libraries yielded these findings: A sample of 440 titles held by eighteen state universities was collected and searched in LIBRUNAM. Sixty-six percent (294 titles) of the sample was found in LIBRUNAM. At present LIBRUNAM can be accessed through the Web page of General Direction for Libraries at: http://www.dgbiblio.unam.mx.

Another union catalog that has been significant for Mexican libraries is the one at the National Library of Mexico. Similar to other national libraries, the National Library of Mexico has among its objectives the conservation and dissemination of national bibliographic production. Addressing this point, Escamilla González (1980, 115) states:

> Bibliographic control of Mexican publications has been for a long time of great interest to the National Library of Mexico and for its researchers and librarians. In January/February 1967, the library started the task of compiling the Mexican contemporary bibliography, with the intention of publishing it bimonthly and including in it monographs published in Mexico. Since then, fascicles were published every two months until its publication was delayed in 1978.

Since 1967 the National Library of Mexico has edited and distributed its collection of cataloging records in the publication *Bibliografía Mexicana* [*Mexican Bibliography*], which, according to Quiroga, Juárez, Ramos, Zahar and Flores (1987, 319-320) has had three periods:

1. In 1958 the current national bibliography began to be published with the title *Bibliographic Yearbook*, of which seven numbers were published, the last one for 1964. Each yearbook has an average of 5,000 cards representing printed monographic works for each year. The great majority of these works are published in the Federal District.
2. In 1967 the publication changed its name and periodicity. Since then, it has been called *Mexican Bibliography*; and its frequency was bimonthly until 1978. One purpose of this change in frequency was to speed up publication without waiting to gather everything together to edit a yearbook.
3. Since 1979 the change has been radical. The periodicity of fascicles continued being bimonthly until the second fascicle of 1981. The number of cards varies. In 1979 there were 500; the first two bimonthly periods of 1980 contained 700 cards; the third, 800; the fourth, fifth and sixth, 1,000. And since 1981 the *Mexican Bibliography* has been monthly, with each fascicle including 750 cards on average.

The *Bibliografía Mexicana* serves as an auxiliary bibliographic tool for cataloging materials published in Mexico. However, it must be remembered that the bibliography does include only a small percentage of all materials published in Mexico. Furthermore, the delay in publication meant that materials published in one year did not appear until the next year's issue. As a result, backlogs developed (Martínez Arellano 1982a). There were attempts to automate the *Bibliografía Mexicana*, but they were not successful. Publication was suspended by the end of the 1980s.

FINAL CONSIDERATIONS

The present article has shown the evolution of cataloging and classification in Mexico during the twentieth century. One of the main problems that Mexican libraries have faced is a scarcity of librarians adequately prepared to catalog and classify their collections. Although schools of library science have been established since mid-century and that number has increased by six in recent years, the number of students is still insufficient to meet the demands of libraries, not only for cataloging and classification but also for other library activities. The lack of librarians is more acute in the states since many of them prefer to work in Mexico City. Thus, libraries in the states have become dependent on using LIBRUNAM as a cataloging and classification source for organizing their collections; nevertheless, the problem of organizing local collections continues, and there are cataloging and classification backlogs in many Mexican libraries.

Moreover, it has not yet been possible to create union catalogs at a national level, which would, of course, support cataloging and classification. The challenge for Mexican librarians and libraries in the twenty-first century will be to develop union catalogs. Likewise, the continuation of *Bibliografía Mexicana* as an important union catalog should be resumed. Automation offers many advantages and possibilities for developing the union catalogs that the country requires.

Although many Mexican libraries use AACR2, it remains necessary for catalogers to strive for better interpretation of cataloging standards. Moreover, it is necessary to promote the expansion of manuals for the same purpose. Additionally, it is important to increase the participation of Mexican catalogers in international meetings and to expand their involvement on committees that discuss AACR. There should also be increased involvement in activities relating to DDC and LCC, the two major classifications in Mexico.

Finally, one of the major problems for organizing bibliographic materials in Mexican libraries has been the lack of a subject headings list to cover local language features and other local needs. Therefore, another challenge for Mexican librarians in the twenty-first century should be the generation of that subject headings list. To accomplish this task, automation and information technologies offer many advantages and opportunities that should be used jointly with the experience of large libraries.

REFERENCES

Abell Bennett, Roberto. 1975. Aplicación de la clasificación de la Biblioteca del Congreso en bibliotecas mexicanas: basada en la ponencia del Prof. Pedro Zamora [Application of the Library of Congress classification in Mexican libraries: based on the paper of Professor Pedro Zamora]. In VI Jornadas Mexicanas de Biblioteconomía: *Integración del servicio nacional bibliotecario* [VI Mexican Conference on Librarianship: *Iintegration of the national service*], 320-324. México: Asociación Mexicana de Bibliotecarios.

_____. 1988. *Manejo y aplicación de la clasificación de la Biblioteca del Congreso de Estados Unidos a la historia: clases C, D y E-F* [*Management and application of the Library of Congress Classification in History: Classes C, D, and E-F*]. México: UNAM, Centro Universitario de Investigaciones Bibliotecológicas.

_____. 1989. *Manual para el manejo y aplicación de la clasificación del Congreso a la geografía, antropología y recreación: clase G* [*Manual for Management and Application of the Library of Congress Classification in Geography, Anthropology, and Recreation: Class G*]. México: UNAM, Centro Universitario de Investigaciones Bibliotecológicas.

_____. 1992. *Manual para el manejo y aplicación de la clasificación del Congreso al Derecho Europeo, subclases KJ-KKZ* [*Manual for management and application of the Library of Congress Classification in European Law: Class KJ-KKZ*]. México: UNAM, Centro Universitario de Investigaciones Bibliotecológicas.

Abell Bennet, Roberto, and María Luisa Garza Avalos. 1989. *Memoria de las cuatro reuniones nacionales sobre la normalización del uso en México del sistema de clasificación de la Biblioteca del Congreso de Estados Unidos (LC)* [*Proceedings of the four national meetings on normalization for use of the Library of Congress Classification (LC)*] México: UNAM, Centro Universitario de Investigaciones Bibliotecológicas.

Adelman, A., and S. Ortega Salazar. 1995. *An international students guide to Mexican universities*. México: Secretaría de Educación Pública.

Armendáriz Sánchez, Saúl. 1996. La producción de información compactada: seis años de edición de CD-ROMs en México [The production of compact information: six years of CD-ROM production in Mexico]. In XXVI Jornadas Mexicanas de Biblioteconomía: *Memorias* [XXVI Mexican Conference on Librarianship: *Proceedings*], 103-114. México: Asociación Mexicana de Bibliotecarios.

Chávez, Tobías. 1957. Clasificación y reclasificación [Classification and reclassification]. In Primeras Jornadas Mexicanas de Biblioteconomía, Bibliografía y Canje: *Informe final* [First Mexican Conference on Librarianship, Bibliography and Exchange: *Final report*], 230-234. México: Asociación Mexicana de Bibliotecarios.

Chávez Campomanes, María Teresa. 1957. Unificación de las normas de catalogación [Unification of cataloging norms]. In Primeras Jornadas Mexicanas de Biblioteconomía, Bibliografía y Canje: *Informe final* [First Mexican Conference on Librarianship, Bibliography and Exchange: *Final report*], 244-248. México: Asociación Mexicana de Bibliotecarios.

Datschkovsky, Raisa. 1957. Encabezamientos de materia [Subject headings]. In Primeras Jornadas Mexicanas de Biblioteconomía, Bibliografía y Canje: *Informe final* [First Mexican Conference on Librarianship, Bibliography and Exchange: *Final report*], 235-238. México: Asociación Mexicana de Bibliotecarios.

Díaz Mercado, Joaquín, and Atenógenes Santamaría. 1945. Tres sistemas de clasificación: ponencia presentada al III Congreso Nacional de Bibliotecarios [Three classification systems: paper submitted to the III National Congress of Librarians]. In M. M. Hardman [i.e., Herdman]. *Clasificación Bibliográfica Decimal: manual compendiado del Instituto Internacional de Bruselas: manual preliminar [Decimal Bibliographic Classification: abridged manual of the International Institute of Brussels: preliminary manual].* México: Antigua Librería Robredo.

Escamilla González, Gloria. 1976. *Reglas de Catalogación Angloamericanas, texto norteamericano: capítulo 6, monografías publicadas independientemente, incluye capítulo 9, reproducciones fotográficas y de otra índole y está revisado de acuerdo con la International Standard Bibliographic Description (monografías) [Anglo-American cataloging rules, North American text: chapter 6, separately published monographs, incorporating chapter 9, photographic and other reproductions, and revised to accord with the International Standard Description (monographs)].* México: UNAM, Instituto de Investigaciones Bibliográficas.

_____. 1979. *Interpretación catalográfica de los libros [Cataloging interpretation of books].* México: UNAM, Instituto de Investigaciones Bibliográficas. Reimpreso en 1987.

_____. 1980. Las servicios de la *Bibliografía Mexicana* a los usuarios [Services of the *Mexican Bibliography* to the users]. In XI Jornadas Mexicanas de Biblioteconomía, *"El usuario": memorias* [XI Mexican Conference on Librarianship, *"The user": proceedings*], 107-121. México: Asociación Mexicana de Bibliotecarios.

_____. (1981). *Manual de catalogación descriptiva [Manual of descriptive cataloging].* México: Consejo Nacional de Ciencia y Tecnología. Reprinted in 1988 by the Instituto de Investigaciones Bibliográficas.

_____. 1985. El sistema de autoridades de la Biblioteca Nacional de México dentro del marco del sistema internacional de la IFLA [The authorities system of México's National Library in the framework of the IFLA international system]. In II Coloquio de Investigación Bibliotecológica: *Memorias*, ed. E. Morales Campos [II Coloquium of Library Science Research: *Proceedings*]. México: UNAM, Centro Universitario de Investigaciones Bibliotecológicas.

Flores, Gustavo, and Victórico Rodríguez Reyes. 1991. Proyecto Colima [Colima Project]. In XXI Jornadas Mexicanas de Biblioteconomía: *Memorias* [XXI Mexican Conference on Librarianship: *Proceedings*], 177-193. México: Asociación Mexicana de Bibliotecarios.

García López, Carlos. 1999. El trabajo de control de autoridad en línea de la Dirección General de Bibliotecas de la UNAM. [Online authority control work at UNAM General Direction for Libraries]. In *Control Bibliográfico Universal: el control bibliográfico en América Latina y el Carbe hacia el tercer milenio,* ed. R. Garduño [*Universal Bibliographic Control: bibliographic control in Latin America and the Caribbean near the third milenium*], 216-230. México: UNAM, Centro Universitario de Investigaciones Bibliotecológicas.

García López, Carlos. 2000. Technical processes and the technological development of the library system in the National Autonomous University of México. *Cataloging & Classification Quarterly* 30, no. 1: 73-90.

Garduño Vera, Roberto. 1996. Uso de tecnologías de la información en el control bibliográfico [Use of information technologies in bibliographic control]. In

XXVI Jornadas Mexicanas de Biblioteconomía: *Memorias* [XXVI Mexican Conference on Librarianship: *Proceedings*], 175-186. México: Asociación Mexicana de Bibliotecarios.

Garza Avalos, María Luisa. 1979. Introducción a la clasificación de Ciencias: Clase Q en el sistema de la Biblioteca del Congreso de Estados Unidos [Introduction to the Science classification: class Q of the Library of Congress system]. Thesis (licentiate) in library science, Escuela Nacional de Biblioteconomía y Archivonomía.

Iguíniz, Juan. B. 1954. Apuntes para la enseñanza de la biblioteconomía en México [Notes for teaching of librarianship in México]. *Boletín de la Escuela Nacional de Bibliotecarios y Archivistas* 2(3-4): 13-17.

Lira Luna, Daniel. 1999. Gloria Escamilla González: principal traductora, principal promotora de las Reglas de Catalogación Angloamericanas, ahora en su 2ª edición revisada, 1988, con modificaciones de 1993 [Gloria Escamilla González: main translator, main promoter of the Anglo-American Cataloging Rules, now in its 2nd. revised edition, 1988, with 1993 modifications]. *Liber: Revista de Bibliotecología* 1(1): 17-22.

Martínez Arellano, Filiberto Felipe. 1979. Algunos problemas en el manejo y aplicación del sistema de Clasificación L. C. en materiales latinoamericanos [*Some Problems in the management and application of L.C. Classification in Latin American materials*]. Thesis (licentiate) in Library Science, Escuela Nacional de Biblioteconomía y Archivonomía.

_____. 1982. LIBRUNAM como apoyo a las actividades de catalogación y clasificación en las bibliotecas mexicanas [LIBRUNAM as a support tool for cataloging and classification in Mexican libraries]. *Ciencia Bibliotecaria* 5(1): 38-43.

_____. 1982a. Análisis del uso de la *Bibliografía Mexicana* en el Departamento de Procesos Técnicos de la Dirección General de Bibliotecas de la Universidad Nacional Autónoma de México [Use analysis of the *Bibliografía Mexicana* in the Technical Processes Department of the General Direction for Libraries, National Autonomous University of México]. In XII Jornadas Mexicanas de Biblioteconomía: *Memorias* [XII Mexican Conference on Librarianship: *Proceedings*], 53-62). México: Asociación Mexicana de Bibliotecarios.

_____. 1987. *Ampliación a la parte de instituciones educativas de México (LE7-9) dentro de la clasificación de la Biblioteca del Congreso de los Estados Unidos* [*Expansion to the section for Mexican education institutions (LE7-9) in the Library of Congress Classification*]. México: UNAM. Centro Universitario de Investigaciones Bibliotecológicas.

_____. 2000. Library science education in México. *Journal of Education for Library and Information Science* 41(2): 147-157.

Martínez Arellano, Filiberto Felipe, and Roberto Abell Bennet. 2002. Manejo y aplicación de las tablas para el Derecho Latinoamericano en el Sistema de Clasificación L.C. [*Management and application of tables for Latin American Law in L. C. Classification*]. México: UNAM, Centro Universitario de Investigaciones Bibliotecológicas. [Also available on compact disc].

Martínez Arellano Filiberto Felipe, and Carlos García López. 1989. *Manual de codificación para catalogadores* [*Codification manual for catalogers*]. México. UNAM, Centro Universitario de Investigaciones Bibliotecológicas.

Martínez Arellano, Filiberto Felipe, and Alejandro Ramírez Nieto. 1990. The data banks of the General Direction of UNAM Libraries. In NIT 9O, 3rd International Conference New Information Technology: *Proceedings*, ed. C. Chen, 209-216. West Newton, Mass.: MicroUse Information.

Martínez Arellano Filiberto Felipe, Carlos García López, and Jorge Briseño Gómez. 1992. Los procesos técnicos en las bibliotecas mexicanas: situación general en 1991 [Technical processes in Mexican libraries: general situation in 1991]. In *La bibliotecología en el México actual y sus tendencias* [*Library science in the current México and its trends*], 105-132. México. UNAM, Dirección General de Bibliotecas.

Morales Campos, Estela. 1984. Estudio comparativo de los códigos de catalogación más usados en México [Comparative study of the cataloging codes more used in México]. México: UNAM, Centro Universitario de Investigaciones Bibliotecológicas.

———. 1988. *Educación bibliotecológica en México 1915-1954* [*Library science education in México 1915-1954*]. México: UNAM, Centro Universitario de Investigaciones Bibliotecológica.

Ocampo, María Luisa. 1957. La necesidad del establecimiento de un centro bibliográfico nacional [The necessity for the estabishment of a national bibliographic center]. In Primeras Jornadas Mexicanas de Biblioteconomía, Bibliografía y Canje: *Informe final* [First Mexican Conference on Librarianship, Bibliography and Exchange: *Final report*], 177-180. México: Asociación Mexicana de Bibliotecarios.

Ornelas, C., and D. C. Levy. 1991. México. In *International higher education: an encyclopedia*, ed. P. G. Altbach, 943-945. New York: Garland.

Quijano Solís, Alvaro, Pilar Maria Moreno Jiménez, and Reynaldo Figueroa-Servín. 2000. Automated authority files of Spanish-language subject headings. *Cataloging & Classification Quarterly* 29, no. 1-2: 209-224.

Quiroga, Luz Marina, Aurora Juárez, Martín Ramos, Juana Zahar, and Gerardo Flores. 1987. Una nueva etapa en la historia de la *Bibliografía Mexicana*: su automatización [A new era in the history of the *Bibliografía Mexicana*: its automation]. *Boletín del Instituto de Investigaciones Bibliográficas* 2 (Época 1): 319-344.

Rodríguez Gallardo, Adolfo. 1996. Vasconcelos y las bibliotecas [Vasconcelos and the libraries]. In Mesa Redonda "Las Bibliotecas en la Vida de México de Carranza a Nuestros Días" [Round Table "Libraries in the Life of Mexico's from Carranza to the Present Day"]. Mexico: UNAM, Centro Universitario de Investigaciones Bibliotecológicas.

———. 1998. Hacia la recuperación humanística del bibliotecólogo [Toward the humanist recovery of the librarian]. Doctoral thesis, Universidad Nacional Autónoma de México.

Salas Estrada, Eduardo. 1983. Pedro Zamora Rodríguez: apuntes para la biografía de un bibliotecario eminente [Pedro Zamora Rodríguez: notes for the biography of an eminent librarian]. In XIV Jornadas Mexicanas de Biblioteconomía: *Memorias* [XIV Mexican Conference on Librarianship: *Proceedings*], 19-20. México: Asociación Mexicana de Bibliotecarios.

Solís Valdespino, Ofelia (1980). El Colegio de Bibliotecología y Archivología [The College of Library and Archive Sciences]. (Licenciate thesis, Universidad Nacional Autónoma de México).

Solís Valdespino, Ofelia. 1984. La problemática del asiento de autores personales, nombres geográficos, autores corporativos y títulos uniformes en cinco unidades de procesos técnicos en la Ciudad de México. [*The problems of entry of personal authors, geographic names, corporate authors, and uniform titles in five technical processing units in México City*]. México: UNAM, Centro Universitario de Investigaciones Bibliotecológicas.

Tecuatl Quechol, María Graciela Martha. 2000. Los Bibliotecarios del Distrito Federal: una análisis social [Federal District librarians: a social analysis]. Master's thesis in libraru science, Universidad Nacional Autónoma de México.

Unión Panamericana. 1957. Compilación de una lista al español de ecabezamientos de materia para uso en la organización de bibliotecas [Compilation of a Spanish subject headings list for use in the organization of libraries]. In Primeras Jornadas Mexicanas de Biblioteconomía, Bibliografía y Canje: *Informe final* [First Mexican Conference on Librarianship, Bibliography and Exchange: *Final report*], 239-243. México: Asociación Mexicana de Bibliotecarios.

Vela de la Sancha, Juan. 1983. Bases teórica-practicas para la revisión y corección del catálogo de materias: el caso de El Colegio de México [Theoretical-practical foundations for review and correction of the subject catalog: the case of El Colegio de Mexico]. Thesis (licentiate) in library science, Escuela Nacional de Biblioteconomía y Archivonomía.

Zamora Rodríguez, Pedro. 1957. Catálogos central y en depósito: bases para su organización [Centralized and union catalogs: foundations for their organization]. In Primeras Jornadas Mexicanas de Biblioteconomía, Bibliografía y Canje: *Informe final* [First Mexican Conference on Librarianship, Bibliography and Exchange: *Final inform*], 254-260. México: Asociación Mexicana de Bibliotecarios.

_____. 1975. Sistemas de clasificación de bibliotecas académicas, bibliotecas especializadas y bibliotecas públicas grandes [Classification systems of academic libraries, specialized libraries, and large public libraries]. In VI Jornadas Mexicanas de Biblioteconomía: integración del servicio nacional bibliotecario [VI Mexican Conference on Librarianship: integration of the national service], 306-319. México: Asociación Mexicana de Bibliotecarios.

Three Book Collectors of Imperial Spain

Ruth C. Carter

SUMMARY. During the sixteenth and seventeenth centuries, Spain's Empire flourished. This article discusses leading Spanish bibliophiles of its golden age with detailed attention on the private libraries of Don Fernando Colón; Diego Sarmiento de Acuña, Count of Gondomar; and Gaspar de Guzman, Count-Duke of Olivares. Their libraries are known today through extant portions of collections and/or catalogs describing each item. Colón, whose collections approached 30,000 items, established detailed procedures for catalog entries by author, title, and subject and placed an emphasis on facilitating use of his collection. *[Article copies available for a fee from The Haworth Document Delivery Service: 1-800-HAWORTH. E-mail address: <getinfo@haworthpressinc.com> Website: <http://www.HaworthPress.com> © 2002 by The Haworth Press, Inc. All rights reserved.]*

KEYWORDS. Bibliophiles, book collectors, catalog rules, private collection catalogs, Imperial Spain, sixteenth century Spain, seventeenth

Ruth C. Carter, PhD, MS, MA, is Editor, *Cataloging & Classification Quarterly* and *Journal of Internet Cataloging* and Co-Editor, *Journal of Archival Organization.* She is retired from the University of Pittsburgh Library System where she held many positions including Assistant Director, Automated and Technical Services; Head, Archives Service Center; and Curator of Historical Collections.

Address correspondence to: Ruth C. Carter, 121 Pikemont Drive, Wexford, PA 15090-8447 (E-mail: rccarter@nauticom.net).

The author thanks Michael Carpenter for providing critical information related to Don Fernando Colón and for commenting on this paper.

[Haworth co-indexing entry note]: "Three Book Collectors of Imperial Spain." Carter, Ruth C. Co-published simultaneously in *Cataloging & Classification Quarterly* (The Haworth Information Press, an imprint of The Haworth Press, Inc.) Vol. 35, No. 1/2, 2002, pp. 255-264; and: *Historical Aspects of Cataloging and Classification* (ed: Martin D. Joachim) The Haworth Information Press, an imprint of The Haworth Press, Inc., 2003, pp. 255-264. Single or multiple copies of this article are available for a fee from The Haworth Document Delivery Service [1-800-HAWORTH, 9:00 a.m. - 5:00 p.m. (EST). E-mail address: getinfo@haworthpressinc.com].

255

century Spain, Fernando Colón, Gaspar de Guzman, Count-Duke of Olivares, Diego Sarmiento de Acuña, Count of Gondomar

Spain's days of greatest glory took place in the sixteenth and seventeenth centuries. During its golden age its citizens included many individuals who amassed outstanding personal libraries. Among the most famous bibliophiles of the era were Don Fernando Colón; Diego Sarmiento de Acuña, Count of Gondomar; Gaspar de Guzmán, Count-Duke of Olivares; Don Fernando Afan de Ribera, Duke of Alcalá; Luis Benanides de Carrillo y Toledo, Marquis of Caracena; Nicolás Antonio; and a Doctor Casante. Several other influential bibliophiles were cardinals or archbishops. King Philip II (b.1527, r. 1556-1598) influenced the sixteenth century surge of libraries and private collecting in Spain through his love of books and desire to have the library at El Escorial become the best in the world.[1]

Following is a look at three of the men listed above and their book collections with attention given, where known, to the organization and cataloging of the collections. Colón, Gondomar, and Olivares lives span the years 1488 to 1646, and, in effect, witnessed Spain's rise as an imperial power and the beginning of its rapid decline. Their background and personal wealth varied somewhat, but all had connections with the court of the Spanish monarchs. Olivares, in fact, was the most powerful person in the Spanish Empire at the height of his power. Undoubtedly, their positions of association with the court, the travels they made, and the personal contacts which they formed gave these men special opportunities to pursue their book-collecting interests.

DON FERNANDO COLÓN

Don Fernando Colón, the first of the three chronologically, was born in Cordoba on August 15, 1488, four years before his famous father, Cristóbal Colón [Christopher Columbus] left for his first voyage of discovery. The elder Colón took particular interest in Fernando, his second son, and especially in his education.[2] Fernando accompanied his father on the fourth voyage to the New World in 1502. Later he made two additional voyages to the Western Hemisphere. These were followed by journeys to Asia and Africa as well as many travels throughout Europe as part of the court of Charles V (b. 1500, r. 1516-1556) [Charles I of Spain]. Colón, a diligent, talented man with good judgment, used these opportunities to acquire profound knowledge in geography, navigation, and natural history. Following his inclination to studies and friendship with books, he formed a select and copious library of more than

20,000 volumes of printed works and manuscripts.[3] Francisco Vindel, writing in the twentieth century, termed Fernando Colón the best bibliophile [of Spain] not just in his time, but ever.[4] Before Colón's death in 1539 he had begun work on the establishment of a College of Mathematics in Seville that Charles V had authorized. Unfortunately, Colón died prematurely, before he had completed his plans for the college.[5]

During his lifetime Fernando Colón frequently spent time with the intellectuals of his day, and they presented him with many copies of their books. "His taste was catholic and his books represent to an unusual degree the culture of the day. One finds there the dramatic works of that century [the sixteenth], the poetry, letters and pamphlets on the Reformation, on the coronation and on the plague; prognostications for the coming year, . . . and many little novels and romances of chivalry."[6] Furthermore, the books of Cristóbal Colón, a priceless treasure, constitute an immensely important component of the contents of his collection. These bear the admiral's own marginal notes.

One interesting category of material unfortunately no longer exists; however, from Don Fernando's catalogs it is known that he had many loose sheets on the science of his time. He was very methodical in his collecting as he made a careful record of both gifts and purchases. On the first or last page of each book, he noted its source and the price he paid both in foreign money and Spanish gold if it was purchased.[7]

Perhaps most significantly for the future of libraries and cataloging, Don Colón established detailed procedures or rules for the entries in the catalogs and indexes of his collection and any subsequent additions. These rules were set forth in Colon's later days in a letter memorandum to the Spanish King, the Hapsburg Emperor Charles V. Colón envisioned a library that would hold books in all languages, in all disciplines, and from all parts of the world. He specified that scholars should have access to his collection, for he had nothing hidden in it.[8]

In setting forth principles for maintaining his collection and its access in perpetuity, Colón specified the following separate indexes or catalogs:

- By author alphabetically and within author alphabetically by title of the work.
- By title in alphabetical order under general topic such as Theology, Canonical Law, Civil Law, etc.
- By subject alphabetically in alphabetical order and within subject alphabetically by author with a notation of whether the subject is treated briefly or in depth.
- By numerical sequence a summary of the contents of each book and its main argument.[9]

Each book received an accession or sequential number and the entry in the list with summary contents also included various coded symbols according to a complex table. Don Fernando, for whom his library was his only preoccupation, painstakingly handwrote the catalogs and indexes.[10] Not all remain today, but those that do are part of the Columbine Library in Seville.

In his will Fernando Colón left his library intact to his oldest nephew, Don Luis Colón, with the condition that each year a certain amount be spent on its maintenance. Don Luis, a youth of nineteen years in 1539, did not have his uncle's interest in and love of books, and he allowed the collection to change hands. Finally after several transfers, in 1552 the collection and Colón's detailed manuscript registers or catalogs became the permanent possessions of the Cathedral at Seville.[11] By this time most of the Spanish texts were lost.[12] However, while the remaining collection is perhaps only fifty percent of its original size, at the time Edwards wrote in 1859, it still contained approximately 18,000 volumes, including an especially precious manuscript "in which Cristóbal Colón tried to satisfy the Inquisition that his discovery had been spiritually predicted. The collection also has some books that were his cabin companions, and bear the Admiral's MS notes."[13]

Because the Columbine Library, which has been termed the grandest library [private] of its time,[14] is extant today as a separate entity, it, of the three private collections compiled by bibliophiles of Imperial Spain that are considered herein, has the most direct significance to us almost five centuries later. Colón's library is invaluable because "it reveals to us the intimate character of a courtier and diplomat of the sixteenth century and his relation to the thought of his time."[15] Perhaps even more significant to the history of cataloging, its collector Don Fernando Colón, the most famous, methodical and meticulous bibliophile of his time,[16] established detailed procedures for catalog and index entries that presaged formal cataloging rules of future centuries.

DIEGO SARMIENTO DE ACUÑA, COUNT OF GONDOMAR

In 1567, nearly thirty years after the death of Don Fernando Colón, Diego Sarmiento de Acuña, Count of Gondomar was born in the province of Galicia to one of its leading families. As his parents hoped to enter him into public life, they saw to it that he received the best possible education.[17] There is no doubt his youthful exposure to some of the scholars of the day and many books helped create his intense interest in building his own library.

After Sarmiento held a number of provincial governmental posts, King Philip III (b. 1579, r. 1598-1621) made the Galician a count and appointed him ambassador to the Court of King James I of England in 1613. In that position he had ample opportunity to display his diplomatic talents. Further, he was completely devoted to the concepts of the greatness of the Spanish monarchy and the supremacy of the Roman Catholic Church. Despite being a master of the diplomatic method, Sarmiento was considered "too prejudiced and unsympathetic to be a statesman."[18]

His prejudices carried over into his attitudes toward printing and the contents of books current in the early seventeenth century. At one point Sarmiento suggested the creation of a board to censor contents of books that were to be printed and/or distributed. In the count's opinion, too many disorderly books were being printed and published each day. He considered it necessary that only positive aspects of the Spanish monarchy ever see print. This would ensure the perpetuation of the heroic deeds and virtues of the monarchs as well as the valor and loyalty of their subjects and thus the honor of the nation.[19]

Yet, despite whatever opposition he may have had to the contents of some of the books of his day, the Count of Gondomar built up a great personal library. He and other contemporary nobles prided themselves on their patronage of the arts, including assistance to writers.[20] His library was famous in his own day and was even characterized as being "princely."[21] However, no matter how much the ruling class of Gondomar's generation supported Spain's literature, that same generation probably must take a good sized share of the blame for the collapse of the Spanish Empire. Due in part to the narrow-minded attitudes of men like Gondomar, which were characteristic of the "closed" Spain of the seventeenth century, their society "lost the strength that comes from dissent, and they lacked the breadth of vision and the strength of character to break with a past that could no longer serve as a reliable guide to the future."[22]

Apparently Gondomar's library did not remain intact although details as to its contents or disposition could not be located.[23] Presumably, in addition to collecting in Spain, his library would have had significant holdings obtained during the nearly ten years he spent in England. Its holdings also no doubt included his own correspondence. Until relatively recent years the private library of the Spanish Crown had many of his letters, including those "received from the lords, ladies and gentlemen [of England] whom he bribed for Philip III. . . ." Together with his own letters on lighter social subjects they form a treasure for the study of the Shakespearian period.[24]

GASPAR DE GUZMÁN, COUNT-DUKE OF OLIVARES

Gaspar de Guzmán, Count-Duke of Olivares, was the favorite and leading minister of King Philip IV (b. 1606, r. 1621-1665) of Spain. An aristocrat from Andalusia, he was born in 1587 in Rome, Italy, where his father served as the ambassador from Spain. Originally destined for an ecclesiastical career, Guzmán received a university education at the University of Salamanca. The death of his older brother Don Jerónimo turned Don Gaspar's education at the university to an education at the court under his father's tutelage.[25] Eventually he gained office as a gentleman of the chamber to Prince Philip. Olivares was a restless, dynamic, and forceful figure. Yet his inner conflict between his idealistic and practical impulses always hampered his achievements.[26] Despite his failings, his contemporaries were unanimous in acknowledging his eloquence and erudition. His breadth of knowledge was amazing with his personal library being one indicator of his learning. G. Marañón, in his biography of Olivares, summarizes the importance of books and learning to the count as follows [in translation]:

> The Count-Duke had, in effect, a passion for books. It was inherited, without doubt, from his father "el papelista"; initiated in his childhood residence in Rome and Naples; later in his university years at Salamanca; and, finally, in the period of literary life, above all in Seville, where he was intimate with so many writers and poets, Olivares became one of the illustrious bibliophiles of the Spain of his time. Afterwards, absorbed in affairs of the State, he not only never forgot his youthful likings but always considered his magnificent library the principal ornament of his house and to which he dedicated special words of love even in the solemn hour of his last will.[27]

A catalog remains of Olivares' library. It included at least 2,700 printed works and 1,400 manuscripts predominantly in the Latin language or the Tuscan dialect. Many of the books were about history, travel, or politics. Some concerned theology and religion.[28] His library was intended for studying; and although Olivares possessed many novels, tales of chivalry and verses, in his collection, those he preferred most were the classical works. The influence of the latter pervaded his personality, his concepts of Spain's future, and most of his actions. Many of these derived from his readings that stimulated a desire to imitate the great persons of antiquity. Without doubt, the count-duke was a reader and not just a collector of books. Further, Olivares' library held a great many works on geography and maps.[29]

An erudite monk named Father Alaejos authored the catalog of Olivares' library entitled "Biblioteca selecta del Conde-Duque de San Lucar, Gran Chanciller. De materias hebreas, griegas, arabiga, latinas, castellanas, francesas, tudescas, italianas, lemosinas, portuguesas, etc." The catalog was divided into two parts. The first included access by author arranged alphabetically within each different language of the texts with printed books and manuscript books listed separately. Secondly, there was an integrated author listing for both types of books regardless of language. Each book had a number; and its size, octavo or quarto or folio, was indicated.[30] Olivares gave minute instructions for the arrangement of the volumes and the method of searching for them. He took great pride in the luxurious binding of each volume, which included the coat of arms of his family on the book cover.[31]

Olivares inherited many of the books he owned from his father. Many others he acquired when bookstores broke up or dissolved. He also bought many items in his collections of Greek and Latin manuscripts from the humanist Alvar Gómez de Castro. Olivares acquired some of his papers through an evident abuse of power in which he simply ordered the confiscation of desired materials, particularly those of an archival nature. Apparently this was not an uncommon method of acquisition used by book lovers who became high ranking ministers. Though their methods were questionable, Olivares and others thus conserved many public documents that might otherwise have been lost.[32]

Through 1641 Olivares governed Spain with an iron hand as Philip IV had little interest in politics and allowed his chief minister to have free reign. But by early 1642 Olivares had made too many enemies, and the king reluctantly forced him to retire at the end of January.[33] Having time now, welcome or not, the Count-Duke concentrated on making provisions for his library after his death. Olivares left instructions regarding the disposition of his library in his will dated 1642. He specifically wanted his library to remain intact for posterity and thereby perpetuate the fame of his erudition through the ages. Unfortunately, the books did not have the same value to his widow that they had for the count-duke. In her eyes they primarily represented the means of raising money to pay for masses for herself and her husband. As a result, many of the books passed to several convents in Spain while others ultimately reached the hands of various book lovers of Spain and other countries. Today many books from Olivares' collection have reached official libraries, including the Biblioteca Nacional in Madrid. Probably those items from the collection now in The Escorial are the largest quantity in any single location.[34]

SIGNIFICANCE OF THE BOOK COLLECTORS OF IMPERIAL SPAIN

Spain in the sixteenth and seventeenth centuries had numerous bibliophiles who devoted a great deal of time and effort in building their personal book collections. Unfortunately, not many of the collections have survived intact. But in most cases when the books are still extant, no matter how widely dispersed, some records of ownership still exists; and, consequently, it is possible to compile data on individual collections, for example the collection of the Count of Gondomar. In some cases, while a library may be scattered, a catalog of it remains. These extant catalogs are invaluable. By providing bibliographic descriptions of items in the libraries of private collectors, they facilitate documentation of existing items and their collector(s). Additionally, in the role of the catalog as history and bibliography, they, including the catalogs of the library of Don Fernando Colón and the Count-Duke of Olivares, provide information about books and manuscripts that no longer exist. From what is known of the various collections today it is possible to gain an understanding of the material available in print and manuscript in Imperial Spain as well as the personalities of the men who built the collections. The latter is of particular significance because in many cases men like Gondomar and Olivares played prominent roles in shaping the policies and destiny of Spain and, therefore, indirectly, Western civilization. Colón, with the largest personal library, thought about how users would approach his catalogs and formally proposed giving access by author, title, and subject. Those access points remain central to catalogs five centuries later and are part of the heritage of Imperial Spain and its book collectors.

NOTES

1. Francisco Vindel, *Los bibliófilos y sus bibliotecas: desde la introducción de la imprenta en España hasta nuestros días* (Madrid, 1934), 20-21.

2. Rudolfo del Castillo, "Documento inédito del Siglo XVI referente a D. Fernando Colón," Real Academia de la Historia, *Boletin* 33 (1898): 115.

3. *Diccionario enciclopedico hispano-americano.* s.v. "Colón, Fernando."

4. Vindel, 16.

5. *Diccionario enciclopedico.*

6. Mary Louise Foster, "Three Great Spanish Libraries," *Library Journal* 56 (1931):10-11.

7. Ibid., 11.

8. Henry Harrissee, *D. Fernando Colón, historiador de su padre: ensayo crítico,* Sociedad de bibliófilos andaluces, ser. 1, no. 3. (Seville: D. Rafael Tarasco, 1871), 44, 117-120.

9. Ibid., 117-121. (Also in Harrisse, *Bibliographie de quatre cents pièces gothiques, françaises, italiennes & latines du commencement du XVIe siècle non décrites jusqu'ici* (Paris: H. Welter, 1877), 284-286.

10. Harrissee, *D. Fernando Colón,* 23.

11. Archer M. Huntington, *Catalogue of the Library of Ferdínand Columbus: Reproduced in Facsimile from the Unique Manuscript in the Columbine Library of Seville* (New York: 1905), pref.

12. Foster, 11.

13. Edward Edwards, *Memoirs of Libraries* (1859; reprint, New York: Burt Franklin, 1965), 553.

14. Rafael Altamira y Crevea, *Historia de España y de la civilización española,* vol. 3 (Barcelona: Herederos de Juan Gili, 1906), 548.
15. Foster, 11.
16. Harrissee, *D. Fernando Colón,* 22-23.
17. Francis Hamilton Lyon, *Diego de Sarmiento de Acuña, conde de Gondomar* (Oxford: Blackwell, 1910), 8-9.
18. Ibid., 10-11.
19. Diego de Acuña, conde de Gondomar, *Cinco cartas de D. Diego Sarmiento de Acuña,* Publicados de la Sociedad de bibliófilos españoles, vol. 4 (Madrid: Impr. de M. Rivadeneyra), 114-115.
20. J. H. Elliot, *Imperial Spain, 1469-1716* (New York: New American Library, 1966), 314.
21. G. Marañon, *El conde-duque de Olivares: la pasión de mandar.* (Madrid: Espasa-Calpe,1936), 153.
22. Eliot, *Imperial Spain,* 376.
23. Francisco Vindel does not discuss Gondomar's collection in his essay on the bibliophiles of Spain and their libraries.
24. Edwards, 549.
25. J. H. Elliott, *The Count-Duke of Olivares: The Statesman in an Age of Decline* (New Haven, CT: Yale University Press, 1986), 18.
26. Elliot, *Imperial Spain,* 319-321.
27. Marañon, 153. [Translation by R. Carter]
28. Ibid., 154.
29. Ibid., 155.
30. Ibid., 416.
31. Ibid., 154.
32. Ibid., 156.
33. J. H. Elliott, 643-651.
34. Marañon, 418.

REFERENCES

Altamira y Crevea, Rafael. *Historia de España y de la civilización española,* vol. 3. Barcelona: Herderos de Juan Gili, 1906.

Cánovas del Castillo, D. Antonio. *Estudiós del reinado de Felipe IV.* Madrid: A. Perez Dubrull, 1888-89.

Castillo, Rudolfo del. "Documento inédito del Siglo XVI referente á D. Fernando Colón," Real Academia de la Historia, *Boletín* 33 (1898): 114-122.

Castro, Adolfo de. *El conde-duque de Olivares y el Rey Felipe IV.* Cadiz: D. Vicente Caruana, 1846.

Edwards, Edward. *Memoirs of Libraries.* New York: Burt Franklin, 1859 (reprinted 1965).

Elliott, J. H. *The Count-Duke of Olivares: The Statesman in an Age of Decline.* New Haven, Conn.: Yale University Press, 1986.

⸻. *Imperial Spain 1469-1716.* New York: New American Library, 1966.

Fernandez de Navarret, D. Eustaquio. "Noticias para la vida de D. Hernando Colón." In *Colección de documentos ineditos para la historia de España,* Vol. 16. Madrid: Viuda de Calero, 1850: 289-483.

Foster, Mary Louise. "Three Great Spanish Libraries." *Library Journal* 56 (1931): 9-12.

Gondomar, Diego Sarmiento de Acuña, Conde de. *Cinco cartas politico-literarias de D. Diego Sarmiento de Acuña.* Publicados de la Sociedad de bibliófilos españoles, Vol. 4. Madrid: Impr. de M. Rivadeneyra, 1869.

Harrisse, Henry. *Bibliographie de quatre cents pièces gothiques, françaises, italiennes & latines du commencement du XVIe siècle non décrites jusqu'ici: Précédée d'une histoire de la Bibliothèque colombine et de son fondateur.* Paris: H. Welter, 1877.

_____. *D. Fernando Colón, historiado de su padre: ensayo crítico.* Sociedad de bibliofilos andaluces, ser. 1, no. 3. Sevilla: D. Rafael Tarasco, 1871. (Also available in facsimile: Sevilla: Colegio Oficial de Aparejadores y Arquitectos Técnicos, 1989?).

Hernandez Diaz, Jose, y Antonio Muro Orejon. *El testamento de don Hernando Colón y otros documentos para su biografía.* Publicaciones del Instituto hispano-cubano de historia de America. Seville: Impr. editorial de la Gavidia, 1941.

Huntington, Archer M. *Catalogue of the Library of Ferdinand Columbus: Reproduced in Facsimile from the Unique Manuscript in the Columbine Library of Seville.* New York: n.p., 1905. Reprint, New York: Kraus Reprint, 1967.

Lyon, Francis Hamilton. *Diego de Sarmiento de Acuña, conde de Gondomar.* Oxford: Blackwell, 1910.

Marañón, Gregorio. *El conde-duque de Olivares: la pasión de mandar.* Madrid: Espasa-Calpe, 1936.

Vindel, Franciso. Los bibliófilos y sus bibliotecas: desde la introducción de la imprenta en España hasta nuestros dias. Madrid: n.p., 1934.

SPECIAL FORMATS OR TOPICS

Cultural Reassertion
of Alaska Native Languages and Cultures:
Libraries' Responses

Tamara Lincoln

SUMMARY. During the past thirty years, scholars in many fields have written voluminously on the maintenance and significance of Native languages among ethnic minorities. Language endangerment and erosion is viewed as a tragic phenomenon on a global level. Yet, it is in the circumpolar North that these losses have been especially poignantly felt. This essay will address those aspects of the history of Alaska Native languages and language loss as it has unfolded within the broad spectrum of socio-cultural forces affecting Alaska Native cultures. Evidence suggests that the legacy of language loss has been substantial. Throughout the spectrum of Alaska Native cultures, this tragedy is felt profoundly as it has brought about a sense of irreplaceable loss and left many questions

Dr. Tamara Lincoln is Associate Professor of Library Science, Curator of Rare Books and Maps, and Curator and Arctic Bibliographer, Elmer E. Rasmuson Library, Alaska and Polar Regions Department, University of Alaska Fairbanks (E-mail: fftpl@aurora.alaska.edu).

[Haworth co-indexing entry note]: "Cultural Reassertion of Alaska Native Languages and Cultures: Libraries' Responses." Lincoln, Tamara. Co-published simultaneously in *Cataloging & Classification Quarterly* (The Haworth Information Press, an imprint of The Haworth Press, Inc.) Vol. 35, No. 3/4, 2003, pp. 265-290; and: *Historical Aspects of Cataloging and Classification* (ed: Martin D. Joachim) The Haworth Information Press, an imprint of The Haworth Press, Inc., 2003, pp. 265-290. Single or multiple copies of this article are available for a fee from The Haworth Document Delivery Service [1-800-HAWORTH, 9:00 a.m. - 5:00 p.m. (EST). E-mail address: getinfo@haworthpressinc.com].

unanswered. Have the outside forces working within been the primary causes of this erosion or, perhaps, have the victims of this tragedy also played a role of enablers in this process? The recognition of this condition has triggered strong, positive reactions throughout the state of Alaska and its Native communities. These culturally integrated responses indicate tenacity, courage, wisdom and hope for a renaissance. How can libraries become more sensitive and culturally responsive in this emerging milieu? We do not want to be perceived, as libraries often are, as a component of a white, European imperialist institution but rather as supportive partners in this process of cultural reassertion. Thus, our methodologies of selection, preservation, classification, access, and dissemination may need to be refashioned and explained in terms that fit into the vision and philosophy of connectivity to Alaska Native cultures. *[Article copies available for a fee from The Haworth Document Delivery Service: 1-800-HAWORTH. E-mail address: <getinfo@haworthpressinc.com> Website: <http://www.HaworthPress.com> © 2003 by The Haworth Press, Inc. All rights reserved.]*

KEYWORDS. Elmer E. Rasmuson Library, University of Alaska Fairbanks, Alaska and Polar Regions Collections, Oral History Program UAF, Alaska Native Language Center UAF, Arctic minority languages endangerment, Native language loss–Alaska, Alaska Native people–history, Alaska Native people–assimilation, Circumpolar Regions–Library collections, bilingual education, Alaska cultural reassertions, culturally responsive libraries

Our languages
the most northerly of al phoenixes
we rise brilliantly
from the ashes–
deeply buried from neglect . . .
hidden among the filth of lies and deception.
Venturing above
the stench of suppression
Slowly–with measured calculation
each voice finds
our song
our rhythm–
our natural cadence . . .
born from generations of meaningful time.

Twenty voices–
vapor locked with our ancestor's voices
speaking as real people.
Hear us loudly
hear us clearly
hear our pride of resolution
Wear the plume of confidence with honor!

–Mishal Tooyak Gaede, *"Twenty Perfect Phoenixes"*[1]

INTRODUCTION

"Alaska" is a name bequeathed to us from an Aleut word referring to the Alaska Peninsula, interpreted by Europeans to mean "the Great Land." It was the official name adopted by the United States following the purchase of Russian America in 1867. The Native heritage found within these 586,412 square miles is rich and multi-faceted. Alaska is the homeland of twenty intriguing and complex Native languages that are still spoken to a smaller or a larger degree. They represent an irreplaceable cultural wealth, which is becoming endangered.

This rich, multi-ethnic, multi-cultural society found within these boundaries faces incredible challenges. It needs to devise political and spiritual guidelines that will enable it to reconcile them in a just, sensitive, and collectively acceptable manner. It needs to foster a strong sense of unity and common belonging among its citizens. If this is not done, it cannot act as a united community able to make and enforce collectively binding decisions to resolve conflicts. Paradoxical, indeed, as this seems, the greater and deeper the diversity in a society, the greater the unity and cohesion it requires to hold itself together and nurture diversity. A weakly fused society feels threatened by differences and thus lacks the courage, confidence, and, above all, willingness to welcome and be enriched by them. A multi-cultural society, such as Alaska, cannot ignore the demands diversity places on it. Diversity is the soul of its life and as such it cannot be suppressed, legislated, or wished out of existence.

We are shaped by the richness of our cultures and its nuances. Our source of pride and self-identity is intimately fused with that heritage. Our mother tongue, native language or languages, as the case may be, becomes the very life-blood that empowers and nourishes cultural pride in us. Yet this does not always happen. Countless immigrants to the United States have, for reasons of social mobility, sacrificed their children's linguistic heritage to the altar of assimilation. Because I also started out as a discoverer of this new land, the issues affecting the Native People of Alaska, their cultures and languages, have always interested me deeply. Though I am an outsider, being neither an Alaska Native nor a native-born American, I understand intolerance and assimilation. As a child, I was victimized by these forces, as ridicule and unspeakable cruelty were inflicted upon my uncomprehending young soul.

In a society dominated by one culture, tolerance is not enough to sustain diversity either in the public or private domain. Public institutions, federal and state governments, community and family members within the domestic milieu need to play a very active and supportive role.

As a nation of immigrants, the United States has long insisted on policies of swift assimilation of its aliens into a language and culture that came down to us from the builders of the republic. Dominated and driven by the idea of a single suitable American identity, culture and belief system that supposedly constituted the core of Americanism, the country welcomed many diverse peoples, but did not necessarily accommodate diverse cultures. The history and the fate of the Native People of America serves as a testament to this tragic act, and the wounds inflicted have scarred this magnificent landscape.

While I stand in awe of the Statue of Liberty to this day, the idea of the great American "melting pot" still remains an alien concept. Instead, I prefer to envision the United States as a powerful tree, reaching outward while being deeply rooted–each branch with its distinctiveness extending the life of a tree.

As Alaska cast its spell on my life, another powerful symbol began to permeate my imagination. Whenever I waited for the northern lights to appear, it seemed that this eternal, pulsating force pushing through the skies and the land itself was an appropriate symbol of strength and vibrancy of the ancient cultures inhabiting this land. Within this spectrum, the linguistic heritage of Alaska became a powerful magnet for me.

After all, two great North American language families originated in Alaska–the Eskimo-Aleut and the Na-Dene. Both of these language groups have in time expanded far beyond the Alaskan boundaries.[2] Inupiaq Eskimo migrated to Canada and Greenland and the Athabaskan Na-Dene to Canada and the Southwestern United States.[3] The greatest diversity of these language families is found in Alaska. Within these boundaries, one finds both Aleut and Eskimo and with Eskimo, both Yupik and Inupiaq. The Na-Dene family incorporates Tlingit as well as Eyak and about ten or eleven other Athabaskan languages.[4] In Alaska we also find representatives of two other important language families: Haida and Tsimshian.

HISTORY

Even though Alaska is the forty-ninth state of the Union, like Hawaii, the fiftieth state, it shares no common borders with the "lower 48." The image of

Alaska, to many outsiders may still be clouded in mystery, if not dread. Envisioned both as *terra incognita* or *terra nulla*, it has remained for many a sweep of vastness, enrobed in unbearable cold and perpetual darkness. Perhaps this landscape might be enlivened with an occasional igloo, a caribou herd, or a dog-team and maybe even a polar bear! Hollywood bears its share of responsibility in creating absurd images of both the people and the place. Until the 1920s, the dominant idea about Eskimos was that, like other Native Americans, they would not endure. Since then, an unprecedented political and cultural renaissance has taken root. Films and videos about the Alaska Native people since the 1970s stress authenticity of voice, cultural integrity, and self-determination.[5]

To the American imagination, the North is also the "last frontier." This image has been adapted by Alaskans themselves, as they take pride in their personal freedom, courage, bravado, and machismo. Even the new millennium and cyberspace have not altered this image. But, looking at the same land through a different set of eyes, we are presented with a vision of the frontier period as an aberration, though it left lasting imprints.[6] For Native cultures in Alaska, the last century has meant denigration, oppression, and hardship.[7] The last thirty years, however, have brought some hope, as traditional beliefs and practices are being increasingly reaffirmed.

To fully comprehend the intricate network of Alaska Native languages, a short historical synopsis may be helpful. The outside world first learned of Alaska following the 1741 voyage of exploration led by Vitus Bering. The earlier voyages made by Russian seaman Dezhnev in 1648 or Mikhail Gvozdev in 1730 remained largely unknown in Europe.

Generally, one may divide the Russian era in Alaska into three distinct segments.[8] The first period (1775-1785) represents the rather brutal interactions of the Russians with the Aleuts and their conquest. Exploitation of the rich furs available in the Aleutians began almost immediately. The second period (1786-1824) witnesses the establishment of the Russian-American Company under Shelikov at Kodiak; and by 1799 the Russian American Company began operating as a monopoly, serving as the seat of government in Alaska. Firmly established by its colorful first-governor, Alexander Baranov (1790-1818), it was very successful for a time, based on its fur trade with China. However, it is the third Russian period (1825-1867) that is considered to have been of crucial importance to the development and history of the Alaska Native languages. Michael E. Krauss sees the Russian period as "being not only more beneficial in the history of Alaska Native languages and cultures than the earlier Russian periods, but also more beneficial than any of the following American periods."[9]

The strength of this statement is defensible if we remember that not any of the Alaska Native people had a written language before the third Russian period

(1825-1867). At that time, a remarkable man, Ioann Veniaminov, appeared in Alaska. His outstanding humanitarianism, intellectual acumen, and educational and political abilities left a lasting imprint on Alaska. Veniaminov's manifold contributions were very much recognized by the Russian Empire as well, for he became the Metropolitan of the Orthodox Church in Russia and was subsequently canonized, receiving the name of St. Innokentii, or St. Innocent. The linguistic contributions that he made particularly affected the Aleut languages–Aleutian and Aluutiq, and to a lesser extent central Yupik, Eskimo and also Tlingit. Veniaminov worked closely with his companion and collaborator, Ivan Pankov, the Chief of Krenitzin Islands.

Orthographic development of these languages followed; and in 1834 the first Aleut catechism was published, which was followed by other significant works. Veniaminov's enthusiasm was infectious, as indicated by the important linguistic contributions made by other dedicated figures, such as Tyzhov, Zyrianov, Uchilishev, and Netsvetov. As Richard Dauenhauer, an Alaskan linguist, poet, educator, and philosopher, explains, the "Russian Orthodox Church sought to instill a sense of pride in the Native language and strongly fostered literacy in it. As a result, a proud, bilingual, bicultural population emerged."[10]

Throughout this period the Russian Orthodox Church was instrumental in expanding literacy and education among the Alaska Native people through its support of the philosophy and practice of bilingual education. This philosophy, however, differed markedly from the one pursued by the Americans. It has been stated: "The Russians were worse for the people than for their languages, whereas the Americans were worse for their languages than for the people."[11]

When the Americans took control of Alaska in 1867, they did not make their presence felt for about twenty years. So, the American reign started unobtrusively and the impact of any cultural change for the Alaska Native people was imperceptible. The Russian Orthodox Church continued to dominate educational development especially after the arrival of other missionaries in the area. Development of literacy continued, especially in the Yupik and Aleut languages. It was not until the 1890s that some segments of the Native population began to feel the oppression of American presence, as the fishing industries and canneries developed in southern coastal areas and mining operations appeared in many parts. Thus, vast changes appeared between 1887 and 1910. During this period Alaska's multitude of riches were rediscovered, bringing forth an incredible assortment of greedy humanity, as criminals and adventurers heard the call of the wild and envisioned the lure of gold.

After the sale of Alaska in 1867, the federal government almost completely ignored Alaska Natives for the first seventeen years. The Orthodox schools continued on a diminished scale well after the sale in 1867. Before and during the gold-rush years, other churches and missions combined with the federal government to provide an expanding educational system. There has been much debate about the role of missionaries and their long-term effects on Alaska, but many among them misunderstood and failed to respect traditional belief systems. Assimilation and complete cultural substitution became the goal. So, the milieu changed between 1883 and 1903. At that time, the more liberal educational policies upheld by the Orthodox ministries and the missionaries succumbed to the anti-Native, conservative philosophies upheld by men such as Sheldon Jackson and S. Hall Young. Sheldon Jackson eventually became the U.S. Commissioner of Education to Alaska; and from about 1910 on, the use of Native languages in American and mission schools became forbidden by law.[12] Children were punished and physically and mentally abused for speaking their Native languages. Their mother tongues became a mark of shame and fear. As they were being ridiculed, mouths were taped; and frequently, bitter substances were even placed into their mouths. Many of these recollections echo through present day memories of numerous elders and others who had attended the boarding and mission schools established by the Bureau of Indian Affairs (BIA). Such physical and psychological abuses struck at the very foundation of ethnic pride and identity. The BIA strongly believed that teaching an Indian youth in his own barbarous dialect was a positive detriment to him. In view of such philosophies, parents were strongly encouraged to speak only English at home. Fearful of punishment, many complied, realizing that their command of English was not strong enough to successfully carry out the task. As a government policy, it may have fostered formal education, but it served as an alienating force, separating children from their culture and heritage. English, after all, was not presented as a useful skill to acquire but rather as a moral necessity, superior to their own language and culture. These negative implications caused attitudinal shifts; and many parents were reluctant to pass on their language, as the pride in it had been tainted.

It is remarkable that within this period linguistic work on these languages continued steadily in the United States and Europe. This is well illustrated by the works of such scholars as Franz Boas, John Reed Swanton (1886-1910), Francis Barnum and John Hinz (1944), John Wight Chapman (1914), Julius Jetté, Velten, Waldemar Bogoraz, Waldemar Jochelson, and others.[13]

GLIMPSES AT THE PRESENT

How has the milieu changed in the present? Without tracing all the developments, we can positively say that from the legal aspect of language learning, some positive events have taken place. In 1991 Senator Murkowski introduced the Alaska Languages Preservation and Enforcement Act; and Governor Knowles signed Senate Bill 103 into law, effective July 1, 2000.[14] The Alaska Native Language Education Act mandates each local school board, in the district in which the majority of students are Alaska Natives, to establish a local Native language curriculum advisory board. If the advisory board recommends the establishment of a Native language curriculum, the school board may imitate it within the K-12 limits. Such a program, if established, must include Native languages traditionally spoken in the community. For the purposes of this measure, "Native" was defined as someone of one-fourth degree or more Alaskan Indian, Eskimo, or Aleut blood. Such programs must also be evaluated and reviewed annually.[15]

In the meantime, what is the status of the state's bilingual regulations? The whole intent of the bilingual education programs is to improve the English language capacities of the student, while exiting them out of the program as soon as possible. These regulations imply that in order to have a two-way immersion program, at least 50 percent of the incoming students must speak the Native language!

For community empowerment, the Alaska Federation of Natives, in their "Call for Action Report" (1990), sees the children and their education as the most important segment of any community. Their education must span two value systems. The first skills to be mastered are those that will enable them to succeed in traditional Native life ways. The other skills must prepare the youth to succeed also in Western society. Thus they must be empowered in both cultures. The skills, values, and languages are inseparable in this process.

This ideal of the integrated education has not been achieved yet, but there are positive philosophical and social forces that are moving it into the right direction. An empowered community is envisioned as one in which all the education and learning systems, formal and informal, accommodate the present and the future needs of their students, incorporating a strong foundation of the child's culture and language. The words of John Pingayak of Chevak serve as reminders that "Our ancestral ways are always best for the future. Never forget them and learn them well."[16]

CHANGING ATTITUDES AND NEW HOPE

A significant philosophical shift has occurred within the last decade in many northern countries, whether we examine the forces that are reshaping the fate of the "Small Peoples of the Russian North," the Saami, the Inuit of Northern Canada, or Alaska Natives. The government policies of some of these areas have moved toward a more tolerant philosophy, and they are giving increasing support for the indigenous minority languages and people. The effect of this momentum is infectious. Communities, people themselves, parents and elders and children are active participants in this process of cultural revitalization. From the mouths of parents, grandparents, and elders, the language and its wisdom are transferred to the "mouths of babes." A poignant example of these efforts can be seen in the emergence of "total immersion programs," "spirit camps," and "academies of elders" that are appearing across Alaska.[17]

A powerful example of this momentum is the establishment of the Alaska Rural Systematic Initiative: Native Pathways to Education, which is sponsored by the Alaska Federation of Natives, the University of Alaska, the National Science Foundation, and the Alaska Department of Education. The purpose of this initiative is to document Native indigenous knowledge systems of the Alaska Native People and designing educational curricula, applications and technologies that would incorporate "indigenous knowledge and ways of knowing" into formal educational systems, including the libraries so that "traditional knowledge systems, ways of knowing and world views" can be more effectively utilized as foundations in the total learning process.[18] This initiative embraces many facets, such as: teacher leadership development programs, establishment of regional and local curriculum clearinghouses, designing and developing cultural documentation initiatives, and establishing cultural standards and guidelines for education and other facets of life.

Through these initiatives, educators, parents, elders and children are recognizing the power held in their cultural arsenals. As stories are retold and written, drummed and enacted through song and dance, pride and hope emerge, reinforcing the power of Native languages as the bridge that can connect the oral tradition and the written record.

FORMAL DEVELOPMENTS IN THE CURRENT HISTORY OF ALASKA NATIVE LANGUAGES

The 1960s and 1970s can be considered another period of renaissance for Alaska Native languages. According to Michael E. Krauss, numerous social and political factors laid the foundation for this phenomenon. Changing philosophical attitudes toward racial and ethnic minorities, as reflected by the Civil Rights Movement, the disruption of the American society brought about by the war in Vietnam, the entire philosophical reevaluation of the accepted American value systems, and the influx of a large number of immigrants from Asian, Hispanic and other communities changed the ethnic mapping and attitudes in the United States.

In 1961, for example, the University of Alaska, Fairbanks took the first step in recognizing its interest in Alaska Native cultures and languages, as the first academic courses were offered in these areas.[19] Compared to the United States, interest in Eskimo linguistics and literacy had been a serious concern in Denmark and in Russia for a much longer period. Bilingual education of the Asiatic Eskimo minorities in the former Soviet Union was an essential tool for political reeducation; thus a significant amount of excellent linguistic work was accomplished in the 1930s. Denmark also shared an enlightened attitude towards their Eskimo minorities residing in Greenland. The University of Copenhagen, for example, has had a recognized department of Eskimo linguistics for many years; and in 1968 the University of Aarhus also established a Department of Greenlandic.[20] Thus the path was set for similar developments in Alaska.

THE ALASKA NATIVE LANGUAGE CENTER AT THE UNIVERSITY OF ALASKA, FAIRBANKS

In Alaska, the Alaska Native Language Center (ANLC) has been and continues to be the strongest and most effective torchbearer in the study, preservation, and dissemination of the Alaska Native languages. Under the tireless and brilliant leadership of Michael E. Krauss, the ANLC was formally established in 1972 by state legislation. Outstanding scholars, such as: Jeff Lear, Irene Reed, Steven A. Jacobson, Lawrence D. Kaplan, Edna Ahgeak Maclean, James Kari, and others are also equal contributors to the success of this institution.

Alaska Native languages also benefited from certain paramount political events, which created positive legislative changes: for example, the Federal Bilingual Education Act of 1967, which permitted the re-introduction of bilingual education, and Senate Bill 421 (passed in 1972),[21] which made bilingual education mandatory in those state-operated schools where Native languages were spoken. Concurrent with these developments, another Senate bill authorized and funded the establishment of a Native Language Center at the University of Alaska, Fairbanks. The passage of the Alaska Native Land Claims Settlement Act in 1971 provided the additional impetus for continued development in this area.

The primary purpose for the establishment of the Alaska Native Language Center in 1972 was to document the Native Indian and Eskimo languages of Alaska. The Center's extensive multi-level program has included the training of Native bilingual teachers and other specialists. It supports a broad publication and documentation program, translating documents and texts, publishing Native language materials, and offering leadership in this field at national and international levels. Considering the weight of all of these responsibilities, the Center could not continue to assume the total responsibility for all of these functions. Other local agencies, such as the National Bilingual Materials Development Center (Anchorage), the Inupiat Materials Development Center at Barrow, and others, became involved in sharing these responsibilities. With such well-sustained efforts, the publication record in these areas has increased and is increasing voluminously. With its voluminous 10,000 item archival collection, the Center offers Academic degree programs in Yupik, Inupiaq, and Athabascan; and it also offers certificates in Native language education. Thus it acts as a powerful foundation for the development of Alaska Native languages and cultures. The Elmer E. Rasmuson Library's Alaska and Polar Regions Collection has, over the years, benefited from the support and counsel of these centers. Working together, we have been able to build a stronger bridge connecting the needs of Alaska Native cultures.

ALASKA NATIVE LANGUAGE COLLECTION OF THE ELMER E. RASMUSON LIBRARY

Alaska Native languages and cultures are encompassed under the Alaska and Polar Regions Collection. The collection is circumpolar in nature and multilingual. It incorporates materials in the field of humanities, social sciences, technology, and physical sciences and to a smaller degree biological and geophysical sciences, as those collections exist outside of the Rasmuson Library. Native cultures of Alaska and the Circumpolar Region including Siberia form the primary foundation. The primary inclusion is geographic as the library attempts to acquire all significant literature relating to Alaska, Canada north of 50 degrees, Greenland, Northern Provinces of Norway, Sweden, and Finland as well as the northern parts of Russia and Siberia and the Russian Far East. The collection is internationally recognized and, as such, represents the major research collection in the United States in these areas. As the collection has grown in recognition and volume to incorporate about 90,000 monographs and serials, providing timely, culturally appropriate access and delivery of these materials has always been a major concern.

As a linguist, upon my arrival in Alaska in 1976, I was entrusted with the task of reformulating Library of Congress' arrangement used for the "Hyperborean languages of America and the kindred languages of Arctic Asia." Its alphabetically arranged verbal designators were misleading, out of date, and simply linguistically inappropriate. Inconsistencies, errors, and misrepresentations appeared throughout the categories, which did not consider geographical, ethnic, or linguistic accuracy.[22] The Native language materials constitute an extremely valuable component of this collection; therefore, a linguistically and culturally more appropriate approach had to be developed.

THE LINCOLN REVISION

A new approach to the system was developed in 1979 by this author, in consultation with Michael E. Krauss. "Guidelines for the Application of the Classification for Alaskan and Other Arctic Native languages: Lincoln Revision" provided an improved grouping of languages while adhering more closely to the Library of Congress framework. The boundaries acceptable for the revision were narrow. It had to ascertain the inclusion of all Alaska Native languages within the classification scheme and, at the same time, create as much linguistic unity as possible. In this process logical locations had to be found for formerly undesignated languages, and some transpositions had to be made that would not violate the established LC schedule. Dialectical variants, separately listed by the Library of Congress, were brought into the immediate vicinity of their major language families; and all erroneously included languages were systematically excluded.

METHODOLOGY

Several major steps were taken. First, the established LC designators for the Alaskan, some Canadian and related Siberian Arctic languages, and the Arctic Indian languages were examined to determine their current linguistic and ethnic relevancy. Second, the currently acknowledged Arctic languages of North America and their related Siberian languages were compared to the LC classification and listing, noting the existing discrepancies and geographical mislocations. Those currently recognized Alaska Native languages that were not identified by LC were incorporated into the scheme in a compatible manner. Through transposition and correction, more linguistic unity was created. This was accomplished by consultation with the Alaska Native Language Center as they are the internationally recognized authority in the field. In addition, this study also utilized the most current (1982) edition of the map published by the Center: "Native People Languages of Alaska," which is considered the national standard.

USE OF GEOGRAPHIC DESIGNATORS

The revision tried to fit orphaned languages into geographically suitable locations, as indicated by LC terminology. For example, Central Yupik, one of the most widely used major Eskimo languages, was one of the linguistic orphans that needed to be placed within a proper sequence. Upon examination of the LC schedule, the decision was made to place it into the PM 21 Aglemiut class number, since the term Aglemiut, although it appears to be an erroneous linguistic designator, does at least refer to an extinct Bristol Bay Area tribe of Central Yupik Eskimos. The other major Yupik language of Alaska, known as Siberian Yupik, spoken on the St. Lawrence Island in the communities of Campbell and Savoonga, presented similar location problems. Not only does Siberian Yupik represent a separate language, which is not inter-changeable with Alaskan Central Yupik, but it also needed to be separated from the Russian Siberian Central Yupik. For clarification, the entire Siberian Yupik branch of Eskimo is linguistically divided into two primary language groups, which are in turn subdivided. The groups are:

A. Chaplino-Naukanskii languages
    1. *Naukanskii of East Cape* (Russia)
    2. Central Siberian Yupik group, subdivided
       a. Siberian Yupik of the Chaplinskii area, Chukotskii Peninsula, Siberia
       b. St. Lawrence Island Yupik, Alaska
B. *Sirenikskii language of Siberia*

Though structurally similar to St. Lawrence Island Yupik, the Siberian Yupik of the Chaplinskii area needed to be separated in classification from its Alaskan counterpart because it is written in the Cyrillic alphabet, whereas St. Lawrence Island Yupik uses Roman orthography.

NOTATION FOR DIALECTS

The Library of Congress has chosen a Russian ethnic term used for Siberian Eskimos in general (**Yuit-PM94**) as the only designator for the Central Siberian Yupik spoken on the Chukotskii Peninsula. To accommodate the placement of St. Lawrence Island Yupik, we utilized the **PM94: Yuit or Yugat** classification. Since these languages had to be separated, some additional internal notation was used for subdividing languages by dialects. As a result, monographs written in St. Lawrence Island Siberian Yupik were classified under **PM94.Z9L3** and Siberian Yupik materials were to be classed under **PM94.Z955**.

DISTINCTIONS FOR VARIANT LANGUAGES

The **PM61-64: Eskimo** designator created additional problems. The term Eskimo is obviously too broad to be used successfully because of the large number of variant languages in existence. However, in the revision, **PM61: Eskimo** was used for general comparative Eskimo linguistics, whereas **PM64** was borrowed to be used for another major distinct group of languages: the Innuit-Inupiaq languages, spoken in variant forms in Canada and Labrador and in Greenland. As a separation had to be created for these languages, while maintaining proximity, internal notation was used, as had been done with Siberian Yupik. **PM64.Z9L3** was used for Labrador, and **PM64.Z9G7** was used for Greenlandic Inuit. Another distinction remained to be made for the Alaskan Inupiaq variants that had not been specifically provided for by LC. The Library of Congress had used **PM73: Kopagmiut or Chiglit** as a designator, and geographically it encompasses some of the Alaskan Inupiaq language area. Kopagmiut refers to contemporary Kuuvagmiut, which means "Kobuk River People"–as mentioned earlier in the list of languages and Chiglit refers to an extinct tribe of the Mackenzie River Delta.

Because Alaskan Inupiaq is spoken in the general area of the Kobuk River, Kopagmiut was chosen as a possible location for these Inupiaq languages. In this revision, Kopagmiut or Chiglit was divided into four separate regional Inupiaq dialects: Malimiut (**PM73.Z9M3**), North Slope Inupiaq (**PM73.Z9N6**), Qauiaraq (**PM73.Z9Q3**), and Wales Inupiaq (**PM73.Z9W3**).

Sugpiaq is yet another Yupik Eskimo language that was placed into the new revision. Since LC had used the label Kaniagmiut (also known as Kadiaskii Aleut) for **PM73**, the revision adopted this location for Sugpiaq, as Kadiaskii Aleut means the Aleut spoken on Kodiak Island. Thus, at least geographically, the region coincided with the area where Sugpiaq is spoken. We retained the use of **PM89** for the somewhat confusing Uglakmiut or Ugalennyi language, since it represents a distinct variant of both Eyak as well as Sugpiaq.

ALASKA NATIVE INDIAN LANGUAGES

Within the Alaska Native Indian languages, changes also had to be made. As mentioned earlier, the Library of Congress **PM** schedule had designated twenty-one numbers and languages for the classification of Arctic Indian languages of Alaska and Canada. Numerically the range assigned was broad, but it did not reflect contemporary status or knowledge about these languages. The problematic areas within this range reflected similar difficulties to those experienced within the Eskimo language categories: erroneous concepts and lack of representation for existing tongues.

To reflect linguistic unity and currently recognized languages, the revision used the same methodology as was done for handling Arctic Eskimo languages of North America and their related counterparts. **PM641: Athapaskan** presented a problem since it refers to a whole group of closely knit but often geographically widely separated languages; there are eleven Athapaskan languages in Alaska, twelve in Canada, seven in Oregon-California, and five Apachean in the American Southwest.

The Athapaskan group was also subdivided, accommodating Alaskan Athapaskan languages that had not been placed within the scheme, as well as relocating its related languages and placing them under its wings. All the related displaced languages were absorbed through internal subdivision: **PM641.Z9T3** (Tanacross), **PM641.Z9T4** (Tanana), **PM641.Z9U6** (Upper Kuskokwim), **PM641.Z9U7** (Upper Tanana). **PM2455** (Tlingit) underwent a similar subdivision, incorporating all its related dialects under the major language family. In this process, Henya was relocated from LC's **PM1325.H4** to **PM2455.Z9H4**; Huna, LC's **PM1357.H3**, was moved into the Tlingit family as **PM2455.Z9H8** and Hutsneuvo from LC's **PM1367.H5** to **PM2455.Z9H82**. A similar method was adopted for LC's **PM1271-1274** (Haida). **PM1271** was used for general and comparative Haida, depending on internal dialectical subdivision as prescribed by LC for incorporating its regional language variants–the Canadian Masset, Skidegate, and the Alaskan Kaigani. The LC designator **PM1393** (Kaigani) was not used at all, and the dialect was moved into the immediate proximity of its language family **PM1271.Z9K3** (Haida). Other relocations involved the utilization of the LC's **PM1561** (Knaiakhotana) for the unplaced Tanaina, as Knaiakhotana represents a nineteenth-century term used for a dialect of that language. In a 1983 edition of *Additions and Changes,* the Library of Congress did place Tanaina into a separate number. However, the "Lincoln Revision" does not reflect it.

To achieve clarity and correctness, several LC-designated languages were not used at all. These included Kake (**PM1411**), which is an abandoned Tlingit village without linguistic distinction; Kutchakutchin (**PM1615**), which is indistinguishable from Kutchin; and Niska (**PM2026.N3**), which is a small dialectical variant of Chimmesian. Eyak, a distinct and significant, though almost extinct, Tlingit-related Alaska Native language for which placement had not been provided. As a somewhat independent offshoot of the Athabaskan language family, the revision incorporated Eyak into the classification assigned for Tinne (LC's **PM2453**), since *Tinne* is a general alternate term for the entire Athabaskan language family.

This overview of the classification problems of the Alaska Native language materials and the related Arctic languages of Canada, Greenland, and Siberia indicated that more inconsistencies and inaccuracies were present in the Library of Congress's handling of the Arctic Indian languages of North America than in their treatment of Eskimo languages. Corrections, transpositions, and new placements were imposed on both linguistic groups. The completed revision created a more uniform, logical system of bibliographic control for these materials. The linguistic transpositions, created within the accepted LC parameters, established more linguistic and geographic unity; reflecting linguistic interrelationships based on contemporary understanding of these languages.

The needs of the Elmer E. Rasmuson Library and those of other libraries in the University of Alaska system were the primary motivators for the creation of this alternate classification plan for Alaska Native language and related languages materials. The library system in a state where more than one-fifth of the state's non-military population is Native must serve the needs of its multicultural, multi-ethnic population. There has been a continuous geometric increase in the amount of Alaska Native language publications of grammars, dictionaries, story collections, and school texts for bilingual programs. Therefore, considering the fact that our collection in this field represents a major research resource in this area, the Rasmuson Library continues to bear a special responsibility for the enrichment, access, and dissemination of this collection on a national and international level.

The revision design presented in this work was implemented in 1980 at the Rasmuson Library. It has been used continuously, as all the holdings on Alaska Native language materials were reclassified according to the revision. We have shared our results through bibliographic networks with other Alaska libraries, other states, and with other American as well as Canadian libraries. As the primary collectors of Alaska Native language materials in the University of Alaska System and the state (excluding the ANLC), the redesigned **PM** schedule continues to be used by those libraries within the state that wish to do so or can do so.

Creating a collection that encompasses the past, harnesses the present, and envisions the future is a formidable task, not only philosophically but also technically. The library needs to continue to provide additional access to its unique resources in a wide variety of formats, including those in the Alaska and Polar Regions Collection. Access is as much a problem of awareness as it is of intellectual approach. The recent rapid development of Internet-based information resources such as online indexes, links to full-text periodical articles, and Web-based services has enabled the library to serve users in many locations across the state. For rural residents and students at community campus sites around the state, online library services and databases now provide access to materials that were once difficult or impossible to obtain.

Kuskokwim Consortium Library (Kuskokwim Campus, Bethel), Northwest Campus Resource Learning Center (Nome), and Chukchi Consortium Library (Kotzebue) are administered by the College of Rural Alaska. While these have no direct budgetary or administrative connections with the Rasmuson Library, they have access to the library services offered; and they are heavy users of the Alaska and Polar Regions Collection. The UAF Interior-Aleutians campus is headquartered in Fairbanks and has six rural learning centers. Those at rural sites use a variety of Internet and telecommunications library services. Thus the Rasmuson Library serves a broad constituency through our online catalog GNOSIS and the Alaska Periodical Index, SLED, and other online resources. Even with shrinking budgets we must continue to expand and coordinate the intellectual tools that provide better access to our resources.

RELATED AREAS OF CONCERN

The best methodologies for access and dissemination must at all times be coupled with collection enrichment, in whatever format, that reflects cultural sensitivity and awareness of the emerging social and political realities of the region. As the issues of interconnectivity of Alaska Native cultures, sovereignty, and cultural reassertion are exploding across Alaska, we may need to continually re-examine other Library of Congress classifications and subject access.

For example, just as the revised **PM** classification scheme clarified linguistic, cultural, and geographic relationships making them more ethno-culturally acceptable, another cloud has appeared on the horizon, which has caused misunderstandings. This category is of particular concern to the Alaska and Polar Regions Collection, as it deals directly with the Native cultures. The **E99.E7** or **E99.A-Z** category, as it stands now, creates a giant mixture of unrelated materials, arranged in alphabetical order. This area has, indeed, become a true "melting pot" for America. This is also a category that has expanded beyond all reason, as it contains an enormous range of materials. Its wide expanse covers a wide range of topics including building fishnets, sledges, beadwork, Eskimo dolls, etc. Many of the monographs in this class area are in assorted Native languages appearing singly or in parallel texts.

It is a heavily used and confusing category, which is also viewed often as being culturally insensitive. Over the years countless errors and misreadings have crept into this category. Even the subject headings, which depend heavily on the skill of the person assigning them, cannot be relied upon. This illogical treatment of **E99.A-Z** still reflects the Eurocentric attitudes prevailing when the LC classifications were created. This issue needs to be addressed at another time and place.

The importance of the value of these Native language and cultural resources cannot be underestimated at this time, especially in the light of the language losses that are occurring not only globally but in the minority languages of the Arctic in particular. Therefore, we must continue to pursue methodologies that will enhance access to these materials in the most appropriate formats available, transforming the nature of cataloging and its effect on handling unique materials and languages.

OUTSOURCING

As have many libraries in the United States, the Elmer E. Rasmuson Library has embraced the concept of outsourcing. Organizational changes, ever-increasing budgetary constraints, lack of staffing, and the growth of uncataloged materials have contributed to this decision. Contrary to initial expectations, outsourcing has not had a wholly detrimental effect on the quality of cataloging although special attention has been paid to materials dealing with Alaska. As an in-depth discussion is beyond the scope of this discussion, I would like only to address the issue as it relates to Alaska Native language materials and materials in the other minority languages of the Arctic.

These materials cannot be outsourced. If no previous cataloging for these materials is available, they are currently placed into the backlog. Clearly, this issue needs a resolution. In consultation with the Head of the Bibliographic Access Management Department and this author and based on a previous recommendation mentioned by Michael Krauss of the Alaska Native Language Center, we might seek grant support. Grant funding would enable the hiring of recommended Native students, for limited periods, as indicated by need, who would translate, if necessary, and provide subject identification. This would provide an on-going support system for the cataloging of these important resources.

Present State of Alaska Native Languages, Ethnic Population Estimates, and the Estimated Number of Speakers[23]

Languages and researchers	Total population Alaska	Alaska number of speakers	Documentation
Eskimo-Aleut			
1. Inuit ANLC, E. MacLean, L. Kaplan, Arctic Sivumnum Illsagvic and the Commission on Inupiat History, Lang., Culture (North Slope)	13,500	3,100	fully documented studied comprehensively
2. Alutiiq	3,000	400	fully documented studied comprehensively

Languages and researchers	Total population Alaska	Alaska number of speakers	Documentation
Eskimo-Aleut			
3. Central Alaskan Yupik ANLC, J. Lear, S. Jacobson, E. I. Reed	21,000	10,000	fully documented studied comprehensively
4. Central Siberian Yupik ANLC, S. Jacobson, M. Krauss, D. Orr	1,100	1,000	fully documented studied comprehensively
5. Aleut ANLC, Univ. of Oslo: K. Bergsland **Athabaskan - Eyak - Tlingit** ANLC, M. Krauss	2,000	300	fully documented studied comprehensively
6. Kutchin ANLC: J. Lear, L. Garnett, K. Sikorskii, K. Peter	1,000	300	extensive documentation for Alaska dialects
7. Han Yukon Native Lang. Center, ANLC	50	8	considerable, but not full documentation
8. Upper Tanana Yukon native Lang. Center, AK Native Lang. Center	300	105	considerable, but not extensive documentation
9. Tanacross ANLC: J. Kari, M. Krauss	220	65	one of the most weakly documented AK languages
10. Tanana ANLC: J. Kari, M. Krauss	380	30	considerable to extensive documentation
11. Upper Kuskokwim ANLC, R. Collins, P. Petruska	160	40	considerable documentation
12. Koyukon ANLC: E. Jones, J. Kari	2,300	300	comprehensive lexical and grammatical documentation
13. Holikachuk ANLC: J. Kari	200	12	extensive but not comprehensive documentation
14. Ingalik ANLC: J. Kari	275	40	extensive but not comprehensive documentation
15. Tanaina/Denàina ANLC: J. Kari	900	75	comprehensive documentation
16. Ahtna ANLC: J. Kari	500	80	comprehensive documentation
17. Eyak ANLC: M. Krauss		1	comprehensive documentation
18. Tlingit ANLC: J. Leer	10,000	500	comprehensive documentation
19. Northern Haida ANLC: J. Enrico	600	15	comprehensive documentation
20. Gitskan ANLC	1,000	100	fully documented

Speaker = defined as active, fluent speaker.

The realistic summation given above of the linguistic reality facing Alaska Native languages presents a somber projection for the future. Bilingual education cannot perform miracles; it merely serves as a band-aid, a cover-up for a more serious condition. It gives lip service to language retention, but anyone who has experienced a forty-five-minute daily "immersion" in a language knows that it is not a thorough experience. The immersion has to start at home and in the community and has to occur at an early age. There is hope expressed throughout Alaskan communities that if there is a will, there will be a future, and it is the right of every child to take part in it.[24] In the words of a Yupik leader, educator, and philosopher, Dr. Angayuqaq Oscar Kawagley:

> How is it that we "stabilize indigenous languages?" I think that we must once again speak the Native languages in the home a majority of the time. If we expect only the school to do it, it will surely fail. The school must become a reflection of a Native speaking family, home and community. During the waking hours of the day, the children must hear the Native language being spoken–in the home and in school. The one-to-one and family conversation in the local language must be the standard of the day. The community, family, parents and especially the children must begin to know place. How is this to be done? By the Elders, parents and community members speaking to one another in their own language and from the Yupiaq perspective. To know self, one must learn of place. How does one learn of place? You begin by telling quliraat, the mythology, stories of distant time, which are powerful teaching tools still applicable to the present.[25]

BUILDING CULTURALLY RESPONSIVE LIBRARIANSHIP: PRESENT AND FUTURE PERSPECTIVES

Cultural reawakening is recognized in many ways. The state of indigenous librarianship is stirring not only across Alaska but also throughout the United States, and in September 2001 at the State Board of Education meeting "Culturally Responsive Guidance for Alaska Public Libraries"[26] was endorsed. The document was sponsored by the Alaska State Library and with support from the Alaska Native Knowledge Network (ANKN). It was developed by a group of Alaska public library directors under the leadership of Dr. Lotsee Patterson. The document examines how libraries can respond to the educational, informational, and cultural needs of Alaska Native people and communities and offers good building blocks to create that connective link between oral and written traditions of documenting and accessing knowledge.

The document echoes and articulates many of the philosophies that have guided the growth and development of the Alaska and Polar Regions collections for many years. To be constantly vigilant and alert and sensitive to the peoples of the Native cultures that enrich Alaska is our mantra. This often leads a curator to uncommon paths and sources. The grey literature is not only elusive but also often politically sensitive and difficult to obtain diplomatically. Thus personal networks and contacts, built on trust, are essential. Collectively, the State Library, the Alaska university and private libraries, the public libraries, and even several school libraries contain an impressive corpus of cultural and language materials. Following is a partial list of libraries, which are our partners in this endeavor.

Anchorage:	Alaska Pacific University Library
	University of Alaska Consortium Library
	Z. J. Loussac Municipal Library
Barrow:	Tuzzy Consortium Library
Bethel:	Kuskokwim Consortium Library
Fairbanks:	Noel Wien Library
	UAF E. E. Rasmuson Library
Juneau:	Alaska State Library
	Public Library
	University of Alaska Southeast: William A. Egan Library
Ketchikan:	Public Library
Kotzebue:	Chukchi Consortium Library
Nome:	Kegoayah Kozga Public Library
Palmer:	Matanuska Susitna Community College Library
Sitka:	Kettleson Memorial Library
	Sheldon Jackson College: Stratton Library
Valdez:	Consortium Library

UAF RASMUSON LIBRARY–
ALASKA AND POLAR REGIONS DEPARTMENT

The Alaska and Polar Regions Department acquires, preserves, and provides access to materials that document the past and present of Alaska and the Polar Regions. The following pathways can lead you to many unique, irreplaceable resources:

- The **Film Archives** has moving images on film or videotape detailing many aspects of life in the North from 1925, including both amateur and professional footage.
- The **Historical Manuscript Collections** consist of two miles of business records, journals, diaries, scrapbooks, and other papers documenting the political, social, and economic history of Alaska and its neighbors.
- The **University Archives** contain significant historical records of the University from its beginning in 1917 as the Alaska Agricultural College and School of Mines, as well as records of the Statewide Office.

- The **Historical Photograph Collections** contain over 7,000,000 images from the 1870s forward. Prints, slides, and digital images are available from our photo lab.
- The **Rare Book Collection** has over 5,000 volumes of early exploration accounts and studies of the Polar Regions from the fifteenth to early twentieth centuries. It is one of the world's leading collections on Russian America.
- The **Rare Map Collection** is especially strong in maps of Alaska from sixteenth century speculative cartography to the gold rush era.
- The **Manuscript Map Collection** consists of more than 18,000 maps, plats, and charts emphasizing twentieth century Alaskan development. Topics include mining claims, cannery sites, and land use planning.
- The **Alaska Periodical Index** covers articles on Alaskan and polar subjects from over 500 magazines and journals received by the Library. Coverage is current and retrospective.
- The **Alaska and Polar Regions Printed Monographic, Serial, Journal, Newspaper Collection** is a multilingual circumpolar world-class collection including multiple formats.
- The **Wenger Anthropological Eskimo Database** (CD-ROM, version 2.0) is available at UAF and other libraries internationally. This is an electronic full-text database containing books and articles regarding the first contacts and first observations of Inuit-Eskimos in Chukota, Alaska, Canada, and Greenland. A search engine retrieves text, subjects, and images from about 260 published books and articles, including many out-of-print sources not easily accessible. The database includes voluminous information on language: bilingualism, classification, borrowing, dialects, distribution, grammar, innovation, integration, orthography, writing systems, translation, vocabulary, etc.
- The **Oral History Program** was established in 1981 to collect and curate audio and video recordings that relate to Alaskan history and its peoples. The collection contains over 8,000 hours of individual recordings, including interviews with politicians, pioneers, and Native elders. Key collections include "Alaska Native Songs and Legends" by the Alaska Library Association, "Early Day Alaskans" by the Tanana-Yukon Historical Society, "The Alaska Native Elders-In-Residence Program" by the UAF Alaska Native Studies Department, and "On the Road: Recordings with Old Timers."

"The Alaska Native Elders-In-Residence Program" is especially significant to the history of Alaska Native cultures and languages and the serious retention issues facing them. As these tamed voices capture memories of lives lived, the panorama of events described may move the listener through the power of shamans, traditional beliefs and Native knowledge in all of its spheres. Topics include such subjects as polygamy, rabbit and caribou hunts, survival techniques, marriages and losses, northern lights, tribal law, etc. But, most important, we hear about the richness of the language as it is used and spoken, how place names are determined in a cultural context, and of how suddenly the Native languages became forbidden and became a mark of shame. School memories echo painfully as assimilation became the order of the day.

PROJECT JUKEBOX: GIVING VOICE TO ORAL HISTORY

It must be recognized that the words recorded in an interview, powerful as they may be, are only indicators of the communication that took place. Through Project Jukebox, the researcher/recorder/documenter emerges as someone responsible for going beyond recording the speaker's words to preserving as much as possible of the meaning that was conveyed in the interview. This is done with context statements, excerpts from written and oral documents. The emphasis is on the interplay of many recordings available in a jukebox, telling various stories. Enhancements such as a map showing the places described in an interview, a picture of the activity or subject described, or a statement made by someone remembering a particular storyteller, or perhaps a story told in its original language can provide an incredible bridge of understanding for those watching and listening.

Project Jukebox thus is an ambitious effort led by Dr. William Schneider and others to preserve full-length audio recordings in digital form with associated maps, photos, and supporting text either in English or in the appropriate Native languages, sometimes with parallel English texts. The programs feature interviews with narrators, who describe their experiences and various parts of the state and Native communities. The basic framework for each Project Jukebox computer program is the same although each has its own personal variations. Each Jukebox has a variety of materials: transcripts, interviews, photos, maps, or a searchable topic list. In some cases, materials are cross-referenced within the program. In others, each type of resource must be looked at independently. In the last ten years, over twenty-five multi-media CD-ROM Project Jukebox programs have been developed. Internet access is still limited, but this sensitive issue is being addressed. There is a great push to go online, but caution signs appear everywhere–many Natives view this as an invasion of privacy and as exploitation. Delicate balancing of the public versus the private domain remains a challenge.[27]

Walking through these innovative doorways leading to Alaska history and culture has enabled us to re-examine the paths we have taken and the direction we are moving in. Juxtaposing the recommendations made in "The Culturally Responsive Guidelines for Alaska Public Libraies,"[28] upon our "roadmap," revealed that as the major academic research library serving the state of Alaska, our compass is pointing in the right direction.

Cultural responsiveness is the core of the philosophy of the Alaska and Polar Region Collections of the Rasmuson Library. As the collection also has a circumpolar focus, the cultural responsiveness extends across wide ethnic and geographic perimeters. We attempt to provide guidance, recommendations, and access to the best current and retrospective resources on a national and international level. Exceptional, unique and elusive materials are made available via the best delivery methods. Sensitivity and awareness to the current socio-political milieu plays a paramount role in the curatorial efforts, as an attempt is made to provide access to these materials through the most appropriate formats: traditional, electronic, and digital. We welcome and seek counsel from appropriate faculty and organizations. We try to seek recommendations from the inner circles of Native leadership and communities, through personal and professional contacts. We want to be active participants in the cultural reassertion that is enveloping Alaska. Our vistas are expanding to embrace new approaches as we seek to celebrate and honor the richness of Native cultures in Alaska and throughout the circumpolar world. This will strengthen the bridges of acceptance so that we may be viewed not as outsiders "looking in" but as valuable partners in the process of seeking knowledge. The work that lies ahead is challenging and rewarding.

CONCLUSION

Language and nationality policies of a country are an official as well as a symbolic reflection of its prescribed attitude towards ethnic minorities. Indigenous people, such as the Alaska Natives, are part of that construct. "Language policies can become even more confusing when viewed in relation to the ambiguities expressed in the existing bilingual education regulations . . . This to have and have not stance leaves us waiting and questioning . . ."[29] As Willie Hensley, an Inupiaq Eskimo, expressed: "In 1971, we fought for the land because it represents the spirit of the people, because it represents an intimate knowledge of the environment our people grew up with for ten thousand years . . . our first fight for it was a fight for survival . . . we cannot look to corporate political life to fill the void of a century of psychological depression . . . a renaissance of our language and culture will give us the basis for the renewal of our people."[30]

Echoing Michael Krauss: "We may now hope that the North may yet keep at least its share of mainland languages." And, this is also the hope held for Alaska Native languages. As libraries, research centers, curators, and scholars we must do all we can to be active, believing participants in this effort. As we do so, we will continue correcting past errors and misconceptions in our theories and methodologies as we seek out better ways to serve future needs. Providing the best, culturally appropriate service in all aspects of our endeavors is an essential step in this journey.

REFERENCES

1. Anthony M. Kaliss, "European and Native Peoples: A Comparison of the Policies of the United States and Soviet/Russian Governments Towards the Native Peoples on Both Sides of the Bering Strait" (Ph.D. diss., University of Hawaii, 1999), 265.

2. Michael E. Krauss, *Alaska Native Languages: Past Present and Future*, Alaska Native Language Center Research Papers, no. 4 (Fairbanks, Alaska, 1980), 1.

3. Ibid.

4. Ibid.

5. Ann Fienup-Riordan, *Freeze Frame: Alaska Eskimos in the Movies* (Seattle: University of Washington Press, 1995), 6.

6. Eric Heyne. *Desert, Garden, Margin, Range: Literature on the American Frontier* (New York: Twayne Publishers, 1992), 9.

7. Ibid., 10.

8. Tamara Lincoln, "Ethno-Linguistic Misrepresentations of the Alaskan Native Languages as Mirrored in the Library of Congress System of Cataloging and Classification," *Cataloging & Classification Quarterly* 7, no. 3 (Spring 1987): 71.

9. Krauss, *Alaska Native Languages*, 25.

10. Richard Dauenhauer, *Conflicting Visions in Alaskan Education* (Juneau: Tlingit Readers, Inc., 2000), 7.

11. Michael E. Krauss, "The Eskimo Languages in Alaska, Yesterday and Today" in *Eskimo Languages: Their Present Day Condition*, ed. Bjarne Basse and Kristen Jensen (Aarhus: Arkona, 1979), 40.

12. Ibid., 42.

13. Krauss, *Alaska Native Languages*, 25.

14. *Information Exchange 2000* 28, no.12 (May 12, 2000): 2.

15. Ibid.

16. Kaliss, 162.

17. Ibid., 163.

18. Beth Leonard, "Documenting Indigenous Knowledge and Languages: Research Planning Protocol," *Sharing Our Pathways* 6, issue 5 (Nov/Dec 2001): 1.

19. Krauss, *Alaska Native Languages*, 24.

20. Regitze Margarithe Soby, "Language Identity in Thule," in *Eskimo Languages: Their Present Day Conditions*, ed. Bjarne Basse and Kristen Jensen (Aarhus: Arkona, 1979), 147.

21. Michael E. Krauss, "Alaska Native Language Legislation," *International Journal of American Linguistics* 40, no.2 (April 1974): 150.

22. For a full discussion of these issues, see: Lincoln, 69-89.

23. Michael E. Krauss, "The Indigenous Languages of the North: A Report on Their Present State," in *Northern Minority Languages: Problems of Survival,* ed. Hiroshi Shoji, Juha Janhuen (Osaka: National Museum of Ethnology, 1997), 32-33.

24. Ibid., 30.

25. Oscar Angayuqaq Kawagley, "Nurturing Native Languages," *Sharing Our Pathways* 7, issue 1 (Jan/Feb 2002): 3.

26. "Culturally Responsive Guidelines for Alaska Public Libraries," *Sharing Our Pathways* 6, issue 5 (Nov/Dec 2001): 6-8. The text of this document is also available on the ANKN Web site at: http://www.ankn.uaf.edu/standards/library.html [cited 31 May 2002].

27. For a discussion of this issue, see "Guidelines for Respecting Cultural Knowledge" at http://www.ankn.uaf.edu/standards/CulturalDoc.html [cited 31 May 2002].

28. See note 26.

29. Kaliss, 210.

30. Ibid., 311.

Descriptive Standards
and the Archival Profession

Susan E. Davis

SUMMARY. Studies of professions emphasize various means by which an occupation increases its authority over areas of activity within its jurisdiction. Development of standards and codification of knowledge are important stages in professionalization for any occupation. As technology became a more prevalent component of library bibliographic access, archivists began to seek ways to develop standards for archival description that would support information exchange and allow archives and manuscripts collections to be included in bibliographic utilities. This article describes the evolution of archival descriptive standards, beginning in the late 1970s, within the context of the development of the archival profession. *[Article copies available for a fee from The Haworth Document Delivery Service: 1-800-HAWORTH. E-mail address: <getinfo@haworthpressinc.com> Website: <http://www.HaworthPress.com> © 2003 by The Haworth Press, Inc. All rights reserved.]*

KEYWORDS. Archival description, archives, MARC formats, Research Libraries Group (RLG), Society of American Archivists (SAA), Library of Congress, online cataloging, professions

Susan E. Davis is a PhD candidate and lecturer, School of Library and Information Science, University of Wisconsin, Madison, and an archival educator (E-mail: sedavis@students.wisc.edu).

[Haworth co-indexing entry note]: "Descriptive Standards and the Archival Profession." Davis, Susan E. Co-published simultaneously in *Cataloging & Classification Quarterly* (The Haworth Information Press, an imprint of The Haworth Press, Inc.) Vol. 35, No. 3/4, 2003, pp. 291-308; and: *Historical Aspects of Cataloging and Classification* (ed: Martin D. Joachim) The Haworth Information Press, an imprint of The Haworth Press, Inc., 2003, pp. 291-308. Single or multiple copies of this article are available for a fee from The Haworth Document Delivery Service [1-800-HAWORTH, 9:00 a.m. - 5:00 p.m. (EST). E-mail address: getinfo@haworthpressinc.com].

INTRODUCTION

Description is integral to the archival mission to collect, preserve, and make accessible records and papers considered to have enduring value. All archives undertake descriptive work in its various manifestations so that changes in the theory and practice of description have a profound impact on professional activities. The advent of automation in libraries and archives transformed the ways in which archivists carried out their responsibilities in the area of description and supported the codification of archival knowledge and the development of the profession's first standards of practice. This transition sheds light on the ways in which a profession moves towards greater control over its jurisdiction.

The archival profession is one of several groups devoted to the care of information resources. Archivists differ from other information colleagues in that archivists focus on unpublished records and papers, created in the course of ongoing activity, rather than published information packages created for consumption by others. Archivists work mostly with aggregate groupings of records and papers, not individual items, and description of the collections is a primary function of the profession. This article examines the evolution of archival description and descriptive standards between 1977 and 1990 and analyzes the ways in which this single issue shaped the profession.

This period during which archivists first developed standards for description coincided with the growing use of technology in libraries and other information agencies and the increasing availability of graduate archival education, both of which encouraged unification within the field. The convergence of a variety of factors and events created an environment conducive to the kind of collaborative work necessary to achieve consensus on professional issues. The period since that time has built on the patterns established during the initial decade. The emergence of Encoded Archival Description (EAD), and its subsequent development and promulgation, has been supported by the combination of grant funding, workplace initiatives, association subgroups, and continuing education that characterized the adoption of the Machine Readable Cataloging (MARC) format and the first generation of descriptive standards.

In order to evaluate the leadership roles played by individuals, archival repositories, and professional associations in the development of description and descriptive standards, it is important to understand some of the approaches used in studying professions, leadership, and the history of archival practice, as well as the series of events and projects that took place within the archival profession, primarily in the 1980s.

PROFESSIONS, KNOWLEDGE, AND STANDARDS

Considerable literature exists relating to the history and sociology of professions, and various schools of thought have evolved over time.[1] Consensus seems to exist in certain areas. Scholars agree that a profession is "an occupational group with some special skill . . . usually this was an abstract skill, one that required extensive training. It was not applied in a purely routine fashion, but required revision case by case."[2] A profession also has a set of general dimensions. The cognitive dimension is based on a body of knowledge and techniques. The normative dimension relates to the profession's service orientation and ethical aspects, and the evaluative dimension compares a specific profession with other professions in the context of autonomy and prestige.[3]

Unfortunately, these dimensions are fairly vague; it is not clear how much training is necessary, how long the training should last, or how specialized the knowledge must be. Because of the difficulty inherent in defining the specific criteria for a profession, Freidson suggests that, instead of trying to define the specific characteristics of a profession that distinguish it from all other occupations, it would be more effective to focus on the process by which occupations move towards what might be construed as "profession" status:

> Professionalization might be defined as a process by which an organized occupation, usually but not always by virtue of making a claim to special esoteric competence and to concern for the quality of its work and its benefits to society, obtains the exclusive right to perform a particular kind of work, and control training for and access to it, and control the right of determining and evaluating the way the work is performed.[4]

This approach allows one to look at the ways in which an occupation develops coherency as a group, and over time progresses towards the necessary links between the creation of specialized knowledge and the authority to maintain control over the ways in which the knowledge is applied.

One constant that appears in all the theories of professions is the importance of the codification of professional knowledge and the development of standards through which that knowledge is applied. Whether the body of esoteric knowledge and authority and monopoly over its application is considered a trait, an element of power, or a jurisdictional issue, the existence of a distinct body of theory and practice is integral to an occupation's status as a profession. In the case of the archival profession, the attention focused on description and the formulation of standards for descriptive practice resulted from circumstances both external and internal to the profession. Description, however, is clearly the first area in which the profession moved deliberately towards establishing distinct standards and parameters for application of those standards.

THE ARCHIVAL PROFESSION

The community of American archivists is a twentieth century phenomenon. Archivists have been educated and worked in Europe for centuries, but the transition to American institutions was slow and took a shape somewhat different from their European counterparts. In the United States the archival tradition has two sets of roots. The first is the historical manuscripts tradition, shaped by private collectors and antiquarians, who concentrated on collecting historical materials. The curators of these collections used techniques borrowed from libraries and combined an historical perspective with library techniques of cataloging and item-level control. The Massachusetts Historical Society, established in 1791 by the historian and minister Jeremy Belknap, was the earliest institution of this type.[5] The American Historical Association (AHA) established a Historical Manuscripts Commission in 1895.

The second set of antecedents derives from European public archives. From the French came the principle of *provenance*, which emphasizes the connection records have to the agencies that created them. Prussian archivists formulated the concept of *Registraturprinzip* or *original order*, which means that records accumulate in a pattern that provides evidence of the function and purpose of the creating offices. These archivists were not interested in collecting historical materials but only in the management of an institution's own records. The AHA established a Public Archives Commission in 1899, an action that indicates that the organization distinguished between public records and historical manuscripts. Between 1900 and 1912, the Commission surveyed state archives around the country and reported on their programs. The concepts of *provenance* and *original order* soon became two of the fundamental principles of archival theory on which the core of the profession's expert knowledge is based. These concepts now apply to both publicly and privately generated materials.

Initially the historical manuscripts tradition dominated in the United States, which delayed the adoption of distinct archival practices. In Europe, archivists believed that records were created by an organization in the course of ongoing activity, and preserved and made accessible by that organization, but should not be collected by a separate institution. The archivist's role was thus tied to the creating agency, and archivists developed a distinct occupational identity. In contrast, American archivists initially linked their work to that of librarians and historians, which postponed the development of an independent occupation. The profession thus needed to find middle ground between the historical manuscripts and public archives traditions, and this ongoing debate continued well into the twentieth century.[6]

In the 1930s a series of events took place that shifted the direction of the archival profession. The National Archives was established in 1934, and the Society of American Archivists (SAA) was founded in 1936. Once SAA existed, AHA disbanded its Public Archives Commission. AHA originally intended to sponsor an institute for the leading practitioners, but it was recognized that such an institute would be too limited to meet the broader needs that a full professional association could serve.[7] From that point on, archivists had in the National Archives a visible institution focused on protecting the nation's documentary heritage and one around which professional development could evolve.

The National Archives played a leading role in the early years of the American archival profession and SAA because it constituted the single largest and strongest professional repository. This situation did not change until the late 1960s and 1970s when a growing number of colleges and universities began to set up archival programs that frequently encompassed both institutional records and the private papers of faculty and alumni. It is estimated that two-thirds of the college and university archives listed in the 1980 *Directory of College and University Archives in the United States and Canada* had been established since 1960.[8]

The college and university archives acted out the conflict between public records and manuscripts in that they frequently sought to preserve both the official records of their schools and the broader informational documentation of institutions of higher learning. Their growing numbers increased the membership in SAA, and their identification with a profession and not just their employing institution shifted the dynamic among archivists. In addition, college and university archives were frequently organizationally situated within the library, thus increasing the ties between archivists and librarians. As library practices changed, archivists felt increasing pressure to accommodate automation and more uniform practices. Since the late 1970s, this has manifested itself in description.

The Research Libraries Group (RLG) played a very important role in the work of college and university archives. Established in 1974 as a "not-for-profit corporation devoted to the mission of 'improving access to information that supports research and learning,' " this powerful consortium combined the resources of a group of distinguished research libraries in a variety of cooperative ventures.[9] RLG hosts the Research Libraries Information Network (RLIN), which created one of the first bibliographic utilities providing centralized access to research library collections around the world. RLG and its member libraries were major actors in the development of the MARC AMC (Archives and Manuscripts Control) format and its implementation by college and university archives. The resources and influence of RLG represented the only significant coalition of archival workplaces, in contrast to the norm of archival practice occurring in small institutions, and RLG's contributions to archival descriptive practice have been considerable.

The contemporary archival community continues to represent a diverse constituency. Archivists work in a wide range of institutions: governments at all levels, colleges and universities, public libraries, historical societies, museums, religious groups, corporations, labor unions, and a diverse array of not-for-profit organizations. At approximately 40 percent, college and university archivists represent the largest membership group within SAA, and almost two-thirds of the SAA membership work in small repositories (one to three FTE). Solo practice (or "lone arrangers," as single practitioners have often been called) is not uncommon.[10]

The fact that so few archivists work in large archival institutions places a far greater emphasis on the role of the professional associations than might be expected for other professions. In contrast, fewer librarians work alone, and the vast majority work in places familiarly labeled as libraries. Librarians thus have more access to colleagues and professional identification within their institutions than do archivists. SAA, as the national association, is the most visible, but archivists also join regional associations around the country. Archivists invest a great deal of energy in these professional associations, which facilitate colleague communication, career satisfaction, visibility, credibility, professional identity, continuing education, and advancement of the profession. And within the professional associations the opportunity for leadership is often greater than it is within a specific workplace, where the archivist frequently is isolated. Approximately 25-30 percent of the individual members of the Society of American Archivists attend the annual meeting each year, indicating that members strongly value this professional connection.

The structure of SAA, the largest and most influential of the professional associations, supports a network of decentralized activity.[11] An elected Council appoints task forces and standing committees that undertake both ongoing activity and special projects. Membership overlaps open sections and roundtables through which various interest groups pursue specific agendas. While the names of these groups have changed over time, both appointed and open membership groups devote attention to issues of description and standards development. Members of those groups represent both the professional association and the institution for which they work. Individuals bring the archival experience from their jobs to these SAA units, collaborate in ways that are often not possible in small repositories, gain knowledge, and develop consensus that informs both the profession and the practices in individual work-places. This symbiotic framework represents the context within which archivists have developed descriptive practice and standards.

HISTORY OF ARCHIVAL DESCRIPTION

The evolution of archival description and descriptive standards represents the single most important innovation undertaken by the profession. Not only did this work profoundly alter the way archivists performed a fundamental professional function, but it also fostered communication between archivists and other information professions. Archivists began to codify their own body of knowledge that extended across institutional and record types within the archival world, and they also claimed jurisdiction over this expertise as it overlapped with other related occupations.

Prior to the advent of the computer in archival practice, archivists viewed description as the production of *finding aids*, or narrative descriptions of the source, scope, and content of collections along with box/folder lists. Archivists tended to use the unique nature of their collections as reasons for developing and maintaining nonstandard, often idiosyncratic repository-level practices for arranging and describing collections. Repositories shared information on related collections through printed guides and informal channels, and there seemed to be little potential benefit in developing standardized practices.[12]

The ability to automate catalog entries and other finding aids and the potential of using bibliographic utilities for the ongoing management of archival collections shifted the emphasis of description to *control,* both intellectual and physical. Unlike library materials, archival collections contain a variety of formats and tend to change in size and shape after repositories acquire them. Donors continue to add to collections, and archivists weed and discard materials, reformat and rebox portions of the collections. The responsibilities of managing quantities of primary source materials requires archivists to maintain fairly meticulous records of their work, including the connection between the creators of the records and the records themselves, to respect *provenance*. Automation of description promoted a more active system of management than previously possible. In an automated system, descriptive records can easily be modified and updated as changes occur. It also became apparent that a commonality of practice existed, despite archival protests to the contrary. Archivists were following similar arrangement and description procedures, compiling similar information and producing comparable results, even if the formatting and labeling differed.

During the 1977-1990 period, three major projects occurred that stimulated the series of events credited with changing archival description. First, SAA Council established a National Information Systems Task Force (NISTF) in 1977. Then, the National Endowment for the Humanities (NEH) awarded SAA two consecutive automation grants between 1985 and 1988 that supported the use of the MARC AMC format through workshops, presentations, and publications. And in 1988 the National Historical Publications and Records Commission (NHPRC) funded the Working Group on Standards for Archival Description, composed of a number of archivists from various repositories, facilitated through Harvard University. RLG participated in all of these projects and initiated its own agenda of centralized access that both led and reinforced these other efforts.

These initiatives served as a focal point around which both the national and regional professional associations and a number of archival repositories engaged in related activities. Each represents a stage in archivists' efforts to grapple with changes in the profession and the environment in which the profession operated. Combined, these efforts constitute a major change for the archival profession and the first formal codification of professional practice. Individual leaders emerged from these various projects, whose accomplishments contributed to the shape of the modern archival profession.

Phase 1: NISTF

SAA Council established NISTF during the 1977 annual meeting to study the problem of constructing a national information system for archives and manuscript collections. In its charge to the Task Force, SAA applauded efforts by the *National Union Catalog of Manuscript Collections (NUCMC)* and the NHPRC's national guide project in this area, but pointed out that the profession itself tended to think on the repository level and had not devoted enough attention to the impact such programs had "on professional standards and techniques, on individual and institutional members and their descriptive activities, and on the resources available for archival needs."[13] After issuing its initial report, NISTF struggled with its broad mission. In 1979, membership was altered, and the next year NISTF received funding to study and assemble data on descriptive elements. That funding was later extended to 1983 to support the Task Force's continued efforts.

NISTF's work had three goals: to provide intellectual access to archives and manuscripts sources in American repositories; to establish a framework for "describing and improving access to archival resources"; and to facilitate adoption of automated techniques.[14] Meetings held in July 1980, October 1980, and January 1981 resulted in a position paper that defined an important role for the archival profession in the development of this national information system for archives and manuscripts repositories, and SAA Council approved it in January 1981. NISTF concluded that "archival and manuscript descriptive practices, while varying from repository to repository, employ a common set of descriptive elements which could be codified into a standard format."[15] This finding enabled the Task Force to recommend the establishment of a standard format as the first step towards national information systems. This common format would serve as a link among one or more databases, created by a variety of repositories.

These conclusions set the stage for the next phase of NISTF activity: to define standard data elements. NISTF completed "Data Elements Used in Archives, Manuscripts and Records Repository Information Systems: A Dictionary of Standard Terminology" (known in brief as the "Data Elements Dictionary") in early 1982 and circulated it among the profession for testing and feedback by repositories. The document defined the units of information used by archivists to describe archives and manuscripts in a way that would facilitate communication across different systems. The "Data Elements Dictionary" proved to be one of the foundations of the MARC AMC format because it codified terms and categories of information.

NISTF eventually concluded that a single national information system was problematic. *NUCMC*'s scope and format excluded government and institutional archives and was based on library practices. NISTF raised several questions about the viability of the proposed NHPRC guide. NHPRC's commitment to its own data base, NISTF assumed, could bring it into political and financial conflict with other proposed developments in archival automation that would seek Commission funding. Attention to such a massive project would also deflect the NHPRC's attention from its other important contributions, which also could benefit the larger goals. NISTF also expressed doubt about the role of a government agency in the creation of a national information resource, and the Selective Permutation INDEXing (SPINDEX) software program on which the NHPRC database depended was proving to be appealing only to government repositories. Manuscripts repositories were not adopting SPINDEX.[16]

NISTF's charge expired in 1983, and a new SAA standing committee, the Committee on Archival Information Exchange (CAIE), took over its ongoing responsibilities. ALA's Committee on Representation in Machine-Readable Form of Bibliographic Information (MARBI) approved the US MARC format for Archival and Manuscripts Control (MARC AMC) in 1983; the Library of Congress published the format in 1984. In 1983 the Library of Congress also published Steven Hensen's first edition of *Archives, Personal Papers, and Manuscripts: A Cataloging Manual for Archival Repositories, Historical So-*

cieties, and Manuscript Libraries, which interpreted the MARC format for archivists. SAA committed itself to the ongoing maintenance of both the NISTF Data Elements Dictionary and the MARC AMC format. Representatives from NISTF, RLG, CAIE and other interested parties met at the Hoover Institution, Stanford University in March 1983 to discuss what had been accomplished up to that point and to set an agenda for the future.

In retrospect, NISTF's work had both short- and long-term ramifications. The Task Force constituted the first orchestrated effort to examine changes in the information professions and the potential place of archivists within that world. While the members began with the goal of constructing an information system for archives and manuscripts, they quickly realized that, due to a lack of both resources and autonomy, such a system was beyond the reach of archivists. They also realized that the National Archives was not going to take a leadership role like the Library of Congress did for the library profession. Instead, pioneering efforts in descriptive information systems had to come from college and university libraries, and particularly RLG member institutions. Realistically, albeit somewhat reluctantly, NISTF concluded that the best way to pursue archival descriptive standards was through an adaptation of MARC cataloging and that active participation in that process might yield a satisfactory result over which archivists could maintain some measure of control. Instead of one national information system, repositories utilizing consistent descriptive formats and standards could contribute to a multitude of bibliographic systems.

The long-term consequences of this decision were considerable. Instead of pursuing the national information system, NISTF focused on the development of the "Data Elements Dictionary" that would encompass what archivists believed was important for efficient and effective description of archives and manuscript collections. This entailed a codification of professional knowledge that could become a component of these larger, library-oriented systems. In a larger political sense, NISTF chose the route that would dominate the next decade of archival descriptive work and would characterize the nature of that work. Archivists would not develop a totally independent descriptive practice but instead would work in close collaboration with other information professions, especially library and information studies. NISTF also recommended that SAA play a leadership role in the process.

The existence of NISTF was timely for the archival profession for another reason. In the early 1980s, several other professional groups had taken on related tasks. RLG's Advisory Committee on Archives and Manuscripts worked on a data elements dictionary as a first step towards RLG systems development. The National Archives established an internal working group to develop data elements. The Library of Congress established a Committee on Specialized Cataloging. NISTF included all these groups within its meetings and discussions. While NISTF often served as a lightning rod for the frustrations others felt at the slow pace of developing a format that would serve the more immediate needs of archivists, the Task Force did provide opportunities for discussion and a driving force for grappling with these large and thorny issues.

The individual members of NISTF represented both their institutions and the larger profession. They brought professional expertise gained through their positions to the table and thus could see both the benefits and pitfalls of the proposed descriptive systems. They were also positioned to test the new descriptive formats in their repositories and share those results with their colleagues at home and in the larger professional arena. Archivists working in RLG libraries had the added benefit of RLG's intense interest in the MARC format, and RLG contributed both financial and political support. Some of these individuals, including Steven Hensen (Library of Congress), H. Thomas Hickerson (Cornell University), Nancy Sahli (NHPRC), and David Bearman (consultant) continued to play important roles in the other professional projects undertaken during the 1980s. Their sustained involvement in archival description led to their identification as leaders in this process, providing continuity between initiatives and bridging the gap between archival repository and professional association.

Phase 2: RLG and SAA

If NISTF served as the catalyst to define the problem and outline the desired approach to developing automated archival descriptive systems, RLG and SAA provided the means to disseminate that information to the profession at large. By 1983, when NISTF was transformed into a standing committee, CAIE, the archival profession had chosen a specific direction for the development of descriptive standards. The larger political decisions had taken place. Deliberations turned instead to the logistics of implementing that format within archival repositories and the accumulation of a sufficient number of bibliographic records to evaluate the application of this new format to actual collections of archival materials.

RLG took an early active interest in development of the MARC AMC format. RLG saw the implementation of the format as integral to the development of its online catalog, RLIN, and by 1984 had already made the necessary enhancements to RLIN to incorporate the format. The consortium directors realized that simultaneous access to primary source materials enhanced access to traditional library holdings. Thus, their goal was the integration of research library holdings on specific topics, including books, recordings, visual materials, and manuscripts. To achieve this, RLG/RLIN supported the development of seven different files for different material formats, each with related MARC fields that could be searched independently or in combination.[17]

RLG had established an Archives, Manuscripts, and Special Collections Task Force in 1983 in order to solicit broad-based participation in the automation of archival description through this new format. Members of this Task Force participated in some of the NISTF discussions as well as those at the Library of Congress, whose Joint Committee on Specialized Cataloging was working on revisions to three chapters of the *Anglo-American Cataloging Rules (AACR2)*. The RLG Task Force subsequently became the Archives, Manuscripts and Special Collections Program Committee which monitored this activity until 1992. In fact, several NISTF members and the majority of the seven initial members of CAIE were employed by RLG member institutions.[18] The combination of professional goals and institutional incentives supported the activity of these individuals as they collaborated on a series of task forces and grant projects over the next few years, all aimed at refining the format, developing descriptive standards, and increasing the number of automated catalog records for archival collections.

Independently and through its member institutions, RLG obtained a series of Department of Education Title II-C (Strengthening Research Library Resources Program), NEH, and NHPRC grants that funded both the development of the format and the entry of thousands of bibliographic records into RLIN. For example, RLG received an NEH grant in 1981 to support development of a functional requirements document for archives and manuscripts enhancements to RLIN. They also successfully applied for Title II-C funding to work on external design of the archives and manuscripts system. That system development began in 1983, and Yale University entered the first bibliographic record in January 1984. In 1981 Yale received Title II-C funding to develop an automated format for cataloging archival collections, and in 1986 Yale received additional Title II-C money for the development of workstation based MARC AMC. In 1986 RLG received NHPRC funding for what became known as the Seven States Project. This project sought both to make available over 25,000 state records series through RLIN and to develop consistent functional appraisal standards for the records of state agencies.[19]

RLG's importance in automated archival description continued to grow as more and more research libraries became members. In 1985 RLG had thirty-two regular member institutions, as well as ten associate and eighteen special members. Currently over 160 universities, national libraries, archives, historical societies and other institutions participate in RLG's varied services.[20] In contrast, the Online Computer Library Center's (OCLC) equivalent application of the MARC AMC format was less successful, due both to the nature of the institutions involved and greater limitations for their version of the

MARC AMC format. The National Archives remained a marginal player in the national discussions, leaving RLG the strongest advocate for archivists within archival institutions. RLG's clearly articulated priorities strengthened the efforts of archivists, who otherwise would be more isolated within small repositories.

SAA provided the other constant and vocal influence for archivists in the development of automated description and descriptive standards. As the national professional association, SAA had served as the forum for publication and communication for the profession. Through NISTF, CAIE, and other membership groups devoted to archival description, archivists had been meeting regularly to discuss both activities within their institutions and the larger issues surrounding changing professional theory and practice. In 1986, SAA established an RLIN Users Roundtable, which served as an annual venue for discussion of the specific attributes of the system.

Professional associations generally play a significant role in a profession's progress, but the diffuse nature of the archival work environment placed a greater emphasis on SAA's ability to coordinate activity. Individual archivists brought both their own experiences and the priorities created by their job responsibilities to the elected and appointed positions they assumed in SAA, and the benefits they derived from this larger collaboration often served the interests of their employing institutions. In the case of MARC AMC, SAA provided a means for the archivists in RLG-affiliated institutions to "spread the word" to their colleagues through publications, membership groups, and the annual meeting. As such, links between workplace and professional association were forged and strengthened.

NISTF was the first SAA group to undertake an automated archival description project, but it would not be the last. Archival institutions looked to SAA for guidance in local implementation of the MARC AMC format. In response, SAA successfully sought funding from NEH for an Automated Archival Information Program, established in 1985. The grant project contained three parts: (1) workshops to train archivists in the application of the MARC AMC format, (2) a clearinghouse to publicize archival automation efforts, and (3) research and development activities in the area of archival automation.

In 1985 two publications appeared that provided detailed explanations of the format and examples of its application by several repositories. In October 1984 NHPRC supported a conference in Madison, Wisconsin, attended by thirty-six people representing twenty-two institutions, "to share experiences and understanding of the format."[21] The State Historical Society of Wisconsin published *MARC for Archives and Manuscripts: A Compendium of Practice* in 1985, and the same year SAA published a companion volume by Nancy Sahli, *MARC for Archives and Manuscripts: The AMC Format.* These were the first major attempts by the profession to disseminate widely the ways in which institutions applied the specific MARC fields to their own archives and manuscripts collections.

SAA began offering MARC AMC workshops in February 1986 and by mid-1987 had held seven workshops attended by 170 people representing over 140 repositories.[22] The success of this work encouraged NEH to extend the funding for a second two-year period to expand the workshop program and to underwrite a revision of Steven Hensen's *Archives, Personal Papers, and Manuscripts*. This new edition incorporated changes and clarifications in the format developed as a result of its widespread adoption by archival repositories around the country.

By the time the NEH funding ended in 1989, SAA had strengthened its position as a focal point for archival automation and descriptive activity. Articles in its bi-monthly newsletter frequently highlighted the status of projects undertaken by SAA and those underway in repositories staffed by SAA members. SAA had its own standing committee, CAIE, which focused on descriptive standards and information exchange, in addition to several informal groups which met and shared information. Sessions at annual meetings, and articles in the *American Archivist*, SAA's official journal, focused on descriptive and automation issues, and SAA had official liaisons with other relevant groups involved in these areas.

Phase 3: Working Group on Standards for Archival Description

Despite the support RLG and SAA lent to a variety of description-related activities, the profession had still not found an effective way to address standards development and implementation. RLG had successfully launched RLIN, which by August 1, 1986 contained over 70,000 archives and manuscripts bibliographic records.[23] These records, however, revealed many inconsistencies in the interpretation of MARC fields. And as a membership organization, RLG mainly benefited a select group of research institutions, rather than a broad cross-section of the profession. SAA had sponsored publications, meetings, and workshops that reached many archivists, but SAA, as a voluntary association, had little enforcement authority; its members balance professional interests against job responsibilities.

In 1988, a group of archivists representing SAA, the Library of Congress, and the National Archives, and their individual institutions convened "to consider questions relating to descriptive standards and to try to provide a conceptual framework within which the profession can consider these issues." In addition, they hoped to make recommendations to SAA regarding procedures for systematic standards development and approval.[24] They sought funding for this work from the NHPRC, and in June 1988, Harvard University received a grant "to convene a working group of archivists to assess the current status of archival description standards; to identify standards that need to be developed; and to identify other issues and problems relating to standards developing and implementation that need to be addressed."[25]

Led by Lawrence Dowler of Harvard University, the working group met twice over the next year, and their discussions reframed the scope of archival description. The group drafted a new definition of description that incorporated its ongoing nature and focused more on the process than on the end result of specific finding aids. In addition, the Working Group developed a matrix that articulated the levels of description, and the relative strengths, and sources of the varied archival descriptive standards. This matrix clarified areas of professional autonomy for archivists as well as areas where archivists derive expertise from related fields. The matrix also provided criteria for the evaluation of existing and proposed standards.

The significance of this project was twofold. In pragmatic terms, it succeeded in raising the theoretical and practical issues of standards development and implementation for the archival profession. By this time the profession had accepted the MARC AMC format, but the nature of automated systems necessitated a more consistent approach to the way individual repositories structured their bibliographic records. The Working Group addressed these issues, and in a double issue of the *American Archivist* they publicized the results of their discussions to the archival profession.[26] Furthermore, the Working Group also represented a significant milestone for the profession. It was not SAA or RLG or the Library of Congress that successfully applied for this funding; it was a group of professional archivists who took the initiative and tackled this important issue. Each individual on the Working Group had associations with both his or her employing institution and the larger archival profession. The ability to carry out a project of this duration and complexity signified a maturing of the profession and a consensus on its forward direction. The importance of description and descriptive standards was the catalyst for this activity.

CONCLUSION

A major challenge for any profession is the maintenance of control over the basic aspects of its work. For archivists, this challenge was evident as automated systems began to alter the shape of the information professions. Librarians embraced the MARC format in large measure because of the cost benefits of shared cataloging. This factor was inconsequential to archivists for whom cataloging was an element of larger, complex descriptive systems. Instead, the development of the MARC AMC format offered archivists a way to find common ground, to strengthen professional practice, and to codify the knowledge of a fundamental archival function.

The process by which archivists progressed toward the goal of descriptive standards was significant not just for its end results, but also for the ways in which the profession coalesced. Individual archivists, representing both their employing institution and their profession, participated in the committees, task forces, roundtables, and workshops that led to the creation and dissemination of the MARC AMC format. By the end of the 1980s, the archival profession had collaborated on a set of descriptive standards that gave the profession control over a fundamental area of activity and facilitated the inclusion of archival holdings in the online catalogs that were becoming prevalent in the library world.

The prominence of organized networks played a significant role in the events of the 1980s. RLG set a high priority on the development of the MARC format and the unification of its libraries' varied holdings. RLG resources also supported the leadership roles played by archivists employed by consortium institutions in the other professional projects. SAA constituted a consistent forum for the development and diffusion of professional knowledge. Their efforts laid the groundwork that enabled the Working Group on Standards for Archival Description to take what had been established and build it into a coherent framework. The result was a codified body of expertise, a process for developing and approving archival standards, and a more unified and proactive profession.

ABBREVIATIONS

AHA	American Historical Association
AACR2	*Anglo American Cataloging Rules*, 2nd edition
CAIE	Committee on Archival Information Exchange
EAD	Encoded Archival Description
MARBI	American Library Association Committee on Representation in Machine-Readable Form of Bibliographic Information
MARC	Machine Readable Cataloging
MARC AMC	MARC Archives and Manuscripts Control Format
NEH	National Endowment for the Humanities
NHPRC	National Historical Publications and Records Commission
NISTF	National Information Systems Task Force
NUCMC	*National Union Catalog of Manuscript Collections*

OCLC	Online Computer Library Center
RLG	Research Libraries Group
RLIN	Research Libraries Information Network
SAA	Society of American Archivists
SPINDEX	Selective Permutation INDEXing

NOTES

1. See the Introduction chapter in Andrew Abbott's *The System of Professions* (Chicago: University of Chicago Press, 1988) for an excellent review of this topic.

2. Ibid., 7.

3. Magali Sarfatti Larson, *The Rise of Professionalism* (Berkeley, CA: University of California Press, 1977): x.

4. Elliot Freidson, "Professions and the Occupational Principle" in *The Professions and Their Prospects* (Beverly Hills, CA: Sage Publications, 1973), 22.

5. Mattie U. Russell, "The Influence of History on the Archival Professions in the United States," *American Archivist* 46: 3 (1983): 279.

6. Luke Gilliland-Swetland, "The Provenance of a Profession: The Permanence of the Public Archives and Historical Manuscripts Tradition in American Archival History," *American Archivist* 54:3 (1991): 166.

7. J. Frank Cook, "The Blessings of Providence on an Association of Archivists," *American Archivist* 46: 4 (1983): 375.

8. Ibid., 394.

9. <http://www.rlg.org/rlg.htm> [cited 8 April 2002].

10. In many respects archivists "self-identify" as members of the profession. There is no official control over entry, no legal licensure, and no accreditation of graduate archival education. A program of individual certification, established in 1989, remains controversial.

11. Each year SAA elects three members of Council, who serve three-year terms and a Vice-President who serves one year as Vice-President and the subsequent year as President. The Treasurer is also elected to a three-year term. All twelve elected officials have votes, and the President does not have veto power.

12. "Report of the Working Group on Standards for Archival Description," *American Archivist* 52: 4 (1989).

13. Charge to NISTF, 15 March 1978, Box 135 (unprocessed), The Society of American Archivists. Records, 1936-[ongoing]. UWM Manuscript Collection 172. Golda Meir Library. University Manuscript Collections. University of Wisconsin-Milwaukee.

14. Society of American Archivists, *Newsletter* (May 1981): 6-7.

15. SAA grant proposal to NEH, "Definition of Descriptive Elements for Archives and Manuscript Collections," 1980, Box 135 (unprocessed), The Society of American Archivists. Records, 1936-[ongoing].

16. NISTF Response to NHPRC Proposal, January 1981, Box 135 (unprocessed), The Society of American Archivists. Records, 1936-[ongoing].

17. The seven formats are Archival and Mixed Collections, Books, Maps, Recordings, Scores, Serials, and Visual Materials.

18. NISTF Members included: Richard Lytle (Smithsonian Institution), Maynard Brichford (University of Illinois), John Daly (Illinois State Archives), Charles Dollar (National Archives), Lawrence Dowler (Harvard University), Max Evans (State Historical Society of Wisconsin), Steven Hensen (Library of Congress); H. Thomas Hickerson (Cornell University), Charles Palm (Hoover Institution, Stanford University), Nancy Sahli (NHPRC). CAIE initial members included: Lewis Bellardo (Kentucky Dept. of Library and Archives), Kathy Hudson (Yale University), William L. Joyce (The New York Public Library), Lydia Lucas (Minnesota Historical Society), William Wallach (University of Michigan), Vicki Walch (National Archives).

19. The seven states are Alabama, California, Minnesota, New York, Pennsylvania, Utah, and Wisconsin.

20. <http://www.rlg.org/rlg.htm> [cited 8 April 2002].

21. *MARC for Archives and Manuscripts: A Compendium of Practice* (Madison, Wisconsin: State Historical Society of Wisconsin, 1985), 1.

22. Society of American Archivists, *Newsletter* (March 1987): 7.

23. H. Thomas Hickerson, "Archival Information Exchange and the Role of Bibliographic Networks," *Library Trends* 36:3 (1988): 553.

24. Lawrence Dowler and Richard Szary to Participants, 29 August 1988, Box 53 (unprocessed), The Society of American Archivists. Records, 1936-[ongoing]. Working Group members included: Lawrence Dowler (Harvard University), David Bearman (Archives and Museum Informatics), Lynn Bellardo (National Archives), Jean Dryden (United Church Archives), Steven Hensen (RLG), H. Thomas Hickerson (Cornell University), Marion Matters (SAA), Fredric Miller (NEH), Harriet Ostroff (*NUCMC*), Kathleen Roe (New York State Archives and Records Administration), Leon Stout (Pennsylvania State University), Richard V. Szary (Yale University), Sharon Gibbs Thibodeau (National Archives), Nancy Sahli and Lisa Weber (representing the NHPRC) and Vicki Walch, project coordinator.

25. Resolution on the Report of the Working Group on Standards for Archival Description, 1988, Box 80 (unprocessed), The Society of American Archivists. Records, 1936-[ongoing].

26. *American Archivist* 52:4 (Fall 1989) and 53:1 (Winter 1990) contain the Report and Recommendations of the Working Group, as well as all the background papers and lists of additional resources. The Working Group also won SAA's Fellows Posner Prize for the most outstanding essay published in the 1989 *American Archivist*.

Foundations of Government Information and Bibliographic Control in the United States: 1789-1900

John A. Shuler

SUMMARY. A history of classification and bibliographic control of government information is, by necessity, a tangled tale that involves the complex evolution of governments, the regularization of official publishing, along with the growth of professional librarianship. For the purposes of this article, the main argument will draw its narrative largely from the historic evolution of bibliographic control and U.S. government information during the nineteenth century. The standards and practices developed in the United States during this period remain a common framework for the discussion of any government in the world. It is further argued that these bibliographic arrangements remained in play until the 1980s when the advent of distributed computer networks began to undermine the traditions of what had largely been a print culture. *[Article copies available for a fee from The Haworth Document Delivery Service: 1-800-HAWORTH. E-mail address: <getinfo@haworthpressinc.com> Website: <http://www.HaworthPress.com> © 2003 by The Haworth Press, Inc. All rights reserved.]*

John A. Shuler, MLS, is Associate Professor and Department Head/Documents Librarian, University of Illinois at Chicago (E-mail: alfred@uic.edu). He serves as an editor and editorial board member of *Government Information Quarterly*, is editor of *Documents to the People*, quarterly publication of the American Library Association's Government Documents Roundtable, and writes a column for the *Journal of Academic Librarianship*.

[Haworth co-indexing entry note]: "Foundations of Government Information and Bibliographic Control in the United States: 1789-1900." Shuler, John A. Co-published simultaneously in *Cataloging & Classification Quarterly* (The Haworth Information Press, an imprint of The Haworth Press, Inc.) Vol. 35, No. 3/4, 2003, pp. 309-334; and: *Historical Aspects of Cataloging and Classification* (ed: Martin D. Joachim) The Haworth Information Press, an imprint of The Haworth Press, Inc., 2003, pp. 309-334. Single or multiple copies of this article are available for a fee from The Haworth Document Delivery Service [1-800-HAWORTH, 9:00 a.m. - 5:00 p.m. (EST). E-mail address: getinfo@haworthpressinc.com].

KEYWORDS. Government information, government publications, U.S. Government Printing Office, government information bibliographic control, government publishing, government information resource management, depository libraries

THE NATURE OF GOVERNMENT AND ITS INFORMATION NEEDS

Bibliographic control of government information, as with other communication artifacts collected and organized by libraries through the centuries, seeks several critical outcomes. First, there is a need to describe and list. Second, there is a need to place the individual publications within a larger context of other relevant publications, as well as within government processes. Third, there is the need to access this complexity of information over a period of time and geography. However, any serious attempt to try to explain the historical evolution of cataloging and bibliographic standards as they apply to official publications must begin with the understanding of political culture and bureaucratic development. Simply, a "government publication" is just one example from a wide variety of communication artifacts produced and distributed through public processes; it is not a creation often borne from discrete (or single) authorship. And this is, perhaps, the primary reason why government publications are considered by many librarians to be such difficult artifacts to collect, organize, catalog, and service. It is a rare government publication that can stand apart from the policy or political world that created it.

When a government sets policy, or pursues the execution of its culture's legal, economic, and political ends, the official record created by these public acts contain no meaning if there is no larger understanding of what the government means to accomplish with these policies, regulations, court decisions, or enacted laws. In other words, remove government publications from the context of public policy formation or divorce their relationships to other government information services, and they are rendered unintelligible. They are serial publications, although our present-day cataloging rules treat many official publications as such. Although this argument applies to any government system operating around the world, the U.S. system usually stands as a model of how librarians have sought methods or establish practices to solve the essential problems of bibliographic control.

FROM THE CRADLE OF CIVILIZATIONS AND COMMUNICATIONS

Governments, as complex organizations, rely on a dynamic combination of power, technology, and tradition to control and command resources through time and place. The more a government could know on how to motivate a growing population of unrelated people, the more effective it might be to achieve the necessary support (if not the complete obedience) from the masses. This governing motivation can be found in the ancient cultures of the Americas, Asia, and the Indian subcontinent as well as the Middle East; and this impulse to control and organize drew upon an accumulated store of society's collective customs, rules, regulations, religious beliefs, sanctions, and knowledge of the physical conditions of a particular geography (tides, floods, astronomy to measure time, awareness–if not direct knowledge–of other cultures). Early "libraries" of these civilizations were little more than collections of the oral traditions and customs written down through evolving systems of writing. These written records were kept close to the government's seat of power and/or religious activity. As one author describes the practices of the Sumerians (around 3000 BC), organized collections of laws, by-laws, and important events were recorded on clay tablets and stored in rooms found in centralized government/temple complexes. As these physical spaces became regulated, particular individuals (scribes, archive organizers, technicians to create and prepare the various surfaces used to record the writing) were also trained to care for the collections. Early systems of classification, to judge from the archeological record, indicate that lists of tablets found in these collections were organized not by title but by first line.

A good deal of this organized knowledge remained intimately linked to predominant religious beliefs and were part of the effort to spread faith and train new leaders in understanding the reality of the local religious codes. Military knowledge (necessary intelligence and strategic observations of both an enemy's capability and terrain) was often kept in these collections, as well as the necessary statistics and accounting methods that supported these early cultures' evolving economies as they moved from informal exchanges or barter systems to symbolic systems of money. Nowhere else is this intricate weaving of civic and religious missions more evident than in the several hundred years of Egyptian civilization. Egyptian libraries were among the first to exploit the possibilities of a new medium: papyrus. As the civilization spread its influence beyond the Nile River Valley, the portability of paper and the expressiveness of Egyptian hieroglyphics divided writing into three categories: religious (hieroglyphic); hieratic (read by the priests); and epistolographic or demotic (for everyday uses). Obviously this expanded the demands of classification and storage, and the complexity of the library physical structure reflected this. Egypt civilization, from the evidence of archeological findings, also appears to be one of the first to foster a true mass reading culture. In other words, societies around the world moved from a framework of cultural understandings that were largely driven by spiritual needs of divinely appointed rulers to one that focused on the individual and materialism of this present world.[1]

Over the thousands of years, then, as governments developed increasingly sophisticated systems of command and control, a comparable expansion in the complexity of their information systems took place. However, it would not be until the cultural and political revolutions that began in the late fifteenth through the eighteenth centuries, when the ideas of capitalism, republicanism, and democracy destabilized the ancient rules of religion and royalty, that the modern sense of government information and bibliographic control came into existence. Governments could no longer take as a given that their actions, words, or edicts would be simply accepted by the masses. The spread of literacy, the creation of an economic system that fostered more efficient means of production and distribution (which in turn led to a population explosion for many cultures as more individuals had access to stable food supplies), along with the evolving sense that personal destiny is a matter of individual choice, not accepted as a fate already foretold.[2] Certainly, a principal agent of change during this period was the development of paper and print on an early industrial scale. As printed books captured current scientific and commercial developments, manuscripts from the ancient civilizations of the Near East and Asia were rediscovered.

The idea of mass education and literacy was reborn. And governments responded in kind by creating publications and documents that did more than just record official acts but actually began to explain and argue why these actions were necessary in the first place. What's more, the spread of literacy and printing fostered the ability of larger segments of society to talk back to the government, expressing their desires and choices in some very profound ways. One of the first acts of bibliographic control during this period was the creation of edited "papers" from the early assemblies or parliaments of Europe. Although these were not officially organized (or broadly distributed) in a useful way until the mid to late 1700s, the idea that a government would preserve a record of its actions to be read by the masses at some point in the future or geographically distant from the government's seat of power was a critical element in the development of bibliographic control. It remains an essential element in any discussion of cataloging and classification that we are talking about the need to organize a written record fractured by both time and geography.

THE GROWTH OF BIBLIOGRAPHIC CONTROL IN THE UNITED STATES

In many ways the sense of bibliographic control in terms of government information largely depends not so much on the professional practices of librarians, but rather on the shape and force of a government as it attempts to implement its policies and programs. For the first century of American government, production, identification, and access of government information were largely by-products of unrelated government programs. This should not come as a surprise, really, for the traditions of bibliographic control do not fare well in a political culture where the diffusion of knowledge and information directly feeds the political agendas of ruling political elites.

The political traditions and practices established during the American and French revolutions of the late eighteenth century became the first models of modern public information practice. These new forms of representative governments demanded a greater reliance on written records and civic accountability within a geographically dispersed population. Early constitutions from this period specifically mention records and sharing information to support the government as well as to inform the citizenry. These new societies also expected a greater literacy among the people and the expectation that they understand and participate in the decision-making process. More important, these forms of government built a new relationship between their citizens and official organizations. There are three distinct policy conflicts within the federal government's bureaucratic development.

The first conflict, **constitutional**, stems from the shared and divided responsibilities among the three branches, which are, in turn, leavened by individual civil rights contained in the first ten, and subsequent, amendments to the constitution. Because this policy disunity remains embedded in the national government's very fabric, each branch sought, managed, and implemented its own public information distribution needs independently from one another. At the same time, the legislative branch attempted to influence, and sometimes control the information policies of executive and judicial offices.

The second conflict, **political**, evolves from an expansive definition of citizenship and a concurrent increase in the influence of national political parties. After the Civil War, these political forces would shift from a strident network of national and regional partisan political newspapers to a more commercialized mass media. These newspapers grew to depend less on the economic lifeblood of lucrative public printing contracts and more on the economic vitality of paid advertising, subscribers, and other publishing ventures. With the expansion of the right to vote beyond the limits of white male property owners, the newly enfranchised ex-slaves and other poor whites sought and received their political information from other sources, usually demanding the basic information directly from the government or their elected representatives. Cultural institutions, such as public schools, libraries, and other community and civic associations, assumed a primary role in the political education of new citizens.

The third, **economic**, reflects the significant investments in the growing public infrastructure. Subsidies would be at the heart of continuous national debate over the federal government's proper role in building roads, turnpikes, canals, harbors, postal routes, and early telecommunications technologies. The rough interplay among these constitutional responsibilities, political rights, and economic developments remains the foundation of the American public information regime. Over time internal and external financial demands pressured the federal government to find increasingly rational solutions to meet its growing demand for durable, economical, and efficient information resources. Some of this capacity comes through bureaucracy building; some, by contracts or partnerships with private market forces.

Furthermore, the government's support of particular information policies is either passive or active. If passive, public authorities play no direct role in the distribution of information or the creation of communication channels. Other public associations, private organizations, or individuals set the necessary standards or expectations. However, the government may step into the process to stand against unnatural monopolies, to prevent criminal acts, or to insure no direct harm to the "public good." The national press, as it evolved under its constitutional protections, clearly reflects this passive influence. The government intrudes only when there has been a clear case of libel or when it perceives a serious threat to the nation's security and welfare. If active, the federal government moves among the policy players as a positive (some would argue profoundly negative) change-agent. The public authorities work for the "equal" distribution of resources, sometimes choosing among the conflicting demands of its private citizens to meet the public's interests. In the area of telecommunication, this positive influence would be represented by the concept of universal service.

These prescriptive policies, in turn, frame a deeper dynamic parity among three other civic contexts: civil rights, economic resources, and technological development. Perceptions of injustice and inefficiency evolve when a government policy or program fails to keep these three conditions working in tandem for the betterment of individuals and organizations. The public information regime, reinforced by the individual rights embodied by the first amendment (the freedom of speech and print, as well as the right to peaceable assembly and to petition the federal government) creates a rather fractious environment of public debate regarding the performance of public officials and the effectiveness of government programs.

Individual political rights. Promised through the explicit and implicit guarantees of the Bill of Right's first ten amendments, these encompass the seventeenth and eighteenth century expectations of how the interests of citizens would be protected from, as well as advanced by, a popular government. These liberties survive through a dynamic interdependency between a government's centralized administrative powers and the distributive constitutional powers of citizens to actively change that government structure. Citizen involvement through the electoral process, the easy and wide exchange of public information, and the ability of citizens (and non-citizens) to organize collective responses to governmental actions energize this relationship.

Individual and collective economic resources. These are best captured through the assertion in the Declaration of Independence of the individual's primacy (or individuals acting as a collective) to seek property and wealth through unfettered "Life, Liberty, and the pursuit of Happiness." The Declaration envisions a commonwealth of economic beings happily pursuing their separate destinies and, through the fortunes of combined or common interests, sustaining a productive society for everyone's benefit. Furthermore, the people, acting through an informal system of unregulated social, political, and economic associations, shall ensure a rough form of economic justice and wealth distribution. The government plays a minimum role in this scenario and will not disrupt this natural process with unwise taxes or with unreasonable regulation of free trade and commerce unless approved by the people.

Technological innovations. In many ways, this category is an amalgamation of the first two conditions mentioned previously. Through Section 8 of the Constitution, Congress is given the power to "promote the Progress of Science and useful Arts, by securing for limited Times to Authors and Inventors the exclusive Right to their respective Writings and Discoveries." This is the basic right for the government to recognize, grant, and protect copyrights, trademarks, and patents. This is a most explicit recognition of the economic power and security individuals may enjoy from the application of their ideas and/or inventions. This power to "promote" the sciences and development of "useful" inventions also led the central government to become actively involved in the creation and application of new technologies.

The construction of turnpikes, canals, highways, postal roads, harbor improvements, and other public works ensured the consistent and economical exchange of public and private goods. This national infrastructure also transported people and ideas, creating a demand for a national communication system. Newspapers, handbills, books, broadsides, letters, and other written or printed matter moved from one part of the country to another through a nationally subsidized postal system, which in no small way supported the distribution of public documents. According to John, ". . . Congress bombarded the public with newspaper accounts of its proceedings, pamphlets, reprinted speeches, and reports and documents of all kinds. By 1830, these publications, along with the publications of the individual states, made up fully 30 percent of all imprints in the United States . . ."[3]

The creation of locally controlled education systems fostered a national demand for common ideals and expectations about the purpose and scope of citizenship. As this system of transportation, communication, and social facilities expanded during the nineteenth century, it created what Beniger calls a "control revolution":

> . . . the beginning of a restoration–although with increasing centralization–of the economic and political control that was lost at more local levels of society during the Industrial Revolution . . . now control came to be reestablished by means of bureaucratic organization, the new infrastructures of transportation and telecommunications, and system-wide communication via the new mass media.[4]

If parity among these three conditions exists, citizens' ability to exercise free speech and civic participation remain independent of their individual economic or social conditions. This parity depends further on an equitable distribution of technological innovations throughout society. However, the parity would never be achieved because of uneven national economic development; lack of universal access to the increasing speed and sophistication of the emerging information technologies, the episodic development of enfranchisement, as well as a general lack of large bureaucratic structures to enforce the national policies.

Of all the civil rights sought and debated by the British colonists before the American Revolution, free press and speech were considered cornerstones of all other civil rights. Taking from their cultural heritage in England, American colonists repeatedly linked a nation's prosperity and the free distribution of ideas. Many writers marked the wide spread of knowledge as a hallmark of progress; serving as both a bulwark to freedom and the first barrier to tyranny. The argument is simple, clear, and compelling, even three hundred years later. Give a rational and freedom-loving individual enough information, and his or her decisions will not only be more enlightened (as compared to not having the information) but in the best interests of those around them (i.e., society). Examined this way, it is a rough cousin to the economic argument of an "invisible hand" metaphor used in classic economic theory. The founders of the new nation's constitutional order expressed comparable, if somewhat more cynical, expectations about the power of a popular free press and wide discussion of the public matters. But these jaundiced expectations were tempered by understanding how easily public discussion could be twisted to further the ends of an unjust government. Thomas Jefferson, in a January 16, 1787, letter to Edward Carrington, said:

> I am persuaded for the moment that the people are the best army . . . They may be led astray for a moment, but will soon correct themselves. The people are the only true censors of their governors; and even their errors will tend to keep these to the true principles of their institutions. To punish these errors too severely would be to suppress the only safeguard of the public liberty. The way to prevent these irregular interpositions of the people is to give them full information of their affairs thro' the channel of public papers, & to contrive that those papers should penetrate the whole mass of the people. The basis of our governments being in the opinion of the people, the very first object should be to keep that right; and were it left to me to decide whether we should have a government without newspapers or newspapers without governments, I should not hesitate to prefer the latter. But I should mean that every man should receive those papers & be capable of reading them . . .[5]

And although his faith in newspapers was thoroughly shaken by his rough treatment as president at the hands of the Federalist partisan press, his support for the diffusion of knowledge through active social and political instruments would not waver.

Comparable sentiments of democracy, a broad diffusion of public information, and the betterment of the general public are found in the creation of other cultural institutions during the first 150 years of American history, including social and public libraries, literary or historical societies, scientific associations, colleges and universities, the public mails, and social reform organizations. Contemporary analysis considers these organizations to be a "great good place"[6] a chance for individuals or small groups to meet, reflect, debate, and communicate concerns, ideas, and plans. These institutions, whether begun by elite groups or fashioned from a common need to serve the less fortunate in a community, are social and economic levelers between society's high and low. From the perspective of early development of public libraries, a preamble found in the 1851 draft of Massachusetts's library statute puts the matter plainly:

> Whereas, a universal diffusion of knowledge among the people must be highly conducive to the preservation of their freedom, a greater equalization of social advantages, their industrial success, and their physical, intellectual and moral advancement and elevation; and, Whereas it is

requisite to such a diffusion of knowledge, that while sufficient means of a good early education shall be furnished to all the children in the Common Schools, ample and increasing sources of useful and interesting information should be provided for the whole people in the subsequent and much more capable and valuable periods of life; and, Whereas there is no way in which this can be done so effectively, conveniently, and economically as by the formation of Public Libraries, in the several cities and towns of this Commonwealth, for the use and benefit of their respective inhabitants . . .[7]

At least until the 1880s, then, these cultural institutions were the primary forms of bibliographic control and "cataloging" of nearly all types of government information.

By the 1780s, America's elected officials experimented with several methods to procure official printing and distribution of their public papers, which included finished public documents, necessary forms, paper, subsidies for legal advertising, and publishing enacted laws in local newspapers. The first decade of the federal government was a heady mixture of both tradition and innovation. Indeed, the first few years under the Constitution, the new government looked to the familiar practices favored by the Continental Congress or the government under the Articles of Confederation: procuring paper and printing from private printers located in whichever region the government was holding session. This expediency and mobility fostered an expectation among officials that their staff, secretaries, or aides would arrange for the proper inquiries and selection of acceptable printers. A handful of printers, realizing the political and commercial opportunities of meeting the new government's publishing needs, followed it from New York to Philadelphia and on to Washington, D.C.

At the heart of these experiments, Congress held the greatest influence, primarily through its constitutional powers, to appropriate funds, shape the structure of new federal programs as a partner with the president, and its power to appointment. Few printers enjoyed exclusive political connections with either the legislative or executive and would offer their technology, trained work force, or financial resources to meet the somewhat hectic and chaotic scheduling of the public's printing and publication demands. And just as private printers struggled to obtain and sustain the necessary resources, the newly elected and appointed members of the legislative, executive, and judicial branches shared a comparable challenge in mustering its administrative talents to the effort of creating a government under the bare bones of the constitution. In his analysis of the Federalists' administrative structure, White outlines the fundamental reasons why so many of these early administrative policies and practices were either ad hoc or expedient:

The stage in the development of administrative and technical skills reached by the American people in the years 1790-1800 was still relatively rudimentary. The business of local government and private enterprise with which they were familiar was simple in character. The level of administrative competence the world over was not high . . . The capacity of the Americans to forge a nation was untested and problematical; their attention had been focused on liberty and rights, not on organization and discipline.[8]

The basic elements necessary for the creation of a "government publication" (and, therefore, the need to print it) were difficult to find and maintain during the first decade of federal government in either New York or Philadelphia. These elements included stenographic skills, record-keeping routines, predictable schedules of correspondence, and managing personnel, as well as the necessary office space and supplies. While in New York or Philadelphia, the public's servants enjoyed a comparatively rich commercial infrastructure to support these needs: printers, supplies, and a relatively stable transportation system within the close confines of a "central city." Outside the few urban centers along the eastern seaboard and when public officials found themselves traveling in the vast under-populated territory of the several states, such amenities were greatly missed. This lack of administrative resources further complicated the government's move to the new national capital carved out of the Virginia/Maryland wilderness. In the early winter of 1800, its first citizens found little to recommend either its cultural amenities or its location. Isolated and devoid of the civilized comforts taken for granted in Philadelphia or New York, most of the District's buildings were either primitive, under construction, or only just being sketched out on drafting boards. The District was surrounded by swamps and wetlands that only added to the misery of summer's humidity with a plague of disease-carrying insects.

It is little wonder, faced with this scarcity of administrative talents and limited resources, White points out, that the first generation of federal officials, following the example of their counterparts in the nascent commercial and business sector, preferred "committees rather than single executives."[9] Legislative and executive leaders repeatedly created management arrangements and administrative solutions in an attempt to overcome the difficulties of long distances between the nation's settlements. These include private/public partnerships designed to improve or build roads, canals, and turnpikes, as well as improvements in such public facilities as harbors and rivers. These collective approaches were further strengthened by Congress, and its evolving committee structure, as it took an early leadership role in managing the affairs of administration of the newly created executive departments, especially through its appointment powers, appropriation committees, and through the direct management of building the nation's system of postal roads, stations, and federally subsidized postal deliveries to citizens.

Indeed, the first laws enacted to manage the public's printing and publications distribution contained the basic ingredients of Congressional administrative control and a scheme of decentralized executive arrangements to get the information to the people through a variety of increasingly redundant schemes and methods. According to Harris,

> . . . legislative control of administration, and its purposes may be stated as follows:
>
> 1. To determine whether legislative policies are being faithfully, effectively, and economically carried out, so that appropriate legislative action may be taken to correct any shortcomings of administration;
> 2. To determine whether legislative programs are accomplishing their desired objectives, and if any further legislation is needed;
> 3. To ascertain that the laws are being administered in the public interest, and to encourage diligence on the part of administrative officers;
> 4. To discover any abuses of discretion, arbitrary actions, or gross judgment by administrative officers;
> 5. To check on the systems of internal management and control established by the department heads and the chief executive, to ascertain that they are adequate and effective;
> 6. To hold responsible executive officers accountable to the legislature for their use of public funds and other resources put at their disposal.[10]

Within these conditions of legislative oversight of the executive, the early printing and publishing acts fashioned the earliest layers of duplication, as well as the first foundations of bibliographic control. Early policy choices regarding federal printing and publishing followed very specific points: what was to be printed, how many copies would be printed, how it was going to be paid for, who was going to do the printing, as well as who was going to get copies of publications. The scope of these decisions was both practical and political. Distribution (who was going to get the document) was considered to be first a political decision largely made by the good judgment of congressional members and deeply rooted in the early formation of service traditions to their constituents. In this sense, government publications became "gifts" or benefactions bestowed on individual citizens or their congressional districts. In a world where owning books, much less a library of any significant size, was considered to be a sign of wealth or achievement, these government publications held a certain political and social value not easily understood in today's information-rich environment. Through these laws, Congress created a policy tradition of several distinct (and overlapping) methods for the printing and distribution for both the executive and legislative branches. By 1794, the legislature and the executive began to express some dissatisfaction with earlier practices of decentralized printing contracts and publishing enacted laws in various newspapers. In this year, Congress regularized the funding of printing for the legislature and executive by including specific lines in their budgets to handle the expected printing for each session. As important as the printing would be to perform the public's business, it was still considered to be a matter of "housekeeping" rather than of serious national import. According to the Congressional *Annals*, the lawmakers designated "for the expenses of firewood, stationery, and public printing, and all other contingent expenses of the two houses of Congress, ten thousand dollars." This act was the first to end one of the traditions left over from the years of government under the Continental Congress and Articles of Confederation, a tradition that granted the Congress nearly exclusive claim to be the printer and publisher of all the government's documents.

By 1795 Congress decided to discontinue the practice of printing laws in at least three newspapers in each state, for it found the lack of newspapers in many of the states' rural areas hindered the desired wide distribution of the laws. The mechanics of the documents distribution process was left largely to the direction of the House Clerk, Senate Secretary, or the Department of State (or other executive departments until 1895). Before 1813 Congress did not allow for any formal distribution of public documents to other institutions outside the officers of the various federal and state governments. Other than the State Department's Library (the Library of Congress was not formed until 1800 and did not begin to receive federal government publications until 1804), libraries and other cultural institutions obtained public documents either through private printers, as gifts from public officials, or through other donations or purchases. The modern concept of a "depository library" was not fully embraced until the mid-nineteenth century; and before then, legislators chose to deliver government publications either directly to the citizens through the public mails using their postal franking privileges, through other government agencies (at the federal and state level), or through the popular press. Libraries, historical societies, and colleges were gradually included in the distribution schemes as the federal government began to produce an excess of publications that could not be distributed through the relationships established during the late 1700s and early 1800s. This excess of government publications came about because of the growing number of copies Congress legislated into existence to meet what appeared to be a demand from the public.

> with the governors, in turn to be responsible for having the laws deposited "... in such fixed and convenient place for each county, or other subordinate civil division of such state or territory, as the executive or legislative thereof shall deem most conducive to the general information of the people . . ." The act required the laws of each future session of Congress to be distributed in the same manner.[11]

Within six years of its first legislative action on the public's printing, Congress increased the number of copies available to the public by nearly tenfold, from six hundred to five thousand. Congress attempted to solve the problem of government publication distribution and availability by increasing the number produced rather than find ways of improve the distribution system. There was really no good evidence offered on why Congress considered that state governors or officials would be better distributors than newspapers. Their actions would have two further, perhaps unintended, consequences. First, by increasing the annual printing orders to five thousand copies, Congress added to the economic value of its printing contracts. At the time, as the House Clerk and Senate Secretary managed the contracting process, there was no formal bidding process that awarded the job to the lowest bidder. This effort at economy would come ten years later. Instead, based on discussions between the printer and the clerical staff of Congress, a price was negotiated before the job was started. If the printer could deliver under the dollar amount given by Congress, the remaining money would be pure profit; eventually these profits became political kickbacks to the congressional ruling party for awarding the contracts to favored publishers and their partisan newspapers. Second, by increasing the number of copies available, Congress created the first of a "surplus document" problem that plagued the printing and distribution policies for the next two hundred years.

At first, this surplus would find its way into the nation's library collections, either through formal arrangements or donations. But, as Congress began to legislate in earnest, increasing the number of copies for not only the Acts and its Journals, but a growing number of other titles as well, the document rooms in the halls of Congress, the offices of the Executive, and basements of libraries would be awash with multiple copies of unwanted publications. Furthermore, it would be the first time in the area of printing and publication policy that Congress would bind the decisions of current legislative members to those who would follow. This practice of creating a specific set of rules and guidelines from one legislative session to the next would be more fully developed by the mid-1840s when, in response to the rampant corruption in the public's printing, Congress created the Joint Committee on Printing and gave it the power to take appropriate measures to remedy "any neglect of delay" affecting the public's printing. This practice of rules and regulation would also be codified in the development of the House and Senate manuals, which outlined many of the acceptable (i.e., traditional) approaches to these matters.

Two years later, Congress restored the State Department and Secretary of State to the management of the contracts to publish the laws in state and territorial newspapers as well as the distribution of the printed laws to various federal and state agencies. Many regional newspapers actively sought the State Department as official publishers, both as an economic benefit and to be associated with this imprint of federal authority. Printers and publishers sent eager petitions to their congressional delegations, the president, the secretary of state, or any public officer they thought would give them the printing contracts. As White points, this created some political difficulties from the start:

> Jefferson thought this quite inadequate and "altogether too partial and perishable." Pickering [then, John Adam's Federalist Secretary of State] appointed Philip Freneau's brother, a prominent Republican, and his partner to publish the laws in South Carolina, but as time passed the selection of printers became a partisan act. Pickering asked a Kentucky correspondent to nominate a printer suitable "for correctness in typography, intelligence, and *real*, not boasting & *professing*, patriotism.[12]

By the early years of the eighteenth century, selection of the newspapers, congressional printers, and executive printing contracts evolved into a system of spoils and rewards of the growing number of newspapers that grew out of the national political parties. Add to this the obvious economic benefits of subsidized postal deliveries and the concurrent wide distribution of many regional newspapers to a growing national audience of readers, and it is not hard to understand how the private press and public officials became such easy partners (as well as adversaries).

By 1801 Jefferson and the Republicans inherited a loose arrangement of policies and laws administrating the public printing procurement and publication distribution. These practices were plagued by high costs, badly executed printing, undue political influence, and little policy direction. But the legislative and executive officers could not come to any agreement on its relative importance, and because of this lack of direction, a three-tiered system of printing and publishing policy would be fashioned from political expediency over the next five decades. Printers sought public printing contracts as due reward for their newspapers' support of successful candidates. Regardless of what private printers wanted to do in Washington, D.C., their facilities proved inadequate to meet the needs of Congress, which had the greatest demand on time and volume for its printing, given its often chaotic and short legislative schedule. Committees waited for weeks to have important documents printed, often stalling their committee deliberations and floor debates. By 1801, the House appointed a committee "to expedite the printing of the House." Its report recommended that better economy and speed could be achieved if

> . . . the heads of departments be requested to inspect carefully such documents, reports, and statements as are directed by law to be annually laid before the House, and it was directed that a printer for the House be appointed. The first suggestion in the report was carried; that relating to a public printer was lost.[13]

By 1803 concerns over printing resurfaced again during floor debates in both chambers, sparked by Jefferson's decision to send a written message to Congress, rather than appearing in person before a joint session. Some members were outraged by the extra expense, but Congress voted the extra funds to print the presidential publications. A year later, a joint resolution authorized the House Clerk and Senate Secretary to discontinue exclusive contracts with one printer and to award the printing to the lowest bidder to meet the congressional needs for printing, fuel, and stationery. In 1805 Congress voted to include the Library of Congress within these general distribution schemes. As a result, three hundred copies of the laws and journals printed since 1789 were ordered to be deposited in its care; and it was directed that future copies should also be delivered. By 1809, the act was amended to include all the printed reports and documents considered by Congress during each session.

By the eve of the second war with Great Britain, Congress and the President had begun to hammer out some broad administrative structures that included committees and party caucuses, and much of the legislature's work was channeled through these bodies for the sake of political amity and administrative felicity. The growth and organization of Congress for the last two decades led to some early efforts to create a comparable rational approach to its own publications and printing needs. Miller gives a very detailed analysis of how Thomas F. Pickering, using his experience as Secretary of State and a longstanding interest in supplying libraries with public documents, introduced a number of successful resolutions to help Congress organize its voluminous output of published matter.[14] Specifically, Pickering's proposal created the first bibliographic structure of organizing the myriad number of congressionally mandated publications within a clear numbering scheme that would be used from one congressional session to another. The numbering schemes created in 1813 continued to evolve, and any sense of comprehensive bibliographic control was lost as the government struggled with the burgeoning problems of printing and distribution.

The federal government, recovering from its second war with Britain, economic upheaval, and keeping a wary eye on the ongoing struggle for empire among the European nations in North and South America, returned to domestic affairs with a renewed sense of purpose, if only briefly put off by the National Bank's 1819 economic crisis, which ended the postwar economic resurgence the country had enjoyed since 1815. In spite of the national economic setback and the cries of "hard times" from both country and city, the United States was a long way from the struggling nation-state created nearly thirty years ago. From thirteen isolated, largely rural colonies huddled along the eastern Atlantic seaboard, the citizens migrated to over nearly two-thirds of the continent that stretched from former Spanish Florida in the Southeast to the vast rainforests of the Oregon Territory in the former British Northwest. The people were moving into vast tracks of land, driving out, with increasing hostility, the original inhabitants from their ancestral lands along the vast stretches of the Midwest and pushing into the colonial holdings of Spain in the Southwest and Far West. With this vast amount of geography to govern, federal and state political leaders, over the next four decades, grew to rely on a number of technological and social innovations to bind the nation's millions of citizens. These innovations took advantage of several road and canal projects begun under previous administrations and congresses. Steam engines to telegraphy were either already near production or about to be tested in some fashion. Public officials and citizens alike sought more active federal intervention throughout a growing national market economy. Rulings from the Supreme Court and other judicial officials began to outline the broad concepts of incorporation, capitalism, and commercial law, allowing many of the early republic businesses, largely family owned and managed, to take advantage of new regulations and funding opportunities within a growing national market of labor, resources, and services.

The parity of national political rights, economic advantages, and technological innovations was radically altered by these larger social and economic movements. The national postal service, representing an early form of federally subsidized information distribution, began to merge with the recent practices in public printing policy, with the contracts and appointments increasingly going to the supporters of the ruling political parties in Washington. Improved printing technologies created new kinds of publications and transformed the national mails from a simple delivery network for personal letters or official parcels into a highly interactive and volatile communication system.

By the 1820s, Kielbowicz argues, the postal service was instrumental in the widespread dissemination of public information and

> . . . had become indispensable to several societal processes. Political par-
> ties needed communication to maintain cohesion and coordinate activi-
> ties. Associations–religious, fraternal, reform, and occupational–used
> publications to foster a sense of community among widely scattered ad-
> herents. And as commerce grew, communication increasingly tied pro-
> ducers and consumers into a national economy.[15]

To manage this increased demand, postal authorities and Congress reexam-
ined rates charged for delivering printed material. Newspapers, by tradition
and practice, enjoyed lower rates than letters. With the growing demand for
magazines, books, and other non-newspaper publications, producers of the
new literature insisted on comparable postal subsidies for their publications.
Some even suggested that the public mails ought to be used as a form of free
national communication. In their bid for reduced postal rates, a group of
Boston publishers testified before congress in 1832:

> Without the means of transmitting knowledge with ease, and rapidity,
> and cheapness, a nation, however free in name must become the blind
> followers of the wealthy and well-informed, or the tools of the designing.
> Every means, therefore, which renders access to knowledge more diffi-
> cult or more expensive directly increases the power of the few, and di-
> minishes the influence of the many, and thus tends to weaken the
> foundations of our government.[16]

Congressional members, more than other citizens, enjoyed the added benefits from the national postal system and used the system to their political advantage in several ways. First, they enjoyed the right of franking–in other
words, the right to send (or receive) material through the mail free of charge as
long as the deliveries supported their public duties. This was a benefit they
would enjoy, in spite of repeated revelations and investigations of abuse, until
the early 1870s. With franking, Congressional members made sure that they,
and their constituents, received newspapers and other publications. Second,
though obviously a growing executive function, Congress continued to control
the creation, designation, and appointments of all postal offices in the country,
including the creation of much needed postal roads. This kind of congressional
administrative control fostered a system of political patronage that fed into the
contracts for public printing and dominated legislative and executive debates
from the late 1820s through the late 1850s. Third, Senate and House members

often sent public documents to their constituents through their franking benefit. John indicates that by the 1850s ". . . the franking privilege accounted for somewhere between one quarter to one-half of the total weight of the mail that left Washington on any given day. In addition to speeches and government documents, congressmen got into the habit of franking of things, including books, dirty laundry, and even pianos . . ."[17] Fourth, postal printing and contracts were mired in a comparable level of patronage and political manipulation as congressional and executive printing, with the awards often going to the same printers each year. Finally, Congress increased the number and types of publications legislated to be printed and sent to its constituents. What began as a modest attempt to get important historical documents printed and distributed to various local academic and cultural institutions in 1813 had, by the late 1820s, become involved in a succession of printing scandals. Indeed, the problems of public printing and its corruption were investigated no fewer than ten times by congressional committees between 1820 and 1860, filling thousands of pages of testimony and debate. Many of the investigations revealed a sophisticated system of political kickbacks, deliberate fraud, and/or gross mismanagement in the execution of the printing contracts.

Congress essentially invited the trouble by not revising some obvious shortcomings in its 1819 resolution. This inability to go back and "fix" a bill is quite common in the political process surrounding the legislative development of any major law, an environment that often invites compromise and expediency. As a rule, however, it was particularly so when it came to congressional action regarding the complexity of printing and publication laws. In the case of the 1819 resolution, congressional inaction stemmed largely from two conditions: the law's requirement to elect the House and Senate Printer (which could be two different printers or the same printer) and the codification of artificially high prices written into the basic law.

Soon after the enactment of the 1819 law, Congress chose to elect and share a single printing firm to handle the business of both chambers: Gales and Seaton, old hands at manipulating the political ways of Washington. The publishers of the *National Intelligencer* also enjoyed the favor of the administration, becoming the house organ for the ruling political party both on Capitol Hill and in the White House. Further, Ames indicates that the 1819 resolution was enacted in order to directly benefit Gales and Seaton and political parties, particularly with an eye towards future presidential elections:

> One of the chief contenders for the office was Henry Clay, and primarily through his guidance the bill was pushed through Congress. Clay, a politician well aware of the necessity to operate from a base of power in order to achieve political office, undoubtedly sought to obtain ties to

Congress as well as to the executive branch of government from the capital's leading political newspaper. In fashioning this new method of awarding printing, Clay had put together one of the richest patronage schemes the country had seen . . .[18]

With this kind of political and economic support, Gales and Seaton built one of the best printing shops in the nation, taking advantage of the latest technology and printing methods, and attracting more contracts from the executive department. Because the prices were fixed according to the cost of printing technology in use before 1820, printers elected to the House or Senate posts in following years enjoyed a larger profit margin between these fixed rates and the rapidly falling production costs gained by innovation and economies of scale as they purchased increasingly larger and faster printing equipment. The 1820s and 1830s saw the addition of new presses and power sources (steam).

Gales and Seaton enjoyed these kinds of profits for the next ten years. Even when they lost either the patronage of Congress or the president, they came up with other large printing projects and petitioned Congress to fund these large series of historical volumes and distribute them to the public. Material for these historic sets came from Gale and Seaton's own archival records and printing plates of the *National Intelligencer*. These massive public printing projects would include the *Register of Debates*, the *Annals of Congress*, and the *American State Papers*. What we now consider to be the "public" record of the earliest years of congressional and executive deliberations are actually privately produced and some of the earliest examples of graft and corruption in the public printing enterprises.

And here lies another great irony for many librarians and other supporters of a rational scheme for distribution of government publications to consider. If these historical sets had not been produced to such excess, it would be very unlikely that a surplus of documents would have been created, thereby eliminating the need to devise schemes and programs to distribute publications among the nation's burgeoning community of public and private libraries.

By the late 1820s, elected printers were expected to return a portion of their profits to the political party in power. The greater portion of congressional and executive printing contracts was awarded to four establishments that would tie their economic fortunes to the political patronage of the ruling majority political party: Gales & Seaton: *The National Intelligencer*; Peter Force: the *National Journal*; Duff Green: the *United States Telegraph*; and Blair & Ives: the *Congressional Globe*. In 1828, and toward the end of President John Quincy Adams' administration, the political elections of the House and Senate printers were openly linked to an active party press and the concept of a president's newspaper (or administration organ). White is careful to make the distinction between a party press and an administration press. The latter, he says,

> . . . had always existed, North, South, and West. An administration press falls in a different class, i.e., one or more newspapers sponsored by the President and his advisers, usually published in Washington, edited by persons enjoying the President's confidence and at times named by him, with special access to official circles, and with financial support from perquisites and profits controlled by the government.[19]

These considerable charges of corruption and political abuse would culminate in the late 1850s and lead to the establishment of the Government Printing Office in 1861. However, the same spirit of reform did not extend to the distribution and access of public documents, and this aspect of bibliographic control continued to be lost in the shuffle over policy and implementation. Until the Printing Act of 1896, both Congress and the president continued to send millions of paper documents to citizens, libraries, and other institutions with little regard for duplication, lack of organized indexing, or even a systematic understanding of which publications are useful to the public. Further, the years prior to the Civil War and after until the new century were times of explosive scientific exploration and technological achievement, which generated their own output of government publications from the Smithsonian Institution, the Department of Interior, and Department of Education, as well as various military expeditions along the country's waterways and overseas. Until the late 1800s, however, there were no consistent numbering schemes or comprehensive indexing for any of this output.

STANDARDS CREATION AND PROFESSIONAL LIBRARIANSHIP AFTER THE CIVIL WAR

From 1865 through 1900, American librarians began to organize on a national scale and work towards the creation of national policies that sought to create bibliographic control and rational indexing and descriptive standards for the expanding number of magazines, books, and other products being created by the industrialization of the printing industry. If libraries of an earlier age were largely institutions of a printing technology limited to small press runs, expensive production costs, and high valued volumes, libraries (and librarians) of the late nineteenth century were awash in printed products. This abundance focused their professional attention on the creation of tools and practices that would work from Seattle to Syracuse. In a telling survey of librarianship during this period, the 1876 congressional report called *Public*

Libraries in the United States of America: Their History, Condition, and Management,[20] the kinds and types of libraries throughout the country were surveyed and evaluated; and, for the first time, consistent statistics about their various conditions were tabulated. Of particular interest to the report's authors was the distribution and access of government publications. In general, they found the situation very difficult:

> . . . In view of the fact that, so far as known, no library in the United States, neither the Library of Congress, nor that of any State or Territory, nor any other public library, contains a complete set of the public documents of the General Government, it may be regarded as unfortunate that the provisions of the law are not availed of to the fullest extent. Fifty years hence, it should not be as difficult for the student to find all the public documents of the present as it is for an investigator to-day to discover the records of a half-century ago.[21]

For the next twenty years, librarians from around the country worked together to form a national coalition and to agitate for the liberal reform of federal printing and publishing laws in attempt to change these conditions. Also, two new major catalogs of government publications were issued, which became the gold standards for the bibliographic control of government information.[22] During the 1880s and 1890s, librarians petitioned lawmakers in Washington to rationalize the distribution of government information. When the American Library Association officially formed in 1876, one of its first goals was to change these laws; and it was successful in 1894-95, when it convinced Congress to centralize the printing and distribution functions within one agency: the Government Printing Office.

THE REFORMULATION OF THE GPO

Within its first year under the new legislation, GPO still found itself asking for the funding and legislative support to replace its antiquated buildings and the resources needed to take advantage of new technologies. GPO assumed its new responsibilities as the federal centralized printing production and publication distribution agency on January 12, 1895. The Printing Act of 1895 (28 Stat. L. 601-624) reconfigured the institutional arrangements in such a way to lead many lawmakers, bureaucrats, and librarians to think that the "evils" that had infested the public's printing for the last half century were, if not largely settled, then on the proper road to resolution. In certain aspects, especially in the areas of distribution, publicity, ordering, and indexing government publications, they had good cause for their optimism. GPO's new Superintendent of Documents' legislative foundations clearly benefited from the library profession's nearly forty years of debate, legislative agitation, and professional experience. The new legislation fashioned a rational system of government publication distribution and reflected the years of experience and management acumen of John G. Ames and his experience in the Department of Interior's public document. The next great cataloging and indexing tool created under the new Superintendent was the *Monthly Catalog of Government Publications*, which would serve as the single reference and cataloging standard for federal publications for the next hundred years. Improvements would be made in terms of the *Catalog*'s production and distribution. GPO would struggle mightily through the twentieth century to include all manner of government publications within its pages, but in the end it would fail because of changes in information technology that allowed executive and judicial agencies to publish and distribute their material outside the centralized control of GPO. In the policy area of printing production and procurement, however, the new law really changed very little. It simply froze the complicated century-long policy debate over disputed public printing procurement and production responsibilities shared between executive and legislative agencies along current bureaucratic arrangements and technological capabilities. It assumed that a form of government dominated by congressional will and administrative control would continue indefinitely, and the executive would simply acquiesce to this legislative mandate. This was the law's single most serious flaw: an institutional failure to accommodate a fundamental shift in the political and technological resources from the legislative to the executive over the next seven decades.

In the nineteenth century's last few years, the art and technology of printing was still a "slow and tedious business at best, notwithstanding the many and diversified improvements which have been invented to facilitate the rapid production of printed matter."[23] Since the early 1860s, GPO overcame this lack of speed through a carefully managed concentration of many printing presses, as well as through a rational distribution of labor among the many steps in the production process, with its greatest concentration in the office's vast type-composing rooms. The speed and efficiency of the printing presses were further enhanced by new power sources (steam and electricity) as well as by the management decision to commit large numbers of printing presses to work on specialized printing jobs. Following this methodology, the printing production managers could schedule the office's daily production work load in the most efficient fashion, leaving the fastest, and usually the most modern, press machines to produce the Congressional *Record* and other legislative publications. The composition process, which includes the production, selection, and arrangement of individual typefaces needed to make up pages of printed material, was the least automated. Typesetting machines, specifically the monotype and linotype, were found in most large newspaper printing shops in major cities since the early 1880s but would not be purchased by GPO until 1904. In this sense, then, GPO's singular bureaucratic strength was managing a careful blend of human and machine power. The 1895 Printing Act's one bright spot and promise of success in the legislation was the Superintendent of Documents. Specifically, the Superintendent was given broad responsibilities for the distribution and sales of all publications processed through GPO. Under the legislation, the Superintendent's duties included four separate, but interdependent, areas:

- Bibliographic control and indexing; the creation of monthly catalog of government publications. Additional duties included annual and biennial indexes of all congressional documents and publications for use by congressional members and the public.
- Reprinting, sales, and distribution of publications to the public.
- Management and oversight of the depository library system. Superintendent responsible for communicating and managing a system of around 500 libraries that were sent everything the Superintendent processed through his office. The libraries were supposed to keep everything they were sent. The office was also given "enforcement" capabilities to make sure that the documents were kept in good order and available to the public.

Through the decades of the twentieth century, the Superintendent of Documents would use the *Monthly Catalog* and the depository library system as a one-two punch to solve the problem of bibliographic control and distribution of government information. And as long as the GPO remained the biggest information producer and distributor in the federal government, it was a powerful combination. But GPO's hegemony would end shortly after the Second World War. Even with the advent of automated bibliographic records creation through MARC in the mid-sixties, as well as the complete automation of the *Monthly Catalog* in 1976, the Superintendent of Documents never recaptured the authority or ability to be the single source of cataloging for government publications. Agencies, through the last half of the twentieth century, were creating their own index systems; private firms such as the Congressional Information System in the early 1970s were carving off huge portions of GPO's traditional turf by turning out far superior indexing and distribution systems for high volume areas of government information that included congressional information, regulations, and statistics.

CONCLUSION

GPO and the Superintendent of Documents have been forced to play both administrative and bibliographic catch-up since the early 1900s. Indeed, the 1895 system of depository libraries became a further fail-safe system that enabled GPO to avoid the serious flaws of production and distribution inherent in the 1895 law. As long as it was sending these publications to designated libraries and as long as these libraries were organizing and servicing these collections within their local communities, issues about national bibliographic standards could be sidetracked by the more pressing administrative concerns of managing a national depository. After all, everyone involved in the policy process, from librarians to the managers of GPO, could point to the depository system, along with the *Monthly Catalog*, and say that, for the most part, the government's information was getting into the hands of the people. And this game might have gone on indefinitely had it not been for the formation of the World Wide Web. For the first time in over 150 years, librarians must deal with a situation where they have to reconstitute their relationship with the government based on changes in technology and political expectations. Government agencies at all levels of government now consider their Web pages and electronic services to be the natural successors to the system of printed libraries created over a century ago.

Depository libraries and centralized bibliographic control are no longer the gold standards in a world dominated by a global information network of computers.

NOTES

1. Konstantinos Sp. Staikos, *The Great Libraries: From Antiquity to the Renaissance (3000 B.C. to 1600)* (London: Oak Knoll Press & British Library, 2000).

2. Fernand Braudel, *The Structures of Everyday Life: Civilization and Capitalism 15th through 18th Centuries,* 3 vols. (New York: Harper and Row, 1979). Braudel's volumes on the interchange between individuals and society during this critical historical epoch remain among the best general discussions of the cultural revolutions that gave birth to our modern sense of what constitutes a library.

3. Richard John, *Spreading the News: The American Postal System from Franklin to Morse* (Cambridge, Mass.: Harvard University Press, 1996), 57.

4. James R. Beniger, *The Control Revolution: Technological and Economic Origins of the Information Society* (Cambridge, Mass.: Harvard University Press, 1986), 7.

5. Thomas Jefferson, *Writings* (New York: Library of America, 1984), 880-881.

6. Ray Oldenburg, *The Great Good Place* (New York: Paragon House, 1991). An interesting volume that discusses the importance of "gathering places" in American society.

7. Sydney Ditzion, *Arsenals of the Democratic Culture: A Social History of the American Public Library Movement in New England and the Middle States from 1850 to 1900* (Chicago: American Library Association, 1947), 18-19.

8. Leonard D. White, *The Federalists: A Study in Administrative History, 1789-1800* (New York: Macmillan, 1949), 466.

9. Ibid., 472.

10. Joseph Pratt Harris, *Congressional Control of Administration* (Washington: Brookings Institution, 1964), 1-2.

11. Sarah Jordan Miller, "The Depository Library System: A History of the Distribution of Federal Government Publications to Libraries of the United States from the Early Years of the Nation to 1895" (DLS diss., Columbia University, 1980. Ann Arbor, Mich.: University Microfilms International, 1980), 63.

12. Leonard D. White, *The Jeffersonians: A Study in Administrative History, 1801-1829* (New York: Macmillan, 1951), 506.

13. Laurence F. Schmeckebier, *The Government Printing Office: Its History, Activities, and Organization,* Institute for Government Research. Service Monographs of the United States Government, no. 36 (Baltimore, Md.: Johns Hopkins University Press, 1925), 3.

14. Miller, 189-308.

15. Richard Burket Kielbowicz, *News in the Mail: The Press, Post Office, and Public Information, 1700-1860s* (New York: Greenwood Press, 1989), 57.

16. Ibid., 59.

17. John, 57.

18. William E. Ames, *A History of the* National Intelligencer (Chapel Hill: University of North Carolina Press, 1972), 110-11.

19. Leonard D. White, *The Jacksonians: A Study in Administrative History, 1829-1861* (New York: Macmillan, 1954), 284.

20. U.S. Department of the Interior. Bureau of Education, *Public Libraries in the United States of America: Their History, Condition, and Management* (Washington, D.C.: Government Printing Office, 1876).

21. Ibid., 283.

22. Benjamin Perley Poore, *A Descriptive Catalogue of the Government Publications of the United States, September 5, 1774-March 4, 1881,* United States. Congress. Washington: Govt. Print. Office, 1885, Series: [U.S. 48th Cong., 2d sess. Senate. Misc. doc.; 67]. John G. Ames, *Comprehensive Index to the Publications of the United States Government, 1881-1893,* United States. Dept. of the Interior. Division of Documents. Washington: Government Printing Office, 1905, Series [58th Cong., 2d sess. House. Doc. 754].

23. R. W. Kerr, *History of the Government Printing Office (at Washington, D.C.) with a Brief Record of the Public Printing for a Century: 1790-1881* (Lancaster, Penn.: Inquirer Printing and Publishing Co, 1881), 1.

Characteristics of Material Organization and Classification in the Kinsey Institute Library

Liana Zhou

SUMMARY. Dr. Alfred C. Kinsey's landmark research in the 1940s and 1950s made his name synonymous with the scientific study of sexuality. The extensive resources collected by Kinsey and his research team provided a foundation of library and special collections at the Kinsey Institute, located on the Bloomington campus of Indiana University. A library of books, articles, periodicals, and other materials is valuable to scholars and users only if the materials are organized with a practical classification scheme and retrievable by unique subject headings. In the 1960s the Institute librarians applied the Dewey classification system to the realm of sexuality. In the 1970s the Kinsey Institute developed a monograph of controlled vocabulary, *Sexual Nomenclature: A Thesaurus,* for cataloging the diverse materials at the Institute. Now more than 95,000 items are available via KICAT, the online database, consisting of monographs, journals and reprints, manuscripts, and audiovisual materials that represent all disciplines in the social and behavioral sciences as well as literature, art, and folklore. The library also has significant holdings in such areas as erotic novels, popular sex magazines, nudist publications, pseudo-scientific works, comic books, and tabloids. This article will trace the history of

Liana Zhou is Head of the library, Kinsey Institute for Research in Sex, Gender, and Reproduction, Indiana University, Bloomington, IN 47405 (E-mail: zhoul@indiana.edu).

[Haworth co-indexing entry note]: "Characteristics of Material Organization and Classification in the Kinsey Institute Library." Zhou, Liana. Co-published simultaneously in *Cataloging & Classification Quarterly* (The Haworth Information Press, an imprint of The Haworth Press, Inc.) Vol. 35, No. 3/4, 2003, pp. 335-353; and: *Historical Aspects of Cataloging and Classification* (ed: Martin D. Joachim) The Haworth Information Press, an imprint of The Haworth Press, Inc., 2003, pp. 335-353. Single or multiple copies of this article are available for a fee from The Haworth Document Delivery Service [1-800-HAWORTH, 9:00 a.m. - 5:00 p.m. (EST). E-mail address: getinfo@haworthpressinc.com].

bibliographic control of the library collections over many decades, and describe the approaches and efforts in providing organization and access to these rich and unique collections. *[Article copies available for a fee from The Haworth Document Delivery Service: 1-800-HAWORTH. E-mail address: <getinfo@haworthpressinc.com> Website: <http://www.HaworthPress.com> © 2003 by The Haworth Press, Inc. All rights reserved.]*

KEYWORDS. Alfred C. Kinsey, Kinsey Institute, Kinsey Institute library, KICAT, sexuality, cataloging of sex-related materials, sexual nomenclature

BIRTH OF A SEXOLOGICAL LIBRARY AND AN OVERVIEW OF THE LIBRARY COLLECTIONS

Kinsey the Researcher, Collector, and Classifier

For all that Dr. Alfred C. Kinsey accomplished with collecting and organizing sexually related materials, he could well be described as the first librarian of the Institute that he founded for conducting sex research. Kinsey, a Harvard-trained biologist, authority on the gall wasp, and an Indiana University professor, searched for publications on sexuality while preparing for a class he co-taught at the university in 1938 when the University agreed to offer a new course on marriage as a result of a petition from the Association of Women Students on the Bloomington campus. Kinsey, as one of the faculty sponsors of the petition, was asked to coordinate the course. His subsequent discovery of little scientific literature on sexuality piqued his interest in sex research, and thus he embarked on his world-renowned research on human sexuality. Not only did he collect individual sexual records, but he also set out to collect social evidence of sexual behavior, which confirms, as he states in *Sexual Behavior in the Human Male*, that there was no aspect of human behavior about which there have been more thought, more talk, and more books written. From the dawn of human history and from drawings left by primitive peoples and throughout the development of all civilizations, men have left a record of their sexual activities and their thinking about sex. The printed literature is tremendous, and the other material is inexhaustible.

Kinsey recognized the importance of erotica collections as resource materials for researchers. His discovery of a lack of research data in sexuality led him to begin collecting sexual data himself by interviewing first his students, their families and friends, and, eventually, people throughout the United States. The publication of *Sexual Behavior in the Human Male* (1948)[1] and

Sexual Behavior in the Human Female (1953)[2] made Kinsey a household name in the United States. He amassed interview data on some 18,000 subjects, including answers to hundreds of questions and thousands of materials that he purchased for his research. These data and collections comprised the primary holdings of the newly established institute and library. He emphasized that his team were recorders and reporters of facts, not judges of the behavior that they described, and practiced his principles of objectivity and a non-judgmental approach in both surveying sexual behaviors of Americans and collecting sexological materials, including erotica, from around the world.

The Institute for Sex Research and Its Library

In order to guarantee confidentiality for the interview records and to clarify ownership of the growing collection of sex-related materials, the Institute for Sex Research[3] was established as a private non-profit corporation in Indiana. Because of this incorporation, the Kinsey Institute's library and special collections are privately owned by its Board of Trustees instead of being part of a public university's records. Royalties from the first two publications were used to augment the collection. Kinsey also received items from many of his research subjects, who knew of his interest in collecting materials for data. Since those early days, there has been a steady stream of donations from individuals all over the world, particularly those who had been collectors themselves and saw the Kinsey Institute as a place where their collections would be valued, secure, and well used. The size and breadth of the collections today are due to the generosity of these many donors.

The initial goal of the Library was to support Kinsey and his staff in their research program. Kinsey felt that it was crucial that he and his staff have access to a wide range of materials depicting and describing human sexuality and the various ways in which societies of the past and present have responded to it. He believed that this access would immeasurably enhance the scientific and scholarly work of the Institute staff. In the early 1960s the collections were made available to a wider readership of qualified scholars, professionals, and students. However, because of the legal restriction of the Institute collections, the Library is not open to the general public.[4]

In 1957 the United States District Court, Southern District of New York, ruled in favor of the Institute that U.S. Customs and postal authorities, which since 1950 had been confiscating sexually explicit materials addressed to the Institute, could no longer interfere with the Institute's research. That decision,[5] a landmark in the history of the relationship between science and the law, empowered the Institute to import for research purposes any sort of sexual materials and allowed such materials to be sent through the U.S. mail.

The Vastly Varied Collections

The Kinsey Institute Library's collections[6] reflect Dr. Kinsey's view that sexual materials provide valuable insights into a culture's interests and that a sex research library should contain materials from a wide range of fields, including biology, medicine, psychology, sociology, anthropology, counseling, religion, history, law, literature, the arts, and erotica. The primary focus of the collections has been on social and behavioral sciences materials dealing with sexual behaviors and attitudes. There is also an extensive collection of erotic materials. Collections at the Institute include holdings from six continents and include books, serials, data sets, flat art and art objects, photographs, films, biographical materials, and many other items that document sexual behaviors, interests, and values. Items date from 3200 B.C. to the present and represent various cultures.

Jeannette H. Foster served as Kinsey librarian from 1948 to 1952; from 1952 to 1960 the collections were attended by various members of the Institute staff as time permitted. In 1961 Elizabeth Egan became head of the Library and undertook the development of an interdisciplinary classification scheme and a special subject-heading list to serve researchers in the field. In the 1970s Joan Brewer led much of the development of the thesaurus construction and produced published catalogs.

The Kinsey Legacy

Wardell B. Pomeroy, one of Kinsey's colleagues, summarized the significance of the Kinsey Institute library in his book *Dr. Kinsey and the Institute for Sex Research*:

> The library and archives stand as an enduring monument to Kinsey's lifetime of devotion to his work . . . [The] Institute has spent its own funds, saved from book royalties and fees, and it also depends heavily on donors, as it did when Kinsey was alive . . . Anything that is relevant to human sexuality in any way merits consideration for possible inclusion. In addition to virtually all scientific works on human sex research, numerous specialized fields are strongly represented, including physiology, abortion, sex law, prostitution, psychology, marriage counseling and many other related topics. Nonscientific published materials, such as

popular books and articles, are included. The Institute has . . . the largest collection of erotic literature assembled in any one place.[7]

CATALOGING: THE PHYSICAL DESCRIPTION

Pseudonym Rules

Kinsey Library materials have three major components: the social and behavioral studies, erotica, and sexual ephemera. The uniqueness of the collections has determined the characteristics of their organization. While bibliographic control of the social and behavioral studies materials has presented its own set of challenges in terms of providing subject access, they share much similarity with other types of library materials in physical description. Given the development of proper terminology and classification, the social and behavioral materials could be organized and become accessible. In fact, the Library's cataloging tools were first designed for organizing this group of materials.

The characteristics of the erotica and sexual ephemera, however, have presented many problems and challenges for Library cataloging staff and public services staff alike. While scholars, researchers, and the outside world struggle to define "pornography," the Library simply labels as "erotica" all materials produced for the purpose of arousing sexual response or which contains sufficient sexually explicit matter to do so. Creating bibliographic records for these materials is extremely challenging because much of it has no actual authorship and is written either anonymously or pseudonymously. Publishing houses are often fictitious. The intrinsic nature of these underground publications sets them apart from the norms and standards of a regular library collection. Anonymity for authors, publishers, and printers has been the norm for the publishing of erotica. The use of pseudonyms on erotic literature has long been the rule.

Rebecca Dixon in her 1974 unpublished paper, "Bibliographical Control of Erotica,"[8] recounts an examination of her purchases of twenty-two titles, of which only twelve contained traditional imprints, six contained partial information such as series titles and dates, and four did not contain any bibliographic information. Publishers often omit dates so that works can remain on the market for a longer time. Many erotic publications provide imprint information that is fictitious and nearly impossible to verify. There is no standard reference available for erotica, and standard bibliographic sources are of little value. As the Library of Congress does not catalog most of these titles, the Institute Library staff is responsible for a considerable amount of original descriptive cataloging for each publication. OCLC and RLIN offer little help in cataloging or identifying information. In 1980 Ruth Beasley, Head of Information Services, conducted an OCLC trial run of a limited sample that resulted in a hit rate of only 21 percent, and searches of other standard sources obtained similar low rates.[9] On the other hand, descriptive cataloging does not require much time if little bibliographic information is available.

These results were not surprising to the library staff as sex had been a taboo topic for much of social history. Most erotic literature publishers, almost as a general rule and often as underground endeavors, disguise themselves, printing their publications privately for distribution to a small circle of consumers who have the interest and money to acquire such publications. Of the few recognized bibliographies of erotica, almost all of them have been based on private collections and describe primarily nineteenth-century works. Rebecca Dixon, who was head librarian of the Institute in the 1970s, points out that, "Bibliographies and histories of erotica tend to be based on each other, building a body of erroneous information that creates formidable problems for the contemporary scholar."[10]

In the nineteenth century a number of bibliographies of erotic literature were published that provided a record for the contemporary world of what existed at that time. French erotica bibliographer Jules Gay, writing as le C. d'I***, compiled *Bibliographie des ouvrages* (1861).[11] Hugo Nay, a German bibliographer of erotic literature, using the name Hugo Hayn, produced *Bibliotheca Germanorum erotica* in 1875.[12] The first English bibliography appeared in 1877; it was compiled by Henry Spencer Ashbee, a collector of erotic literature. Ashbee, under the pseudonym Pisanus Fraxi, wrote *Index Librorum Prohibitorum*.[13] His second and third volumes, under the same pseudonym, were published in 1879 and 1885: *Centuria Librorum Absconditorum*[14] and *Catena Librorum Tacendorum*.[15]

As a result of general societal attitudes towards erotica, the entire apparatus of erotica production from creating and writing to distribution was well guarded. For example, there are too many authors to list who use pseudonyms. The compilers of the bibliographies of erotica mentioned above all used pseudonyms in their publications. This is a noteworthy characteristic of the literature itself. For obvious reasons the authors of many of these works did not wish to be identified.

Small or Fictitious Publishers and Printer Information

The same attitude of secrecy holds true for publishers and printers producing erotic materials. Works were often privately printed, sometimes by the publishers or printers of more acceptable publications. These persons or companies deliberately disguised their identities by using false imprints, fictitious publishing name, false places of publication, and false publishing dates. For the purpose of marketing, a title with an imprint reading Brussels 1778 might actually have been published in London in 1860. Dixon points out:

> In fact, one of the challenging aspects of cataloging erotic literature involves deciphering a coding system, the key to which has been lost and may never be retrieved. Scholars, who deal with erotic literature, as well as analytical bibliographers, learn to recognize subtleties in typefaces, printing plates, and various decorative treatments of title pages, which were customarily used by certain printers.[16]

In the case of retrospective or historical materials, it has also been possible at times to identify the various imprints associated with one individual. Rarely did a publisher or printer openly acknowledge association with such publications. Because the words were not copyrighted, there was also a high degree of theft among publications. In some cases, the text of a story might be stolen, the title changed, and the same work reissued by a different printer. This practice resulted in a variety of editions of essentially the same work.

Charles Carrington, one of the most prolific publishers of erotica at the turn of the twentieth century, is a good example. Authors of his publications were frequently disguised; and, in fact, several different writers appear to have used the same pseudonym (e.g., Jacob X). Similarly, Olympia Press, a Paris publishing house, produced a large number of erotic novels in English under various trade names in the 1950s and 1960s including its "Traveller's Companion" series, Ophelia Press, Mediterranean Press, and others. The authors of some Olympia Press publications are well-known writers such as Henry Miller and Vladimir Nabokov. Girodias, the owner of the Press, employed a group of writers who collaboratively produced many titles under a variety of pseudonyms. It is almost impossible to know the accurate identification of the authors.

CLASSIFICATION AND SUBJECT ACCESS

From Kinsey's Subject Classification to an Adapted Dewey Scheme

Along with Kinsey's generous donation came the first classification scheme developed by Kinsey himself. It was a system for the practical use of his materials. The examples of Dr. Kinsey's coding and classification reflect the nature of a personal collection serving both purposes of subject analysis and a location code function. In Kinsey's original coding, he used **A** for Artists, **AC** for

Art Collections, **AP** for Art and Photography, **BL** for Bibliography, **BM** for Biology and Medicine, **D** for Dictionary, **E** for Erotica, **F** for pre-twentieth century Fiction, **EM** for Erotic Manuscripts, **GA** for gallant literature, **PO** for Poetry, **SH** for Social history, **WL** for Women and love, and **Gen** for general works, including essays, humor, censorship, etc. Kinsey created a card for each book, just as he did for his gall wasps, identifying it by general subject, author (if any), and title, for both English and foreign titles. The Library had large holdings of French and German and a small but significant Japanese collection. Kinsey had access to many excellent staff to help him translate titles and tables of contents and, occasionally, summarize the contents. While European-language materials were incorporated into his general scheme, Asian materials were coded as **OR-C** for Chinese erotica, **OR-J** for Japanese erotica, and so forth.

In the 1960s Egan applied the Dewey Decimal Classification (DDC) system to the realm of sexuality. Adapted from DDC, the following examples illustrate its usage in the Kinsey Library: class number **0XX** was assigned for general topics, **1XX** for psychological, cultural, and attitudinal aspects of sexuality, **2XX** for religious aspects, **3XX** for legal, educational, or research methodology and prostitution, and **4XX** for languages, linguistics, and sexuality. The class number **5XX**, the most frequently used number in the Kinsey collection, brings together all works on sexual behaviors. This class (**5XX**) has been further expanded: **532** for homosexuality, **532.09** for history of homosexuality, **532.18** for case studies on homosexuality research, **532.8** for female homosexuality but not to include any popularized case studies, **538** for transvestitism, and **54X** for sadomasochism. Class **6XX** is used for medical aspects of sexuality–for example, **613** for family planning, population, and eugenics, **617** for AIDS and sexual behavior, **618** for abortion-related works and studies and further extended for surveys or research of abortion, rights of the fetus, and its legal, moral or religious interpretation of abortion.

Class **7XX** covers the most treasured and rare items related to art and sexuality from all cultures and languages–for example, **704** for collections and anthologies of themes in art and mythology and legend as portrayed in art, **704.69** for sadomasochism in art, **706.3** is assigned for book illustrations and works dealing with sample illustrations of several artists, **706.7** for pin-ups, **707** for homosexuality in art, **708** for guidebooks and catalogs from galleries, museums, and private collections, **709** for historical and geographical treatment of art (for example, **709.44** for French art, **709.52** for Japanese art, etc.), **710** for individual artists, regardless of medium, process, purpose, or subject.

Class **8XX** is used for erotic literature–a large and most complex collection of 14,000 items. The table of classification for this section is further extended chronologically, by language or literary format. For instance, **803** is for dictionaries and encyclopedias that are not limited to any specific language, **808** for collections of literary criticism from various languages, **808.07** for collections from various languages of the nineteenth century, **808.7532** for collections from multiple languages on homosexuality, **820** for English-language erotic literature (including **820.3** for dictionaries and encyclopedias), **821** for collections of poems by multiple poets, **822** for works of drama, **822.3** for individual fifteenth century playwrights, **823** for collections of erotic fiction, **823.8** for fiction of individual twentieth century authors, **830.3** for German erotica, **840** for French-language literature, **870.3** for Latin-language literature, and **880.3** for Greek-language literature. For anonymous works, of which there are many, the period of composition is considered when assigning a classification number.

Sexual Nomenclature: A Thesaurus

The Kinsey Library uses its own in-house developed thesaurus, *Sexual Nomenclature*, which is perhaps the most comprehensive thesaurus in the field of sex research. The thesaurus's origin can be traced back to Kinsey's subject access codes. Egan is credited for her expansion of Kinsey's subject areas/codes to include more than 300 headings, in addition to her adaptation of DDC for the collections. In 1970 the Institute staff realized the critical need for a tool that would organize the existing collection and also provide a searching tool for users. The Institute received a grant from the National Institute of Mental Health to organize the Institute collections and to establish an information service. In order to provide access to the data contained in the Institute's large collection of reprints, the development of a controlled vocabulary, the construction of the thesaurus and nomenclature of sexual terminology, was begun. The development of controlled vocabularies was a welcomed phenomenon in library science in the 1970s. The *Education Resources Information Center (ERIC) Thesaurus* was developed at this time, and a draft of the *American National Standard: Guidelines for Thesaurus Structure, Construction, and Use* (ANSI Z39.19-1974) became available. The Institute's goal was to construct a thesaurus of sexual terminology that would achieve a satisfactory level of specificity in retrieval. Work for this project started in 1971.

Joan Brewer, a librarian at the Institute in the 1970s, led a group of library staff to define subject areas and construct hierarchical relationships among the terms, based on the ANSI guidelines. Medical or general references consulted included *Dorland's Illustrated Medical Dictionary* (24th-25th eds., 1965, 1974) and *The Random House Dictionary of the English Language*

(1971). The subject areas are based on Egan's developed detailed subject files as well as literature holdings of the collection. Many of the terms or concepts were directly borrowed from the *Library of Congress Subject Heading* (*LCSH*) list. Thesaurus terms are listed alphabetically. It originally had about 2,000 descriptors with 250 references from unused to used words or phrases. Each descriptor entry includes its hierarchical relationships to other descriptors, cross-references that have been made to it, if any, and a scope note that defines the term or limits its use. For ease of use, a permuted index has also been included. This index provides alphabetical access to individual words in the multi-word descriptors.

Because the thesaurus was constructed at a time when manual cataloging was a common practice, many pre-coordinated terms were included in order to achieve better relevancy retrieval. Multi-word concepts and extensive pre-coordination of terms were chosen. For example, the term **Homosexual Body Build Research** is a pre-coordinated term for research attempting to correlate homosexuals with certain types of body builds. **Prostitution Slang** is another pre-coordinated, multi-word term, intended for discussions or research on the underground terminology used by prostitutes and/or pimps.

This locally developed thesaurus differs from *LCSH* in many ways, with its most notable feature being lack of structure for free subdivision for subject headings. Instead, fixed subdivisions, or breakdowns, are applied. The fixed subdivisions include gender, age, historical period, and geographical location. These breakdowns include parameters important for researchers and users, and provide another way of pre-coordination of terms. For "Age" breakdown, for example, there are eight defined terms: Infant–from birth to approximately 2.9 years; Child–from approximately 3 years to puberty; Adolescent–from puberty to approximately 17.9 years; College Student–from approximately 18-24.9 years for those who are enrolled in a college or university; Young Adult–for non-college, approximately 18-24.9 years; Adult–for approximately 25-44.9 years; Middle Aged–for approximately 45-64.9 years; and Aged–for age 65 or older.

The historical subdivision **Hist.** is broken down as: Antiquity (up to and including the fall of Rome, 476 A.D.), Dark Ages (500-1099), Medieval (1100 to 1399), Pre-Columbian (American continents before 1500), Renaissance, Reformation, 15th Century, 16th Century, 17th Century, 18th Century, 19th Century, and 20th Century. Breakdowns may be used only where they are indicated in the thesaurus and in the order as indicated in the thesaurus. For example, the term **Interfaith Marriage** has both geographical and historical subdivisions whereas the term **Sex Offenders** is allowed for age and geographical subdivisions. The term **Sex Education** covers discussions of what is involved in educating people about sex and can be used with all four breakdowns in the following order: age, male or female, geographical, and historical.

A piece on adolescent boys' sex education in Switzerland in the 1970s, for instance, can be assigned this subject heading: **Sex Education (Adolescence) (Male) (Switzerland) (20th Century, 1960-)**. It is essential for catalogers to recognize that some breakdowns contain important information and must be included. For example, an article on the lesbian community would translate to **Homosexual Community (Female)** with the female breakdown being significant. Similarly, if an article presents study or research on a certain age group of people, such as children or seniors, the relevant breakdowns are essential to the heading.

Objectivity, a guiding principle for Kinsey and his research associates in conducting surveys, also was a goal for the thesaurus development by the library staff. The term **pornography**, while it is widely used, was not chosen as the controlled term in the thesaurus. Instead, the term **Erotica** is used for materials of pictorial or written text that is intended to produce sexual arousal in readers and viewers. The term **Coitus** is used instead of **Intercourse** for heterosexual, penile/vaginal coitus. **Homosexuality (Male)** and **Homosexuality (Female)** are used but not **Gayness** and **Lesbianism**. Similarly, **Homosexuals (Male)** and **Homosexuals (Female)** are used instead of **Gays** and **Lesbians**. The term **Sex Variations** is used for sexual behavior that is statistically deviant from the norm and/or has legal consequences.

It took about two years to complete the initial construction of the thesaurus. By the fall of 1973 the first draft was completed and was immediately put to the test by the Institute cataloging staff, who began using it to provide subject indexing for the Institute's collections of social and behavioral materials.

Applying the Terms and Classification to Cataloging

Proper use of the thesaurus requires familiarity with its concordance, grasp of broader/narrower/related terms concepts, understanding of the breakdowns, and correct reading of the scope notes. For instance, an author may use the term **Celibacy** when discussing people who for no religious reason have decided to abstain from sexual intercourse. The thesaurus, however, defines **Celibacy** as "religious restriction against marriage." The required term in this case is **Continence**, which the thesaurus defines as "self-restraint, specifically in refraining from sexual intercourse." The Library staff has developed documents to further explain or regulate the application of the terms. For instance, there is no maximum set of thesaurus terms assigned to a document or a book;

there can be as many terms as necessary to provide adequate subject access to the material. Each cataloging worksheet is checked by at least two other staff, a process which serves as a quality-control mechanism for the application of terms. The descriptor terms are to be listed with the most important concept first. It is also recognized that there will not always be a most important concept; and when this is the case, the order of the terms is not important. However, when there are one or two descriptors that are more significant than others for retrieving an article, they should be listed first on the list of descriptors. In the 1970s all recommended new descriptors and new breakdowns were submitted to a committee of librarians for discussion, and it was decided whether new terms were actually needed or whether post-coordination of several terms would be sufficient to describe a given document.

Special Codes for Special Collections

Even though DDC has been valuable in organizing the library collections, there are materials that do not seem to fit the classification precisely. These ephemeral publications include "girlie" magazines, nudist publications, tabloids, underground publications, homosexual magazines, pulp novels, and other publications that are collected by few, if any, other libraries. These collections give a fair representation of the type of materials available to the general public at a given time. These collections of erotica have been divided into sub-categories based on the physical format, time period, publishing houses, or themes. For these special collections a further location is defined for organization and access purposes. For practical reasons many of the original Kinsey abbreviations were inherited because of the need to group certain types of materials. For example, **SM** has been used for sadomasochistic erotica.

Pulp Fiction. Pulp fiction is a genre of fiction dealing predominantly with sex-oriented themes. Such literature was published with soft covers and became known as "soft-core pornography." This term was used because these works of fiction, though dominated by sexual themes, stopped short of deliberate, explicit description of sexual activity. According to Egan, since about 1967, "soft-core pornography" has been replaced in the erotica market by "hard-core pornography," which is devoted exclusively to the explicit description of sexual activities. All pulp fiction titles in the Kinsey Library are cataloged with literary classification numbers and include a specific location symbol (*) to indicate that they are part of the pulp fiction collection.

Sex Magazines. Because graphic materials seem to impose greater concern to censors than written words, sex magazines with explicit pictures are an even greater problem for bibliographic control than erotic novels.[17] Publishers of such magazines will go to great lengths to disguise themselves. The more than

2,000 individual titles of adult magazines at the Library, also known as "girlie" magazines, were not cataloged but simply listed on serial cards that indicated title and holding information. In 1994 a pilot project identified ninety titles to be entered into the Institute's online catalog using the USMARC serial format. The project completed descriptive cataloging and subject analysis, established necessary authority work for series/uniform titles, and created holdings records. In the process the Library staff encountered great difficulty in establishing titles and locating publication histories because of the scarcity of reference sources and the unavailability of most titles in OCLC or RLIN. Of the ninety titles, nineteen were found in OCLC and four in RLIN.[18]

By 1970 the influence of Danish and Swedish sex periodicals was visible in "girlie" magazines published in the United States. An explosion of new titles, each labeled "volume 1, number 1," often with no date and no publisher's imprint, appeared in adult bookstores. Similar situations exist with homosexual and nudist magazines. Publishers of these magazines appear to be more apprehensive about content than publishers of novels. Greater care is exercised in disguising source information. Often it is difficult to distinguish a magazine from a catalog. For example, publishers of strictly sadomasochistic publications include advertisements for their products. Irving Klaw issued a series of bulletins in the 1950s advertising photo sets, films, and magazines depicting various sadomasochistic activities. Other publishers and producers of similar material have issued catalogs that have featured photo sets, devices, and a few publications. "Girlie" magazines in the Kinsey Library are assigned the location code **J**.

Pseudo-Science Materials. Erotica titles often pose problems in that they have no relationship to the contents of the actual publications. These works use research-sounding titles and become a marketing device and are sensationalized to attract customers. Pseudo-scientific works contain little research or scholarship and are simply fiction in disguise. The Institute puts all research-sounding pseudo-science titles under the symbol # and shelves them together.

Authority Files, Identifiers, and Geographical Files

As in any other library that uses classification and subject headings to provide the foundation for material organization, it is necessary to have additional tools for cataloging efficiently and consistently. Before automation when tools and files had to be created and maintained manually, the library staff put forth great effort in maintaining these resources that are necessary for a consistent organizational system and an effective public catalog. The Library developed procedures and policies with regard to filing, indexing, cataloging, and following cataloging standards such as AACR2 as closely as possible.

Authority Files. This file is particularly important given the prevalence of pseudonyms in the Kinsey Library. This file is a record of the names of all authors represented in the books, reprints, and journal collections. The Library policy has been to establish names in the fullest forms possible. Sources such as an in-house directory and published directories of various professional organizations are checked. Cross references are created as needed.

Identifier File. An identifier is a proper name used as a subject tracing but not incorporated into the thesaurus as a descriptor. This file consists of identifiers used in cataloging and their proper forms of entry. Common examples of identifiers are names of drugs, names of questionnaires, and names of people needed for biographical articles. It serves the same function as the authority file–to insure that every time an identifier is used, it is used in the same way. The information to establish these names can usually be ascertained from the documents being cataloged, but sometimes it is necessary to check in other sources. For corporate bodies full names are preferred to initials or acronyms unless the bodies are clearly better known by their acronyms than by their full names.

Geographic File. Because geographic locations are used only in pre-coordinated terms by means of the breakdown **Geog.**, there is no access to geographic locations by their names. With the thesaurus format, the only way of locating such information is to check all the terms that are listed in the thesaurus as having geographic breakdowns. The way to circumvent this problem has been to keep a file of each geographic location and indicate where specific locations have been used in conjunction with thesaurus descriptors. The Institute Library has used the "Geographic and Socioeconomic Areas Hierarchy" from *Population/Family Planning Thesaurus* by Caroline Lucas and Margaret Osburn.[19]

Analytical Cataloging

Because of the interdisciplinary nature of sex research, it is not surprising to see that many journal articles and monographs suitable for the Institute's library collections are written by scholars from a variety of disciplines. For an effective retrieval of journal articles, book chapters, or papers in conference proceedings, the Library provides analytical cataloging for each item.

Reprints. The Institute Library subscribes to numerous journals such as *Archives of Sexual Behavior, Forum, Journal of Sex Research, Medical Aspects of Human Sexuality, Sexology,* and *Sexualmedizin.* Before the various online full-text databases or indexes became available, journal contents were accessible only by using vague standard tools such as *Psychological Abstracts* or *So-*

ciological Abstracts or by looking through each journal. Because the field of sexology comprises many subjects and is derived from many other disciplines including law, psychology, sociology, anthropology, medicine, biology, history, and folklore, most documents are in the form of research or general journal articles; but there are also curricula, bibliographies, and various other types of documents represented. Reprints are classified with a single Dewey-style number and are accessible by that classification number or by the first author under whose name card was filed into the reprint file. The indexing of reprints is considered as important as the cataloging of books and is designed to provide greater access to the reprint literature. Indexers keep in mind such questions as: What is the piece about? What is the intended audience, or who will use the article? What is the level of the article? Does it report on research? Is it from a psychoanalytic viewpoint? Is it law or about law? Is it a certain identifiable form? Is it about something that is a proper noun and therefore requires an identifier?

Analytical cataloging also includes articles in books, which are marked as either **"from"** (when the Library does not hold the host item) or **"in"** (when the Library holds the host item), and determines book titles, book editors, pages covered by the articles, places of publication, publishers, and dates of publication. A card as well as a label is created for each analytical entry–for example: In Sexual Problems: Diagnosis and Treatment in Medical Practice, ed. by Charles William Wahl. p. 228-237. New York, Free Press, 1967. Later, in the library database, unpublished papers have been cataloged as in this example: Prison and homosexuality. Paper presented at Western Psychological Association, San Francisco, May 1967, Mimeograph, 9 p.

Detailed Descriptive Cataloging

Institute catalogers, ever aware of the rarity and uniqueness of the library's holdings, strive to make the collections as accessible as they can. One means of providing this access is to include detailed notes in the catalog records. For example, notes are generated to alert researchers to the existence of certain materials in appendices. A research instrument, such as a questionnaire, an interview schedule, or a related policy statement or document, may exist only in the appendix of a monograph.

Subject Literature Analysis

Providing subject analysis for the erotic literature collection was one of the goals of a grant-supported project on literature cataloging that was undertaken in the early 1980s. Cataloging the 14,000 items in this collection was time-consuming and labor-intensive, but subject analysis provided a unique benefit to library users. The subject headings for these literary works were taken from the Institute's own in-house thesaurus *Sexual Nomenclature*. Those records are clearly identified in the notes area as fictional works and not works of social studies or non-fiction.

Other Collections and Their Organizational Structures

Art, Artifacts, and Photography. In terms of its comprehensiveness and depth, the strongest part of the visual art holdings is the photography collection. The Institute's founders placed great value on the cultural importance of visual representation. The subject code for this photographic collection was developed by Kinsey and his associates, including, for example, **ANAT** for anatomical, **BNDG** for bondage, **BR** for breast, **CINE** for cinema, **CLERIC** for images of clergy, and **CLOSE** for close-up views.

Archival Collections. Kinsey corresponded with an enormously wide range of people, from the famous to many ordinary individuals contacting him for advice. He answered all of the letters and kept copies. They discussed all sorts of issues, often private problems and concerns. There are also reports, field notes, unpublished manuscripts, and personal diaries in the archival collections. The archives are a gold mine for social historians. The 65,000 pieces of correspondence are organized by the correspondents' names and indexed in an MS Access database, with information on the piece counts, the affiliation of the correspondents, and dates. In addition, the personal archival and manuscript collections are alphabetically arranged. The Institute's archival records are arranged chronologically. The archives also include the records of 18,000 interviews conducted during Kinsey's collection of sexual histories for his research as well as archival collections of many significant researchers including Magnus Hirschfeld, Harry Benjamin, and John Money.

Catalogs and Databases

The Institute has produced many reference tools. Two of the most prominent catalogs are the *Catalog of the Social and Behavioral Sciences*[20] in 1975 and the *Catalog of Periodical Literature in the Social and Behavioral Sciences Section*[21] in 1976. The *Sex Studies Index*[22] appeared in 1982.

The Institute developed an in-house database (ACROBAT), designed on the University's mainframe in 1980, with a grant from NEH. The system was designed for MARC cataloging all types of materials. Cataloging of the Institute's social and behavioral sciences acquisitions were also input during this time. Tom Albright, computer analyst at the Institute, designed an indexing format compatible with both the Institute's database as well as with cataloging conventions. By 1984 all materials, including art and art objects, were cataloged into ACROBAT system.

In 1995 KICAT, a NOTIS-based online catalog, become available. In 2001, the database was converted to the Sirsi library automation environment. The online database provides access to books, journals, and journal articles. A user, for example, can retrieve articles from a known journal by searching MARC field 773. A more efficient search can use the call number of a journal, given that the journal is analytically cataloged. A user can also browse through individual journal articles. For example, when searching the call number **J532 J68** for *Journal of Homosexuality*, the result would be a list of all cataloged articles in this cluster since all related articles share the same call number as the journal. This searching mechanism is indeed an important service to the users of the Kinsey Institute. Even though the library has closed stacks for security reasons, a well-conducted call number search under any of the classification areas would generate a shelflist of what was included in that portion of the collection.

CONCLUSION

Institute funds for the support of the acquisition and organization of publications and other media for its collections are precarious. Active purchasing has been directed to the more critical needs in the social and behavioral sciences collection of the library. The result is a less-than-comprehensive contemporary erotica and ephemera collection. Gift collections of erotica have been a major source of new acquisitions. Each year, there are 400 to 600 research visits by qualified scholars, scientists, professionals, media representatives, and students with a demonstrable research need who are at least eighteen years old. Some materials in the collections have additional donor restrictions. For instance, some materials are inaccessible until fifty years after the donor's death. Because of the Institute's efforts in organizing and providing access, researchers have been able to use the collections to address topics ranging from sex and aging, gender identity disorder, and lesbian pornography to honeymoons, health reform eras, and white slavery in Victorian England.

NOTES

1. Alfred C. Kinsey, Wardell B. Pomeroy, and Clyde E. Martin, S*exual Behavior in the Human Male* (Philadelphia: Saunders, 1948).

2. Alfred C. Kinsey et al., *Sexual Behavior in the Human Female* (Philadelphia: Saunders, 1953).

3. In 1981 the Institute for Sex Research, which has been known informally as the Kinsey Institute, officially changed its name to the Alfred C. Kinsey Institute for Sex

Research. In 1982 the name was changed to the Kinsey Institute for Research in Sex, Gender, and Reproduction.

4. For information on how to apply for access, read the Collections Use Policy at the Institute's Web site at http://www.kinseyinstitute.org.

5. As a result of this legal decision, the Institute won the right to import erotic materials for research purposes and to send such materials through the mail. A portion of that decision restricted the use of the collections to qualified scholars with demonstrable research needs. For a detailed discussion of the case, see: Jennifer Yamashiro, "In the Realm of the Sciences: The Kinsey Institute's 31 Photographs," in *Porn 101: Eroticism, Pornography, and the First Amendment*, ed. James Elias (Amherst, N.Y.: Prometheus Books, 1999): 32-52.

6. For the study of human sexuality, the Kinsey Institute has the richest and possibly the largest collections of research materials in the world. The collections include 95,000 books, journals, and scientific articles; over 7,000 art and objects; approximately 75,000 photographic images dating from 1880 to the present; around 6,500 reels of film; and a variety of objects spanning more than 5,000 years of human history. The emphasis in collection is contingent upon the nature of current research projects of the Institute. For example, the Library collects exhaustively in the areas of homosexuality and sex education. Literature on sex laws, sex crimes, prostitution, contraception, fertility control, abortion, and STDs are all represented in the collection but vary in the degrees of comprehensiveness. Reprints and journal articles come to the Institute either as a result of ongoing subscriptions or though an elaborate acquisition process that includes writing to authors to request copies of their papers or writing to journals for specific items of interest.

7. Wardell B. Pomeroy, *Dr. Kinsey and the Institute for Sex Research* (New York: Harper & Row, 1982), 458-459.

8. Rebecca Dixon, "Bibliographical Control of Erotica" (unpublished paper, Kinsey Library, 1974).

9. Ruth Beasley, "Another Look at OCLC's Potential for Special Libraries" *Journal of the American Society for Information Science* 31, no. 4 (July 1980): 300.

10. Dixon, 30.

11. Jules Gay, *Bibliographie des principaux ouvrages relatifs à l'amour, aux femmes, au mariage: indiquant les auteurs de ces ouvrages, leurs éditions, leur valeur et les prohibitions ou condamnations dont certains d'entre eux ont été l'objet* (Paris, 1861).

12. Hugo Nay, *Bibliotheca Germanorum erotica: Verzeichniss der gesammten deutschen erotischen Literatur mit Einschluss der Uebersetzungen: Nachschlagebuch für Literaturhistoriker, Antiquare, und Bibliothekare* (Leipzig, 1875).

13. Henry Spencer Ashbee, *Index librorum prohibitorum: Being Notes Bio-biblio-iconographical and Critical on Curious and Uncommon Books* (London, 1877).

14. Henry Spencer Ashbee, *Centuria librorum absconditorum: Being Notes Bio-biblio-iconographical and Critical on Curious and Uncommon Books* (London, 1879).

15. Henry Spencer Ashbee, *Catena Librorum Tacendorum: Being Notes Bio-biblio-iconographical and Critical on Curious and Uncommon Books* (London, 1885).

16. Dixon, 10.

17. Ibid., 23.

18. Liana Zhou and Susan Heusser-Ladwig, "Cataloging Pilot Project for the Adult Magazines at the Kinsey Institute Library" (unpublished paper, Kinsey Library, 1994).

19. Caroline Lucas and Margaret Osburn, *Population/Family Planning Thesaurus* (Chapel Hill: Technical Information Service, Carolina Population Center, University of North Carolina at Chapel Hill, 1975).

20. Institute for Sex Research Library, *Catalog of the Social and Behavioral Sciences, Monograph Section of the Library of the Institute for Sex Research, Indiana University, Bloomington, Indiana*, 4 vols. (Boston: G. K. Hall, 1975).

21. Institute for Sex Research Library, *Catalog of Periodical Literature in the Social and Behavioral Sciences Section, Library of the Institute for Sex Research, Indiana University: Including Supplement to Monographs*, 1973-1975, 4 vols. (Boston: G. K. Hall, 1976).

22. Alfred C. Kinsey Institute for Sex Research, *Sex Studies Index*, 2 vols. (Boston: G. K. Hall, 1982).

Development of a Universal Law Classification: A Retrospective on Library of Congress Class K

Jolande E. Goldberg

SUMMARY. The creation of a law classification schedule at the Library of Congress has been under development since the late 1930s and has continued to the present. The law schedules have been published over the past thirty-five years. Class K delineates all laws and legal systems on global, regional, and jurisdictional levels and provides links between historical and religious systems as well. This article also discusses historical and political aspects of the development of law classification. *[Article copies available for a fee from The Haworth Document Delivery Service: 1-800-HAWORTH. E-mail address: <getinfo@haworthpressinc.com> Website: <http://www.HaworthPress.com> © 2003 by The Haworth Press, Inc. All rights reserved.]*

KEYWORDS. Library of Congress Class K, law classification, jurisdictionality, civil law, common law, Anglo-American law, law of American Indians, law of the United States, German law, regional law, regionalism, European law, law of the world

Dr. Jolande E. Goldberg is Senior Law Classification Specialist, Cataloging Policy and Support Office, Library of Congress (E-mail: jgol@loc.gov).

[Haworth co-indexing entry note]: "Development of a Universal Law Classification: A Retrospective on Library of Congress Class K." Goldberg, Jolande E. Co-published simultaneously in *Cataloging & Classification Quarterly* (The Haworth Information Press, an imprint of The Haworth Press, Inc.) Vol. 35, No. 3/4, 2003, pp. 355-436; and: *Historical Aspects of Cataloging and Classification* (ed: Martin D. Joachim) The Haworth Information Press, an imprint of The Haworth Press, Inc., 2003, pp. 355-436. Single or multiple copies of this article are available for a fee from The Haworth Document Delivery Service [1-800-HAWORTH, 9:00 a.m. - 5:00 p.m. (EST). E-mail address: getinfo@haworthpressinc.com].

OUTLINE

INTRODUCTION

The recent implementation of KBR (History of Canon Law, 2001) and KBU (Law of the Roman Catholic Church. The Holy See, 2001), subclasses of KB-KBX for Religious Legal Systems within Library of Congress Class K:

Law, signals the end of the law classification development with respect to comparative and uniform private and public international law on the global and regional level, as well as domestic law on the jurisdiction level. At the same time, it is the keystone of the century-old Library of Congress Classification system (LCC), the manifest of LC collection policy.

Implementation of the vast Class K began in 1967-1969 with subclass KF (Law of the United States), which was designed as the model for all common law jurisdictions, in particular for the subsequently written schedules KD (Law of the UK and Ireland, 1973) and KE (Law of Canada, 1976), forming together the core of classification for the common law. During the development of the classification of German law (KK-KKC) as a model for all civil law jurisdictions beginning in 1972 (published in 1980), early patterns of parallel classification began to emerge in the patterning of KKA (Law of East Germany). The schedule for another major civil law system, the law of France (KJV-KJW, 1985), marked the end of full law classifications for individual jurisdictions.

Already, during work on the dual schedules KZ (Law of Nations, 1998) and JZ (International Relations, 1998), which together replaced the obsolete LC Class JX, parallel classification was introduced bridging over to particular areas of subclass K (Law. General, 1977), which was simultaneously redesigned and published in 1998 under its new title "Law in general. Comparative and Uniform law. Jurisprudence." KBR and KBU, subclasses of the currently developed Class KB-KBX (Religious Legal Systems), are fully based on the principles of parallel classification.

A study of the regionalism policy, the extension of the initial jurisdictionality principle, during the development of KJ-KKZ (Law of Europe, 1989), laid the basis for classification of comparative, uniform, and organization law for the regions of the world, completed with the regional classification for Asia, Africa, Pacific Areas, and Antarctica (KL-KWX).

In summary, these schedules, published in succession over the past thirty-five years, form the Library of Congress Law Classification as it is known today. The conceptual outline or matrix of Class K reveals at a glance how all laws and legal systems are delineated, or integrated, on the global, regional, and jurisdictional level, as shown in Figure 1, providing elegant interlinks between the historic and religious legal systems as well.[1]

1. THE EARLY YEARS OF LIBRARY OF CONGRESS COLLECTING AND CLASSIFYING (1801-1901)

The history of Class K cannot be written without examination of the formative years of LC collection building and retrospective organization, or reclassi-

FIGURE 1

CLASS K: SYMMETRICAL MNEMONIC

Main Class	K	(Global) Comparative/uniform law
Sub Class	KJ	(General: Region Europe)
‖	KJC	(Regional comparative/uniform law)
‖	KJE	(Regional organization)
‖		Countries w/harmonized tables
‖		
‖	KM	(General: Region Asia)
‖	KMC	(Regional comparative/uniform)
‖	KME	(Regional organization)
‖		Countries w/harmonized tables
‖		
‖	KQ	(General: Region Africa)
‖	KQC	(Regional comparative/uniform)
‖	KQE	(Regional organization)
‖		Countries w/harmonized tables
‖		
‖	KZ	(Global) Law of Nations

fication, of these collections between 1900 and the 1930s with a new tool for collection design, the Library of Congress Classification (LCC) for subjects A-J and L-Z. The letter K for the subject law is still missing. Since then, the law classification, implemented class by class, has become for several of the LC classes the younger shadow companion. For the older LC collections on political and social sciences as well as for humanities and religion, it is the switch or linking mechanism.

1.1 Setting the Stage: The American Century

The study of the older collections offers interesting insights into the initial period of Library of Congress acquisitioning folded in with the first period of political history and historiography in the first half of the nineteenth century, the American century. This period was defined by the struggle for colonial independence on one end and the westward expansion over Indian territories, boundary settlements, territorial solidification in the Northwest and to the

South, and the Civil War on the other end. Each step to nationhood was recorded and interpreted by the historians, tasked firstly to create the nation's common heritage, a common national history subordinating the role of the individual colony or state to the story of the nation and, secondly, to create a common national bond guided by the desire to see the U.S. acquire "American character."[2] Since the mid-1800s, one can observe in the United States a steadily rising number of local historical societies, including those in the new frontier territories,[3] which provided the historiographer with collections of personal papers, accounts of lawyers, businessmen, pioneer settlers, colonial offices, etc., and treatises on American institutions. This still echoes in LC's mission statement proclaimed by Librarian of Congress John Russell Young (1897-1899)[4] in his Annual Report 1898, to "... bring it [the Library] home to the people as belonging to them–a part of their heritage–to make it American, in the highest sense, seeking ... whatever illustrates American History ... varied forms of American Growth ... Commonwealth, Building, Jurisprudence, Peace and War ... ," which was adopted in principle by his successor, Herbert Putnam,[5] who envisioned the Library of Congress as a clearing house for Americana.

Many chapters have been written in the past about Library of Congress collections, recording the beginnings, expansions, and losses, which should be recited here in only a few sentences: one year after establishment of the Library, the holdings were 740 volumes and three maps. In 1802, the first catalogue is a printed list of 964 volumes arranged by size and nine maps.[6]

Annual reports, memoranda, letters, and the early catalogues allow tracking the initial growth and the character of the collections. From 1808 on, collecting had concentrated on government documents, laws and legislative (Congressional) journals,[7] official and diplomatic correspondence, and treaties. In response to the destruction of the Library in August 1814 by the British, Jefferson offered to sell his library; by the acquisition of Jefferson's Library in 1815, the scope of LC's collection was broadened for the first time.[8] In 1817, LC received its first copyright deposits;[9] in 1837, the Joint Library Committee supported international exchange of public documents[10]–all materials of contemporary value and sources of history as well. Critics, however, concerned themselves still with the rather narrow scope of these collections. The Secretary of War, Lewis Cass, one of the noted voices, publicly opened the window to Europe. In an address to the American Historical Society in 1836,[11] he urged the expansion of LC collections to cover all subjects of human learning and ". . . elevate it to an equality with those great repositories of knowledge which are among the proudest ornaments of modern Europe."

Thomas Jefferson's classification scheme was introduced at the Library of Congress with the acquisition of his collection.[12] This classification was applied until the introduction, in 1861, of the new general catalogue for the collection, then totaling 79,214 volumes. Although the classification was steadily expanded to accommodate the fast growing library, its division of knowledge into the three principal classes–history, philosophy and fine arts (poesy)[13]–was preserved until development of the new LC Classification, the LCC.

1.2 Expanding General Collections: The Window on Europe

The second phase of LC's collection development witnesses major changes in treatment of the subject history. In the U.S., writing of history changed to critical/historical exploration, establishing, in particular after the Civil War, the national past as the basis for the reunion (which in turn became the justification for the Civil War). From Germany, the scientific, or seminar, method of study and writing of history was brought back around 1884 to the U.S. by scholars trained in German seminars, where government and international law formed part of the history curriculum. This so-called new historical movement perceived history as a study and record of social evolution. The best of these scholars, viewing themselves as political scientists, would establish departments for history and political science at American universities. The foundation of the American Historical Association under authority of the American Social Science Association is one of the most interesting testimonies.[14] The border between the two disciplines had begun to blur.

The following accounts are much defined by the politico-cultural climate of the second half of the nineteenth century, the citizens' century: Humboldt's declaration of *freedom of study and teaching* in Germany, underpinned by major achievements in the arts and sciences; the archeological endeavors of the Germans and the English in the Middle East, deepening the interest in antiquity and classical studies (*Altertumswissenschaften*) relating to Hellas and Rome. A critical factor was the new industrial wealth, which was to lay the foundation for public collections, mostly libraries and museums, as well as botanical and zoological gardens, open to all citizens. This was the time when the best of America's industrial upper class had their agents for buying and acquisitioning in Europe: the DuPonts, Frick, Vanderbilt, and the Pittsburghers were competing with the old continent. So, too, did LC.

Although the LC collections in this period expanded in a major way by the formalized exchanges of foreign government documents (1867-1875), by establishment of exquisite foreign collections (up to 1890) either through congressional appropriation or by bequest and gift, among them the Rochambeau collections, the Turkish collection, and other European purchases, acquisitioning had never lost sight of the perceived "American character" of the Library. Examples are congressional requests for deposit of all documents by the states' governors (1866); the invitation to twenty-six leading American cities to send city documents to LC (1872); or purchases of documents such as the collections relating to the 1783 Treaty of Paris.[15] The most significant expansions of the Americana collections occurred by American copyright deposits, secured by the copyright act of 1870.[16]

The beginning phase of Library of Congress Classification, initiated in 1897 by Librarian of Congress John Russell Young,[17] marks the end of LC's first collecting period, which spanned the nineteenth century—the collections now being up to the one million mark.

1.3 A New Classification for the Library of Congress

The sequence of classification development was predetermined by both size of the collections that had been building and the political and intellectual atmosphere of this moment in time. The thought is arresting that this intellectual endeavor coincided with the Dakota Indian or Sioux War (1890-1891), including such events as the Wounded Knee Massacre and death of Chief Sitting Bull (1890).

Because of its importance for the planned massive reclassification, Class Z (Bibliography and Library Science) was the first class developed and implemented between 1898 and 1902. To follow were the first subject classifications, notably Classes D (Universal and Old World History), E-F (America: History and Geography), [18] which, although finished and applied in draft form in 1901 to the most extensive of LC collections of the day, were published almost fifteen years later (1916). Class D was significantly revised tracking national and international developments after World War I.[19]

The draft schedule for Class H (Social Sciences and Economics), basically completed and applied since 1904 at the Library, was published first in 1910. In the same year, the political science classes J-JX, in company with Naval and Military Science (V and U), were published as well. Class P (Language and Literature) was constructed between 1909 and 1931. The established priority shows clearly two things: first, Putnam's vision of LC as "a bureau of information for Americana,"[20] which aligns with the philosophy (American orientation) of his predecessor, John Russell Young, and, second, the prevailing general comprehension of that period, which treated history as an all-inclusive field in subject matters, still residual today in the curricula of many schools of higher learning—because the work of American historians, the analysis and authentication of national constitutional, economic and socio-cultural data with a keen eye on international implications, had procured political justifications and status for the young nation. Here lies in part the explanation for the glaring meagerness of the law collections overall and absence of a class for law although this was clearly mandated in the early outlines of the LCC.[21]

Classes E-F and D included:

- the recorded manifestations of U.S. westward expansion and territorial dominance over the Indian territories; the Indian wars; [22] customary law (and treaties) of the American Indians;
- boundary questions and treaties, both relating to the narrower subject of a state's territory and sovereignty;
- geography;
- works on wars and peace, together with the peace treaties; and
- the first regional development leading eventually to the formation of the Organization of American States (OAS), a subject belonging by definition to regional comparative law.

In addition, Class D, with its numerous branches, had absorbed eminent sources of ancient law and peoples. But then, legal history was never recognized in U.S. law school curricula as a subject of legal study but was treated, instead, as a subset of general history.

Classes J-JX (Political Science) and Class H (Social Science) shared to an even larger extent in the legal spoils:

- official gazettes (a primary source of the law);
- legislative papers; and
- texts of constitutions of the world together with constitutional history; the whole of classic concepts of international law were, in accord with the philosophy of the time, welded together with the subject international relations. A standard note in pertinent areas of Class JX instructed the cataloger "to prefer Classes D-F in case of doubt."

Class H probably harbored most of the legal subjects since laws deal with every social and economic aspect of life and are classed in the proper place " . . . by virtue of the application of the rule . . . that a book on the law of a subject should be classed with the subject . . . ,"[23] a sentiment voiced repeatedly by the General Reference Division. Class HV included under Social Pathology a large development for administration of criminal justice and for crimes and offenses (as a subset under criminology, in most systems part of criminal law and procedure). Although LC classification was mostly completed by 1948, the letter K in the official outlines of the LCC appears still in brackets; the Outline of 1955 finally shows "K Law (in preparation)."[24]

2. BREAKING GROUND FOR LAW: CLASSIFICATIONS FOR THE DISCIPLINE AND ITS LITERATURE

It is well known that publication of legal materials in the United States has originally focused on a few particular forms such as periodicals, dictionaries and encyclopedias, statutes, court reports, and digests. The latter two were of special import to lawyers operating under common law, while treatises, the product of legal research, played a minor role in the profession. It is estimated that the general categories or forms make up about 90 percent of a medium-sized law library collection, while monographic treatments on a legal subject are traditionally arranged in alphabetical order (A-Z).[25]

The discussion of law classification in the United States reached back into the nineteenth century and must be understood as two different things: the classification of law as a science and classification of legal materials as a product of legal thought, study, and activity by the legal profession and the courts. The latter, the question of systematic arrangement of legal literature, comes in at the tail end of the larger dialogue of law classification and was folded in with the early explorations of library classifications, especially the LCC.[26]

There was a strong movement for classification of law in the latter part of the nineteenth century, probably spurred by the European law codification movement and supported by the legal profession, notably under the authority of the American Bar Association (ABA) in search of a standard classification for law principally as a tool to organize legal knowledge or as basis of restatement of law or codification. Committees on classification of the law–in sequence established and dissolved between 1888 and 1917–were tasked to develop a workable concept of law classification, subsequently broadened to a "systematic classification and restatement of the law" during cooperation with the American Academy of Jurisprudence. This concept was pursued for a short time around 1923 by the American Law Institute, which was active in restatements of some parts of the law. However, by ABA's openly stated policy, all attempts at developing or sponsoring a classification for the law were abandoned. The reason: ". . . the absence of a generally accepted classification . . . has been a source of discouragement, for [it is useless] to attempt a collation of related principles and rules upon a logical basis and a historical, philosophical and scientific restatement of the law . . . The very lack of a classification . . . has produced an absence of scientific interest and study of the law in the profession, and it has caused the law to be looked upon, and treated by many, not as a science, but as a livelihood."[27]

The New York State Bar Association took up the challenge where the ABA had dropped it. But its efforts, undertaken by a Committee on Classification and Restatement of the Law, failed in the same way, mostly because of indifference of the profession or its opposition against various proposals.[28] Despite these glaring failures the fires were not put out, as the need was many times over restated by men of the law profession, unsatisfied with the disagreeable state of affairs–the disorganized field of learning reflects on publishing practices and impacts negatively on organization of physical collections of legal materials as well: "The constant business of the lawyer is to search text books, digests, and indexes. But he finds in these the most heterogeneous arrangements of matter. What one compiler classes under contracts, is placed by another under evidence . . ."[29] And: "The present method of alphabetical arrangement, with the hackwork of digesting according to the fact, unimportant details and in minute cross-sections, often in disregard of the legal principles involved, as now efficiently undertaken by our enterprising publishing companies, leads yet to greater chaos from year to year . . ."[30]

The law librarians were next in the receiving line after the practitioners for the fallout of the aborted law classification. They are the ones in charge of, and confronted with, the "vast and ever increasing mass of reported decisions" on one side and the body of American law without a transparent conceptual order or presentation of its concepts and principles on the other. What would it take to come up with a systematic and serviceable arrangement for collections and the user of these collections? Was it a wonder then that law librarians resorted to book arrangements dictated by local convenience rather than scientific comprehension of the legal subject? And that they perpetuated classification of law books together with the subjects in Classes A-Z, while only those works "which are both general and technical"[31]–i.e., do not fit easily in any one subject category–are set aside for law? This principle was embedded in several classification systems, among them notably the Library of Congress Classification.

In defense, this principle was early on combined with several other "principles," e.g., that ". . . general libraries are to serve all groups of readers equally well and the need of the *general reader* in particular . . . [thus] law affecting the interests of certain groups should be classed with nonlegal materials affecting the same interests."[32]

What a strange assumption this was that the "general reader" should dictate the principles or method of arranging library collections. In fact, the general reader, the end-user, is irrelevant for design of different classifications addressing both the general and the specialized library collection. The "service to the reader principle" appears as merely a justification in hindsight for a convenient but unscientific practice. However, the much-invoked general reader would never leave the classification theater. He reappeared in different coats on every committee during the evolving collection disputes between different custodial departments at LC. This issue brought the law classification development almost to a halt in its initial phase and has interfered ever since.

The second widely pronounced credo in classification of that time (in fact, the introductory statement of Benyon's law classification),[33] that law addresses all aspects of life and for that should be classed as *legal aspect* of every subject, has also a real flaw of argument. It dismisses the differentiation of several and distinct aspects of law: namely, law as snapshot of socio-economic and cultural conditions at a given time in the life of a nation; the theory or science of law outlining and defining philosophical concepts or ethical standards, which underlie all prescriptions for conduct on the personal and public level; and, last, enforcement of such conduct through a finite catalog of sanctions.

2.1 The Early Proposals for a Law Book Classification

Actual law classification proposals for use *intra muros* at the Library of Congress appear to have been first made around 1939, triggered probably by Columbia University Law Library's Classification of Foreign Law.[34] This brought the need for organization of law libraries with large foreign law collections at once to the attention of the broader library community, marking the beginning of systematic law classification by institutions independently from LC. It is consistent as well with the observation that until then in Anglo-American law, monographic literature on particular subjects was hardly published in contrast to the mass of European monographic literature on the civil law, which serves doctrinal development, research, and study of law.[35]

A committee of librarians, appointed by the Librarian of Congress to survey the situation at LC, delivered its findings and the recommendation that (1) the "very rough classification schedule without notation" presently in use at the Law Library only and gradually expanding there to absorb new *forms* of legal materials, should be translated into symbols, and that (2) ". . . law classification should be assigned to the Processing Department." In 1939, the Chief of LC's Classification Division assumed that a shelf arrangement could be readily adopted by a classification system "which need not be a uncompromisingly scientific classification for law." It was estimated then that, assuming the hiring of some additional staff, the whole work on a law classification could be completed by the end of fiscal year 1940.[36]

In 1941 the Chief of the Subject Cataloging Division prepared statements for the Processing Department, subsequently shared with the Librarian of Congress,[37] with a specific recommendation on two questions: whether a library should (1) devise a systematic classification for its holdings, or (2) stay with a simple shelf arrangement by broad categories? In this statement, a distinction was made whether collections are used only by attorneys ". . . satisfied with arrangements by codes, session laws, digests, court reports . . ." and the like, or by researchers interested in treatises on theory, legal history, comparative law, etc. Since the Law Library is used by both groups, it should be fully classified. To provide notation to the existing shelving device would "be a makeshift classification at best." It also was proposed that a committee of three or four experienced classifiers and assistants with legal training would work on a first draft of a law classification scheme devised according to LC classification practices under the direction of the Chief of the Subject Cataloging Division and that the draft would be reviewed by the Law Librarian.[38]

By the end of 1942, the subject cataloging of law had been transferred permanently to the Subject Cataloging Division; in an instruction to the Chief, "all law materials which lend themselves to be classed in A-J and L-Z, should be so classified. This would embrace all law except for procedure and *non-classifiable works*. No provision was made then to assign these books to the Law Library."[39]

In 1944, the Committee on the Facilities of the Law Library of Congress of the ABA concerned itself with the ". . . situation existing in the Law Library of Congress with regard to location and custody of legal publications which elsewhere are found in law libraries, but which are excluded from the Law Library of Congress by the classification . . . of LC set up many years ago . . . This extraordinary situation . . . would seem to require the consideration of the administration of the Library of Congress."[40] Around that time, on request of the Chief Assistant Librarian, Dr. Luther H. Evans, the Law Library offered its opinion: that it was strange that LC never developed Class K, even though it appeared in the LC Classification outline from the beginning. Instead, legal treatises and legislation on virtually every subject, including texts of constitutions, and the official gazettes (for foreign law the primary source material), which one expects to find in the Law Library, are scattered throughout LC's classification A-Z. This may pass in a general library with a few law books, but where an organized law library is established, they ought to be found in that library. He added on a detailed list of LC classes where the highest number of the legal materials are to be found and concludes with the strong recommendation that ". . . as a matter of policy and in the interest of a functional organization and efficient library management, *custodial responsibility* should be laid upon the department rendering service and that facilities used by such a department should not be scattered . . . but brought together . . . at the point of service."[41] This statement, with the key word "custody" in the center, was the distant trumpet for the coming campaigns inside LC between the two principal departments, the Reference Department and the Law Library.

2.2 Expanding Law Collections: The Second Window on Europe

From 1945 on, critiques and proposals poured into LC, notably from the American Association of Law Libraries (AALL), dealing with LC's underlying policy of treating legal material as a *form division* in other classes rather than as material pertaining to the field of study "Law." On top of this and in keeping with certain directives, it became known that numbers were created, particularly in the H and J schedules, to receive legal materials.[42] This practice deprived the Law Library of materials essential to its services, or even of those purchased from the Law Library's own appropriations, and reduced the scope of the projected class to a rudimentary collection of residual materials that would not fit in with other subjects.

When in 1945 Dr. Luther H. Evans, a political scientist, took office as Librarian of Congress (1945-1953), the focus of collection and selection policies shifted to the World War II European Theater. His "Mission in Europe," which aimed at obtaining "multiple copies of European publications for the war period"[43] for distribution to American libraries and research institutions, accounted for an unprecedented expansion of LC's collection due to the massive inflow of foreign materials up to 1949, including legal materials. This meant serious business for the Law Library. Not only the size but the increasing use of the collections was such that the Law Library was forced to explore solutions of how best to service scholars and practitioners familiar with foreign legal systems. In an interesting letter of November 1947 to the Librarian of Congress, the aforementioned Miles O. Price of Columbia University points to the ". . . duty which the Library of Congress owes to the law libraries of the country. The interest . . . is on the increase, it is real, and it is in my opinion one which you should satisfy . . ." In his opinion, the Library of Congress should develop, rather than adopt, one of the existing law classification schemes, which would be "well done . . . and which . . . will be a standard classification . . . adopted by other libraries . . ." because of ". . . the prestige enjoyed by LC and the competence with which it performs its job . . ."[44] The law library community outside LC had begun to assemble arguments and gather its forces. Slowly, reasoning point by point, all of the so far involved parties acknowledged–supported each by ever shifting alliances–that the time had come to separate authoritatively the scope of law from other disciplines of study. Inside

LC, a law classification was now expected to possibly bring the custodial and service responsibilities of the two principle departments into harmony.

Thus, in February 1948, instructions from the Processing Department to the Subject Cataloging Division were issued to assign henceforth **LAW** to all acquisitions anticipated to fall within the perimeters of the anticipated Class K.[45] Consequently, about 400 groups of class numbers in existing schedules were blocked off, i.e., discontinued. This new policy was announced at the New York convention of the American Association of Law Libraries of the same year, which also was addressed by the Librarian of Congress, Dr. Evans, who formulated his views on law classification for the assembly: ". . . I personally believe that classification of knowledge is essential for adequate library administration . . . There is some point in having a system that covers all knowledge rather than trying to follow the pattern of letting each special interest [of users of reference collections] organize the world around a new point of interest . . . I am full of hope that . . . classification will be one that will place things in Schedule K which properly belong in Schedule K . . ." He suggested that the Association appoint a committee to cooperate with LC in defining the policies on scope and content of Class K, as well as the principles for the technical development of the schedule.[46]

For a better understanding of the bilateral–intellectual and administrative–disagreements accompanying the "Class K Project," as it became known, it is worthwhile to quote in the following some of the remarkable historic utterances of the women and men contributing to it. In the heyday of law classification development, the members of such dashing think tanks as the LC Committee on the Classification Schedule for Law, the AALL Committee to Cooperate with LC on Law Classification, the Interdepartmental Committee on Class K, and the Joint Advisory Committee on Anglo-American Law (AALL and LC), to mention a few, would address each other politely as Messieurs or Messers, but the records are full of harsh words. Class K development was a worrisome prospect for all who realized its possible scope, and could have been easily put aside without the astonishing foresight and ceaseless campaigning of its chief promoters, Dr. Werner B. Ellinger, Senior Subject Specialist (Law) at LC, and Miles O. Price, Law Librarian at the Columbia University Law School Library. Indeed, only at the Library of Congress, because of its established authority and leadership in the field and, to a large degree, because of its uniting force for adoption of common rules and standards, could a central law classification system as a basis for later cooperative enterprises in the library community be brought about. The magnitude of the task is well documented in the Class K records, now residing with the Cataloging Policy and Support Office (CPSO) at LC.

2.3 The Law Classification Theater and the Players

In March 1949, the Librarian of Congress, Dr. Evans, appointed the Committee on the Classification Schedule for Law (LC Committee)[47] to explore theoretical and administrative implications. At the same time, the AALL appointed a Committee to Cooperate with LC on Law Classification (AALL Committee). One of its members was Elizabeth V. Benyon of the Law Library, University of Chicago.[48] The classification scheme (Class K– Law) she had recently developed, "based on the principles of the Library of Congress system . . ." (as stated in her Introduction), for the Chicago University Law Library was published by LC in August 1948 as a manuscript for comment.[49] This draft was introduced into the deliberations of the two committees as a possible point of departure for LC's development.

Obviously in anticipation of the arbitrations yet to come, Ellinger summarized in an article, published in the *Library Quarterly* of April 1949,[50] all current concepts and principles of classification design for law, with a sampling of contemporary thought on the subject. His masterly crafted essay, including the analysis of all known classification systems at that time with regard to "law," was a critique on the current practice (i.e., to fold legal materials in with other classes) as well as an impassioned plea for *systematic* classification. A detailed analysis highlighted and, at the same time, disqualified Benyon's classification for adoption at LC since it was conceptualized by the author as a "supplement to the LC scheme for law materials which form part of the general collection and not for an autonomous law library." In other words, it signaled preservation of the status quo.[51] The Benyon draft provided for division of "primary materials" in Class K, subarranged in an Anglo-American and foreign law section, and "secondary" (i.e., "general and special" monographic) literature in seven divisions (for regions of the world, with its countries) in classes KA-KG, to be subarranged by author A-Z. Added on is an alternative design, arranging broad subject categories that are again subdivided by "General works" and "Special topics, A-Z." [52] Benyon's philosophy of classification is clearly stated in her introduction: ". . . Since law is part of every field of human endeavors, it may rightly be considered as a subdivision of every subject . . . as recognized [by LC] by designating specific numbers for law materials under many of the classes in its system . . . No attempt has been made to indicate that the K class should be used in preference to the non-K classes. In the event that subject classification is not desired, a detailed arrangement for authors [A-Z] is indicated in the classes for secondary materials . . ."[53]

It was unfortunate that Benyon had built her scheme upon this confusion of original LC policies and current thinking. Miles O. Price, the most distinguished of the AALL Committee members, pointed with his criticism of the

Benyon scheme to the envisioned direction of Class K development, anticipating the principles that were later established by the joint committee:

> . . . [the Benyon classification] destroys the organic unity of individual legal systems, and forces incongruous legal systems into the same class numbers . . . The differences between common and civil law are sufficiently great to render two parallel but in many respects quite different classifications necessary. There are many concepts in each that find no counterpart in the other, and the fact that Civil lawyers proliferate so much more with fine code-point monographs serves the point to absurdity of trying to fit both into the same mold . . . As to Benyon's A-Z devices: no classification can anticipate all future needs, and something must be left to the intelligence of the classifier. However, alphabetical devices that go beyond and are consistently used to take care of well known subjects properly classifiable with stated subjects prove that a subject classification is insufficiently developed . . .[54]

After in-depth studies of the scheme and its implications, the plan of using it was abandoned. On May 12 of the same year, the LC Committee recommended to the Librarian of Congress that LC develop its own classification scheme based on the principles that have governed the construction of all other LC classifications because the Benyon scheme "is adopted only to a small law collection, does not sufficiently provide for all legal literature, is particularly inadequate for foreign law, and is built too much upon the theory of dispersion of legal materials."[55] On May 16-17, 1949, the famous joint session of the AALL and LC Committees took place, during which the guiding principles for classification of law were hammered out, later to be published as the "Interim Report" of June 10, which has remained the governing document for the development of Class K.[56] Accordingly, the projected K schedule would include:

- legal source materials,
- books dealing with subjects in terms of legal principles involved, and
- materials which would be grouped with law materials because of their relevance to the practice of the legal profession and by generally accepted canons of classification.

Supporting documents, such as a "Proposal Draft" for the discussion on May 16-17 and a "Guide to the Interpretation of the Joint Interim Report,"[57] prepared much later by the Subject Cataloging Division for deliberations of the so called Interdepartmental Committee, projected adjustments to be made in other classes:

- Legal topics and bibliography now provided for in Classes A-J and L-Z will become inoperative.
- Class K will provide for the classification of materials on constitutional law (including constitutional history) and colonial law and, further, for the law of local and municipal government, which were then classed in JA-JV.
- Private international law in JX will be blocked off and transferred to K.
- JX will be revised and expanded by utilizing numbers that fall vacant, thus providing adequate treatment for all materials that are presently classed with history or other branches of knowledge, and will be transferred to JX.

The *Guide to the Interpretation of the Interim Report* provides first-time definitions for individual categories of legal materials that were in fact reviewed for development of Subclass KK (Law of Germany) and again scrutinized for the development of the schedules KJ-KKZ (Law of Europe):

- In foreign law, the term **source materials** includes statements of usages and customs and privately recorded customary laws (Custumals) as well as early treatises and compilations (anteceding constitutional government) which have gained authoritative status.
- Characteristic sources for the **common law** are ancient reports and such writings as those by Bracton, Littleton, Coke, or Fleta.
- For the **civil law** systems, e.g., German law, such works as the *Rechtsbücher*, Urbaria, and other rolls are typical; as are for the French law the *Coutumiers*. For the medieval law of Europe (*ius Romanum Medii Aevi* and *ius canonum*) the writings of the glossators and commentators have to be considered.

Still during the AALL annual convention 1949, the "Interim Report" made the issue of a panel discussion. During the session, Dr. F. H. Wagman, at that time director of the Processing Department, pointed to problems emanating from the development of the K classification, namely structural changes in the rest of LC classification and to custody:[58]

> . . . I should like it kept in mind . . . that the Library of Congress must maintain an encyclopedic collection of materials, and consequently, must maintain an encyclopedic classification of knowledge. Classification of law with us is no different from the classification of economics or the classification of material in political science or medicine. In the case

of certain of these disciplines we have custodial divisions, but that fact has no influence upon our classification of knowledge . . . We are *not intent upon developing a classification for whatever it might suit the purposes of a special division or department to have it in its collection* [emphasis added]. We are intent on developing a classification for law as a segment of the whole field of knowledge . . .

Then Dr. Wagman turned to the question of reclassification: Since the question of how to finance the project of reclassification of law materials was not clear yet, the Library was not ready to give an answer to the question although it considered the reclassification "with the materials in their right places as a long range objective."

How severe the financial problems were is shown in a "Report" of the American Bar Association of 1949.[59] In its budget estimates for fiscal 1949, the Law Library had asked Congress for an appropriation sufficient to add four positions to the staff, since the workload in the Foreign Law Sections and American-British Law Section had increased to such an extent ". . . that it is imperative to have these positions as a minimum to enable the Law Library to carry on its workload." In its appropriations for 1949, Congress not only did "not grant the four positions, but also declined to provide funds for reinstatement of two positions, those of the Law Librarian and of the Chief of the British Law Section."

At last, in 1952, Werner B. Ellinger of the Subject Cataloging Division was tasked to develop the law classification, assisted by, and reporting to, the simultaneously reconstituted staff Advisory Committee on the Development of Class K (Law)[60] [henceforth Development Committee]. The jurisdiction overall for Class K development has rested from the beginning with the Subject Cataloging Division, in this function the successor of the original Classification Office, and after reorganization of LC's processing operations in 1992, with the new established Cataloging Policy and Support Office within the Cataloging Directorate.

Since the consensus among law librarians was that a classification of foreign law deserved highest priority, Ellinger prepared, between 1952 and 1959, a set of systematic outlines (without notations) for the major legal systems, the so-called *Working Papers*, which were printed and distributed by LC in limited edition as a basis for upcoming deliberations, starting off with *Working Paper No. 1: German Law (Outline)*, completed in 1953.[61] Although the area specialists in the Law Library were, from 1953 on, regularly consulted and invited to contribute to legal subjects arrangements for other European and East European jurisdictions, the management of the Law Library never took an active role in the development.

2.4 Structure and Scope of the Anticipated Class K Jurisdictionality

The ground of the initial phase of Class K development was roughly staked out by the relatively few policy statements made by LC, by the few general principles agreed upon inside and outside LC, and by general procedural principles governing the development of all other LC classes, in particular: analysis of legal systems, reduction to its basic structure in a skeletal outline, and filling in of detail delivered by the legal literature. The schedules should reflect LC holdings and be kept current (i.e., expanded or revised) by newly cataloged materials. Finally, the schedules should be arranged in the alphanumeric fashion of notation common to all LC classes. Alphabetical arrangements of branches and subjects were kept to a minimum. Reasons are readily and widely acknowledged.[62] Which language in foreign law classification should be used for alphabetical arrangements for accessing foreign, Roman or canon law collections? Or collections in other than Roman script?

Nomenclature is not uniform; legal terminology changes as swiftly as legal axioms or institutes change, as fields of study mature, as laws become obsolete. And it is "particularly disturbing when blanket alphabetical arrangements form parts of subject subdivision tables designed for uniform topical arrangement under many jurisdictions."[63] If uniform nomenclature is not recorded and observed, classification of similar or the same topics under different terms is almost certain. The strongest argument, however, is the purpose of classification, namely grouping of related materials together, while the function of the subject heading (index term, key word) is to describe the content of a work without expressing relationships to similar materials. Developed in this fashion, a systematic classification scheme offers invaluable aid for several purposes: for a classed catalog, for acquisitioning, and for comparative studies, while a blanket alphabetical subject list is practically useless, especially when indiscriminately applied under a number of different jurisdictions.

As a part of LC's encyclopedic classification system, Class K was to follow general LC cataloging practices and principles established for classification development: "The philosophy of Class K is an obvious one–it is a class similar in all respects to the other classes A-J and L-Z. It fills a gap in the LC classification system, a system for general libraries, by adding a schedule for the field of knowledge designated 'Class K–Law,' not supplying a schedule for a law library . . . [Therefore] the schedule is to be prepared as though it were being prepared at the same time as the schedules for classes A-J and L-Z, that is, it is to include provisions for *all* legal materials whether or not provisions were made, in the light of the knowledge of fifty or more years ago, for them erroneously in schedules prepared for other classes by library experts untrained in law . . ."[64]

One basic difference distinguishes the whole of Class K: arrangement by jurisdiction, which was preferred over a tabular grouping of subjects. This decision was made because of differences in legal systems from one jurisdiction to another and also due to the problems that would be created by superimposing legal concepts or nomenclature on one jurisdiction that are valid only for another. Law and legal principles of nations are neither static nor interchangeable; they are the true reflections of the social, economic, and cultural tradition. They are indicators of constitutional transformation by internal and external forces, as well as documents of changes in the legal order. Methodology, the techniques of reasoning, and interpretation reflect the caliber of a nation's legal science.

Since the legal literature in its forms and groupings of topics reflects long-standing legal traditions, development of law classification has aimed at subject arrangement in a systematic order, tracing the peculiarities of each legal system and showing the historic layers of its institutes and their relationships. While this concept did not allow for development of one subject model for the entire class oriented on a single legal system, it was understood at the primary stages of the Class K Project that not every jurisdiction would require a fully developed scheme.[65]

The early discussions focused on the order in which jurisdictions should be arranged. The option to design for classification purposes groupings of such countries (jurisdictions) that belong to the same legal system, as so-called "law families" (e.g., one for all civil law countries, one for all common law countries, one for all socialist law countries, and so forth), was quickly dismissed. Instead, it was agreed that for a relatively stable arrangement (which would not be subject to obsolescence because of fast political changes) the world should be arranged in a geographic rather than political order, first by continent (region) and second within the continent (region) in alphabetical (or linear) order by jurisdiction, with the exception of the United States and Great Britain.

The *Class K: Law. Draft Outline* [henceforth *Class K Outline*],[66] which was to be Ellinger's last task, showed in its 1970 published form that for some reason it had deviated from this original plan in that it arranged all jurisdictions more in line with the true historic evolution of a region and showed past and current constitutional interdependence of states in such a region.[67] Shortcomings of such an arrangement were first detected during the preliminary work on Class KK (Law of Germany).

The geographic principle underlying the arrangement of jurisdictions by region (continent) was then still viewed as a mere ordering device, or rather a bracket, which provided for all individual schedules that were intended to be developed for most of the Western Hemisphere and countries like Russia, India, China, and Japan. Most of the jurisdictions perceived at that time as "less important," predominantly in Africa, Asia, and Pacific Areas, were thought to be easily accommodated by smaller general tables. "Regionalism" as a workable principle for subject classification introduced itself much later in the Project.

3. THE CODE vs. THE COURT REPORT: MODEL SCHEMES FOR CIVIL AND COMMON LAW

The initial plan was to create first the schedule for German law. In the introduction to the outline for the German law schedule, the so-called *Working Paper No. 1*, Richard S. Angell, then Chief of the Subject Cataloging Division, remarked: "The first jurisdiction chosen for development was modern German law. An important consideration leading to this choice was the fact that the system underlying German law has been widely adopted by other countries . . . Accordingly, an outline for modern German law can also serve as far as possible as a master scheme for legal systems other than Anglo-American."[68]

Modern German law doctrine as it had developed and was codified in the second half of the nineteenth century had indeed set the patterns for the legislation of a number of modern jurisdictions. For that reason, a German law classification schedule had, from the beginning, been expected to serve as a model schedule for other schedules in the realm of civil law. This and the fact that German legal material constituted the largest body within the foreign law collections of the Law Library was a determining factor for the sequence in which law schedules should be prepared. According to an account of early 1956, the Law Library had a collection of ca. 170,000 volumes. Of this number, only ca. 12,000 were U.S. titles; ca. 158,000 were foreign titles, of which ca. 40,000 were German law, plus an estimated 20,000 titles from Classes A-J and L-Z thought to be re-allocated to the Law Library.

3.1 The Washington Dialogues: Law for Law

The method of law schedule construction was debated for about ten years. Should a schedule be based on the actual library holdings? Or should it be developed on a strictly theoretical basis? As demonstrated in the past, the Library had considerable experience in classifying existing collections; the Class K development should be handled in exactly the same manner as previous classes. So, in 1953, Ellinger wrote: ". . . Far from being a 'theoretical' classification, Class K is being developed as a tool to control the law collections of the Library of Congress. Since 1949, this division [i.e., Subject Cataloging Division] has been under instructions by the Director of the Processing Department to assign LAW to all materials which under the terms of the Interim Report on Class K would fall in this Class . . . Whether or not the Law Library wants for custody a certain publication is a question which is properly decided after a book is classified; it is not a question which should decide the classification . . ."[69] This reflected in tenor the opinion of the Development Committee. The accumulated record for the initial seventeen years of the *Class K Project*–measured from the appointment of Ellinger to the Project (1952) until publication of the preliminary edition of KF (1969)–consists of correspondence, memoranda, and carefully kept minutes of meetings, in-house or in the public, and is in itself a unique collection on the tension between library science and library administration and of the confusion of theoretical library classification issues with collection custody issues. The observation is quite unsettling that classification for law, in contradistinction to other classes, was expected for some time to come as a remedy for problems springing from custodial jealousies among several curatorial units, which, in a way, seems to be inherent in any administrative departmentalization.

The real impact of certain decisions concerning the expected application of Class K, already felt by the Law Library, was now being studied in several meetings of the Processing Department, the Law Library and the staff Development Committee. As the scope of Class K was being worked out in more detail, the Law Library was flooded "by legislative bills, hearings, reports, as well as official gazettes, delegated legislation (administrative regulations, etc.), compilations of statutes," which the Law Library then could not handle "because of the lack of staff and shelf space." Therefore, it was viewed by the Law Library as reasonable to delay transfer of such materials until Class K would be completed. ". . . There seems to be no good reason not to continue to route this material to the Government Publications Reading Room and to Class J." Thus, the Law Library suggested "not to reclassify and transfer to the Law Library materials now in Classes A-J and L-Z without specific reason, but only receipts of materials from its own purchases and currently received materials destined for a later Class K." Enclosed was a detailed list of items wanted by the Law Library, mostly serial publications.[70] Now, this added, on the Law Library side, another interesting twist to the issue: that only those items should be classed in law which are *bought or selected* by the Law Library–just one more instance of *custodial want* to be decided by classification. How does this compare against the Reference Department's spirited view that the subject-oriented law materials under its custody should remain there because it serves the reader best?

"Dual classification," i.e., assigning two class numbers to an item, was already dismissed in 1949 as too expensive on the one hand; and on the other hand, it was maintained that this has nothing to do with logic of classification but rather with custody and service, which would have to be resolved by "placing duplicate copies, though classed in K, in the general collections."[71] Other ideas, such as "split classification," were explored (e.g., to place in Class K a work of which the earlier edition remains in Class H) to be "indicated on cards of all LC Catalogs, Shelf list and Serial Record."[72] From 1954 on, requests were made to reconstitute the Advisory Committee on Development of Class K: Law since the members of the current committee stuck to their positions unwilling, or unable, to resolve their problems. Other "disturbing encounters" were reported, e.g., that a major revision and expansion of schedule BM (Judaism) 490-646, incorporating Jewish law, were undertaken by the Hebrew Section/Orientalia Division without consultation of the Law Library as to the placement of the law materials. It appeared also as a reasonable idea that the new committee would include outside advisers, also for a subcommittee on Anglo-American law to be established, because the responses to the first set of *Working Papers*, which were widely distributed to profiled professionals in the law community, were disappointingly meager.[73]

To move things forward, the Development Committee recommended in March 1956 to mount a pilot project and apply the *Draft Outline for German Law (Working Paper No. 1)*, to all German law holdings in both general and Law Library collections, which in combination were considered "highly representative of German law."[74] The Law Library would produce the duplicate shelf list. This prospect, of cause, put the Reference Department in a heightened state of alert.

3.2 In Search for Common Ground

On the outside, however, things had begun to change. During the AALL convention in July 1956, the Executive Committee of the Association charged the Standing Committee on Cataloging and Classification with developing a classification for law. During the following panel discussion, existing classifications were again analyzed. William B. Stern, Los Angeles County Law Library, championed the Benyon scheme, used at the LA County Law Library, on which further development of a law classification should be based. In a major debate, strong misgivings were voiced, in particular by Miles O. Price, Columba University Library, against an "Association schedule," with regard to adoption and maintenance. Following up with a letter to Elizabeth Benyon, he strongly objected to any other scheme than one developed by the Library of Congress. Back at LC, contradictory reports were pouring in. Ellinger pointed out that the interest of AALL had now totally changed in favor of a schedule for American law.[75]

During several conferences convened by the Librarian of Congress, the same questions were once more revisited: Does LC benefit from a K schedule? Was this not primarily in the interest of other libraries? Would LC ever be able to undertake the development of Class K because of its financial constraints? And was the Library committed to develop the Class because it was publicly announced? And which parts of the Library holdings should form the basis of the schedule: only Law Library holdings? Or Law Library holdings and General Collection holdings combined? According to an estimate of the Law Library, there were between 300,000 and 600,000 items, or more, in the general classified collections, which should come under Class K. It seemed that, at last, all had concurred that a full schedule could not be developed without the materials in the general collections. In a special meeting, held on July 1, 1958, by the Chief Assistant Librarian, Rutherford D. Rogers, with a delegation from AALL, the representatives of AALL indicated their desire that Anglo-American law should be developed first. But would LC be willing to proceed with Anglo-American law, without "assurance that the whole of Class K would ever be developed?" The Librarian then agreed to proceed with the assistance of AALL. A committee would be appointed by him, this time including also prominent jurists and university librarians. Funding for its work was discussed as well. During the annual convention of that same year, AALL and LC appointed the joint Advisory Committee on the Development of a LC Classification Schedule for Anglo-American Law (henceforth Anglo-American Law Advisory Committee). At the same time, the AALL Committee on Cataloging and Classification voted to abstain from any further classification development work.[76]

While Ellinger continued working on his *Working Paper No. 8: Classification of American Law (WP8)* in conjunction with the outline for American law book classification,[77] LC administrators worked on ramifications and finances for a ". . . joint committee of specialists in law and in library classification . . . ," inviting now the three institutions–American Association of Law Schools, the American Bar Association, and the American Law Institute–to nominate one representative each. It took a year, though, to get all projected members on board.[78] Eventually, the Library had also secured funds from the Council on Library Resources, Inc.,[79] to reimburse members of the Anglo-American Law Advisory Committee for their expenses connected with the meetings at LC.

The charge to the committee was (1) to study all factors of a library classification on American law, which was envisioned also as a possible model for other common law schedules; and (2) to serve as a conduit to other prominent experts in the field of law.

This swift change delayed the development of schedules for the civil law group for many years, although the broad and very fine collections on German law were of great interest to government and other users for the study of German law and politics and the past roles of Germany in the European Theater (at the time of the classification deliberations still "Germany. Territory under Allied Occupation"). It would also add tens of thousands of new titles to the unclassified foreign law collections in the Law Library during the major impact years of acquisitioning under the Higher Education Act of 1965.[80]

In the end, the delay for the civil law schedules proved to be to the advantage of the overall structure of Class K. It permitted a relatively smooth restructuring of the original *Class K Outline*, completed by 1983, and a revision of principles and methodology during development of the regional classifications. The increasing activities of the United Nations and European Communities had changed the politico-legal landscape all together, and, being prolific legal publishers, had contributed significantly to the European and international law collections of the Library of Congress as well, since it is a depository library for materials of these organizations.

3.2.1 The Committee Dialogues: Joint in Dissent

In order to ease the situation at LC between the General Reference Division and the Law Library, the Librarian of Congress appointed the Interdepartmental Committee to explore the differences in interpretation of criteria for assignment of law materials. It seems, however, that on this new platform the administrative disagreements intensified: law materials were classified by subject in the past because of the absence of a law classification, but, more significantly, by virtue of the application of the rules which implied that a book on the law of a subject should be classed with the subject. And the Reference Department felt this should be continued because and above all ". . . the first concern is service of the material to the reader. . . ," who wants to find his material in one place, which should not be ". . . governed by opportunism and shifting demands of the Law Library."[81] The Law Library challenged the status quo, because "a systematic classification does not distribute materials according to reader usage" and insisted that ". . . the long term effects of this procedure will be the complete removal of all legal materials from other classes and their reclassification in Class K. . . . The rate and pattern for this transfer are realistic not opportunistic . . ."[82] On closer examination, the fundamental disagreements were rooted in the lack of an authoritative interpretation of what constitutes legal materials, including for the first time investigation of the character of constitutions, constitutional history, international organizations and treaties, all in Class J and E-F–a question which seems to have perplexed the Library administrators for many years. It was an extraordinary demonstration of the prevailing confusion of abstract parameters that were setting apart one discipline from another by inherent criteria with jurisdictional parameters created by competing operations based on heterogeneous criteria. Late in 1959, yet another detailed *Guide to the Interpretation of the Joint Interim Report on Class K of June 10, 1949,* was drafted and distributed to the members of the Interdepartmental Committee.[83]

Interestingly, dual classification was revisited several times as a possible solution to the situation at LC. There was some sympathy for "classification of an item in two schedules if such a principle was carefully and sparingly applied," a method much later used in design for redevelopments or parallel developments of older LC social and political science classes in relation to Class K. One point, though, was proved: namely, that conflicts for the classification designer and classifier alike do not arise from a conceptualized class of reader but stem from such materials which include information pertaining to different disciplines, i.e., different classes. The final decision as to which class is the preferred one has to be made by the classifier, book by book, on the general as well as on the specialized level. In a meeting called by the Librarian in anticipation of the first session of the new Anglo-American Law Advisory Committee,[84] the Librarian attempted to clarify all the points raised over the last few years. He supported Ellinger's thesis that classification must follow the organization of knowledge itself and not user interest; but even without a Class K, legal materials, nevertheless, should be assigned to the Law library. Considering LC's needs, he questioned whether LC could develop a schedule that serves both LC and other libraries. He still did not regard LC as irrevocably bound to develop the schedule if it were not useful for LC or financially and otherwise not feasible–let alone the fact that the Law Library had never made a strong case for it! He decided, however, that the official gazettes, bills, hearings, reports (previously in Class J) and monographic literature on legal subjects would have to be assigned to the Law Library. Period.

The first set of meetings of the Advisory Committee under Chairmanship of the Chief Deputy Librarian, Rutherford D. Rogers, took place at LC on December 3-4, 1959.[85] Ellinger's *Working Paper No. 9 (Law of the United States; WP9),* had been distributed beforehand. During the meeting general points of classification were discussed. The advisors took the view that this particular classification would not be used so much by librarians but by patrons of libraries expecting to find things in logical order. A second interesting point was brought up by Miles O. Price: that borderline materials should go either into Law or alternate parallel classifications should be devised. A library could then use either classification, according to its preference. Several committee members favored parallel classification. The differences of opinions over the structure of the scheme, however, were such that the Library felt compelled to send to a select group of experts Ellinger's *Working Paper No. 8,* a summary report on the various and aborted attempts for a standard classification of American law. It was hoped that this study would clarify the "potentialities and limitations" of a classification for American literature, and that current efforts could possibly avoid the pitfalls of those past efforts. It included the outline of classifications by such jurists as:

- David Dudley Field, the drafter of the civil code of New York State, which (although vetoed by the Governor of New York) was the basis for several civil codes, including the California civil code (showing patterns and concepts of a civil law code);
- John William Salmond and his classification outline;
- Henry H. Terry, with his classification outline; and
- Roscoe Pound, the reporter of the American Law Institute (founded 1923 for the purpose of law classification), with his outline of American law.

Pound's own "pessimism towards limits of a law classification" might have contributed to the failure of the American Law Institute to proceed with the development of a law classification. In any case, it was an interesting exercise and proved that classification of law in America was a manifestation of individuality. Many of the proposals were, in both concept and inclusiveness or exclusiveness of topics, incompatible with one another, and even if categories for the outline of arrangement corresponded, the content within categories–under the same nomenclature–differed in meaning because of lack of a common terminology.[86]

Comments of engaging frankness would come in after the revised *WP9* was sent out, on request of Rutherford D. Rogers, to an additional set of scholars, whose names had been solicited from the advisers.[87] Professor Lawrence Friedman of Saint Louis University Law School, was one of the first to agree on a review of *Working Paper No. 6 (English law; WP6),* the companion common law classification outline to *WP9,* and provided a detailed critique on both. The fundamental differences of opinion concerning hierarchy and priorities of subject classes in the schedules surfaced at once. His evaluation actually demonstrated ". . . that there is no generally accepted, or traditional, classification of the law in American jurisprudence (or science of law) on which to base a classification of legal literature . . ."[88]

The second set of meetings, May 12-13, 1960, was disrupted by such disagreements that the chair asked the advisers to meet separately and hand in a written rearrangement proposal. Friedman wanted both schedules for English and American law closer aligned, which Ellinger rejected, since in his opinion, "organization of subject matter in the exposition of American law . . . assumed too different a shape from that of English law for us to try to force both systems into the same pattern of classification . . ." Therefore, arrangements in *WP9* with those in *WP6* could be achieved only to a degree.

Severe objections had been raised also against the "private-public law dichotomy" of the draft schedule, and the complete hierarchic arrangement of substantive administrative law was rejected as a bunch of "miscellany" in the wrong place! The advisors favored the assignment of regulatory aspects to those private law subjects they pertain to. "Public property" was suggested to follow "Real estate." Placement of the Constitution and constitutional law in the schedule proved even more delicate. Separate developments of federal U.S. law and state law were contested. Solutions had to be found for state law; one solution seemed to place the states A-Z under each subject in the federal scheme. Convenience for the practitioner was frequently quoted, too. Pollack and Friedman urged the Library not to adopt a system that will be obsolete before it is issued. They prepared their "Rearrangement" proposal for *WP9* along these lines, which was reproduced the next day for discussion.[89]

Ellinger, in a twenty-seven page point-by-point rebuttal, identified those parts of the draft that could be adjusted. But he would not compromise those sections that were grounded in closely observed modern developments. In particular, he proved that administrative law in the U.S. was, indeed, a rubric of public law and a discipline *ipso iure* with a general procedural and a special substantive part. He cautioned emphatically against introduction of an arrangement into the classification of legal literature "that would not take its departure from a recognized system."[90] He is in good company of jurists, such as:

- Justice Felix Frankfurter (". . . administrative law is hardly given *de iure* recognition by the English speaking-bar although . . . now . . . in the vocabulary of the Supreme Court");[91]
- Bernard Schwartz (". . . failure to take cognizance of administrative law as a recognized rubric of Anglo-American law did not prevent . . . administrative law from developing . . . [but did] . . . make an orderly development of the system more difficult . . .");[92] and
- Ernst Freund,[93] the latter pioneering modern administrative law in the U.S., following the continental tradition of procedural and substantive administrative law. He recommended following this approach and not dispersing it among other branches of the law.

These documents–*Comments on Working Paper No. 9, as Rearranged by Prof. Friedman*; the minutes of the May meeting; and a synopsis of major transpositions in the draft called *WP9* (revised)–were sent to the advisers, consultants, and committee members with the ". . . hope and expectation, that the October meeting can be the last." Without waiting for a return of answers, the LC management decided to adopt *WP9* (revised), since the advisors' opinions were perceived "as very little useful to the lawyers using the law library."[94]

After these two sets of meetings of the Anglo-American Law Advisory Committee, the Librarian established the in-house Committee on Development of Class K, by General Order No. 1724,[95] which formally replaced the 1952 reconstituted Advisory Committee on the Development of Class K, and a Law Processing Committee, which was to be in charge of descriptive legal cataloging and interdepartmental and inter-divisional routines concerning law cataloging.

3.3 The Anglo-American Law: Model KF (Law of the United States)

Then the letters of the consultants came in. Ervin H. Pollack, in general siding with Miles O. Price, was still objecting to the treatment of the "Administrative procedure and Substantive administrative law" treatment, thinking that Ellinger might be misguided by outdated legal authorities (in particular Ernst Freund). However, Price, although urging to adopt the *WP9* (revised) ". . . rather than risk collapse of this vital project,"[96] was mildly critical of Ellinger for ". . . trying somewhat too much to translate the civil law concepts into common law." This is the tenor of Friedman's letter as well: Ellinger may have been the "victim of his Continental background" and "that it is clear from Ellinger's notes, that there is no meeting of the minds between him and the consultants."[97] In contrast, Mortimer D. Schwartz, Associate Professor of Law at the University of Oklahoma, concluded his evaluation of the work done with a sharp note: "I do not believe that the simplest thing is to merely accept the working paper. However, I do believe that it is the *best* thing to accept this working paper, because no one can do a better job than Werner."[98] Interesting enough is the strong support for Ellinger's coherent arrangements for topics of "Administrative procedure and Substantive administrative law" that came from Charles J. Zinn, Law Revision Counsel to the House Committee on the Judiciary:[99] "If this classification were for lawyers and for law libraries, one would have to stick with the terminology and classification of lawyers." Public land law, for example, was not a subject of private real property. He also would prefer the term "Substantive administrative law" over "Regulation of industry, trade and commerce" because it is the term for "a very new field." He deplored the narrowing down of administrative law to administrative process. The ". . . reluctance to include substantive administrative law in Administrative law . . ." is in his opinion to be attributed to the ". . . *unfamiliarity of law school teachers with the body of substantive administrative law* [emphasis added]." In his view, they teach, as a consequence, administrative procedure and arbitrary courses on federal trade regulations and other regulatory topics without relating them to administrative law proper.

All in all, it was an ill foreboding for the upcoming meeting. In a pre-conference meeting on clarification of LC's final position, the Library decided to go with Friedman's proposed changes "in a spirit of graceful compromise," basically in the interest of cooperation with other AALL constituencies.[100] During the Anglo-American Law Advisory Committee meeting the deal was settled: *WP"9F,"* as the Friedman update was named, would be the basis for the full development of the KF schedule. Thus, the distinction of "Public law" and "Private law" was dropped from the hierarchy of the outline. A good number of categories of the administrative substantive law, the rules and "regulations of industry, trade and commerce" were to be fitted by " topical affinity" next to the "private law" section of the *WP"9F."* Courts, procedure, and criminal law dropped to the very end of the federal arrangement while a separate arrangement for law of the states was approved.

To be sure, though, LC would seek further input to this final draft from yet another set of "legal scholars, practicing lawyers, law librarians, and others competent in this field,"[101] among them William B. Stern, Foreign Law Librarian at the LA County Law Library. Instead of writing an evaluation of *WP"9F,"* he invited an LC delegation and other librarians and scholars (to be named by LC and himself) for discussion of law classification issues with which "LC as the National Library aroused national interest" and with the expectation of coming up with common policies or joint work.

This meeting concerning the Relationship of the Library of Congress Class K Development Work with "Class K–Law" (the LA County Law Library scheme) was set for May 25-26, 1961, at the LA County Law Library.[102] It would add yet another volume of disagreements to the LC records. The hosts felt that *WP"9F"* was unserviceable without major changes since it followed only the American Digest theorem classification, which does "not involve analysis of law or law in books but is simply an arrangement device."[103] Also asked was whether LC had really done analytical work on other successful classifications, for example *Class K–Law?* The position that the LC delegation took was the same as before–namely, that classification ought to be an "organization of law which is based on scientific and educational consensus" and that LC wanted a homogeneous arrangement of topics missing in the present alphabetical arrangements of *Class K–Law,* a hybrid of the Benyon scheme. The arguments, smoldering underneath since1949, were kindled anew. Stern, supported by Carleton W. Kenyon, State Law Librarian of California, pointed to the functional approach of *Class K–Law* in contrast to the theoretical but deficient attempt of *WP"9F."* Among many other objections which spread into committee meetings at the AALL convention that same year, the LA County law librarians urged reversing the placement of constitutional law to the top of the hierarchy of the outline. The "insistent and widespread campaign . . . for the adoption by LC of the LA County Law Library classification . . . entirely or in part . . ." had begun.[104] The LA County Law Library, backed up by Ms. Benyon, would not easily give up making the constitution the first topic on the ". . . criterion of *dignity*, because it is the source of law of a jurisdiction."[105]

Why should a common law schedule, the door to the American law collections, open with a subject hierarchy stemming from "civil" law? Was this the democratic question versus the continental imposition? True, *Persons, Domestic relations, Inheritance*, and *Contracts* are the core of what is commonly perceived as civil/Roman law, transmitted since Bologna in a long line of "civil law" jurisprudents and the Catholic Church and fanning out over Europe and England. But does it matter in substance whether law is expounded by the professors or decreed by rulers and princes, legislated by parliaments, or dealt by the bench? And after all, law book classification, any classification, though a "science" in itself, does not strive to re-invent legal doctrines that have been formed by centuries of legal scholarship. Classification provides merely the order for manifestations of legal thought and activity.

The meeting of the Advisory Committee in March 1962 included several guests, among them William B. Stern, who would set the tone. He confronted LC with the observation that, against all prior policies, LC disregarded other classifications in the country instead of developing a uniform system of classification that would be acceptable to other libraries. Pointing towards the LA meeting, he thought that there was general agreement to use the expertise of others who had worked for many years in this area (i.e., the LA County Law Library). In an attempt to cool the issue, Mortimer Schwartz addresses the two contending positions as follows: (1) The *hierarchical* or *organic* approach, considering constitutional law as of the highest dignity, places literature on constitutional law at the beginning of the schedules. (2) In contrast, the *subject* or *logical* approach considers constitutional law just as any other subject of law and is placed where the classification schedules prescribe.[106] To put this in context of *WP"9F,"* it seemed to him that the latter would be the better approach for LC: the hierarchical/organic approach is a fallacy since it ignores the criterion of universality. LC's collections consist of books from many countries, and the outlined placement of constitutional law in *WP9* "must be retained if such books are to be properly shelved at LC."

Nevertheless, all those siding with the subject-logical approach were appalled. No legal systems, be it Roman, canon or common law, would open the subject hierarchy with "constitutional law" because the sources do not provide constitutional law. Constitutional law was a new development of the late eighteenth and early nineteenth century, oriented on American and French revolutionary ideas and constitutional documents, the formula for other constitutions to follow. And because of the purpose of the constitution, with very few exceptions (e.g., in the socialist sphere of law), constitutions are not the source of substantive law. The document is an outline of government's power and separation of powers, organization of government and territory, and government acts, including those concerning themselves with people residing in the territory. In other words, constitutional law has to be treated as a subject and should stay where it is.

Next to follow would be administrative law. As a field of legal studies *sui generis*, it is still younger; its evolution is tied to the evolution of the civil or citizens state (under the constitution) and the society. In tension between these two entities, state and society, administrative law gained contour. The area in which the state operates in steadily increasing measures over the past eighty years in the U.S. and abroad is constituted of the private economic sector, the social sector including social insurance, welfare, public health, and education. Of course, in a civil law culture with the tradition of systematic categorization, administrative law will be embedded as a distinct and complete subject in the larger scientific structure of law under defined categories or rubrics, with adapted or harmonized terminology. But, then, this was the "Continent." In the U.S., books should be arranged in the way that the lawyer looks at them and how they have been developed in this country. Thus, the component of the substantive administrative law should be fitted closest in proximity to the subject the regulations pertain to.

There was no middle ground on these issues. It appeared that LC and its advisors had arrived at the same intersection of dead-end streets as had the different committees on the "American law classification" a quarter century earlier, when they could not agree on the same points as those at issue now. And once proclaimed, the distrust towards the jurisprudent raised in the continental civil law tradition that now was operating in the common law environ of American *couleur* would linger on and never go away. It did not further the cause that LC tried after the meeting to widen the circle of the "knowing" by such icons as Roscoe Pound, Felix Frankfurter et al., some of whom were forever connected with the failed "American law classification." All but a handful who had some advice or a few encouraging words to spare declined to get involved. In the end, it had to be LC's decision.

Most of all, it was the "hands-on" work, the analysis of the collections, that completed the task. During his tour of duty between 1962-1964 as a member of the Anglo-American Law Advisory Committee and now as consultant to the "Class K Project," Miles O. Price had spent considerable time on retrieval of what he pronounced for the record as "misclassed " titles from classes A-J and L-Z, and off the record as "manifest absurdity"; these titles were, of course, not mistakenly allocated to the wrong classes at all but classed according to earlier LC perceptions.[107] In his opinion, only a combination of the Law Library shelflist and catalog records of legal works in the other LC classes would deliver the topical detail for the new K schedule. A look at the numbers seemed to confirm this assumption. Shelflist figures quoted for U.S. federal law materials at that time showed that the Law Library shelflist count stood at 16,000 titles and the General Collections shelflist at 29,000 law titles, almost double the number.

Numbers speak! With a shelflist that was now reproduced inclusive of all U.S. law titles at LC, development of the notation and fuller subject hierarchies in *WP"9F"* was set in motion, scrutinized at every step by a vigilant, competent, and vociferous law and law library community.

In April 1963, Carleton W. Kenyon, with years of experience at the LA County Law Library, joined Miles O. Price and the staff as consultant to the project. For a while, sanguine point-by-point opinions were exchanged on subject arrangements in a wide range of intellectual temper. Irreconcilable differences–basically Kenyon's "utter conviction that the LACLL classification, essentially an alphabetical arrangement of very broad categories, was far superior to the detailed *WP"9F"* scheme"–continued until the departure of Kenyon.[108] It was unfortunate, though, that only a very limited trial run (reclassification of selected materials to test the schedule) was granted to the new schedule KF between implementation of the manuscript in 1967 and the schedule's publication in 1969, a very short period considering practices in developing other LC classes.[109]

Ellinger, from his perspective, considered KF as a "compromise," a document of reconciliation of differing views on several proposals,[110] which could in part also be attributed to the changing membership on the Advisory Committee. Nevertheless, the original bi-polar division of the KF hierarchy into private and public law (although not expressly stated in the captions) was saved. The opening chapter of Class KF was written for the centuries–proven "civil" concepts of prime import for the family of man first; second, for man's fellowship on the individual private level as well as on the public communal level–inherent, after all, in both the civil and common law traditions. And the closing part is written for the doctrine and catalog of society's sanctions for misconduct.

Just as controversial laws, once promulgated, gain their own momentum, KF upon implementation took on its own life. In the thirty years of application, the schedule has almost doubled in size. Judging from its wide adoption by the federal and local government institutions, by the courts, universities, by private law firms in ever growing number, and by many institutions abroad, one cannot help wondering whether the law book classifier in fact completed what the legal scholar had left unfinished: to classify American law as it presents itself in various manifestations and to put it in time-proven rubrics on the shelf and in databases, from where it can be retrieved by the law profession in its proper class.

Following in short sequence and relatively unencumbered were the other two schedules for common law jurisdictions, based on the KF overall patterns as far as applicable, as well as on their own complete shelflists: KD (Law of the United Kingdom and Ireland, 1973), which was in the main designed by Dr. John Fisher,[111] and KE (Law of Canada, 1976), for which Class KF with appropriate adjustments in the hierarchy had set the patterns and which was developed in a cooperative effort between LC and the National Library of Canada by E. Ann Rae. The subject content of the KE schedule reflected at that time the holdings of the Canadian library as well.[112] The section on the law of the Province of Quebec, which is grounded in French law, was developed by Guy Tanguay at the University of Sherbrooke. Schedule KE has only in recent years found wider application in Canadian institutions, among them the Parliamentary Library of Canada, the National Library in Ottawa, and the University of Toronto.

One further common law mutation, based on the "pattern pool" of KF in combination with KD, are the uniform subject tables for other common law jurisdictions of the world, classed in KL-KWX (Law of Asia, Africa, Pacific Areas and Antarctica), implemented in 1991.

3.4 Law of the American Indians

A number of orphan classes were left, though, without a systematic place in the schedule, notably the American Indians. The author of a recently published paper wonders whether the position of the classes for American Indians (KF8201-KF8228) following Military law, was deliberately chosen because of the "original handling of federal Indian affairs within the War Department."[113] In fact, it is both coincidental and a deliberate choice. The major collections on the subject are classed mainly in Classes E and F[114] together with the history of American westward expansion, the Indian wars, and history of the frontier territories. By placing creation of schedule KF in the appropriate time frame of American history, Indian affairs–compared against the civil rights movement of the 1960s–were not an urgent piece of legal speculation but rather a subject "for which any location would have to be arbitrary!"[115] Indeed, the "subject" appeared and disappeared throughout the various drafts of KF but was always envisioned to conclude the federal law section of the schedule until, for pragmatic reasons, "Courts and procedures" was dropped down to the end. The "Indian lands," on the other hand, have a different classification history. They can be traced in Class HD[116] from the first edition (1910) to the third edition (1950) in HD231-234, a subdivision under "Public lands." A revision of HD converted the subject to a reference to E93, from where it migrated into the first KF draft under the section of "Public property," still valid today as class KF5660+. The classes for law and Indian treaties, still Class E94-E95 in the 1958 edition, were blocked off at the time of the KF development and referred to as the new Class KF. To recognize indigenous peoples, historic or contemporary, as sovereign jurisdictions would have meant grouping them with the U.S. states and territories.

The situation for other North American indigenous peoples–Indians and Eskimos (Inuit) of Canada–is not different since KE is based on KF blueprints; they are classed between "National defense. Military law" and "Courts and procedure."

"Jurisdictionality" for indigenous peoples was much later adopted as a bona fide concept in the classifications for Asia, Africa, and Pacific Areas.[117] Indigenous peoples are, in each of the mega-regions, established as independent jurisdictions on equal footing with all other jurisdictions in these regions.

4. THE CIVIL LAW: MODEL KK (LAW OF GERMANY)

From 1966 on, while the finalizing work on the projected schedule KF was underway, Ellinger was requested to lay out the sequence of subclasses to be developed in the larger frame of Class K and come up with a detailed schedule for the "enormous logistics" and manpower estimates, and, by the end of 1967, with a "Crash Program to complete Class K." Since pressure was mounting during this period to revise JX, increasingly unserviceable with regard to international developments and intensifying UN activities, international and comparative law had to be folded into the overall plan as well. Looking at this Herculean task, Ellinger cautioned that all had ". . . to relinquish the half-hearted and uncertain approach to the preparation of Class K that prevailed earlier . . ." and as a first step establish ". . . an *official statement of policy . . .* governing the development of Class K as a whole . . . [It should also] serve as a manual which . . . would lay out . . . Classes and notations . . . [and] outline the structure of those legal systems that are to serve as models for systems patterned after them." The *Class K Outline*, though not the policy statement Ellinger had requested, was completed by him in 1970. Work by then was also under way on subclass K (Law general) in order to set parameters for materials intended for the new subclass on comparative and uniform law and JX (International law).[118] It was not until 1970 that preliminary work, with many interruptions and only as a detail assignment, could be started for the first civil law schedule.[119]

The first decision was the assignment of the class letter. Criteria were that (1) Germany, a federal jurisdiction like the United States, warranted a two-letter combination for the imperial and federal law and a notation expansion to three-letter combinations for its past and present states,[120] and (2) her "alphabetical position" among the other European jurisdictions that would determine preceding as well as following class letters, which called at once for a re-examination of the letter combinations assigned to Europe in the *Class K Outline.*

The original layout had KJ assigned to general works and regional federations of Europe, followed by Western European countries under three class letters–e.g., KJB Portugal, etc. The next breakdown began with KK for "General works" on Central Europe. Germany led the procession of countries with KKC to KKG, followed by Switzerland, Austria, Hungary, Czechoslovakia, and Poland, arriving in Southeastern Europe already at class letter KL (now the initial class for Asia), ending at KM for the Soviet Union, and so forth.

The changes of the *Class K Outline,* no matter how extensive, were in itself a delicate task which had to be undertaken in consultation with the library community since many institutions had begun in 1970 to assign the letter combinations to their foreign collections, which were provided in the *Class K Outline.*[121] It was, however, in principle agreed that the classification scheme could never be a true historic portrait of intricate constitutional fluctuation patterns linked to the physical realities of an entire region or should not be since it might compromise the flexibility of the schedule. Therefore, the *Class K Outline* revision utilized the original plan, filing all jurisdictions (historic and current) of a continent/region in plain alphabetic sequence with alphabetical extensions up to three class letter combinations and with enough "room to grow."

This principle was, in analogy, first tested with Class KK-KKC (Law of Germany) including the German Empire and Republic and East Germany. In this arrangement, Germany was treated as a "quasi"-region with an alphabetical arrangement for the masses of jurisdictions, historic and current, which were in constant political flux and changing patterns of sovereignty within her boundaries over the course of history.

In outlining the structure of the schedules, a number of other problems were encountered peculiar to the situation of Germany after World War II. The reunification of the country under either West or East regimes, speculated and discussed for so many years, had not materialized yet. Instead, East Germany passed through a rapid sequence of constitutional changes since her status as "Soviet Zone" and emerged as a sovereign socialist state manifested in her third constitution of 1974.[122] The principle of jurisdictionality in law classification required for East Germany a separate scheme. Furthermore, a rationale had to be found for subdividing the multitude of German states, provinces, and territories past and present, as well as the German cities between East and West since many did not neatly align with one or the other side after the political divide.

4.1 The Historic German Split and History of Law

A decision also had to be made as to where to incorporate history of German law, an important field of legal and comparative study, represented in LC by a significant collection of rare sources and monographs, now mostly in Class DD (History of Germany). Constitutional history relating to both West and East German states, the most recent division in a long line of German territorial divisions and resulting sovereignty questions, had also to be related to the larger scores in the European theater because of their baggage of post-revolutionary nineteenth century constitutional developments. Part of the answer could be found only through analysis of historical events and examination of constitutional and other documentation before and after 1949, the year of proclamation of East German and West German constitutions.[123]

The politico-legal and constitutional problems following the breakup were almost insurmountable, which is documented in the growing contemporary legal literature.[124] There was never a peace treaty with the Allies. In West Germany, the complex coexistence of German law and occupation law, formulated first in the *Occupation Statute* (*Besatzungsstatut*) of August 6, 1949, together with a control organ of the three Western Allies, the Allied High Commission, was a seed bed of competing theories and interests during the evolution of the new constitutional law, in the center: sovereignty questions, government powers, government acts, and liability.

In East German government, major changes occurred from 1952 on. The states, i.e., the federal structure, were liquidated and state governments and parliaments were dissolved. Constitutional offices of the Republic were abolished [124] in a concerted effort to centralize the power of the state and to create a central state apparatus. During the same period of time, commencing with the Soviet sequestration order in 1945, East Germany completed the phase-by-phase nationalization of natural and industrial resources and property. These events were reflected in rapidly changing legal nomenclature, concepts, institutions, and in the law itself.

Without consideration of reunification speculations, the varied politico-philosophical theories amidst the uncertainty of state succession after the

Deutsches Reich did not aid the classifier in the decision of which of the two states would "inherit" the legal and constitutional history.[125] At the end, the decision was based on the observation that West Germany had retained and preserved the major body of German statutory law and doctrine, while East Germany abolished all earlier law.[126]

Although the law in West Germany had undergone revision and judicial review, only those parts not in accord with the 1949 constitution were abolished. For these reasons it was decided that KK, the schedule for the German Federal Republic, should include the entire body of German law. It should also incorporate all legal materials stemming from the 1945-1949 period, since then the whole of Germany (Deutsches Reich) was still Territory under Allied Occupation with an undecided constitutional future.

At the same time, the development of a separate schedule for history of law, as proposed by Ellinger's *Working Paper No. 3*,[127] was abandoned. Instead, KK incorporated the history of German law as well, beginning with the tenth century. The *divisio imperii* in Charlemagne's political testament (806), the distribution of government and powers among his sons, had by then resulted in a final territorial division–or beginning of European fragmentation–into a West and East Empire, the latter being known henceforth as the Holy Roman Empire.[128] All materials of the earlier history, primarily relating to the Germanic period and to the Frankish Empire (including *Volksrechte, capitularia,* etc.) were designated for the history section of the European law classification to be developed later. This principle was implemented for the development of other schedules of the European region, in particular France and Italy, in order to prevent massive duplications and cross references. The resignation of Emperor Francis II in 1806, which was the formal dissolution of the Holy Roman Empire, set the demarcation line: all legal materials prior to 1806 were assigned to history of law.

The nineteenth century studies on the German "common" law (*Gemeines Recht*) and works of the nineteenth century *Pandektenwissenschaft* (i.e., elaborations on the Roman-civil law) were set aside to be classed later in a Roman law schedule. Left alone for the moment was the decision where to class the mass of literature from the mid-nineteenth century on, founded in legal scholarship and in the spirit of the national federation movement, providing towards the end of the century the unified empire with a body of uniform law.[129]

4.2 KF and KK Comparatively

Arrangement of subjects stirred little controversy. The two broadest subject categories, "Private" and "Public" law, represent a division formally adopted in the West during the eighteenth century. Implementation of KF had cleared the way for the overall pattern with regard to this issue for the rest of the classification–namely, placing "private" law subjects first but without the explicit caption "Private law."

4.2.1 Private Law: Mixed Aspects

In the block of private law, the subject sequence was determined by patterns of the three codes: civil, civil procedure, and commercial code. In all areas governed by a code, the enactment dates of the codes have drawn the line between materials belonging to the sources of legal history and those of modern law. However, most of the scholarly comparative literature forecasting the codes was classed together with the legislative history of the respective code. The rationale lies in the legal system that has to be seen in its historical context. Codification is not exclusive but inclusive, rather, of axioms, principles, and concepts of Roman, Germanic, and canon legal provenance, which form, perpetuated by the scholars, the core of civil law. Thus:

1. The **civil code** is overall an "apparatus" of central concepts and principles. Civil marriage, the larger part of family law, and rules for consanguinity and affinity are for the first time codified as civil law and only after the imperial chancellor Otto v. Bismarck, in a powerful struggle with the Catholic Church (*Kulturkampf*), achieved secularization of marriage.
2. The **commercial code** covers every aspect of business and commerce including corporation law and even maritime law and freightage. Most subjects in KF are covered under "Contracts," followed by "Association" and "Bankruptcy." In KF, "Regulation of industry, trade and commerce" has been placed in close vicinity of the "Private law" subjects "for the convenience of the practitioner," as it was argued then, although it is straight regulatory (administrative) law. In contrast, KK classes all regulatory aspects of industry, trade, and commerce in the large class "Economic law" (*Wirtschaftsverfassungs- und Verwaltungsrecht*) as part of administrative law, regulating all aspects of the economic sector.
3. **Copyright**, in KK, reflects the German "democratic" attitude of the beginning of the twentieth century; it is a complementary law to the civil code in order to place intellectual property under the same legal umbrella as the tangible property that is taking up a lot of room in the bourgeois civil code, the latter often criticized as the *fin de siècle* creation of the possessing upper class. In KF, "Intellectual property," in particular "Copyright" and "Patent law," is wedged between "Regulation of industry, trade, and commerce" and "Social legislation."

4. **Social legislation and Labor law** in KK was viewed as transition to the area of public law since this branch of law is grounded in the new constitutional proclamation of social justice *(Sozialer Rechtsstaat,* in rejection of the absolute or police state and totalitarianism).[130] Social insurance, mandatory health insurance and corporate pension plans, and detailed welfare laws have a long reform history. Thus does "Education law" since the Bismarck era at the end of the nineteenth century when education in the broadest sense was constituted as one of the state's mandates.

5. **Civil procedure** is governed by the code of civil procedure and complementing civil law as well as the court organization statute for the regular courts, which are the last subjects before "Constitutional law." In German law, they are separated from "Criminal law, courts and procedure."

There are, on the other hand, certain concepts adopted by German law that may seem alien in a civil law system. For example, *stare decises*, the doctrine that similar cases should be decided similarly, is by definition a common law concept but has made its entry into the German judicial process since the end of the nineteenth century. The authoritative decisions of the Reichsgericht (Imperial Supreme Court) with its historic function of finite interpretations of statutes had a certain latitude among all courts even in instances where Reichsgericht decisions were not binding on the lower courts. Particularly after World War II, decision-making has gravitated towards uniformity of law application in the interest of certainty of the law *(Rechtssicherheit)*.

Judge-made law *(Richterrecht)* is another of those concepts seemingly inconsistent with the principle of separation of powers, judicial and legislative, in the civil law country. It is the law created by analogy and interpretation by the judge in order to substitute for *lacunae (Gesetzeslücke)* in cases where the codes or statutes do not respond to fast changes of modern life. In these instances, the judge participates in law development and formulation of the so-called pre-eminent doctrine *(herrschende Meinung)* in the same way as the legal scholars.

4.2.2 Constitutional and Administrative Law: Mixed Messages

Public law proper begins with constitutional law; major subdivisions are:

• **Sources**, i.e., all constitutions and other fundamental laws relating to the constitutional periods covered by Class KK.

• **Constitutional history**, beginning with the early and progressive constitutionalism (yielding the first constitutions of German states around

1820) and the federation movement in the German region after dissolution of the Empire (1806). All materials before are classed with legal history. Laws, legislative, and government documents and related materials of individual German states, falling in the period between 1806 and 1870, did not present a problem as they were generated by independent sovereign states in the German "region" and are classed under the respective jurisdiction in subclasses KKB-KKC.

The Empire of 1871, Weimar Republic (1918), and the Third Reich (1933-1945) are the most interesting periods showing transitions and changes in the philosophy of the state. External and internal forces in the twentieth century had impacted on society in unprecedented ways. Social conditions were reshaped. The evolving social state transcends the individualistic state; terms such as "public interest," "public good" (*Gemeinwohl*), "socialization," and "social reform" are manifests of this phenomenon in contradistinction to "enjoyment" of the highly individual "private rights and property" and "pursuit of happiness."

The last period, concluding constitutional history, is the interim between 1945 and 1949 with the bulk of military government and occupation law.

- **Modern constitutional law** begins with the constitution of 1949, which is similar to KF in human and civil rights and other areas with typical democratic content, safeguarded by the Federal Constitutional Court (Bundesverfassungsgericht). To see Germany as a decentralized republic with powers divided and competences distributed throughout the federal structure was clearly an objective of the Western Allies (notably the United States) though the federation model had been around since the early nineteenth century in European constitutional law. During the sessions of the Constituent Assembly (Parlamentarische Rat) in Herrenchiemsee (Bavaria), the Military Governors introduced a number of proposals concerning the substantive matter of the constitution.[131]

Still, the catalog of basic rights of the citizens, counter-balanced by civic duties, as well as the set of programmatic declarations (*Programm-Sätze*) and the detailed prescriptions for government mandates together with the organizations in execution of those mandates, are firmly grounded in the German constitutional past and the new political conscience. They go far beyond the American model.

- **Administrative law,** all-inclusive of the catalog of regulated substantive branches under their prescribed departments and agencies, closely tracks constitutional law. On equal footage with the other branches of German law, it was completed with a Federal supreme court, the Bundesverwaltungsgericht.

This is a major difference between KF and KK. Here lies also one of the pronounced compromises in the common law model KF, its administrative law reduced to a minimalist procedural section. Subsequently, substantive administrative-regulatory law was treated as many unrelated, independent subjects. It was theoretically unfounded, as Ellinger advised many times, and had nothing to do with KF being the model schedule for common law or his being a civil law jurist. Administrative procedural and substantive law had developed simultaneously on both sides of the Atlantic in answer to the wars and driven by progressive science, technology, and aggressive markets in the company of new hazards for community and environment. The administration, casting policies into regulations, is the ordering hand of government in the private sector. Many aspects of the national economy–the corporate sector including public utilities, transportation and communication; health, welfare, and education–are government liabilities in the interest of healthy communities and are as such a large component of public law.

4.3 KKA (Law of East Germany): Classification by Comparison

During the development of KK, classification structures for overarching concepts of law were already explored in view of a subject classification for law of the German Democratic Republic, beginning in the year 1949.

Acting on the assumption that, although modified by socialist/Soviet doctrine, enough of the German legal structure had survived to try for derivation of numbers from the KK model scheme, the impact areas of Soviet/socialist law on the German legal system had to be identified. East Germany had literally re-codified every major branch of the law[132] and adjusted constitutional law to her current ideological and political agenda.[133] In civil law, ownership, possession, family and community were redefined. Progressively, one segment after another of commercial law was eroded and abolished.

The most recent constitution (1974), signed into law while the work on KK was progressing, was at the apex of the complex hierarchical system of laws and normative legal acts and provided the governing principles and concepts which are the foundation of the Socialist way of life.[134] Their implementation–together with the superimposition of the Soviet model on areas of civil and public law–had modified German legal concepts significantly. The result was a composite system made up of elements of both civil law and socialist party doctrine.

First, it was determined what special provisions and how much detail were required for the schedule KKA. Second, the numbers necessary to construct the skeleton of schedule KKA for the individual branches of the law were derived from the number base of the KK model scheme. Third, those features of the law peculiar to the legal system of East Germany were entered in detail in the text of the derived scheme, i.e., the impact areas of socialist doctrine, using numbers of the KK model that were free. For a harmonized classification system, it is essential to identify the common denominators, the essence of the dogma by comparison, which is, in other words, the method of numerical alignment in the new class with hierarchies in the same subject area of a related class.[135]

The technique can be best described by a few examples, particularly from constitutional law.[136] For major areas in both German post-World War II constitutions, the Weimar Constitution (1919) had served as the model. Despite many changes in the social fabric of West Germany, the constitution guaranties law and order of a basically post-monarchic state; high values are placed on a form of life which is deeply rooted in socio-cultural traditions; on undisturbed enjoyment of possession and ownership, and on the freedom of the individual to exercise personal and political rights without infringement of the state. From the socialist East German point of view, fundamental rights safeguarding citizens against infringements of the state is an anachronism; by socialist doctrine, the interests of state, society, and individual are identical since the state is the instrument of the workers, by and through which they exercise their power and participation in government. Socialist fundamental rights (civil rights) thus are not devised to protect the individual from the state. They are defined as personality rights to participation, co-determination, and self-realization by active cooperation with the state. These rights also organize a basic social process–the development of the individual to the socialist personality. They provide guidelines for social behavior and guarantee basic cultural and material goods for a person, paired with corresponding socialist duties.[137] In general, the reduction of constitutional rights to personality rights in contrast to the state's almost limitless power, reminds one of the absolute pre-enlightenment police state. There is no constitutional court and no protection of the individual against government acts (judicial review).

Nevertheless, it was interesting to uncover the underlying cultural blueprint: stripping from the rights and duties the socialist embellishments; except for few instances, the KK numbers for the entire area of cultural, political, and economic rights could be applied in structuring KKA. In both systems, right to work, cultural and educational rights, especially to education and occupation, are high on the list. Eastern emphasis, though, is on duty because through labor the individual establishes human relationships binding him more closely to enterprise and community. Work is not a personal achievement but rather a group effort or socializing force aiming at the fusion of individuals to the collective and ultimately extinction of individuality. Duty to physical fitness corresponds in the West to inviolability of life and health; both constitutions guarantee protection of motherhood, social assistance in old age and invalidism, as well as the common catalog of freedoms. The outline of rights and guaranties, even proclamations, are the framework of the administrative infrastructure as well.

Civil law, represented by two new codes, the civil code and the family code, was not difficult to align with the West German code since, despite ideological pronouncements, the legal principles in the code were German law. The real area of concern was property and real property. The West German system defines property and ownership as the exclusive right to possess, use, or dispose of a thing and exclude interference. This is modified by the doctrine of social obligation inherent in property. East German doctrine, embedded in the constitution,[138] supplies different forms of property: socialist public property in co-ownership with socialist collectives, property of socialist organizations, and private property for satisfaction of material and cultural need. Generally, property is a social relationship of man to production conditions. It is not an abstract doctrine but rather a dynamic process of man's acquisition or occupancy of nature by means of production.[139] His position in society results from his productivity. The East German code of 1975 provided a list of property (some verbatim repetitions of articles of the constitution) as wages, savings, and intangibles as patents, copyrights, innovations, etc., the last group not contained in the West German civil code, which had given the code attributes in the East such as "immoral," the product of capitalist greed, mostly concerned with material possessions and patriarchal rights! Marriage law and child-parent relations and education are other examples of the law, which on the surface is written with the same letters as in the West and is comparable by class. However, the intangible spirit of the law and immeasurable impact on society are beyond capture in any classification.

4.4 German States and Territories

The subclasses KKB and KKC provide for the German *Partikularrecht*, the law of German states, provinces, and territories past and present; they are arranged in one file thus treating the entire German Territory as one region.[140] The jurisdictionality principle in law classification requires that all jurisdictions be treated equally, regardless of their political or cultural mission and economic importance and regardless of whether they are historic (i.e., extinct) or modern jurisdictions. Of course, there was always concern over possible future changes on the political map affecting recognized jurisdictions. However, if a state merges with another, is annexed, or divides into independent jurisdictions, the jurisdiction once established by LC remains under its given name, letter, or number on the list; and the newly emerging jurisdiction(s) will be entered under its/their appropriate name(s), letter(s), or number(s) with connecting references or scope notes.

Historical materials in this arrangement are classed with the subject, provided in a uniform table similar in concept to the table for the states in KFA-KFZ. This arrangement proved surprisingly stable and allowed for a smooth transition following the reunification of East and West in 1991, at which point KKA became a "historic" jurisdiction, and her provinces were, under their current names, introduced in the file of German states KKB-KKC. This principle has been adopted for the arrangement of jurisdictions in most regions throughout Class K as reflected in the restructuring of the *Class K Outline*, still awaiting the final layout at completion of the Class KK-KKC implementation in 1980[141] but reflecting the direction of the regional European law classification.

In hindsight, the creation of Classes KK-KKC was a much easier project because it allowed the classifier, without external interference, the careful tracking of doctrinal developments and historico-constitutional realities which delivered the definitive outline as well as the content for the German law classification.

5. THE REGIONAL LAW: MODEL KJ-KKZ (LAW OF EUROPE). REGIONALISM

The organization of an enormously complex body of legal thought emanating from a single region such as Europe seemed best achieved by dividing the schedule into sections that are coherent either by definition or by function. Obvious divisions are by historic time periods or by territory. Both of these divisions are recognized in the development of the schedule for the law of Europe. KJ-KJA reflects the European legal history. The harmonized tables for European comparative and uniform law (KJC), European organization law (KJE), and the uniform subject table for the European jurisdictions KJG-KKZ were all based on the civil law model KK.

The regional classifications had originally evolved in response to financial and manpower shortages at LC and the wish to finish–or, rather, shortcut–the development of Class K with some tables of broad applicability for its own steadily growing foreign law collections. On the outside, the legal community considered lack of bibliographic control always as a roadblock for networking and effective delivery of information. The critique on the Law Library of Congress by the American Bar Association and the 1981 call "for redirection . . . [of it] to a library dedicated to serving the legal information needs of the entire nation,"[142] notably by the Standing Committee on the Facilities of the Law Library of Congress, had once more moved Class K into the spotlight and under intensified pressure for completion.

Already from 1980 on, the law classification specialists had conducted reviews of the European, Asian, and African collections, and had begun to construct a control file for the European law schedule by selecting catalog records of materials classed in various subclasses of H (Social sciences), J (Political sciences), D (History. General and Europe), and in the unclassified Law (General) collection. Included in this operation was the Law Library's own shelflist for collections, which were to a large extent not under any bibliographic control. At the end of 1981, equipped with a good overview of the collections, the law classification specialist prepared, on request of the Processing Department, a timetable and action plan for finishing Class K.[143] The formula, the regionalism principle for a European law classification, took shape.

Based on the control file, the outlines for the individual subclasses of the European schedule were drafted by the end of 1982.[144] During this time, work on the schedules for the Law of the Americas and the West Indies, KDZ, KG-KH, was nearly completed. This class contained for the first time a table for regional comparative and uniform law as well as a uniform subject table for all the countries of the continent/region patterned on KF and KK. Those patterns for creation of uniform subject tables for general comparative law and for the law of European countries were still studied comparatively with those of the draft schedule KDZ, KG-KH.

In 1983, before the schedule for the Americas went to press, the table developed for European intergovernmental organizations was modified to be applicable to the Organization of the American States (OAS) and was added to the schedule. This caused major consternation in the Serials Division, which considered "service to the user of paramount importance . . . and a disservice to the . . . patrons to change custody . . . ," especially of the OAS Official Record. It was only the beginning of the "Official Records" debate. Other intergovernmental organizations, such as the European Communities, Council of Europe, Human Rights Commission, and the entire organizational construct of the U.N. in the frame of the coming JX revision, loomed large on the horizon. Not even mentioned yet were the African and Asian organizations! Nevertheless, while collections of official gazettes and official records were studied, the schedules for the Americas, for the law of Europe, and the first part of KJV-KJW (Law of France) were ready for the final editing process early in 1984.[145]

The appointment of the latest, and last, Advisory Committee falls in that year during a visit with the LC leadership of AALL's Special Committee on a National Law Library together with members of the ABA Standing Committee on the Facilities of the Law Library of Congress.[146]

The first detailed drafts, attacking classification now with the new regionalism approach for speedier completion of Class K, were discussed in 1985 at the first meeting of the Advisory Committee on Library of Congress Foreign Law Classification held at LC.[147] The 1984 *Class K Outline* revision had returned to the original concept, a breakdown first by continent (i.e., region) and second by countries (i.e., jurisdictions), historic and present, within each continent or region. Now, the function of the first level in the original geographic hierarchy, the continents or regions, was more closely examined. At the beginning of law classification in the early 1950s and still in 1970 at the completion of the *Class K Outline*, the full development of a specific subclass for the law of a region was considered rather meaningless unless the region were to issue laws or was governed by a common body of law. Such political developments, as large-scale interstate cooperation in a region, accompanied by the emergence of intergovernmental organizations (IGOs) and courts, was at that time a phenomenon not yet fully recognized.

This extension of the past geographical principle to the new emerging regionalism principle meant two things in law classification: the regional arrangement recognizes a region as a geographically defined area in which (1) historical, religious, and prevailing socio-economic or ethnic similarities, as reflected in the laws and treaties emanating from the area, allow for creation of refined uniform tables that can be applied to a multitude of jurisdictions in the same region, and (2) cultural, scientific, and economic interests have led to the formation of regional intergovernmental organizations, which, modeled after the United Nations, spread throughout the regions or sub-regions of the world and which created the supra-national, i.e., regional law for the region in which they operate. In both cases, comparative legal investigation secured such concepts and patterns, which were found to be common to the largest number of jurisdictions, for design of a refined frame on which detailed subject classification could be mounted. Once the regionalism principle was introduced into law classification, the hierarchical structure of Class K, the interdependence of all its subclasses, had to be re-evaluated and adjusted as well.

5.1 The Resulting New Hierarchy

In classification for law, which is traditionally part of social sciences, policies have set exterior demarcations to Classes H (Social Sciences) and J (Political Sciences). Now, within Class K, principles and policies have to define the provinces of its own subclasses, structuring the hierarchy. The main class (first caption in the hierarchy) is represented by the single letter K and is the definitive classification schedule for comparative and uniform law, private international law and jurisprudence (universal, i.e., supra-regional in scope) and for supra-regional, or global, intergovernmental organizations (IGOs) as far as they do not belong to Class KZ (Law of Nations).

Opposite K, on the same level of the hierarchy, is Class KZ (Law of Nations),[148] the definitive classification schedule for public international law, also universal/comparative in scope and application, including the supra-regional, or global, IGOs belonging in the realm of public international law.

Second in the hierarchy, one step down, are the regional classes. They include all works with regional aspects covering not only private international and comparative law limited to the region, as well as the regional IGOs based and operating in the region, provided that the organizations' activities are not exclusively political, i.e., devoted to international order and security. The treaties establishing these regional organizations are classed with the organizations since in all instances these instruments provide the internal order of the organization (*organogram*) as well as the government of the organization:

K: Law	[Main Class]
KJ: Law of Europe	[Subclass Region Europe]
KJJ: Law of Austria	[Subclass Jurisdiction in Europe]
1-9999	[General to specific topics, expressed by integral numbers]

Because in LC's encyclopedic classification the subject has priority over form or any other criteria, such organizations created to regulate specific activities or interests are to be classed with the subject area.

Separated from KZ and classed henceforth in the regional subclass with the subject area are treaties between two or more countries in the same region. Only the universal treaty collections (e.g., U.N. treaty sets) and comprehensive treaty collections of individual countries regardless of region or subject and treaties on subjects pertaining truly to public international law, such as peace, boundary, and arbitration treaties, will be classed in KZ.

Thus, the adopted regionalism policy singles out a substantial part of international law from KZ: the law of regional organizations and their treaties, as well as the regional treaty law, incorporating it in the regional K subclasses as part of comparative and uniform law.

Constitutional and legal history, with its pertinent body of sources, is always classed with the appropriate jurisdiction in a region if so identified. Both are classed with the region if the sources have been identified as law in force throughout the region. Under the latter category fall Germanic, Slavic, and Roman law as the major historic systems in operation throughout the European region. Non-legal works will be classed in subclasses D, PA and J subclasses, in particular JC, JF and JN.[149]

5.2 European Legal History: A Comparative Discipline

A comprehensive classification scheme that organizes the works produced by a legal culture must account for the historical development of that culture. The complex phenomenon called "European legal culture" is rooted in the Roman Empire and in Christianity and is equally impacted by the legal-ethical catalog of the corporate Germanic culture. The latter provided new ethical standards to early medieval civilization, culminating in the feudal system, which determined the territorial-jurisdictional development in Europe. Roman law survived as an intellectual achievement and created a universal jurisprudence in Europe, based on the teachings of the jurists of Bologna. This Germanic-Roman dualism has to be understood in order to comprehend the periods of European jurisprudence and the values fed into the European legal order from these two major sources.[150]

Comparative legal studies on the European continent have always included comparisons of subjects stemming from, or systems covering, different historical periods; such studies are the links to modern comparative law. In order to facilitate comparative research, a scheme for legal history cannot be limited to individual jurisdictions *in* the region but has to comprise all existing source materials emanating at various times *from* the region at large. These faceted lists of historic European materials in the regional (comparative) classification schedule form the essential catalog of sources commonly underlying most modern European legal systems.

The division of the source materials between classes for the region and those for individual countries follows the principles stated already in the schedules KK (German law) and KJV (French law): the established demarcation for regional and national sources is set by Charlemagne's partition of his empire in A.D. 806, the beginning of *national* history of law. This provision of regional legal history in the classification for Europe, was reflected in the *Class K Outline* revision by closing the original classes KBB (Ancient law) and KBD (Roman law).

Regional legal history consists of two parts: (1) Class KJ: History of law (General) and Germanic law. It includes all the sources relating to the

East/West Germanic nations and the North Germanic/Scandinavian nations, treated as the sources of autonomous peoples; and (2) Class KJA: Roman law. It contains the three major periods as established by European scholarship: Pre-Justinian, Justinian (focused on the *corpus iuris civilis*), and the post-Justinian periods (sixth to fifteenth centuries, the so-called *Ius Romanum Medii Aevi*, and sixteenth to eighteenth centuries, the common law period of Europe).

This was unanimously supported by the Advisory Committee on LC Foreign Law Classification during the meeting on January 6, 1985, in Washington. However, the Law Library objected to the layout of the schedules with regard to the historic legal systems, in particular to inclusion of Roman law, and requested that opinions of legal scholars be solicited. Basically, the Law Library's European Law Division wanted to retain custody over those collections, which would fall under the second part of KJA classification, the so-called "Medieval Roman law," including the *consilia* collections, because of the "particular needs for use or service to users"; however, classical Roman law, including the Justinian period, should be moved back to KBD and be stored in the new compact shelf system. From the scholarly and the classification point of view, this was a non-position and went into arbitration inside LC and in the scholarly arena. The outcome was inconclusive, and LC management decided to go with the schedule as developed because of outside clamor for the schedules "no matter where Roman law was classed." Nevertheless, the intervention had delayed the final processing for publication of the schedules and distribution to the outside user libraries for several years.[151]

5.3 KJC Regional Comparative and Uniform Law

Works on the law of two or more jurisdictions appear in different forms. They can be parallel presentations without actual comparisons (e.g., collections). On the other hand, they will be encountered as true comparative investigations of legal systems or subjects. Such in-depth studies are often conducted in the legislative or treaty-making process and are especially found in the juridical process. For example, decisions of the European Court of Justice (ECJ) on the question of identifying general legal principles common to all legal systems (*principes généraux du droit*) that are the essence of comparative interpretation, analogy, or abstraction are quite numerous. Employment of such scientific-deductive methods by courts or legal scholars for law finding or development has become generally accepted practice for European Union/European Community law as well.

The same refining process based on patterns of KK was used for creation of schedule KJC (Regional comparative and uniform law). It comprises the treaty law of the Conseil de l'Europe and of regional IGOs other than the EC/EU and comparative works on the law of two or more jurisdictions of the region Europe at large, including now those of the European Union.

The European jurisdiction (countries KJG-KKZ) is assigned one of two uniform tables which are derived from the civil law model KK with various modifications to fit all European jurisdictions.

5.4 KJE Regional Organization and Integration

The KJE schedule is organized in two principal parts: Classification for intergovernmental organizations *other* than the European Community (e.g., the Council of Europe, Benelux Economic Union, and the Council for Mutual Economic Assistance (COMECON/CMEA), among others) and the European Communities. The core section of schedule KJE is designed for the law of the European Community (to 1993) and its successor, the European Union (EC/EU).

It is recognized in principle that the European Union is not yet a full-fledged federal state and therefore does not have sovereignty in the strict sense; neither did its predecessor, the European Community. Nevertheless, treaty law binds the contracting parties, the member states, to the inclusion or exclusion of rights and functions as laid down in the agreement. This treaty law replaces general international law for the sphere of EU jurisdiction.

In pursuit of its final goal, creation of greater security and stability within the union (or federation) of states, the contracting member states had furnished the organs of the EC with *compétence d'attribution,* which is partial sovereignty,[152] applying to the EU as well. Thus, within its jurisdiction, the organs of the EU have law-making power. Their acts are official acts, and a great number have laterally binding force for all the member states upon enactment; this part of the legislation is considered supranational. Therefore, the EC and its successor, the EU, in structure and function of its organs, were considered, generally speaking, as a federally organized state-like jurisdiction for which schedule KJE was designed based on the civil law model KK (Law of the German Federal Republic).

The main categories of EC/EU law[153] are primary law and secondary law. Primary law consists of constituent treaties of the EC; the treaty work expanding the European Community to the Union, the Single European Act, 1982; the Treaty on European Union, Maastricht 1992; and the Protocol to the Treaty, Amsterdam 1998. Secondary law includes the treaties concluded by the European Community/Union; further, the regulations, decisions, directives, and other legal measures by the organs, which are legally binding upon all member states, or a particular addressed member state, of the Union or Community; and the non-binding recommendations and opinions at large.

6. REGIONAL CLASSIFICATION:
KL-KWX ("THE REST OF THE WORLD")

The draft of the regional law classification system for subclasses KL-KWX (Asia, Africa, Pacifica, and Antarctica) was introduced in 1989 into the discussion of the Advisory Committee on LC Foreign Law Classification. The outlined principles were supported by the Advisory Committee[154] and restated as follows:

- **Arrangement of countries within the various regions** will disregard sub-regions (e.g., West, Central, or East Africa) in alphabetic sequence, including historic jurisdictions such as colonial areas or regions.
- **Regional comparative and uniform law** will have a place in all regions of the world. The pattern established by KJC (Regional and Uniform law of Europe) will be carried over into schedule KL-KWX and will be always indicated by the letter "C": e.g., KMC (Middle East), KNC (South, Southeast, and East Asia), KQC (Africa), and KVC (Pacific Area).
- **Regional intergovernmental organizations** are established with each region. A fifty-number table applied first in KJE for the classification of regional organization and integration is refined for the Asian, African, and Pacific area regions, following closely the established policies for distribution of materials. This table is applied to all regional classes in the schedule governed by the letter "E": e.g., KME (Middle East), KNE (South, Southeast, and East Asia), KQE (Africa), and KVE (Pacific Area).
- **Law of indigenous peoples**. These were recognized as independent jurisdictions and thus equal with other jurisdictions in the region.[155] The same principle was applied for the historic states of the pre-colonial period, especially in Africa. In almost all instances, it will be difficult to locate them within the political borders of one modern state; therefore, they reside now in the list of jurisdictions in the region, preceding the modern states. Thus, the first class in the region Asia (KM) and Africa (KQ) is reserved for indigenous developments. Where it is deemed necessary or useful because of close territorial affinity of the indigenous or historic jurisdiction to a modern jurisdiction, *confer* notes have been made. Indigenous law provided a particular challenge, where either the indigenous people form the larger part of the population in a country (as the Maori New Zealanders, KUQ) or where jurisdictions, by physical constitution, are in fact continents or sub-continents, as India (KNS-KNU) and Australia (KU-KUN). Although these three countries are by definition states under common law, in classification they are now, with regard to their indigenous populations, considered regions.

- The **Antarctic Treaty System** (ATS), now more frequently referred to as Antarctic Legal Regime, has the character and structure of a legal institution with jurisdictional quality comparable to other intergovernmental organizations like the EC/EU. It is created and internally organized by treaty and operates through a decision-making process.

The ATS is a strong framework for conducting activities in Antarctica in a peaceful, cooperative, and environmentally sound way. To achieve those goals, it provides the mechanism and the organizational framework with organs and agencies comparable to the EC/EU. Therefore, the subject classification KWX of the organizational part, was modeled on KJE.[156] However, the Antarctic Legal Regime had other functions and did not develop in isolation. It has to be seen in the broader context of the international commons regimes, such as the regimes for the high seas and for outer space that were shaped over the same period of time by the same politico-ideological processes. The regime theory, cast originally by political scientists in the 1960s in a search for international conflict resolutions, had further evolved into the legal framework for operations of the international community in the sphere of international commons.[157]

The development of the doctrine of "common heritage (or patrimony) of mankind" is an achievement of the legal scientist–the doctrine that certain areas designated as common spaces are beyond the limits of national jurisdiction–in law classification applied first for KWX. This has set the pattern for other so-called international commons such as the high seas (KZA: Law of the sea) and outer space, including the moon and other celestial bodies (KZD: Space law. Law of outer space).[158]

These subclasses, KL-KWX, concluded the subject classification for works on regional comparative and uniform law, and the entire body of law emanating from, or governing, individual jurisdictions identified with the regions Asia/Eurasia, Africa, Pacific Area, and Antarctica. In concept and structure, this new group of schedules is governed by the same set of policies laid down for development of its forerunner, *Law of Europe*, and does not markedly stray from the overall design formula developed for the European schedules. However, the scope as well as the structural flexibility of the generalized tables had to be greatly enhanced in areas of expected expansion, if they were to serve successfully a multitude of different jurisdictions (see Figure 2).

Since the Advisory Committee, during the 1989 session, stated its satisfaction "with the quickest progress in history" of the Class K development, the committee members examined an LC budget proposal for editorial work by commercial contractors. The possibility was entertained to enhance LC re-

FIGURE 2

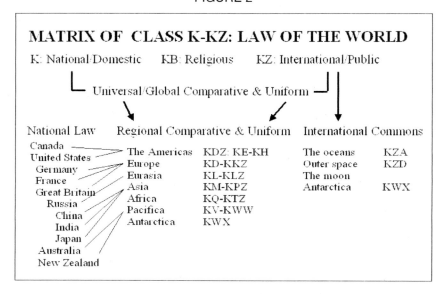

MATRIX OF CLASS K-KZ: LAW OF THE WORLD

K: National/Domestic   KB: Religious   KZ: International/Public

Universal/Global Comparative & Uniform

National Law   Regional Comparative & Uniform   International Commons

Canada	The Americas	KDZ: KE-KH	The oceans	KZA
United States	Europe	KD-KKZ	Outer space	KZD
Germany	Eurasia	KL-KLZ	The moon	
France	Asia	KM-KPZ	Antarctica	KWX
Great Britain	Africa	KQ-KTZ		
Russia	Pacifica	KV-KWW		
China	Antarctica	KWX		
India				
Japan				
Australia				
New Zealand				

sources by outside contributions in order to speed up the publication of the law schedules.[159] Consequently, a Consortium of Law Libraries collected over the next few years a fund that at the 1993 session of the Advisory Committee[160] was reoriented to the conversion of the major part of the K Classification to the electronic format, now open on the LC Web site for the public.[161]

CONCLUSION

It is unfortunate, though, that the existing Library of Congress law collections, large and of incredible diversity, interest, and rarity, were to be the only collections at the Library of Congress not brought in range of the new classifications. Shortage of funds and personnel, but mostly space to receive large blocks of materials on the Law Library side and resistance by custodial units to part with materials on the general collections side, barred not only the "reunification" of law materials in one physical collection under service of the Law Library but also the re-examination of the law titles dispersed throughout classes A-J and L-Z, once expected to form the basis for subject developments.

The classification of law materials was henceforth limited to current receipts, a policy still in effect, as stated in the preface of every law classification schedule issued by the Library of Congress. Of course, this shift in classification policy had provided the opportunity to design the K classes not tied to existing collections, custodial or other preferences, but rather as an ideal-conceptual knowledge organization for the large and diverse body LAW.

NOTES

1. Class K Outline 2002: The Matrix of Class K

K	Law in general. Comparative and Uniform law. Philosophy of law and Jurisprudence (1977; 1998 rev.)
	Including all legal periodicals
	Historic legal systems
	Ancient law, see KL
	Celtic, Germanic, and Slavic law, see KJ
	Roman law, see KJA
KB-KBX	Religious legal systems
KB	General. Comparative religious law
(KBL)	Hindu jurisprudence, see KNS
KBM	Jewish (Mosaic) (2002)
KBP	Islamic (Mohammedan) (2002)
KBQ	*Buddhist*
KBR-KBX	Law of the Christian Churches
KBR	History of Canon law (2001)
KBS	*Canon Law of Eastern Churches*
	Oriental Orthodox Churches
	Orthodox Eastern Canon law. Nomocanon
KBU-KBV	The Catholic Church
KBU	Law of the Roman Catholic Church. Holy See (2001)
	History of Canon law, see KBR
KBV	*Oriental Canon law (Catholic Oriental Rites)*
KBX	*Anglican Communion and Protestant Churches; and Other Christian Denominations or Sects*
KD	United Kingdom and Ireland (1973; 1999 rev.)
	The Americas
KDZ 1-1000	America. North America (General)
2000+	Individual countries
KE	Canada (1976; 1999 rev.)
KF	United States of America (1969; 1999 rev.)
KG 1-1000	Latin America (1984; 2000 rev.)
3000+	Central America
KGA-KGH	Individual countries
KGJ	West Indies. Caribbean Area
KGK-KGZ	Individual Islands and Island Groups
KH	South America (General) (1984; 2000 rev.)
KHA-KHW	Individual countries
	Europe (1989. 2000 rev.)
KJ	History of Law (General). Celtic Law. Germanic Law. Slavic Law

KJA	Roman Law
KJC	Regional Comparative and Uniform Law
KJE	Regional Organization and Integration. European Union
KJG-KKZ	Individual countries
	England, see KD
	France, see KJV-KJW
	Germany. West Germany. East Germany, see KK-KKC
	Russia. Soviet Union, see KLA-KLB
KJV-KJW	France (1985; 1999 rev.)
KK-KKC	Germany (1982; 2000 rev.)
	Asia and Eurasia. Africa. Pacific Area. Antarctica (1993; 2001 rev.)
KL	Ancient Law. Law of the Ancient Orient
	Eurasia
KLA	Russia. Soviet Union
KLB	Russia (Federation, 1992-)
KLD-KLW	Other Countries
	Asia
KMC-KMY	Middle East. Southwest Asia
	South Asia. Southeast Asia. East Asia
KNN	China
KNP	China (Republic, 1949-). Taiwan
KNQ	China (Peoples Republic, 1949-)
KNS-KNU	India
KNX-KNY	Japan
KPA-KPW	Other Countries
	Africa
KQ	History. Law of Indigenous Peoples
KQC	Regional Comparative and Uniform Law
KQE	Regional Organization and Integration
KQG-KTZ	African Countries
	Pacific Area
KU-KUN	Australia
KUQ	New Zealand
KVB-KVC	Regional Comparative and Uniform Law
KVB	Australia and New Zealand
KVC	All other Area Jurisdictions
KVE	Regional Organization and Integration. Pacific Area Cooperation
KWX	Antarctica. The Antarctic Treaty System. Antarctic Legal Regime
KZ-KZD	Law of Nations. Law of the Sea. Law of Space (1998)

2. David D. Van Tassel, *Recording America's Past: An Interpretation of the Development of Historical Studies in America, 1607-1884* (Chicago, IL: Univ. Chicago Press, 1960), 31-34 (hereinafter *Recording America's Past*).

3. Ibid., 95-102.

4. John Y. Cole, *For Congress and the Nation: A Chronological History of the Library of Congress* (Washington, DC: Library of Congress, 1979), 70 (hereinafter *For Congress and Nation*).

5. Ibid., 66-67. Herbert Putnam took the oath of office as the eighth Librarian of Congress (1899-1939).

6. Ibid., 5. For a sample page of the 1802 catalog prepared by Librarian John Beckley (1802-1807), see **Appendix 1**.

7. Ibid., 6. See **Appendix 2**.

8. John Y. Cole, *Jefferson's Legacy: A Brief History of the Library of Congress* (Washington, DC: Library of Congress, 1993), 13 (hereinafter *Jefferson's Legacy*).

9. Ibid., 19. Since 1846 the Library has received copyright deposits.

10. *For Congress and Nation* (supra note 4), 17.

11. Ibid., 16.

12. See **Appendix 3** for a sample page of Jefferson's classification scheme as it appears in the "Catalogue of the Library of the United States" (Washington: Printed by Jonathan Elliot, 1815). *Thomas Jefferson's Library: A Catalog with the Entries in His Own Order*, ed. James Gilreath and Douglas L. Wilson (Washington, DC: Library of Congress, 1989), ix.

13. "Tree of classification," based on Jefferson's classification. *For Congress and Nation* (supra note 4), 69. See **Appendix 4**.

14. *Recording America's Past* (supra note 2), 171-79.

15. *For Congress and Nation* (supra note 4), 29-42.

16. *Jefferson's Legacy*, 19. The copyright law of 1870 contributed significantly to the collections of Americana. Around 1897, over 40 percent of the 840,000 volumes and about 90 percent of the music, graphic art, and map collections had come into the Library as copyright deposits.

17. Under Charles Martel, who was hired in December 1987 as assistant to the superintendent, J. C. M. Hanson, of the Catalogue Department, work begins for the expected reclassification. *For Congress and Nation* (supra note 4), 59-62.

18. Samples (see **Appendix 5**) taken from Class E show the finely crafted encyclopedic articles, introducing the user to the historic development of the new territories and states. This material has been removed from the schedule. The Chief of the Subject Cataloging Division, Richard S. Angell, writes in his Introduction to the 3rd revised edition (1958): ". . . the schedule for America . . . entitled *America: History and Geography. Preliminary and Provisional Scheme of Classification, January 1901* . . . was prepared by Charles Martel, the Chief Classifier and later Chief of the Catalog Division. In 1913–the collection of Americana having more than doubled in size–the second edition appeared, prepared . . . by Charles A. Flagg, head of the *Americana section* [emphasis added] . . . The third edition incorporates the revisions and expansions required by the growth of . . . a collection of more than 300,000 volumes . . . that has taken place . . . in a period of rapid and extensive historical developments . . . In the interest of *maximum economy of presentation* [emphasis added], two features of earlier editions have been omitted: the historical summaries under countries, regions and states; and the cross reference entries to persons under historical periods . . ."

19. Following is a sample of Class D revision of 1921 that shows how treaties and other peace-related legal documents were incorporated into this expanded class:

D	European War	
....		
641		Armistice
		Peace
642		Sources and documents. Collections
643		**Treaty with Central powers**
		Germany
.A3-4		Preliminary discussions

.A5	Texts and drafts, by date
.A51	Protocols, etc.
.A55	Reservations, by date
.A6	Official discussions, hearings, etc., by date
....	
.A8-Z	Other,

        e.g. **Austria**
           .A8   Texts, by date
           .A9   Discussions, etc.
           Bulgaria
           .B5   Texts, by date
           .B6   Discussions, etc. ...

20. *For Congress and Nation* (supra note 4), 70.

21. Lois Mai Chan, *Immroth's Guide to the Library of Congress Classification*, 4th ed. (Englewood, CO: Libraries Unlimited, 1990), 8-11. See **Appendix 6**.

22. See **Appendix 7** for samples of classification for westward expansion and Indian territories in Class F with reference to Class E.

23. Taken from a Memorandum of Henry J. Dubster, Chief, General Reference and Bibliography Division, to the Chief Assistant Librarian (15. December 1958; on file with the Library of Congress Cataloging Policy and Support Office; hereinafter CPSO).

24. Library of Congress. Classification Outline Scheme of Classes, 1909, 1914 (rev.) and 1955 (Washington, DC: Library of Congress, 1910, 1914, 1955).

25. Werner B. Ellinger, "Subject Classification of Law," *Library Quarterly* 19, no. 2 (1949): 79 (hereinafter "Subject Classification of Law").

26. Ibid., 93-98. The author gives detailed accounts (with subject outlines) in particular of the *"Schema des Realkatalogs der Königlichen Universitätsbibliothek zu Halle,"* Germany, and of Prof. A. Arthur Schiller's subject classification for the Columbia University Law Library; both had been studied in depth during the initial development periods of the K Classification.

27. Werner B. Ellinger, *Working Paper No. 8: Classification of American Law: A Survey* (Washington, DC: Library of Congress, 1959), 78 (hereinafter *WP8*).

28. Ibid., 2-7, lists all the committees established over the course of thirty years.

29. Ibid., 77.

30. Ibid., 79.

31. "Subject Classification of Law" (supra note 25): 81.

32. Ibid.

33. Elizabeth V. Benyon, *Classification. Class K: Law,* with preface of David J. Haykin, Chief Subject Cataloging Division, Library of Congress (Washington, DC: Library of Congress, 1948), 6 (hereinafter Benyon's *Classification*).

34. A. Arthur Schiller, "The Reclassification and Supplemental Cataloging of Books in the Columbia University Law Library: A Survey" (New York: Columbia University Law Library, NY, NY, 1938, mimeographed). A revised edition was published later: *Foreign Law Classification in the Columbia University Law Library* (Dobbs Ferry: Oceana Publications, 1964).

35. It is interesting to note here some of the law libraries with their foreign law holdings around 1949: Law Library of Congress, 698,100 v. total (of which about one-third were foreign law); Harvard University Law Library, 656,000 vol.; Columbia University Law Library, 280,000 vol.; Yale Law School Library, 305,000 vol.; University of

California at Berkeley Law School Library, 87,072 vol.; University of Chicago Law Library, 122,000 vol.; Library of the Law School of the Northwestern University, 131,234 vol., and Bar Association of the City of New York, 268,000 vol. Cf. "Subject Classification of Law" (supra note 25): 81.

36. "The Librarian's Conference: Agenda Item 57-16," issued August 21, 1956, was an extensive background paper for the Development of the Law Classification project and covers, with several revisions, the years 1939-1956 (hereinafter "Librarian's Conference 1956 Agenda"). Statement of the Chief of the Classification Office, C. K. Jones, to the record (December 19, 1939). (On file with CPSO).

The outline, which had been applied by the Law Library of Congress for shelving of U.S. law and foreign law, is not a classification but rather an arrangement by form of publication. Since it is still in use for the unclassified law collections at LC, it should be mentioned, as follows:

1. Session laws, annual laws (chronological)
2. Compilations, revisions, collections of general laws (chronological)
3. Codes (chronological)
   (1) Civil
   (2) Civil procedure
   (3) Criminal
   (4) Criminal procedure
   (5) Commercial
   (6) Political
4. Official editions of laws on special subjects, arranged alphabetically by subject.
5. Court reports.
6. Treatises (alphabetical by author).
7. Miscellaneous, e.g., departmental decisions and reports, decisions of quasi-judicial agencies. The resulting notation consists of the name of the country, followed by the number for the "form" and the first three letters for name of the agency, etc., or author. Constitutional law, municipal and local law, and international law were classed in J-JX. Special or historic laws (e.g., Roman or Canon, etc.) as well as comparative law and legal philosophy (Law. General) form special collections.

37. Statements prepared by David J. Haykin for the Librarian of Congress, at that time Archibald MacLeish (1939-1944), and L. Quincy Mumford, Director of the Processing Department (4 April and 13 May 1941). (On file with CPSO).

38. Statement prepared by David J. Haykin (3 September 1941). (On file with CPSO).

39. Memorandum of Werner B. Ellinger to the Chief, Subject Cataloging Division (hereinafter SCD), Richard S. Angell (24 June 1958). (On file with CPSO).

40. Ibid., 4.

41. "Librarian's Conference 1956 Agenda" (supra note 36), 2-3.

42. "According to a directive of Processing to Subject . . . legal material is classed whereever there seems a good place for it–mainly for administrative, i.e. custodial reasons. In keeping with this directive, numbers were created in the H and J schedules to receive legal materials . . ." Stated by Werner B. Ellinger in a memorandum to the Processing Department (27 November 1945). (On file with CPSO).

43. *For Congress and the Nation* (supra note 4),121.

44. "Librarian's Conference 1956 Agenda" (supra note 36), 3.

45. This instruction was reissued in 1951. Memorandum from the Director of the Processing Department, Dr. F. H. Wagman to David J. Haykin, Chief, SCD (28 February, 1951). (On file with CPSO).

46. "Librarian's Conference 1956 Agenda" (supra note 36), 4; and excerpts of Dr. Evans's address, attached to a draft for a department memorandum by Werner B. Ellinger to Dr. F. H. Wagman, Director of the Processing Department (26 February 1951; on file with CPSO).

47. "Librarian's Conference 1956 Agenda" (supra note 36), 4. The committee was chaired by Leo LaMontagne, then Assistant Chief of the Subject Cataloging Division, and included, besides Werner B. Ellinger, Deputy Law Librarian Francis X. Dwyer, and other staff of the Law Library.

48. The committee was appointed by AALL President Hobart Coffey. Members were William R. Roalfe, Northwestern University (chairman); Elizabeth V. Benyon, University of Chicago; Catharine Campbell, University of Michigan Law Library; Thomas S. Dabagh, Los Angeles County Law Library; Elizabeth Forgeus, Yale University; Julius J. Marke, New York University; Miles O. Price and Professor A. Arthur Schiller, both Columbia University. Announcement in the *LC Information Bulletin* (November 1948): 9.

49. Benyon's *Classification* (supra note 33), 5.

50. "Subject Classification of Law" (supra note 25), 79-104.

51. Ibid., 100.

52. For a sample page of Benyon's *Classification,* see **Appendix 8.**

53. Benyon's *Classification* (supra note 33), Introduction, 6.

54. Letter of Miles O. Price to the Director of the Processing Department, Dr. F. H. Wagman (7 April 1949). Major statement with the same conclusion came in from A. Arthur Schiller (21 March 1949), followed by evaluations of the other committee members. (On file with CPSO).

55. Excerpts from the minutes of the Librarians Conference of 12 May 1949. (On file with CPSO).

56. For the text of the report, see: Leo LaMontagne, *American Library Classification, with Special Reference to the Library of Congress* (Hamden, Conn.: Shoe String Press, 1961), 336-338 . The purpose of this report was not so much to determine the internal structure of Class K as to resolve disputes about distribution of materials that had traditionally been assigned to other classes. Amended was an outline for all the subclasses of the law classification. (On file with CPSO).

57. "Draft Proposal for the Interim Report" (6 May 1949) with accompanying documentation and "Guide to the Interpretation of the Joint Interim Report of Class K of 10 June 1949" (dated 1959). (On file with CPSO).

58. *Law Library Journal.* 42 (1949): 218. Dr. F. H. Wagman's statement.

59. American Bar Association *Report* 74 (1949): 286.

60. Members of this reconstituted Advisory Committee on the Development of Class K (replacing the committee appointed in 1949) were: Leo LaMontagne, of the Subject Cataloging Division (chair); Dr. W. Lawrence Keitt, Law Librarian; Francis X. Dwyer, Assistant Law Librarian; Dr. Werner B. Ellinger and Dr. Charles C. Bead, of SCD. Excerpt of memorandum from John W. Cronin, Director, Processing Department, to the Librarian of Congress (23 January 1952). (On file with CPSO).

61. Werner B. Ellinger, Library of Congress, Subject Cataloging Division, *Class K: Law. Working Papers.* They were published in the following sequence: no. 1: *German Law* (1953); no. 2: *Roman Law* (1953); no. 3: *History of German Law* (1954); no. 4:

Canon Law (1955); no. 5: *Law of China* (1955); no. 6: *English Law* (1956); no. 7: *Law of Japan* (1958); no. 8: *Classification of American Law; A Survey* (1959); and no. 9: *Law of the United States* (1959, rev. 1960). (Washington, DC: Library of Congress, 1953-1960; on file with CPSO).

62. "Subject Classification of Law" (supra note 25): 85.

63. Ibid.: 85. This was a clear critique on Benyon's scheme.

64. Statement of Frances X. Dwyer, Assoc. Law Librarian, to members of the Advisory Committee on the Development of Class K (3 November 1958). (On file with CPSO).

65. Memorandum of Werner B. Ellinger to Richard S. Angell, Chief SCD (25 July 1961). (On file with CPSO).

66. Memorandum of Ellinger to Dr. Charles C. Bead, Chief SCD, submitting the *Class K: Law. Draft Outline* (6 March 1970). (On file with CPSO).

67. Memorandum of Ellinger to Bead, discussing: ". . . that one should consider moving letter combinations again to allow for more expansion." (7 March 1970). (On file with CPSO).

68. Richard S. Angell, "Preface" to *Working Paper No. 1: German Law* (Washington, DC: Library of Congress, 1953). (On file with CPSO).

69. Memorandum of Werner B. Ellinger to Richard S. Angell, Chief SCD (26 February 1953). (On file with CPSO).

70. Memorandum of Frances X. Dwyer, Associate Law Librarian, to John W. Cronin, Acting Director of Processing (12 September 1952). The Law Library's proposition was adopted by the Advisory Committee in its meeting of 29 October 1952, and communicated to the Director of the Processing Department on 10 November 1952. (On file with CPSO).

71. Minutes of the Librarian's Conference (21 December 1949); extract from Committee on Classification of Law (11 April 1949). (On file with CPSO).

72. Memorandum of Dr. Charles C. Bead to the Chief SCD, Richard S. Angell (3 February1953). (On file with CPSO).

73. Memoranda of Werner B. Ellinger to Leo LeMontagne and John W. Cronin (17 and 19 August 1954). (On file with CPSO).

74. Advisory Committee on the Development of Class K. "Meeting minutes" (16 March 1956). (On file with CPSO).

75. Appendix to the *LC Information Bulletin* (2 July 1956); letter of Miles O. Price to Eizabeth V. Benyon (19 July 1956); memorandum of Werner B. Ellinger to Richard S. Angell and John W. Cronin (17 August 1956). (On file with CPSO).

76. Minutes of the Librarian's Conferences, no. 131-133 (19 June, 26 June, and 3 July 1958). (On file with CPSO). Notes on a special meeting of 1 July 1958, held by the Chief Assistant Librarian, Rutherford D. Rogers with the following attendees: for AALL, Carol Moreland, University of Pennsylvania; Ervin Pollack, Ohio State University; Miles O. Price, Columbia University; from CLR, Inc., Verner W. Clapp; from LC, L. Quincy Mumford; John W. Cronin, Dr. W. Lawrence Keitt, Francis X. Dwyer, Dr. Werner B. Ellinger, Leo LaMontagne, Richard S. Angell. (On file with CPSO).

AALL *President's Newsletter 1958-1959*, no.1 (Oct. 1958). Announcement of the Advisory Committee's establishment. AALL representatives are quoted as: Miles O. Price, Mortimer Schwartz, and Arthur A. Charpentier. "*To broaden the Committee and draw talent from related groups, ABA, ALI and AALS are being invited to appoint one member each to the Committee.*" (On file with CPSO).

Extract from a memorandum of Mortimer Schwartz, Chairman of the AALL Committee on Cataloging and Classification (22 October 1958): ". . . Instead, the Committee will concentrate its efforts on policy matters relating to classification . . ." (On file with CPSO).

77. *WP8* (supra note 27); *WP9* (supra note 61).

78. Members of the expanded Advisory Committee on Classification for Anglo-American Law under the Chairman Rutherford D. Rogers, Chief Assistant Librarian were: **LC,** Richard S. Angell, Dr. Werner B. Ellinger, Francis X. Dwyer, and Leo LaMontagne; **AALL,** Arthur A. Charpentier, Librarian Bar Association of New York City; Miles O. Price, Law Librarian of Columbia University; Mortimer Schwartz, Law Librarian of the University of Oklahoma; Ervin H. Pollack, College of Law Library at Ohio State University; **AALS,** Professor Judson F. Falkner, NYU Law School; **ALI,** Professor Warren A. Seavey, NYU Law School. Seavey declined later, as did another nominee, Prof. Austin W. Scott. The ALI was, therefore, without representation on the Committee. *LC Information Bulletin* 17, no. 49 (1958): 682.

79. Press release no. 62-58 (2 July 1962). (On file with CPSO).

80. The Librarian of Congress, L. Quincy Mumford (1954-1974), Special Announcement 86 (18 November 1966): ". . . The new National Program for Acquisitions and Cataloging, resulting from the requirements of Title II-C of the Higher Education Act of November 8, 1965, is placing on the Library of Congress unprecedented responsibilities for the acquisition of all library materials currently published throughout the world which are of value to scholarship and for their prompt cataloging . . ." For fuller detail see: John W. Cronin, "The Library of Congress National Program for Acquisitions and Cataloging" *Libri* 16 (1966): 113-117.

81. Interdepartmental Committee on Class K was appointed on 11 July 1958; members were, under the Chairman Rutherford D. Rogers, Chief Assistant Librarian: Henry J. Dubester, Chief, General Reference and Bibliography Division; Richard S. Angell, Chief SCD; Dr. Werner B. Ellinger, Senior Subject Cataloger (Law); and Francis X. Dwyer, Assistant Law Librarian. Minutes of the Committee Meetings from 26 August 1958 to 30 November 1959. (On file with CPSO).

82. Position papers of Frances X. Dwyer, Associate Law Librarian, submitted to Rutherford D. Rogers and to the Interdepartmental Committee members (27 October and 3 November 1958). (On file with CPSO).

83. Draft paper (7 May 1959) and Memorandum (18 December 1959). (On file with CPSO).

84. Minutes of meeting called by the Librarian of Congress (30 November 1959). (On file with CPSO).

85. Minutes of the meeting, 3-4 December 1959. Besides the Committee members, Frances Farmer, then President AALL, attended as did the Librarian of Congress (for the opening session). Announcement in the *LC Information Bulletin* 18, no. 49 (1959): 722. (On file with CPSO).

86. *WP8* (supra note 27),13-35 (outlines), 41; 72-76.

87. Letter of Rutherford D. Rogers (27 January 1960) to the advisers to name additional legal scholars who would likely consent to examine the *WP9*. (On file with CPSO).

88. Prof. Lawrence M. Friedmann's "Observations on Working Papers Nos. 6 and 8" (10 March 1960; comments of Ellinger on Friedman's "Observations" (3 May 1960). (On file with CPSO).

89. Minutes of the meeting, 12-13 May 1960. (On file with CPSO).

90. Ellinger's comments on *"WP9 as Rearranged by Prof Friedman"* (29 August 1960), 9-12. (On file with CPSO).

91. Ibid., 21.

92. Ibid., 24.

93. Ibid., 6.

94. The three documents were sent out to advisors and members of the Advisory Committee (29 August 1960). *WP9 as Rearranged by Friedman*, who was then the driving force, was–after adoption by the Committee and LC–quoted as *WP"9F."* Meeting was called by the Chief Assistant Librarian, before the letters of consultants had come in (Note to the record; 11 October 1960). (On file with CPSO).

95. General Order No. 1724 (12 July 1960). The composition of the Law Processing Committee, which was supposed to deal with interdepartmental and interdivisional routines involved in the cataloging of law, was: Chief of the Descriptive Cataloging Division and Associate Law Librarian (chair and vice-chair); Assistant Chief of the Subject Cataloging Division and a senior subject cataloger, and Principal Cataloger of the Descriptive Cataloging Division. (On file with CPSO).

96. Letters of Ervin H. Pollack (13 October 1960) and Miles O. Price (11 October 1960) to the Chief Assistant Librarian. (On file with CPSO).

97. Letter of Lawrence M. Friedman (14 October 1960) to the Chief Assistant Librarian. (On file with CPSO).

98. Letter of Mortimer Schwartz (19 October 1960) to the Chief Assistant Librarian. (On file with CPSO).

99. Memorandum of Ellinger to Richard S. Angell and Rutherford D. Rogers (19 October 1960). (On file with CPSO).

100. Minutes of the meeting of 20 October 1960; minutes of the Advisory Committee meeting of 21-22 October 1960. (On file with CPSO).

101. *LC Information Bulletin* 19, no.43 (1960): 613. By personal letter from Librarian L. Quincy Mumford or Law Librarian W. Lawrence Keitt and Associate Law Librarian Frances X. Dwyer, the following scholars, judges, and law librarians were invited for comment on *WP"9F"*: Wolfgang Friedman, Columbia; Bernard Schwartz, NYU; Dean Roscoe Pound; Dean Jefferson B. Fondham, University of Pennsylvania; Justice Felix Frankfurter, U.S. Supreme Court; Judge E. Barrett Prettyman, U.S. Court of Appeals for D.C. Circuit; Charles J. Zinn, Law Revision Counsel to the House Committee on the Judiciary; Earl C. Borgeson, Harvard; Arthur A. Charpentier, Bar of N.Y. City; Max Rheinstein; J. Myron Jacobstein; K. Howard Drake; A. Arthur Schiller, Columbia; Marvin P. Hogan, Dept. of Justice Library; Paul Howard, Dept. of the Interior Library; members of the AALL Standing Committee on Cataloging and Classification; and, among others, William B. Stern, LA County Law Library, and Fred B. Rothman, previously NYU and law book dealer. Letters were sent out during March and April 1961. (On file with CPSO).

102. Stern writes in his letter of invitation (6 April 1961): " . . . We have no intention to rub it in . . . but state for the record . . . that our 10-year experience with Class K–Law . . . and communications with the 25 libraries which use our Class K, has given us the background to give you advice of substantial importance." The Minutes of the meeting (3 June 1961) show in attendance: William B. Stern, Phil Wesley, and Forrest S. Drummond of LA County Law Library; Richard S. Angell of LC; Miles O. Price, Columbia Law Library; Ervin H. Pollack, Ohio State University, College of Law Library; Frances S. Holbrook, UCLA Law Library; Dan F. Henke, UC at Berkeley

Law Library; and Carleton W. Kenyon, California State Library. Lawrence M. Friedman could not attend. (On file with CPSO).

103. Letter of Carleton W. Kenyon (6 June 1961). (On file with CPSO).

104. Travel reports (AALL Convention) of Werner B. Ellinger (18 July 1961) and Richard S. Angell (6 July 1961) to Librarian of Congress L. Quincy Mumford. Letter of Werner B. Ellinger (12 February 1962) to Rutherford D. Rogers. (On file with CPSO).

105. Memoranda of Werner B. Ellinger (25 July and 14 August 1961) to Richard S. Angell and Rutherford D. Rogers. (On file with CPSO).

106. Minutes of the Advisory Committee meeting of 2 March 1962. The advisors were joined by Arthur A. Charpentier, Librarian of the Bar of N.Y. City; other invited guests attending were Elizabeth Finley, President AALL; Earl C. Borgeson, Librarian, Harvard Law School; Vaclav Mostecky, Assistant Librarian, Harvard Law School. Letter of Mortimer Schwartz (20 December 1961) to Richard S. Angell. (On file with CPSO).

107. Memorandum of Miles O. Price (19 March 1964) to Richard S. Angell. (On file with CPSO).

108. Memoranda of Miles O. Price and Werner B. Ellinger to the Chief SCD, Richard S. Angell, with regard to Carleton W. Kenyon's letters and statements on particular points, especially on the position of constitutional law in the schedule, and arrangement of civil law subjects with regard to Persons, etc. (21 February 1962, 12 December 1962, 12 February 1963, 5 June 1963). Minutes of meeting on Development of Class K (7 June 1963), chaired by Rutherford Rogers, attended by the consultants Miles O. Price and Carleton W. Kenyon (before his departure). (On file with CPSO).

109. Memorandum of Ellinger (19 September 1964) to Robert R. Holmes, then Acting Chief SCD, on publication of KF as manuscript without actual application to the collections. He gives a status report of the project and protests publication as "unprecedented in the LC history of classification." He pointed to Leo Montagne's account of application of individual classes, which were published only after the drafts were applied to the collections for their reclassification, in some instances for six years, in others for fifteen or twenty-three years, depending on the size of the collections. (On file with CPSO).

110. Werner B. Ellinger, "Classification of Law at the Library of Congress 1949-1968," *Law Library Journal* 61 (1968): 226, 229 (hereinafter "Classification of Law").

111. Originally at the Law Library of Congress, Dr. Fisher served from 1962 to 1969 as assistant to Ellinger in the development of KD. The schedule was published and available by 1973. *LC Information Bulletin* 31 (1972): 441. He succeeded Ellinger in 1972 as law classification specialist.

112. E. Ann Rae was at the National Library of Canada during the development of the KE schedule and is currently Chief Librarian, University of Toronto.

113. Nancy Carol Carter, "American Indians and Law Libraries: Acknowledging the Third Sovereign," *Law Library Journal* 61(2002): 24.

114. Library of Congress. "Classification. Class E-F America" (Washington, DC: Government Printing Office, 1913; typescript). See **Appendix 8** for samples of classification for Indians in Class E.

115. "Classification of Law" (supra note 110): 229.

116. Library of Congress. *Classification. Class H. Social Sciences. Subclass HD Agriculture and Industry* (Washington, DC: Government Printing Office, 1950).

117. See Section 6 below: Regional Classification: KL-KWX. ("The Rest of the World").

118. Memoranda of Ellinger to William J. Welsh, Associate Director Processing Department (7 November and 22 November 1966) and to Robert R. Holmes, Chief SCD (20 December 1967).

In his "Report on Attendance at the 1970 AALL Annual Meeting" (6 July 1970), he stated that at a special meeting of KF users, there was consensus at revision of JX taking "priority over development of most of the jurisdictions." (On file with CPSO).

Library of Congress. Processing Department. Subject Cataloging Division. *"Classification. Class K: Law. Draft Outline,"* prepared by Werner B. Ellinger (Washington, DC: Library of Congress, 1970).

119. Ellinger, "Draft Progress Report on Class K" to Charles C. Bead, Chief, Subject Cataloging Division (after March 1970). Dr. Jolande E. Goldberg, then subject cataloger in the Subject Cataloging Division, was assigned on an irregular basis to organize the shelf list (ca. 60,000 cards that were reproduced for this purpose) in the anticipated order of the new class for German law. (On file with CPSO). To organize the shelflist in this fashion took two and one-half years.

120. At the height of German political and territorial division or fragmentation on the eve of the mediatization and secularization in 1803 (*Reichsdeputationshauptschluss*), about one thousand independent jurisdictions existed.

121. Rearrangement of the *Class K Outline* was carried out in sections during the development of Class KK, roughly between 1974 and 1978, also with an eye on revisions in Class JN (Constitutional history), later to be renamed "Political institutions and public administration." At the AALL Annual Convention in 1978, the Subject Cataloging Division announced that a ". . . substantive restructuring of the outline may now be in order." Memoranda of Goldberg to Ed Blume, Chief SCD, (19 April 1974) and Mary K. D. Pietris (18 April 1978 and 6 June 1979). (On file with CPSO).

122. June 6, 1973, treaty between East and West Germany concerning the basis of the relations between the two States (Vertrag über die Grundlagen der Beziehungen zwischen der Deutschen Demokratischen Republik und der Bundesrepublik Deutschland). In that same year, September 18, both nations took seats in the United Nations.

123. Theodor Maunz, *Deutsches Staatsrecht* (München: C. H. Beck'sche Verlagsbuchhandlung, 1951), 10-12 (hereinafter *Staatsrecht*).

124. The office of the Staatspräsident in 1960; the office of the Ministerpräsident in 1968, the former replaced by the Staatsrat, the latter by the Ministerrat.

125. *Staatsrecht* (supra note 123), 16-18.

126. These were the new codifications in East Germany: 1961, Labor law; 1965, Family law; 1965, Education law; 1965, Contract system; 1968, Criminal law and procedure; and 1975, Civil law and procedure.

127. Werner B. Ellinger, *Working Paper No. 3: History of German Law* (Washington, DC: Library of Congress, 1959).

128. The division in Charlemagne's political testament (806) was intended to be only a division of government among his three sons, not a physical division of the empire. Among his grandsons Lothar, Ludwig the German, and Karl, the empire's physical division became final (Treaty of Verdun, 843).

129. Richard Schröder and Eberhard Frh.v. Künssberg, *Lehrbuch der deutschen Rechtsgeschichte*, 7. ed. (Berlin und Leipzig: Verlag Walter de Gruyter, 1932), 1010-1015.

130. *Staatsrecht* (supra note 123), 45-46.

131. Ibid., 10. Introduced into the work of the Assembly were in particular recommendations and drafts addressing the judiciary and independence of judges, the whole complex federal-state system of concurring or exclusive legislative and administrative competences, and the civil service. Allied interferences endangered at times the entire process.

132. See supra note 126.

133. In the preamble of the East German constitution of 1974, for the first time reference is made to the Marxist-Leninist ideology and its realization as a national goal.

134. Article 4 of the Constitution of 1974.

135. Memorandum of Goldberg (19 August 1980) informing Mary K. D. Pietris, Chief SCD, that the drafts for KK and KKA were completed. The memorandum points to the possibility of finishing Class K in a reasonable time by using this new technique of derivative scheme development: ". . . Since there have never been established guidelines for the implementation of principles governing the structure of Class K as whole, my concern for future development and conclusion of Class K . . . is on workability of derivations . . . KKA can stand as an example for future . . . scaled down [schemes but] . . . according . . . to subjects peculiar to a system . . . Looking at Class KK-KKC from that point of view they may present the possibility to complete Class K at reasonable speed and expense without abandoning the original concept and commitment . . ." (On file with CPSO).

136. For a fuller discussion of the East and West German systems comparatively, see the analytical study by Jolande E. Goldberg, "Classification of German Law at the Library of Congress: a Study in Comparative Law," *International Journal of Law Libraries* 9 (1981): 145-161. A detailed review of the topical arrangement of the two schedules KK and KKA is included in the author's "Library of Congress Classification System for German Law: a New Approach," *Law Library Journal* 74 (1981): 619-631.

137. As early as 1958 (5th Party Congress of the Sozialistische Einheitspartei Deutschlands), Walter Ulbricht (1893-1973) stated the change from fundamental rights to personality rights "as in accord with the Party doctrine." Dietrich Müller-Römer, *Die Grundrechte in Mitteldeuschland* (Köln: Verlag Wissenschaft und Politik, 1965), 59-99.

138. Article 12 of the East German Constitution of 1974 states: ". . . All natural resources, mines, the continental shelf, all waters, dams, power plants, industrial enterprises, banks and insurance enterprises, agricultural land holdings, all land and water ways, all kinds of transportation, communication, and the postal service are *Volkseigentum* (Socialist public property). Private ownership is prohibited."

139. Johannes Klinkert, Ellenor Oehler, and Günther Rohde, *Eigentumsrecht, Nutzung von Grundstücken und Gebäuden zum Wohnen und zur Erholung* (Berlin: Staatsverlag der Deutschen Demokratischen Republik, 1979), 13+.

140. At the height of fragmentation, the "German region" had more than a thousand jurisdictions. Treating Germany as a region, geographic and territorial relations or connections are disregarded as are constitutional interdependencies or divisions, such as personal and real unions, or unions by succession, etc.

141. Memoranda of Goldberg to Mary K. D. Pietris, Chief SCD (19 August, 1 October, and 14 October 1980), on implementation of KK-KKC, layout of the European law classification, and statements on the restructuring of the *Class K Outline*. (On file with CPSO). Report of Diane Hillmann on the meeting of Heads of Cataloging Departments in Large Law Libraries Discussion Group during AALL 1981 Convention,

Technical Services Law Librarian 17, no.1 (1971): 14. Announcement in the *LC Information Bulletin* 39, no.5 (1980): 478.

142. In the larger frame of its activities to encourage and support "the creation by an enactment of the United States Congress of a National Law Library as an independent, separate department of the Library of Congress . . . ," members of the Law Library Committee of the American Bar Association's Section on Legal Education and Admission to the Bar met with members of AALL in 1982 to discuss this and related issues. In that same year, AALL (President Leah Chanin) appointed a Special Committee on a National Law Library. This committee visited in 1982 with the leadership of the Library of Congress and was invited to present a list of priorities for services of the Library to the legal profession. First in priority ranking was completion of Class K and retrospective application to the LC Law Library's collections. George S. Grossman, "The Special Committee on a National Law Library: A History," *Law Library Journal* 77 (1984-85): 621-625 (hereinafter "The Special Committee").

143. Memorandum of Jolande E. Goldberg to the Chief SCD, Mary K. D. Pietris (9 December 1981). Projections are made according to size of collections and manpower available. From the several proposals the Director for Cataloging, Lucia Rather, and the Assistant Librarian for Processing Services, Joseph H. Howard, supported the regional development and communicated the decision to the Law Librarian, Carleton W. Kenyon. Memoranda (13 and 18 January 1982). (On file with CPSO).

144. Memoranda and meeting notes from the period between July 1981 and November 1982 show the progress on the European schedule. By 9 November 1982, all the subclasses for the European schedule had been turned over for editorial processing. At that point Goldberg proposed to implement the "regionalism principle," which would also be employed for the next regional classifications in the "Rest of the World" schedule (Asia, Africa, Pacific Area and Antarctica). Memorandum of Goldberg to Mary K. D Pietris (9 November 1982). (On file with CPSO).

145. Memoranda of Goldberg to Mary K. D. Pietris, Chief SCD (31 January 1983, 13 September 1983, 14 February 1984, 17 July 1984, 3 December 1984). Memoranda and notes "to the record" concerning meetings between Goldberg, the Law Librarian and area specialists of the Law Library, and the senior documents specialists in the Serial Division from 7 February 1984 to 14 February 1984. Progress report on Class K by the Chief SCD Mary K. D. Pietris to Lucia Rather, Director for Cataloging (26 March 1984). Studies on LC's government document collections were conducted for some time by the Foreign and International Documents Team, a subgroup of the ad hoc Government Publications Project Team. The team contributed its findings and recommendations concerning the document collections of intergovernmental organizations (IGOs) to the report and executive summary of the Government Publications Project Team Steering Committee (30 September 1991). (On file with CPSO).

146. The meeting was held on 30 January 1984 and included a luncheon with the Librarian of Congress, Daniel J. Boorstin; William J. Welsh; Donald C. Curran; Carleton W. Kenyon and Division Chiefs of the Law Library; the President of AALL, Kathleen Price; and Roger F. Jacobs, the Librarian of the U.S. Supreme Court. The advisory group held its constituent meeting during the AALL Annual Convention in San Diego in 1984. The first members were Jane L. Hammond, Margaret A. Leary, Phyllis Marion, Heinz Peter Mueller, and Thomas H. Reynolds. Lucia J. Rather and Carleton W. Kenyon co-chaired. "The Special Committee" (supra note 142): 626.

147. Since its inception, the Advisory Committee convened annually at LC between 1984 and 2002 or, in a few instances, biannually. Law librarians and professors of law

who served on this committee over its duration were **for AALL**: Phyllis Marion of Case Western School of Law and M. Kathleen Price of New York University; **for ABA**: Jane Hammond of Cornell University, Margaret Leary of the University of Michigan, and Gail Daly of Southern Methodist University; **for AALS**: Heinz Peter Mueller of Brigham Young University, Robert Oakley of Georgetown Law Center, Laurent Mayali of the Robbins Collection, and Frank Vogel of Harvard University; **for RLG, Inc**: Thomas Reynolds of the University of California at Berkeley. **Chairs** of the Committee, representing the Processing Department (later Cataloging Directorate) at LC, were Lucia Rather, Dr. Sarah Thomas, and Beacher Wiggins.

148. For history of KZ (Law of Nations) and its parallel, or "shadowing" schedule JZ (International relations), which together replaced the abandoned LC Class JX, see Jolande E. Goldberg, *Library of Congress Classes JZ and KZ: Historical Notes and Introduction to Application* (Washington, DC: Library of Congress, 1997) (hereinafter *JZ and KZ: Historical Notes*).

149. Certain materials, such as Cicero's works *De legibus, De iure civili in artem redigendo,* and *De republica* or Aristotle's *Politika* and *De republica Atheniensium,* have traditionally been classified with original languages in subclass PA (Classical philology) and will now remain there. Numerous legal works are in PJ (Oriental literature) that actually should be reclassed to KL (Law of the Ancient Orient) or in PK (Indo-Iranian literature) that belong in KNS (Law of India).

150. Franz Wieacker, *A History of Private Law in Europe with Particular Reference to Germany,* trans. Tony Weir of *Privatrechtsgeschichte der Neuzeit,* 2d ed. 1967 (Oxford: Clarendon Press, 1995).

151. Between January 1982 and May 1985, the layout of the European schedule was discussed in detail with specialists in the European Law Division of the Law Library before the classification for European law was completed. Per memorandum of 13 August 1985, the Law Librarian handed to the Assistant Librarian for Processing Services a list of twenty-eight American professors who should be consulted; these professors specialized in Roman law and taught at law schools with strong Roman law collections. The law classification specialist was asked independently for review of the list and additional names, if so desired. From this list of thirty-one scholars, the Law Librarian and the law classification specialist were asked to select six each: Alan Watson (University of Pennsylvania), Stephan Kuttner (U.C. at Berkeley, Robbins Collection), Giles Constable (Princeton Institute for Advanced Study), Rodolfo Batiza (Tulane University), Byron Cooper (Library Director, University of Detroit), Charles Szladits (Columbia University), Peter Stein (Queen's College, Cambridge, England), John Henry Merryman (Stanford Law School), Shael Herman (Tulane University), Robert L. Oakley (Library Director, Georgetown Law Center), Thomas H. Reynolds (Associate Director, U.C. at Berkeley Law School). The incoming evaluations were as follows: one person abstained; six others preferred the location of Roman law next to canon law; five preferred the location of Roman law in the schedule for the law of Europe. Several other University law libraries had already urged LC to go forward and not hold up the schedule, notably Berkeley, Harvard and Georgetown. No additional staff was added to the project to assist in preparation of new schedules. Between 12 and 24 March 1986, the arbitration was settled between Deputy Librarian of Congress William J. Welsh, Assistant Librarian for Processing Henriette D. Avram, and Law Librarian Carleton W. Kenyon, who conceded with "grave reservations." (Memorandum, 12 March 1986, with notes and signatures). (On file with CPSO).

152. Albert Bleckmann, *Europarecht: Das Recht der Europäischen Wirtschafts-gemeinschaft* (Köln: Carl Heymanns Verlag, 1976), 10-12.

153. Ibid., 71.

154. Margaret Leary, ABA representative. Minutes for the session of 14 November 1989 (15 November 1989). (On file with CPSO).

155. Jolande E. Goldberg, Library of Congress, Cataloging Policy and Support Office, *Classification: Subclass KL-KWX, Law of Asia and Eurasia, Africa, Pacific Region and Antarctica* (1993), "Introduction," viii.

156. Jolande E. Goldberg, "Antarctica: Economic War Zone or World Patrimony? Festschrift Dr. Walter Witzenmann," in *Konstanten für Wirtschaft und Gesellschaft* (Konstanz: Labhard Verlag, 1993), 94-95.

157. *JZ and KZ: Historical Notes* (supra note 144), 22-26.

158. Library of Congress, Cataloging Policy and Support Office, *Classification: Subclass KZA: Law of the Sea,* and *Subclass KZD: Space Law. Law of Outer Space* (1993).

159. Margaret Leary's minutes (supra note 153) included the stated anticipation of further budget cuts for LC. Thus the Advisory Committee "supported the concept of bringing the budget for outside work to the RLG Law Program Committee's January meeting." Thomas H. Reynolds, RLG representative. Report on the 14 November 1989 meeting to the members of the RLG Law Program Committee. It is a strong appeal in support of LC: ". . . While some might complain that the nation's law libraries appear to be paying LC to do its own job, the realities of the situation, the costs of the project and the lack of support staff at LC and its own serious budget difficulties dictate a more open approach on the part of the Law Library Community" (15 November 1989). The "possibility of support for accelerated work on the law classification" was already brought, in October 1988, to the attention of the National Legal Resources Committee in Washington, DC (On file with CPSO).

160. Thomas H. Reynolds, Report on the meeting of the Advisory Committee on 7 February 1993 (18 February 1993). The understanding was reached that the ". . . funds will be spent to convert Class K to an automated version with a caveat that there will be a completion of KZ and KB and revised JX . . ." (On file with CPSO).

161. Announcement of the LC Cataloging Distribution Service: "Classification Web Service to begin June 1, 2002!" See http://www.loc.gov/cds/classweb.html.

APPENDIX 1. Sample Page of the 1802 Catalog Prepared by Librarian John Beckley (1802-1807)

C A T A L O G U E.

Nº.	FOLIO's.	No. of Vols.	Value, as near as can be estimated.	
			WHOLE SET.	EACH BOOK.
			Dollars.	Dollars.
1	FATHERS PAUL's Council of Trent,	1	4	
2	Blair's Chronology, . (not to issue,)	1	35	
3	Helvicus's Chronological Tables, -	1	3	
4	Booth's Diodorus Siculus, - - -	1	10	
5	Appian's History of the Civil Wars of the Romans, - - - - -	1	4	
6	Machiavel's Florentine History, -	1	3	
7	Duncan's Cæsar, - - - - - -	1	32	
8	Du Halede's History of China, -	2	24	12
10	De Soli's Conquest of Mexico, -	1	4	
11	Rapin's History of England, - -	5	50	10
16	Lord Herbert's Life of Henry VIII.	1	2	
17	Rushworth's Historical Collections, ·	8	24	3
25	Lord Clarendon's History of the Rebellion, - - - - - - - -	4	24	6
29	Guthrie's Geography, - - - -	1	13	
30	Bayle's Dictionary, - - - - -	5	30	6
35	Postlewayte's Dictionary of Commerce,	2	24	12
37	Beawes' Lex Mercatoria, - - -	1	12	
38	Domat's Civil Law, - - - - -	2	12	6
40	Grotius, by Barbeyrac, - - - -	1	14	
41	Puffendorf, by ditto, - - - - -	1	24	
42	Sidney on Government, - - - -	1	10	
43	Bacon's Works, - - - - - -	5	55	11

The first page of the 1802 catalog, prepared by Librarian John Beckley and printed by William Duane of Washington City. Volumes were listed by size. As described in the catalog, the Library's 964-volume collection consisted of 212 folios, 164 quartos, 581 octavos, and 7 duodecimos, plus 9 maps and charts. Rare Book and Special Collections Division.

APPENDIX 2. Outline of the 1812 LC Classification Scheme with 18 Classes, an Excerpt of the Philadelphia Scheme Comprising 31 Classes

LIBRARY OF CONGRESS CLASSIFICATION 1812

A. HISTORY

    1. SACRED HISTORY
    2. ECCLESIASTICAL HISTORY
    3. CIVIL HISTORY (chronology, biography, antiquities, etc.)
    4. GEOGRAPHY. TOPOGRAPHY. VOYAGES

B. PHILOSOPHY
    5. LAW
    6. ETHICS. MORAL SYSTEM. THEOLOGY. MYTHOLOGY
    7. LOGIC. RHETORIC. CRITICISM
    8. DICTIONARIES. GRAMMARS. EDUCATION
    9. GENERAL AND LOCAL POLITICS. POLITICAL ECONOMY, ETC.
    10. TRADE AND COMMERCE
    11. MILITARY AND NAVAL TACTICS
    12. AGRICULTURE. RURAL ECONOMY
    13. NATURAL HISTORY. NATURAL AND EXPERIMENTAL PHILOSOPHY
    14. MEDICINE. SURGERY. CHEMISTRY

C. FINE ARTS

    15. POETRY. DRAMA. FICTION. WIT, ETC.
    16. ARTS AND SCIENCE. MISCELLANY

D. FORMS

    17. GAZETTES
    18. MAPS. CHARTS. PLANS

APPENDIX 3. Sample Page of Thomas Jefferson's Classification with Its 44 Subdivisions

BOOKS may be classed according to the faculties of the mind employed on them: these are—
I. MEMORY.   II. REASON.   III. IMAGINATION.

Which are applied respectively to—
I. HISTORY   II. PHILOSOPHY.   III. FINE ARTS.

					Chapt.
I. HISTORY	Civil	Civil Proper	Antient	Antient History	1
			Modern	Foreign	2
				British	3
				American	4
		Ecclesiastical		Ecclesiastical	5
	Natural	Physics		Natural Philosophy	6
				Agriculture	7
				Chemistry	8
				Surgery	9
				Medicine	10
		Nat. Hist. Proper	Animals	Anatomy	11
				Zoology	12
			Vegetables	Botany	13
			Minerals	Mineralogy	14
		Occupations of Man		Technical Arts	15
II. PHILOSOPHY	Moral	Ethics		Moral Philosophy / L. of Nature & Nations	16
		Jurisprudence	Religious	Religion	17
			Municipal	Equity	18
				Common Law	19
			Domestic	Law Merchant	20
				Law Maritime	21
				Law Ecclesiastical	22
			Foreign	Foreign Law	23
		Oeconomical		Politics	24
				Commerce	
	Mathematical	Pure		Arithmetic	25
				Geometry	26
		Physico Mathematical		Mechanics	27
				Statics	
				Dynamics	
				Pneumatics	
				Phonics	
				Optics	
				Astronomy	28
				Geography	29
III. FINE ARTS	Architecture			Architecture	30
	Gardening			Gardening	31
	Painting			Painting	
	Sculpture			Sculpture	32
	Music			Music	33
	Poetry			Epic	34
				Romance	
				Pastorals	35
				Odes	
				Elegies	
				Didactic	36
				Tragedy	37
				Comedy	38
				Dialogue	39
				Epistles	
	Oratory			Logic	40
				Rhetoric	
				Orations	
	Criticism			Theory	41
				Bibliography	42
				Languages	43
Authors who have written on various branches				Polygraphical	44

The classification scheme Jefferson devised for his collection as it appears in the Catalogue of the Library of the United States (Washington: Printed by Jonathan Elliot. 1815). The Library of Congress adopted Jefferson's organization of knowledge, using it to classify its growing collection of books for most of the nineteenth century.

APPENDIX 4. Tree of Classification

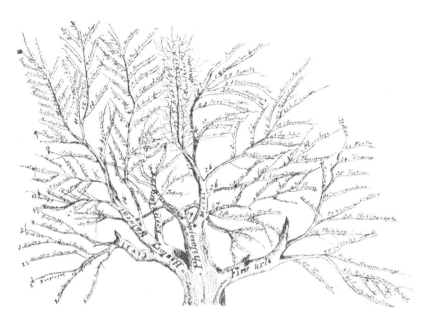

This "tree of classification," anonymously penned in the 1890's, illustrates the classification system used in the Library of Congress until 1897. Its caption reads: "The Library is divided into 44 chapters. The system of classification was originally prepared by President Jefferson, but has been modified since. It is based upon Lord Bacon's division of knowledge, the subjects classed according to the faculties of the mind employed on them."

69

APPENDIX 5a-b. Two Sample Pages of Class F with Encyclopedia Articles Introducing the User to the Historic Development of the New Territories

F   BRITISH NORTH AMERICA—CANADA   F

Ontario.
1059   Regions. Counties. Boundaries—Continued.

.05   Ontario Co.
.06   Lake Ontario region, Ont.
      Cf. F 556.
.091 Ottawa River and Valley, Ont.
      Cf. F 1054.09.
.P3   Perth Co.
.P4   Peterborough Co.
.Q3   Queen Victoria Niagara Falls park.
      Cf. F 127.N8.

.S3   Lake St. Clair region, Ont.
      Cf. F 572.S34.
.S4   St. Lawrence River and Valley, Ont.
      Cf. F 1050.
.S6   Simcoe Co.
.S9   Lake Superior region.
      Cf. F 552.
.T5   Thunder Bay region.
.W4   Wentworth Co.
.Y6   York Co.

1059.5 Towns. Cities.

1060 The Canadian Northwest (Region to the west and northwest of the ancient New France). Hudson Bay. Hudson's Bay company. Rupert's Land. Northwest company of Canada. Northwest Territories.

This region, though visited in its southern parts by French explorers was never colonized or actually governed by that power. By virtue of discovery by Frobisher and Hudson it was claimed by Great Britain and in 1670 the crown chartered the Hudson's Bay company to control the region about Hudson Bay and to the west, and this claim was ultimately recognized by the French, early in the 18th century. Outside the company's own domain, Rupert's Land or the region watered by the rivers flowing into Hudson Bay, it received temporary renewable leases of the western territory to the U. S. and the Pacific (the Northwest Territories). British Columbia was lost to the Company on its organization as a Crown colony in 1858, and in 1869 all the rest of the Company's holdings outside certain reservations were surrendered to the Dominion of Canada. In 1870 this region, excluding the district of Keewatin, was made a separate government as the "Northwest Territories." In 1882 it was subdivided by the formation of the provisional districts of Assiniboia, Saskatchewan, Alberta and Athabasca. (In 1905 these four districts were consolidated and admitted to the Dominion as the provinces of Saskatchewan and Alberta.) In 1895-97 the remaining unorganized territory in British North America was subdivided into the districts of Ungava, Franklin, Mackenzie and Yukon, of which the last was made a territory the following year. The present Northwest Territories, so-called, include Mackenzie, Keewatin, Ungava and Franklin.

Boundaries.
U. S. boundary   F 597, 880, 854.
Alaska boundary   F 912.B7.
Ontario boundary   F 1059.B7.
Canadian Rocky Mts.   F 1090.
Polar regions   G 575-726.
Northwest passage   G 640-665.

F THE WEST INDIES **F**

1901–1981 **Haiti (Island).**

Discovered by Columbus in 1492, named Hispaniola or Española and at once settled by the Spaniards. It was the seat of the Audiencia of Santo Domingo and the centre of the Spanish colonial empire in America in the early 16th century. Even after the erection of separate governments in Mexico and Peru, it was still the capital for the West Indies and northern South America for a century more. In the early part of the 17th century bands of adventurers, chiefly French, obtained a foothold in the northwest of the island and out of this grew the French colony of Saint Domingue, occupying the western end of the island (corresponding to the republic of Haiti today). This was formally recognized as a French possession by Spain in 1697. Early in the French revolution, in 1791, the home government passed and then repealed an act granting civil rights to negroes in Saint Domingue. This caused a revolution which the French were unable to put down. The situation was further complicated by the incursion of an English force (that country being at war with France) which maintained itself on the western end of the island from 1793 till its final expulsion in 1798. In 1795 Spain withdrew from the island, ceding to France her colony in the east, which the latter power was unable to hold. By 1801 the native leader Toussaint Louverture had succeeded in restoring order in all parts and inaugurated a constitutional government, which he desired to have recognized and guaranteed by France. He was treacherously seized and taken to France, but Dessalines his successor (who had himself proclaimed emperor as Jacques I) finally expelled the French in 1803, declared the island independent 1804, under the aboriginal name of Haiti, and maintained his supremacy till his death in 1806. His empire was divided between the rival generals: Christophe who maintained himself in the north 1806–1820 and proclaimed a monarchy as King Henry I; and Pétion who ruled in the south 1806–1818, and was succeeded by Boyer. The latter annexed the dominion of Christophe in 1820 and in 1822 drove out the Spaniards who had regained their foothold in the east a few years before. He continued ruler of the entire island till 1843.

The eastern or Spanish part of the island then asserted its independence and organized the Dominican Republic the following year. About 1869 there was a strong movement toward annexation to the U. S.

The French or western end of the island, the Republic of Haiti, was a prey to anarchy for several years, one of her rulers, Soulouque, proclaiming himself king, as Faustin I, in 1849.

1901 Comprehensive works. Description of the whole island.

1909 Antiquities.

1911 History (of the island). Spanish colony, 1492–1795.
Spanish colony 1804–1822 F 1931.
Union of the whole island 1822–1843 F 1924.

APPENDIX 6a-b. Two Samples of Classification Outlines Showing in Progression the Treatment of Class K

Cutter's Outline[17]		Hanson's First Outline (1899)		
A	Reference and General works	A	1-200	Polygraphy; Encyclopedias; General Periodicals; Societies, etc.
B	Philosophy	A	201-3000	Philosophy
BR	Religion & Religions (except the Christian and Jewish)	A	3001-B9999	Religion; Theology; Church history
C	Christian and Jewish religions			
D	Ecclesiastical history			
E	Biography	C	1-9999	Biography; and studies auxiliary to history
F	History and subjects allied	D	1-9999	General history; periods; and local (except America) with Geography
		E-F		America; history and geography
G	Geography and travels	G		Geography; general; and allied studies (e.g., Anthropology and Ethnology)
H	Social sciences	H	1-2000	Political science
		H	2001-9999	Law
I	Sociology	I	1-8000	Sociology
J	Government, Politics			
K	Legislation. Law. Women. Societies	I	8001-9999	Women; Societies, clubs, etc.
		J	1-2000	Sports; amusements
		J	2001-9999	Music
		K		Fine arts
		L-M		Philosophy & Literature

THE NEW LIBRARY OF CONGRESS CLASSIFICATION

The 1903 outline:		The 1904 outline:	
A (in part)	Polygraphy. General works	A	General works. Polygraphy
A501-3000	Philosophy	B-BJ	Philosophy
A3001-B	Religion & Theology	BL-BX	Religion. Theology
C	Biography; Studies auxiliary to History	C	History — Auxiliary sciences
D	History (except America)	D	History & topography (except America)
E-F	America. History and Geography	E	America General and U.S. General History
		F	U.S. Local and America Outside U.S. History
G	Geography; & allied studies: Anthropology; etc.	G	Geography, Anthropology, Sports
H	Statistics. Economics	H-HA	Social Sciences. General Statistics
		HB-HJ	Economics
J	Sociology	HM-HX	Sociology
		J	Political Science
K	Law	K	Law
L	Education. Sports. Amusements	L	Education
M	Music	M	Music
N	Architecture. Graphic Arts	N	Fine Arts
P	Philology (Language and literature)	P	Philology (Language and literature)
Q	Science	Q	Science
R	Medicine	R	Medicine
S	Agriculture. Plant and animal industry	S	Agriculture. Plant and animal industry
T	Technology	T	Technology
U	Military Science	U	Military Science
V	Naval Science	V	Naval Science
Z	Bibliography	Z	Bibliography

APPENDIX 7a-c. Three Sample Pages of Class F on U.S. Westward Expansion, Indian Territories, and Indian Wars

F   UNITED STATES LOCAL HISTORY   F

676–690   **Kansas**—Continued.

687   Regions. Counties. Boundaries.

.A4	Allen Co.	.L4	Leavenworth Co.
.A7	Arkansas River and Valley, Kan. Cf. F 417.A7.	.L7	Lincoln Co.
		.M6	Missouri River and Valley, Kan. Cf. F 598.
.B2	Barton Co.		
.B5	Big Blue River, Blue Valley.	.M7	Montgomery Co.
		.N3	Nemaha Co.
.B7	Boundaries.	.N4	Ness Co.
.B8	Brown Co.	.N8	Norton Co.
.C5	Cheyenne Co.	.P8	Pottawatomie Co.
.C6	Cloud Co.	.R4	Republic Co.
.D6	Doniphan Co.	.R5	Riley Co.
.D7	Douglas Co.	.R7	Rooks Co.
.E3	Ellis Co.	.S4	Sedgwick Co.
.E4	Ellsworth Co.	.S5	Shawnee Co.
.G3	Geary Co. (formerly Davis Co.)	.S9	Sumner Co.
		.W2	Wabaunsee Co.
.L2	Labette Co.		

690   Topics.

.S2   Scandinavians.

691–705   **Oklahoma** (a).

All of the present state of Oklahoma, except the westernmost strip, was included in the Louisiana purchase 1803. It formed part of the District (later Territory) of Louisiana 1804–1812, and territory of Missouri 1812–1819. In 1819 it was included in the new Arkansas Territory, but by acts of Congress in 1824 and 1828 was detached from Arkansas and thenceforth formed part of the Indian country, or the unsettled region west of Arkansas and Missouri. It was not till after the close of the civil war that the government succeeded in bringing to it all the Indian tribes destined to occupy the territory; no territorial government in the ordinary sense was granted. In 1890 the northwestern part, having been purchased by the government from its Indian owners, was organized as Oklahoma Territory; No-man's land, north of Texas and west of 100° being added to the new territory. Meanwhile the Indian Territory continued its existence till the two territories were reunited and admitted as the state of Oklahoma in 1907.

696   Antiquities.

Indians of Indian Territory and Oklahoma   E 78.O45.
The Five civilized tribes (collectively)   E 78.I5.

697   The "Indian country" (that part of the Louisiana purchase, west of Ark., Mo. and the Missouri River). Indian Territory before division in 1890.

698   Indian Territory, 1890–1907.

699   Oklahoma Territory, 1890–1907.

700   1907–   State of Oklahoma.

Table of subdivisions (a), (b), (c), or (d) under each state may be found on pages 85–87.

F UNITED STATES LOCAL HISTORY F

476-485   **The Old Northwest.** Region between the Ohio and Mississippi rivers and the Great Lakes.

First explored by the French from New France in the latter part of the 17th century, and various trading posts established. On the formation of the province of Louisiana, the entire Mississippi Valley with the Illinois country was incorporated in it, the northern and eastern portions of the Old Northwest (the Great Lake region and Ohio Valley above modern Louisville) continuing under New France. Certain of the English colonies, notably Virginia, had charter claims to this region, and the dispute over jurisdiction helped to bring on the French and Indian war, one result of which was to transfer all territory east of the Mississippi River to England. But the claims of the individual colonies were ignored by the mother country, and the region west of the Alleghanies as far south as the Ohio was annexed to the province of Quebec in 1774. Then came the Revolution, with Clark's conquest of the Northwest, which led to the abandonment of the British claim in the peace of 1783. New York, Virginia, Massachusetts and Connecticut all ceded their claims to the general government, 1781-1786; and 1787 there was passed an ordinance organizing the "Territory of the United States Northwest of the Ohio". The British posts, however, were not surrendered till 1796. In 1800 the Territory was divided by a line drawn north from the mouth of the Kentucky River, the eastern portion retaining the old name, and including all of Ohio, eastern Michigan and a strip along the eastern edge of Indiana; the western part received the name of Indiana Territory. 1803 Ohio was admitted as a state with substantially its present limits, the remainder of the Northwest Territory being annexed to Indiana Territory.

Upper Mississippi Valley   F 597.

Louisiana   F 366-380.

Ohio Valley   F 516-520.

476   Periodicals.   Societies.   Collections.

477   Gazetteers.   Dictionaries.

478   Biography.   Genealogy.

479   General works.

480   Miscellaneous.

481   Antiquities.

482   To 1763.

New France   F 1030.

Mackinac region; Michilimackinac   F 572.M16.

Detroit, 1701   F 574.D4.

Illinois country   F 544.

Ohio company, 1749   F 517.

French and Indian war, 1755-1763   E 199.

Table of subdivisions (a), (b), (c), or (d) under each state may be found on pages 85-87.

133

APPENDIX 7a-c (continued)

F   LIBRARY OF CONGRESS   **F**

856–870   **California.**

868   Other regions. Counties. Boundaries—Continued.

.S15	San Diego Co. Colorado Desert. Escondido Valley. Imperial Valley.	.S3	Santa Cruz Co. California redwood park.
		.S4	Sequoia national park.
.S156	San Francisco Bay. region.	.S49	Shasta Co.
		.S495	Shasta Mountains.
.S17	San Joaquin Co.	.S5	Sierra Nevada Mountains.
.S173	San Joaquin River and Valley.		(Donner party F 868 .N5.)
.S18	San Luis Obispo Co.	.S6	Siskiyou Co. Butte Valley.
.S19	San Mateo Co.		
.S22	Santa Ana River and Valley.	.S66	Solano Co.
		.S7	Sonoma Co.
.S23	Santa Barbara Co.	.S8	Stanislaus Co.
	Cf. F 868.S232.	.S9	Sutter Co.
.S232	Santa Barbara Islands (Channel Islands) collectively. The individual islands belong to Santa Barbara, Ventura and Los Angeles cos.	.T3	Tehama Co.
		.T8	Tulare Co. Mt. Whitney. Cf. F 868.S4.
		.T9	Tuolumne Co. Cf. F 868.C14.
		.V5	Ventura Co.
		.Y6	Yosemite national park. Yosemite Valley.
.S25	Santa Clara Co. Santa Clara Valley.	.Y8	Yuba Co.

870   Topics.

.C5	Chinese.	.J3	Japanese.
.F8	French.	.M6	Mission buildings.
.I6	Irish.	.P8	Portuguese.

871–885   **Oregon (c).**

The "Oregon country" in the later 18th and early 19th century comprised the region between New Spain (Upper California) and Russian America (Alaska); from 42° to 54° 40′. Both Spanish and British claimed it by right of discovery and exploration. In 1792 Capt. Gray explored the Columbia River, laying the basis of the American claim. In 1818 a treaty of joint occupation between the U. S. and Gt. Brit. was made. The Spanish treaty of 1819 (Florida treaty) also surrendered to the U. S. all Spanish claim to the Pacific coast above 42°. The joint occupancy of the two countries was terminated in 1846 by agreement to divide the territory on the line of 49° and the Straits of Fuca. The territory of Oregon was organized 1848, consisting of all the region north of 42° not included in the old Louisiana purchase (Oregon, Washington and Idaho and parts of Montana and Wyoming). The northern part of the region was organized as Washington Territory in 1853, and when Oregon was admitted as a state in 1859, the eastern part of Oregon Territory was added temporarily to Washington Territory.

Table of subdivisions (a), (b), (c), or (d) under each state may be found on pages 85–87.

APPENDIX 8a-b. Two Sample Pages, Reproduced from the Original Edition of Elizabeth V. Benyon, *Classification, Class K: Law*, with Preface of David J. Haykin, Chief Subject Cataloging Division, Library of Congress (Washington, DC: Library of Congress, 1948)

```
KB      JURISPRUDENCE. LEGAL HISTORY. LEGAL INSTITUTIONS, ETC.
            COLLECTED WORKS. TREATISES, ETC.

                        ANGLO-AMERICAN.

 1      PERIODICALS.
            Cf. KA1-2.

 3      YEARBOOKS. ANNUALS.

        BAR ASSOCIATIONS AND LAW SOCIETIES.
            United States.
 4          General.
 5          State and other local.
 6          Great Britain.
 7          Other, by country, A-Z.

 8      CONGRESSES AND CONFERENCES.

 9      COLLECTED WORKS.

10      ADDRESSES, ESSAYS, LECTURES.

11      ENCYCLOPEDIAS.
            Cf. KA22.

12      DICTIONARIES.
            Cf. KA23+

13      DIRECTORIES.
            Cf. KA25-26.

15      BIOGRAPHY.
            Cf. KA28-29.

18      LAW AS A SCIENCE (JURISPRUDENCE).
            Cf. KA30-35.

        GENERAL AND SPECIAL WORKS.
            (Decisions and opinions, see KA29, KB15).
            (By subject. See alternate subject classification following KB6935).
20-6831     By author (including anonymous works by title, and corporate authors, A-Z.
            Under each:
                .A1         Collected works, by date.
                .A2         Selected works and selections, by editor, A-Z.
                .A21-.27    Separate works, by title. Titles beginning "the law of,"
                                "the law and practice of," "a treatise on the law of,"
                                etc. are cuttered from the subject dealt with, and not
                                the first word of the title.
                            Under each:
                                .0      Texts, by date.
                                .1      Selections, by editor, A-Z.
                                .2-29   Translations, by language.
                                            E.g.  .22  French.
                                                  .23  German.
                                .3      Criticism, by author, A-Z.
                .28A-Z      Criticism, by author, A-Z. Cf. KA29, KB15.

                                    52
```

APPENDIX 8a-b (continued)

```
KB                     ALTERNATE SUBJECT CLASSIFICATION
                        FOR GENERAL AND SPECIAL WORKS
                               in Class KB

        PUBLIC LAW.
                Governmental regulation of economic activity (continued).

57              Industries, A-Z., including agriculture, mining, and
                    state industries.  Cf. KB75; HD; S; T.
60              Labor law.  Cf. HD7801+; HD7960.
                Patents, trademarks, copyrights.  See KB157-163.
61              Professions.  Cf. L; N; M; R.
                    .A1    General works.
                    .A2-Z  By profession, A-Z.
62              Public utilities.  Cf. HD2763.
63              Pure food and drug laws.
65              Securities regulation.  Investments.
                Unfair competition.  See KB157.
68              Other, A-Z.

        Other governmental or administrative regulation.
71              Atomic energy.
72              Education law.
73              Liquor law.  Prohibition.
74              Medical jurisprudence.
75              Natural resources.  Conservation.
77              Public hygiene.  Public health law.  See also KB63.
78              Public welfare law.  Social insurance.  Old-age security.
                    Charities, etc.
79              Other, A-Z.
                    E.g.:  .B6    Birth control.
                           .G2    Gambling.
                           .I6    Indians.
                           .L6    Libraries.
                           .L8    Lotteries.
                           .P85   Prostitution.
                           .S7    Speculation.
                           .V4    Veterans.

        Public finance.  Taxation.  Cf. HJ.
80              General works.
                Special.
81                  Tariffs.  Customs.
                    Taxation.
82                      National taxation.
83                      Local taxation.
84                  Other topics, A-Z.

        Administration of justice.  Courts: Systems and structure.  Cf. JF-JQ.
85              General works.
                Special.
86                  Judges.  Selection and tenure.  Impeachment.
87                  Legal aid.
88                  Police.  Detectives.  Police courts and administration.
89                  Other, A-Z.
                        E.g.:  .J85  Judicial councils.
                               .J9   Jury.
```

114

The Evolution of Bibliographic Control of Maps

Rebecca L. Lubas

SUMMARY. Although maps have been used for thousands of years, they have not been maintained or organized as well as printed books until relatively recently. Maps were often treated as ephemeral material. Early attempts at map cataloging are much more scattered than book cataloging, and printed catalogs of early libraries often omitted the mention of maps. It was only after map use became commonplace and thematic maps increased in number that cataloging and classification attempts began in earnest. The classification and cataloging of maps started to come together in the early part of the twentieth century. This article will examine how maps were organized in early collections and some of the advice provided for catalogers of map collections from the end of the nineteenth century and the first half of the twentieth. *[Article copies available for a fee from The Haworth Document Delivery Service: 1-800-HAWORTH. E-mail address: <getinfo@haworthpressinc.com> Website: <http://www.HaworthPress.com> © 2003 by The Haworth Press, Inc. All rights reserved.]*

KEYWORDS. Map cataloging, map catalogers, maps, bibliographic control

The differences between maps and books are numerous and fundamental. In approaching the problem of map cataloging, it is therefore not in

Rebecca L. Lubas is Special Formats Cataloging Librarian, Massachusetts Institute of Technology Libraries (E-mail: rll@mit.edu).

[Haworth co-indexing entry note]: "The Evolution of Bibliographic Control of Maps." Lubas, Rebecca L. Co-published simultaneously in *Cataloging & Classification Quarterly* (The Haworth Information Press, an imprint of The Haworth Press, Inc.) Vol. 35, No. 3/4, 2003, pp. 437-446; and: *Historical Aspects of Cataloging and Classification* (ed: Martin D. Joachim) The Haworth Information Press, an imprint of The Haworth Press, Inc., 2003, pp. 437-446. Single or multiple copies of this article are available for a fee from The Haworth Document Delivery Service [1-800-HAWORTH, 9:00 a.m. - 5:00 p.m. (EST). E-mail address: getinfo@haworthpressinc.com].

437

the interest either of the specialist in library science or of map users who are to be the catalog's beneficiaries to begin with the assumption that maps are to be regarded as if they were simply books in another format.[1]

Map collections seem to be the last to receive attention from catalogers. Large libraries often have every other format cataloged before directing efforts to cartographic resources. The reasons for this historical neglect lie in the history of map creation, publication, usage, and collecting practices. The treatment of cartographic materials as publishing and collecting exceptions added to maps' delayed entry into the cataloging mainstream. Once the need for organizing map collections was felt, they were thought of as separate from books. Map collections were individually organized, outside of the early bibliographic control schemes. Organization of maps evolved very slowly over the centuries, out of necessity as map usage increased. A single sheet map is referred to in the first Bodleian catalog.[2] Even as late as the twentieth century, map collections were described as "both rare . . . usually very incomplete or ill arranged."[3] The earliest printed catalogs make mention only of books and manuscripts.[4] The historical study of early libraries also neglects maps themselves in the collections, let alone cataloging practices for maps. *The English Library*, a major study of early libraries, does not even have an index listing for maps.[5]

Medieval monasteries were the sites of well-known early library collections. As the purpose of these collections was to serve religious instruction and meditation, maps would have been of little use.[6] Geography was not among the classical subjects in which the monastic catalogs organized their collections.[7] Medieval catalogs served much more as inventories of valuable property than as finding aids. Recording donors was also an important goal of these catalogs.[8] Perhaps if maps did have some small place in these libraries, they were not considered valuable enough to inventory. Early map usage does provide some indication that maps would not be considered as precious as books, or at least not in the same manner. Had a map been displayed on a library wall, the need for a map shelflist would hardly seem necessary as the item was in plain sight. Medieval books often contained severe curses against defacing or theft such as "the damnation with the traitor Judas," but the individual maps that have survived contained no such warnings.[9] By the fifteenth century, non-religious libraries, such as court libraries and private collections, began to flourish. However, none of these budding libraries was devoted solely to maps.[10] Mapmakers did keep inventory of their stock, so there is some record of which maps existed.[11] Publishers' map inventories exploded in number when the age of exploration began, for then there was a demand.[12]

The lack of map cataloging in early libraries, however, may belie their actual presence. We cannot know for certain in every case that they were not there; they may simply not have survived. A sheet map is fragile, and a collection of sheet maps could easily be obliterated in a single fire or flood. They were most likely stored differently from books, such as being hung on walls for decoration or reference.[13] A few maps that were mentioned in medieval library catalogs were rolled maps.[14] These possibly were inventoried to reflect separate shelflists. Conversely, they may have been so valued that they were hidden away. Sir William More, for example, kept his most prized maps in a closet.[15] Thus many collections of maps may have existed but were not clearly accounted for. Most of the maps that have survived from the Middle Ages did not come as sheet maps but were "coddled in the protective wrapping of books, cradled in the written word."[16] Maps may not have been cataloged as separate entities because they were not meant to be used separately. Diagrams were intended to be used with texts and human instruction, and maps would have been considered diagrams. Often a map would be removed from a book, increasing the odds that it would be lost. Other maps that have disappeared include wall maps and maps made of precious materials, melted for their base value.[17]

There may have been more maps in medieval libraries than the surviving evidence shows at first glance. There is no specific word meaning "map" used in the catalogs. *Mappa* means "cloth," *carta* means "document," and *pictura* or *figura* could be any drawing or diagram. The maps would be listed in these general terms if they were listed at all. Another reason that maps may have slipped through the bibliographic cracks was a lack of popular subject headings. Geography would not have been considered a classical discipline. Geography texts that have survived from the Middle Ages rarely contain maps. This could be because the maps by themselves were considered useless, as the human component of instruction provided knowledge, not the maps. The cartographic drawings may have also existed as wall maps and were long since separated from their text. The treatment of accompanying material has historically been problematic. Texts of lectures exist that clearly indicate reference to maps, but the maps themselves are not usually with the lectures. Maps may have also migrated, being detached from the original text and appended to another.[18] Perhaps the transitory nature of the map made it not worth mentioning in a catalog or inventory. The medieval value of committing knowledge to memory may have also worked against the recording of maps in inventories.[19] Maps were secondary to books in another way. Often the draughtsman had never personally surveyed the area but drew a map from information written in a book.[20]

The importance of cartographic resources in collections grew as usage grew. Once usage increased, the importance of inventories and catalogs finally received attention. This trend continued to happen slowly, though. Maps would have been used for travel, but very few members of society traveled—only government officials, some high-ranking church officials, and military. As the movements of common people were extremely localized, maps were simply not a necessity to everyday life. Sea travel was important, but the routes were so jealously guarded as trade secrets that they were often not recorded on purpose, so as not to risk theft. A sailor would not have dreamed of having his sea routes inventoried. There was a thriving business in personal guides to cities. Again, knowledge was a professional secret and not committed to map or book. Around the mid-fifteenth century, routes finally began to be written down by merchants who may have had others make journeys for them. Royals retained route planners, who may or may not have documented their plans. When shipbuilding technology improved, ships became faster and more numerous. Sailors no longer had the luxury of committing routes to memory; there was too much to memorize. The earliest sailing directions to survive are from 1486, for a route from Britain to Gibraltar. There are no distances recorded, but rather the soundings were written out for the journey.[21]

The first major collections of directions for travel were held by political advisors. Lord Burghley, advisor to Elizabeth I, held road lists kept with a portfolio of maps. Many of the maps in this collection were annotated. These maps existed mainly for political information, not for physical geographical information. Government repositories of maps began to increase as the number of government agencies using maps increased. These collections increasingly required inventories. Formal postal systems were one example of agencies needing maps.[22]

By the mid 1500s, road-book publication expanded. These books often contained, or were meant to contain, foldout maps. As travel became more accessible, the publication of maps and publishers' inventories increased. Exploration became big business, and navigation charts improved in quality and increased in number in the sixteenth century. The charts that were actually used on voyages rarely survived though copies held in state collections were preserved. It is at this point that maps were more widely treated as resources in collections, important for the work they represented alone rather than to be used alongside other print resources.[23]

Maps also became status symbols. They were purchased, even commissioned, to impress rather than to be used.[24] A map of an estate showed social standing and authority. These maps were more decorative and treated more as artwork than as information resources. The ornamentation of these maps was critical to the commissioner of the map, and they usually had elaborate renditions of the coats-of-arms of the estate-holders. These maps would often show manor houses pictorially, hand-colored. These works were probably not used as practical maps. Institutions, such as colleges, may also have commissioned maps to show status rather than for practical use. Further evidence of the map not quite being considered a regular library resource was the placement of map display cases. In the 1800s, elaborate display cases were built into bookcases for maps, but these cases were often placed in dressing rooms, rather than in libraries, in unlikely places for a catalog to reach.[25]

While map collections were finally evolving, it still took a long time for them to be recognized as important segments of libraries. Map rooms appeared in the eighteenth century, such as the one for the collection of the Library of Saxony, which held 117 atlases and 200 maps, totaling 10,000 sheets.[26] But recognition came slowly; the British Map Room of the British Museum, for example, did not become the Map Library of the British Museum until 1973. A contributing factor, along with the difficulty of handling the material and their inconsistent placement, may also be that maps were not entirely considered reliable sources of information. Maps frequently sacrificed precision for a more "pictorial cartographic style" and took on the "more imaginative and symbolic qualities of a work of art, rather than a scientific document." Printing techniques were not applied to cartographic resources until the 1600s, and even after that maps may still have been made by the draughtsman's hand.[27]

The growing private map collections of the seventeenth and eighteenth centuries often belonged to royalty. George III had a topographic map collection as well as maritime charts. These collections sprung up as government use of maps increased. By the nineteenth century, national libraries that had sizable map collections were finally being inventoried and even cataloged. Catalog entries improved in description and increased in number.[28]

By the nineteenth century, maps were produced primarily for utilitarian purposes rather than for decoration. Official agencies of colonial powers had much use for maps. Interest in the social sciences gave rise to thematic maps. In the Victorian era, social trends, crime rates, religions, and other data began to appear in cartographic form. Now, maps started to require subject consideration, in addition to the geographic regions covered. Maps with medical information began to appear in official reports in the first half of the nineteenth century, such as the reports of the cholera epidemic in 1832. As the insurance business boomed, fire insurance maps became some of the most accurate, precisely detailed cartographic resources in the late 1800s.[29]

The first union list for maps appeared at the University of Chicago in 1936.[30] It is a union list of map holdings of libraries in the Chicago area. However, maps were still not being cataloged in a uniform, consistent manner. R. A. Skelton, who conducted major studies of maps and map collections, wrote that "description of the map in a form intelligible to other students and permitting comparison with other maps described in the same form" was a goal of map cataloging. Skelton's studies revealed that cataloging should include the mathematical construction (projection), the accuracy of the map, the design, representational technique and symbols used, lettering and decoration, mode of preparation (drawing or engraved), method of engraving, and state of the plate or block. The location and movement between collections of maps ought to also be recorded. Additionally, he believed that every map in a collection should be examined for its value as art.[31]

Skelton also concerned himself with improving access to cartographic resources by describing their locations. He wrote that there should be survey guides for single collections, union catalogs for regions, complete catalogs for national libraries and special collections, and catalogs of manuscript maps. "All such catalogues should be kept up to date, and we should not bite off more than we can chew" was Skelton's overarching advice. He thought that a partial catalog was not of much use.[32] His principles challenge us even today.

At the turn of the twentieth century, maps in special collections began receiving both cataloging attention and preservation. The Lenox Branch of the New York Public Library described in the *Library Journal* in 1897 that it had actively organized its maps collection. The maps were arranged in geographic, alphabetic order. The Lenox Library recommended a separate indexed catalog for maps in atlases. Attention to the sheet level should be extensive; every sheet in the library was wrapped in paper to give it some protection from tearing.[33]

A few years later in 1902, Thomas Letts recommended in the *Library Journal* some methods of making the cataloging process more efficient. He found that pre-preparing catalog cards with lines for place and publication, date, size within border, scale, engraving method, whether the map was plain or colored, and sheet size (description) sped the cataloging process. The title of the map should be written on the card; and if there was no title, one should be supplied. He also detailed practical problems of recording titles. On old maps, for example, the dedication portions of titles could be very long, often requiring many cards. He did not emphasize the names of individuals responsible. The cataloger was advised to add every draughtsman, surveyor, editor, and compiler only if it would mean not having to use more than one card! Maps were entered under title, not under an author. Letts dismissed the importance of place of publication and publisher of an individual map and was concerned with place of publication only for collections. Dates were important in this catalog due to chronological arrangements. Because of this importance of dates, they were estimated, if unknown, with the supplied dates marked on the maps themselves in green pencil. "You will find the chronological arrangement of each place is far more valuable than any other." Letts stressed the importance of the scale, a detail even more important than the actual size of the map. Other physical characteristics recorded included the engraving process. He cautioned that if one did not have time for this ideal cataloging of a map collection, one should simply arrange them by region, name of country, date, and style or mounting. A simply organized collection is better than a collection that has only parts organized and cataloged in detail.[34]

In 1896 Herbert Fordham completed a catalog of Hertfordshire maps, which was printed in 1901. He gave an individual description of every original engraved map of the county and their reprints from 1579-1900. Fordham described the standard he created in this process. The goal of the catalog should be to allow the reader to identify an individual map from reading the catalog entry. He carefully stressed the importance of distinguishing reprints from originals. Fordham also believed that chronological order was essential in a map collection and its catalog. The year of publication should be "the foundation fact." "If an undated book is a nuisance, an undated map . . . is a proper subject of something more than annoyance," wrote Fordham, identifying a problem that has persisted in map cataloging to the present. He suggested using watermarks to help date maps. Fordham also devised a method to distinguish reprint dates, by marking them with asterisks.[35]

Fordham, like the Lenox Library, was irked by the lack of titles on many maps. He gave preference to author over title in the case of maps taken from books. Fordham's entry, to be contained within a paragraph, consisted of the dimensions of the map, then the scale, the name of the engraver or the draughtsman, and a note about the original, if applicable, with the date of the original. Descriptive details should include the border, orientation, prime meridian, and latitude and longitude. Notes should be made if political divisions, watercourses, centers of population, or details such as churches, parks, mills, woods, lakes, houses of note, or hills were shown. While color was an interesting detail, Fordham did not think it worth mentioning if a map was hand-colored. He was interested mainly in a map's original state. He favored the idea of cataloging inset maps as their own titles. Fordham also recommended that, ideally, each map of an atlas be cataloged separately. Such entries should always include the title of the source atlas. He also recommended that a catalog of maps have a chronological index, a title index, and an index of authors, engravers, printers, and publishers. He stressed again the importance of the chronological information.[36]

By 1927 Cambridge University Library's *Rules for the Catalogues of Printed Books, Maps & Music* stated that rules for maps were "not widely different from those which obtain for the cataloging of books." This statement is in contrast with the Lenox Library's and Fordham's special treatments. The *Rules* advised that the main entry for cartographic resources be for the name of the place. Abridged entries for the author, draughtsman, or compiler should be arranged within one alphabet that also contained the main entry. Abridged entries for insets, authors, and surveyors should also be made. The *Rules* gave detailed instructions on the determination of the main entry. If there is more than one region on the map, one should choose the first place name in the title for the main entry, and use abridged entries for the remaining place names (a practice map catalogers follow today with many 246 fields). If there was no title, a cataloger should supply one that describes the entire region of the map. The *Rules* were also concerned with standardization of place names; they recommended using the *Lippincott Gazetteer* for deciding the matter. If the name of a country had changed, the *Rules* specified use of the form of name on a map, but if the name of a town changed, they opted for the most current name. Supplied titles were placed in square brackets. The description, according to the *Rules,* included title, author, scale, projection, edition, and insets. They also provided for series names and number of sheets. The *Rules* cautioned that scale be included only if stated on the map, a policy which has persisted in current common practice. The chronological arrangement became subordinate to the geographical arrangement in this system. Despite the *Rules'* insistence that maps are not that different from books, the topical matter, the geographic subject, distinguishes that format from other items.[37]

Samuel Whittemore Boggs addressed the American Geographical Society in 1937 on the subject of library classification of geographical material. His goal was to get geographers to understand that general classification schemes such as Dewey Decimal or Library of Congress should be applied to maps and that subject headings of interest to geographers should also be assigned. Geographic subjects should usually be subordinate to larger subjects such as commerce or history. Boggs advocated a now familiar arrangement: geographic resources should be arranged by area first. However, he placed subject and author or publisher ahead of date for subordinate arrangements. Boggs recommended this treatment for all materials with geographic subject matter–books, articles, and maps. Boggs also proposed a subject system that he believed to be simpler than Dewey or Library of Congress.[38]

In 1945 Boggs published, with Dorothy Lewis, *The Classification and Cataloging of Maps and Atlases.* The authors cited the 1941 ALA cataloging rules in this manual. Boggs and Lewis stressed the importance of the date of situation of the map, not merely the date of publication or reprinting.[39] The order of importance for entry was area, subject, date, author, and, lastly, title.[40] The subjects of maps had finally become critical, even though thematic maps had been produced regularly for over a century. Boggs and Lewis stressed all the descriptive elements that their predecessors had, and they specified more detailed notes.

Before 1950 the foundations of current map cataloging practice were laid within the geographic information and the library communities. A tradition of considering the geographic place and the date of the information was established, and maps began to appear in catalogs with increased regularity.

REFERENCES

1. Samuel W. Boggs and Dorothy Lewis, *The Classification and Cataloging of Maps and Atlases* (New York: SLA, 1945), 1.

2. Catherine Delano-Smith and Roger Kain, *English Maps: A History.* (Toronto: University Press, 1999), 242.

3. Herbert George Fordham, *Studies in Carto-Bibliography* (Oxford: Clarendon Press, 1914), v.

4. Raymond Irwin, *The English Library: Sources and History* (London: Allen & Unwin, 1966), 166-167.

5. Delano-Smith, 289.

6. James Westfall Thompson, *The Medieval Library* (New York: Hafner, 1939), 30-31.

7. Ibid., 272.

8. Ibid., 613.

9. R. A. Skelton, *Maps: A Historical Survey of Their Study and Collecting* (Chicago: University of Chicago Press, 1972), 37.

10. Ibid., 38.

11. Ibid., 45.

12. Ibid., 40.

13. Delano-Smith, 241-243.

14. Evelyn Edson, *Mapping Time and Space: How Medieval Mapmakers Viewed Their World* (London: British Library, 1997), 1.

15. Delano-Smith, 243.

16. Edson, viii.

17. Ibid., ix, 1.

18. Ibid., 2-13.

19. Ibid., 133.

20. Delano-Smith, 247.

21. Ibid., 142-146.

22. Ibid., 148-164.

23. Ibid., 149-154.

24. Ibid., 162.

25. A. Sarah Bendall, *Maps, Land, and Society* (Cambridge: University Press, 1992), 177-184.

26. Skelton, 46.

27. James Elliot, *The City in Maps: Urban Planning to 1900* (London: British Library, 1987), 7-9.

28. Skelton, 47-55.

29. Elliot, 67-85.

30. Skelton, 97.

31. Ibid., 103-106.

32. Ibid., 105-106.

33. W. Eames, "The Care of Special Collections," *Library Journal* 22 (Oct. 1897): 51.

34. Thomas Letts, "Notes on the Cataloging of Maps," *Library Journal* 27 (Feb. 1902): 74-76.

35. Fordham, 94-97.

36. Ibid., 98-103.

37. Cambridge University Library, *Rules for the Catalogues of Printed Books, Maps & Music* (Cambridge: University Press, 1927), 53-55.

38. Samuel Whittemore Boggs, "Library Classification and Cataloging of Geographic Material," *Annals of the Association of American Geographers* 27 (1937): 52-54.

39. Boggs and Lewis, 24.

40. Ibid., 20.

Monastic Cataloging and Classification and the Beginnings of "Class B" at The Library of Congress

Lawrence Simpson Guthrie II

SUMMARY. This work explores the influence of medieval monastic libraries on the modern university, the break of monastic libraries from antiquity, and the cataloging and classification methods of medieval times, their influence on today, and their template for later historical eras. *[Article copies available for a fee from The Haworth Document Delivery Service: 1-800-HAWORTH. E-mail address: <getinfo@haworthpressinc.com> Website: <http://www.HaworthPress.com> © 2003 by The Haworth Press, Inc. All rights reserved.]*

KEYWORDS. Monastic cataloging and classification, medieval libraries, Library of Congress classification schedule B

MONASTIC INFLUENCE ON UNIVERSITY LIBRARIES

To have walked in the monastic libraries of the Middle Ages[1] is to have literally walked with saints. The history of these libraries and Catholic Church

---

Lawrence Simpson Guthrie II, BS, MA, MSLS, is Law Librarian, Covington & Burling, Washington, DC (E-mail: lguthrie@cov.com). He was educated by the Benedictines, Augustinians, and Jesuits and dedicates this work to Fr. Royden B. Davis, S.J. (1923-2002).

[Haworth co-indexing entry note]: "Monastic Cataloging and Classification and the Beginnings of 'Class B' at The Library of Congress." Guthrie, Lawrence Simpson, II. Co-published simultaneously in *Cataloging & Classification Quarterly* (The Haworth Information Press, an imprint of The Haworth Press, Inc.) Vol. 35, No. 3/4, 2003, pp. 447-465; and: *Historical Aspects of Cataloging and Classification* (ed: Martin D. Joachim) The Haworth Information Press, an imprint of The Haworth Press, Inc., 2003, pp. 447-465. Single or multiple copies of this article are available for a fee from The Haworth Document Delivery Service [1-800-HAWORTH, 9:00 a.m. - 5:00 p.m. (EST). E-mail address: getinfo@haworthpressinc.com].

history are synonymous. And, in that many of these traditions and library procedures have in some fashion continued, a librarian of today is following in the footsteps of saints. One such saint was Jerome, who made reference to the earliest documented church collection. It is in the basilica of St. Lawrence, known as *chartarium ecclesiae Romanae,* and is documented under the reign of Pope Damascus (A.D. 366-384). This collection anticipated the first official library project of Pope Agapetus (A.D. 535-36): the building of the Library of St. Gregory.[2]

Jumping ahead to the end of the twelfth century and looking at the overall impact of seven centuries (A.D. 500-1200) of monastic libraries on the formation of universities and their libraries, one can conclude that the church and monasticism had substantial influence on the founding of most subsequent Western libraries, including those in universities. Regarding the transition from monastic to university libraries, J. W. Clark noted in his famed Rede Lecture of June 13, 1894:

> The collegiate system was in no sense of the word monastic, indeed it was to a certain extent established to counteract monastic influence; but it is absurd to suppose that the younger communities would borrow nothing from the elder–especially when we reflect that the monastic system had completed at least seven centuries of successful existence before Walter de Merton was moved to found a college (Oxford).[3]

He further notes that many of the founders of colleges at the time were churchmen, if not actually monks, and that there were monastic colleges, for example, at both Oxford and Cambridge. So, monastic cataloging and classification have influenced university cataloging from the beginning, leading up to today's practices, especially classification schemes.

The first Western university was the medical school at Salerno, Italy, in the ninth century; next at Bologna in the late eleventh century and a school of law in the twelfth century; the University of Paris between 1150 and 1170; and Oxford at the end of the twelfth century.[4]

From the monastic perspective, St. Benedict established his "Rule," which required the monks to study; and many of the same requirements were established at the first colleges. "An examination of the statutes affecting the library in the codes imposed upon the colleges of Oxford and Cambridge shows that their provisions were borrowed directly from monastic Customs. The resemblances are too striking to be accidental."[5] And so, too, library practices.

Although the influence of the church on shaping university and library practices may not be so apparent today, such influence was present, for example, in the founding of Harvard College in 1636. Kelly Monroe in her 1998 book,

Finding God at Harvard, notes that the Harvard motto reflects the original dedication of the college: *In Christi Gloriam* ("In the glory of Christ") and later *Veritas Christo et Ecclessiae* ("Truth for Christ and the Church"), now abbreviated on school symbols merely as *Veritas* ("Truth").[6] The dropping of the reference to the authority of Christ and the Church, furthermore, was significant enough for Shaunti Feldhahn to write a novel with this decision at the center of it: *The Veritas Conflict.*[7]

EARLY MONASTIC HISTORY

"Monasticism" (Greek, *monos*: "alone") evolved to refer to men or women living under religious vows in seclusion from the world. Monasticism began on the Nile in Egypt at Tabennisi in the monastery of St. Pachomius (ca. A.D. 290-346), who specified rules for the care of books.[8] These Christian hermits "were men who believed that to let oneself drift along, passively accepting the tenets and values of what they knew as society, was a disaster. The fact that the Emperor was now a Christian and that the 'world' was coming to know the Cross as a sign of temporal power only strengthened their resolve."[9] St. Isidore of Pelusium (d. ca. A.D. 450) wrote extensively about his library, and he had access to the profane authors in Latin and Greek. Other monastic libraries in Egypt included the hellenized Coptic monastery of Athribis in Upper Egypt and St. Epiphanius at Thebes. There were also monasteries in the Nitrian Desert in Libya. Western European monasticism began under Cassiodorus (A.D. 485-580) and Benedict (A.D. 480-543).[10]

The order of St. Benedict, the Benedictines, consisted of independent monasteries united by following the "Rule of St. Benedict." Benedict was born at Nursia in A.D. 480 and died at Monte Cassino in A.D. 543 where he is buried.[11] Although current scholars speculate that the "Regula Benedicti" was an adaptation of the an earlier "Regula Magistri," the "Rule of St. Benedict" remains the most prominent. But of all the written documents that have influenced the preservation of books, the text of the "Rule of St. Benedict" is the most important. Upon this is chiefly based that love of learning distinctive of the great monastic orders. The "Rule" states: "Idleness is an enemy to the soul, and hence at certain times the brethren ought to occupy themselves with manual labour and at others with holy reading . . ." And after specifying the hours to be devoted to reading at various seasons, the "Rule" further lays down:

> During Lent let them apply themselves to reading from morning until the end of the third hour . . . And in these days of Lent let each one receive a book from the library and read it all through in order. These books are to

be given out at the beginning of Lent. Above all let one or two seniors be appointed to go round the monastery at the hours when the brethren are engaged in reading and see that there be no slothful brother giving himself to idleness or to foolish talk and not applying himself to his reading, so that he is thus not only useless to himself but a distraction to others. If such a one be found (which God forbid) let him be corrected once and a second time . . .

In commenting on this passage from the "Rule," the *Catholic Encyclopedia* continues: "[A]nd the Rule adds that if all this be ineffectual, the delinquent is to be chastised in such a way as to strike terror into others. That these principles were fully taken to heart, and bore fruit in the respect shown for books and in the zeal displayed to acquire them, was nowhere more clearly proved than in England."[12]

To a certain extent, most monasteries and convents followed a version of the "Rule of St. Benedict" regarding the care of books. The Cluniacs put books under the charge of the *armarius* (librarian). The Carthusians kept the principle of lending. The Augustinians and the Premonstratensians followed the Cluniacs and Benedictines. The Cistercians caution the librarian about locking the press (bookcase).[13] "The most valuable of the texts copied for Charlemagne in Italy was that of the 'Regula' of St. Benedict done at Monte Cassino, where Benedict's autograph version was kept."[14]

MEDIEVAL LIBRARIES

By the fifteenth century most monasteries dedicated special rooms for books.[15] Libraries as a special separate entities were afterthoughts in older colleges as they had been in monasteries. For example, at Merton College (Oxford), founded in 1264, the library was started in 1377. Also at Oxford, University College was founded in 1280, but the library was established in 1440.[16]

All medieval libraries were essentially public in the later Middle Ages, and monastic libraries sometimes lent books. Houses such as St. Victor in Paris were open to the public on certain days of the week. The Papal Library and those at Urbino and Florence were also public. Oxford and Cambridge lent books.[17] Earlier, however, "[t]he precious manuscripts of a monastic library were secured against unauthorized borrowing or tampering with the threat of excommunication. This extreme measure of library administration was condemned by the reforming Council of Paris (1212)."[18] In another example, Pope Sixtus V (1585-1590) said: "No one shall have the authority to remove or draw out therefrom, or carry away elsewhere the books, manuscripts, and rolls of this Vatican Library–neither the librarian, the custodians, the scribes, nor any others of whatsoever rank or office–except by the hand-written permission of the Supreme Pontiff."[19]

There was little medieval inter-library cooperation except for the great Franciscan union catalog in fourteenth-century England, the *Registrum liborum Angliae*.[20] However, a number of monasteries exchanged their respective catalogs; and the monks of St. Arnulf Cloister in Metz collected catalogs of other cloisters.[21] Inter-library cooperation of another sort, based on the influence of St. Benedict, occurred: "Coming together to be read to also became a necessary and common practice in the lay world of the Middle Ages."[22]

MONASTIC CATALOGING AND CLASSIFICATION

As stated in my previous work, "The medieval monastic libraries broke from the traditional procedures of the libraries of antiquity by following the regulations of religious orders, such as the 'Rule of St. Benedict.' "[23] Karl Christ goes on to say that even the highly developed libraries of antiquity had little influence on medieval libraries because of the total adherence to these monastic rules of behavior.[24] The break may also be attributed to the monastic mission of breaking with contemporary and established culture by fleeing from the influences of the city (Rome) and establishing in seclusion a rule of living they believed more consistent with goodness and the teachings of Christ. St. Benedict, the patriarch of Western monasticism, "was repelled by the licentiousness of Rome and retired, coincidentally for the history of learning, to a cave at Subiaco."[25]

On the taking of inventories and the cataloging of manuscripts, Karl Christ says, "There are no known examples of formal, written rules from the Middle Ages describing how a catalogue of books was to be made. Nothing of this type has survived, either from many of the religious orders or from Charlemagne and his successors; it is possible that none ever existed."[26] So, what we know must be inferred from the few surviving inventory lists, which do not show a consistent arrangement, format, or logic.

Medieval catalogs were more like inventory lists with simple listings of authors and titles, if known. If not, a description of a book's exterior or the opening words of the text might serve to identify it. Multiple volumes on various subjects were often bound as one to save binding costs. Valuable manuscripts were frequently bound into catalogs or into a Bible to protect them from theft. Ownership marks were inscribed on books.[27] Clark calls these " . . . attempts to snatch from oblivion libraries, which though probably according to our ideas insignificant, were centres of culture in the darkest of ages. . . ."[28] These monastic libraries were indeed the stewards of knowledge through these Dark Ages from the end of the Roman Empire to the tenth century.

The number of volumes in medieval collections was small. Medium-sized libraries had a few hundred, and smaller monasteries only a few dozen. By the ninth century larger collections held 300-500 volumes with Bobbio, the largest, holding 700 codices. The tenth century Lorsch catalog lists 590 manuscripts. The twelfth century Cluny Library contained 500-600, not counting liturgical books. The famous monastery collections of Reichenau and St. Gall had 100 codices in A.D. 1100. Even at the end of the Middle Ages, 2000 was an impressive size at the papal library at Avignon and the Sorbonne in Paris.[29]

As mentioned, the break from antiquity coincided with the establishment of Christianity. "A shift of emphasis was introduced from the end of the fourth century, when Christendom was definitely established and organized. In previous times, religion had been neglected altogether, and a certain impartiality could be discerned when authors reviewed the theories of various philosophers. On the contrary, the close of the fourth century saw a change in that the main concern of scholars became the study of theology, and all other fields considered as parts of a preparation for theological knowledge."[30] This theme is crucial and set the tone for all of monastic cataloging and classification throughout the Middle Ages. Each example is a variation of prioritizing theology among the other categories of human knowledge. This also constitutes a basis of the break from antiquity in the Middle Ages. In the organization of the writings of antiquity, religion was not emphasized. From the beginning of the Middle Ages, however, Christian writings became central and of highest priority in organizing Western writings.

Cassiodorus (ca. A.D. 490-ca. 583) was a Roman senator who retired and founded two Christian monasteries on the Benedictine model near Squillace in Calabria. He provided the brothers with profane as well as religious texts.[31] A romanticized painting of the history of Christianity in the Laurentian Library in Florence (assumed to be from A.D. 716) was presumably influenced by Cassiodorus, who followed St. Benedict in founding his monastery at Vivarium. In the painting a book press (bookcase) depicts the following classifications: "OCT Lib. (Octateuch: 5 books of Moses plus Joshua, Judges, and Ruth); HIST. LIB.; SALOMON; EVANG. IIII; ACT. APOSTOL.; REG.; PSALM. LIB.; PROPH.; EPIST. XXI."[32] Although the exact origin of this painting is not known, the presumed influence of Cassiodorus shows primacy and exclusivity of the Biblical classifications.

The library of St. Isidore, Bishop of Seville, was classified. "There were fourteen presses arranged as follows: I. Origen; II. Hilary; III. Ambrose; IV. Augustine; V. Jerome; VI. Chrysostom; VII. Cyprian; VIII. Prudentius;

IX. Avitus, Juvencus, Sedulius; X. Eusebius, Orosius; XI. Gregory; XII. Leander; XIII. Theodosius, Paulus, Gaius; XIV. Cosmas, Damian, Hippocrates, Galen.[33] The order of these classifications likely indicates the importance of the authors to Isidore.

Isidore's classification of philosophy emphasized three categories, the first being physics, which is subdivided into three categories, the first including arithmetic, geometry, music, astronomy, astrology, mechanics, and medicine; the second, dialectic; and the third, rhetoric. The second category is logic and the third ethics. One can see that the cataloging applied to that specific collection of books, but the classification could apply to many collections then and in the future.

One can infer from these early collections that classification is one of the most fundamental of human instincts. With Isidore we observe that the classification of materials is based on the authority of the authors. Authority is an important type of classification used in monastic cataloging. Much as modern U.S. law is based upon authority from the Supreme Court down through the lower courts, these early writings are grouped on the established respect for the authors. Such appeals to previous higher authority follow through the ages. The vanguard of great movements in history, such as the classification of knowledge or the beginnings of the United States of America, all draw strength and guidance from the notion of authority. In these two cases the authority is religious and Biblical. For example, the Liberty Bell appeals to the authority of the Bible with the inscription "Leviticus XXV X" ("Proclaim Liberty").

Boethius (ca. A.D. 480-ca. 525) was a Roman statesman and scholar affectionately called "the last of the Romans." He was accused of trying to re-establish "Roman Liberty" and was imprisoned and executed, possibly as a Christain martyr. During his imprisonment he wrote his work *De consolatione philosophiae (On the consolation of philosophy)*. Further, scholars even until the twelfth century relied entirely on Boethius for their study of the doctrines of Aristotle.[34] In Boethius's classification of knowledge, he introduced the term *quadrivium* to classify philosophy. In his system, philosophy was divided into theoretical and practical. The theoretical included physics, mathematics (quadrivium), and theology with mathematics subdivided into arithmetic, geometry, music, and astronomy. The practical (philosophy) was subdivided into moral science, political science, and economics. Boethius's classification influenced the Benedictines through Cassiodorus, the Augustinians through Hugh of St. Victor, and the Dominicans through Vincent of Beauvais.

These types of classification systems anticipated those of today. The cataloging rules of the Middle Ages were more like a would-be modern catalog of china in a kitchen–i.e., tea cups on second shelf; saucers over refrigerator; etc.

Items are grouped together by classification (tea cups) but are located geographically (on second shelf). Similarly, in the medieval library books were associated with geographic locations. These books were generally grouped together by subject in those locations.

Whereas in the Middle Ages catalogs listed titles and authors and referred patrons to desks or bookcases where the items were located (often chained in place), today the call number system locates books in relation to other books by subject and number. They are geographically independent, but the call numbers establish locations among other books. The medieval classification schemes placed sacred writings and most respected Church Fathers at the top of the classification scheme out of respect for their religious authority. "The order of entries in a typical medieval catalog began with the Bible and portions of the Bible, followed by the writings of the Church Fathers in varying sequence, then medieval theologians, then ancient authors, and finally works on the liberal arts."[35]

EXAMPLES OF MONASTIC CATALOGING AND CLASSIFICATION BY RELIGIOUS ORDER

Augustinians

This treatise discusses the Augustinian order, founded in 1256, along with all inspired by the "Rule" of St. Augustine (A.D. 354-430). Hugh of St. Victor (1096-March 11, 1141) was a philosopher, theologian, and mystical writer who is referred to as *alter Augustinus* because of his expertise with the works of St. Augustine.[36] He joined the Canons Regular of St. Augustine at Hamerleve and arrived at the monastery of St. Victor in Paris in 1115. He developed a classification scheme in his *Didascalicon de studio legendi*, in it he theorized that philosophy and knowledge were the avenue for humans to recover perfection lost at the time of the fall from grace.[37] The *Catholic Encyclopedia* notes that "at the same time he held an erroneous view as to the reviviscence, after a fall, of previously pardoned mortal sins (*De Sacr.*, Bk. II, P. XIV, c. viii)."[38] Hugh divided knowledge into four categories, stating that "[p]hilosophy is divided into theoretical, practical, mechanical, and logical. These four (divisions) comprise all knowledge" (*Didascalicon,* II, ii). Each category was broken down as follows: (1) Theoretical, which contains arithmetic, music, geometry, and astronomy; (2) Practical, which is subdivided into ethics, economics, and politics; (3) Mechanical, which is subdivided into fabric-making, armament, commerce, agriculture, hunting, medicine, and theatrics; and (4) Logic, which includes grammar, dialectic, and rhetoric.[39] He elaborated in detail on these four divisions and also addressed the "problems that still face the classificationists of today. For instance, he realized that one and the same topic may appear in various contexts, and he was therefore faced with the problem of the reoccurrence of such topics under various headings throughout his scheme."[40] At the conclusion of his section on Medicine, Hugh says: "Let no one be disturbed that among the means employed by medicine I count food and drink, which earlier I attributed to hunting. For these belong to both under different aspects. For instance, wine in the grape is the business of agriculture; in the barrel, of the cellarer, and in its consumption, of the doctor. Similarly, the preparing of food belongs to the mill, the slaughter-house, and the kitchen, but the strength given by its consumption, to medicine" (*Didascalicon,* II, xxix). "Hugh's scheme departed from tradition in so far as it provided a new synthesis of knowledge. It thus did not follow Plato's view, which prevailed until the twelfth century, of a three-fold division of philosophy within Hugh's own system of thought."[41] Hugh cataloged each book as associated with a particular desk, e.g., A, B, C (first row); AA, BB, CC (second row); etc.[42] The books also had ownership marks.[43] Once again, the cataloging system associated a book with a particular desk, a specific location (perhaps chained in place) while the classification system could apply to his collection or a collection in the future.

In his history of the Augustinians, Fr. David Gutierrez comments on the extent of Augustinian libraries: "For the libraries, the years between 1357 and 1518 were not years of decline. In the registers of the Generals, in abundant medieval inventories preserved today, and in other reliable references, mention is made of more than 140 Augustinian libraries throughtout Italy, Germany, Belgium, and England . . . also . . . in the major Houses of Spain, Portugal, Poland and Hungary."[44]

The Augustinians also maintained convents such as the one at Cascia where St. Rita (1386-1456) died. Another one at Siena in 1360 listed an inventory in Latin with the following catalog entries: (1) "Imprimis in bancha A sunt isti libri videlicet; (2) Infrascripti sunt libri affixi et cathena (ti) in Bancha B videlicet; (3) Infrascripti sunt libri dicti conventus affixi in bancha C videlicet; and (4) Infrascripti sunt libri affixi super bancha D videlicet."[45] Most of the titles under these categories are religious; and the cataloging system once again gives specific locations on benches.

The kinds of books kept in Augustinian houses in the late Middle Ages included liturgical books kept in the sacristy; books of government (constitutions, capitular definitions) kept by the prior of each house; books recording the religious profession of each member; record books of receipts, expenditures, and debts; record books of the transgressions that the superior had not been able to punish (keeping in mind "love for the man and hatred for the sin");

complete inventories of the goods of each house; and books listing the friars of each community.[46] In addition to the types of books described above, there also exist personal catalogs. One such catalog is that created in Latin by the Augustinian historian and archaeologist Onofrio Panvinio, O.S.A. (1529-1568).[47]

Dominicans

The Dominicans, founded by St. Dominic (1170-1221), who is buried at the cloister of St. Domenica in Bologna, was solemnly approved in 1216. They were the earliest Catholic order to set out rules of study for its members and also followed the "Rule" of St. Augustine in both the convents and monasteries.[48]

Vincent of Beauvais (c.1190-1264) joined the Dominicans in Paris about 1218 and lived all his religious life as a Dominican friar at the monastery at Beauvais. "A man of industry, he undertook a systematic and comprehensive treatment of all branches of human knowledge."[49] His work *Speculum Majus* (*Greater Mirror*) (ca.1259) reflects the world. His *Speculum Doctrinale* catalogs human doctrines or sciences: (1) Scientiae, (2) Ethics, and (3) Mechanical. "Scientiae" is subdivided into language, grammar, and logic (or dialectic), which is further subdivided into rhetoric and poetry. "Ethics" was divided into monastic sciences (general ethics, practical ethics, special problems of ethics), economics, politics, law, and crimes (against God, against one's neighbor, or oneself). The third mirror is "Mechanical," which is subdivided into mechanical arts (fabric-making, architecture, metal work, armament, military, theatrics, navigation and commerce, hunting and agriculture, alchemy) and medicine (practical and theoretical). There are separate categories for (4) Physics or Natural Philosophy; (5) Mathematics, including Metaphysics and (6) Theology.[50] The *Speculum Doctrinale* also contains glossaries of approximately 2,300 grammatical terms.

The Dominicans had a presence at the Sorbonne. The first Paris college was founded in 1180, but the Sorbonne, founded by Robert de Sorbon in 1250, was the best. The Dominicans, like other orders, founded houses at the Sorbonne for their members who were studying in Paris. The main Dominican house was St. Jacques; and older monasteries such as Notre Dame, Ste. Geneviève, St. Victor, St. Germain des Prés, and St. Bernard also invited students.[51]

Peter L. Goodman, acting head librarian and cataloger at the Dominican College Library in Washington, D.C., summarizes the cataloging practices of the Dominican Order in the Middle Ages (1216-1500) as follows: Humbert of Romans, O.P., who was fifth prior-general of the Order from 1254-1263, wrote *Instructiones de officiis Ordinis Praedicatorum*, which contains a chapter on library cataloging as well as other information about organizing and running a proper library. Humbert stated that a model catalog for an ideal Dominican collection would reflect an earlier age, heavy on theology and philosophy. The library catalog, such as it was, consisted mainly of a simple list of titles and locations. Some inventories were more extensive and included precise information on each title, opening words of the second folio, and other notations of value. There was a wide variety of practice depending on the needs of the institution. For example, we have lists from English Dominican houses which present information about books and their location.[52] One list contains this entry: "Thomae summa contra gentiles. [7m armarium]." Later lists in the period (1400-1500) give more detail, e.g., "Thomae summa contra gentiles 7m armarium fol. Scriptum de Frater Dominicus de Langley." This citation provides the same information plus the author and the size of the item.

Dominican monks arranged their libraries according to standard medieval practice, classifying their books according to fields of interest and and the intellectual traditions of the order. The basic fields of study included: Scripture and biblical exegesis, speculative theology, philosophy, patristics, jurisprudence, moral theology, homiletics, history, hagiography, and rhetoric. The friars used presses (shelves), which held an average of ten books. Chaining, entitling, and pressmarks were also used to aid in the location and security of the collection. Humbert stated in his *Instructiones* that it was the librarian's duty to create and maintain a catalog. Provincial chapters (meetings of the order) in Italy and France during the thirteenth and fourteenth centuries also charged the brothers with keeping inventories of the collections and providing the books with ownership marks.

Medieval inventories survive from the fourteenth to sixteenth centuries, mainly from Italian houses based in Lucca, Venice, Milan, and Rome although Fr. Martin Purlwasser also wrote out an inventory for the Viennese Dominicans in 1513. These were simple lists. In a number of cases cited in Hinnebusch,[53] the catalogs or inventories also served as circulation lists, letting brothers know which brother had which book.[54]

Jesuits

The Jesuit Order was founded in 1540 by Ignatius Loyola upon the approval of Pope Paul III. According to Fr. Joseph N. Tylenda, S.J., Director of the Woodstock Theological Center at Georgetown University, there is no set Jesuit classification scheme. The systems in Jesuit libraries in Europe are all homemade, that is, the creation of the individual who was the first librarian. Fr. Tylenda states that he has worked in various European Jesuit libraries and found that each one had its own system. As for Jesuit libraries in the United

States, depending on the time when they came into existence, some follow the Dewey system and others LC. "We at the Woodstock Library follow the Dewey system; however, the 200 section (Bible and theology) had been expanded and enhanced to meet the needs of Catholic theology. This expansion was done by one of the Woodstock librarians and has not been published. The Dewey system was sufficient to take care of Protestant theology, but inadequate for Catholic and that of the Oriental Churches. Hence you will find no set cataloging practices of the Jesuits from the beginning of the 1500s. Rather you will come upon great diversity."[55]

In the post-medieval period, the Jesuits continued individualized classification schemes in their libraries. For example, the library of the Jesuits at Rheims, which was constructed in 1678 and served as such until 1764 when the order was expelled from France,[56] was arranged in the following categories: (1) Miscellanei, (2) Historia Sacra, (3) Philologi, (4) Oratores Sacri, (5) Philologi, (6) Historia Profana, (7) Grammatici, (8) Poetae, (9) Oratores Profani, (10) Ius Utrumque, (11) Mathematici, (12) Philosophia Nova, (13) Philosophia Antiqua, (14) Ascetici, (15) Theologi Morales, (16) Theologi Controversistae, (17) Deus Scientiarum Dominus est 1 Reg.c.9, (18) Theologi Scholasti, (19) Ascetici, (20) Patres Latini, (21) Patres Graeci, (22) Scriptura et Interpretes.[57] Fr. Tylenda also notes that the Jesuit Library in Rome is arranged so that a patron looks up a book by title or author and is referred to a particular shelf for its location, e.g., **A 317**. For instance, there are twenty classes under **Jesuit Biography**. While the Jesuits are not specifically a monastic order, their tremendous influence on learning merits a look at their classification system.

Franciscans

St. Francis of Assisi (1181-1226) founded the Franciscan Order in 1209. The friars were forbidden to own any property, including books of any type, even prayer books. Nor could a brother or sister write books for money. However, within thirty years after Francis's death, the order had decided that the ownership of some books was necessary.[58] The parent house of the Franciscans in Assisi had a large library with a catalog in 1381.[59] This catalog represents the best example of medieval librarianship. Also, as early as 1231, Franciscans Alexander of Hales and Robert Grosseteste were the most famous professors at Paris and Oxford.[60]

Cistercians

At the parent-house of the Cistercians at Citeaux, a catalog of late fifteenth century by Abbot John de Cirey indicates that its 740 books were scattered throughout the house in any bookcase or spare corner. This no doubt caused significant friction among the brothers as they searched every room for specific books while interrupting the occupants of the rooms. This situation clearly shows the necessity of a good cataloging system.

EXAMPLES OF CATALOGING AND CLASSIFICATION IN SPECIFIC LIBRARIES AND TYPES OF LIBRARIES

Abbey of Saint-Pons-de-Thomières

The small Abbey of Saint-Pons de Thomières, founded by Raymond, Count of Toulouse, in 936, and run by the monks of St. Géraud d'Aurillac, in 1276 had a catalog of 300 volumes arranged in fifteen classes: (1) De textu Biblie, (2) De Gregorio, (3) De libris Augustini, (4) De libris Hieronimi, (5) De libris Isidori, (6) De libris beati Bernardi, (7) De collationibus abbatum, (8) Item sunt XXXVIII volumina in catenis minimus qui non sunt magni valoris, (9) De libris accomodatis, (10) De libris artis grammatice, (11) De libris logice artis, (12) De libris rhetorice artis, (13) De libris astronomie, (14) De libris medicine artis, (15) Sequitur de libris ecclesie in qua invenies . . .[61] Of particular interest in this classification is the listing of Gregory before Augustine showing the respect for the former in contrast to most medieval catalogs that list Augustine first among Church Fathers. This arrangement shows authority as a classification.

Vatican Library

The catalog of the Vatican Library from 14 September 1481, under Pope Sixtus IV (1471-1484), identifies the location of the library's books, each chained in place. The catalog divides the library's 3,499 books into four categories: (I) Latin library (Bibles and commentaries), Hieronymus, Augustinus, Ambrosius, Gregorius, Ioannes Chrysostomus, Thomas, In theologia, In divino officio, Ius canonicum, Ius civile, Philosophi, Astrologi, In medicina, Poetae, Oratores, Historici, Grammatici. (II) Greek Library (subdivided). (III) Inner library, subdivived into (A) *Banchi* (benches), (B) *Armarium* (press), (C) *Capsae* (chests), and (D) *Spalera* (settle). (IV) Bibliotheca Pontificia, subdivided into (A) *Banchi* and (B) *Spalera*. The classification is by location in a room, and the catalog refers the patron to the shelf area where the book is located. Although the Vatican Library is not a monastic library, its prominence as the Pope's own library merits consideration of the classification scheme.

Cathedral Libraries

Another category of libraries was the libraries associated with cathedrals rather than monasteries; while usually not monastic, cathedral libraries were important during the Middle Ages. For example, Richard de Fournival (ca. 1190-1260) was chancellor of Amiens Cathedral from 1246 and among the group of scholars at the Sorbonne in Paris. In his document *Biblionomia,* he outlined several subject areas. He offered three divisions: (1) Philosophy, subdivided grammar, dialectic, rhetoric; geometry, arithmetic, music, astronomy; physics, metaphysics, ethics, poetics; (2) Lucrative sciences, comprised of medicine and law (civil and canon); (3) Theology. He associated call numbers of sorts (e.g., AA, BB, CC) with the location of books at particular tables, and the books were generally arranged geographically by subjects.[62] This system of call numbers developed a labeling method using letters in various forms–capital, uncial, miniscule, angular script, and rounded script in addition to varying the colors to identify subject areas: blue, violet, red, and green for philosophy; silver for the lucrative arts; and gold for theology. His classification also was unique for its time, and he inscribed on each book a call letter identifying its reading desk location.[63]

University Libraries

King's Hall (later part of Trinity College at Cambridge University)[64] in 1394 held only 87 volumes and had 122 volumes in 1424 (chained and lent). They were classified as: general theology (54), scholastic theology (*theologica disputata*) (15), moral philosophy (5), natural philosophy (12), medicine (*medicinalis philosophia*) (5), logic (1), poetry (0), *libri sophisticales* (1), grammar (6), history (*libri cronicales*) (0), and canon law (23) for a total of 122.[65] This classification scheme is consistent with other medieval schemes that list sacred works before leading to more secular studies.

THE END OF THE MIDDLE AGES

The fifteenth century was a great era for monastic libraries in Europe as well as for libraries in cathedrals, universities, and secular institutions. Christ, for example, lists over eighty medieval library catalogs in the index to *The Handbook of Medieval Library History.*[66] However, there had been setbacks along the way. The ninth and tenth century Viking attacks had destroyed the monastic libraries of Ireland. None of the thirty *libri Scottice scripti* (books in Scottish script) of St. Gall can be identified with certainty, and more old Irish manuscripts are on the continent than in Ireland, saved by fleeing monks.[67]

Between 1536 and 1539, the monastic system had been largely destroyed. In France the Huguenots were responsible for the destruction of monasteries, churches, and their libraries.[68] In England King Henry VIII (1491-1547), denied an annulment by Pope Clement VII, summoned the Reformation Parliament in 1529 and broke from Rome through law, not social outcry. By 1536 every ecclesiastical and government official was required to approve in public the break from Rome and take an oath of loyalty. Thomas Cranmer, Archbishop of Canterbury, was in charge of the dissolution of the monasteries. The holdings of approximately 800 monastic libraries were destroyed, from the 2,000 volumes of Christ Church at Canterbury to small libraries with only a few volumes. By 1540 the only libraries remaining were those of Cambridge and Oxford and the cathedrals of the old foundations. "So the monastic libraries perished, save a few hundred manuscripts which have survived to give us an imperfect notion of what the rest were like."[69] In *English Medieval Books: The Reading Abbey Collections from Foundation to Dispersal*, Alan Coates traces the fate of some of these manuscripts.[70] And yet much has survived. The monastic libraries effectively preserved and delivered the Western world of learning from the Dark Ages to the next guardians of learning: the universities and the printing press invented by Johannes Gutenberg in 1452.

INFLUENCE OF MEDIEVAL CLASSIFICATION SCHEMES

That the classification schemes of the monastic libraries were influential on modern schemes can be seen in the Library of Congress classification scheme, which uses twenty-one of the twenty-six letters to represent subject areas. Philosophy and religion are classified in **B**, near the top of the listings, in rank comparable to the earliest monastic classification schemes, which placed holy writings and the Church Fathers first. The 1812 Library of Congress system placed sacred history and ecclesiastical history as the top two of eighteen classes. The 1903 LC classification scheme placed religion and theology in A3001-B.[71] The current LC scheme places philosophy and theology near the top (after general works) of the alphabetical classes, no doubt harkening back to the schemes of the monastic libraries and thus forming the basis of Class **B** of the Library of Congress System.

The fascinating aspect of the monastic classification schemes is not necessarily that books were cataloged primarily for geographic locations but rather for the subject classifications. Even though individual monastic libraries early on held only enough books to fill perhaps six modern bookshelves, monks, such as the Dominican Vincent de Bouvais, undertook the ambitious task of a comprehensive classification of all human knowledge for all times, which to a large extent could apply today. It is hard to imagine what he would think of his system applied to the almost 50,000,000 items in the OCLC database in May 2002 and to the millions of current and developing Web sites, among which are such sites as the Hill Monastic Manuscript Library[72] and the Pontifical Institute of Medieval Studies.[73] Their basic ideas also apply to today's establishing of taxonomies of Web sites, that is, a hierarchial classification scheme of content. "When the definition is applied to digital content, it usually includes software that uses auto-catagorization algorithms to find, screen, and classify information. The approach often involves sample documents categorized manually and then used to train a taxonomy system to classify other information automatically."[74] So, the monastic classification schemes are still having an influence on taxonomies for the Web as we transition more fully to the electronic medium.

Another interesting paradox is that the driving force behind the first monastery was similar to that of the founding of America. St. Benedict retired from what he saw as the evil in Rome to establish in seclusion a shining example of the Christain life. Similarly, John Winthrop and the Pilgrims in 1588 sought to expand the British Empire and Christainity and to preserve themselves from the corruption of an evil world by sailing to America. In his mid-voyage sermon, "A Model of Christain Charity," Winthrop likened America to a "city on a hill" from Matthew 5:14[75] to be a shining example for the world.[76] One can envision the medieval monastery on a hill, windows aglow like a Thomas Kinkade painting, and monks inside reading and writing and imagining a world of learning for the ages.

NOTES

1. The Library of Congress dates the Middle Ages from 600 to 1500.

2. *The Catholic Encyclopedia* online, s.v. "Libraries." Available on the WWW at http://www.newadvent.org/cathen/.

3. John Willis Clark, *Libraries in the Medieval and Renaissance Periods* (Chicago: Argonaut, 1968), 32.

4. *New Encyclopaedia Britannica*, Vol. 12 Micropaeda (Chicago: Encyclopaedia Britannica, 1998), 165.

5. Clark, 33.

6. Kelly Monroe, ed., *Finding God at Harvard: Spiritual Journeys of Christian Thinkers* (Grand Rapids, Mich.: Zondervan Pub. House, 1996).

7. Shaunti Feldhahn, *The Veritas Conflict: A Novel of Spiritual Warfare* (Sisters, Ore.: Multnomah Publishers, 2001).

8. *Encyclopedia of Library and Information Science*, s.v. "Monastic libraries."

9. Thomas Merton, *The Wisdom of the Desert* (Boston: Shambhala, 1994), 2.

10. *Encyclopedia of Library and Information Science,* s.v. "Monastic libraries." The College of St. Benedict, St. John's University, has a good online outline of monastic history. [cited 26 April 2002]; available at http://www.csbsju.edu/library/internet/theomons.html.

11. Benedict was followed by Cassiodorus, who adhered to Benedict's pattern in founding monasteries; and by St Isidore, Bishop of Seville (ca. A.D. 560-636), who called himself "Protector of Monks."

12. *The Catholic Encyclopedia* online, s.v. "Libraries."

13. John Willis Clark, *The Care of Books: An Essay on the Development of Libraries and Their Fittings from the Earliest Times to the End of the Eighteenth Century* (Cambridge: University Press, 1901), 73. A note about book presses: The book press (*armarium*) was a piece of furniture that would hold rolls (*volumina*) as well as books (codices). It eventually became a bookcase. This evolved from the book box or *capsa* that was a rounded container to hold Roman rolls. These were under the care of the librarian (*armarius*). Cf. Clark, 37.

14. Karl Christ, *The Handbook of Medieval Library History* (Metuchen, N.J.: Scarecrow Press, 1984), 125.

15. Clark, *Care of Books,* 106.

16. Ibid., 143.

17. Ibid., 240.

18. *Encyclopedia of Library and Information Science,* s.v. "Catholic libraries and collections."

19. Ibid.

20. Ibid.

21. Christ, 43.

22. Albrecht Classen, ed., *The Book and the Magic of Reading in the Middle Ages* (New York: Garland,1999), xiii.

23. Lawrence Simpson Guthrie II, "An Overview of Medieval Library Cataloging," *Cataloging & Classificatiion Quarterly* 15, no. 3 (1992): 93.

24. Christ, 16.

25. *Encyclopedia of Library and Information Science,* s.v. "Monastic libraries."

26. Christ, 35.

27. Ibid., 36, 40.

28. Clark, *Care of books,* 45.

29. Christ, 14.

30. Alain Besson, *Medieval Classification and Cataloguing: Classification Practices and Cataloguing Methods in France from the 12th to 15th Centuries* (Biggleswade, Beds.: Clover Publications, 1980), 5-6 (quoting Picavet 31-41).

31. *Encyclopedia of Library and Information Science,* s.v. "Monastic libraries."

32. Clark, *Care of books,* 41.

33. Ibid., 45.

34. *The Catholic Encyclopedia* online, s.v. "Boethius, Anicius Manlius Severinus."

35. Christ, 39.

36. *The Catholic Encyclopedia* online, s.v. "Hugh of St. Victor."

37. Besson, 9-10.

38. *The Catholic Encyclopedia* online, s.v. "Hugh of St. Victor."

39. Besson, 10.

40. Ibid., 16.

41. Ibid., 16-17.

42. Clark, *Care of books,* 166-167.

43. Christ, 40.

44. David Gutierrez, O.S.A., *History of the Order of St. Augustine,* vol. 1, pt. 2, *The Augustinians in the Middle Ages, 1357-1517* (Villanova, Pa.: Augustinian Historical Institute, Villanova University, 1983), 142-143. I thank Fr. Karl A. Gersbach, O.S.A., Director of the Augustinian Historical Institute at Villanova University for providing me with this citation.

45. David Gutierrez, O.S.A., "De Antiquis Ordinis Eremitarum Sancti Augustini Bibliothecis," *Analecta Augustiniana* 23 (1954): 301-310.

46. Gutierrez, *History,* vol. 1, pt. 2, 146.

47. Balbino Rano Gundin, "Las mas antiguas reglas conocidas de los Agustinos/as seculares," *Analecta Augustiniana* 52 (1989): 51-76.

48. Christ, 22, 260.

49. *The Catholic Encyclopedia* online, s.v. "Vincent of Beauvais."

50. Besson, 21-22.

51. Christ, 241, 243.

52. K. W. Humphreys, ed., *The Friars Libraries* (London: British Library in Association with the British Academy, 1990), 195-206.

53. William A. Hinnebusch, O.P., *History of the Dominican Order,* vol. 2, *The Intellectual and Cultural Life to 1500* (New York: Alba House, 1973), 214-215.

54. Summary of comments from Goodman in an e-mail communication of March 17, 2002.

55. Fr. Joseph N. Tylenda, e-mail interview with author, February 5, 2002.

56. Clark, *Care of books,* 287.

57. *Encyclopedia of Library and Information Science,* s.v. "Monastic libraries." Also Clark, *Care of books,* 288.

58. Clark, *Care of books,* 72.

59. Ibid., 73.

60. Christ, 257-258.

61. Besson, 49.

62. Besson, 26-27.

63. Christ, 298.

64. For background on the history of Cambridge University after suppression of Dominican, Franciscan, and Benedictine monasteries by Henry VIII, see "A Brief History: The 'New' University of the Sixteenth Century" at the University of Cambridge Web site [cited 29 April 2002]; available at http://www.cam.ac.uk/cambuniv/pubs/history/16c.html.

65. Clark, *Care of books,* 144.

66. Christ, 481.

67. Ibid., 95.

68. Clark, *Care of books,* 245.

69. Ibid., 246.

70. Alan Coates, *English Medieval Books: The Reading Abbey Collections from Foundation to Dispersal* (Oxford: Clarendon Press, 1999).

71. Lois Mai Chan, *Imroth's Guide to the Library of Congress Classification,* 3rd ed. (Littleton, Colo.: Libraries Unlimited, 1980), 16, 23.

72. "Hill Monastic Manuscript Library," [cited 18 May 2002]; available at http://hmml.org/Default.htm; Internet.

73. "Pontifical Institute of Mediaeval Studies," [cited 18 May 2002]; available at http://www.pims.ca/; Internet.

74. Thomas Pack, "Taxonomy's Role in Content Management," *Econtent* (Mar. 2002): 26.

75. Matt. 5:14: "Ye are the light of the world. A city that is set on a hill cannot be hidden."

76. "John Winthrop–An American Nehemiah," [cited 18 May 2002]; available at http://www.gospelcom.net/chi/GLIMPSEF?Glimpses/glmps022.shtml; Internet.

Classifying and Cataloguing Music
in American Libraries:
A Historical Overview

Carol June Bradley

SUMMARY. This paper presents an account of the development of music classifications, cataloguing codes, and subject heading lists in the United States. It also discusses pertinent activities within the Music Library Association, particularly the efforts of Eva Judd O'Meara, music librarian at Yale University from 1924 to 1952. *[Article copies available for a fee from The Haworth Document Delivery Service: 1-800-HAWORTH. E-mail address: <getinfo@haworthpressinc.com> Website: <http://www.HaworthPress.com> © 2003 by The Haworth Press, Inc. All rights reserved.]*

KEYWORDS. Music cataloguing, music classification, music subject headings, cataloging of records, music librarianship, Music Library Association, Eva Judd O'Meara

Classifying printed music and books about music was a major issue for American librarians adding such material to their collections. The influential, much-used Dewey Decimal Classification (DDC) was the automatic choice of many; several librarians, however, were dissatisfied with its provisions. First,

Dr. Carol June Bradley, Emerita, was Associate Director, Music Library and Co-Director of the double master's program in music librarianship, State University of New York at Buffalo (E-mail: muscarol@acsu.buffalo.edu).

[Haworth co-indexing entry note]: "Classifying and Cataloguing Music in American Libraries: A Historical Overview." Bradley, Carol June. Co-published simultaneously in *Cataloging & Classification Quarterly* (The Haworth Information Press, an imprint of The Haworth Press, Inc.) Vol. 35, No. 3/4, 2003, pp. 467-481; and: *Historical Aspects of Cataloging and Classification* (ed: Martin D. Joachim) The Haworth Information Press, an imprint of The Haworth Press, Inc., 2003, pp. 467-481. Single or multiple copies of this article are available for a fee from The Haworth Document Delivery Service [1-800-HAWORTH, 9:00 a.m. - 5:00 p.m. (EST). E-mail address: getinfo@haworthpressinc.com].

only ten numbers–780 to 789–were provided for all music materials. Second, there was no differentiation between printed music and literature about music. Oscar G. T. Sonneck, who developed the Library of Congress' *Class M* found the DDC to be "the work of a gentleman not sufficiently familiar with music. It is incoherent, illogical, and quite a number of musical terms are misused."[1]

Sonneck met Herbert Putnam, Librarian of Congress, early in 1902. Sonneck, who had been using the Library's Newspaper Division, walked into Putnam's office to offer his manuscript, "Bibliography of Early Secular American Music," for publication by the Library.[2] Putnam immediately recognized Sonneck's potential for the Library and offered him the position of Chief of the Music Division. Raised and educated in Europe, Sonneck had the skills to develop the Library's "collection on the scholarly side, and to assure a scholarly conduct of it."[3] Sonneck's first assignment was the development of a classification for music materials. Already collected at the Library were documents detailing the classifications of the Brooklyn Public Library, the Boston Public Library, the Peabody Institute, the Lenox Branch of the New York Public Library (NYPL), the Newberry Library,[4] Harvard University,[5] the Dewey *Decimal Classification*,[6] and C. A. Cutter's classification in use at the Forbes Library.[7]

Before reporting for work at the Library of Congress in October of 1902, Sonneck spent two months revisiting European libraries to study their classifications.[8] On 31 October Sonneck presented his report on "the classification of music and of literature on music . . . ," a significant review of extant classifications. He critiqued several of the schemes listed above. As noted, he dismissed the DDC. Of the NYPL system he wrote: "Neither the classification nor the notation contains much to recommend it."[9] He identified three chief peculiarities of the Harvard classification.[10] First, most books were arranged in subdivisions by accession number

> with no attempt at alphabetical order. Second, nevertheless, "important and growing divisions are given alphabetical numbering by the use of 26 running figures." That is to say, there is practically a return in the smaller sections to the discarded practice of the [Dewey] D. C. . . . . The third characteristic is that all the scores of individual composers are arranged in one alphabet of composers and are not put in classes according to their musical form. . . . Harvard puts individual biography and criticism with each composer's musical works.[11]

That is, the Harvard plan intershelved biography and criticism with the scores, "an attractive idea" with the "practical inconveniences" of combining large, deep musical editions with small books. Cutter had tried such a scheme at the

Forbes Library for three years but "the longer we tried it the less we liked it." That experimentation had also revealed "the majority do not want a piece of music at the same time with the life of its composer."[12]

The Newberry plan classed scores by musical form or medium, similarly to publishers' catalogues. Biography and criticism were shelved as books; thematic catalogues were classed with composers' collected works (*Gesamtausgaben*). Classes were arranged alphabetically by genre, medium, and instruments without regard to "relative importance, family, and musical logic. It goes without saying that this arrangement, not being elastic and expansive, will occasionally disclose similar disadvantages as a fixed shelf notation."[13] There is no evaluation of the other American schemes.

Among European libraries he noticed

> very little attention has been paid . . . to the problem of music classification . . . The system adopted by the Königliche Bibliothek in Berlin is, as far as completed, the most scientific, logical, and practical of which I know. However . . . I have not considered it advisable to literally adopt [it]. [*L. 4*]

The problem lay in the nature of LC's collection:

> Whereas the music collections in the Harvard, Newberry, Boston Public, New York public and other libraries are enlarged by the purchase of what is generally considered desirable music, the Library of Congress is obliged by the copyright laws to embody within its collection not alone the desirable music but also the undesirable. This latter constitutes at least nine tenths of the entire musical output, and is written largely in forms, for instruments, and instrumental combinations to which the above mentioned institutions need pay no attention. It follows that a musical classification, if suitable for the Library of Congress, will essentially differ from the systems elsewhere in use. It is bound to more minute, expansive, complicated. It will resemble the systematic catalogues of those who publish undesirable music. . . . Certainly, if classification is to count for anything it will not be based upon the composer arrangement as main principle, for this would mean to our Music Division the indiscriminate interweaving of desirable and undesirable matter. [*L. 5*]

Sonneck concluded his classification should be

> peculiar to the needs and nature of the Library of Congress. . . . Experienced criticism and a trial only will show if it deserves to be introduced

permanently, where important alterations will have to be made, and where it is to be broadened or condensed. [*L.* 7]

Sonneck appended a typewritten "Classification of Literature on Music" with handwritten class numbers and a typewritten "Classification of Music," also with handwritten class numbers. He imitated Berlin's "running-leaping numbers," that is, a numerical sequence with gaps of unassigned, skipped numbers for future use. Putnam referred the proposal to Charles Martel of the Catalogue Division. Martel critiqued the proposal in a 12 November 1902 memo to Putnam. He, too, considered the character of the music collection, the relationship of the proposed classification to the other classes in the Library, and some "details of the scheme" by which he meant classing vocal and instrumental methods as literature rather than music. In sum, Martel found Sonneck "has planned his scheme so harmoniously and has worked out the details so well that it impresses itself upon the mind clearly and without effort like a birds [*sic*] eye view" [*L.* 10]. After some negotiations between Sonneck and Martel, Putnam approved the classification 16 December 1902.[14] A little more than a year later the classification was published. A revised, second edition was published in 1917. In that edition Sonneck recommended the classification to other institutions which

> might wish to adopt it with modification as their own needs would suggest. A classifier of fair talent and skill could without much difficulty "telescope" our scheme into a suitable instrument for any collection of any size, by canceling unnecessary subdivisions, by substituting subdivisions needed for his special purposes, and by rearranging at his convenience the sequence of certain entries. [*P.* 6]

Other institutions did indeed adopt the scheme, many reclassifying from Dewey to LC. Sonneck intended to create a version of *Class M* for other libraries that did not have the copyright deposit circumstance nor the special collections unique to LC.[15] He never got to do it; in 1917 he left the Library of Congress to assume new responsibilities at G. Schirmer, a New York City music-publishing firm.

Another classification for printed music is that developed by George Sherman Dickinson of Vassar College. Dickinson was appointed assistant professor of music history and theory at Vassar in 1916. For the next thirty-seven years he provided impetus and direction to the Department of Music.[16] In 1927 Dickinson was appointed music librarian; for his departmental library in the music building he created a classification[17] by which it is possible to construct specific schedules appropriate to the different types of music libraries:

1. Loan and performance libraries where classification is by *actual* medium of the piece in hand.
2. Reference and musicological libraries where classification is by *original* medium of the piece in hand with indication of arranged medium, if appropriate. There are three possible refinements within this option.
3. and 4. General or small libraries where classification may be by *actual* medium but with simplified call numbers or by general class only with further simplified call numbers.[18]

The principal characteristics of the classification parallel some of those sought by Sonneck for the Library of Congress:

1. The separation of original compositions from arrangements.
2. The separation of collections from individual compositions–which Dickinson was able to manage within the *same* classification number by varying the title marks on the third line of the call number in the reference and musicological option.
3. Dickinson was concerned with medium whereas Sonneck was required to note form because of copyright deposits.
4. The separation of general from specific–especially Class 0, Miscellaneous, in the Dickinson classification.
5. A systematic arrangement by instruments and voices similar to that used in publishers' and dealers' catalogues. Dickinson's systematic arrangement progresses from music for a single keyboard instrument through the most grand stage presentations.[19]

The particulars of the Dickinson classification in its musicological option of classification by original medium are detailed in the author's *American Music Librarianship*, pp. 89-98.

As academic music libraries proliferated in the 1950s and 1960s, some adopted the Dickinson classification. Among them are Brooklyn College, Connecticut College, California State University at Hayward, and the State University of New York at both Albany and Buffalo. Earlier, Radcliffe College had adopted the classification in its pre-publication version.[20] When Richard Angell was appointed music librarian at Columbia University in 1935, he constructed a version of the classification that is known as the "Vassar-Columbia" scheme. That scheme and its companion implementation manual were published in 1955.[21]

Essentially, older libraries, which had developed unique classifications in the nineteenth century, continued their local schemes. Many libraries originally using Dewey reclassed all or parts of their collections to the Library of

Congress *Class M*. Some academic libraries, newly created or permitted to reclassify, adopted the Dickinson classification.

Historically, music cataloguing has been an ample and challenging field for the want of rules applicable to the special problems of music and for the want of adequate bibliographies and thematic catalogues for ready identification.[22] Similar to the classification issue, individual libraries worked out local solutions to cataloguing problems. Elizabeth Schmitter, the first music cataloguer (1922 to 1949) of the Sibley Music Library, Eastman School of Music, described the situation: "We were certainly pioneers. . . . We had to find our own way."[23]

In 1904 Sonneck published a set of rules for cataloguing music in the fourth edition of Cutter's *Rules for a Dictionary Catalog*,[24] but they were inadequate. In particular, they did not address the issue of title-page transcription of musical editions. A single symphony could have many different title-page titles because of language variants, for instance: *3te Symphonie (Es dur), Dritte Symphonie, Sinfonia eroica, Symphonie III, Symphonie no. 3, Symphony no. 3, Third Symphony, Troisième Sinfonie*. Librarians in other subject areas were also struggling with title-page transcription. Eva Judd O'Meara of Yale University described the situation:

> Every library met up with the problem. I remember one of the very good cataloguers from University Library coming over and seeing what I had run into: That the same thing might have had a dozen different titles and that the title printed on the title-page might have very little to do with what was in it and what would we do? And so, for us, and the University Library [which] in its catalogue was giving bracketed titles–what we spoke of as bracketed titles–for such things as Shakespeare and Dickens. You know, some of the Dickens titles begin with half a dozen different words: *The Long and painful story of . . . Oliver Twist*, things of that sort. So that we tried to put in, at the beginning [of the card] a title that would bring all the similar things together.[25]

As nearly as recollection could be dated, O'Meara was into the problem and solution of title-page transcription before 1930. O'Meara, who had joined the Cataloging Department of the Yale University Library in January, 1914, was named librarian of the School of Music Library in June of 1924. She recalled, "the more I catalogued [music], the more I found these problems."[26]

An ALA publication, *Pamphlets and Minor Library Material: Clippings, Broadsides, Prints, Pictures, Music, Bookplates, Maps*[27] was published in 1917. The music treatment, only five pages, was superficial; indeed, it was little more than a list of the problems of music in libraries. In 1920 William

Warner Bishop published a "Report of the [ALA] Committee on Catalog Rules: Rules for Cataloging Musical Scores,"[28] in search of comments and criticism of the "provisional" rules.

The breakthrough came in 1927 when the work of a subcommittee of the ALA Committee on Cataloging was published as *The Care and Treatment of Music in a Library*.[29] A cooperative work, the volume represented the current practices of many contributors. Produced in only two years, December 1924 to February 1927, the speed with which the questionnaires and circularized text were treated by participating libraries surely indicates the urgency of the issue. Not restricted to cataloguing issues, it does offer guidance in the formation and use of bracketed titles (pp. 20-23). By its guidelines, the bracketed title for the symphony cited above would be [Symphony no. 3], inserted between the composer statement and the title-page transcription. By this device, all editions of the work would file within a single alphabetical sequence.

In June of 1931 the Music Library Association was formed during the American Library Association meetings at New Haven, Conn. O'Meara and Carleton Sprague Smith of the New York Public Library instigated the MLA meetings.[30] One of the major concerns of the newly affiliated music librarians was improvement in several aspects of music and record cataloguing.

There needed to be a standard code that resolved the problems involved in cataloguing music and records. The Library of Congress should be persuaded to print cards for music. Some method of exchanging the detailed, analytical cataloguing of the composite sets, the *Denkmäler*, had to be worked out.

The lack of standardized cataloguing rules was the most persistent issue. Description adequate to identify a unique musical composition was difficult with extant cataloguing codes. Although bracketed titles[31] had been used in all "the larger libraries for many years, no rules for their formulation [had] been worked out."[32] There needed to be a standard that was "scholarly, adequate and practical." Yet there was the danger that those working only with music would "disregard the established principles and practices of cataloguing" and adopt "practices which would result in cards so irregular that they would not be accepted for general library catalogues."[33] A code for the cataloguing of music . . . was sorely needed and . . . the Music Library Association was the logical group of librarians to prepare it.[34] To that end, W. Oliver Strunk, President of the MLA, appointed O'Meara Chairman of a committee to prepare such a code. Catharine Keyes of the New York Public Library, Harold Spivacke of the Library of Congress, Margaret Mott of the Grosvenor Library in Buffalo, and Richard Angell of Columbia University were the members. O'Meara and Keyes were already involved in the work of the ALA Committee which was revising the 1908 code,[35] O'Meara as chairman of the Music Section. Of immediate question, then, was the relationship of the forthcoming ALA code to that proposed by the MLA. O'Meara suggested "very few rules be included" in the ALA code; its user would be "referred to a proposed special pamphlet on the subject to be issued by the Music Library Association."[36]

Shortly after the 1936 MLA meeting, O'Meara explained the MLA's action and her proposal to Rudolph Gjelsness, Chairman of the ALA Catalog Code Revision Committee:

> A thorough study of the problems of music cataloging is needed. At the present time there is little in the way of an accepted standard; each library has worked out its own way of doing–in many cases with little regard for general cataloguing principles. The lack of uniformity, or consistency, is making co-operative work among the music libraries very hard, and it causes confusion when cards for music are to be filed in union catalogues.
>
> In the desire to bring about a better state of things the Music Library Association is ready to take responsibility for the preparation of a handbook on music cataloguing, to be put out first in tentative form and to be revised after two years or so of use and criticism. With this to supplement the A.L.A. Code, entries for music in the Code could be limited to a few headings: the most necessary, those on which there is some degree of unanimity, and those [where rulings on other subjects] must be extended to cover musical works. Reference could be made from the Code to the fuller treatment in the handbook. The advantage would be that in the handbook topics could be treated at greater length than would be possible in the concise style of the Code. . . .
>
> I hope there is nothing in this that will give the impression that I am setting aside the work of the A.L.A. committee for that of the Music Library Association. I hope the two will work together and bring about a much better result than the code rules alone; and I hope the plan will meet with your approval.[37]

Gjelsness agreed, and O'Meara presented the plan of action to the MLA at the Columbia University meeting on 22 June 1937.

The members of the two committees worked intensely and long; it was not until June 1939 that O'Meara could report to then MLA President Dickinson that the ALA "Committee on Code Revision has given general approval to the rules as we have them."[38] The original plan to split publication between the new ALA code and a preliminary MLA handbook was still valid. The author rules were published in the *A.L.A Catalog Rules* as "Appendix VIII. Music: Entry and Heading" (pp. 354-71).[39] Approval of a bracketed title inserted between the author statement and transcription of the title page was included.

The *Code* was published by the Music Library Association as individual chapters, 1941-42: "Chapter 2, Title," was issued in 1941. "Chapter 3, Imprint," is dated February 1942. "Chapters 4 and 5, Collation and Notes," bear a preface dated 23 November 1942.

In 1946 a Joint Committee[40] of the Music Library Association and the American Library Association was formed to revise the O'Meara committee's MLA *Code* and to write a handbook of music cataloguing. The following year the Library of Congress also appointed a Music Processing Committee to examine the original MLA *Code*, the revision developed by the Joint Committee, and LC's own rules for cataloguing music based on the original MLA *Code*. The reports of the committees, Virginia Cunningham for the joint MLA-ALA Committee and C. Sumner Spalding for the LC Music Processing Committee, were presented at the Chicago MLA meeting on 30 December 1948. At stake were cataloguing rules written and approved by the MLA rather than LC and ALA. Cunningham recalls:

> MLA wanted to revise the MLA *Code* and the expectation was that MLA would go ahead and revise it [with] the hope that then, once it was revised, LC would adopt it as part of the descriptive cataloguing rules that were then in the process of being developed at LC . . . under Lucille Morsch's direction. . . . The big showdown was at a meeting in Chicago. . . . I got up and talked about what the MLA was directed to do and what we had expected to do. Sumner Spalding got up and talked about what LC was planning to do. . . . The question was: What does MLA want to do? Shall we proceed? Should we just turn it all over to LC and go along with what LC wants to do? . . . The decision was that MLA would proceed. But eventually, somehow or other, Lucille was able to take that over so that the MLA never did actually finish a revision of the Code. . . . How much hard feeling there was about it I don't know but I felt very badly that I had somehow let down MLA.[41]

In 1958 the *MLA Code for Cataloging Music and Phonorecords* was actually published. Rather than a revision of its own work as the MLA had originally intended, it was a compilation of chapters[42] drawn from the ALA *Cataloging Rules* (1949) and LC's *Rules for Descriptive Cataloging* (also 1949) accepted by the Joint Committee "in the interest of one cataloging practice for one category of material."[43] That *Code*, in turn, has been superseded by the various editions of the *Anglo-American Cataloging Rules*.[44]

A second lacuna in music cataloguing was printed LC cards for music. Again, O'Meara was in the forefront! She submitted her catalogue copy for the *Denkmäler deutscher Tonkunst, 1. Folge*, to the ALA Cooperative Cataloguing

Committee to be printed by the Library of Congress as part of the cooperative cataloguing project. Her copy was accepted in June of 1934, almost as submitted. The printed cards were an unqualified success; purchasing libraries and the ALA Committee were equally pleased. O'Meara was immediately asked to supply copy for the *Denkmäler deutscher Tonkunst, 2. Folge* and the *Denkmäler der Tonkunst in Österreich* if enough subscriptions could be solicited to justify printing cards.

But the MLA membership also sought less formal, less expensive ways of exchanging catalogue data. (In those Depression years, printed Library of Congress cards were relatively expensive.) At the January 1935 MLA meeting, O'Meara was named chairman of a committee[45] to determine which libraries were analyzing which series so that exchanges could be arranged. She thought the simplest way to share catalogue copy "would be for the library analyzing a serial to make an extra copy of the main card with all subjects, added entries and references traced, and let it be known that these cards would be lent to other libraries or duplicated for them."[46]

Questionnaires revealed that responding libraries preferred printed cards. The reasons mentioned were the "thorough revision," that is, standardization, of the printed cards; centralized rather than cooperative cataloguing; and the economy of purchased cards for libraries with limited reference collections. Eight libraries favored outside cataloguing to that carried on in their own libraries. In 1943 LC expanded its "cataloging program" to print cards for "all types of music" and in 1953 began "the cataloging and printing of cards for sound recordings."[47]

At a meeting of the ALA Cooperative Cataloging Round Table in Richmond, May 1936, both O'Meara[48] and Catharine Keyes[49] read papers that emphasized the need for bracketed titles. Keyes's paper reported her work at the New York Public Library as Chief of the Music Cataloguing Section, Preparation Division, 1934-38. Beginning in 1933, staff of the NYPL Music Division indexed the collected works of the major composers. Those index cards are among the first NYPL printed music cards to include bracketed titles although the Library's *Preparation Division Notes* 3 (1930) describes the procedure for devising such titles for Shakespeare, Bunyan, and "classical authors."[50] The papers convinced the group to allow, "as an experiment," an extra space "directly below the author heading . . . to be used for the insertion of . . . standard titles."[51] In addition,

> O'Meara also addressed the issue of a musical form note in English, even if it repeats information already given . . . in another language. We have here a condition peculiar to works of music. There is a general cataloguing maxim that a title is not to be translated, the person who

cannot read the title cannot read the book, and it is not for him. But a musician might make nothing of title-page or introduction and still be very much concerned with the substance of the volume.[52]

When MLA President Strunk appointed the committee to prepare a code for cataloguing printed music, October 1936, he also named one to prepare a code for cataloguing phonograph records. Philip L. Miller of the New York Public Library's Music Division was chairman, with the members of the committee being Gladys Chamberlain of the NYPL's Music Library and Daisy Fansler of the Free Library of Philadelphia. Several articles addressed the issues of record cataloguing. Harold Spivacke's "The Cataloging of Folk-song Records,"[53] established the principle that the music, *not* the physical record, was the unit to be catalogued. Ethel Louise Lyman published the Smith College record classification scheme in the *Library Journal*.[54] Miller published a subsequent article, also in *Library Journal*, upon which the MLA code was built.[55] Published "as an integral part of the larger 'Code,'" MLA's *Code for Cataloging Phonograph Records* was issued in 1942. It, too, was never revised by the MLA; record cataloguing guidelines were incorporated into the ALA/LC publication described above (n. 42).

Although there has been a consistent effort to make records accessible to their users in such a way that their full potential will be realized, there has been little agreement about how best to accomplish this.[56] Indeed, there are "almost limitless" ways to arrange records. Perhaps the best overview of the situation is the Stevenson article quoted above (n. 55). Prepared from a questionnaire survey of hundreds of libraries, the various arrangement options are identified, their local variations described.

Providing subject access to music materials was no easier than any of the other issues of music in libraries. Extant subject heading lists[57] combined headings for both music and literature about music with general, non-musical headings. A first step, then, was to extract the music headings to create lists specific to printed music and music literature. The lists,[58] extracted from the LC list at Yale University, were duplicated at the Sibley Music Library, Eastman School of Music, for the members of the Music Library Association. The headings, not actually used by LC's Music Division, did not meet the needs of the various types of libraries represented by the MLA membership, many members representing libraries that had created their own local lists.

To achieve some uniformity, MLA President Edward N. Waters appointed a committee in 1942 to prepare a suitable list. Inger M. Christensen, who had drawn up the NYPL list, was named chairman. Her first step was to ask ten libraries,[59] in addition to LC, for copies of their lists. But the task did not lend itself to committee work, so Christensen resigned, convinced the task should be "a job done by one person."[60] It was, by Helen E. Bush at the Library of Congress. In the Introduction to *Music Subject Headings Used on Printed Catalog Cards of the Library of Congress* (Washington: Library of Congress, 1952), David Judson Haykin, Chief of the Subject Cataloging Division, took care to note that "The present list of music subject headings is not in any sense a revision of the two provisional lists published by the Music Library Association in 1935 and 1937 [*sic*; actually 1933 and 1935]. . . . The work of compilation was accomplished by Dr. Helen E. Bush, to whom credit is due for her constant and continuous interest in the list" (pp. III, VI).

But the LC-oriented list did not meet the needs of "special music libraries." The headings for music, which LC did not use in the Music Division, were devised "for general, public libraries."[61] Some academic libraries followed the practice of LC's Music Division by using a public shelflist as their subject approach to music.

The headings for books about music were equally problematical. First, many started "with the words 'Music' or 'Musical'–quite pointless in a special catalog consisting exclusively of books on music."[62] Other problems were terminology that did not satisfy musicological usage; a lack of sufficient subdivisions by historical period, place, type of music, etc.; and a preponderance of headings that were really subheadings for larger subjects.[63] The end result was that music libraries continued their individual lists tailored to local needs.

"Local solution" of the various aspects of music classification and cataloguing may be the appropriate summation of the efforts of America's first music librarians. They met together within the Music Library Association but reached individual resolutions to the problems music presented.

NOTES

1. Oscar G. T. Sonneck, "Report on the Classification of Music and Literature on Music," Oct. 31, 1902, Music Division Files, Library of Congress, Washington, D.C.

2. Details of this encounter are reported in the author's *American Music Librarianship: A Biographical & Historical Study* (Westport, Conn.: Greenwood Press, 1990), 71.

3. Herbert Putnam, "Remarks . . . at the Funeral Services, November 1st, 1928, for O. G. Sonneck," *Musical Quarterly* 15 (1929): 1-2.

4. The Newberry Library was originally classified according to a scheme developed by its first director, William Frederick Poole. That scheme was used only from 1890 to 1895 when the Library converted to "the Cutter Expansive Classification with a specially devised notation." See William Landram Williamson, *William Frederick Poole and the Modern Library Movement* (New York: Columbia University Press, 1963), 168. A précis of the Poole classification is printed on p. 167.

5. Clarence W. Ayer, "Shelf Classification of Music," *Library Journal* 27 (1902): 5-11.

6. Melvil Dewey, *A Classification and Subject Index for Cataloguing and Arranging the Books and Pamphlets of a Library* (Amherst, Mass., 1876).

7. C. A. Cutter, *Expansive Classification* (Boston: C. A. Cutter, 1891-93). [Part I: The First Six Classifications]; (Boston, Northampton, Mass.: C. A. Cutter, 1894?-1914?) [Part II: The Seventh Classification].

8. Sonneck studied eleven libraries: Berlin, Königliche Bibliothek; Bologna, Liceo Musicale; Brussels, Bibliothèque du Conservatoire royal de musique de Bruxelles and Bibliothèque Fétis; Dresden, Königliche Öffentliche Bibliothek; Leipzig, Musikbibliothek Peters; London, British Museum; Munich, Hof- und Staatsbibliothek; Paris, Bibliothèque nationale, and Bibliothèque de L'Opera; Vienna, Hofbibliothek. He collected both their written classification tables and explanatory letters from librarians.

9. Memo to Putnam, Nov. 7th, 1902.

10. Sonneck credited Prof. J. K. Paine with the authorship of the Harvard classification but Ayer, in his "Shelf Classification of Music" cited in n. 5, writes: "Of the systems of music classification that have come especially to my notice, I may claim familiarity from experience with two–that of the Dewey Decimal classification, longest and best known throughout the country, and that of the Harvard College collection which I helped to make–a newcomer of only four years' standing" (p. 5). Contemporary research at Harvard has not yielded additional information about the authorship of the classification.

11. Quotations from Sonneck's memo, which itself quotes C. A. Cutter's *Library Journal* critique of the Harvard scheme: "Shelf Classification of Music," 27 (1902): 68-69.

12. Ibid., 69.

13. Sonneck memo, *L.* 3.

14. For a detailed account of the Sonneck-Martel negotiations, see the author's "The Genesis of American Music Librarianship, 1902-1942" (Ph.D. diss., Florida State University, 1978), 1: 230-34.

15. For instance, compositions which accrue to the Music Division from the various competitions sponsored by the Coolidge Foundation are classed in M29 rather than by medium. (For a brief description of the Coolidge Foundation and its activities, see the author's *American Music Librarianship*, 22-23.) Songs of various wars are classified as special topics under secular vocal music rather than by medium: Civil War songs, for example, are separated into Union (M1639-40) and Confederate (M1641-42).

16. Bradley, *American Music Librarianship*, 84.

17. George Sherman Dickinson, *Classification of Musical Compositions: A Decimal-Symbol System* (Poughkeepsie, N.Y.: Vassar College, 1938). A reprint edition is included in the author's *Dickinson Classification: A Cataloging & Classification Manual for Music* (Carlisle, Pa.: Carlisle Books, 1968).

18. Bradley, *American Music Librarianship*, 88.

19. Ibid.

20. Ibid., 122.

21. Columbia University Music Library, *Manual for the Classification and Cataloging of Music Scores (1955 revision): The "Vassar-Columbia" Classification Scheme Integrated with the Cataloging Procedure Manual of the Columbia University Music Library*; expanded and revised by Virginia G. Haft (New York, 1955).

22. Naomi Edwards Held, "Another Ample Field: Music Cataloging at UCB [University of California at Berkeley]," *Cum Notis Variorum* 83 (June 1984): 29.

23. Elizabeth Schmitter, interview with author, Northampton, Mass., 2 October 1973.

24. "Music," in Charles A. Cutter, *Rules for a Dictionary Catalog*, 4th edition (Washington: Government Printing Office, 1904), 138-40; reprint, *Reader in Music Librarianship*, ed. Carol June Bradley (Washington: Microcard Editions, 1973), 146-47.

25. Eva Judd O'Meara, interview with author, New Haven, Conn., 11 June 1973.

26. Ibid.

27. *Preprint of Manual of Library Economy*, chap. 25 (Chicago: ALA, 1917), 17-21.

28. *ALA Bulletin* 14 (1920): 295-96.

29. Ruth Wallace, Chief of the Cataloging Department of the Indianapolis Public Library, was the editor (Chicago: ALA, 1927).

30. For a detailed account of this historic event, see the author's *American Music Librarianship*, 158-62.

31. "Bracketed titles" are variantly known as conventional, filing, standard, or uniform titles.

32. O'Meara to George Sherman Dickinson, 14 March 1941, O'Meara Papers, MLA Archive, University of Maryland. Hereafter referred to as O'Meara Papers.

33. O'Meara to T. Franklin Currier, 7 December 1935, O'Meara Papers.

34. Unpublished minutes, Music Library Association, New Haven, Conn., 23 and 24 October 1936, O'Meara Papers.

35. *Catalog Rules: Author and Title Entries*, compiled by a Committee of the American Library Association and the [British] Library Association, American ed. (Boston: ALA, 1908).

36. Unpublished minutes, Music Library Association, New Haven, Conn., 23 and 24 October 1936, O'Meara Papers.

37. O'Meara to Rudolf [*sic*] Gjelsness, 23 December 1936, O'Meara Papers.

38. O'Meara to George Sherman Dickinson, 27 June 1939, O'Meara Papers.

39. Chicago: American Library Association, 1941; preliminary American 2nd edition, in 2 parts.

40. Members: Virginia Cunningham, Chairman; Sarah H. Beck, Inger Christensen, Amelia Krieg, Gertrude Oellerich.

41. Virginia Cunningham, interview with author, Chapel Hill, N.C., 14 January 1979.

42. Chapter I is rule 12 of the *ALA Cataloging Rules*; II and III are Chapters 9 and 9a, respectively, of the *LC Rules for Descriptive Cataloging*. Chapters on "Simplified Rules" and "Filing Rules for Conventional Titles" complete the volume.

43. *Notes: Supplement for Members*, no. 14 (March 1951): 9.

44. Portions of this account of the development of cataloguing codes for music are reproduced from the author's *American Music Librarianship*, 113-14, 115, 116, and 162.

45. Members of the committee were Harold Spivacke of the Library of Congress and Margaret Mott of the Grosvenor Library in Buffalo.

46. O'Meara to Harold Spivacke, 18 May 1935, O'Meara Papers.

47. Quotations from John W. Cronin, "Introduction," in U.S. Library of Congress. *Library of Congress Catalog: Music and Phonorecords; A Cumulative List of Works Represented by Library of Congress Printed Cards*, 1953-1957, iii. Two articles describe the beginning of LC cards for records: Lucile M. Morsch, "Printed Cards for

Phonorecords: Cataloging," *Notes* 10 (1952-53): 197-98, and Richard S. Angell, "Printed Cards for Phonorecords: Subject Headings," *Notes* 10 (1952-53): 198-200.

48. "Cooperative Cataloguing of Music," unpublished document, O'Meara Papers.

49. "Use of Standard Titles on Printed Catalog Cards," cited in unpublished document, 9 June 1936, O'Meara Papers.

50. See the author's *American Music Librarianship*, 36-39, for a detailed discussion of the Music Division's conversion to bracketed titles.

51. Unpublished document, 9 June 1936, O'Meara Papers.

52. Ibid.

53. *Notes*, 1st series, no. 5 (November 1937): 9-16.

54. "Arrangement and Care of Phonograph Records," *Library Journal* 62 (1937): 150-54.

55. "Cataloguing and Filing of Phonograph Records," *Library Journal* 62 (1937): 544-46.

56. Gordon Stevenson, "Classification Chaos," *Library Journal* 88 (1963): 3789-94; reprint, *Reader in Music Librarianship*, ed. Carol June Bradley (Washington: Microcard Editions, 1963), 274-78; quote from 274.

57. American Library Association, *List of Subject Headings for Use in Dictionary Catalogs*, 3d. ed. (Chicago: American Library Association, 1911); Minnie E. Sears, *List of Subject Headings for small Libraries*, 3d ed. (New York: H. W. Wilson Co., 1933); U.S. Library of Congress. Catalog Division. *Subject Headings used in the Dictionary Catalogues of the Library of Congress*, 3d ed. (Washington: Government Printing Office, 1928).

58. Music Library Association, *A Provisional List of Subject Headings for Music*. Based on the Library of Congress Classification. Mimeographed for the Music Library Association, 1933. *Subject Headings for the Literature of Music* (From the Library of Congress *Subject Headings Used in the Dictionary Catalogues of the Library of Congress*, 3d ed. and supplements to date). Mimeographed for members of the Music Library Association, 1935.

59. The Carnegie Library of Pittsburgh, the Sibley Music Library, Columbia University, the Boston Public Library, Yale University, the NYPL Music Library at 58th Street, radio station WOR in New York, Minneapolis Public Library, Vasssar College, and the Free Library of Philadelphia.

60. Bradley, *American Music Librarianship*, 176.

61. Harriet Nicewonger, "Subject Approaches in the Music Library at UCB [University of California at Berkeley]," *Cum Notis Variorum* 75 (September 1983): 5.

62. Ibid.

63. Summarized from Nicewonger, "Subject Approaches," 6-7.

Cataloging and Classification of Pacific and Asian Language Materials at the National Library of Australia

Peter Haddad

SUMMARY. From its inception early in the twentieth century, the National Library of Australia has included in its collections materials in the languages of the Pacific region. Following the Second World War, the Library began to collect materials in the languages of East and Southeast Asia. This collection policy presented the Library with a number of choices in the cataloging, classification, and organising of its collections. Early difficulties in controlling materials, many in non-roman scripts, showed the need to be consistent in bibliographic standards and practices. A concern for the needs of specialist readers led the National Library to provide innovative solutions for accessing script materials in the automated environment. *[Article copies available for a fee from The Haworth Document Delivery Service: 1-800-HAWORTH. E-mail address: <getinfo@haworthpressinc.com> Website: <http://www.HaworthPress.com> © 2003 by The Haworth Press, Inc. All rights reserved.]*

KEYWORDS. Asia, bibliographic organization, cataloging standards, Pacific, transliteration

Peter Haddad, BA, Dip. Lib., is Director, Technical Services Branch, National Library of Australia, Canberra, ACT 2600, Australia (E-mail: phaddad@nla.gov.au).

[Haworth co-indexing entry note]: "Cataloging and Classification of Pacific and Asian Language Materials at the National Library of Australia." Haddad, Peter. Co-published simultaneously in *Cataloging & Classification Quarterly* (The Haworth Information Press, an imprint of The Haworth Press, Inc.) Vol. 35, No. 3/4, 2003, pp. 483-489; and: *Historical Aspects of Cataloging and Classification* (ed: Martin D. Joachim) The Haworth Information Press, an imprint of The Haworth Press, Inc., 2003, pp. 483-489. Single or multiple copies of this article are available for a fee from The Haworth Document Delivery Service [1-800-HAWORTH, 9:00 a.m. - 5:00 p.m. (EST). E-mail address: getinfo@haworthpressinc.com].

INTRODUCTION

The primary collecting responsibility of the National Library of Australia is Australian materials in keeping with its role of ensuring that a comprehensive record of Australian history and creative endeavour is collected and preserved for the nation. The Library has built a comprehensive collection of Australian materials deposited under the terms of the *Copyright Act 1912* and the *Copyright Act 1968*. However, it is not possible for even the most narrowly focused national collection to remain untouched or unaffected by the formative influences shaping the nation, the cultural diversity of its society and the geographical location of the country. From the outset, the National Library's collections contained both Australian material and the records of British and European civilisation on which the institutions and customs of the Australia of one hundred years ago was so heavily based.

PACIFIC COLLECTIONS

To build a national collection worthy of the name, the fledgling National Library of Australia relied on the acquisition of large formed collections amassed by bibliophiles and scholars. Two of the National Library of Australia's formative collections of Australiana also included books dealing with New Zealand and the Pacific.

The Petherick Collection, which the National Library acquired in 1909, contained around 1,000 books on New Zealand and Polynesia, including works on the languages and customs of indigenous peoples. Sir John Ferguson's large collection came to the Library progressively between 1937 and 1970 and was particularly rich in religious material from the islands of the Pacific, including many early publications in the languages of the region. The oldest item in the collection in a Pacific language is the 1820 translation by John Davies of the Gospel according to St Matthew in Tahitian: *Te Evanelia Mataio no Iesu Christ to tatou fatu*. A third collection, acquired from Sir Rex Nan Kivell, also added a number of items in Pacific languages and Maori materials from New Zealand.

Geographical proximity to the Pacific and its strategic and economic importance to Australia have ensured that the National Library has continued to give a high priority to collecting material from Oceania. The Library's collections of Papua New Guinean materials are also strong. Australia administered Papua New Guinea until it became an independent nation in 1975, and throughout the colonial period its publications were subject to legal deposit with the National Library of Australia.

ASIAN COLLECTIONS

Prior to the Second World War, the National Library collected little from Asia. Its focus was on Australiana and the literature of Europe. During the war, the rapid Japanese advance through Southeast Asia to the borders of Australia itself and the resulting need for information and intelligence revealed the paucity of Australian library holdings on Asia. After the war, with the former colonial powers withdrawing from the region, Asia assumed a new importance and prominence in Australian consciousness. Harold White, the National Librarian at the time, was quick to sense this and to realise the role the National Library could play in building up its Asian collections. The Chinese, Japanese, Korean, and Thai collections built up during the 1950s became the core languages of the Library's Orientalia Section, established in 1962. They have since grown rapidly with the Chinese and Japanese collections becoming the largest in Australia while the Korean collection is one of the few Korean collections in the region. Reporting to the Library's Bibliographical Services Section, the Orientalia Section functioned as a library within a library, with its own acquisitions procedures, card catalogues, and reading room.

Collecting from Asia was also expanded during these years to encompass Indonesia, the former Dutch East Indies. In 1972 the National Library established an acquisitions office in Jakarta, a move that was instrumental in allowing the Library to build an outstanding Indonesian collection. During the 1970s collecting from a number of other countries of Southeast Asia was expanded. Publications from Burma, Cambodia, Laos, and Vietnam were acquired for the collections and continue to be collected today.

As in the National Library's earliest years, formed collections were used as a way to add depth and richness to the Library's holdings and to acquire older historical publications in addition to the more recent publications representing the bulk of the Asian collection material. In the field of Asian studies, the Library was fortunate to secure a number of significant personal collections belonging to scholars and academics. Among these were the acquisitions of the collection of Walter Percival Yetts, one time Professor of Chinese Art and Archaeology at the University of London, Harold Williams (Japan), Professor Gordon Hannington Luce (Burma), Professor George Coedes (Indo-China), Professor Henry Otley-Beyer (Philippines), Jose Maria Braga (Macau and Hong Kong), and Mrs. Jessie McLaren (Korea). The Library also purchased the Chinese language holdings of the London Missionary Society, which included a number of scarce nineteenth century Chinese imprints.

BIBLIOGRAPHICAL CONTROL

The acquisition of materials from Asia and the Pacific presented the National Library with a number of decisions to be made in the cataloguing, classification, and organising of the collections. Materials in Maori and the Polynesian and Melanesian languages of the Pacific presented fewer problems as they used the Roman alphabet and could be readily incorporated into the Library's card catalogues. Their cataloguing, requiring language expertise in numerous Pacific languages, was more difficult, and for many years the cataloguing was basic, consisting of transcription data from the publication, without subject headings, and a Dewey Decimal Classification number. It was only many years after the acquisition of these materials that a cataloguer with the required language expertise and contacts with academics working in the field of Pacific linguistics completed the task by entering full cataloguing data into the on-line catalogue that had succeeded the card catalogue. Wherever subject headings were found to be lacking for the material in hand, proposals for new Library of Congress subject headings were submitted.

In a similar way, materials from East and Southeast Asia using the roman script were relatively easily accommodated in the Library's general collections. Materials from Indonesia, Malaysia, and Brunei required the services of specialist cataloguers but were catalogued using the same standards used for the general collection of the Library: *Anglo-American Cataloguing Rules, Library of Congress Subject Headings*, and Dewey Decimal Classification. Authority headings, and to a large degree the subject descriptors required by the materials, could be handled perfectly well using the existing standards. Because of the depth of its collections from Southeast Asia, the National Library expanded the geographic area codes for Indonesia, Malaysia, and Papua New Guinea in the early 1980s to be able to code subjects at the provincial level as well as at the national level. Vietnamese language materials presented some problems with the early generation of automated systems. Although using the roman script, the diacritics used, and particularly the practice of using more than one diacritic with a letter, could not always be accurately represented in the output from the systems.

VERNACULAR SCRIPTS

Materials in non-roman scripts, however, presented the National Library with a series of challenges as records for these materials could not readily be integrated into card catalogues using the roman script, nor could the materials be easily interfiled with most of the other resources of the Library. The standards for descriptive and subject cataloguing remained the same (*AACR* and *LCSH*); specialised classification schemes were applied to these materials, such as the Harvard-Yenching classification for Chinese, Japanese, and Korean materials. While the card catalogues in the Orientalia Section contained cards in the Chinese, Japanese, and Korean scripts, romanized headings were constructed and filed in the catalogues. The transliteration schemes used were Wade Giles for Chinese, the modified Hepburn system for Japanese and the McCune-Reischauer system for Korean. American Library Association (ALA) transliteration tables were also used for Burmese, Khmer, Lao, Thai and Tibetan. During the 1980s the Library's Asian collections moved from bibliographic control via card catalogues to control using automated systems. From 1985 romanized records for Asian script materials were made available on automated systems and began to appear in the Library's microfiche catalogue and its online network. Today they continue to appear in the Library's online catalogue as part of the highly integrated approach that has always been taken towards the cataloguing of its collections.

AUTOMATION AND VERNACULAR SCRIPTS

The Library has always regarded the use of romanization as a necessary mechanism for constructing card catalogues and later in building online catalogues, but it has never been seen as an ideal solution. Transliteration is cumbersome and time consuming for the cataloguing staff and is difficult and in some cases impenetrable to the native speaker.

During the 1980s the National Library followed overseas developments in the automation of vernacular scripts with great interest. In 1992 a study revealed that 78 out of 180 Australian libraries surveyed held materials in vernacular scripts, the largest collections being those in Chinese, Japanese, and Korean. An automated system for resources in these languages was envisaged not only to control the National Library's own collections but also with the potential to serve as a national network for all Australian libraries wishing to use it.

THE AUSTRALIAN NATIONAL CJK SYSTEM

In 1995 the Library began planning for a Chinese Japanese Korean System based on the INNOPAC software and which would allow the input and display of vernacular script characters. The National CJK system that was launched in 1996 was a co-operative project involving seven Australian university libraries and the National Library to build a union catalogue of CJK materials and to provide a ready source of copy cataloguing. The aims of the system were to allow libraries to create catalogue and authority data for the CJK materials they held, to include CJK characters in the data, and to share the data. Library users and staff would be able to search for CJK materials using vernacular script in the search terms, and search results would contain vernacular script. The resultant database would provide a union catalogue of Chinese, Japanese, and Korean materials held in Australia. The Australian National CJK system has been very successful in achieving these aims. Use of the CJK system has provided the National Library with the means to allow both cataloguing staff and readers to work in the relevant language and to reduce reliance on romanization.

One of the key features of the system was the provision of parallel databases for Chinese records, one containing Chinese records using the Wade-Giles system and one using pinyin. The parallel databases reflected the romanization situation in Australia at the time. Older libraries generally used the scholarly and widespread Wade-Giles scheme, while newer libraries had generally adopted the pinyin system favoured by the Chinese government. However, the time had arrived for many libraries to move from Wade-Giles to pinyin. For Australian libraries considering the change, the Australian National CJK System project staff developed a migration process using a computer program devised in-house and based on the work of Karl Lo at the University of California, San Diego. This mechanised conversion process was later adopted by the Library of Congress in making a similar change. The CJK system currently operates with twenty-three libraries around Australia and no longer maintains its parallel databases.

FUTURE DIRECTIONS

Bibliographic control of Asian and Pacific language materials within the National Library of Australia has been greatly aided from the beginning by the high degree of adherence to internationally recognised cataloguing and classification standards. While the Library has developed and expanded means of access to its collections, it has preferred to seek these enhancements through the existing bibliographical infrastructure and within the standards framework. This has enabled the widest possible opportunity to share data and has made it possible for the Library to undertake retrospective conversion of its data relatively easily. Today, the Library's catalogue is available via the Internet, and the Library's website at http://www.nla.gov.au contains substantial information about the Library's language collections.

Although Canberra is the capital city of Australia, it has a relatively small population, and it is geographically distant from the major centres of the population. One of the National Library's objectives is to take advantage of the new technologies to open up its collections to people living elsewhere in Australia and, indeed, the world. With the widespread introduction of personal computers and their ability to display fonts in a wide range of scripts, library user expectations are increasing. The ability of the personal computer to display a range of fonts in a range of non-roman scripts creates the expectation that library systems will be similarly sophisticated and efficient. The National Library of Australia's experience with the bibliographical control of its Chinese, Japanese and Korean materials through the CJK system has been a positive one. The Library's remaining large collections in script languages are Thai, Lao, Burmese, and Khmer. It is part of a wider vision of the Library to be able to allow users direct access to these materials, and to integrate the cataloguing records in these vernacular scripts into the national bibliographic database.

BIBLIOGRAPHY

Biskup, Peter; and Henty, Margaret. *Library for the Nation.* Canberra: Australian Academic & Research Libraries, National Library of Australia, 1991.

Burmester, C. A. *National Library of Australia: Guide to the Collections.* Canberra: National Library of Australia, 1974-1982.

Cochrane, Peter, ed. *Remarkable Occurrences: The National Library of Australia's First 100 years 1901-2001.* Canberra: National Library of Australia, 2001.

Groom, Linda. "Converting Wade-Giles Cataloguing to Pinyin: The Development and Implementation of a Conversion Program for the Australian National CJK Service." *Library Resources and Technical Services*, 41, no. 3 (1997): 254-263.

Kenny, Janice. *National Library of Australia: History and Collections.* Canberra: National Library of Australia, 1984.

Description and Access
in Rare Books Cataloging:
A Historical Survey

Beth M. Russell

SUMMARY. Rare book cataloging codes and practices have been shaped by a constant interplay between the tradition of descriptive bibliography and the evolution of library cataloging codes. At the same time, technological changes, such as the emergence of bibliographic databases and online catalogs, have led to promises of increased flexibility and usability in records for rare books. This article will focus on the development of modern Anglo-American rare book cataloging, highlighting special access points that often appear to exist outside the mainstream of library cataloging. By focusing on the treatment of several "hallmarks" of rare book records in codes published during the second half of the twentieth century, the development of rare book cataloging and its relationship to the traditions of bibliography and general library emerge. *[Article copies available for a fee from The Haworth Document Delivery Service: 1-800-HAWORTH. E-mail address: <getinfo@haworthpressinc.com> Website: <http://www.HaworthPress.com> © 2003 by The Haworth Press, Inc. All rights reserved.]*

KEYWORDS. Rare books cataloging, Anglo-American cataloging rules, cataloging history

Beth M. Russell, MA, MLIS, is Head, Special Collections Cataloging, The Ohio State University Libraries, Columbus, OH 43210-1286 (E-mail: bethrussell@osu.edu).

[Haworth co-indexing entry note]: "Description and Access in Rare Books Cataloging: A Historical Survey." Russell, Beth M. Co-published simultaneously in *Cataloging & Classification Quarterly* (The Haworth Information Press, an imprint of The Haworth Press, Inc.) Vol. 35, No. 3/4, 2003, pp. 491-523; and: *Historical Aspects of Cataloging and Classification* (ed: Martin D. Joachim) The Haworth Information Press, an imprint of The Haworth Press, Inc., 2003, pp. 491-523. Single or multiple copies of this article are available for a fee from The Haworth Document Delivery Service [1-800-HAWORTH, 9:00 a.m. - 5:00 p.m. (EST). E-mail address: getinfo@haworthpressinc.com].

491

INTRODUCTION

"Anything written on rare book cataloging just now is bound to be controversial."[1] These words were written, surprisingly, in 1951, a time of stability and tradition compared to the modern library environment. The fact that an expert believed rare book cataloging to be controversial at mid-century underscores the forces that have shaped description and access for rare books through the present day.

This article will explore the development and character of modern rare book cataloging codes and practices, highlighting the constant tension between descriptive bibliography and library cataloging. The focus will be on the modern Anglo-American cataloging tradition, particularly as North American cataloging has developed distinctly from other traditions. Although cataloging codes have focused on descriptive cataloging, discussion of access is warranted in light of the different historical practices which, from the point of view of the uninitiated, often result in a multitude of unfamiliar access points and long, confusing bibliographic records. These differences become particularly significant when considering the relationship between rare book cataloging and special collections cataloging as well as the relationships between rare book cataloging practices and the application of those practices to other formats.

Finally, although theoretically descriptive cataloging codes are distinct from those practices dictated by bibliographic database requirements, practicing catalogers know that creation and editing of records are often based, not on intellectually correct goals of creating records, but on the exigencies of time, money, and the shared environment. Along with other environmental changes in libraries, rare book cataloging practices have accommodated the changing technological landscape, while catalogers have simultaneously attempted to benefit from the possibilities.

Although the history of the development of mainstream Anglo-American cataloging codes is a fascinating story, it will not be recounted here. Readers unfamiliar with the tradition are referred to surveys of the development of *Anglo-American Cataloging Rules* in its many manifestations.[2] In addition, while previous articles have highlighted special aspects of rare book cataloging practices, such as the emergence of electronic indexes corresponding to special files,[3] these valuable surveys have not always examined the intertwined aspects of description and access to rare materials. In addition, the ever-changing nature of library technology means that even the most complete survey is in need of constant revision.

WHAT IS RARE BOOK CATALOGING?

The term "rare book cataloging" is used for many different activities, ranging from full bibliographical description of an item, including quasi-facsimile transcription of the title-page, to the creation of bibliographic records with more than the usual number of notes. In the special collections world today, the term is usually applied to bibliographic records created using a set of descriptive rules specifically for rare books. It has been said, in another context, that "an unfamiliar convention often appears to be more difficult than it really is,"[4] and in this case, rare book cataloging codes, which are often unfamiliar to other librarians, have acquired the reputation of being inherently more difficult to understand and apply.

A helpful analysis of why separate cataloging codes for rare books are needed is provided by Laura Stalker and Jackie Dooley, who propose that there are two purposes for rare book cataloging rules:

1. To enable the precise identification of books on the basis of characteristics that do not relate solely to the works or texts they contain; and
2. To justify and explain access points which allow the user to identify books which possess these intellectual and physical characteristics.[5]

Although these aims do not differ in theory from the purposes of cataloging rules in general, it can be argued that the fundamental difference between mainstream cataloging codes and rare book codes is that "the object of description is essentially different"[6]: a printed book, pamphlet, or single-sheet publication produced either during the handpress period (before 1801 in the Western world) or using the techniques common during that period. This artifactual difference therefore accounts for special practices of description.

Received library history suggests that ancient and early medieval cataloging practices evolved primarily to inventory treasures, rather than to identify intellectual works.[7] Exceptions, such as library finding aids and catalogs of remarkable sophistication, do exist, however, and catalogers (to use the term anachronistically) were able to make intriguing use of the technology at their disposal to provide description of and access to the works in their care.[8]

Nonetheless, the need for elaborate cataloging codes and practices only truly emerged with the explosion of printing and the growth of libraries. Originally inherently local in nature, these practices reflected the priorities of individual libraries and collections. As libraries grew, there were always some "treasure" books of historical significance or high monetary value that may have been described in a different way than the rest of the collection. However, the movement to create standardized cataloging, coupled with the growth of descriptive bibliography as a scholarly endeavor, were necessary for the emergence of true rare book cataloging rules.

HALLMARKS OF RARE BOOK CATALOGING

The province of rare book cataloging has traditionally been the descriptive areas of the bibliographic record, although these often go hand in hand with additional access points, which will be discussed below. Understandably, in the pre-computer library, the goal of providing adequate description was often in tension with the reality of limited card catalog space. While modern library systems make this less of a problem, the time, money, and effort necessary to describe materials must be balanced with the realities of contemporary library administration.

Before the emergence of cooperative cataloging standards, libraries treated rare books in their collections in any number of ways, and even today, codes and practices recognize the need for institutional flexibility. The entire bibliographic record is, in fact, potentially different in rare book cataloging from mainstream cataloging. Nonetheless, four representative elements of departure between rare book codes and general cataloging codes will be highlighted to focus the discussion and exemplify the philosophical differences underlying the codes.

Transcription of Title Page Elements

As title, author, and other information usually found on any book's title page is considered essential to identifying the piece, transcription of this information is not inherently different in purpose. However, the fullness or faithfulness of such transcription forms one of the more easily noticeable differences between rare book and "regular" cataloging records. Especially in early printing, typeface, exact wording of statements (such as the address for printers), line breaks, and other details distinguish among various editions, states, and printings of a title. Abbreviating publishers' names, for example, as is common in mainstream cataloging, can obscure valuable clues as to the identity and creation of the piece in hand. Other common practices, such as transcribing early letter forms in their modern equivalents ("v" to "u," for example) create more comprehensible records, but do not represent the text found in the book in hand.

Although it is often thought that rare book transcription is more time-consuming and difficult because it is more exact, Laura Stalker and Jackie Dooley suggest that faithful transcription provides "an accurate 'picture' of the object *and* is simpler to learn and practice than the transposition and normalization" mandated by mainstream descriptive codes.[9] It is also worth noting that full transcription does not mean "quasi-facsimile transcription," a convention of descriptive bibliography which seeks to reproduce the appearance of the printed title page (as much as possible with modern typographical symbols) complete with capitalization, notation of borders and line endings, etc. The value of this practice is somewhat controversial, even among bibliographers.[10] As we shall see, even though rare book cataloging codes have insisted on faithful transcription of title page elements, what constitutes such transcription has varied considerably.

Format and Collation

Handpress books were assembled using specific formulae related to the manner in which pages were printed. This formula is marked by signatures, "the letters (or, in some modern books, numerals) printed in the tail margin of the first leaf (at least) of each gathering or section of a book, as a guide to the binder in assembling them correctly."[11] Recording both the signatures and the format of the book ("the size of a volume in terms of the number of times the original printed sheet was folded to form its constituent leaves")[12] provides another method of distinguishing among manifestations of a title. Additionally, complicated formulae for recording such practices as removing and replacing leaves allow comparison of the copy in hand to both an "ideal copy" and to other copies known to exist. The system for recording collation is, in theory, rather simple, but becomes necessarily more complex as anomalies such as removal or addition of leaves, unsigned gatherings of leaves, and the like are accounted for in collational statements.

Notes

To many people, one of the most obvious signs of a rare book record is the number and length of notes. Indeed, the means of production of handpress era books, in particular, ensure that more distinctive physical information is available to the cataloger and therefore will be recorded because of its value to users. At the same time, authoritative published descriptions in bibliographies for many geographic areas, time periods, or subjects make it common to record citations to these bibliographies (currently using MARC 510 field). Such notes, in combination with transcription and collation, can provide valuable evidence of the history of a particular book.

Copy-specific information is also more likely to be recorded although these conventions can be used in mainstream cataloging as well. Binding descriptions, provenance ("the pedigree of a book's previous ownership"),[13] inscriptions, or annotations may convey important information in the context of a particular library or collection.

Added Access Points

Although descriptive cataloging codes have, until recently, confined themselves to the physical description of material, much of what is common in rare book cataloging practice also depends on added access points. Historically, rare book libraries often maintained special files tracing donors, types of bindings, or other characteristics that would not be searchable in traditional catalogs but which could be very useful to researchers working with the collection. The continued evolution of the MARC format allows for many of these access points to be indexed, even when the rare book records form part of a larger library catalog. Also, the development of specialized thesauri for providing controlled vocabulary access to terms outside the broader realm of sources such as Library of Congress subject headings allowed the application of these thesaurus terms as tracings within records. This combination of electronic access and standardized vocabulary gives "increased visibility–and perhaps respectability–to many of the features that were important reasons for the material to having been collected in the first place and which special collections librarians have always intuitively known were important bibliographic access points."[14]

These are by no means the only differences between Anglo-American rare book cataloging rules and general cataloging rules developed during the twentieth century. The degree to which they appear in cataloging codes and manuals through the last half of the twentieth century makes them particularly symbolic of the approach of rare book cataloging.

RARE BOOK CATALOGING AND BIBLIOGRAPHY

It could be argued that there could have been no rare book cataloging on a national or international scale had there been no explosion in the field of descriptive bibliography during the late nineteenth and twentieth centuries. As scholars became increasingly interested in researching the physical attributes of books, it became desirable to record more of this information in catalog records. At the same time, bibliographers were developing sophisticated ways of communicating information about the physical structure and appearance of books that crept (and continue to creep) into rare book records. Two representative discussions will illustrate this point.

In his essential essay on the subject, G. Thomas Tanselle argues for cooperation and mutual understanding between bibliographers and catalogers, lamenting that the development of two separate specializations has resulted in more divergence between practices than in their compatibility. Writing in the late 1970s, Tanselle was aware even then of the role computers would play, both in the creation of union catalogs and in the spirit of cooperative cataloging that has since become a reality. He even goes so far as to argue for the emendation of the (then current) *Anglo-American Cataloging Rules* to include "the contributions which descriptive bibliography might make."[15]

Nonetheless, Tanselle maintains the distinction between catalogs and bibliographies and, therefore, between the activities of cataloging and creating bibliographies. He enumerates the now-familiar distinction between a "catalogue," broadly defined as a record of the particular copies of books in a given collection, exhibition, etc., and a "bibliography" which concerns books which are related to each other but not with specific copies of those books. Bibliography, therefore, is concerned with the "ideal copy," which represents "a standard form of the book as published," and is, therefore, inherently an abstraction. This distinction has no relation to the amount of detail included in either a catalog or a bibliography although that difference has sometimes been advanced as well.[16]

Tanselle goes so far as to claim that both catalogs and bibliographies may result from certain types of bibliographic activity (e.g., "reference bibliography" wherein the concern is for works or "physical bibliography" wherein the concern is actual books), depending on the overarching purpose.[17] In the areas of overlap, therefore, it is essential for cataloging and bibliography to be compatible.[18] Indeed, Tanselle enumerates two related approaches in attempts to reconcile at least the terminology used by bibliographers and catalogers: bibliographies "taking up the problems of description for those concerned with the physical book" and librarians writing "about the physical details appropriate for inclusion in the catalogue entries for certain classes of materials." An illuminating survey of the results of these two streams of writing follows.[19]

Rather than suggesting what information can be added to routine catalog records to make it useful for the purposes of physical bibliography, Tanselle instead argues that whichever physical details are presented in any catalog entry be intelligible, or at least not misleading, to the physical bibliographer.[20] "Library cataloguers, for instance, need not employ the full pagination formulae of descriptive bibliography; but their formulae should then be unambiguously focused on the content of the books, so that no one will mistake them for attempts to record physical facts."[21] This recognition that more is not necessarily better is essential to understand the requirements for a good rare book record.

Michael Winship also ties the distinction between bibliography and cataloging to one of purpose–in this case, to how well a catalog fulfills its objects. In terms of assisting the patron in finding or choosing particular books, Winship asserts that "a cataloging record will never reproduce the text in its entirety or satisfy the scholar's needs for the original, nor can it provide access to every possible point of scholarly interest." He would prefer catalogers focus on creating "short, accurate and clear records of a library's entire holdings" instead of "long, elaborated ones that conceal, and to some extent cause, a tremendous backlog."[22] Therefore, the relationship between bibliography and rare book cataloging should not focus on trying to create records that are as long, complicated, or detailed as entries in some bibliographies but rather on producing accurate and comprehensible records so that scholars, researchers, and even casual users can interpret them.

DESCRIPTIVE CATALOGING CODES AND MANUALS

Many general rules about description have remained more or less constant and will be familiar to anyone with knowledge of current cataloging codes and standards; this discussion will highlight rare book specific rules or interpretations rather than summarize entire contents of the codes. Before the 1980s, "various catalogs, handbooks, treatises and cataloging codes that could be used in whole or in part with profit in treating rare books," as well as "general rules in which little or no attention to rare books was given" (such as the American Library Association's rules of 1908, 1941, and 1949) were available, but these were not applicable to most libraries' entire collections, resulting in the proliferation of local practices.[23] Nonetheless, it is worth examining both the specialized literature which fell short of full descriptive codes and the general codes, which paid little attention to rare books in order to understand the development of rare book cataloging practices.

In 1951 Paul Shaner Dunkin's *How to Catalog a Rare Book* appeared, specifically aimed at generalist librarians needing guidance in handling rare materials. This manual provides a very level-headed and practical approach to cataloging, acknowledging the parallel needs to create records that are useful to experts and intelligible to other users. Dunkin also recognizes the realities of time and money constraining the work of the cataloger, even at mid-century. After discussing transcription, notation, and other practices in detail, illustrated with examples from rare books, he finishes his text with a summary of his approach so succinct and deliberate it merits quotation verbatim:

You can catalog almost any rare book adequately if you have an intelligent skepticism. The important thing is not so much what you do to the card as what you do to the book.

You will examine the book as a physical entity, and as you do so you will keep asking three questions: (1) Is everything what it seems or professes to be? (2) What features are significant? (3) Is the book complete?

Then, briefly and clearly, you will tell of every way in which that book may differ from all other editions and issues of that particular title and all other copies of that particular edition and issue. This means that you will give: (1) rather full title noting line endings, rules, and ornaments; (2) collation by gatherings in simple language; (3) collation by pages, the full contents, and sometimes other descriptive notes.[24]

In 1973, a new edition responded directly to the growing influence of descriptive bibliography upon rare book cataloging.[25] In this edition, Dunkin responds to the transcription and collational formulae promulgated by writers such as Fredson Bowers in his *Principles of Bibliographic Description.*[26] Through the middle years of the century, developments in bibliography exercised an increasing influence on rare book cataloging practices. Dunkin argues that bibliographers will have examined all copies of a given book, unlike catalogers, who do not have the luxury of such close examination.[27] The idea that bibliographers and catalogers are doing fundamentally different things in describing books would continue to be echoed by other writers. Dunkin believes a simpler method of handling collational formulae than the system articulated by Bowers is "quite enough"[28] to convey the necessary information.

In discussing title page transcription, Dunkin suggests that catalogers take a "calculated risk," attempting to represent the *content* of the title page rather than taking the time and effort to construct elaborate systems to identify text.[29] This practical recognition of the limits on the cataloger is also used to justify spot-checking of contents in order to identify copies although he acknowledges that "probably there is no such thing as a duplicate of an early book printed on the handpress."[30] Dunkin's work continued to influence rare book cataloging before and after the development of cooperative Anglo-American descriptive codes.

Anglo-American Cataloging Rules (AACR1)[31]

The publication of *Anglo-American Cataloging Rules* in 1967 did not, of course, represent the beginning of a codified approach to creating bibliographic records but rather built on earlier work. The preface acknowledges that

AACR1 (as it is now known) is based on general principles that have been followed as consistently as possible, rather than a code-based set of rules such as earlier publications.[32]

AACR1 description serves two purposes: to make it possible to distinguish one work from another and also one edition of the same work from another. Annotation may be required to explain the nature and scope of the publication and its bibliographical relationships. The elements to be presented in the body of the entry are enumerated: title, author statement, edition statement, imprint, collation, series statement, and (if needed and if they can be stated succinctly) number of volumes, illustration statement, and the statement naming other persons, such as a translator. All other statements on the title page that contribute to the identification of the work should be presented "only if they are grammatically inseparable from other elements presented there, or if separation would require repetition of data in the body of the entry" (*AACR1* 130A-130B). All other information should be presented as notes (*AACR1* 132.A.1). Appendices list guidelines for capitalization, punctuation, and abbreviations.

Regarding the hallmarks of rare books cataloging discussed above, *AACR1* was a forerunner for later cataloging practice in a number of ways. The title proper should be recorded "exactly as to order, wording, spelling, accentuation, and other diacritical marks (if possible), but not necessarily as to punctuation and capitalization" (*AACR1* 133A). "Typographical peculiarities" such as the use of "v" for "u" in nineteenth and twentieth century works are disregarded. Long titles are abridged "if this can be done without loss of essential information." Marks of omission are required. The use of line endings is allowed "only if all other methods of distinguishing two editions or issues of a rare book are inadequate," although there is no specific guidance about what might constitute such a situation. Author statements are transposed in most cases to their required position in the body of the text, according to rule 134B. The recording of numerals is spelled out in Appendix IV: as a rule, Roman numerals should be translated to Arabic, except in "the recording of a title or author statement, in the recording of pagination and references to pages, and in citing quoted matter."

One point of possible confusion in applying *AACR1* to rare books is the edition area. "Edition," so important in library cataloging, is not defined in the glossary and has often been understood in different ways, particularly when the concept is translated across languages. Representing the edition, along with states and printings, may be the essential element of the printing history of the book, and "an edition statement in a work is always included in its catalog entry, the impression or printing only in the case of items having particular bibliographical importance" (*AACR1* 135A). Interestingly, "no attempt is made to describe works in detail sufficient to identify them as issues" (that is, further discriminating than edition) except "in certain cases of rare books."[33]

The "imprint" area shows place of publication, name of the publisher and the date (*AACR1* 138). A discussion outlines which parts of the publisher statement are essential and which are not, although neither is generally applicable to rare book cataloging (*AACR1* 140B-140C).

AACR1 also offers a potentially confusing use of the word collation: "the cataloger's description of the physical work and consists of a statement of the extent of the work in pages, volumes, or volumes and pages, the important illustrative matter, and the size" (*AACR1* 142). The ambiguity between "work" and "book," as exemplified in this statement and others in the code, has not escaped comment.[34] Examples of the pagination statement correspond to modern usage, for the most part; this does not address problems related to the sequences of unnumbered pages frequently found in rare books.[35]

In the note area, a note "to identify the work or edition and distinguish it from others" is considered the first of a list of "indispensable notes" enumerated in rule 144B1. Other type of notes that might be encountered in rare book cataloging, such as notes "to supplement the physical description in the collation" and "to provide bibliographical history of the work" are considered "important but not indispensable notes" (*AACR1* 144C2; 144C4).

Although technically limited to incunabula ("books produced in the infancy of printing," i.e., before 1500 in Western Europe),[36] *AACR1*'s Chapter 8 "Incunabula" provides a model that might logically extend to early printed books in general given the lack of explicit guidance in handling later rare books. The first assumption is that incunabula often lack title pages or traditional "title page information," making it impossible to apply general rules of description. The second is that detailed descriptions of most incunabla have been published in standard reference works. These assumptions justify short-title entry, pointing to a fuller description elsewhere, rather than the detailed description common today. This desire to abbreviate was likely driven by the reality of space limits in card file catalogs.

Rules 180A and 102A guide recording of the title for incunabula. Interestingly, the title preferred is that found in a "competent authority," and only if that is not found should the title found in the work be used. The title printed in the piece itself, if it differs from the conventional form of the title, is to be recorded in a note (*AACR1* 184A). Also, imprint information is to be given in the form used as catalog entry, with the form used in the book itself following "if notably different." Dates, including the "exact date of publication, including day and month" if available, are recorded "according to modern style of chronology" (*AACR1* 182A; 182C). References to printed descriptions are required by rule 184B. They are to be given in a "brief but unmistakable form." Rule

184C allows for "elaboration of collation," including signatures "if the account is not given in a bibliographical source cited." "Peculiarities of the copy in hand" are suggested by rule 184E. Clearly, the catalog record is to be shorthand for the full bibliographical citation; transcription of information takes second place to standardized, intelligible access in catalog entry, and, in some ways, echoes manuscript cataloging practice more than book cataloging.

AACR1 formed the foundation of modern Anglo-American cataloging codes. Some apparent inconsistencies, such as "blind" references to rare books and a specific chapter applicable only to incunabula, must have been frustrating to those attempting to reconcile the cooperative rules with existing traditions of rare book cataloging.

The advent of the computer age in libraries saw the publication of another "non-manual" for cataloging rare books, *The Cataloguing Requirements of the Book Division of a Rare Book Library*.[37] Josiah Bennett modestly begins his work by stating that if a "practical manual to cover all rare book operations could be prepared," he would not be the person to do it, referring "those who would like to see a fine example of rare book principles adapted to specific books and reduced to manual form" to the *AACR1* chapter on incunabula.[38] Despite his deference, however, Bennett did compile a thorough overview of the issues involved in determining practice for rare book cataloging, focusing on university libraries' special collections.

He argues for an even briefer description in the catalog entry than Dunkin: "In almost any field in which reputable bibliographies exist . . . it should be obvious that citation of authorship and location of the reference, with a short identification of the state if called for, and description of the binding, will take care of the great majority of books." The extra time and effort put forth in cataloging will pay for itself in savings down the road, since recataloging or repeated investigation of the book will not be necessary.[39] Bennett's practicality extends to his near revolutionary recommendation that "all wordage not essential to the identification of the work and all wordage duplicated or to be introduced more efficiently elsewhere" be removed from the transcription. This is, of course, to be coupled with references to standard bibliographies for identification. Bennett also argues that there are many instances "in which accurate title-page transcription in detail may be of great importance bibliographically–and in which the library cataloguing form of transcription is of no use whatsoever."[40] His attitude extends to the imprint, where he calls for consulting speakers of unfamiliar languages in order to avoid transcribing unnecessary information; transcription, if preferred, should be "with free use of the ellipsis."[41]

While acknowledging that elaborate collation is rarely necessary, he does state "the reduction of the page collation to the mere recording of the last page number found has absolutely no place in rare book or special collections cataloging." He goes so far as to emphasize the importance: "ALL COLLATIONS OF EVERY TYPE . . . *MUST* REPRESENT WHAT IS ACTUALLY PRESENT, *NOT* THE IDEAL COPY."[42] Despite his disclaimer, the book emerges as a true manual of rare book cataloging, focusing on the brevity of records so important in a card catalog age. Bennett's work does seem to assume, however, that establishing the bibliographic identity of a book is a relatively simple matter, and that the cataloger can easily record such information in an intelligible way.

Anglo-American Cataloguing Rules, Second Edition (AACR2)[43]

A major development in rare book cataloging came with the inclusion in the second edition of *AACR* (published in 1978) of specific rules designed to allow description of early printed monographs, not just incunabula. Rule 2.12 specifies the scope of their application: "books, pamphlets, and broadsides published before 1821 in countries following European conventions in bookmaking." They are designed to supplement rules in Chapters 1 and 2.1-2.11 (the corresponding sections of the "Books, Pamphlets and Printed Sheets" chapter) and are to be used "only when the conditions they state apply to the early book, etc., or when, as in 2.16, they contain instructions different from previous rules." The inclusion of such rules in a mainstream catalog code is so important it merits close scrutiny.

Rule 2.13 provides for a hierarchy of choices to be consulted as the chief source of information when the book has no title page. This is a departure from the general rule (*AACR2* 2.0B1) that states only to use "the part of the item supplying the most complete information." Instructions as to the abridgement of long titles proper found in 2.14B call for the omission of alternative titles, which contradicts later rare book rules. Rule 2.14E covers transcription of early letter forms, calling for a degree of modernization one might expect in a mainstream cataloging code. For example, when the text does not distinguish between "v" and "u," the rule calls for transcription as "u," suggesting this is the most common modern usage. Edition statements are to be transcribed "as . . . found in the item," with the option to use standard abbreviations and Arabic numerals "if an exact transcription is not desired."

Rules governing the publication, etc., area would be familiar to rare book catalogers today. Examples include treating the bookseller, bookseller-printer, or printer as a publisher if appropriate (*AACR2* 2.16A), transcribing the place of publication as found in the item (*AACR2* 2.16B), adding the full address or sign of the publisher, printer, etc., "if it aids in identifying or dating the item" (*AACR2* 2.16A). Rule 2.16H calls for recording the date of publication or printing "including the day and month," although Roman numerals are to be changed to Arabic in recording the year. An option allows for "formalization" of a very long date statement. The format is recorded in abbreviated form after its dimensions (*AACR2* 2.17C).

The identification purpose of rare book cataloging is clearly acknowledged in the section on notes. In addition to the requirements that certain types of notes be made in records for incunabula, rule 2.18A instructs: "If the formalized description of the areas preceding the note area does not clearly identify the edition or issue being catalogued, make all notes necessary for unambiguous identification." Catalogers experienced with rare books might wish it were that easy to provide unambiguous identification. Bibliographic references and signatures/foliation are prominently mentioned (*AACR2* 2.18C-2.18D). Rule 2.18F, corresponding to 2.7B20 for non-rare books, shows a greatly expanded set of examples for copy-specific notes, including imperfections, binding, inscriptions, etc.

The inclusion of special rules, however brief, for early printed materials was an important first step in the development of special rare book rules within the Anglo-American cataloging tradition. The special chapters in *AACR2* designed for other formats attempted to provide a unified approach to describing the growing universe of library materials, and rare books (defined solely by age, in this case) took their appropriate place. Despite the philosophical coherence signaled by this change, these rules would shortly prove to be inadequate.

ISBD(A): International Standard Bibliographic Description for Older Monographic Publications (Antiquarian)[44]

Parallel to the development of Anglo-American cataloging codes was the development of the standards issued under the auspices of the International Federation of Library Associations, *International Standard Bibliographic Description (Monographic Publications)* or *ISBD(M)*. In response to dissatisfaction among those working with rare books with the revised draft *ISBD(M)*, an explicit statement was added in the published version: "*ISBD(M)* is primarily concerned with current publication. It therefore makes no provisions for the special problems of older books."[45] At this time records for older materials tended to exist in separate catalogs, and, in 1973, "there was little demand for machine-processing of records for any but current items."

The growth of large cooperative databases for antiquarian materials, however, led to the realization that electronic manipulation of bibliographic data could be just as useful to those working on handpress era books as to current cataloging. A draft version of *ISBD(A)*, (with the "A" standing for Ancien, Antique, Antiquarian, Alt, etc., conveniently encompassing most European languages) emerged from an IFLA working party in 1975, but at the same time, the entire framework of the ISBD was being revised. The Rare Books and Cataloguing Sections of IFLA therefore established a Working Group to examine the applicability of *ISBD(M)* to description of older books. The Working Group assumed that:

> descriptions of older books are usually formulated for a somewhat different purpose from that guiding the professional skills of those recording current information . . . older books are considered as artifacts to be described in such a way as they can be clearly distinguished for the purpose of comparison with other copies and other editions of the same work. The aim of the rare book librarian here is not only description of an antique, but, more important, the clarification of the transmission of the text and the "points" which distinguish editions.[46]

Without resorting to title-page transcription, ("that is for the literary bibliographers,") "such descriptions should pay close attention to detailed accurate transcription of the two areas of the title and the imprint and give an exact statement of the extent of the work as published." Therefore, it is not a book's age which makes *ISBD(M)* unsatisfactory, but the distinct characteristics of the hand-printed book, which dominated in Western Europe until around 1820. Later publications produced by hand "or by methods continuing the tradition of the hand-produced book" are also within the scope of the rules (*ISBD(A)* 0.1.1). Title, imprint and collation are therefore the three areas in which *ISBD(A)* departs from *ISBD(M)* "in detail, but not in principle." This scope signals the growing importance of modern fine printing and other types of special collections beyond purely antiquarian books.

International dialogue and comment followed the drafting and revision of the rules, and they were approved (with one exception) by the Standing Committees of the IFLA Sections on Rare and Precious Books and Documents and on Cataloguing in January 1980. Clearly defining the roles of cataloging vs. bibliography, the introduction states "The ISBD(A) is intended to provide for the description of older books in *general* catalogues, bibliographies and data-bases containing records of approximately equal detail for books, and other library material, of all periods . . . It is not, therefore, a set of rules for the full bibliographical description of older books . . ." Options are given to allow flexibility based on institutional needs. ". . . [F]or those items which appear to defy any rules, I can offer only the advice to act by the spirit of ISBD(A) and employ common sense."[47]

One of the major contributions to cooperative cataloging from the development of the ISBD concept is that punctuation which has come to be known by its name. For rare books, "ISBD punctuation" becomes even more significant. Rule 0.4.1 introduces what is commonly, but mistakenly, called "double punctuation." "Bibliographic agencies . . . may wish to record a full description incorporating the full punctuation, i.e., the exact punctuation as found on the item and as given in the sources of information. When full punctuation is recorded . . . the prescribed punctuation is also given, even though this may result in double punctuation." Rules governing the options in this case have led to confusion among catalogers ever since; punctuated information within the framework of ISBD signals the type of information, while transcription dictates punctuation based on the usage of the piece in hand.

The title is to be recorded "exactly as to wording but not necessarily as to capitalization or punctuation . . . Exceptionally, a very lengthy title proper *may* be abridged in the middle or at the end" with marks of omission (*ISBD(A)* 1.1.2). "Initials indicating membership of societies, academic degrees, etc., and statements of positions held and qualifications following an author's name are generally omitted from the statement of responsibility," unless necessary for grammar, identification, or for providing context (*ISBD(A)* 1.5.3.1). Explanations of the relationship between the statement of responsibility and the title "*may* be used within square brackets to link the title and statement of responsibility" (*ISBD(A)* 1.5.1.1). "Statements on the title-page or title-page substitute which are not connected with responsibility for the intellectual or artistic content of the work(s) contained in the publication and do not constitute other title information . . . are omitted." These would include mottoes, dedications, statement of patronage, etc. (*ISBD(A)* 1.5.10).

Transcription of early letter forms is covered by rule 0.8. Where practice is not consistent, "i" and "j" are transcribed (in most cases) as "i," "u" and "v" as "u." An initial "u" or "v," is to be transcribed as a "v," and specific rules apply to other instances, as well. This departs from guidelines given in *AACR2*. Another early printing convention covered is the virgule (/) used as a comma. It is to be transcribed as a comma, and "in case of doubt the usage of the text of the work is followed."

"The names of publishers, etc., are given as they appear in the publication in the full orthographic forms and the grammatical case (with necessary preceding works and phrases) in which they are given in the preferred principal source of information." Provision is made to add addresses "when they aid in identifying or dating the publication" (*ISBD(A)* 4.2.2.1). Detailed rules govern transcription of names for various functions of printer, publisher, bookseller, etc. (*ISBD(A)* 4.2.24-4.2.26). "Dates are given as found in the publication, including the day and month. Years of the Christian era and dates taken from a chronogram are, however, given in Arabic numerals. Phrases such as "printed in the year . . ." and "anno . . ." are omitted. Very long statements *may* be formalized. Dates not of the Christian era are transcribed, with the equivalent added in square brackets (*ISBD(A)* 4.4.2).

Signatures are first mentioned in rule 5.1.2.6.C, which allows for a statement of extent by signatures as one option in a wholly unpaginated or unfoliated work. In other cases, "the register of signatures *may* be given in a note." Rule 5.3.2 states: "the bibliographic format of the item is given in the terms of a numeral (including a fraction) followed by a raised **o** or similar abbreviation," followed by the item's height.

In discussing the inclusion of notes in the bibliographic record, *ISBD(A)* acknowledges that the enumeration of notes cannot be exhaustive but should or may include such types as the bibliographic reference note (*ISBD(A)* 7.1.1.1). Notes on the edition area and the bibliographic history of the publication (*ISBD(A)* 7.2) allow for description of earlier manifestations of the text as necessary. Notes can also provide clarification or expansion of publication, distribution, etc., information (*ISBD(A)* 7.3).

An attempt to include an analog to the International Standard Book Number concept in rare books allows for the optional inclusion of the fingerprint, which "consists of a number of characters drawn from a number of uniform places in the text of the publication, followed by a number indicating the source of one or more of the characters, and/or a letter indicating the direction of the chain-lines, and/or the date as it appears in the imprint." The use of a fingerprint "has been considered as a substitute for the standard number for older publications," but no definitive formula had been determined (*ISBD(A)* 8.1.1-8.1.3). The limitations of the fingerprint as a standard led to its rarity in North American bibliographic records. *ISBD(A)* included no provisions for creating headings or uniform titles (*ISBD(A)* 0.1.3), as it was designed as a purely descriptive code.

Bibliographic Description of Rare Books (BDRB)[48]

As the second edition of *AACR2* was being prepared, rare book catalogers and librarians realized the brief section on rare printed materials at the end of the second chapter "might benefit from some expansion and elaboration to address in a more complete way the often troublesome questions of rare book description." Since there was not enough time to incorporate most of the provisions of *ISBD(A)*, published in first draft in 1977, into *AACR2,* the progress of *ISBD(A)* through drafts was watched with interest. It became obvious that what was needed was "a single cataloging standard, based on *AACR2* but approaching the cataloging of rare materials with the thoroughness of *ISBD(A)*."[49]

At the same time, the importance of electronic cataloging in the context of rare books was becoming greater. The Eighteenth-Century Short Title Catalogue (ESTC) project was being planned, along with Independent Research Libraries Association's Ad Hoc Committee on Standards for Rare Book Cataloging in Machine-Readable Form.[50] In June 1979, the Library of Congress began to prepare rules for descriptive cataloging of rare books under *AACR2*, combining Chapters 1 and 2 plus *ISBD(A)* rules. *Bibliographic Description of Rare Books* was published in 1981 as "the Library of Congress' interpretation of *AACR2* Chapter 2 for its own cataloging of older printed materials." Contributions and comments were made by many other groups and libraries.

One of the primary assumptions of the rules that emerged is that "elements of data from a publication are generally transcribed as they appear, frequently without transposition of the other forms of intervention practiced by catalogers of ordinary books under *AACR2*."[51] This necessitates using other forms of entry (such as uniform title) to allow access by strings that would be expected to retrieve the records, had more familiar rules been used. Also, the rules apply to "any printed books, pamphlets, broadsides, and single sheets requiring special description," based on the following criteria: date of printing, place of origin (particularly where books are printed by hand), and administrative policy of the institution. In this way, the application of the rules may vary from library to library, within libraries by particular collections, or even book by book. The Library of Congress applied *BDRB* for books printed before 1801, with *AACR2* being used for later books (*BDRB* 0A). Libraries could, of course, apply *BDRB* much more broadly.

Rule 0E allows recording all punctuation, giving the prescribed punctuation as well, although the Library of Congress will omit punctuation in source if application of *ISBD* punctuation would result in "double or duplicate punctuation." Rules for the transcription of early letter forms were similar to those in *ISBD(A)*, yet allow for even more variation based on capitalization (*BDRB* 0H). Rule 0J2 calls for expansion of marks of contraction, with supplied letters (or words) enclosed in brackets. Apparently conflicting with the goal of exact transcription, however, initials, initialisms, and acronyms are to be recorded without internal spaces, "regardless of how they are presented in the source of information" (*BDRB* 0K).

A potential source of confusion through the code, particularly for those not working with it on a regular basis, is the seemingly arbitrary decision of when omissions are to be shown with marks of omission and when such marks are not to be used. The title and statement of responsibility area allows omission (without mark of omission) of information that is neither title nor statement of responsibility information (*BDRB* 1A2). Familiar rules cover transcribing, supplying, etc., the title. The title proper is, in general, not to be abridged, but when abridged "in exceptional cases" marks of omission must be used (*BDRB* 1B8). Acknowledging the differences in broadsides, rule 1F provides rules for recording titles of single sheet publications, usually beginning with first line of printing.

Rule 1G calls for transcription of statements of responsibility "in the form in which they appear" including titles, honorifics, etc., although the statement can be transposed if it appears above title, for example. Initials, degrees, etc., are to be omitted in most cases according to rule 1G8, with the same exceptions applying as in *ISBD(A)*.

An important difference between *AACR2* and *BDRB* is that the edition statement is to be recorded in the form in which it appears (*BDRB* 2B1). Exact wording is to be used unless the statement is taken from a source other than the title page, in which case it can be abbreviated and standardized.

"Because these rules are for both early printed books, for which the modern functions of printer, publisher, and distributor are often still undifferentiated, and for later books, in which information about the printer may be of particular importance or interest, the name and location of the printer are here given equal status to those of the publisher and distributor" (*BDRB* 4). This results in longer, more detailed transcriptions of imprint than *AACR2*. The place of publication is to be transcribed as it appears, and it can include prepositions, larger jurisdiction names, exact transcription of abbreviations, etc. (*BDRB* 4B1-4B4). If necessary to distinguish among places, further information such as state or province can be supplied, as in *AACR2* 23.2A, although when supplying such a name, *BDRB* calls for using "name or form appropriate to the date of publication." This avoids anachronistic phrases placing a publication in a nation not yet in existence. If publication information is given, the printer can be recorded in a note (*BDRB* 4E1). Rule 4D covers date; date of publication is recorded "as found in the publication" although Roman numerals are to be changed, as usual, to Arabic. Some phrases, such as "printed in the year" are to be omitted. Optionally, the information can be transcribed exactly "if it is considered important to retain in the catalog record the exact wording of imprint information," in which case, Roman numerals can be used with Arabic added in square brackets afterwards. Special explanation (as in *ISBD(A)*) is given for historical calendars, expanded beyond the scope of *AACR2* to account for their incompatibility with the modern Western calendar during various time periods.

In the description area of the record, (*BDRB* 5B), blank leaves are generally counted. Advertisements are included "if they clearly belong to the publication." Unnumbered pages or leaves are counted, in appropriate terms. Also, if they interrupt a numbered sequence, the record should make this explicit. When a whole volume is unnumbered, pages are to be counted, contrary to *AACR2* rule 2.5B7. Several sequences are "preferably" to be recorded, although the option of using the phrase "various pagings" still exists.

After the publication's size, the bibliographical format is to be added, in abbreviated form, and if it can be determined. This is required for publications before 1801 and optional for later publications (*BDRB* 5D1).

BDRB provides for similar notes as in *ISBD(A)*: Rule 7C9 instructs "make a note giving details of the signatures of a volume, if desired,"[52] according to the formula published in Philip Gaskell's *New Introduction to Bibliography*.[53] Therefore, one of the most visible clues in a bibliographic record that rare book rules have been used is actually optional. The reference to Gaskell's important treatise also underlines the influence of bibliography on rare book cataloging.

Rule 7C14 calls for references to published descriptions to be recorded in a standard and abbreviated form; the Standards Committee of the Rare Books and Manuscripts Section of ALA, in cooperation with the Library of Congress, was noted as preparing a list which should be used in any note. A short list of sources which should be recorded includes standard American and British bibliographies.[54] This type of short list of standard bibliographies would eventually develop into a reference for not only the bibliographies, but also standardized forms for citations to them.[55]

"Copy specific information," often forming the bulk of a bibliographic record, is discussed in rule 7C18. *BDRB* states that the Library of Congress will not use fingerprint technique as an analog to standard numbers (*BDRB* 8).

The code concludes with ten examples of catalog records constructed according to the rules, plus a very brief glossary. Some definitions are taken from another article by Tanselle,[56] highlighting the overlap between rare book cataloging and bibliography. Although no index was included in *BDRB*, the subsequent publication of an index by David M. Rich suggests it was very useful to be able to find information in this manner.[57]

Another result of *BDRB* was to serve as the impetus for other specialized codes to be used with rare materials,[58] including graphic materials,[59] archives and manuscripts,[60] and rare serials.[61] As we shall see, these related cataloging codes followed paths of revision and updating much the same way as *BDRB* itself. Since *AACR* included rules for all formats, this development paralleled in many ways the evolution of format-based codes, acknowledging the insufficiency of general codes to provide enough guidance to catalogers in handling specialized, non-book formats.

Anglo-American Cataloguing Rules, 2nd ed., 1988 Revision (AACR2R)[62]

Along with other changes in the 1988 revision of AACR2, rules 2.12-2.18 were revised. The scope rule (*AACR2R* 2.12) includes a specific injunction to "consult specialized reference materials for more detailed treatment of early printed books, etc.," acknowledging that the circumstances governing printing, binding, distribution, and other facets of the book trade cannot adequately be understood without further study.

The transcription of early letter forms rule (*AACR2R* 2.14E1) was simplified. "U" is transcribed as "u," but as "v" if the first letter of the word. "V" is also transcribed "u" in this case, unless it is the first letter. This may still be confusing to those not used to working with early letter forms and orthography. The publication, etc., area was overhauled considerably, and simplified. The overarching principle in the 1988 revision is to "give the rest of the details relating to the publisher, etc., as they are given in the item" (*AACR2R* 2.16D). With the 1988 revision of *AACR2*, the importance of special rules for rare book cataloging was confirmed, along with movement in the direction of faithful transcription, despite the exigencies of mainstream cataloging rules.

ISBD(A) was also revised soon afterwards.[63] The general theme of this standard is the same as its earlier edition, for example, in seeking exact transcription but attempts to conform more to the other *ISBD* standards. It, along with other revised *ISBDs*, also accounts for non-Roman scripts and languages.[64]

Descriptive Cataloging of Rare Books (DCRB)[65]

By the early 1990s, the influence of electronic cataloging was being felt in rare book cataloging codes in an explicit way, indicating the increasing prevalence and sophistication of bibliographic databases and integrated library systems. Subsequent codes would acknowledge this reality, as well as moving towards integrating concepts of description and access in ways unknown in previous codes.

Nearly ten year's experience with *BDRB* by rare book catalogers along with the revision of *ISBD(A)* prompted review of the code,[66] marked by cooperation between the Library of Congress and the Bibliographic Standards Committee of ACRL/RBMS. A survey distributed in 1989 by the BSC generated a great number of responses, including feelings of confusion about some provisions of *BDRB*, particularly early letter forms, inconsistencies in transcription rules, and the need for general updating and indexing. The code which resulted from these revisions, although called a second edition, was named *"Descriptive Cataloging of Rare Books"* instead of *"Bibliographic Description of Rare Books"* as an effort to address the ongoing confusion between bibliography and rare book cataloging.[67]

The committee decided to proceed with two basic assumptions: "a rare book cataloging code should be driven by the characteristics of early printed books" and "harmony among related and analogous codes is desirable." Following this thinking, "a separate descriptive code for rare books, and each particular rule within it, can be justified only if it results in catalog records that are used in ways that general catalog records for books are not." Therefore, while not fundamentally contradicting the prevalent cataloging code (*AACR2*), rare book codes differed in numerous ways. "It can be maintained that the fundamental difference between *AACR2* and *BDRB* is that the object of description is essentially different." Usually, the difference is based on criteria (bibliographical or artifactual value) related to age (pre-1801).[68] Of course, for libraries with small collections of rare materials, it would likely be too difficult to apply multiple codes; most of these libraries would use *AACR2*'s provisions, rather than a separate rare book code.[69]

Another problem with *BDRB* acknowledged by the committee was the proliferation of options designed to allow flexibility based on local needs; these actually had the result of making identification of items (one of the primary goals of a catalog) difficult, since libraries could have cataloged the same item in many different ways. This is especially confusing in bibliographic databases, resulting in multiple records. Internal consistency was another goal of the revision. Some inconsistencies remain between *DCRB* and *ISBD(A),* such as transcriptions of early letter forms, prescribed source of information for edition statement, and the placement of bibliographic format in description area.[70] Nonetheless, cataloging at the Library of Congress (and, by extension, those libraries following LC practice) must follow the rules (*AACR2*) rather than the standard (*ISBD(A)*), and *DCRB* allows them to do that.[71]

Perhaps the most important change in the revision was the evolution toward creating a cooperative rare book cataloging manual, instead of a descriptive code, including advice on access points, serials, MARC coding, etc.[72] The resulting publication has several appendices: title access points, early letter forms, rare serials, minimal-level records, *DCRB* code for records (used in the 040 field to indicate rules used in constructing the record), concordance between *DCRB* and *AACR2* rules, and a glossary, much expanded from *BDRB*.

Appendix A: Title Access Points, is the first indication that *DCRB* is going beyond the scope of descriptive rules. The creation of additional title access is necessary because *DCRB* calls for transcription without "transposition or the other forms of interventions practiced by catalogers of ordinary books under *AACR2*." Characteristics of the early books themselves, such as a lack of title page or the use of contractions, also make it essential to provide additional access in order to identify and locate books. The subsequent rules, arranged to correspond with parts of the description, provide a suggestive rather than exhaustive list of entries with the goal of providing "thorough access by title."[73]

Another departure from past codes was the inclusion of Appendix C: Rare Serials, expanding on guidelines published in 1984 and incorporating changes from the CONSER Operations Committee and CONSER Operations Coordinator.[74] The scope of application is all serials published before 1801 and later ones for which a more detailed level of description is desired (*DCRB* Appendix C, 1.1). In sum, the rules call for liberal application of notes, more faithful transcription of serial designations, and addition of bibliographic format where appropriate. The United States national serials database's need for consistent records (in choice of title) led to the admonition to *not* apply the *DCRB* provision in rule 1B1 that allows including within the title proper statements that appear before the chief title on the title page. Provisions for cataloging individual issues of serials are also provided, largely calling for treatment as monographs, along with guidance for linking such records to the master serial record (*DCRB* 3.1-3.5).

The text of *DCRB* itself begins with a list of works cited that forms a short list of "rare book cataloging tools."[75] The need for this type of primer for rare book cataloging, especially referring novices to sources of more detailed information on book production, binding, etc., continues even today.[76] Appendix E makes a clear distinction between rare book cataloging and "special collections cataloging," defined as "fuller use of notes, access points, and other elements that are not specifically called for in AACR2 or its predecessors, but that follow the spirit of DCRB without following its rules exactly."[77] Confusion often clouds this distinction, particularly for those unfamiliar with bibliographic records for special collections material.

While in some ways, *DCRB* was a more complete manual than its predecessor, it could not include all things necessary to catalog rare books. The examples of full bibliographic records which had appeared in *BDRB* were removed, but the subsequent publication of a separate volume of examples proved much more ambitious.[78] Work on this volume began almost immediately after *DCRB*'s publication. The examples were aimed at illustrating *DCRB*, with particular emphasis on unusually complex rules. They also illustrate options, showing how different applications would appear in real bibliographic records.

The justification for such a volume was that "variations in printing practices, lack of standardized title pages in early works, range of languages, and the artifactual aspects of rare books can all pose problems for the cataloger. Through use of examples, these potentially difficult areas can be clarified." The examples were never meant to be used as substitutes for the rules which they illustrate. The examples are MARC coded, using "generic USMARC" instead of local applications used by OCLC or RLIN. Subject headings are omitted from the records since subject access is essentially the same for rare books and other books, but some additional access points are included to illustrate particular rare book practices.[79]

Another spin-off of *DCRB* was the eventual emergence from "Appendix D: Minimal-Level Records" to the "Core Standard for Rare Books," which was approved in January 1999. This standard is the rare book component of a core record project devised under the direction of the Program for Cooperative Cataloging (PCC), administered by the Library of Congress with input from libraries throughout the world. Simply put, most notes allowed for in *DCRB* have been omitted, and, where options exist, areas are abbreviated. The *DCRB* standard differs from the PCC "Core Bibliographic Record for Books" in a few ways: there is no requirement for a nationally standard classification since many libraries use local call numbers for rare books; notes are to be recorded "as to method" more like *DCRB* records than *AACR2*, although, of course, they can be abbreviated; citations are encouraged where appropriate; and genre terms are to be used if local policy requires.[80] The use of this standard will fulfill one of the major needs seen by Melissa Flannery in 1986: minimal standards of completeness so that "records contributed to databases on a national and international level will have enough consistency to provide accurate information for the online retrieval of various lists and indices which technology has made possible."[81]

As of this writing, the ARCL/RBMS Bibliographic Standards Committee is engaged in a revision *DCBR* with the long-term goal to produce a series of volumes more appropriately titled *DCRM: Descriptive Cataloging of Rare Materials,* with separate portions for books; music; serials; cartographic materials; ancient, medieval, and early modern manuscripts; etc. Work on these modules is underway, with appropriate bodies being consulted, or, in some cases, creating rules in consultation with BSC.[82]

This emerging North American standard for all rare materials will solve one of the perceived shortcomings of descriptive codes up to this point: their focus on the book format. Since catalogers often work in specific formats independent of age or rarity of materials, expanding provisions to capture important artifactual or bibliographic information about these formats will provide a useful tool for catalogers, particularly those used to working with a specific format chapter of *AACR2*. The ongoing process of revision continues the drive for consistency and for removing confusion that undergirded revision of *BDRB* into *DCRB*.

ACCESS POINTS

Descriptive records do not exist in a vacuum. Most libraries also classify and provide subject access to their collections; but, for the most part, this practice will not differ substantially for rare books from the practice used for mainstream materials. (Obviously preservation needs may prevent marking of books, and other local conventions may apply, but the principle nonetheless holds true.) These basic types of access points, however, are often not seen as sufficient to point researchers toward specific types of material.

Josiah Bennett referred to a common practice in administering rare book libraries, "set[ting] up specialized files in non-subject areas for more efficient scholarly and bibliographical use of rare books. Tracing to such files often has the great value of reducing the detail on the catalogue card, making a specific aspect of the book traceable in its own right." Suggestions for special files include imprint files, association files, printers' files, and binders' files.[83]

One of the most visible ways in which the English-speaking North American rare book cataloging community has strived to make possible access to specialized types of information in bibliographic records is the creation and ongoing maintenance of several thesauri. Here, as in the construction of descriptive rules, the Bibliographic Standards Committee of ACRL/ALA has been the driving force. Beginning in the 1980s and continuing today, assembly and revision of several thesauri for rare books cataloging have provided standardized vocabularies,[84] supplementing the "mainstream" vocabularies produced under the auspices of the Library of Congress. The first thesaurus to appear centered on terms to describe bindings, highlighting the importance of this type of information in traditional rare book records.[85] The introduction of field 755 ("Physical Characteristics Access") into MARC in 1984 necessitated a controlled vocabulary if such characteristics were to be described in a uniform way. *Binding Terms* "presents terms for the description of bookbindings and includes descriptors relating to techniques for binding construction, and to the style, materials, and decoration of bindings."[86]

A similar need to standardize access points based on emerging technology drove the publication of *Genre Terms* in 1983:[87]

> Many rare book libraries maintain files of certain categories, or genres, of works found in their collections. These files include both intellectual or literary genres which characterize works (e.g., Courtesy books) and physical genres which characterize physical manifestations of works (e.g., Miniature books). The files are especially useful when an item is sought not through conventional author, title, or subject approaches, but rather through a term descriptive of the category into which it falls. Indeed, many items in rare book libraries are chiefly of interest to researchers as representatives of intellectual or physical genres.[88]

These terms were aimed at exceeding the depth and specificity allowed by using Library of Congress subject headings as form/genre terms. The development and use of MARC field 655 allowed for automated retrieval of this type of information, rather than relying on manual files. Its use was acknowledged to be voluntary and selective.[89] Arguably the most used of the thesauri, a new edition of *Genre Terms* was published in 1991.[90] Other thesauri produced include vocabularies for printing and publishing evidence,[91] provenance evidence,[92] paper terms,[93] and type evidence.[94] The ongoing process of revision of these thesauri includes submission and public comment under the auspices of the Bibliographic Standards Committee.[95]

In addition to the rare book thesauri, catalogers have available to them other vocabularies designed by specific communities, usually based on format of materials. For example, the *Art & Architecture Thesaurus* might be used to describe works of art or material culture.[96] While use of these vocabularies allows for a greater breadth and depth of access for special collections, the lack of reconciliation between vocabularies means that, in reality, the collocation features of standardized terms may be lost.[97]

Added name entries assume a special prominence in rare book records based on the tradition of tracing many more names associated with items than in mainstream cataloging. Scholars might use such tracings to reconstruct the work of a given printer or bookseller or to study the development of illustrative techniques by searching for the work of a particular engraver or lithographer. In addition, copy-specific tracings for former owners, donors, and the like are often traced. *AACR2R* allows functions to be added to tracings: "In specialist or archival cataloguing, when desirable for identification or file arrangement, add designations from standard lists appropriate to the material being catalogued" (*AACR2R* 21.0D1). This justifies the inclusion of names (either personal or corporate) in a bibliographic record in an intelligible way. For North American rare book catalogers, the standard English-language list is the relator terms maintained by the BSC.[98] The MARC codes which correspond to these terms are incorporated into the "MARC Code List for Relators, Sources, Description Conventions" maintained by the Library of Congress.[99]

A final type of special access has been alluded to previously: title access. As has been acknowledged since *BDRB,* the exact transcription called for by rare books rules requires added entries in order to facilitate retrieval by title. Uniform titles are also likely to play a large role, especially in early printed books. Format integration has, not surprisingly, broadened the possibilities of providing access to titles in useful ways. Although acknowledging that this problem is not unique to rare books, Bennett, for example, opined: "While our learned friend may turn immediately to the cards for *Travels into several remote Nations of the World,* we must also serve those who will look first under *Gulliver's Travels.*"[100]

BIBLIOGRAPHIC DATABASES
AND INTEGRATED LIBRARY SYSTEMS

Increasingly, the structure and functioning of library integrated systems are responsible for how individual bibliographic records are retrieved, displayed, and organized. The de facto national (or international) databases of OCLC and RLIN have rules and procedures that govern when new records can be added as well as how local information can be presented. In OCLC, in particular, the traditional library cataloging function of describing the copy in hand becomes less clear since the master record ought to retain little of the copy specific information so valuable in rare book records. Particularly for catalogers working in larger institutional contexts, the choice of when and how to create a bibliographic record may be governed by these databases rather than by specialist codes.

At the same time, local integrated library systems play a huge role in the creation of rare book records as well. Obviously, the increasing sophistication of such systems has provided many outstanding ways to provide access to collections. Theoretically an unlimited number of indexes could be provided without the manual work required in card catalog days, allowing for tracing of donors, printers, engravers, and others types of names. Additionally, keyword searching promises retrieval based on even those fields which are not indexed, as long as someone knows how to find what is being sought. The possibility of multiple call number indices can address the need for "virtual browsing" of closed stack collections, accommodating the local classification schemes that are often used for rare book collections. Davis' predictions of incompatible system requirements, duplication of work, and other problems associated with a lack of standardization among library systems appeared early on to be coming true,[101] but the emergence of international standards for information exchange such as Z39.50 and other market factors have caused some resolution of these issues.

An important difference between manual and electronic files is the way in which computer systems read catalog records. For example, in filing cards, insertions such as "[sic]," or expansions of contracted words can be ignored, but these types of characters will affect retrieval in computer indexing. It becomes even more necessary, then, to provide additional forms of access based on the actual information transcribed as well as on the implied sense of that information. At the same time, it is possible to easily create headings for multiple interpretations of titles so that cataloger judgment, user knowledge, and even descriptive rules can be augmented with multiple search strings to retrieve records based on anachronistic spellings, expanded abbreviations, and the like.

In order to address some of these issues, the BSC led a study examining the expectations rare book catalogers had for their local systems.[102] Results also appeared in the "Guide to Rare Book Records in Online Systems."[103] It outlines the minimal requirements on a local system for how it indexes, retrieves, and displays the type of information provided in rare book records. It is heartening to observe that many of these desiderata, which were uncommon or prohibitively expensive just a few years ago, are now becoming available in many cataloging systems. Because the market for library catalogs is rarely driven by small special-interest audiences, it is only now becoming possible to handle the information already provided for in USMARC, for example, with any degree of sophistication.[104]

Many of the objections raised in regards to bibliographic records for special collections materials are now, finally, being overcome. It is increasingly easy for anyone, not just a technologically savvy scholar, to search imprint fields, to gain access to the databases of OCLC and RLIN, and to manipulate data in catalogs without the need for complicated truncation strategies or delimiters required in years past.[105] Nonetheless, it is important to continually keep in mind the limitations of rare book cataloging, even in the most sophisticated environment, particularly as the quality and consistency of any computer system still depends on the information provided by a human being.

The issue of retrospective conversion of rare book records, although not strictly related to codes and practices, does merit at least a brief mention because of its influence on the number, quality and character of bibliographic records for special collections material over the past several decades. Guidelines for the retrospective conversion of rare books catalogs, desired by some,[106] did not materialize, with the result that many libraries found themselves "reinventing the wheel" when it came time to face the issue. One response to this situation indicates that retrospective conversion and the cleanup necessitated by it will continue to be a challenge for libraries for quite some time.[107] This limitation must be borne in mind when formulating procedures for the use of descriptive rules since it is likely that earlier rules led to the construction of records in different ways than would current rules.

CONCLUSION

The creation of bibliographic records for rare books has a rich tradition and heritage, encompassing masterpieces of description and access that have served scholars well for generations. While this tradition has, in some ways, existed outside the mainstream of library cataloging, descriptive codes have come to acknowledge some of the special issues present in rare book cataloging, at least bringing them to the attention of generalist catalogers. While the impossibility of a single Anglo-American cataloging code for all formats of information has been acknowledged, the continuing evolution of rare book codes has provided, in some ways, "one-stop shopping" for description and access.

At the same time, modern information technology offers amazing possibilities, such as linking bibliographic records to digital images of title pages and the simultaneous indexing of unlimited fields of information. Such possibilities are tempered by reality of costs, the need to handle large volumes of materials, and often a cooperative environment within or external to the library that imposes its own requirements. Nonetheless, the integration of rare book records into online catalogs for larger library collections has provided a degree of visibility, accountability, and cooperation unheard of in the early part of the twentieth century, when rare book cataloging practices were inherently localized. In this way, Anglo-American rare book cataloging has become an acknowledged part of the cataloging mainstream while maintaining its own conventions and purposes.

ABBREVIATIONS

AACR1   *Anglo-American Cataloging Rules* (North American Text). 1967.
AACR2   *Anglo-American Cataloguing Rules*, 2nd ed. 1978.
AACR2R   *Anglo-American Cataloguing Rules*, 2nd ed., 1988 revision, amended 1993.
BDRB   *Bibliographic Description of Rare Books: Rules Formulated Under AACR2 and ISBD(A) for the Descriptive Cataloging of Rare Books and Other Special Printed Materials.*
BSC   Bibliographic Standards Committee (Rare Books and Manuscripts Section/Association of College & Research Libraries).
DCRB   *Descriptive Cataloging of Rare Books (DCRB)*, 2nd ed.
IFLA   International Federation of Library Associations.
ISBD(A) *ISBD(A): International Standard Bibliographic Description for Older Monographic Publications (Antiquarian).*
ISBD(M) *ISBD(M): International Standard Bibliographic Description for Monographic Publications.*

NOTES

1. Paul Shaner Dunkin, *How to Catalog a Rare Book* (Chicago: American Library Association, 1951), 1.
2. For example: Ingrid Parent, "Building Upon Principles; Building Upon Success," *International Cataloguing and Bibliographic Control* 29, no. 1 (2000): 9-12.
3. Susan A. Adkins, "Automated Cataloging of Rare Books: A Time for Implementation," *Collection Management* 16, no. 1 (1992): 89-94.

4. G. Thomas Tanselle, "Descriptive Bibliography and Library Cataloguing," *Studies in Bibliography* 30 (1977): 55.

5. Laura Stalker and Jackie Dooley, "Descriptive Cataloging and Rare Books," *Rare Books & Manuscripts Librarianship* 7, no. 1 (1992): 9.

6. Ibid., 10.

7. James Westfall Thompson, *The Medieval Library* (Chicago: University of Chicago Press, 1939), 611.

8. Beth M. Russell, "Hidden Wisdom and Unseen Treasure: Revisiting Cataloging in Medieval Libraries." *Cataloging & Classification Quarterly* 26, no. 3 (1998): 21-30.

9. Stalker and Dooley: 11.

10. G. Thomas Tanselle, "Title-page Transcription and Signature Collation Reconsidered," *Studies in Bibliography* 38 (1985): 45-81.

11. John Carter, *ABC for Book Collectors,* 7th ed. (New Castle, DE: Oak Knoll Books, 1995), 193.

12. Ibid., 106.

13. Ibid., 171.

14. Stephen Paul Davis, "Bibliographic Control of Special Collections: Issues and Trends," *Library Trends* 36, no. 1 (1987): 115.

15. Tanselle, "Descriptive Bibliography," 1-3.

16. Ibid., 4-5.

17. Ibid., 11.

18. Ibid., 14.

19. Ibid., 36-43.

20. Ibid., 45-46.

21. Ibid., 54.

22. Michael Winship,"What the Bibliographer Says to the Cataloger," *Rare Books & Manuscripts Librarianship* 7, no. 2 (1992): 102.

23. John B. Thomas, III, "The Necessity of Standards in an Automated Environment, *Library Trends* 36, no. 1 (1987): 129-130.

24. Dunkin, 82.

25. Paul Shaner Dunkin. *How to Catalog a Rare Book,* 2nd ed. (Chicago: American Library Association, 1973).

26. Fredson Bowers, *Principles of Bibliographic Description* (Princeton, N.J.: Princeton University Press, 1949).

27. Dunkin, 2nd ed., 92.

28. Ibid., ix.

29. Ibid., 36-39.

30. Ibid., 100.

31. *Anglo-American Cataloging Rules (North American Text)* (Chicago: American Library Association, 1967).

32. *AACR1,* 2-4.

33. Ibid., 191.

34. Tanselle, "Descriptive Bibliography," 18-19.

35. Ibid., 19-24.

36. Carter, 125.

37. Josiah Q. Bennett, *The Cataloguing Requirements of the Book Division of a Rare Book Library* (Kent, Ohio: Kent State University Libraries, 1969).

38. Ibid., 11.

39. Ibid., 10.

40. Ibid., 15-16.

41. Ibid., 18.

42. Ibid., 19.

43. *Anglo-American Cataloguing Rules*, 2nd ed. (Chicago: American Library Association, 1978).

44. *ISBD(A): International Standard Bibliographic Description for Older Monographic Publications (Antiquarian)* (London: International Federation of Library Associations and Institutions, 1980).

45. *ISBD(M): International Standard Bibliographic Description for Monographic Publications* (London: IFLA, 1974), 1.

46. *ISBD(A)*, vii.

47. Ibid., viii-ix.

48. *Bibliographic Description of Rare Books: Rules Formulated Under AACR2 and ISBD(A) for the Descriptive Cataloging of Rare Books and Other Special Printed Materials* (Washington, D.C.: Library of Congress Office, 1981).

49. Ibid., [v].

50. Thomas asserts that ESTC cataloging practice, although not generally applicable to other institutions or projects, developed as it did due to the lack of a cooperative code: 131.

51. *BDRB*, [v]-vi.

52. Ibid., 49.

53. Philip Gaskell, *A New Introduction to Bibliography* (New York: Oxford, 1972).

54. *BDRB*, 51-52.

55. Peter M. VanWingen and Stephen Paul Davis, *Standard Citation Forms for Published Bibliographies and Catalogs Used in Rare Book Cataloging* (Washington, D.C.: Library of Congress, 1982).

56. G. Thomas Tanselle, "The Bibliographical Concepts of Issue and State," *Papers of the Bibliographical Society of America* 69 (1975): 17-66.

57. David M. Rich, *Index to Bibliographical Description of Rare Books* (Providence, R.I.: John Carter Brown Library, 1987).

58. Thomas, 132.

59. Elisabeth W. Betz, *Graphic Materials: Rules for Describing Original Items and Historical Collections* (Washington, D.C.: Library of Congress, 1982).

60. Steven L. Hensen, *Archives, Personal Papers, and Manuscripts: A Cataloging Manual for Archival Repositories, Historical Societies, and Manuscript Libraries.* (Washington, D.C.: Library of Congress, 1983).

61. "Rare Serials," *Cataloging Service Bulletin* 26 (Fall 1984): 21-25.

62. *Anglo-American Cataloguing Rules,* 2nd ed., 1988 revision (Chicago: ALA, 1988, amended 1993).

63. *ISBD(A): International Standard Bibliographic Description for Older Monographic Publications (Antiquarian),* 2nd ed. (New York: Saur, 1991).

64. Ibid., xii.

65. *Descriptive Cataloging of Rare Books (DCRB)*, 2nd ed. (Washington, D.C.: Cataloging Distribution Service, Library of Congress, 1991).

66. Stalker and Dooley, 8.

67. *DCRB*, v.

68. Stalker and Dooley, 9-10.

69. *DCRB*, viii.

70. Stalker and Dooley, 11-13.

71. *DCRB*, viii.

72. Stalker and Dooley, 15.

73. *DCRB*, 67-68.

74. Ibid., 71.

75. Ibid., xii-xiii.

76. See, for example, BSC's "Rare Materials Cataloger's HelpNet," available on the World Wide Web (http://www.library.yale.edu/bibstand/resource.html) [cited 22 March 2002].

77. *DCRB*, 77.

78. *Examples to Accompany Descriptive Cataloging of Rare Books* (Chicago: Association of Research Libraries, 1993).

79. Ibid., iii-v.

80. "Core Standard for Rare Books (DCRB Core)," available on the World Wide Web: (http://lcweb.loc.gov/catdir/pcc/dcrbcore.html) [cited 19 March 2002].

81. Melissa C. Flannery, "A Review of Recent Developments in Rare Books Cataloging," *Cataloging & Classification Quarterly* 7, no.1 (1986): 59.

82. The RBMS Bibliographic Standards Committee Revision Homepage chronicles the development of the project. Available on the World Wide Web: (http://www.folger.edu/bsc/dcrb/dcrbrev.html) [cited 19 March 2002].

83. Bennett, 38-39.

84. For a discussion of the development of changes to the MARC format related to these fields, see Thomas, 132-138.

85. *Binding Terms: A Thesaurus for Use in Rare Book and Special Collections Cataloguing* (Chicago: Association of College & Research Libraries, 1988).

86. Ibid., v.

87. *Genre Terms: A Thesaurus for Use in Rare Book and Special Collections Cataloguing* (Chicago: ACRL, 1983).

88. Ibid., i.

89. Ibid., iii.

90. *Genre terms: A Thesaurus for Use in Rare Book and Special Collections Cataloguing*, 2nd ed. (Chicago: ACRL, 1991).

91. *Printing and Publishing Evidence: Thesauri for Use in Rare Book and Special Collections Cataloguing* (Chicago: ACRL, 1986).

92. *Provenance Evidence: A Thesaurus for Use in Rare Book and Special Collections Cataloguing* (Chicago: ACRL, 1988).

93. *Paper Terms: A Thesaurus for Use in Rare Book and Special Collections Cataloguing* (Chicago: ACRL, 1990).

94. *Type Evidence: A Thesaurus for Use in Rare Book and Special Collections Cataloging* (Chicago: ACRL, 1990).

95. "RBMS Thesauri for Use in Rare Book and Special Collections Cataloging," available on the World Wide Web: (http://libweb.uoregon.edu/catdept/home/genreterms/main.html) [cited 19 March 2002].

96. *Art & Architecture Thesaurus*, available on the World Wide Web: (http://www.getty.edu/research/tools/vocabulary/aat/) [cited 22 March 2002].

97. Thomas, 129.

98. "BSC Relator Terms," available on the World Wide Web: (http://www.folger.edu/bsc/relators.html) [cited 19 March 2002].

99. "MARC 21 Code List for Relators, Sources, Description Conventions," available on the World Wide Web: (http://lcweb.loc.gov/marc/relators/) [cited 19 March 2002].

100. Bennett, 15.

101. Davis, 117.

102. Henry Raine and Laura Stalker, "Rare Book Records in Online Systems," *Rare Book and Manuscript Librarianship* 11, no. 2 (1996):103-118.

103. Available on the World Wide Web (http://www.folger.edu/bsc/guide.html) [cited 19 March 2002].

104. Adkins, 89-102. Adkins, although enthusiastic about the possibilities of automated rare book cataloging, was still realistic about the limitations on technology in the early 1990s. Many of these limitations no longer apply.

105. Winship, 102-105.

106. Davis, 116.

107. "Summary Results of the Retrospective Conversion Survey of Rare Materials," available on the World Wide Web: (http://www.library.yale.edu/bibstand/survey98.htm) [cited 22 March 2002].

Posthumously Plagiarizing Oliva Sabuco:
An Appeal to Cataloging Librarians

Mary Ellen Waithe
Maria Elena Vintro

SUMMARY. The Biblioteca Nacional of Madrid and the U.S. National Library of Medicine, followed by libraries worldwide, have changed the authorship of the 1587 *Nueva filosofía de la naturaleza del hombre* from Oliva Sabuco to her father, Miguel Sabuco y Alvarez. The authors present arguments offered by others supporting this change and examine newly uncovered archival documents to show that the change of named author to Miguel Sabuco is founded on mistaken arguments based on misconstrued evidence and that the burden of proof has been met to restore the attribution of this work to Oliva Sabuco. *[Article copies available for a fee from The Haworth Document Delivery Service: 1-800-HAWORTH. E-mail address: <getinfo@haworthpressinc.com> Website: <http://www.HaworthPress.com> © 2003 by The Haworth Press, Inc. All rights reserved.]*

KEYWORDS. Attribution, authorship, women authors, Oliva Sabuco, Miguel Sabuco y Alvarez, sixteenth century Spanish authors, history and philosophy of medicine

---

Mary Ellen Waithe, PhD, is Professor of Philosophy, Cleveland State University, Cleveland, OH 44115 (E-mail: m.waithe@csuohio.edu). Maria Elena Vintro has an MA in philosophy from Cleveland State University (E-mail: mecvintro@aol.com).

[Haworth co-indexing entry note]: "Posthumously Plagiarizing Oliva Sabuco: An Appeal to Cataloging Librarians." Waithe, Mary Ellen, and Maria Elena Vintro. Co-published simultaneously in *Cataloging & Classification Quarterly* (The Haworth Information Press, an imprint of The Haworth Press, Inc.) Vol. 35, No. 3/4, 2003, pp. 525-540; and: *Historical Aspects of Cataloging and Classification* (ed: Martin D. Joachim) The Haworth Information Press, an imprint of The Haworth Press, Inc., 2003, pp. 525-540. Single or multiple copies of this article are available for a fee from The Haworth Document Delivery Service [1-800-HAWORTH, 9:00 a.m. - 5:00 p.m. (EST). E-mail address: getinfo@haworthpressinc.com].

BACKGROUND

Oliva Sabuco was born in 1562 in the town Alcaraz, in Albacete Province, Spain, the child of Miguel Sabuco y Alvarez and Francisca de Cosar. (Due to the disappearance of Book 1 of the Baptismal Records of the Church of Santisima Trinidad from the Archivos Historicos Diocesano in Albacete (AHDA), we rely on the only author claiming to have seen the original: Marco e Hidalgo.)[1] In 1587 *Nueva filosofia de la naturaleza del hombre (NF)* was published in Madrid under Oliva Sabuco's name.[2] The second edition of *NF* appeared in 1588, as did a pirated reprint of that edition. A third edition, probably the last undertaken by Sabuco herself, appeared in 1622. In this article, we will describe the scholarly evidence that led to Spain's Biblioteca Nacional (BNE) and the U.S. National Library of Medicine (NLM) attributing authorship of *NF* to Miguel Sabuco rather than to the named author, Oliva Sabuco.

BNE AND NLM AUTHORSHIP ATTRIBUTION PROCESSES

In the 1970s the Biblioteca Nacional de Espana (Madrid) changed its attribution of authorship of *NF* from Oliva Sabuco to "Miguel Sabuco, *antes* [formerly] Doña Oliva." The BNE suggested that we consider the 1987 publication of the Instituto de Estudios Albacetenses (IEA) in which various arguments were offered towards the change of authorship, Oliva Sabuco to "Miguel Sabuco, formerly Doña Oliva."[3] At NLM a nearly identical process occurred. The only American copy of the 1587 edition of *NF* is in the History of Medicine Collection of NLM. Internal documentation provided to us by the chief bibliographic librarian at NLM indicates that NLM's decision to change the bibliographic listing of authorship of *NF* from Oliva to "Miguel Sabuco y Alvarez, formerly Oliva" is based on Marco e Hidalgo's evidence, and upon authorities other than those affiliated with IEA. Each of NLM's cited authorities[4] relies either upon assumptions that a woman could not have written *NF* or on Marco e Hidalgo's established texts of Miguel Sabuco's will, power of attorney, or promissory note, or upon Marco e Hildalgo's analysis of these documents.

THE BURDEN OF PROOF

The burden of proof is on catalogers who attribute a book's named author to another party to ground the reattribution in arguments which are founded on clear and convincing evidence. We argue that reattributions of authorship by BNE and by NLM were based on misconstrued evidence compiled into deficient arguments.[5] Because these errors were so significant, the burden of proof has not been met to warrant attributing authorship of *NF* to Miguel Sabuco rather than to Oliva Sabuco, its named author. We will introduce new evidence and argue that it supports the view that Oliva Sabuco, not her father Miguel Sabuco, was the true author of *NF*.

MISCONSTRUED EVIDENCE, DEFICIENT ARGUMENTS

In 1903 José Marco e Hidalgo, the Registrar of the City of Alcaraz, established and published texts of three documents: the last will and testament of Miguel Sabuco y Alvarez,[6] a power of attorney executed by him, and a promissory note executed by his son and son-in-law. Marco e Hidalgo's establishment of the text contains numerous errors and omissions. Our establishment of the text is based upon examination of the orginal at the Archivos Historicos Provinciales de Albacete (AHPA). Of these documents, only the will survives. In the will Miguel Sabuco claimed authorship of *NF*. Since then, many scholars including Marcos,[7] Solana,[8] Granjel,[9] Guy,[10] Palau y Dulcet,[11] Munoz Alonso,[12] Rodriguez Pascual,[13] Abellan[14] and Mellizo[15] have repeated Marco e Hidalgo's findings. Of these, none claim to have seen the presumably lost promissory note or the power of attorney. Some scholars who concur with Marco e Hidalgo's attribution of *NF* are affiliated with the Instituto de Estudios Albacetenses (IEA) in Albacete, Spain. In its journal[16] IEA scholars confirm Marco e Hidalgo's conclusion that Miguel Sabuco and not Oliva was the author of *NF*. This support is partially grounded on Miguel Sabuco's testamentary claim of authorship and copyright, which, he claims is backed up by notarized documents. Further support for IEA attribution of authorship to Miguel Sabuco is based on assumptions that the clergymen who witnessed Miguel's will would not swear to a falsehood and upon other highly speculative claims.

MIGUEL SABUCO'S TESTAMENTARY AUTHORIAL CLAIM TO NF

Miguel Sabuco's will is a six-page document penned by a scribe. Immediately preceding the notarial paragraph identifying the testator and witnesses appears the following paragraph whose text has been established and translated by the authors based on examination of the original:

> Item, I also clarify that I composed a book entitled *Nueva filosofia o norma* and another book that were printed, in which everyone took and I put as author the mentioned Luisa de Oliva my daughter, only to give her

the name and the honor, but I reserve for myself the fruits and profits that could result from the said books by me.[17]

The claim made by Miguel Sabuco is unverifiable and akin to claiming authorship of *Don Quixote*: a statement of a claim does not constitute proof that the claim is true. Moreover, Miguel refers to his book as *Nueva filosofia o norma.* Why? The title of the book is *Nueva filosofía de la naturaleza del hombre.* And what are we to make of the curious reference to "another book"? Why does the testator, who in his will is claiming to be the author of *NF*, not correctly remember the title of the just completed work that culminates his lifetime career as a pharmacist? Why can he not remember the names of the several treatises constituting *NF*? None has the title *o norma.* Self-attribution of authorship does not rise to the level of proof of authorship.

TESTAMENTARY CLAIM OF COPYRIGHT

In his will Miguel Sabuco further claims that he is "reserving fruits and profits conferred by the privilege" to himself. As we shall see, his claim to having the privilege, the equivalent of a modern copyright, is also deficient. Let us assume, hypothetically, that Miguel Sabuco and not Oliva composed the book. He has just completed the arduous process of obtaining permission to publish it. To obtain a privilege, an author must appear before representatives of the Consejo Real (Royal Council) to explain the subject matter of its contents. False statements to the Council or publishing a work without a privilege placed both author and publisher in grave peril. Serious violations were punishable by death and confiscation of the author's and publisher's worldly goods. Lesser violations were punishable by confiscation of the publication run and the imposition of a fine equivalent to the value of all the printed copies.[18] Publishing an unauthorized work in 1587 was a dangerous activity. Why, then, would Miguel Sabuco acknowledge in a sworn, witnessed instrument that he had intentionally deceived the royal authorities who granted Oliva the privilege for "his" book? Such an admission could have cost him his life. By making his claim only in his will, Miguel assured that his deception of the authorities would be discovered only after his death, i.e., when the will was probated. Upon discovery of the will, Oliva, who would have been expected to survive him, would have been exposed to prosecution. Alternatively, we might think that Miguel Sabuco was hiding behind his daughter's skirts and betting that a woman would not have been prosecuted by the Consejo Real.[19] Neither explanation assures that while alive Miguel would receive financial proceeds of the book.

NOTARIZED "PROOF" OF MIGUEL SABUCO'S AUTHORSHIP

The above-cited testamentary paragraph continues: ". . . I have established evidence of how I am the author and not she. Which information is in a legal document that I executed before Villareal the Notary." What is the evidence held by Villareal? The authors have meticulously examined the *Protocolos Notariales* for Villareal.[20] The promissory note and power of attorney are no longer amongst those papers. According to Marco e Hidalgo, the only scholar who claims to have seen the documents to which Miguel Sabuco refers, Miguel Sabuco gave his son Alonso a power of attorney to take the book to Portugal for printing there under Miguel's name. Marco e Hidalgo mentions a second document he found in Villareal's protocols: a promissory note purportedly executed by Alonso Sabuco. Because the originals are missing, we rely upon Marco e Hidalgo's establishment of the texts of both documents. According to Marco e Hidalgo, in the promissory note Alonso agreed to repay Miguel for travel expenses that Alonso would incur while attempting to have *NF* published in Portugal. This obligation was subject to Miguel "actually having the said privilege." However, the privilege printed in *NF* clearly grants Oliva exclusive rights to publish in all the Spanish realms including Portugal and the New World. The Portuguese printer apparently refused Alonso's request. In 1588 Spain still dominated Portugal, and violation of Oliva's copyright could be enforced there. Alonso failed to have *NF* published under Miguel's name. He never repaid Miguel as evidenced by the fact that Miguel's notary, Villareal, continued to hold the note. If we can rely on Hidalgo's established text, the note was neither destroyed nor marked paid.[21]

The authors of this article have examined dozens of "notes of indebtedness" executed in Alcaraz during the period. Those that are paid are crossed out and the date of payment noted in the margin. Often the debtor's signature is cut from the document. Oliva's brother Alonso was no fool; he made the promissory note conditional upon Miguel's "actually having the said Privilege" because he had no intention of reimbursing his father for the travel expenses related to running a fool's errand.

PRIMA FACIE *EVIDENCE*
TO SUPPORT OLIVA SABUCO'S AUTHORSHIP

Several pieces of *prima facie* evidence support Oliva Sabuco's authorship of *NF*. These include the privilege, the levy, the letter of dedication to the King, the poems by Juan de Sotomayor, and the invocation of protection from the President of Castilla.

The Privilege

Oliva Sabuco held the privilege for the publication of *NF*. Much of the following analysis of the nature of a privilege and the procedure for obtaining one relies upon Amezúa y Mayo's[22] well-documented account. In 1586 privileges were granted only at San Lorenzo de L'Escorial. This is the King's primary residence and court: a large isolated walled compound halfway up a mountain 40 km north of Madrid. Alcaraz, where the Sabuco family lived, is 80 km southeast of Madrid. Part of La Mancha, or desert, made famous by Oliva's contemporary Cervantes in *Don Quixote de la Mancha* lies between the two towns. After negotiating with the publisher, Pedro Madrigal of Madrid, the author of *NF* would have traveled northward to San Lorenzo with the manuscript to obtain the license from the Royal Council. The Council appointed a committee of one or two censors who gave close scrutiny to new authors. Although frequently priests, censors were in the employ of the Crown. The procedure typically took months. Obtaining the privilege is comparable to receiving a modern copyright. It authorizes only the author to print the book. Privileges normally were given for a period of ten years and only for the Realm of Castilla. The terms of the privilege given to the author of *NF* are better than those given Cervantes for his work *Primera Parte de La Galatea*, 22 February 1584. Cervantes's copyright was for "in these our kingdoms," i.e., Spain and Portugal.[23] Oliva Sabuco's privilege extended beyond these kingdoms to Spanish territories in the New World. The privilege allows the printer to set type. Once the book, as censored, has been set in type, a copy as well as the original must be resubmitted to the Committee of the Royal Council for verification that the author has complied with the requirements of the censors. Then, the author added the *errata* pages, the "Prologue to the Reader," and the poetic elegies.

The Levy

The unbound proofs were required to be taken from the printer in Madrid and submitted in person to the office of the Corrector General in San Lorenzo. There was a final step to be completed before bound copies could be distributed: the addition of the levy statement. On February 12, 1587, Christoual de Léon, Notary of the King's Chamber, executed a two-page statement verifying that the authorities were satisfied with the corrections to the book "*New Philosophy* composed by Doña Oliva Sabuco." The levy set the price for paper-bound editions of the book (the author was permitted to add a surcharge for finer bindings). The levy includes a statement that it must be affixed to the front material of each printed copy of the book. Upon the completion of all the front material, the publisher and author were legally permitted to begin the production run. Obtaining the privilege and levy required the author to personally appear before the authorities.

How could Miguel have impersonated Oliva? Indeed, how could anyone other than the author of the book have such an intimate understanding of the contents of *NF* needed to survive interrogation by the Committee of the Royal Council regarding the details of the arguments offered in the tome? The issuance of the privilege and levy, considered in light of the book production process in sixteenth century Spain, constitute a persuasive argument that Oliva Sabuco, not her father, was the author of *NF*.

The Poems

Two poems that praise Oliva's abilities and theories appear among the front material of *NF*. The poetic tributes are identified as having been written by a Juan de Sotomayor. There were at least three individuals named Juan de Sotomayor living in Alcaraz during Oliva Sabuco's lifetime. The author of the poems appearing in *NF* could be any of these. The first mention of this name appears in an undated entry[24] made between 5 and 7 October 1572. This priest/attorney remained attached to the Church of Santisima Trinidad, the largest church in Alcaraz, throughout his life, writing many of its legal documents, including the 1585 document settling the estate of Oliva's mother.[25] This is the only individual by that name whose acquaintance with Oliva Sabuco has been documented. However, there was a second Juan de Sotomayor living in Alcaraz. He was the father of a third Juan de Sotomayor, who married Maria de Peralta in 1581.[26]

Dedicatory Letter to the King

The author's dedicatory letter to the King contains several mentions of the author's sex:

> A humble female serf and vassal, on her knees, absent for she can not be present, dares to speak: It gave me this boldness and bravery that ancient law of gallant chivalry: to which the great Lords and cavaliers of noble lineage, of their own free will, bound and obliged themselves so that women would always end up favored in their endeavors. . . .

> And may Your Honor receive this pledge from a woman, for I think it is of higher quality than any others by men, by vassals or by Lords who had vowed to serve Your Majesty. And even if your Cesarean and catholic

Majesty has had many books dedicated to Him from men, only few and rare were from women, and none about this subject matter. . . . This book is as unique and new as its author.

. . . this humble female serf of yours expects great and extraordinary mercies from Your Majesty whose hands I kiss, and I wish You great prosperity, health, grace and eternal glory.[27]

These repeated mentions of the author's gender bring attention to the fact that the author is female. Given the status of the addressee, misrepresentation would have been highly risky.

Invocation of Protection from the President of Castilla

The first four pages of the *NF* treatise consist of Oliva Sabuco's invocation for protection of her ideas by Francisco Zapata, Count of Barajas, who was also President of Castilla. This is often an indication that the named party has provided part of the cost for bringing the work to publication. Invoking protection and using the name of the highest official of the state of Castilla could not occur without the official's explicit permission. Permission would not have been granted had there been deception concerning the name of the author. Unauthorized use of Zapata's name would not have gone unpunished. In this invocation for protection by the President of Castilla, the author invites him to have her defend her thesis before a group of educated men. What would have happened if the President accepted the author's invitation and convened such a group? No one other than the woman who was the author of the work could withstand such personal scrutiny.

Prima facie evidence provided by the privilege, the levy, the poems of praise, the dedicatory letter to the King, and letter invoking protection of the President of Castilla all confirm that Oliva Sabuco was the author of *NF*.

NEW EVIDENCE UNDERMINES DEFECTIVE ARGUMENTS

In addition to this *prima facie* evidence supporting Oliva's authorship, we should note that new evidence from the Archivos Historicos Provinciales de Albacete (AHPA) and from the Archivos Historicos Diocesano de Albacete (AHDA) demonstrate serious defects in arguments that support attribution of authorship to Miguel. The most seriously defective argument is based on the premise that Miguel Sabuco's claim to authorship must be true because three priests who witnessed his will would not lie. A second equally defective argument is grounded on baseless assumptions that Oliva Sabuco and her husband left Alcaraz in the wake of public disclosure of her plagiarism or her refusal to admit that her father used her name as his *nom de plume.*

The Curse Three Priests Were Unlikely to Have Witnessed

There is yet another bizarre statement in Miguel Sabuco's will preceding the remarks about the "evidence" he secured with the notary Villareal:

> I order my daughter, Luisa de Oliva, not to interfere in the said privilege, if she wants to avoid my curse, because I have established evidence of how I am the author and not she.

Marco e Hidalgo has argued that it is inconceivable that the three witnesses to Miguel Sabuco's will, all clergy, would swear to the truth of an authorship claim they knew to be false.[28] Although we agree with the argument, we disagree with its suppressed premise that the three pious witnesses had the opportunity to know of Miguel's testamentary claim of authorship.

Invocation of a curse was evidence of the practice of witchcraft. The well-established House of the Inquisition was located a three-minute walk from the house where Oliva Sabuco and her husband resided. (Both are famous landmarks in Alcaraz, indicated on municipal maps and visited by the authors.) The three priests who witnessed Miguel Sabuco's will would have had a duty to report such evidence to the Inquisitor who was in residence there. In a sworn legal document a signatory invokes by implication the name of God as witness to the truthfulness of the testimony presented in the document. For three priests to invoke the name of God in a threat to place a curse on someone would be blasphemous! It is, therefore, highly unlikely, indeed almost inconceivable, that in his will, in the presence of three priests, Miguel Sabuco threatened his daughter with a curse and then convinced the prelates to sign a document that was not only evidence of *their* participation in Miguel's witchcraft but was, in addition, a public, written act of blasphemy! Yet the curse is in the will, and three priests did sign as sworn witnesses to the will. How can this highly unlikely set of circumstances be explained?

Internal evidence causes us to question whether the witnesses Pedro de Llerena, Sebastian de Molina, and Juan de Coca ever saw Miguel's claim to authorship. (There were at least two others by the name of Juan de Coca, one a sandal maker[29] and shoemaker.[30] The second by this name was a carpenter, who in 1595, with his wife Catalina Barbero, became a godparent.[31]) On page five of the will is the requisite statement revoking all prior wills, claiming only this one witnessed below is his authentic will. The remainder of the page contains two paragraphs. The first paragraph clarifies bequests to

Miguel Sabuco's second wife Ana Navara Garcia and their son, also named Miguel. A second paragraph claims Miguel's authorship of *NF* and threatens Oliva with his curse. Physical examination of these two paragraphs suggests that they may have been interpolated into the will after it was signed and witnessed. The hand appears to be somewhat smaller, and the pen nib to be finer. The signatory and notarial paragraphs follow these paragraphs, appearing at the top of page six, again with what appears to be the original size hand and nib. (We exempt from the present discussion the signatures of the testator, witnesses, and notary, which would not have been written by the scribe.) On page six, just below this final portion of Sabuco's will, is a document by the notary's next customer. This second document appears to be inscribed in the same smaller hand and the same smaller pen nib as the two paragraphs following the revocation paragraph of the will.

What are we to make of this anomaly? Several possible explanations come to mind. The first, simplest, and most obvious is that the scribe took a momentary respite after writing the revocation paragraph and accidentally resumed writing with a different pen in slightly smaller penmanship. Then, realizing that the signatory and notarial paragraphs could not possibly fit on the same page, turned to the *verso*, again changed pens and completed his work. This explanation has considerable merit because of the social status of the signatory, Miguel Sabuco as a former official municipal pharmacist, and of the three clergymen who honored Miguel by acting as witnesses. Important figures routinely inscribed large signatures often followed by ornate rubrics. The scribe might insult the signatories if he failed to leave sufficient room for what might be rather large signatures and rubrics.

An alternative explanation would be that the scribe turned to page six to assure adequate space for the signatures and notarial paragraph. All was completed and testator, witnesses, and perhaps even the notary had finished their business for the day. Several inches of blank paper remained on page five, following the revocation paragraph. The next day, a new customer arrived to execute a document. The scribe began this new document immediately following the signatures of Miguel Sabuco, the three prelates, and the notary, using a smaller hand and smaller nib. Perhaps Miguel Sabuco later returned to the scribe to insert the two paragraphs in which the inheritances of his new wife and their son is clarified, and in which he claimed authorship of *NF*. Having much to write and limited space in which to insert the two omitted items, the scribe may have used the same smaller nib and smaller hand with which he had just inscribed the next client's document. Rather than seem far-fetched, this second hypothesis accounts not only for the scribe's change of pen and penmanship, but also explains why three prelates would apparently witness a document that contained a curse. If Miguel Sabuco's claim to authorship had not been inscribed on page five until after the priests had already affixed their signatures on page six, then the priests never saw the paragraph containing the claim to authorship and the threatened curse on Oliva Sabuco!

There is yet a third hypothesis: that the witnesses were brought in only to witness the signing of the will and not to witness the writing of the will. If so, it remains the case that the priests never saw Sabuco's claim to authorship and remained completely ignorant that the document they witnessed invoked a curse on the testator's daughter.

Our hypotheses become all the more attractive in that they also account for the absence of evidence that anyone other than Miguel thought him to be the author of *NF*. The will and its claim to authorship would not become publicly known until it was probated–i.e., until Miguel Sabuco had died. We have learned that Sabuco survived many more years, to witness the wedding in 1602 of the son who was only four years old at the time the will was executed.[32] According to this record of marriage banns, Miguel Sabuco, son of Baccalaureate Miguel Sabuco, was to marry Isabel de las Vacas, the widow of Alonso de Alegria. Our examination of hundreds of Alcaraz records of the late sixteenth to early seventeenth centuries indicates that when one parent of the bride or groom is still living, that parent is named and no mention is made of the deceased parent. When both parents have predeceased the matrimonials of a child, one parent is named and identified as dead. In cases where a widow or widower remarries, the late spouse is named and the survivor identified as a widow. In cases where a slave is married, the owner is identified. As indicated by the marriage banns for his son, Miguel Sabuco y Alvarez died no earlier than 1602, fourteen years after writing his last will and testament.

Oliva Sabuco's Enduring Social Status in Alcaraz

Compelling evidence refutes the claims by Octavio Cuartero[33] and Marco e Hidalgo[34] that Oliva Sabuco and her husband Acacio left Alcaraz in disgrace, never to be heard from again. Our research has yielded documents indicating that the opposite is true. Oliva Sabuco and her husband Acacio de Buedo spent forty years following the publication of *NF* actively participating in the social milieu of Alcaraz's leading citizens and public officials.

On October 2, 1583, Acacio de Buedo was elected Caballero de la Sierra for the Parish of San Pedro in Alcaraz.[35] According to Henares, in October, 1587 Acacio de Buedo was (again) elected Caballero de la Sierra for his parish and re-elected to this post in October 1589.[36] If Oliva Sabuco had been publicly disgraced by claiming authorship of *NF*, how could her husband have retained the confidence of the parish by whose members he was elected? Oliva Sabuco and her husband Acacio de Buedo remained in Alcaraz, he being mentioned in

1595 as "Alcalde mayor (chief Mayor of Alcaraz) Acacio de Buedo Caballero de la Sierra."[37] Oliva and Acacio were asked to do the honors of being godparents at the September 1, 1596, baptism of Miguel de Valleserios (possibly Vallesteros).[38] They also acted as godparents on May 24, 1600, for Pedro, son of Pedro Alvarez and Maria Vazquez, his wife.[39] On December 9, 1612, and again on June 2, 1613, Acacio de Buedo vouched for the residency of a native from Léon, who married a woman from Alcaraz. Oliva's half-brother, Miguel Sabuco, and his wife Isabel de las Vacas were witnesses to that marriage.[40] This suggests that the ties between Oliva and the child of her father's second marriage remained strong.

There may have been a period between 1615 and 1617 when Oliva Sabuco traveled to Portugal to publish the third edition of *NF* in Braga. By this time, Portugal was (again) independent of Spain; and Oliva's now expired 1587 privilege would not have been honored there. Her new publisher, Fructoso Lorenço de Basto, mentions that the Inquisition took an interest in the second (1588) edition of *NF*, necessitating substantial revision to the third (Braga, Portugal) edition.[41] (It is unclear which Inquisitiorial authorities the publisher is alluding to; it is well known that there were numerous committees of the Inquisition operating under somewhat idiosyncratic guidelines, with substantial differences between those in Spain and those in Portugal.) On October 10, 1616, a committee consisting of Bertolameu da Fonseca, Antonio Diaz Cardoso, and Fr. Manoel Coelho authorized Doutor Baltazar Alvarez to verify that the book's contents were as its author claimed. On October 13, 1616, Dr. Alvarez verified that the proofs had been expurgated and corrected as required. Whereupon the original committee consisting of Bertolameu da Fonseca, Antonio Diaz Cardoso, and Fr. Manoel Coelho on October 4, 1616, granted permission to print the book as corrected. In Lisbon, on March 8, 1617, the publisher Fructoso Lourenço de Basto was granted permission to publish the book by Oliva Sabuco, "it having been reviewed by the Holy Office" (of the Church).

Although the manuscript was ready for its production run, it languished, set in type, on the publisher's shelves. This would have meant that valuable type was unavailable for other print jobs, tying up a substantial amount of the printer's equipment. However, the levy was not authorized until October 5, 1622, the year the edition was published. In a three-page dedication appended to the text, the publisher indicates that the book's author died in the interim. The publisher, of course, had a pecuniary interest in completing the publication process. Not only would valuable set type be freed up for other projects, but it may have been the case in Portugal at that time that royalties from posthumous publications accrued to the publisher rather than the foreign heirs of the author.

Other documents belie the publisher's claim that Oliva Sabuco had died by 1622. Oliva Sabuco and her husband both survived to witness the marriage of their daughter, Luisa de Buedo, on August 26, 1629. The marriage banns, preserved in the Archivos Historicos Diocesano de Albacete read:

> Señora Doña Luisa de Buedo, daughter of Señores Acacio de Buedo and Doña Luisa de Oliva y Sabuco married Don Miguel (Sabuco) de Pareja, son of Miguel Sabuco de Penarubia & Señora Doña Madalena de Soto.[42]

The marriage banns and wedding are recorded twice. The first entry omits titles; it is crossed out. The second record appears on the verso and includes the honorifics as mentioned. The identification of all named women with titles Señora and Doña, of all named men with Señor and all (except Acacio de Buedo) with Don indicates elevated social status of both families.

Did Oliva Sabuco and Acacio de Buedo leave Alcaraz, disgraced by her father's accusation that, despite being the named author, she either plagiarized Miguel's work or claimed not to have acted merely as a *nom-de-plume* for Miguel? No. Oliva Sabuco remained in Alcaraz, her husband Acacio de Buedo rising through Alcaraz's political circles to become chief mayor. The couple maintained good relationships with leading Alcaraz families and with Oliva's half-brother Miguel Sabuco y Garcia. Oliva Sabuco and Acacio de Buedo were socially and politically prominent, marrying their daughter Luisa de Buedo into an equally eminent family.

CONCLUSIONS

We have argued that, based upon the evidence of documents discovered by Marco e Hidalgo, several arguments made by him and by other authors are defective. We have introduced new evidence and offered insights into old evidence concerning the misattribution of authorship of *NF* to Miguel Sabuco. His authorship claim is unverifiable. Even the testator cannot correctly recall the title of the just completed book he claims to have written. The copyright that Miguel alleged to be his was not recognized by the Portuguese printer to whom in 1587 his son Alonso had offered *NF*. Clearly, it is improper to construe Miguel Sabuco's testamentary claims as providing sufficient evidence upon which to conclude that he is the author of *NF*. Arguments relying exclusively on those claims are deficient and therefore of no probative value for attribution of authorship to *NF* to anyone other than Oliva Sabuco. Substantial internal textual evidence has been presented to support our conclusion that a woman wrote *NF*. Several pointed mentions of the author's gender are made in the dedicatory letter to the King. Similarly, the invocation of protection from the President of Castilla and the author's offer to defend her thesis before a committee of educated men make it highly unlikely that such a defense could be mounted by a male author or by a female who lacked detailed understanding and intimate knowledge of the author's work. Scholars who examine the relevant pages of Miguel Sabuco's will can view the visible differences in pen stroke and nib size suggestive of an interpolation into the will of material that was not there originally: the bequeathals to Ana Garcia and to young Miguel Sabuco as well as the testator's claim to authorship of *NF*. Consequently, the argument that the clergymen witnesses confirmed Miguel's authorship is moot. There is no evidence that they knew of it. Furthermore, we have introduced ample new evidence that Oliva Sabuco lived not only long enough to complete the preparation of the third edition of *NF* but also that she and her husband Acacio de Buedo remained in Alcaraz. There they joined the ranks of the leading political families. With her husband, Oliva Sabuco remained in Alcaraz for at least forty years following the initial publication of *NF* and married her daughter into one of Alcaraz's most eminent families.

We urge cataloging librarians charged with attribution of authorship to examine our evidence and to reattribute to Oliva Sabuco the authorship of the 1587 philosophy of medicine, *Nueva Filosofía de la Naturaleza del Hombre*.

NOTES

1. José Marco e Hidalgo, "Doña Oliva no fué escritora: Estudios para la historia de la ciudad de Alcaraz," *Revista de archivos, bibliotecas y museos*, 3. época, 9, no. 1 (July 1903): 1-13.

2. Oliva Sabuco, *Nueva filosofía de la naturaleza del hombre, no conocida ni alcançada de los grandes filosofos antiguos, la qual mejora la vida y salud humana* (Madrid: Pedro Madrigal, 1587). Unless otherwise noted, all references are to this edition. *NF* is a comprehensive philosophy of medicine. It develops a theory of human nature that is consistent with a view of the universe. From that view of human nature, Oliva Sabuco accounts for physical, mental, and moral disorders of humankind, shows how the three are mutually interdependent, and how changes in one can effect changes in the other. She then proposes a remedy that is essentially moral in nature. It is a system that recognizes and accepts rather than fights natural processes of growth, development, and decline while promoting health and happiness during that natural life span. She traces the implications of her theory for social and political philosophy as well.

3. Personal correspondence from José Maria Morena, Servicio de Información Bibliográfica, Biblioteca Nacional, Madrid, to Maria Vintro, 22 August 1996.

4. Cited from Wellcome Institute *Library catalogue*: Picatoste y Rodríguez, Felipe. *Apuntes para una biblioteca científica Española del siglo XVI*, Madrid, 1891, entry #719; *Enciclopedia universal ilustrada*, s.v. "Sabuco"; Palau Dulcet, Antonio. *Manual del librero Hispano-Americano*, 2d ed., Barcelona, 1948-1977;

Gallardo, Bartolomé. *Ensayo e una biblioteca española de libros raros y curiosos*, Madrid, 1863-1869; Salvá y Mallen, Pedro. *Catálogo de la Biblioteca de Salvá*, Valencia, 1872; Chinchilla, Anastasio. *Anales históricos de la medicina en general y biográfico-bibliográfico de la Española en particular,* vol. 1, Valencia, 1941: 303-312; and Granjel, Luis. *La medicina española renacentista,* vol. 2 of *Historia general de la medicina española*, Salamanca, 1980, p. 50.

    5. Archival documents viewable at http://www.sabuco.org [cited 29 May 2002].

    6. Archivos Historicos Provinciales de Albacete (AHPA), Protocolos Municipios Diversos/Protocolos Notariales de Alcaraz/Protocolos Notariales: Romero, libro 144, Feb. 20, 1588. The Archivos Historicos Provinciales de Albacete hereafter referred to as AHPA.

    7. Benjamin Marcos, *Miguel Sabuco (antes Doña Oliva)* (Madrid, 1923), 35ff.

    8. Marcial Solana, *Historia de la filosofía española: epoca del Renacimiento,* vol. 1 (Madrid, 1941), 273-288.

    9. Luis Granjel, "La doctrina anthropologico-medica de Miguel Sabuco," in *Humanismo y medicina* (Salamanca, 1956, 1968), 15-74.

    10. Alain Guy, *Les philosophes espagnoles d'hier et d'aujourd'hui* (Toulouse, 1956), 78-83.

    11. Antonio Palau y Dulcet, *Manual del librero hispanoamericano: Bibliografia general española,* vol. 18 (Barcelona, 1966), 213-215.

    12. Adolfo Muñoz Alonso, *Enciclopedia filosofica*, vol. 5 (Firenze, 1967), col. 949-950.

    13. Francisco Rodriguez Pascual, "Una antropologia cosmologica y psicosomatica en el siglo XVI: Nuevo intento de comprension de la obra del bachiller M. Sabuco y Alvarez," *Cuardenos Salmantinos de filosofia 5* (1978): 407-426.

    14. José Luis Abellan, "Los medicos-filosofos: Juan Huarte de San Juan, Miguel Sabuco y Francisco Valles," chap. 8 in *Historia critica del pensamiento español*, vol. 2 (Madrid, 1979).

    15. Carlos Mellizo, "Tres medicos existenciales: Huarte, Sabuco, Sanchez," *Tribuna medica* #890 (Mar. 20, 1981), 35ff.

    16. *Revista de estudios Albacetenses,* 2d época, año 13, #22 (Diciembre 1987). Monografico dedicado a Miguel Sabuco.

    17. AHPA, Protocolos notariales, legajo 132.

    18 Agustín G. de Amezúa y Mayo, "Como se hacia un libro en nuestro siglo de oro" (paper presented at Instituto de España, 23 April 1946) (Madrid: CSIC, 1951), 331-371; also (Madrid: Impr. de Editorial Magisterio español, 1946).

    19. Mary Ellen Waithe, *A History of Women Philosophers,* vol. 2 (Dordrecht, Boston & London: Kluwer Academic Publishers, 1989), 261-284.

    20. AHPA, "Protocolos Notariales," legajo 132, contains Villareal's notarized documents for the years 1587 and 1588. On January 20, 1588, exactly one month before the date of Miguel's will, Alonso Sabuco executed a half page document (an "obligation") to use municipal funds for a public festival. On February 15, 1588, Alonso Sabuco executed a full page "obligation" to travel to the distant Vizcaya (Biscaya) region of the Vascos (Basque) to make various purchases, including some furniture, for the city of Alcaraz. Given the distance and difficulty of such a trip in mid-winter, it is unlikely that Alonso was in Alcaraz at the time his father executed his will.

    21. Waithe, op. cit.

    22. Amezúa y Mayo, op. cit.

23. Miguel de Cervantes, *Primera parte de la Galatea divida en seys partes* (Alcala, 1585).

24. AHPA, Libros de Municipios 245, Alcaraz, Acuerdos del Ayuntamiento 1572-1578, fol. 29.

25. Archivos Historicos Diocesano in Albacete (AHDA), AHDA/ALC-150/ 200-204v, December 27, 1585. Archivos Historicos Diocesano in Albacete hereafter referred to as AHDA.

26. AHDA/ALZ 108 (1581), unnumbered fol.

27. Sabuco, *NF*, fol.1r. Translation from the original by the authors.

28. Marco e Hidalgo, "Doña Oliva."

29. AHDA/ALZ-79/ San Ignacio/2: Bautismos Oct. (24-27), 1573.

30. AHDA /ALZ-79/San Ignacio/2, unnumbered fol. AHDA/ALZ-79/San Ignacio/2: fol. 73-75.

31. AHDA/ ALZ-2/ Bautismos, fol. 46v, Mar. 12, 1595.

32. AHDA/ALZ-108/Amonestaciones, unnumbered fol., Oct. 27, 1602.

33. Octavio Cuartero, "Prólogo," in *Obras de Doña Oliva Sabuco de Nantes (escritora del siglo XVI)* (Madrid, 1888), v-xxxviii.

34. José Marco e Hidalgo, *Biografía de Doña Oliva de Sabuco* (Madrid, 1900), 38.

35. Archivos Municipios de Alcaraz, (AMA) Libro e Actas del Ayuntamiento de Alcaraz 1582-1586, fol. 1068. Archivos Municipios de Alcaraz hereafter referred to as AMA.

36. Original AMA documents missing.

37. AMA Camara de la Justicia, Legajo 498 exp. 9, fol. 8 AMA, and legajo 563 exp. 3, no folio number. These documents are barely legible and not able to be copied.

38. AHDA/ALZ80/ Bautismos San Ignacio Libro 3, fol. 68, Sept. 1, 1596.

39. AHDA/ALZ-80/ Bautismos San Ignacio Libro 3, folio 80, May 24, 1600.

40. ADHA/ALZ-109, Matrimonios Santisima Trinidad, Dec., 1612.

41. Oliva Sabuco, *NF* (Braga: Fructoso Lourenço de Basto, 1622), unnumbered fol.

42. ADHA/ALZ-108, Amonestaciones Santa Maria, August 26, 1629.

Serials Cataloguing in Germany:
The Historical Development

Hartmut Walravens

SUMMARY. This paper outlines the development of serials cataloguing in Germany, which started with entries usually in systematic catalogues. Cataloguing codes were developed first by individual major libraries; the establishment of a Prussian union catalogue called for generally recognized rules, but these focused mainly on sorting and filing. When, in the 1960s, the *Prussian Instructions* were given up in favour of *RAK (Regeln für Alphabetische Katalogisierung)*, ISBD was adopted for the descriptive part. As to modern international cooperation, this paper explains that the main obstacles are not so much different cataloguing codes but the lack of consensus on the definition of a serial title. Recent revision efforts missed the opportunity of accepting an International Standard Serials Title. *[Article copies available for a fee from The Haworth Document Delivery Service: 1-800-HAWORTH. E-mail address: <getinfo@haworthpressinc.com> Website: <http://www.HaworthPress.com> © 2003 by The Haworth Press, Inc. All rights reserved.]*

KEYWORDS. Serials, alphabetical cataloguing, serials cataloguing–history–Germany, *Prussian Instructions*, Prussian Union Catalogue, *RAK*, serials cataloguing, International Standard Serials Title

Hartmut Walravens is affiliated with the Staatsbibliothek zu Berlin–Preussischer Kulturbesitz (E-mail: hartmut.walravens@sbb.spk-berlin.de).

[Haworth co-indexing entry note]: "Serials Cataloguing in Germany: The Historical Development." Walravens, Hartmut. Co-published simultaneously in *Cataloging & Classification Quarterly* (The Haworth Information Press, an imprint of The Haworth Press, Inc.) Vol. 35, No. 3/4, 2003, pp. 541-551; and: *Historical Aspects of Cataloging and Classification* (ed: Martin D. Joachim) The Haworth Information Press, an imprint of The Haworth Press, Inc., 2003, pp. 541-551. Single or multiple copies of this article are available for a fee from The Haworth Document Delivery Service [1-800-HAWORTH, 9:00 a.m. - 5:00 p.m. (EST). E-mail address: getinfo@haworthpressinc.com].

541

ZUSAMMENFASSUNG. Der Beitrag beschreibt die Entwicklung der Zeitschriftenkatalogisierung in Deutschland, die mit Eintragungen gewöhnlich in den Realkatalogen began. Katalogisierungsregeln wurden zuerst von einzelnen grösseren Bibliotheken entwickelt; der Aufbau des Presussischen Gesamtkataloges erforderte allgemein akzeptierte Regeln, doch diese konzentrierten sich grossenteils auf Fragen der Ansetzung und Sortierung. Als in den 60er Jahren die *Preussischen Instruktionen* durch die *RAK (Regeln für die Alphabetische Katalogisierung)* abgelöst wurden, wurde die ISBD für die Titelbeschreibung übernommen. Hinsichtlich der modernen internationalen Zusammenarbeit weist der Beitrag darauf hin, dass das Haupthindernis nicht so sehr unterschiedliche Regeln als vielmehr das Fehlen einer gemeinsamen Definition des Zeitschrfiten-Titels ist. Die jüngsten Revisionsbemühungen haben die Chance verspielt, einen Internationalen Standard-Zeitschriftentitel zu akzeptieren.

SCHLAGWÖRTER. Zeitschriften, alphabetische Katalogisierung, Zeitschriftenkatalogisierung–Geschichte–Deutschland, *Preussische Instruktionen*, Preussischer Gesamtkatalog, RAK, Zeitschriftenkatalogisierung, Internationaler Standard-Zeitschriftentitel

1. INTRODUCTORY REMARK

When I started investigating this subject, I was surprised to notice that there was a considerable amount of publications on serials in Germany but little on cataloguing. To quote just two standard works: The *Lexikon des gesamten Buchwesens* (1937, vol. 3, pp. 611-617) has an informative article on Zeitschrift (periodical), and some others on Zeitschriftenakzession, zeitschriftenartige Reihen, Zeitschriftengestelle, Zeitschriftenhandel, Zeitschriftenkataloge, Zeitschriftenlesesaal, Zeitschriftenteil, and Zeitung (i.e., acquisition, series, periodicals display shelves, catalogues [card files, or lists], periodicals reading room, periodical title, and newspaper, respectively). There is no information regarding the actual cataloguing of serials. The same goes for the renowned *Handbuch der Bibliothekswissenschaft,*[1] which used to be the German librarian's bible; the index gives a number of references to Zeitschriften but, again, most of them deal with selection, acquisition, reading rooms, display, etc. This may be taken as an indication that serials were considered just a different publication form whose challenge lay in selection, management, and access but not necessarily in the field of cataloguing–the same rules applied, with just a few modifications, as to multi-volume works.

2. DEVELOPMENT OF SERIALS IN GERMANY

Serials developed in Germany much as they did in the neighbouring countries, France and Britain. Broadsheets marked the beginning of newspapers, the *Acta Eruditorum* (1682) the beginning of scholarly journals, a little bit later than the *Journal des savants* (1665) and the *Philosophical Transactions* (1665). Most of the earlier German periodicals were not yet called Zeitschrift, a word originally used for chronograms or historical chronological surveys. Popular names were Journal, Monatsschrift, Wochenschrift and Tagebuch. In the beginning people's interests were encyclopedic; there was no specialization yet. This gradually developed in the early eighteenth century: journals for entertainment, theology, and history, later on for law and literature as well as medicine. The second part of the eighteenth century brought a boom in theatre journals. The nineteenth century then offered a wide variety of serial publications focused at individual professions; then came gazettes and specialized scientific journals, starting with medicine, natural sciences, and technology. Illustrated journals, like *Illustrierte Zeitung, Pfennigmagazin,* and *Gartenlaube,* were successful with a large audience. Statistical information is provided by the postal subscription lists, which give 371 titles available through postal delivery in Berlin in 1826 and 3,169 for 1890. The German directory of journals (Sperling) lists 7,173 for 1931.[2]

3. COPING WITH SERIALS

There is little information on serials cataloguing in Germany prior to the nineteenth century. Libraries definitely acquired journals, and the accessions were duly recorded. The usual form of cataloging at that time was to write the data into a catalogue volume that was arranged according to subject; there was usually no alphabetic catalogue–the librarian either knew what was there, or he knew where to look for it. The nineteenth century with its prolific publishing industry provided such a flood of new acquisitions–even if libraries were not able to buy them, there were donations–that librarians devised quite sophisticated systematic catalogues, and they were the pride of the libraries. Alphabetic catalogues were also started mainly in the nineteenth century, and they served as a shortcut to the call number.

Let us take the example of the Royal Library in Berlin, which began preparing its alphabetical catalogue–in book form, of course–as early as 1811. It was finished in 1827 and comprised 162 volumes in folio size. By 1905 it had grown to 1,250 and by 1920 to 2,230 volumes. But the main catalogue was usually the systematic catalogue (Realkatalog), and there the most complete information was given. (See Illustration 1.) In the case of journals, it meant that new volumes had to be added to the records there.[3] The whole procedure changed when a fundamental new development started at the end of the nineteenth century. The decision was made to realize a statewide union catalogue for Prussia. Scholars had become weary of writing postcards to libraries in their search for needed items. The immediate result of this decision was that it was necessary to develop a strategy to file this slightly heterogeneous information from all the university libraries in the country. While there had been individual rules (consuetudines) in major libraries, there was no standard. While the description of a title was still not very important (of course, the title, the place of publication, perhaps the publisher, volumes, etc., had to be listed), the identification of items and their filing became a major issue.

The second result was the decision to publish new acquisitions right away; as of 1892 the *Berliner Titeldrucke* was a great help to other libraries because one might cut the records from the publication (there was a special edition printed on one side of the sheet only) and paste them in one's own catalogues. There was also soon an edition on file cards in the international format. This was remarkable as, so far, catalogues in book form dominated the field. Yes, there were also catalogue cards; but usually they were an auxiliary, a secondary instrument, to build a new version of the systematic catalogue. In Berlin, as in many other libraries, this catalogue was at the same time the shelflist–the most important catalogue of the library.

It was, therefore, a revolutionary decision when the Royal Library was granted permission to keep its card file as an independent alphabetic catalogue; the decision was made by the minister himself (March 31, 1865). If we think of today's already badly outdated filing cabinets, we do not get the real idea. In those days the German format was 19.5 × 15 cm., and often neither cardboard nor thick paper stock was used but instead thin paper. This meant that the file cards were bundled in flat boxes, and they were not suited to stand upright. That was a later development!

There was a third result to the important decision mentioned. Up to this time, most of the work, recording and filing items, was done by staff with scholarly backgrounds. It turned out that it was too heavy a workload, and therefore library training was introduced that led to a diploma. That meant that

ILLUSTRATION 1. Entries from the Alter Realkatalog (Old Systematic Catalog) of the Berlin State Library

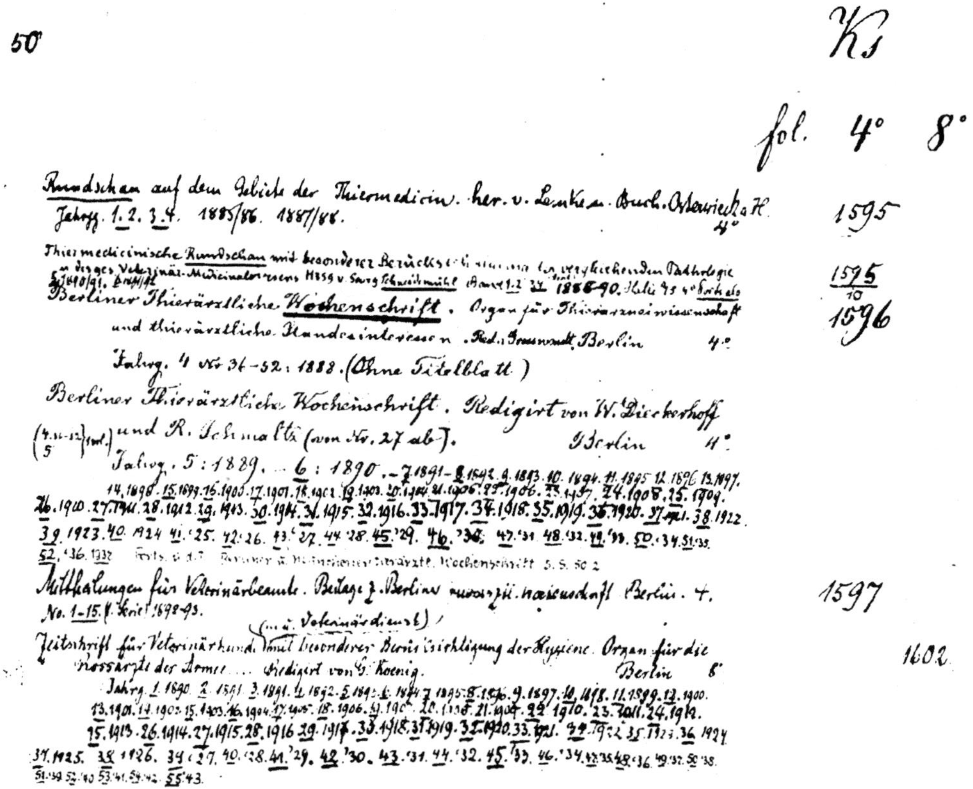
50

Ks

fol. 4° 8°

Rundschau auf dem Gebiete der Thiermedicin. her. v. Lenke u. Buch. Osterwieck a. H. 4° 1595
Jahrg. 1. 2. 3. 4. 1885/86. 1887/88.

Berliner Thierärztliche Wochenschrift. Organ für Thierarzneiwissenschaft und thierärztliche Standesinteressen. Red.: Grosswendt. Berlin 4° 1596
Jahrg. 4 Nr 36–52: 1888. (Ohne Titelblatt)

Berliner Thierärztliche Wochenschrift. Redigirt von W. Dieckerhoff und R. Schmaltz (von Nr. 27 ab). Berlin 4°
Jahrg. 5: 1889. 6: 1890. 7. 1891

Mittheilungen für Veterinärbeamte. Beilage z. Berliner tierärztl. Wochenschrift. Berlin. 4. 1597
No. 1–15. 1892–93.

Zeitschrift für Veterinärkunde (mit u. Veterinärdienst) mit besonderer Berücksichtigung der Hygiene. Organ für die Rossärzte der Armee ... Redigirt von G. Koenig. Berlin 8° 1602
Jahrg. 1. 1890.

a growing group of library professionals was available to cope with the ever-increasing work.

4. CATALOGUING vs. UNION-CATALOGUING

Up to this time, there were some individual libraries that occasionally compiled lists, or brochures, of their serials holdings. This was not a common practice, however. Rare books and manuscripts had a much higher priority. When the Prussian union catalogue was started at the Royal Library in Berlin, serials were not an issue. As work progressed, however, it became clear that it might be useful to create a separate alphabet for serials. As work on the union catalogue proved to be time-consuming, it was decided to publish a representative list of serials holdings of a number of major libraries: the *GZV* or *Gesamtzeitschriftenverzeichnis* comprising approximately 17,000 titles in 357 libraries. (See Illustration 2.) This publication was triggered by the earlier compilation of serials union catalogues in Austria and Switzerland. Only up to four holdings were indicated by a new device, library symbols, or siglas, which had been created for use in the union catalogue. The actual holdings, by volumes or by year of publication, were not given. The following development of serials union cataloguing in Germany, mostly in connection with the need of surveying surviving resources after two world wars, has been treated already in another publication and does not need repetition here.[4]

For our present purpose, it is important to notice that serials cataloguing meant mainly listing titles and holdings, either of individual collections or, better, of many libraries. Another essential aspect was the attempt to classify serials according to topics (usually done by a subject index in the printed serials catalogues) and/or according to places of publication, the latter especially in historical bibliographies and in lists of newspapers. It should be kept in mind that all these catalogues were more or less in the form of volumes. The information from handwritten tomes was copied onto file cards, sorted according to various criteria, added to, and turned again into printed catalogues in book form. Books needed less space than card files, they could be more easily distributed, even worldwide, and were handy to use. Card files clearly fulfilled an auxiliary function only.[5]

5. CATALOGUING CODES

It has been mentioned already that individual libraries had their consuetudines or cataloguing rules. When the Prussian union catalogue was

ILLUSTRATION 2. Page from *GZV (Gesamtzeitschriftenverzeichnis)* 1914

— 102 —

4806 Ephemeris αρχαιολογικη εκδιδ. ὑπο της Αρχαιολογικης 'Εταιρειας. Εν Ἀθηναις.
1: 4° Nw 745. 12: 4° Arch. 52 q. 7. 16.
4807 — Διεθνης, της νομισματικης αρχαιολογιας. Journal internat. d'archéologie numismatique. Athènes. 1: Pi 407.
12: Num. Ant. 55 t. 7. 18.
4808 — epigraphica. Corporis inscriptionum lat. suppl. Berolini. 1: Ph 1552.
12: Arch. 84 zp. 7. 18.
4809 — für semitische Epigraphik. Gießen.
1: Ph 8488/2. 12: Arch. 84 zr. 5. 18.
4810 — της Κυβαργησεως του βασιλειου της Ελλαδος. Εν Ἀθηναις. 1: 4° Ho 24150.
12: 4° H. Gr. 26.
4811 — της ελληνικης και γαλλικης νομολογιας. Εν Ἀθηναις. L 3.
4812 Epigraphia Carnatica. (Archaeol. Survey of Mysore. Mysore Archaeol. Series.) Bangalore. 12: 4° H. As. 182 p.
4813 — Indica and record of the Archaeological Survey of India. Calcutta.
1: 4° Ph 10040. 12: 2° H. As. 192 7. 18.
4814 Epilepsia. Amsterdam & Leipzig.
1: Kh 6410. 12: Path. 871 m.
4815 Eranos. Acta philologica Suecana. Göteborg & Leipzig. 1: Va 9410/7.
12: Philol. 99 i. 7. 18.
4816 Erbe der Alten. Leipzig. 1: Va 9491.
12: Philol. 99 n. 21. 28.
Erdbebenbericht. Observatorium, Batavia. Forts. s. *Bulletin*, Seismological.
4817 Erdbebenwarte. [Nebst] Neueste Erdbebennachrichten. Laibach.
12: Phys. Sp. 207 bk. 24. 90. E 1.
4818 Erde. Weimar. 1: 4° Po 2607. 12. 17. 52.
4819 — Deutsche. [Nebst] Beil. Gotha.
1: 4° Rx 391. 12: 4° Germ. G. 44 ir. 5. 18.
Erdteile, Die fünf s. *Pflug*, Deutscher. Beil.
4820 Erfinderfreund, Der deutsche. (Bremen.)
1: 4° Oo 1598/9.
4821 Erfinderrundschau. München. 12.
4822 Erfindungen, Neueste, u. Erfahrungen auf d. Geb. d. prakt. Technik, Elektrotechnik der Gewerbe usw. Wien & Leipzig.
1: Oo 864. 12: Tech. 54 f.
4823 Ergänzungsmessungen zum bayerischen Präzisionsnivellement. München.
12: 4° Bavar. 647 i.
4824 Ergänzungstaxe der deutschen Arzneitaxe, Berlin. 1: Jn 2776. 40.
Ergebnisse der Anatomie u. Entwicklungsgeschichte s. *Hefte*, Anatom.
4825 — der Arbeiten der Drachenstation am Bodensee. Stuttgart. 2° 21. 24.
— am Aeronautischen Observatorium, Berlin in: *Veröffentlichungen* d. Kgl. Preuß. Meteorol. Instituts.
— des Kgl. Preuß. Aeronaut. Observatoriums b. Lindenberg. Forts. s. *Arbeiten* des Kgl. Preuss. Aeronaut. Observatoriums b. Lindenberg.
— des Samoa-Observatoriums der Kgl. Ges. d. Wiss. zu Göttingen in: *Abhandlungen* d. Kgl. Ges. d. Wiss. zu Göttingen. Math.-phys. Kl.

4826 Ergebnisse der Arbeitsvermittlung in Österreich. Wien. 1. 21. B 17.
— der magnetischen Beobachtungen in: *Veröffentlichungen* d. Kais. Observatoriums in Wilhelmshaven.
— in Potsdam in: *Veröffentlichungen* des Kgl. Preuß. Meteorol. Instituts.
— der meteorologischen Beobachtungen zu Bremen s. *Jahrbuch*, Deutsches meteorol. Bremen.
— Brünn s. *Bericht* der Meteorol. Komm. d. Naturforsch. Vereines in Brünn.
— im Reichsland Elsaß-Lothringen s. *Jahrbuch*, Deutsches meteorol. Els.-Lothringen.
4827 — an den Landesstationen in Bosnien-Hercegovina. Wien. 1: 4° Mw 7941.
12: 4° Phys. Sp. 80 cf. 7.
4828 — der meteorologischen u. magnetischen Beobachtungen zu Clausthal. Saarbrücken. 7. 35.
— der meteorologischen Beobachtungen in Potsdam in: *Veröffentlichungen* d. Kgl. Preuß. Meteorol. Instituts.
— im Königr. Sachsen in: *Jahrbuch* der Kgl. Sächs. Landes-Wetterwarte.
— an 10 Stationen 2. Ordnung usw. s. *Jahrbuch*, Deutsches meteorol. Beobachtungssystem der Deutschen Seewarte.
4829 — im Systeme der Deutschen Seewarte. Hamburg. 1: 2° Mv 2406.
12: 4° Phys. Sp. 80 cbb. 7. 18.
— der Station 2. Ordnung Wiesbaden in: *Jahrbücher* d. Nassauischen Vereins f. Naturkunde.
— in Württemberg in: *Jahrbuch*, Deutsches meteorol. Württemberg.
— der Beobachtungen am Observatorium (Aachen) u. dessen Nebenstationen s. *Jahrbuch*, Deutsches meteorol. Aachen.
4830 — der phaenologischen Beobachtungen aus Mähren u. Schlesien. Brünn.
2. 7. 15. 27.
— der Beobachtungen an den Stationen 2. u. 3. Ordnung in: *Veröffentlichungen* d. Kgl. Preuß. Meteorol. Instituts.
4831 — der Chirurgie u. Orthopädie. Berlin.
1: J 6333. 12: Chir. 88 cg. 2. 16.
4832 — der Deklinationsbeobachtungen des Erdmagnetischen Observatoriums d. Westf. Berggewerkschaftskasse zu Bochum. Bochum. 6. 7. 35.
— der pflanzengeographischen Durchforschung von Württemberg, Baden u. Hohenzollern s. *Jahreshefte* d. Vereins f. Vaterländ. Naturkunde in Württ. Beil.
4833 — der Erdbodentemperatur-Messungen im Garten d. Landes-Wetterwarte zu Dresden. Dresden. 7.
4834 — der Forstverwaltung im Reg. Bez. Bromberg. Bromberg. 1: Oy 5906.
4835 — d. Reg. Bez. Düsseldorf. Düsseldorf.
1: 4° Oy 5908.
4836 — im Reg. Bez. Köln. Köln.
1: 2° Oy 5910.

prepared, it became quite clear that standardization was necessary. The results were the *Instruktionen für die alphabetische Katalogisierung der Preuszischen Bibliotheken vom 10. Mai 1899* (PI).[6] This work became popular with librarians as it filled an urgent need. Practical work showed, however, that amendments and compromises were necessary, and therefore a slightly revised edition was published on August 10, 1908, which remained the authority for at least the next fifty years. When we check the PI for rules on serials we find very little; the reason is that the PI were not concerned about descriptive cataloguing but rather about filing titles in the alphabet of a huge union catalogue. The main rules are:

§ 62.   Periodicals are listed under their titles.

§ 63.   With periodicals only those elements are cross-referenced that have their own title, including an imprint.

§ 229.   If titles change considerably and if this change coincides with the beginning of new numbering, these titles are listed separately and all of them are cross-referenced.

That is almost the extent of periodical-specific information there is in PI!

When after World War II the publishing industry and the libraries boomed, when more and more people had to prepare written examination papers of a certain level, demands for books and serials grew enormously, and readers struggled with the card files (the auxiliary files had turned into permanent and recognized search instruments), librarians realized that a new cataloguing code was necessary.

The PI were devised as an instrument for librarians; what was discussed at the International Conference on Cataloguing Principles in Paris in 1961 brought some new developments for German libraries. Corporate bodies would play a major part in cataloguing, owing both to the growing number of publications of such bodies as well as to an envisaged need for international cooperation. The grammatical filing principle of the PI (for anonymous titles) was discarded and the given word order adopted. The latter measure facilitated the situation considerably for a large audience of readers. It was mainly because of the Copenhagen International Meeting of Cataloguing Experts (1969) that German librarians decided to focus on filing again; descriptive cataloguing should be based on the ISBD to be developed as a cooperative international effort. The new *Regeln für die alphabetische Katalogisierung (RAK)*[7] were finalized in the 1970s and offered many options for various types of libraries–public, academic, special. The basic principle was: You may leave some out but must not change any rules! When we look for serials rules in RAK we find definitions (§ 9-13, periodicals, series, newspapers, loose-leaf publications, etc.), notes on periodicity (§ 165.15), the listing of volumes (§ 176) and a paragraph on main entries vs. references. In order to allow for an automatic exchange of records, MAB (Maschinelles Austauschformat für Bibliotheken) was created. RAK as quoted needed some additions and/or interpretations in order to support serials cataloguing in practice. This was done mainly on the basis of practical cataloguing work, and, again, a union catalogue project was the driving force.[8]

6. A COOPERATIVE SYSTEM: ZDB

After World War II, surveys of existing serials holdings had a high priority. This led to the successful GAZS (Gesamtverzeichnis ausländischer Zeitschriften und Series), later supplemented by GDZS (Gesamtverzeichnis deutscher Zeitschriften und Serien). Automation allowed for the creation of a database that, with the advance of networking options, was turned into a cooperative system. Progress was slow, but owing to the staunch support of the German Research Association, many libraries and the regional library systems joined what became known as Zeitschriftendatenbank. (See Illustration 3). Major steps were the integration of the Bavarian regional network and, after the unification of Germany, the major East German libraries. ZDB comprises only titles with actual holdings in German libraries and archives, and its data (currently more than 1 million titles with 5.5 million holdings) form the basis of all German document delivery services. It is run by the Berlin State Library on PICA software in cooperation with its technical partner, the Deutsche Bibliothek (DDB). It is accessible through an OPAC (http://www.zdb-opac.de) and a CD-ROM edition. Participating libraries are connected to the up-to-date cataloguing version that ensures a redundance-free file. The Berlin State Library (successor to the Royal Library and the Prussian State Library) maintains central editorial offices for titles, corporate bodies, and newspapers that have the responsibility to watch over correct bibliographic data; holdings are managed by the participating institutions, but they form an integral part of ZDB.

These short remarks may make it understandable that today the German cataloguing practice for serials is based exclusively on ZDB, which developed their interpretation of RAK under the acronym of ZETA (Format und Konventionen für die Zeitschriften-Titelaufnahme in der Zeitschriftendatenbank). ZDB participants and the editorial offices cooperate on amendments and changes. The national bibliographic data (created by the national library) do not play a major role as they are not entered in the database; it has been a project of long standing to integrate DDB's extensive holdings in ZDB. ZDB philosophy rests on linked files, including authority files. There are separate files for titles, corporate bodies, and holdings. The linking mechanism ensures the immediate realization of changes or corrections in all respective records. The corporate bodies authority file originally evolved from ZDB and is therefore part of the system.

ILLUSTRATION 3. Entry from Zeitschriftendatenbank (Cataloguing Version)

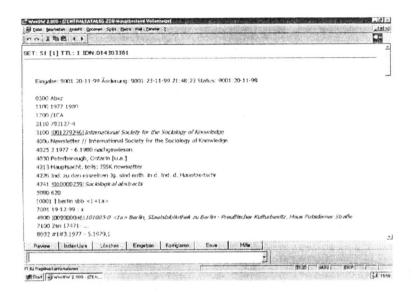

7. PERSPECTIVES

ZDB[9] is working on a number of short- and medium-term projects. Currently an online ordering component is being developed that will make use of the existing document delivery and interlibrary loan structures. This will be particularly important as soon as serials contents databases are linked with the ZDB OPAC. There is a close cooperation with EZB (Elektronische Zeitschriftenbibliothek) Regensburg, which provides up-to-date information on access modalities to electronic journals. Almost needless to say, all EZB titles (and more) are recorded in ZDB. And last but not least, efforts are being made to integrate the serials holdings of the national library in ZDB.

This short survey does not really say much about the actual cataloguing of serials in Germany, for a number of reasons:

- When one really gets down to the details of the cataloguing process, matters become very technical and require much space for explanation.
- While in the past there were rules in individual libraries (mainly requiring the listing of title, volume, imprint and sometimes periodicity), ZDB and ZETA now provide a standardized approach.

• Descriptive cataloguing is based on ISBD(S), and more recently on ISBD(CR).

A discussion has sprung up in Germany about whether it would be a good idea to adopt MARC21 and AACR, with the progressive faction advocating their adoption by 2007. The main reason given is the difficulty in international cooperation and exchange of records. Without commenting on this issue, which is sometimes dealt with in a simplistic way ("let's exchange formats and rules, and the problem is solved"), it may just be pointed out that in the serials field the key issue is of a different nature–it is the definition of the serials title and the determination of title splits. There was some hope that the recent revision and harmonization efforts concerning AACR, ISSN, and ISBD(S) would provide a solution or at least a promising perspective for the future. The most convincing proposal was to use the ISSN key title as the benchmark title. That would have been an acceptable compromise and an excellent perspective for international cooperation in this field. Unfortunately, major players did not agree.

NOTES

1. Rudolf Kaiser, "Die Katalogisierung," in *Handbuch der Bibliothekswissenschaft,* hrsg. von Fritz Milkau (Leipzig: Harrassowitz, 1933): 237-318; Heinrich Roloff, "Die Katalogisierung," Ibid., 2., verm. und verb. Aufl., hrsg. von Georg Leyh (Wiesbaden: Harrassowitz, 1961): 242-356.

2. *Lexikon des gesamten Buchwesens* (Leipzig: Hiersemann, 1937): 615.

3. Richard Fick, "Die Kataloge der Druckschriftenabteilung," in *Fünfzehn Jahre Königliche und Staatsbibliothek* (Berlin: Preussische Staatsbibliothek, 1921): 92-99.

4. Hartmut Walravens, "Anfänge der Gesamtkatalogisierung von Zeitschriften in Deutschland," in *Zeitschriften in deutschen Bibliotheken: Bestand, Erwerbung, Erschliessung, Benutzung,* Bibliothekspraxis, 35 (München: Saur, 1995); Günter Franzmeier, "Zeitschriften-Gesamtkataloge in Deutschland (1945-1970)," Ibid.: 213-219.

5. Rudolf Kaiser, "Der alphabetische Zettelkatalog," in *Fünfzehn Jahre Königliche und Staatsbibliothek* (Berlin: Preussische Staatsbibliothek, 1921): 99-109.

6. Edition quoted: Berlin: Behrend, 1915 (reprinted as *Manualdruck,* 1942).

7. Wiesbaden: Dr. Ludwig Reichert, 1980.

8. Günter Franzmeier, "Die Zeitschriftendatenbank (ZDB)," in *Zeitschriften in deutschen Bibliotheken: Bestand, Erwerbung, Erschliessung, Benutzung,* Bibliothekspraxis, 35 (München: Saur, 1995): 222-234; Franzmeier, "Zeitschriftendatenbank (ZDB): The German National Serials Database," *The Serials Librarian* 35:4 (1999): 119-139.

9. *Die Zeitschriftendatenbank: eine Einführung* (Berlin: Staatsbibliothek zu Berlin, 2002).

The History of "The Work" in the Modern Catalog

Richard P. Smiraglia

SUMMARY. From a historical perspective, one could consider the modern library catalog to be that bibliographical apparatus that stretches at least from Thomas Hyde's catalog for the Bodleian Library at Oxford to the near present. Mai and other recent authors have suggested postmodern approaches to knowledge organization. In these, we realize that there is no single and unique order of knowledge or documents but rather there are many appropriate orders, all of them contextually dependent. Works (oeuvres, opera, Werke, etc.), as are musical works, literary works, works of art, etc., are and always have been key entities for information retrieval. Yet catalogs in the modern era were designed to inventory (first) and retrieve (second) specific documents. From Hyde's catalog for the Bodleian until the late twentieth century, developments are epistemologically pragmatic–reflected in the structure of catalog records, in the rules for main entry headings, and in the rules for filing in card catalogs. After 1980 developments become empirical–reflected in research conducted by Tillett, Yee, Smiraglia, Leazer, Carlyle, and Vellucci. The influence of empiricism on the pragmatic notion of "the work" has led to increased focus on the concept of the work. The challenge for the postmodern online catalog is to fully embrace the concept

Richard P. Smiraglia is Professor, Palmer School of Library and Information Science, Long Island University, Brookville, NY 11548 (E-mail: Richard.Smiraglia@ liu.edu).

[Haworth co-indexing entry note]: "The History of 'The Work' in the Modern Catalog." Smiraglia, Richard P. Co-published simultaneously in *Cataloging & Classification Quarterly* (The Haworth Information Press, an imprint of The Haworth Press, Inc.) Vol. 35, No. 3/4, 2003, pp. 553-567; and: *Historical Aspects of Cataloging and Classification* (ed: Martin D. Joachim) The Haworth Information Press, an imprint of The Haworth Press, Inc., 2003, pp. 553-567. Single or multiple copies of this article are available for a fee from The Haworth Document Delivery Service [1-800-HAWORTH, 9:00 a.m. - 5:00 p.m. (EST). E-mail address: getinfo@haworthpressinc.com].

of "the work," finally to facilitate it as a prime objective for information retrieval. *[Article copies available for a fee from The Haworth Document Delivery Service: 1-800-HAWORTH. E-mail address: <getinfo@haworthpressinc.com> Website: <http://www.HaworthPress.com> © 2003 by The Haworth Press, Inc. All rights reserved.]*

KEYWORDS. Works, catalogs, postmodernism, epistemology, information retrieval

Works (oeuvres, etc.) are intellectual or artistic creations. In knowledge organization, works are considered to constitute the intellectual content of documents or other artifacts that may be collected and ordered for retrieval. Libraries are, of course, collections of works. The importance of works, over the importance of documents, has been understood all through the period in which the modern library catalog was developed. Yet it is only of late that the work-phenomenon–that is, the complexity and extent of instantiation of individual works–has begun to be fully comprehended. In this paper I will assert that there is a distinction between the modern catalog and the postmodern catalog such that the shift can lead us to a better understanding of the importance of the work-phenomenon.

1. ON MODERNISM AND POSTMODERNISM

Modernism and postmodernism are relative terms and are defined in different ways in different domains of scholarship. Modernity is often considered to be the period that followed the Enlightenment, during which arose a humanistic belief that a common denominator somehow underlay everything. In the modern world, scholarship undertook the task of discovering the unity–the common denominator–the description of which would provide a unified theory of creation. Postmodernism, then, is the period following the modern, in which the belief in the approach to unity is challenged by the embrace of diversity. Postmodern scholarship is highly domain- and context-specific, seeking to understand the individual orders that explain specific phenomena without reference to any unifying theory. Postmodern theory replaces empiricism, historicism, and rationalism with the comprehension that everything functions in the reflective manner of signs in language. That is, rather than the modernist approach to a unified explanation, the postmodern approach seeks to understand the systems by which signs are capable of meaning (see Ermarth 1998). Modernism and postmodernism are not precise concepts, but they do provide one lens through which we might view the progress of our own enterprise.

Miksa (1998), Mai (1999), and other recent authors have suggested postmodern approaches to knowledge organization, from which we realize that there is no single and unique order of knowledge or documents. Rather there are many appropriate orders, all of them contextually dependent. Jesse Shera (1950) may have been the first to arrive at this conclusion. In his contribution to the 1950 Conference on Bibliographic Organization, he suggested that the organization of knowledge from Plato to Bliss was founded upon the assumption that (72, emphasis original): "there exists a *universal* 'order of nature' that, when discovered, will reveal a *permanent* conceptual framework of the entirety of human knowledge. . . ." Following an extensive review of the history of classification, Shera concluded that there could never be a universal and permanent classification, but rather, each generation must create its own (1950, 77). Unwilling to completely abandon the concept of a universal order, Shera still pointed to the postmodern concept that human perceptions determine the expression of human experience–that is, that knowledge organizations must be person- and context-dependent. Shera concluded with a call for research to inform the development of new classification schemes, a reexamination of underlying principles, and experimentation in the construction of varying conceptual frameworks. Essentially he set a research agenda that pointed to the postmodern era in which context- and domain-dependent languages can generate the ontologies that underlie classifications.

More recently, Quinn (1994) analyzed the problems inherent in the search for a universal classification, including the inflexibility of discipline-based schemes, and the absence of social relevance in traditional classificatory structures. Beghtol (1998) and Hjørland and Albrechtsen (1999) call for increased interdisciplinarity and multidisciplinarity in classification design, suggesting a postmodern approach can be anchored in discourse communities. Hjørland and Albrechtsen suggest that knowledge organization should be shifted toward a semiotic approach, with a concomitant shift to historical and social understanding of knowledge.

Mai (1999) suggested a postmodern theory of knowledge organization, in which universalism is abandoned in favor of social praxis and the language of the individual communities for which knowledge organizations are created. In essence, Mai's postmodern approach suggested that rather than building concrete schemata for the representation of knowledge artifacts, what is needed are intermediaries that make a knowledge organization transparent for users. He seemed to suggest, though not explicitly, semiotically-derived search engines, with which users might interact using their own person- and situation-dependent languages.

2. ON THE MODERN CATALOG

From a historical perspective, one could consider the modern library catalog to be that bibliographical apparatus that stretches at least from Thomas
Hyde's catalog for the Bodleian Library at Oxford (ca. 1674) to the near present. In this vein we can see the modern catalog as an inventory of documents,
fit together into a unified, superimposed order. Now the modern catalog as we
know it is a marvelous invention, governed by strictly adhered-to principles
for the description of documents and the collocation and separation of headings. When I call this modern catalog an inventory of documents, I do not
mean to give it short shrift, as it is elegant in its conception and, so far as it
went, the modern catalog provided a device for collocation and retrieval vastly
superior to the inventories that preceded it. Ultimately the dictionary catalog
was a most modern invention, being not only a list of documents but also a dictionary of authors and their works. Catalog codes, filing rules, and centralized
catalog card production can be seen as the hallmarks of the modern catalog,
working together to create a virtual universal catalog of documents held by libraries. Each library's own catalog, in essence, was a replica of a segment of
the universal order. But all of this structure was aimed primarily at the identification of known items–books in Cutter's terms or documents in today's parlance. It is my contention that appropriate care of works in the catalog will
signal the occurrence of the fully postmodern catalog.

The postmodern catalog is characterized by domain-specificity, dispersion,
and linkages. The single universal catalog has passed through a virtual filter
into a new age of hyperlinks, metadata schema and their crosswalks, domain-specific internal structures (such as those for archival materials or museum artifacts), and context-specific languages (witness the explosion of
thesaurus and ontology construction). In the midst of this amazing transformation, the near total decentralization of effort has led to the perplexity of a virtual union catalog in the databases of OCLC and RLIN, from which local
web-portals are derived and among which all are interlinked.

3. ON THE TREATMENT OF WORKS

Works are and always have been key entities for information retrieval. Although works have always been comprehended as important, there is something of a checkered past concerning their treatment in the catalog, and,
therefore, in the codes that governed catalogs as well. For the purposes of this
paper, I will take two methodological approaches. First, I will examine the
evolution of the definition of works; in this we will see a progression from a

very modern view to a very postmodern view. Second, I will examine evidence of a very modern phenomenon in the catalog–the attempt to order works uniformly with the uniform title as collocating device.

3.1 Definitions of "Work"

Yee wrote a history of works and their treatment in the catalog in a series of four articles published in 1994 and 1995, and elsewhere I have also compiled a narrative history of works (Smiraglia 2001). Readers are referred to those thorough accounts for the details of this history of the treatment of works. But for our purposes a simple chronology will suffice to demonstrate the role of works in the modern catalog vs. the potential role of works in the postmodern catalog. Table 1 includes critical elements from definitions of works by authors from Panizzi to the present.

The definitions in Table 1 do not constitute an exhaustive list (for which see Yee or Smiraglia). Rather, this compilation was constructed to demonstrate the evolution of the concept of works in the modern catalog. In particular, we can see here the shift toward postmodern ways of thinking among authors of the present day.

Catalogs in the modern era were designed to inventory (first) and retrieve (second) specific documents. This is reflected, not the least, in Cutter's famous "Objects"–first the book, then the work. Panizzi saw the work as the content of a book; he understood that it was the content and not the carrier that interested users, but his perception was of an entity of secondary importance to the physical. Cutter, not too long after, considered a work to be any intellectual creation. But, by the middle of the twentieth century two authors (Pettee and Verona) had posited the presence of a concept called the "literary unit." This was the whole collectivity of editions of a given work. In fact, by Verona's time, it was already clear that the publishing industry was creating a potential nightmare for libraries, because the aftermath of the information explosion of the early twentieth century was a multiplicity of editions of major works. A librarian either had to choose the best among the many or deal with multiplicity in the catalog.

The next phase begins with the Paris Conference in 1961 and hits its stride with the writings of Domanovksy and Wilson. This is the notion that a work is an expression of an abstract phenomenon and that any given instantiation of it is simply one "text" among many. This is the beginning of the notion that a "work" is something much larger than any single document. It is beginning to be clear that a "work" is actually a collectivity of instantiations, among which some degree of variation is frequently to be observed.

TABLE 1. Definitions of a Work

Author	Work Definition
Panizzi (1841)	contents, state, and usefulness of a book, choice among which is to best satisfy reader's needs
Cutter (1876)	any separate intellectual creation
Pettee (1936) and Verona (1959)	literary unit; group of related works
ICCP (1961)	expression of thought in language or symbols for record and communication
Domanovksy (1974)	purely intellectual phenomenon; one constituent of double-sided phenomenon "book"
Wilson (1968 and 1987)	an abstract entity composed or invented; a group or family of texts with one original ancestor
Carpenter (1981) and Smiraglia (1992)	intellectual content of a bibliographic item, two properties: propositions form ideational content, strings express semantic content
Eggert (1994)	phenomenological view: ongoing entities that incorporate across their chronological existence not only physical changes but also reactions of those who encounter them
Yee (1995b)	product of intellectual or artistic activity that has a name
Carlyle (1996)	narrowly, a set of records that share the same primary author and title MARC field contents; a "superwork record set," contains the records of a work and the set of records related to a work
IFLA FRBR (1998)	a distinct intellectual or artistic creation; an abstract entity; commonality of content between and among expressions
Smiraglia (2001)	a signifying, concrete set of ideational conceptions that find realization through semantic or symbolic expression

Wilson's book, *Two Kinds of Power* (1968), was and is an extraordinary manifesto. For the first time, someone had laid out in a very complete way the entire spectrum of bibliographical activity, explaining the divergence between the descriptive domain, the tools we create, and the exploitative domain, where scholarship takes place. Wilson's text is full of dense and complex descriptions of bibliographical phenomena, including a primary focus on works. But perhaps the most important contribution was a rule of efficacy: whatever in the descriptive domain led to exploitation was efficacious, whatever hindered exploitation was not. For the first time there was a way to measure the success of the bibliographic apparatus–i.e., the catalog. This was the opening to empirical analysis, which would pave the way for postmodern approaches.

Empirical analysis of catalogs begins with the major efforts to understand the impact of *AACR2* in the late 1970s–perhaps the most important work being that by Taylor-Dowell (1982), from which we learned that the frequency of name headings in a catalog was amenable to Lotka's law (1926). Among other things, this meant that a certain exact proportion of names in the catalog was unique. The logical conclusion following from this is that those names represent authors who write only one work. But the rest of the names, around 30 percent, represent either authors of many works or those whose works appear many times in different instantiations. This was the first clue that empirical evidence of Pettee and Verona's literary units might be available. The next major empirical contribution was Tillett's (1987) dissertation from which we learned that the extent of interrelationship among library documents was great. Tillett also offered a taxonomy of relationships that has spurred continuing research ever since.

Selecting Tillett's taxonomical category of "derivative relationship," I studied the extent to which works in an academic library catalog might have relatives in the bibliographic universe (Smiraglia 1992). The remarkable result was that nearly half of the works in the academic library collection had other instantiations, and that half of those relationships were not explicit in the catalog. Yee (1994a-b and 1995a-b) and Vellucci (1997) studied the work phenomenon among films and music respectively. They both discovered dramatic proportions of works with multiple instantiations. Later empirical work reported in Smiraglia (2001) has extended our understanding of the work-phenomenon.

About the time Yee was undertaking her research with films, Eggert (1994) posited a phenomenological view of works of art, suggesting that works are actually ongoing entities that change in time in response to their cultural acceptance. That is, if a work becomes associated in the popular mind in a certain way, it then is replicated over and over but changes slightly or dramatically with each replication. Smiraglia (2002c) has demonstrated this effect repeatedly. But here we reach the limits of empiricism and must turn instead to epistemological analysis–the arrival of postmodern thought. We will return to this sequence in the next section of the paper.

3.2 Uniformity

An essential feature of the modern catalog is a conception that a universal order underlies everything. A logical consequence of this conception is the attempt to impose a universal order on phenomena in question. In the early twentieth century, for works with multiple instantiations, this was accomplished through complex filing rules: original editions first, then translations, then selections, then commentaries, for instance. Eventually the uniform title as collocating device took over this function. Used at first mostly for musical works, laws, and scriptures, after *AACR2* the uniform title became the ubiquitous device for imposing order on the collectivity of instantiations of a work that might fall together in a catalog.

The function of uniform title is perhaps best revealed in the cumulation of instantiations in a bibliographic utility. Here we have two examples. Figure 1 includes the uniform titles for English language editions of St. Augustine's *City of God* (originally *De civitate Dei*) that were found in RLIN April 30, 2002. Figure 2 includes uniform titles for Voltaire's *Candide* and its descendents found in RLIN the same date.

There were eighty-nine bibliographic records in the books file in RLIN for this subset of instantiations of Augustine's *City of God*. They were ordered using the ten uniform titles shown below. This, of course, is by no means a complete listing of potential uniform titles for this work. But it is informative, particularly in the way it demonstrates the attempt to impose order on a set of instantiations of this work. Note that there are translations into English, with one grouping of dual English-Latin editions. Note the breakdown of English translations–some by date, some by translator. There are excerpts–selections from the *City of God* published together–and the uniform titles indicate they have been translated into English and are ordered by date. And there are instances of *City of God* included as an excerpt in larger collections of Augustine's work–these are represented by the uniform titles "Selection. English" and "Selections. English. 1990."

For Voltaire's *Candide* there were 500 bibliographic records in RLIN's books file, thirty-seven in the sound recordings file, thirty-four in the scores file, and thirteen in the film-videorecordings file. Sorted, these yield the uniform titles for the various instantiations shown in Figure 2. This example is more complex, but it demonstrates the same attempt to impose a universal order. I have chosen to retain the medium-specific divisions from RLIN for this exam-

FIGURE 1. Uniform Titles Found on Augustine's *City of God*

```
Augustine, Saint, Bishop of Hippo.
[DE CIVITATE DEI. ENGLISH]
[DE CIVITATE DEI. ENGLISH. 1610]
[DE CIVITATE DEI. ENGLISH. 1973]
[DE CIVITATE DEI. ENGLISH. DODS]
[DE CIVITATE DEI. ENGLISH. HEALEY]
[DE CIVITATE DEI. ENGLISH & LATIN]
[DE CIVITATE DEI. SELECTIONS. ENGLISH. 1943]
[DE CIVITATE DEI. SELECTIONS. ENGLISH. 1951]
[SELECTIONS. ENGLISH]
[SELECTIONS. ENGLISH. 1990]
```

FIGURE 2. Uniform Titles for Voltaire's *Candide* and Offspring

Books:

Voltaire, 1694-1778.
[CANDIDE]
[CANDIDE. 1913]
[CANDIDE. CHINESE]
[CANDIDE. ENGLISH]
[CANDIDE. ENGLISH. 1928.]
[CANDIDE. ENGLISH. 1977]
[CANDIDE. ENGLISH. 1978]
[CANDIDE. ENGLISH. 1981]
[CANDIDE. ENGLISH. 1985]
[CANDIDE. ENGLISH. SMOLLET]
[CANDIDE. ENGLISH & FRENCH]
[CANDIDE. ESPERANTO. LANTI]
[CANDIDE. GALLEGO]
[CANDIDE. GERMAN]
[CANDIDE. GERMAN. 1912]
[CANDIDE. GERMAN. SCHNEIDER-SCHELDE]
[CANDIDE. HUNGARIAN]
[CANDIDE. HEBREW]
[CANDIDE. ICELANDIC]
[CANDIDE. ITALIAN]
[CANDIDE. JAPANESE]
[CANDIDE. KOREAN]
[CANDIDE. LITHUANIAN]
[CANDIDE. PORTUGUESE.]
[CANDIDE. RUSSIAN]
[CANDIDE. SPANISH]
[CANDIDE. TURKISH]
[PROSE WORKS. SELECTIONS. 1935]
[SELECTIONS. 1952]
[SELECTIONS. 1983]
[SELECTIONS. ENGLISH]
[SELECTIONS. ENGLISH. 1929]
[SELECTIONS. ENGLISH. 1961]
[WORKS. ENGLISH. 1901]

Bernstein, Leonard, 1918-
[CANDIDE. LIBRETTO. ENGLISH]

Sound recordings:

Voltaire, 1694-1778.
[CANDIDE]
[CANDIDE. ENGLISH]

FIGURE 2 (continued)

Bernstein, Leonard, 1918-
[CANDIDE]
[CANDIDE. SELECTIONS]

Musical scores:

Bernstein, Leonard, 1918-
[CANDIDE]
[CANDIDE. VOCAL SCORE]
[CANDIDE. VOCAL SCORE. ENGLISH]
[CANDIDE. VOCAL SCORE. SELECTIONS.]
[CANDIDE. OVERTURE]

Antheil, George, 1900-1959.
[CANDIDE. VOCAL SCORE. SELECTIONS.]
[CANDIDE. MERRY-GO-ROUND. VOCAL SCORE]

Videorecordings and films:
CANDIDE [VIDEORECORDING]
Bernstein, Leonard, 1918-
[CANDIDE][VIDEORECORDING]
VOLTAIRE PRESENTS CANDIDE--AN INTRODUCTION TO THE AGE OF
ENLIGHTENMENT. [MOTION PICTURE].
CANDIDE--LE TEXTE ET LA VIE DE VOLTAIRE. [FILMSTRIP]

ple, but one could easily interfile the uniform titles, but doing so would lose the critical medium-specific contextual information. The most immediate effect would be the intermingling of audio and text versions of the work and its off-spring. The modern catalog saw books as its central entities, everything else as offspring (or, subordinate entities). Likewise, there are no direct pointers among the access points for the offspring; everything from Bernstein to Antheil to the motion picture is accessed together because of the imposition of the heading "Voltaire . . . Candide" without context-dependent information.

4. ON EPISTEMIC STANCES: THE MODERN YIELDS TO THE POSTMODERN

Birger Hjørland (1998) has given us a basic epistemological approach to the fundamental problems of information retrieval, particularly to the analysis of the contents of documentary entities. Hjørland lists four basic epistemological stances:

- Empiricism: derived from observation and experience;
- Rationalism: derived from the employment of reason;
- Historicism: derived from cultural hermeneutics; and,
- Pragmatism: derived from the consideration of goals and their consequences.

In Hjørland's domain-analytic approach, any given document may have different meanings and potential uses to different groups of users. The essential distinction becomes that between the pragmatic catalog of documents, and the empirical, historical, and rational catalog of works.

From Hyde's catalog for the Bodleian until the late twentieth century, developments are epistemologically pragmatic–reflected in the structure of catalog records, in the rules for main entry headings, and in the rules for filing in card catalogs. Librarians worked in very pragmatic ways to arrange their collections and to provide sophisticated finding tools for those documents. This pragmatism was based on an assumption that there was a correspondence between a book and the work it contained–one item, one work, and vice versa. Once the multiplicity of instantiations became known, the literary unit as a concept arose as rational approach to ordering within an author file. First filing rules, and later uniform titles, emerged as devices to generate both collocation (gathering) and differentiation among instantiations. Yet, the modernist approach to imposing a generic order has yielded the somewhat unsatisfying results we saw above.

Empiricism was and is the turning point between modernism and postmodernism in the catalog. Like Shera, Lubetzky (1953) issued a call for paradigmatic change in the structure of the catalog, noting the importance of works, and relationships among them, over and above the simple inventory of documents. However, Lubetzky tried to work in the context of the unified super-imposed ordering of main entries. It took empiricism to comprehend the extent of the work-phenomenon. Empiricism, or the ordering of phenomena based on the results of empirical observation, by its very nature requires context and domain-specific analyses of phenomena. Wilson's papers (1987 and 1989) on "the second objective"–i.e., works–took up Lubetzky's theme, created a theoretical framework in which efficacy could be evaluated, and pointed to the empiricist shift. From that point developments become empirical–reflected in research conducted by Taylor, Tillett, Yee, Smiraglia, Carlyle, and Vellucci, among others.

In a recent volume, Svenonius (2000) brings us full circle by describing all bibliographic activity as language. She suggests that the point of bibliographic activity is communication, and that each device used to order the records of knowledge can be understood in terms of grammar and syntax. This is a very postmodern idea, suggesting that knowledge organization takes the form of signs in language, leading to the logical conclusion that for any given user, knowledge organization must be person- or context-dependent.

The influence of empiricism on the pragmatic notion of "the work," summarized in Smiraglia (2001), has led to increased focus on the work-phenomenon. This is reflected in IFLA's (1998) *Functional Requirements for Bibliographic Records*, in which a very postmodern point of view about works is proposed. That is, there is a group of documentary entities *works, expressions, manifestations,* and *items* such that a work is a distinct intellectual or artistic creation, an expression is the intellectual or artistic realization of a work (the entities work and expression reflect intellectual or artistic content). A manifestation embodies an expression of a work, which in turn is embodied by an item (the entities *manifestation* and *item* reflect physical form). A work might be realized through one or more expressions, which might be embodied in one or more manifestations, which in turn might be exemplified in one or more items (IFLA 1998, 12-13). The challenge for the postmodern online catalog is to fully embrace the concept of "the work," and finally to facilitate it as a prime objective for information retrieval.

5. CONCLUSION:
ON THE TREATMENT OF WORKS IN POSTMODERN CATALOGS

The modern catalog has had three centuries to bloom; the postmodern catalog is still in the throes of gestation. It is impossible at this point in time to fully comprehend the difference a postmodern approach to knowledge organization will bring to the evolution of the catalog. Empiricism is not a feature of postmodern thought, but we can see in the shift of research from the empirical to the semiotic and qualitative an attempt by scholars to incorporate the postmodern concept of discourse community domain-specificity.

Some trends in the evolution of the definition of a work are very revealing of a postmodern way of thinking. Returning to Table 1, we see that Carlyle moved the definition forward by defining the "superwork record set." This is a totally abstract phenomenon–not an edition (or "progenitor," as I have used the term (for example, Smiraglia 1992) to point to the first instantiation of a work)–rather all of the bibliographic records of a work and of all works related to that work. Figure 2 is an example of the base dimensions of a superwork set.

This is a very postmodern concept, letting the documents in a set determine their own manner of ordering.

Carlyle (1997) has also conducted research on users' interaction to super-work record sets, suggesting that users should have the capacity to design their own displays to meet specific information needs. She reported a qualitative study (Carlyle 2001) in which she analyzed user-clustering behavior. Participants were asked to arrange a set of related objects such that the arrangements would help them remember how to find them at a later time. The most frequently appearing attributes were physical format, language and audience. Note that the order imposed by uniform titles in the examples we saw above completely loses the most important attribute–physical format. The postmodern catalog will require much more research of this nature into person- and context-dependent orders.

Table 1 ends with my own theoretical definition of a work, derived from semiotic analysis. Here a work is no longer seen as a simple entity, but has become a cultural collaborative entity that finds occasional instantiation in physical forms that may be collected and ordered for retrieval. I have recently explored the epistemological nature of works and of musical works (Smiraglia 2002a and 2002b), combining semiotic analysis with Hjørland's epistemological framework to comprehend the ways in which we can see the evolution of works across time and cultures. In recent papers, Andersen (Forthcoming) has explored epistemological understanding of works as informative entities; Morrissey (Forthcoming) has analyzed the semiotic of scientific meaning.

The shift we are observing is that from the perception of a work as mere content of a document in the modern catalog, to a group of instantiations with a collaborative social role in the postmodern. A parallel to this shift is the understanding that a work is more than simply the creative activity of an individual; rather it is the product of intellectual activity spread across time and culture. The modern catalog, in all its elegance, failed to impose a universal order on the elusive work-phenomenon. The challenge for the postmodern catalog is to incorporate the richness of hyper-linkages to fully exploit the informative capability of works.

WORKS CITED

Beghtol, Claire. 1998. Knowledge domains: Multidisciplinarity and bibliographical classification systems. *Knowledge organization* 25: 1-12.

Carlyle, Allyson. 1996. Ordering author and work records: An evaluation of collocation in online catalog displays. *Journal of the American Society for Information Science* 47: 538-54.

_____. 1997. Fulfilling the second objective in the online catalog: Schemes for organizing author and work records into usable displays. *Library resources & technical services* 41: 79-100.

_____. 2001. Developing organized information displays for voluminous works: A study of user clustering behavior. *Information processing & management* 37: 677-99.

Carpenter, Michael. 1981. *Corporate authorship: Its role in library cataloging.* Westport, Conn.: Greenwood Press.

Cutter, Charles Ammi. 1876. *Rules for a printed dictionary catalog.* Washington: U.S.G.P.O.

Domanovsky, A. 1974. *Functions and objects of author and title cataloguing: A contribution to cataloguing theory.* English text ed. by Anthony Thompson. Budapest: Akademiai Kiado.

Eggert, Paul. 1994. Editing paintings/conserving literature: The nature of the 'work.' In *Studies in Bibliography,* v. 47 ed. by David L. Vander Meulen, 65-78. Charlottesville, Pub. for The Bibliographical Society of the University of Virginia by The University Press of Virginia.

Ermarth, Elizabeth Deeds. 1998. Postmodernism. In *The Routledge encyclopedia of philosophy,* Edward Craig general editor, v. 7, 587-90. New York: Routledge.

Hjørland, Birger. 1998. Theory and metatheory of information science: A new interpretation. *Journal of documentation* 54: 606-21.

Hjørland, Birger and Hanne Albrechtsen. 1999. An analysis of some trends in classification research. *Knowledge organization* 26: 131-39.

International Conference on Cataloguing Principles. [1961] 1981. *Report,* ed. by A. H. Chaplin and Dorothy Anderson. London: IFLA International Office for UBC.

International Federation of Library Associations, Study Group on the Functional Requirements for Bibliographic Records. 1998. *Functional requirements for bibliographic records.* München: K. G. Saur.

Lotka, Alfred J. 1926. The frequency distribution of scientific productivity. *Journal of the Washington Academy of Sciences* 16: 317-23.

Lubetzky, Seymour. 1953. Cataloging rules and principles: A critique of the A.L.A. rules for entry and a proposed design for their revision. Washington: Processing Dept., Library of Congress.

Mai, Jens-Erik. 1999. A postmodern theory of knowledge organization. *Proceedings of the 62nd annual meeting of the American Society for Information Science,* ed. Larry Woods, 547-56. Medford, NJ: Information Today.

Miksa, Francis L. 1998. *The DDC, the universe of knowledge, and the post-modern library.* Albany: Forest Press.

Panizzi, Antonio. [1841] 1985. Rules for the compilation of the catalogue. In *Foundations of descriptive cataloging,* ed. Michael Carpenter, Elaine Svenonius, 3-14. Littleton, Colo.: Libraries Unlimited.

Pettee, Julia. [1936] 1985. The development of authorship entry and the formulation of authorship rules as found in the Anglo-American code. In *Foundations of descriptive cataloging,* ed. Michael Carpenter, Elaine Svenonius, 75-89. Littleton, Colo.: Libraries Unlimited.

Quinn, Brian. 1994. Recent theoretical approaches in classification and indexing. *Knowledge organization* 21: 140-7.

Shera, Jesse H. 1950. Classification as the basis of bibliographic organization. In *Bibliographic organization: Papers presented before the Fifteenth Annual Conference of the Graduate Library School July 24-29, 1950* ed. J. H. Shera and M. E. Egan, 72-93. Chicago: Univ. of Chicago Press.

Smiraglia, Richard P. 1992. Authority control and the extent of derivative bibliographic relationships. Ph.D. diss., University of Chicago.

_____. 2001. *The nature of 'a work:' Implications for knowledge organization.* Lanham, Md.: Scarecrow Press.

Svenonius, Elaine. 2000. *The intellectual foundation of information organization.* Digital libraries and electronic publishing. Cambridge, Mass.: The MIT Press.

Taylor-Dowell, Arlene. 1982. *AACR2 Headings: A five-year projection of their impact on catalogs.* Littleton, Colo.: Libraries Unlimited.

Tillett, Barbara Ann Barnett. 1987. Bibliographic relationships: Toward a conceptual structure of bibliographic information used in cataloging. Ph.D. dissertation, University of California, Los Angeles.

Vellucci, Sherry L. 1997. *Bibliographic relationships in music catalogs.* Lanham, Md.: Scarecrow Press.

Verona, Eva. [1959] 1985. Literary unit versus bibliographical unit. In *Foundations of cataloging,* ed. Michael Carpenter, Elaine Svenonius, 155-175. Littleton, Colo.: Libraries Unlimited.

Wilson, Patrick. [1968] 1978. *Two kinds of power: An essay in bibliographical control.* California library reprint series ed. Berkeley: University of California Press.

_____. [1987] 1989. The second objective. In *The conceptual foundations of descriptive cataloging,* ed. by Elaine Svenonius, 5-16. San Diego: Academic Press.

_____. 1989. Interpreting the second objective of the catalog. *Library Quarterly* 59: 339-353.

Yee, Martha M. 1994a. What is a work? Part 1: The user and the objects of the catalog. *Cataloging & Classification Quarterly* 19, no.1: 9-28.

_____. 1994b. What is a work? Part 2: The Anglo-American cataloging codes. *Cataloging & Classification Quarterly* 19, no. 2: 5-22.

_____. 1995a. What is a work? Part 3: The Anglo-American cataloging codes. *Cataloging & Classification Quarterly* 20, no. 1: 25-46.

_____. 1995b. What is a work? Part 4: Cataloging theorists and a definition abstract. *Cataloging & Classification Quarterly* 20, no. 2: 3-24.

Index

Historical Aspects of Cataloging and Classification

_____ in softbound at $52.46 (regularly $69.95) (ISBN: 0-7890-1981-7)
_____ in hardbound at $74.96 (regularly $99.95) (ISBN: 0-7890-1980-9)